# MASTERPLOTS II

## SHORT STORY SERIES
### REVISED EDITION

# MASTERPLOTS II

## SHORT STORY SERIES
### REVISED EDITION

## Volume 3
### Esm–Hor

*Editor, Revised Edition*
**CHARLES MAY**
*California State University, Long Beach*

*Editor, First Edition*
**FRANK N. MAGILL**

SALEM PRESS
Pasadena, California     Hackensack, New Jersey

*Editor in Chief:* Dawn P. Dawson

| | |
|---|---|
| *Editorial Director:* Christina J. Moose | *Assistant Editor:* Andrea E. Miller |
| *Project Editor:* R. Kent Rasmussen | *Research Supervisor:* Jeffry Jensen |
| *Production Editor:* Cynthia Beres | *Acquisitions Editor:* Mark Rehn |
| *Copy Editor:* Rowena Wildin | *Layout:* Eddie Murillo |

Some of the essays in this work originally appeared in *Masterplots II, Short Story Series*, edited by Frank N. Magill (Pasadena, Calif.: Salem Press, Inc., 1986), and in *Masterplots II, Short Story Series Supplement*, edited by Frank N. Magill and Charles E. May (Pasadena, Calif.: Salem Press, Inc., 1996).

∞ The paper used in these volumes conforms to the American National Standard for Permanence of Paper for Printed Library Materials, Z39.48-1992 (R1997).

**Library of Congress Cataloging-in-Publication Data**

Masterplots II : Short story series / editor Charles May. — Rev. ed.

    p.   cm.

Includes bibliographical references and index.

ISBN 1-58765-140-8 (set : alk. paper) — ISBN 1-58765-143-2 (vol. 3 : alk. paper) —

1. Fiction—19th century—Stories, plots, etc. 2. Fiction—19th century—History and criticism. 3. Fiction—20th century—Stories, plots, etc. 4. Fiction—20th century—History and criticism. 5. Short story. I. Title: Masterplots 2. II. Title: Masterplots two. III. May, Charles E. (Charles Edward), 1941-

PN3326 .M27 2004

809.3′1—dc22

2003018256

First Printing

# TABLE OF CONTENTS

# TABLE OF CONTENTS

# TABLE OF CONTENTS

# MASTERPLOTS II

## SHORT STORY SERIES
### REVISED EDITION

# ESMERALDA

*Author:* Roberta Fernández
*Type of plot:* Domestic realism
*Time of plot:* 1958
*Locale:* Texas
*First published:* 1990

> *Principal characters:*
> VERÓNICA LUNA, also called Esmeralda or Ronnie, a young
>     woman
> ISELA, her mother
> CRISTINA, her grandmother
> AMANDA and
> LEONOR, her great-aunts
> ALFREDO, her violent uncle
> NENITA, the thirteen-year-old narrator

## The Story

Verónica, a great beauty of eighteen, is a member of an extended family living in her great-aunt Leonor's house in Texas. She works as a model in a theater, where she simply sits in a booth, her beauty framed by "a round glass house." The narrator, Nenita, first meets her when Verónica and her mother come to live at Leonor's house. Nenita is curious about Verónica because she is so quiet and has a mysterious air. Nenita senses that there is something about Verónica that the family is leaving unspoken. Even more intriguing is the fact that Verónica never visits her former home at her uncle Alfredo's ranch.

After a newspaper columnist writes about Verónica, she becomes a minor public figure and attracts increased attention from men. Troubled by the notoriety that the newspaper column has brought her, she breaks into tears when her cousin Orión teases her by reciting the first line of a famous poem by Federico García Lorca: "Green how I love you green" (*"Verde que te quiero verde"*), which alludes to the columnist's calling her "a shining emerald" (*"una esmeralda brillante"*).

Leonor consoles Verónica and advises her to quit her job at the theater the next day. Leonor points out how men call their *piropos* compliments but that such behavior is "really self-indulgence." Verónica then explains how she came to leave her uncle's ranch five years earlier, when she and a seventeen-year-old worker named Omar were attracted to each other. Gentle and sweet-natured, Omar brought her gifts such as cactus flowers and fruit. Forbidden to see each other, they spoke together through her window at night. One night when the whole house seemed to be asleep, they finally dared to meet on the porch, where they talked and kissed. At that moment, Alfredo appeared. In a rage, he slapped Omar and threw him off the porch, then yanked Verónica around, screaming obscenities and calling her a whore. Verónica believes that Alfredo had Omar killed, but Leonor tells her that he simply had Omar deported.

Taken aback, Nenita asks why Alfredo has interfered. Leonor can only answer that that is how things are. It is further revealed that Alfredo's wife will not leave him herself, but she has seen to it that their five children grow up in other family members' houses, away from him. Reassured by this conversation, Verónica says that she will continue to work at the theater. Later, Nenita and Verónica discuss how Omar was gentle and giving, while the twins Orión and Orso are loud and boorish. On the opposite end of the scale is Alfredo, whose own children openly profess to hate him.

Nenita, who has regularly walked home with Verónica since the latter's notoriety began, arrives late one evening. She runs after Verónica, catching up with her at the same time that the two Mondragón brothers stop the car in which they have been following Verónica. After a struggle, the brothers drive off with Verónica. Nenita runs home to report what has happened. Orión and Orso go off to find Verónica's abductors. Nenita begins to call the police, but is told that they will do nothing. Meanwhile, the Mondragóns rape Verónica, leaving her pregnant.

Afterward, the newspaper columnist prints a condolence for what has happened to Verónica, noting that her assailants were brought to justice, and he apologizes for any part he may have played in what happened. Over the next several weeks everyone helps take care of Verónica. The older women of the family perfume her room, massage her with herbal oils, and encourage her to sleep. They also repeatedly ask her to tell what happened, thereby allowing her to cry and grieve. She recuperates, reflecting on how the family's women have many griefs, largely caused by men. The family women have helped her by telling her their own secret pains. She determines that she will not be a victim. As a final sign of her readjustment, she enjoys a risqué joke with Nenita.

All is not the same as before, however; Nenita senses that Verónica has erected a wall around herself. Verónica meets and quickly marries David, a naïve young musician. In a moment of frankness, Verónica admits that she would like to think that she is happy. After the baby is born, David seems to believe it is his. Nenita has a dream in which the color green figures prominently. Verónica, adored by a crowd, retreats. Nenita passes through rooms reminiscent of the glass booth at the theater and of the colors and scents of the room in which Verónica convalesced. Finally, a stranger, who recalls Omar, approaches Nenita, offering her "half an orange . . . and cactus fruits." She reaches out to accept his gifts.

*Themes and Meanings*

Roberta Fernández's "Esmeralda" is a feminist story in the most basic sense of the term, in that it concerns itself with women and vindicates them. It is about the harm that men do to women, and the ways that women cope. It is also about resisting victimization and is about love. The two epigraphs that introduce the story announce these themes. One is from popular culture, the other from a writer. There is some tension between them; in many respects, they may be reduced to opposites. For example, one may point out that in the story, popular culture speaks with flowery language about love and beauty (the song, the columnist's words), and that, with education and experience, one learns to distrust such messages (Ntozake Shange's poem, Verónica's experience). Fernández, however, is interested in more than sending a message. Her characters and events are rarely simply opposites or symbols. For example, the men are not all bad. The twins Orión and Orso are insensitive and immature, but they—not the police—do what they can to help protect Verónica. Omar and David are loving and gentle. This makes the evil of Alfredo and the Mondragón brothers more believable.

Likewise, Fernández's women characters are not all good. Verónica marries not for love but as a means of escape. She retreats. The story is feminist simply in its advocacy of the women characters and its insistence on the realities of women's experience. Women do get raped; they also fall in love (even with the song's sweet and total surrender).

Another theme that pervades the story can be seen in its numerous acts of revealing and concealing. Family secrets are kept and told; Verónica, who is put on public display, remains quiet and out of reach even to Nenita, and lives a lie with her husband; Alfredo's angry "discovery" of Verónica and Omar uncovers his morally reprehensible, yet unspoken (hidden) desires.

## Style and Technique

Told in twelve fragments, the story is discursive, and it mentions many names of family members only in an offhand way—as if the reader already knows who the characters are. Many times, a character tells a story about a past event that relates thematically to present events but does not advance the plot. Fernández, in short, breaks many of the conventions of how short stories ought to be told. She has excellent reasons for doing so. On a first reading of the story, a reader eager to learn what happens to Verónica may not notice the story's intricacy. It is told in the first person, not in Verónica's voice but in that of one who knew her. What the reader learns about Verónica is what Nenita learns about her. Verónica's story is too much for a typically constructed short story to contain. More than the frame that Nenita provides, it needs a box: the family, the family's stories, the room in which she is displayed, the room in which she convalesces, and the houses in which she is watched. If Fernández had written her short story in a more conventional way, it would not be art but rather a tract or a soap opera. The story's subtleties of narration reward those who reread it.

*Eric Howard*

# ESTHER

*Author:* Jean Toomer (1894-1967)
*Type of plot:* Character study
*Time of plot:* The early twentieth century
*Locale:* Rural Georgia
*First published:* 1923

> *Principal characters:*
> ESTHER CRANE, a black girl growing up in a small town
> KING BARLO, a charismatic black man

## The Story

"Esther" is divided into three parts. The first, titled "Nine," describes the main character, a young black girl who lives in Georgia, at that age. She is first seen walking from her home to her father's grocery store. Esther Crane is almost pretty; her hair does not have enough shine, and her face is too unemotional. Her skin is pale, so that she could be taken for a white girl. As she walks, a strange things happens. King Barlo, a huge, well-proportioned black man, drops to his knees in the street in an area where men spit tobacco juice. White men continue to spit at the spot, hitting Barlo, but he does not notice, as he is in a religious trance. After hours of kneeling in this place, Barlo begins to speak to the large crowd that has gathered to view this unusual scene. He speaks to them of a vision he has had from Jesus, who has told him to tell of an inspired black man of Africa, who, while rapt in a religious concentration similar to Barlo's, was captured by white men and taken to America to be sold as a slave. The blacks in the audience are excited and urge him to continue. Barlo stands up and urges those present to turn to the Lord and greet a new awakening of spirit. That night Barlo leaves town. There are rumors of miraculous events, but all that is known for certain is that a black woman drew a picture of a black madonna on the courthouse wall. Esther is told of these rumors, and her young mind fixes on Barlo as an image of strength.

The second section of the story deals with Esther's adolescence in two sections, titled "Sixteen" and "Twenty-two." In "Sixteen," Esther has two dreams. In the first, she sees the red sunlight on the windows of McGregor's notion shop. She imagines that the shop is burning, and when the fire department puts out the fire, a baby is found, which Esther claims as her own. She cannot think of any way that she might have had the baby except by immaculate conception, but she knows that this thought is a sin, so she stops the dream and replaces it with another, in which people spit tobacco juice on the flames, causing the area to stink. Black and white women lift their skirts to reveal their underwear. Esther rushes in to save the baby and is at first repelled by its blackness but begins to love it as it nurses. The townspeople make fun of her, but she interprets their jeers as envy and is happy with her baby. In "Twenty-two," Esther's daily life as a clerk at her father's store is described. Although her father is the richest black man in town, Esther's emotional life is limited. A young black boy with whom she had an affair while she was in school rejected her because she was cold to him. A white man who was attracted to her dropped her after he found out who her father was. Esther decided that it is the powerful Barlo to whom she is attracted, and she resolves to tell him that she loves him the next time he comes to town. Meanwhile, she grows older, grayer, and plainer.

In "Esther Is Twenty-seven," Esther finally brings the elements of her various dreams together and meets King Barlo. He has returned to town a rich man, having made money on cotton during World War I, and is surrounded by a bevy of beautiful black women. Esther realizes that she will be possessed by an ordinary man if she does not make some sort of advance toward Barlo, but as her resolve increases she begins to be considered strange by the outside world, and people wonder if she is going crazy. Esther sets out at midnight to visit Barlo, who is staying at Nat Bowle's house. She leaves in the middle of the night so that her parents and the other townspeople will not know what she is doing. As she passes McGregor's notion shop, she again imagines that she sees flames in the windows, even though it is night. At Bowle's house, she is sickened by tobacco fumes but goes to the upstairs room containing Barlo and his entourage. She is about to faint, but she revives and sees Barlo before her. She tells him that she has come for him, but Barlo says that this is not the place for her and asks her why she has come. Esther says nothing, but the crowd around Barlo infers her sexual intent and laughs at her. She sees Barlo as an ugly drunk and thinks that conception of a child with such a man would be a sin. Pursued by the jeers of the crowd, Esther goes down the stairs and into the street to discover that the street and the town have vanished.

## Themes and Meanings

To the familiar literary theme of the repressed, young, middle-class woman who is both excited and frightened by her sexual desires, Jean Toomer in "Esther" adds the theme of the person of mixed blood struggling to come to grips with an ethnic heritage that is also both exciting and frightening. Esther Crane looks more white than black, so her fellow blacks reject her. Her black suitor said that "for sweetness he preferred a lollipop," but a white suitor also rejects her because of her blackness. Esther is not torn between two worlds; rather, from the beginning, she can fit into neither.

As befits a middle-class shopkeeper's daughter, Esther's sexual desires are carefully hedged round with the disguises of housewifely duty and religious fervor. Although Esther thinks that she loves Barlo, her dreams disguise his identity in the form of a fire so that even her subconscious can interpret her desires to her conscious mind only in the form of a wish for a baby whose blackness at first repels her. She can accept sexuality only if it is disguised as a component of a respectable life. Barlo first appears in the story as a religious messenger, telling a story of a new age to be led by a new black man. Barlo is as powerful as a god, and the black madonna drawn on the courthouse wall is Esther, who, she imagines, will bear Barlo's child. Tellingly, when she first dreams of having a child with Barlo, she does not even think of sex with him but instead explains her desire through church morality: The baby she bears will be the result of an immaculate conception. However, the same morality that invents a way around the thought of sex traps her again and reminds her that a thought of similarity to the Virgin is sinful. In her second replay of this dream, she sees herself rescuing a black baby from the flames, skipping over the idea of sex altogether.

With such confusion over her motives, Esther's one attempted sexual encounter with Barlo is doomed to disaster. She is reminded of her rejection of half of her heritage when the other blacks, easily accepting sex, make fun of her attempt, saying, "So that's how the dictie niggers does it." When Esther steps into the empty street, it is not the town but her dreams and her future that have disappeared.

*Style and Technique*

"Esther" is heavily freighted with symbols, the first of which is the main character's name. The Esther of the Bible presented herself to a Persian king at his court and was selected to be his new queen. The Esther of Toomer's story also presents herself to a king but is rejected, or perhaps more accurately, does not have the courage to understand and act on her deepest desires and is thereby rejected as not being queenly enough.

There are also echoes of Dante's *La divina commedia* (c. 1320; *The Divine Comedy*, 1802) in the presentation of Esther at the ages of nine and twenty-seven. Dante saw Beatrice, the inspiration for his great poem, when she was nine, again when she was eighteen, and once again after her death, in a vision, when she would have been twenty-seven. As all these numbers are multiples of the Trinity, religious significance is added to the fact of Beatrice's beauty by their use. Esther Crane is also seen at nine, but she is merely a witness to a person who is having a vision. She visits Barlo when she is twenty-seven, when Dante's Beatrice was dead; thus Toomer reinforces the fact that Esther is emotionally and sexually dead, a point he makes by extending the section dealing with Esther's adolescence until she is twenty-two, almost an old maid by rural black standards.

Perhaps even more powerful than the other symbols in the story, including the fire that Esther imagines to represent Barlo's sexuality and blackness, is Toomer's use of images that are not symbolic but which are meant to confront the reader directly with their own emotional impact. Just before Esther goes to visit Barlo, Toomer states, "Her mind is a pink meshbag filled with baby toes," an image that is tender and horrific at once, exactly like the mental state of Esther herself.

*James Baird*

# ETHAN BRAND
## A Chapter from an Abortive Romance

*Author:* Nathaniel Hawthorne (1804-1864)
*Type of plot:* Fantasy
*Time of plot:* Sometime before 1850
*Locale:* Western Massachusetts
*First published:* 1850

*Principal characters:*
> ETHAN BRAND, a philosopher-scientist, formerly a lime-burner
> BARTRAM, a lime-burner
> JOE, his young son
> OLD HUMPHREY, the father of a girl destroyed by Brand's experiments
> THE DOCTOR, a former acquaintance of Brand
> THE JEW, an itinerant German diorama exhibitor

*The Story*

Old Bartram and his young son are burning marble into lime in their isolated kiln when they are disturbed by a strange, mirthless laugh. Soon the laugh is followed by the appearance of a mysterious man who identifies himself as Ethan Brand. Bartram recognizes him instantly, as he has heard village tales of a man by that name who left the village eighteen years earlier in search of the Unpardonable Sin. When Bartram asks if his search has been successful, Brand ruefully confesses that, after all of his wanderings and inquiries, he found the Unpardonable Sin in his own heart.

The lime-burner dispatches Joe to the village tavern to alert the "jolly fellows" there that Brand has returned. Left alone with the stranger, he feels acutely aware of the sins in his own heart responding to this man who "had committed the only crime for which Heaven can afford no mercy." Sins, Nathaniel Hawthorne writes, are "all of one family; they went to and fro between his breast and Ethan Brand's, and carried dark greetings from one to the other." The legends of Brand that seemed comic to Bartram now seem deadly earnest.

Brand, whose search for the Unpardonable Sin actually began with thoughts and speculations during his lonely hours as a lime-burner, stokes up the fire as Bartram recalls tales that he is believed to have evoked the devil from the fire of his furnace. Brand silences his fear by telling him that he no longer has need of the devil, who concerns himself only with such halfway sinners as Bartram. Finishing his chore with the fire, Brand announces that he has looked into human hearts hotter with illicit passions than the fiery furnace, but that he did not find the Unpardonable Sin there. In answer to Bartram's query as to what the Unpardonable Sin might be, Brand announces with pride born of madness,

It is a sin that grew within my own breast. . . . A sin that grew nowhere else! The sin of an intellect that triumphed over the sense of brotherhood with man, and reverence for God, and sacrificed everything to its own mighty claims! The only sin that deserves a recompense of immortal agony! Freely, were it to do again, would I incur the guilt.

Bartram is relieved by the appearance of the villagers, summoned by Joe's account of Brand's return. Brand meets again his old companions from the tavern, who implore him to join their pursuit of the black bottle "in which, as they averred, he would find something far better worth seeking for, than the Unpardonable Sin." Brand is offended by this offer of companionship and rejects their overtures with disdain, but not without momentary doubts that his life has been given to a delusion. The Doctor, spokesperson for Brand's old tavern friends, tells him he is crazy.

Old Humphrey is a pathetic old man who wanders about the hills in search of his daughter, who is believed to have gone off with a circus. Confronting Brand, Humphrey asks if in all of his travels over the world he has seen the girl and if he knows when she is coming back. "Ethan Brand had made the subject of a psychological experiment, and wasted, absorbed, and perhaps annihilated her soul." After this encounter with Humphrey, Brand's self-doubt vanishes and he concludes, "Yes . . . it is no delusion. There is an Unpardonable Sin!"

An old German Jew carrying a diorama now enters the scene. He amuses the crowd more by the shoddiness of his exhibit than its quality. When he has finished his show, he invites Brand to look into the box. After doing so, Brand claims to recognize the old man. When this mysterious figure complains that it was a hard task to carry the Unpardonable Sin over the mountain in his show box, Brand admonishes him either to be silent or "get thee into the furnace yonder," implying that this old Jew might be the devil Brand once invoked from its fiery bowels. This strange scene ends with an ancient dog madly chasing its own tail to everyone's amusement. Brand, "moved, it might be, by a perception of some remote analogy between his own case and that of this self-pursuing cur . . . broke into the awful laugh, which . . . expressed the condition of his inward being."

The fun over, the crowd departs, leaving Brand alone again with Bartram and Joe. He sends them to bed, promising to tend the kiln while they rest. During the night, he recollects his earlier speculations by the fire that gradually turned him from reverence for humanity and pity for the human condition to his search for the Unpardonable Sin. As his intellect grew through isolated philosophical speculation, his heart failed to keep pace and gradually the Idea consumed his whole being. In Hawthorne's words, his heart "had withered—had contracted—had hardened—had perished. It had ceased to partake of the universal throb. He had lost his hold of the magnetic chain of humanity." Brand became a cold scientific observer of humanity, manipulating people to serve the needs of his experiments. "Thus Ethan Brand became a fiend. He began to be so from the moment that his moral nature had ceased to keep the pace of improvement with his intellect."

Having finally found in his own heart the Unpardonable Sin, Brand has no further purpose. Unable or unwilling to rejoin the "magnetic chain of humanity" that might offer him salvation, he chooses instead to consign his body to the flames of the furnace. When Bartram and Joe awaken next morning, they first believe that Ethan Brand has left, allowing the fire to burn down. When the old lime-burner opens the furnace, however, he sees in outline form, on top of the heap of burned marble, the skeleton of Ethan Brand. "Within the ribs—strange to say—was the shape of a human heart."

## Themes and Meanings

Two of Hawthorne's recurrent themes are the violation of a human heart or soul and the tragic subordination of the heart or emotions to the intellect. "Ethan Brand" represents one of the most important expressions of these themes because it is in this story that Hawthorne identifies the Unpardonable Sin—the one sin man might commit for which he cannot be forgiven—as the destruction of another's soul. Ethan Brand is a philosopher-scientist, motivated only by his intellect. His heart has been so subordinated by his thirst for ultimate knowledge that he acts without regard for the sanctity of other people's beings: He is a man without conscience or human sympathy. Thus, while he sets out to find the Unpardonable Sin in the breast of others, whom he apparently manipulates into crimes through his experiments, it is finally in his own breast that he finds what he sought. His own ruthless behavior is the ultimate sin.

Brand himself is a recurrent type in Hawthorne's work. These scientist-philosopher figures—of whom the best known is Chillingworth in his novel *The Scarlet Letter* (1850)—are driven by a coldly empirical curiosity that, if not mitigated by human feeling, can drive them to a form of madness in which the Idea consumes their entire beings. No excess is then too great, no experiment beyond their scope in the pursuit of their goal to achieve ultimate knowledge. Like Ethan Brand, such figures are not bound by the natural sympathy that unites mankind.

## Style and Technique

"Ethan Brand" is subtitled "A Chapter from an Abortive Romance," which may account for its fragmentary nature. More important, however, the subtitle is a reminder of Hawthorne's concept of the romance as a neutral ground where the worlds of reality and fantasy could meet in a dreamlike setting. Thus, against the prosaic world of New England lime-burning, which is presented in realistic detail, there is the story of Ethan Brand's search for the Unpardonable Sin accompanied by such gothic elements as the old Jew, who seems a devil figure, and the fantastic ending, which reveals Brand's heart of marble. It is this careful blending of the real and the fantastic that gives much of Hawthorne's work its unique flavor, and earns for him his reputation as America's greatest romancer.

*William E. Grant*

# EUROPE

*Author:* Henry James (1843-1916)
*Type of plot:* Psychological
*Time of plot:* The late nineteenth century
*Locale:* Brookridge, Massachusetts
*First published:* 1899

*Principal characters:*
THE NARRATOR, an unnamed man
HIS SISTER-IN-LAW
MRS. RIMMLE, an elderly woman who is a friend of his sister-in-law
REBECCA,
JANE, and
MARIA RIMMLE, Mrs. Rimmle's daughters

*The Story*

The unnamed narrator has had a long acquaintance with a family of women. Mrs. Rimmle, the elderly widowed matriarch of the family, controls the lives of her three soon-to-be-old daughters by preventing their much-anticipated trip to Europe—a trip that she and her husband enjoyed in the distant past. The narrator, who is familiar with European culture, encourages the daughters, Becky, Jane, and Maria Rimmle, to make the journey, but soon perceives that their mother is subtly intent on preventing it, using her poor health as an excuse. It is commonly believed that Becky is the daughter most "prepared" and thus most deserving of a journey to Europe, although the narrator intuits that it is Jane who most passionately desires to visit the continent.

As the years go by and Mrs. Rimmle's repeated health crises prevent the European journey, the narrator observes that her daughters' rapid aging is exceeded only by her own aging. However, Mrs. Rimmle always rallies, and she moves toward an advanced age that is treated somewhat comically by the narrator and his sister-in-law, who is his interlocutor in the story. The subject of Europe becomes one that is both embarrassing and amusing for the narrator and the Rimmle daughters, who seem to hold out hope for such a trip, but also seem to understand that their own time is running out as their mother moves into her dotage. Finally, however, the narrator is informed by his sister-in-law that Jane Rimmle has departed suddenly for Europe with a family called the Hathaways, and that the trip has brought about important changes in her personality and demeanor.

The narrator claims not to be surprised, however, when he is told that Jane has become a person whom "no one would know," one who is now described as "obstreperous" and who has "taken to flirting." He later learns that Jane refuses to return to the United States with the Hathaways, whom she informs of her intention to remain in

Europe and even visit the East. Delighted with Jane's metamorphosis, the narrator hopes that the other two daughters will follow her example.

That, however, is not to be. Although Becky approvingly helps finance her sister's continued stay in Europe, both she and Maria devote the remainder of their own lives to their mother, who continues to live long past her time. Becky dies before her mother. Before she dies, she tells the narrator that Jane will never return to them; her mother, barely able to speak, informs the narrator that her daughter Jane is dead. Knowing this is not true, the narrator also pretends to accept as true Mrs. Rimmle's statement that Becky has departed for Europe.

*Themes and Meanings*

Throughout his career Henry James was obsessed with the American experience of Europe; his aptly named short story "Europe" is one of many of his works that take this subject as its major theme. For James, the American response to the social and cultural milieu of Europe is a complex one that usually functions to effect irrevocable changes in the Americans who choose to experience this kind of transformation. To James, Europe often represents a world of greater sophistication, deception, and subtlety for Americans who venture to enter its complex, ambiguous web of social relationships. His characters are generally unprepared for the multilayered reality that they encounter in a European setting.

In "Europe," however, James concentrates on characters who remain in the United States, although Europe still functions symbolically in ways similar to his other fiction. The Rimmle daughters clearly represent what James sees as the major American virtues and defects. They are naïve, puritanical, provincial, and painfully sincere, and, with the exception of Jane, are destined to retain these characteristics because they are denied access to European experience. Jane, on the other hand, reveals her readiness for a personal metamorphosis when she departs hurriedly for Europe and then refuses to return. Rumors of her flirtatiousness and willfulness signal the new freedom from constricting American mores that Europe confers on her, and the narrator's speculation that she has undergone a second youth, or rebirth, in Europe is perfectly in keeping with James's own belief in the cultural and imaginative limitations that American culture imposes.

The theme of aging is closely connected to the theme of Europe in this story, for the narrator's continued focus on the physical and psychological ages of the Rimmle women is one aspect of the American-European dynamic. Mrs. Rimmle, who in her youth had the benefit of a European tour, achieves a preternatural old age that appears to drain the very life out of her daughters, except for Jane, who takes advantage of Europe's rejuvenating powers and apparently does not age like her sisters. Just as America represents the stultifying, self-sacrificing, life-denying power of a culture that is afraid of freedom, Europe symbolizes an escape from the limitations of American experience, an expansive, imaginative stage on which to transform oneself. It seems inevitable that after Becky dies, Maria will slowly sicken and die, while their mother lives to an unheard-of old age and the adventurous Jane flourishes in European capitals.

At an early age James felt the need to escape from what he saw as the cultural provinciality of American society, and although his fiction often depicts Europeans in a less than favorable light, Europe always represents greater self-knowledge and personal growth for his characters. "Europe" is a tale of what its author most feared might have happened to him had he not chosen to live in Europe; the narrator's identification and approval of Jane's choice are also James's.

*Style and Technique*

James is justly famous for his innovations in fictional style and technique, but both these aspects of his work make his writing difficult for the beginning reader. This is particularly true if the work, like "Europe," is written in the "late style," which he developed during the final phase of his writing career. His long and complex sentences contain many embedded clauses and frequently use a periodic structure that delays meaning until the end of the sentence. Such a style provides a challenge for the reader, who also must deal with the ironic, detached tone of many of his narrators.

The narrator of "Europe" is an excellent example of James's style. He is clearly a cultivated, fastidious, and perceptive man; his choice of language and attitude toward the tale he relates are ironic and distanced. He is not an actual part of the story, a fact that enables him to maintain his distance at all times. Indeed, much of the story is told to him by his sister-in-law, a device that creates another barrier between him and the Rimmles and helps to keep the reader from becoming emotionally involved in the story. James enjoys using narrators who have only partial knowledge of the story they tell, limiting the reader to the narrator's perspective and filtering all aspects of the story through the narrator's consciousness. The result is that the narrator's version of the tale becomes as important as the actual persons and events that are described. A close reading of "Europe" reveals perhaps more about the narrator than it does about the Rimmles, a result that James sought in his fiction.

"Europe" also illustrates another important characteristic of James's fiction in its focus on the psychological reality of its characters. Early in his career James abandoned the traditional dependence of fiction on plotted narrative, substituting instead a reliance on the mental and emotional responses of characters. "Europe" has virtually no plot; the events of the story are simply several brief encounters between the Rimmles and the narrator over a period of years. The focus of the story is the narrator's perception of the psychological states of the Rimmles and the changes that take place in them over the years. Like many of James's narrators, he has an almost voyeuristic curiosity about the people around him, a curiosity that enables him to penetrate the psyches of the Rimmles and reward the reader with insights into their psychological reality. It is always the case, however, that several readings of James's work may be needed in order to appreciate the complex artistry of his style and technique, for no aspect of James's fiction is accidental; every phrase, nuance, and irony is consciously crafted.

*Angela Hague*

# THE EVE OF THE SPIRIT FESTIVAL

*Author:* Lan Samantha Chang (1965-    )
*Type of plot:* Ghost story
*Time of plot:* The 1980's through the early 1990's
*Locale:* New York City
*First published:* 1995

> *Principal characters:*
> CLAUDIA, the narrator
> EMILY, her older sister
> HER FATHER ("BABA"), who dies and appears as a ghost
> HER MOTHER, who died when her children were young
> BRAD DELMONTE, head of the father's chemistry department

*The Story*

"The Eve of the Spirit Festival" is a tightly constructed ghost story about two young Chinese American women dealing with the death of their parents. When they are little, their mother dies, forever changing their relationship with their father as they grow up. Once they have become young adults, his death and reappearance as a ghost to the older sister brings the story to a striking close.

The story opens as the girls' mother, who has died from an unspecified illness, has been cremated as part of a Buddhist ceremony. Sitting on the living-room floor of their modest apartment, the narrator, six-year-old Claudia, is comforted by her eleven-year-old sister, Emily. The older daughter is furious at what she sees as her father's tardiness in turning to Western medical treatment and blames him for the death of their mother. As her father enters, Emily ridicules his Chinese customs of mourning the dead by burning paper money for their ghosts and makes him go away.

After forty-nine days of mourning, even their father stops going to the Buddhist temple in their New York City neighborhood. Their mother never appears as a ghost to her children, as Chinese legends say she might. Their father, who has been inviting colleagues to his apartment in order to advance in his career as a university chemist, resumes this practice. He asks his daughters to serve food and drinks to people such as his boss Brad Delmonte, who shows a vague sexual interest in Emily, but she hates the man. Emily promises Claudia that she will leave their father when she turns eighteen.

Four to five years later, the girls' father asks Emily not to go out with her friends on the eve of Gujie, the Chinese spirit festival, when ancestral ghosts are said to visit their surviving family members, who should stay at home to see them. Emily asks Claudia to trim her hair for a night out and defies her father by leaving. Distraught, the father tells Claudia that Delmonte has passed him over for a promotion and that he will no longer socialize with his colleagues. He returns with an urn and lights some incense to protect Emily while she is away from home that night.

Eventually, Emily moves out and graduates from college in California, while Claudia stays home and attends Columbia University. Claudia is a sophomore when she comes home to find that her father has had a stroke. She comforts her father and calls an ambulance, and he asks her to call Emily. Their father dies that night in the hospital, before Emily arrives. Their father is cremated, and Emily decides not to have a Buddhist ceremony but allows only a small reception at their apartment. This is attended by their father's colleagues and two of his Chinese students, who tell Emily that tonight is Gujie again. When the guests leave, Emily asks Claudia to cut her hair really short, in defiance of Chinese beliefs in luscious hair as an ancestral gift, and she obliges. That night, while sleeping in her old bed next to Claudia's, Emily sees the ghost of her father, although Claudia does not share this experience.

*Themes and Meanings*

As a ghost story, "The Eve of the Spirit Festival" derives much of its force from the intergenerational conflict of Chinese American immigrants. For children such as Emily and Claudia, China is associated with a rich lore and belief in the supernatural that pervade the religious, cultural, and social traditions that make up a significant part of their parents' world. In contrast, the United States offers more personal freedom, but also a more impersonal worldview.

At first, the girls' father tries to live according to his beliefs and customs and tries to raise his family according to old precepts and to pass down his heritage to his two daughters. However, the crisis symbolized by the untimely death of the girls' mother challenges their father's strategy. The story never reveals whether the mother could have actually been saved if she had been sent to a hospital sooner. However, the pain that Emily feels at losing her mother finds a ready outlet when she blames her father's ways for her death. The fact that her mother's ghost does not appear to her as foretold by her parents' beliefs serves as a ready proof for the superiority of her seemingly more rational attitude of rejecting religion. However, this view alone is not specific to her situation. The crisis of faith in face of unwarranted personal disaster, such as a parent's tragic death, is also a theme of some universal significance.

The story implies that Emily subconsciously tests the powers of the old beliefs when she continues to defy their rules. Nothing happens to her when she goes out during Gujie. Once she turns eighteen, she can leave home against her father's wishes, and nothing disastrous comes of it. Even cutting her hair does not bring forth ancestral retribution. Only at the end does the story reveal how much Emily is still a child of her parents' culture and religion. It is her, and not the dutiful Claudia, who is visited by her father's ghost. In Chinese custom, ghosts appear to those with whom they have some unfinished business.

Before this dramatic conclusion, Emily has never had a chance to express the double theme of the story: her great, desperate love for her parents and her initial willingness to give tradition a chance. Ironically, Emily rebels because she loves her parents so much. She had wanted her mother to get better but was frustrated by her death in spite of the use of traditional Chinese medicine. She resents her father's friendly treatment of his colleagues when she realizes that they do not treat the Chinese American scientist as their equal. This lingering discrimination is not gratuitous on the part of the author; Eric Liu, in his nonfiction work *The Accidental Asian: Notes of a Native Speaker* (1998), noted that his father suffered in a similar matter.

Emily tries to become the stereotypical American teenager and career woman, but the story suggests that what she really wants is for her parents to be accepted and successful as well. When she defies her religion and her father's ways, Emily reacts against the fact that these things seem to hinder Chinese immigrants in the United States. She senses that no matter how hard her father tries to assimilate, he will still be rejected by people such as Delmonte. When her father's ghost visits Emily, she is given a chance to come to terms with her dual identity.

*Style and Technique*

Telling the ghost story from the limited point of view of the younger daughter, Claudia, allows Lan Samantha Chang to keep the reader guessing at some of the reasons behind Emily's rage at their father and her apparently cruel defiance of him. It also keeps her a bit remote and mysterious, quite befitting to a ghost story. What drives Emily is revealed only gradually, and sometimes implicitly, through Claudia's own musings and the unfolding of the plot.

From its first sentence, the story introduces the world of the Chinese American characters through Chang's masterful control of the language used by her narrator. Claudia tells of the family's Buddhist beliefs and practices in a straightforward, descriptive manner. This form of narration makes ceremonies and religious objects such as chanting and incense look self-evident and normal, despite many readers' unfamiliarity with them. Claudia's narrative also uses specific metaphors that show how deeply she has internalized the Chinese part of her heritage. She likens the stiffness of Emily and her body to that of temple gods and wonders about a secret charm emanating from her sister while she is present in Claudia's daily life.

The dialogue captures the immediate feelings of the characters. In the kitchen with Claudia, Emily cruelly exaggerates their father's Chinese accent to show how unlikely he is to be accepted as equal by his colleagues. There are detailed descriptions of objects with significance for the story, such as Emily's hair.

With remarkable narrative economy, Chang tells a meaningful short story in only eleven pages. From the first to the second death, some thirteen years, key episodes are visited that lead to the climax. The plot follows an interesting doubling, with relevant variations. Two parents die, yet only one reappears to one of the two daughters. Two parties are described, one during and one after the father's earthly life. Emily's hair gets cut twice, both times on Gujie, but with different results. When the father's ghost appears, it is only to Emily. Troubled by love and self-doubt, she needs a second chance to find closure with him and all that he represents.

*R. C. Lutz*

# EVELINE

*Author:* James Joyce (1882-1941)
*Type of plot:* Naturalistic
*Time of plot:* 1900
*Locale:* Dublin
*First published:* 1904

> *Principal characters:*
> EVELINE HILL, a nineteen-year-old Dublin shopgirl
> FRANK, her fiancé, a man who has seen the world and wants to take Eveline with him to Buenos Aires
> MR. HILL, her father, a drunk who forbids her to see Frank
> HARRY HILL, her brother, in the church-decorating business

*The Story*

The story, a psychological study in frustration, is about a young woman who longs to escape from the tyranny of her father and from the responsibilities of surrogate motherhood, thrust on her after the death of her own mother. When she is offered an avenue of escape, she discovers that she lacks the spirit, the courage, and the strength of character to take it.

Although only nineteen years old, Eveline Hill lives in the past, her mind occupied with the way things "used to be" as she sits by the window of her father's house. The world around her has changed, just as the neighborhood has changed. A land developer from Belfast has constructed brick houses on the field where "other people's children" used to play. One of the children who used to play there is now dead, and others have left the area; some have even left the country. Eveline remains. Her brother Ernest, who was "too grown up" to play, is now dead, as is her mother. Her father has turned to drink and is given to violence, particularly on Saturday nights.

Eveline works as a shopgirl at "the Stores," earning a miserable seven shillings a week, which are then given over to her father. She promised her dying mother that she would "keep the house together," rearing the two younger children and contending with her father's bad temper and the drinking that has worsened since her mother's death. She dreams of escaping the dull, routine existence that circumstances have forced on her.

Eveline meets a young man named Frank, who has sailed around the world and represents a means of escape for her. He wants to marry her and take her with him to Buenos Aires, halfway around the world from Ireland. Although she has accepted his offer of marriage and he has arranged her passage by ship, she has second thoughts on the day of her scheduled departure. At first her misgivings at home are centered on a remembrance of her past, as she sits by the window, clutching the letters that she has prepared for her father and brother in order to explain her departure. At the end of the story, she discovers that she is in fact unwilling and unable to leave Ireland. She is a captive of the past; she has no future; finally, she cannot leave.

## Themes and Meanings

If what James Joyce intended to demonstrate in all the stories in *Dubliners* (1914) was the squalor and spiritual impoverishment of typical Irish lives, then "Eveline" is unquestionably in keeping with this general intent. Although still a young woman, Eveline dwells on the past, on the debilitating nostalgia of how things were when her mother was still alive and when her father was "not so bad." She takes solace in childhood memories, dwelling on playmates and siblings who are now either dead or gone. She cannot fully imagine a future away from her family, her neighborhood, or her nation, and when it comes time for her to take her life into her own hands, she is paralyzed and unable to act.

The theme of escape will be a familiar one for those who have read Joyce's semiautobiographical novel, *A Portrait of the Artist as a Young Man* (1916) or its earlier and even more personalized version, *Stephen Hero* (1944), written between 1904 and 1906 and ultimately published as a fragment after Joyce's death. "Eveline," also written in 1904, was inspired by one of the writer's neighbors when the Joyce family lived at 17 North Richmond Street in Dublin. Eveline Thornton, the daughter of Ned Thornton, fell in love with a sailor, whom she married and with whom she ultimately set up housekeeping in Dublin, according to Richard Ellmann, Joyce's biographer. Not only did the prototypical Eveline marry her sailor, but also her mother outlived her. Joyce was writing fiction, however, not biography, and the principal difference seems to be that the husband and wife who served as Joyce's models both ended up being trapped in Dublin.

Joyce turns the sailor into a romantic exile, one who has seen the world and has chosen to live far from Dublin. In other words, Frank in the story becomes a reflection of the young Joyce himself. For Joyce, any young Irishman had to choose between living a life of limited opportunity in Ireland and having to scale down one's expectations, adjusting to the dismal realities and traditions of Irish life, or going out into the world beyond Ireland, which Joyce saw as a world of opportunity and promise.

Buenos Aires, then, represents the ideal of escaping Ireland, of making a clean break with one's nation and family ties, the sort of break that Joyce's own wife, Nora, would make in 1904 when she left her family to go with the writer to Paris. Just as Joyce's *A Portrait of the Artist as a Young Man* romanticizes, with ironic embellishment, the escape of a young man from Ireland, so "Eveline" extends the theme of escape to the case of a young woman who is not nearly so sophisticated as the protagonist of Joyce's novel and who might understandably fear the unknown world that awaits her.

The plight that is described in this story, that of a young woman, overworked and harried by her attempts to hold her family together, Joyce could have observed at home by watching his own long-suffering and tolerant mother, and by also observing the families of his friends and acquaintances. In the story, Eveline is relatively young but is "tired," worn down, old before her time, and very much a captive of routine, conditioned by her father's tyrannical ways. She is offered a means of escape and self-fulfillment, but it is not in her nature, finally, to accept it. She is given a choice between life and a sort of metaphoric death: a new life abroad, or a living death in Ireland, tending after a dying family that, presumably, no longer needs her (even though her father, who is "becoming old," depends on her and for that reason "would miss her"), and working in a demeaning and subordinate position at "the Stores."

*Style and Technique*

"Eveline" is an example of naturalistic fiction in which the protagonist, described at one point as a "helpless animal," responds to internal anxieties and environmental forces, particularly the influences of family life and the responsibilities to which she has been conditioned, and of a working life in Ireland, with its impoverishment, as Joyce imagined it. The way that "Eveline" and other stories of *Dubliners* reflect the details and concerns of everyday life closely observed and raised to significance through art suggests the influence of the Russian writer Anton Chekhov, but Ellmann notes in his biography *James Joyce* (1959) that Joyce claimed not to have read Chekhov at the time that he wrote those stories.

The purpose of Joyce's realistic fiction, however, was not simply the close observation of banal detail. The details are carefully crafted and arranged so as to accumulate in such a way as to give meaning to the story's climax, in keeping with the young writer's theory of the "epiphany." The progression is dramatic in Aristotelian terms, in that the central character is brought to a point of recognition and discovery, as suggested by Aristotle's *Poetics*. Eveline's self-discovery comes at the very end of the story. Her revelation is that she lacks the commitment and perhaps the courage to act on her dream of escape. When forced to choose between staying in Ireland and going to South America, she is also forced to confront her true feelings about Frank, who is "beyond the barrier" at that point, urging her to board the ship: "Her eyes gave him no sign of love or farewell or recognition." Eveline is reduced to a frightened, "helpless animal," as Joyce describes her at the end, who is incapable of exploring "another life with Frank."

*James M. Welsh*

# EVENING IN PARIS

*Author:* Denise Chávez (1948-      )
*Type of plot:* Domestic realism
*Time of plot:* 1960
*Locale:* Southern New Mexico
*First published:* 1986

> *Principal characters:*
> THE NARRATOR, a young girl
> HER MOTHER, a schoolteacher
> HER SISTER

*The Story*

With only three shopping days left before Christmas, the narrator is in a Woolworth's store wondering what to buy her mother. She wants something special. What most appeals to her are the dark blue bottles of Evening in Paris perfume. The cosmetic counter entrances her, although she feels inadequate before its shining glass cases, with their mysterious scents and images of womanhood, and she feels awkward and intimidated by the saleslady. "What help is there for three-dollar realities?" she thinks to herself. Her voice falters as she asks for her treasure, a gift-wrapped package of Evening in Paris cologne and bath water. She considers it her best gift ever to her mother and knows that her mother will like it.

Most of the gifts under the family Christmas tree are from her mother's students. The narrator watches her open them and knows that most of the presents will go into a gift box to be given to others the next year. As the girl waits for her mother to open her special present, she reflects on the passage of seasons, on growth and change, on the special smells and foods of Christmastime, and on the things in her mother's house. Her sister is disappointed that the bright package is not for her. The sister's gift is one that their mother gave the narrator to give to her, a red wallet with a picture of Jesus on it. With eager anticipation, the narrator asks her mother to open the midnight-blue package that she has carefully wrapped in white tissue paper. Her mother says yes, but instead stoops to pick up some stray wrapping paper.

Later it occurs to the narrator that perhaps her mother thought the Evening in Paris gift set was from one of her students. It remains unopened and unused. Maybe her mother prefers her usual Tabu perfume, the narrator thinks, although her mother does use the Avon perfume that a student has given to her.

The narrator feels unfulfilled, empty, inadequate. This attitude continues to haunt her years later, after she has gone to Paris and seen its dark and sad aspects, rather than the romanticized and illusionary world of Eiffel Tower postcards. However, the Paris of magic and lights exists too, she believes.

The following Christmas, the narrator's mother gives her the wallet with Christ's picture; she has forgotten that she used it for the narrator's present to her sister the year before and that her sister put it in the general gift box for other occasions. The wallet reminds the narrator of the previous year, and she thinks her mother perhaps had as little need for perfume on the dusty school playgrounds as the narrator had of a wallet. As the story ends, she stares at the picture on the red wallet, a reproduction of a popular painting of Jesus. She muses that it is a handsome Jesus, one that anyone could love, with his long brown curls and beard, and his deep-set eyes staring out.

*Themes and Meanings*

The most obvious theme of Denise Chávez's "Evening in Paris" relates to the disappointment that the young girl feels after wanting so much to please her mother with a special gift. Her mother scarcely notices the present, even when the narrator eagerly asks her to open it. The present is put in a box with other unwanted items to be given to others during the coming year. The mother never acknowledges the gift from her daughter. She shows no recognition of the love that her daughter feels for her, or the financial and emotional sacrifice that accompanied the material gift. The gift's giver is rejected. The disappointment is especially sharp because it is her own mother whom she dearly loves who ignores her.

The boxed set of cologne and bath water strongly appeals to the narrator; it connotes glamour and the allure of a romantic womanhood yet to be. It appeals to her sister as well, but it clearly does not to the mother, who uses a more expensive scent, Tabu. The mother, however, uses the Avon perfume from a student, a perfume that costs less than Tabu but more than Evening in Paris. The mother clearly judges the Evening in Paris according to her own standards of taste and value, not according to what it means to her daughter. Ironically, the mother does not use a similar criteria of value in giving gifts; she takes items from the unwanted discards to pass out to others, forgets where they came from, and seems to have no concern about whether or not a recipient will like the gift.

The mother also fails to understand that her daughter is on the brink of becoming a young woman, moving from childhood into the stage where she is entranced by the bright cosmetic counter, but still feels shy and out of place before the mysteries of womanhood. The narrator's attention to the various items on her mother's shelf and her listing of several women who had worked in their home as maids reinforce the theme that she is struggling to understand her own place in the world of women. The references to the picture of a handsome Jesus on the wallet suggest that the narrator is moving toward a realm of sexual development in which the emphasis is often on worldly love and outer appearances.

The narrator's mention that years later she traveled to Paris and saw the harsh realism of the city shows that she keeps with her the hard truths that she learned that Christmas as a girl. Gifts—perhaps including Christ's gifts of spiritual love and sacrifice—are not always appreciated or even recognized. Much of life is a series of giving up hopes and illusions. However, the Paris of lights and magic exists, the narrator claims. One must not despair or let the mundane cancel out the beauty. Everywhere there is change and movement toward growth, which offer the opportunity for a higher quality of existence than merely being lured by perfumes and romanticized illusions. The mother fails to notice her daughter's love or even her physical growth. The narrator learns that others often do not react as they should, but the brightest soul is the one that reaches out to others, even without reward.

### Style and Technique

"Evening in Paris" is one of a series of stories in Chávez's *The Last of the Menu Girls* (1986), which together tell the autobiographical history of a protagonist named Rocio Esquibel. Throughout this collection, as Rocio moves from a girl to a young woman, she struggles to understand herself and her relationship to the people around her. The central metaphor of the collection is her home, which expands to the Hispanic community in which she lives in southern New Mexico. It is here that she develops her caring and compassion for others, even for those who do not always respond with love toward her. Rocio decides that she will become a writer and tell their stories as well as her own. She is especially interested in women and the roles that society places on them and wants to write about their lives.

In "Evening in Paris," the narrator's name does not appear. Most of the story focuses on Christmas, 1960, when she is about eleven years old, and is told through the young girl's interior monologue as though she were in the present. The narrative voice shifts, however, as she tells about going to Paris years later and her associations with the Evening in Paris gift that she gave to her mother. It is clear at this point that the narrative voice is of someone older and less naïve than the eleven-year-old girl who loved the bright blue wrapping and the scent of the cologne that her mother ignored. In this story of loss, the adult narrator still believes in a transcendent goodness that goes beyond the response of others. The adult narrator accepts loss, but still believes there is a way to create beauty and to find light and magic in this fallen world.

*Lois A. Marchino*

# AN EVENING PERFORMANCE

*Author:* George Garrett (1929-    )
*Type of plot:* Sketch
*Time of plot:* The mid-twentieth century
*Locale:* The rural southern United States
*First published:* 1959

### Principal characters:

STELLA, a high diver and a mute
A LAME MAN, who accompanies her
ANGEL, a young girl who accompanies Stella and the lame man
A MERCHANT, a local man who sponsors Stella's performance

## The Story

This brief story opens with a description of the promised performance: High atop a tower rising to the clouds stands a plump woman in a spangled bathing suit, poised to plunge into the flaming tub far below. Posters bearing this picture proclaim that "ONE OF THE FABULOUS WONDERS OF MODERN TIMES/ STELLA THE HIGH DIVER" will dive one hundred feet into a "FLAMING CAULDRON." The posters appear suddenly; some are torn down by grumbling citizens and police officers; a few remain for several weeks, silently enticing the residents of the quiet rural town.

Then, one cool and gray October evening, a battered truck parks at the local fairground, and a sagging army-surplus tent rises beside it. Three people have come in the truck: a limping man; a little girl named Angel, shining always in white and unbelievably clean; and a broad, sturdy, red-haired woman who smiles uncomprehendingly and speaks only with her hands. The man does his trading in the town, whose residents watch the family curiously for several days. One morning, the lame man begins to build what appears to be a drilling derrick on the center of the field. Local men gather to watch the stranger working furiously, and the local police officer asks what he is doing. Curtly, the lame man responds that he is building a tower for Stella's dive. On being told that he must purchase a twenty-five-dollar permit to produce an exhibition, the man falls still. As he prepares to admit defeat, a local merchant offers to buy the license for him in exchange for half the profits from ticket sales. The lame man grudgingly agrees and schedules the show for the following evening if the weather is good.

By midafternoon of the following day, the lame man has finished preparations for the evening's performance. Then, a wind rises, bringing rain; the tall, rickety tower sways in the wind. However, wet weather does not keep away the crowd. At dark, a large crowd gathers in a ring around the tower, but Stella refuses to carry out her dive. The merchant, when informed of her unwillingness, insists that she dive despite the risky conditions. Declaring that there must be a trick to the dive, the merchant dismisses danger. The lame man explains simply that the dive is no trick; it is quite dangerous, and Stella hates doing it. On hearing this, the merchant asks in exasperation why they put up posters, build towers, and sell tickets. Because someone must, is the lame man's reply. The merchant gives him five minutes to begin the show.

The lame man turns on the lights around the tower, and Stella appears before the crowd, walks to the foot of the tower, and takes hold of the rope ladder. The lame man addresses the crowd, introducing the woman and explaining that her performance is not magical or mysterious, but based on skill; anyone with "the heart and the skill and the nerve" can do the same. Stella's dive will be "proof of the boundless possibility of all mankind." She climbs the rope ladder to the top of the tower and unfastens and tosses down the rope. As the tower moves in the wind, she signals to the man, who lights the gasoline on the water in the tub below. As he does so, she jumps. She seems to hang gracefully in the air before sliding smoothly into the fiery water. The crowd waits quietly, and she emerges from the water smiling and unhurt. She returns to the tent, followed by the lame man and the merchant. The merchant complains that the brief show seems hardly worth the fifty cents each member of the crowd paid. The lame man responds that Stella's risking her life ought to be enough for one evening; the crowd should be pleased. After failing to change the lame man's mind, the merchant takes his share of the profits and leaves. The crowd departs also.

The next day, all traces of the three strangers are gone, but the memory of the evening performance haunts the small town long afterward. Preachers denounce it, and storytellers embroider on it. A crippled old man says that it was bad for the people because it made them sophisticated, dissatisfied with common marvels. Then the narrative voice, which has recounted only an objective view until now, takes on omniscience and agrees with the old man, who could not even imagine the dreams of unfortunate women now smilingly dreaming of diving from a high tower into a pool of flame.

## Themes and Meanings

The epigraph to George Garrett's short-story collection *In the Briar Patch* (1961), in which "An Evening Performance" is the final story, contains two scriptural passages, the first from Isaiah, and the second from Hebrews:

We roar all like bears, and mourn sore like doves; we look for judgement, but there is none; for salvation, but it is far off from us.

Let brotherly love continue.
Be not forgetful to entertain strangers: for thereby some have entertained angels unawares.

Garrett, a southern writer with a firm Christian understanding of the world, often deals with religious themes in his poetry, novels, and short stories. In "An Evening Performance," Garrett has combined the values of this Christian vision with the regional setting common to his earlier works to produce a short story with a parabolic quality.

The poster that appears at the beginning of the story heralds a coming wonder and is soon followed by the mysterious appearance of three strange travelers who remain curiously aloof from the townspeople. In appearance, the three are far from average: The man limps; the child with the beautifully pure features, Angel, is radiant in her starched white dress (kept oddly fresh and clean despite a nomadic existence); and the strange-looking woman cannot speak. They are not received kindly by the native residents, who hinder and challenge them in their efforts to mount the performance.

The lame man's explanation of why he and Stella, despite her hatred of the dive, continue to travel and perform clearly points toward the lesson that Stella's dive holds: Someone must bring to the lives of ordinary people the possibility of great deeds. As the lame man tells the crowd, anyone—with courage and skill and will—can perform a feat such as Stella's. The merchant's petty reaction to Stella's performance indicates his misunderstanding of the value of life itself; in his obsession with the temporal, he cannot appreciate the spiritual. Still, the performance leaves its mark on the town. With a narrow vision typical of restrictive, organized religion, local ministers decry the strangers' show as the work of the devil. The egocentric drunkards and tellers of tales use the performance as a backdrop for stories of themselves and thereby render themselves trivial.

One "wise man," notably a man with a physical deformity, dimly realizes the true nature of the performance; it was an occurrence that eclipsed the rest of life for the townspeople. No ordinary, safe marvels will satisfy them now. In the end, only the understanding narrator can point out the truly lasting effect of the performance; in their dreams, those who grow older and know no love may see themselves as capable of an act of greatness. The townspeople, like the speakers in the passage from Isaiah, look for judgment and salvation but cannot see the way to either. They have seen among them an Angel and did not understand what they saw. Some needful few, however, retain the vision of the performance; they sleep contentedly with the knowledge that they, too, possess those qualities that allowed Stella to dive gracefully from a great height into the lake of flame.

*Style and Technique*

Although "An Evening Performance" possesses enough development of plot and character to be classified as a short story rather than a vignette, it may be referred to fairly as a sketch. As the title indicates, the story focuses on a single event, one evening's performance; all delineation of characters, all lines of action lead toward the one moment that is the heart of the story. In pointing his reader toward that moment and the lesson contained in it, Garrett writes in the style of the poet that he is. He counters richly evocative language with sparely outlined action.

The story begins with the fiery image of the poster, and as time passes the image dims, "teased by the wind and weather, faded by the still summer-savaged sun and the first needling rains of autumn, the red letters blurring and dribbling away, fuzzy now as if they had been written by a shaking finger in something perishable like blood." When the three people suddenly appear in town, their images rise suddenly in the story, but the reader receives a description of them that seems merely physical, the recollected observations of a narrator who was witness to the scene. The characters remain nameless with the exception of the presciently named Stella (meaning "star") and Angel. Clearly, the reader must derive his or her understanding of the story's events from the descriptive details that the narrator supplies.

The performance itself is the point toward which the narrator is always working. The relating of the act takes only a few pages, but those few paragraphs contain more specifically recounted actions than any other part of the story. Following the performance, the narrator describes local reaction summarily and focuses on a detailed vision, which he projects into the imagination of faceless local women who possess true understanding of the performance's purpose. They see themselves descending in triumph from a "topless tower into a lake of flame."

*Beverly A. Findley*

# EVERYDAY USE

*Author:* Alice Walker (1944-      )
*Type of plot:* Social realism
*Time of plot:* The late 1960's
*Locale:* Rural Georgia
*First published:* 1973

*Principal characters:*
THE NARRATOR, a middle-aged black woman
MAGGIE, her younger daughter
DEE, her older daughter
DEE'S MALE COMPANION

## The Story

"Everyday Use" is narrated by a woman who describes herself as "a large, big-boned woman with rough, man-working hands." She has enjoyed a rugged farming life in the country and now lives in a small, tin-roofed house surrounded by a clay yard in the middle of a cow pasture. She anticipates that soon her daughter Maggie will be married and she will be living peacefully alone.

The story opens as the two women await a visit from the older daughter, Dee, and a man who may be her husband—her mother is not sure whether they are actually married. Dee, who was always scornful of her family's way of life, has gone to college and now seems almost as distant as a film star; her mother imagines being reunited with her on a television show such as "This Is Your Life," where the celebrity guest is confronted with her humble origins. Maggie, who is not bright and who bears severe burn scars from a house fire many years before, is even more intimidated by her glamorous sibling.

To her mother's surprise, Dee arrives wearing an ankle-length, gold and orange dress, jangling golden earrings and bracelets, and hair that "stands straight up like the wool on a sheep." She greets them with an African salutation, while her companion offers a Muslim greeting and tries to give Maggie a ceremonial handshake that she does not understand. Moreover, Dee says that she has changed her name to Wangero Leewanika Kemanjo, because "I couldn't bear it any longer, being named after the people who oppress me." Dee's friend has an unpronounceable name, which the mother finally reduces to "Hakim-a-barber." As a Muslim, he will not eat the pork that she has prepared for their meal.

Whereas Dee had been scornful of her mother's house and possessions when she was younger (even seeming happy when the old house burned down), now she is delighted by the old way of life. She takes photographs of the house, including a cow that wanders by, and asks her mother if she may have the old butter churn whittled by her uncle; she plans to use it as a centerpiece for her table. Then her attention is captured by two old handmade quilts, pieced by Grandma Dee and quilted by the mother and her own sister, known as Big Dee. These quilts have already been promised to Maggie, however, to take with her into her new marriage. Dee is horrified: "Maggie can't appreciate these quilts!" she says, "She'd probably be backward enough to put them to everyday use."

Although Maggie is intimidated enough to surrender the beloved quilts to Dee, the mother feels a sudden surge of rebellion. Snatching the quilts from Dee, she offers her instead some of the machine-stitched ones, which Dee does not want. Dee turns to leave and in parting tells Maggie, "It's really a new day for us. But from the way you and Mama still live you'd never know it." Maggie and her mother spend the rest of the evening sitting in the yard, dipping snuff and "just enjoying."

*Themes and Meanings*

The central theme of the story concerns the way in which an individual understands his present life in relation to the traditions of his people and culture. Dee tells her mother and Maggie that they do not understand their "heritage" because they plan to put "priceless" heirloom quilts to "everyday use." The story makes clear that Dee is equally confused about the nature of her inheritance both from her immediate family and from the larger black tradition.

The matter of Dee's name provides a good example of this confusion. Evidently, Dee has chosen her new name ("Wangero Leewanika Kemanjo") to express solidarity with her African ancestors and to reject the oppression implied by the taking on of American names by black slaves. To her mother, the name "Dee" is symbolic of family unity; after all, she can trace it back to the time of the Civil War. To the mother, these names are significant because they belong to particular beloved individuals.

Dee's confusion about the meaning of her heritage also emerges in her attitude toward the quilts and other household items. Although she now rejects the names of her immediate ancestors, she eagerly values their old handmade goods, such as the hand-carved benches made for the table when the family could not afford to buy chairs. To Dee, artifacts such as the benches or the quilts are strictly aesthetic objects. It never occurs to her that they, too, are symbols of oppression: Her family made these things because they could not afford to buy them. Her admiration for them now seems to reflect a cultural trend toward valuing handmade objects, rather than any sincere interest in her "heritage." After all, when she was offered a quilt before she went away to college, she rejected it as "old-fashioned, out of style."

However, a careful reading of the story will show that Dee is not the only one confused about the heritage of the black woman in the rural South. Although the mother and Maggie are skeptical of Dee, they recognize the limitations of their own lives. The mother has only a second-grade education and admits that she cannot imagine looking a strange white man in the eye. Maggie "knows she is not bright" and walks with a sidelong shuffle. Although their dispositions lead them to make the best of their lives, they admire Dee's fierce pride even as they feel the force of her scorn.

Taken as a whole, although the story clearly endorses the commonsense perspective of Dee's mother over Dee's affectations, it does not disdain Dee's struggle to move beyond the limited world of her youth. Clearly, however, she has not yet arrived at a stage of self-understanding. Her mother and sister are ahead of her in that respect.

*Style and Technique*

The thematic richness of "Everyday Use" is made possible by the flexible, perceptive voice of the first-person narrator. It is the mother's point of view that permits the reader's understanding of both Dee and Maggie. Seen from a greater distance, both young women might seem stereotypical—one a smart but ruthless college girl, the other a sweet but ineffectual homebody. The mother's close scrutiny redeems Dee and Maggie, as characters, from banality.

For example, Maggie's shyness is explained in terms of the terrible fire she survived: "Sometimes I can still hear the flames and feel Maggie's arms sticking to me, her hair smoking and her dress falling off her in little black papery flakes. Her eyes seemed stretched open, blazed open by the flames reflected in them." Ever since, "she has been like this, chin on chest, eyes on ground, feet in shuffle." In Dee's case, the reader learns that as she was growing up, the high demands she made of others tended to drive people away. She had few friends, and her one boyfriend "flew to marry a cheap city girl from a family of ignorant flashy people" after Dee "turned all her fault-finding power on him." Her drive for a better life has cost Dee dearly, and her mother's commentary reveals that Dee, too, has scars, though they are less visible than Maggie's.

In addition to the skillful use of point of view, "Everyday Use" is enriched by Alice Walker's development of symbols. In particular, the contested quilts become symbolic of the story's theme; in a sense, they represent the past of the women in the family. Worked on by two generations, they contain bits of fabric from even earlier eras, including a scrap of a Civil War uniform worn by Great Grandpa Ezra. The debate over how the quilts should be treated—used or hung on the wall—summarizes the black woman's dilemma about how to face the future. Can her life be seen as continuous with that of her ancestors? For Maggie, the answer is yes. Not only will she use the quilts, but also she will go on making more—she has learned the skill from Grandma Dee. For Dee, at least for the present, the answer is no. She would frame the quilts and hang them on the wall, distancing them from her present life and aspirations; to put them to everyday use would be to admit her status as a member of her old-fashioned family.

*Diane M. Ross*

# EVERYTHING IN THIS COUNTRY MUST

*Author:* Colum McCann (1965-    )
*Type of plot:* Regional, psychological
*Time of plot:* The late twentieth century
*Locale:* Northern Ireland
*First published:* 1999

> *Principal characters:*
> KATIE, a tall fifteen-year-old girl
> AN IRISH FARMER, her father
> HAYKNIFE, a British soldier with a scar
> STEVIE, a British soldier who frees the horse

## The Story

"Everything in This Country Must" is a first-person account related by fifteen-year-old Katie, who speaks in a voice that is at once straightforward and poetic. The story begins with Katie and her father working to pull their horse from a flooded river, in which one of its hooves is caught between rocks. Katie pulls on a rope to keep the horse's head above water while her father, who is smaller than she is and afraid of the river, dives beneath the surface to attempt to free the horse's trapped hoof. The threat of losing the Belgian mare carries special significance to her father because he has also lost his wife (called Mammy by Katie) and son Fiachra; later in the story it is revealed that they died after being hit by a British military truck.

When headlights appear in the distance, it appears that help has arrived in the form of a neighbor or friend; instead, the strangers' accents reveal them to be British, and their uniforms suggest that they are soldiers. The farmer's desire to rescue the horse seems to flag at this point, though the soldiers are eager to assist, even risking their lives to save the horse from drowning. When the soldiers treat Katie kindly, lending her a jacket and speaking to her with affection, her father responds by violently pushing one of them away and speaking rudely.

To help save the horse, the soldiers—assuming that the horse is more valuable than a hedge—drive their truck through the hedge, ignoring the protests of the farmer. After the destruction of the hedge, the farmer curses the soldiers and seems to be overcome with grief; the soldiers' easy, thoughtless destruction of the hedge clearly reminds him of the loss of his wife and son. In flashback, it is revealed that nobody was held legally responsible for their deaths.

At this point, the story jumps forward a few hours. The horse has been rescued and is being kept under heat lamps, and at Katie's invitation (and her father's reluctant agreement), the soldiers are enjoying tea in the family farmhouse. The girl describes her complicated tea-making ritual and the soldiers' amusement with it. One of the soldiers, Stevie, smiles repeatedly at her, and her father blanches with disapproval. Katie is confused by Stevie's behavior, even as she is attracted to him. The soldiers' behavior seems innocent, but her father acts as if they are making rude advances toward his daughter. Throughout the conversation, photographs of the dead mother and brother look down from the mantelpiece. When the farmer uses the curtain to dry Katie's hair because all of the towels have been used by the soldiers, the soldier Katie refers to as "Hayknife" offers his towel; her father rudely refuses, and the undercurrent of tension in the room erupts into angry shouting. While the farmer and Hayknife nearly come to blows, Katie sees Stevie looking at the photographs of her dead brother and mother and believes that he understands her father's fear and anger.

After the soldiers have driven away in their truck, the farmer leans his head on the mantelpiece near the photographs and cries. Then he fetches his hunting rifle and leaves the house. Katie hears three shots, and when her father returns to the house, she understands that he has shot his favorite draft horse as it lay under the heat lamps in the barn.

*Themes and Meanings*

Though at first "Everything in This Country Must" appears to be simply a story of rural life, it becomes clear as the history of the family tragedy is parceled out that the story's main theme is the tenuous relationship between the people of rural Northern Ireland and the British military forces that occupy the region. Notably, the story is not overtly political; neither side is praised or demonized. Colum McCann's concern is not with the political tensions in Northern Ireland but with their effects on individuals on both sides.

Katie's father is right to be distrustful of the British soldiers—there is a longstanding history of animosity between the predominantly Roman Catholic rural Northern Irish citizenry and the British soldiers who are charged with keeping the peace. Presumably, soldiers like these, in a truck similar to the one that they drive, accidentally killed the farmer's wife and son. Though his treatment of these soldiers is unfair, it is also understandable. His behavior embarrasses his daughter, but by providing the reader with a context for it in the family's tragic history, the author allows the reader to view her father with sympathy rather than judgment, even when he brutally shoots the horse everyone has worked so hard to save.

Katie, the narrator and protagonist, is clearly central to the story. She is fifteen years old and awkwardly tall. Her father is extremely aware of her fragile adolescent innocence and prepared to defend her against the threat he perceives in the soldiers. For her own part, Katie is clearly charmed by Stevie, the handsome and heroic soldier whose jacket shields her from the rain. She carefully counts the smiles with which he favors her and seems to wish that he would return for the jacket. A sheltered adolescent, she is experiencing feelings she probably has not dealt with before. She views the British soldiers not as her father does, as the brethren of the unwelcome intruders who killed Mammy and Fiachra, but as the heroic strangers who risked their lives to save her father's favorite horse.

The characterization of the soldiers themselves is particularly notable. It would have been easy for McCann to present them as faceless representatives of British authority. Instead, several of the soldiers are given individual characteristics and person-alities. They are under no obligation to stop and help save the horse, but in fact they seem eager to help. These men are human, however, not angels; they respond to the fa-ther's rudeness with human profanity and resentment.

The most difficult question facing the reader is the farmer's motivation for killing the horse. From the moment the soldiers appear on the scene, he seems reluctant to continue trying to save the horse. Based on his experience with the soldier whose carelessness behind the wheel killed half of his family and the legal system that exon-erated the killer, the father's resentment of the soldiers is so great that he would rather kill the horse than owe its life to them. To him, the horse is now unclean; he hopes at least to save his daughter from a similar defilement.

## Style and Technique

The poetic style of "Everything in This Country Must" is typical of McCann's fic-tion. The impressionistic nature of the first-person narrative gives the reader insight not only into the events of the story but also into the imagination, hopes, and dreams of the narrator. Much of her narration focuses on straightforward sensory information about sight, sounds, and sensations. Occasionally, however, an extremely poetic met-aphor or simile lifts the narrative far beyond the mundane reality being depicted.

Rather than being a linear rendering of historical events, the story's chronology re-flects the narrator's growing understanding of the psychological significance of the events as they affect her father. Although she mentions Mammy and Fiachra early on, the story of the accident that killed them both is not spelled out until much later in the narrative. Consequently, the sensitive reader notices the signals that suggest that there is more to the story than meets the eye and begins to reconstruct the story of the acci-dent that changed the family. The narrator's refusal to give a direct account of the two events with the most dramatic potential—the rescue of the horse from the river and the shooting of the horse in the barn at the story's end—suggests that the events have sig-nificance only in how they affect those who perceive them.

Another notable feature of the story is McCann's use of dialect. The rural Northern Ireland dialect of this story is rendered carefully and subtly. The dialect is discernable not in nonstandard spellings and dropped consonants, but rather in the cadence and syntax of the characters' speech (and of course the first-person narration). The En-glish dialect of the soldiers is easily identified because it stands out from the local dia-lect that surrounds it. This just one more way McCann reinforces the subtle web of tensions that connects everyone in the story.

*James S. Brown*

# EVERYTHING THAT RISES MUST CONVERGE

*Author:* Flannery O'Connor (1925-1964)
*Type of plot:* Realism
*Time of plot:* The 1950's
*Locale:* The urban South
*First published:* 1961

> *Principal characters:*
> JULIAN CHESTNY, the protagonist, a self-centered young man
> MRS. CHESTNY, his mother
> A BLACK WOMAN AND CHILD, bus passengers

*The Story*

A middle-aged working woman, the remnant of a once aristocratic, slaveholding family, prepares to go to her YWCA exercise class, recommended for her high blood pressure. She insists that her son accompany her on the bus, for she is afraid to ride the buses alone as they have become integrated. The young man, superficially educated in liberal ideas, is contemptuous of her racial bigotry and fancies himself vastly more enlightened and intellectual than she.

As the story opens, she is undecided as to whether she should wear the new green hat with the purple velvet flaps she has recently bought or take it back to the store. After all, that seven dollars and fifty cents would pay the gas bill. Julian, her son, whose viewpoint dominates the story, thinks the hat is hideous; nevertheless, he insists that she wear it to expedite their departure. His mother, still doubtful, says that at least she will not "meet herself coming and going"; that is, the hat establishes her uniqueness, as befits a lady of quality. The hat attains symbolic importance as an emblem of her true station in life when, much to her son's amusement, a huge black woman boards the bus with her small son and plops down in the seat facing her. The black woman is wearing the exact duplicate of his mother's absurd hat. Julian exults at this magnificent putdown, even though his mother's red face suggests a sudden rise in blood pressure.

His mother, however, seems to recover. She makes up to the little boy, with that peculiar combination of condescension and sentimentality that considers all small black children adorable. The black woman fairly bristles with suppressed anger as the dumpy little white woman fumbles in her purse for a nickel. Nemesis arrives when both women leave the bus and Julian's mother, unable to find a nickel, offers the boy a bright new penny. The black woman explodes with anger and swings at the white woman with her purse, knocking her down. Julian self-righteously berates his mother for her stupidity and insensitivity, even as she sits stricken on the pavement. His superiority and exasperation quickly crumble to infantile panic, however, when his mother shortly after dies of a stroke on the sidewalk.

## Themes and Meanings

This tragicomic tale of social bigotry and fake liberal sentiment is the title story of Flannery O'Connor's last collection of short stories, written before her untimely death at the age of thirty-nine. It displays the author's unique talent for ironic social commentary and grim humor.

With her consummate skill at revealing ordinary people with small minds, she reduces some of the traditional ingredients of southern fiction to the miniature, without sacrificing an iota of their reality. Generational conflict, racial confrontation, sudden death—they are all there, but stripped bare of any aura of honor and glory, displaying themselves either as tawdry and mean-spirited or as absurdly comic.

In spite of Mrs. Chestny's mental and moral limitations, she is a more sympathetic character than her son, and not simply because she, in one sense, dies for her sin of racial bigotry. Unlike her son, she entertains her mindless notions of social superiority without a trace of actual hypocrisy. She truly believes that she is a member of the upper classes, even as she endures and indeed enjoys her thoroughly middle-class struggle to make her own living and put her callow young prince through college. She has absorbed the middle-class work ethic as unconsciously as she internalized her forebears' pride of family, quite unaware of any contradiction of values. Moreover, before she dies, her stroke wipes out her adult memory and she resumes the innocence of childhood, perhaps an indication, if one considers O'Connor's predilection for themes of redemption, of a wiping out of sin along with memory.

Julian, on the other hand, pretends to the most enlightened democratic attitudes toward blacks, but has no real sympathy or understanding for them. He tries to show his intellectual sophistication by striking up conversations with prosperous looking blacks on the bus, a familiarity usually resented by the recipients of his unwanted attention. He does not realize that his behavior is probably perceived as being as condescending as his mother's giving pennies to black children. He daydreams of offering the ultimate insult to his mother by bringing home a beautiful black girl to marry. Indeed, most of his shallow liberality seems to stem from his resentment of his mother and the fact that they are poor.

Although his mother may chatter on complacently about the aristocratic old home of her childhood, it is Julian who looks back with longing to that time when birth, instead of personal effort, luck, character, or ability, established social status. Suspecting, correctly, that he has none of these qualities, he doubts that he can ever compete in a world where idle luxury is not his birthright.

O'Connor's stories are sometimes like Elizabethan secondary plots that provide comic relief for tragedy. The lowlife reenacts in miniature the sins of the tragic hero, such as Wagner dabbling irresponsibly in magic as his master, Dr. Faustus, consigns his soul to the devil.

The title comes from the Catholic philosopher Pierre Teilhard de Chardin, whom O'Connor admired. Teilhard de Chardin based his thought on the conception of evolution as the emergence and perfecting of consciousness. As consciousness becomes more clear in individuals, it projects itself toward some hypothetical maximum development that Teilhard de Chardin called the Omega point. Everything that rises in consciousness must converge in spiritual terms as it approaches nearer the Omega point, which is presumably the end of time. Teilhard de Chardin was trying to avoid a simple pantheistic mysticism in which individual egos simply dissolved again into the impersonal stuff of the universe. The superconsciousness developing at the Omega point is greater than its parts without extinguishing the consciousness of individual selves.

The implications of O'Connor's story are ambiguous with regard to Teilhard de Chardin's conception. One might argue that this ridiculous encounter between a person rising to the middle class and one sinking from aristocracy to that class has only comic overtones, suggesting the not especially lofty homogeneity of the new social order in the South. In this sense, the story may be a parody of Teilhard de Chardin's principle of spiritual convergence in the universe.

Considering O'Connor's propensities for religious themes, however, one suspects that she is suggesting some blundering advancement of consciousness even in such unlikely candidates for wisdom as these. Ironically, in the aging white woman, such purification of soul requires the wholesale wiping out of a lifetime of misinformation about social status and the basis of personal worth. What is left after her stroke is certainly a very immature soul, but one relieved of accumulated error. Meanwhile, her son is forced into the world of guilt and sorrow where he might outgrow his selfishness and accept responsibility for his destiny. This possibility for growth is all that O'Connor usually allows to her sadly human protagonists. She does not concern herself with saints.

### Style and Technique

Besides the creation of unusual symbols, such as the grotesque hat with one purple flap up and the other down, suggesting the social direction of the wearers, O'Connor is a master of dramatic irony. A paragraph of Julian's internal monologue characterizes not only Mrs. Chestny but also the jaded young man himself, who despises his mother for her unreal expectations and blames her for a social situation in which she must sacrifice herself for his welfare:

> She lived according to the laws of her own fantasy world, outside of which he had never seen her set foot. The law of it was to sacrifice herself for him after she had first created the necessity to do so by making a mess of things. If he had permitted her sacrifices, it was only because her lack of foresight had made them necessary. All of her life had been a struggle to act like a Chestny without the Chestny goods, and to give him everything she thought a Chestny ought to have; but because, said she, it was fun to struggle, why complain? And when you had won, as she had won, what fun to look back on the hard times! He could not forgive her that she had enjoyed the struggle and that she thought she had won.

Julian congratulates himself that he has cut himself emotionally free of his mother, as though filial love were some kind of character flaw. He also prides himself on his ability to face facts. His monumental ignorance and immaturity are swiftly brought to a climax in a few sentences, rapidly changing his mode of discourse to one character-istic of childhood. When his mother has a stroke, Julian finds himself "looking into a face he has never seen before."

> "Mother!" he cried. "Darling, sweetheart, wait!" Crumpling, she fell to the pavement. He dashed forward and fell at her side, crying, "Mamma, Mamma!" He turned her over. Her face was fiercely distorted. One eye, large and staring, moved slightly to the left as if it had become unmoored. The other remained fixed on him, raked his face again, found nothing and closed.

Only moments before, he had been flippantly lecturing his mother from his pose of wisdom: "From now on you've got to live in a new world and face a few realities for a change. Buck up . . . it won't kill you."

*Katherine Snipes*

# EXCERPTS FROM SWAN LAKE

*Author:* Peter Cameron (1959-      )
*Type of plot:* Psychological
*Time of plot:* A summer during the 1980's
*Locale:* Cheshire, Connecticut, and New York City
*First published:* 1985

> *Principal characters:*
> PAUL ANDREWS, the young narrator and protagonist
> NEAL, his lover
> MRS. ANDREWS, his grandmother

*The Story*

Paul and his lover Neal prepare dinner for Paul's grandmother in the suburban Connecticut home of Paul's parents. Paul and Neal have moved out of their New York apartment for the summer in order to take care of Mrs. Andrews while Paul's parents cruise around the world. They are interrupted in their work by a visit from a representative from Meals on Wheels—a woman whom Paul calls "Gloria Marsupial" because of his uncertainty about how to pronounce her name. The social services volunteer is disconcerted when Paul answers the door wielding a knife and when she sees the bare-chested, lacto-vegetarian Neal stirring mushroom curry in a wok. In order to make space in the refrigerator for the tray of meat loaf, green beans, and pudding that she has brought for Mrs. Andrews, she pushes aside the men's beer.

The Marsupial woman asks if Mrs. Andrews wants her blood pressure taken, but Paul's grandmother is more concerned about her unreliable memory. Her recollections are very selective. She can no longer identify lilacs and does not remember how many times she has been married, but she can vividly recall one girlhood summer that she spent on a farm. Her memories are triggered by such sensuous details as the sheer physical exuberance of running and the sight of a single mulberry blown into her bowl of mashed potatoes.

In this regard, Mrs. Andrews and Paul are alike. He, too, is engaged more by sensation than by interpretation, more by present experience than by conjecture over the past and the future. Paul is intoxicated by the combined redolence of curry and lilacs; he is made "dizzy" by smoking an occasional cigarette.

Below the surface of domestic routine, however, disharmony lurks. After Mrs. Andrews retires to her bedroom and Paul and his lover are left to rewash the dishes that she has imperfectly cleaned, Neal announces his intention of returning to their apartment in the city. Uncomfortable in this suburban home, he points to the predictable African violets on the windowsill to emphasize his sense of displacement. He is also unable to relax at night when he considers the possibility of the grandmother's confronting both men in bed. No one in the family, it seems, comprehends the true nature of their relationship.

A week after Neal returns to the city, Paul and his grandmother see a television commercial for a coming production of the ballet *Swan Lake*. Because of his grandmother's interest in ballet and her assertion that she has never been to a live performance, Paul purchases three tickets to commemorate her eighty-eighth birthday. Neal drives up from the city to attend the birthday dinner. Afterward, as he puts ice-cream cake back into the freezer, he expresses his fondness for Paul's grandmother and his wish that she knew that Paul and he are lovers.

Later, at the theater, Neal leaves during intermission, still bothered by Paul's apparent inability to see a problem in his refusal publicly to acknowledge his sexual orientation and their relationship. Meanwhile, Mrs. Andrews falls asleep in her seat. The story ends with Paul left to himself. Unamused by the dancing on stage, he is painfully conscious of the contrast between the grace and surety of Prince Siegfried and the Swan Queen and his own clumsiness in matters of the heart.

### Themes and Meanings

Peter Cameron's use in the title and narrative of his story of Peter Ilich Tchaikovsky's ballet *Swan Lake* (1877)—which is often performed in excerpts rather than in its entirety—provides the story's thematic frame of reference. Odette, the ballet's heroine, is a creature of two worlds. By day, she is queen of the swans; by night, she is simply a beautiful young woman. Paul's life is similarly divided between two spheres of existence. In the city, he is a gay man with a live-in lover; in the suburbs, he is a dutiful son and grandson. Like Odette's ill-fated duality, Paul's uneasy balance between two separate identities appears doomed to failure.

In *Swan Lake*, Odette seems to be more at home in the world of sky and water; in the world of humans, she is lost. Odette and her human lover Prince Siegfried are no match for the sorcery of the evil Von Rotbart, who schemes to thwart their romance. No such malevolent figure manipulates the destiny of Paul Andrews, but it can be said that his own maladroitness is the principal source of his problems.

Further textual resonance is derived from the fact that Tchaikovsky, who composed the music for *Swan Lake*, spent most of his adult life fearing that his homosexuality might become common knowledge. His was a closeted existence, akin to Paul's.

Another comparison between the world of ballet and the world of this story stems from their shared emphasis on nonverbal communication. In dance, performers communicate by physical gesture; so too does Paul express himself. When Mrs. Andrews admits that she and Paul had been lonely since Neal moved back to the city and subsequently defers to Paul for corroboration, her grandson remains mute. "I never admit to being lonely," he says. Instead, he communicates by touch. Paul holds hands with Neal or rests his feet on Neal's bare back. These are secretive gestures, however, which Paul hopes to conceal from others. "That's the problem," Neal asserts, Paul's inability to be open about their relationship.

However, romance is a major preoccupation of this tale. Paul's parents are away on a "romance cruise" to the "love capitals of the world." Mrs. Andrews seems fixated on the lilac, a shrub whose fragrant clusters of heart-shaped flowers the poet Walt Whitman used as an emblem of love. There also are, of course, the central emotional attachment between Paul and Neal and the referenced love between Odette and Prince Siegfried. This is an abiding theme in Cameron's fiction: the often ambiguous yearning for or the precarious maintenance of romance.

### Style and Technique

Creating carefully crafted stories that have been compared in subject matter and technique to the works of such modern American writers as Ann Beattie and David Leavitt, Cameron chronicles the lives of modern young people with an understated grace. He is a master of short witty sentences, such as clever correspondents write on postcards that they send from vacation spots. Indeed, the text of the card that Paul's mother sends from Greece is indistinguishable in shape and syntax from the wording of the main narrative.

There is a conscious spareness of language that may be accounted for, in part, by the inability of typical Cameron characters to explicate their feelings. Paul, for example, responds to Neal's discontent by admitting to himself, "I think about answering, but I can't." If he could give full voice to his feelings, perhaps he would say that what really matters is the moment itself as articulated by the senses. Paul tells his grandmother that it does not matter that she cannot remember what year it is or where she is. As each year follows the last, Mrs. Andrews seems to forget more and more; perhaps, thinks Paul, he himself will one day forget what he now thinks is most important. "Someday, I'll forget Neal, just like my grandmother has forgotten the great love of her life."

In acknowledgment of the unreliability of memory and the futility of forecasting the future, Paul leads a life that seems to demonstrate the value of the moment, an existence predicated on direct sensory experience. This may account for the almost lyrical moments in the text, such as when Paul imagines that he is on the balcony of a Mediterranean villa, and not in his parents' suburban kitchen.

Although some critics say that Cameron creates characters who are detached from the world around them, there is actually an exaggerated consciousness of external environment in the typical Cameron narrative. Much value is placed on trademarks and descriptive labels. Perhaps this excessive regard for brand names, such as "Players" cigarettes and "Hostess" cherry pies, and the impulse to enumerate objects, such as the grandmother's repeated queries regarding the identification of items in her immediate surroundings, are the means by which individuals stay connected to their environment and to each other. Specificity provides a sense of surety in a world where less and less is sure.

*S. Thomas Mack*

# EXCHANGE VALUE

*Author:* Charles Johnson (1948-    )
*Type of plot:* Psychological
*Time of plot:* 1980
*Locale:* Chicago
*First published:* 1981

> *Principal characters:*
> COOTER, the narrator, a young, unemployed African American man
> LOFTIS, his ambitious older brother
> ELNORA BAILEY, a neighbor woman

## The Story

Cooter and his brother Loftis break into the apartment of Elnora Bailey, an old black woman whose apartment is down their own hall. The woman has not been seen for a while, and although these two young men are not criminals by habit, they believe she will be an easy mark.

They find that Elnora, who is known around the neighborhood as a beggar, has been hoarding money and material things, including her own feces in coffee cans, for quite some time. They find her body, inflated in death, as well as close to $900,000 and additional wealth in the form of stocks and jewelry. They also discover many years' worth of old junk, including, most disturbing to Cooter, three portions of a tree. An old issue of the *Chicago Defender* tells them that she inherited most of her wealth from a former employer for whom she had worked as a maid.

Cooter urges his brother to forget the money and leave the things where they are, fearing they could be cursed. After Loftis dismisses his fears, the two set about moving everything valuable to their apartment. While they wonder what they should do with their haul, Cooter takes some money and goes on a shopping spree, buying himself new clothes. When he returns, Loftis has changed the locks and rigged a booby trap to protect their new things from anyone who would try to take them.

Loftis is angry that Cooter has spent $250 on clothing and warns him not to spend any more money until he, Loftis, returns from work. After Loftis leaves, the superintendent of the building discovers Elnora's dead body, and as she is being carried away, Cooter looks at her face and thinks that he can see there the poverty she dealt with for many years, and the way the money she unexpectedly inherited changed her. When Loftis does not return for four days, Cooter, obeying Loftis's command not to spend any more of the money, begs for food at a local diner, as Elnora once did.

When Loftis finally comes home, Cooter wants to confront him, but Loftis falls fast asleep. Cooter sees that Loftis has taped to a penny the message, "Found while walking down Devon Avenue." Seeing that Loftis has decided to hoard wealth like Elnora did, Cooter wonders if it has to be this way, but places this newfound penny with the rest of their wealth.

### Themes and Meanings

"Exchange Value" is the second story in Charles Johnson's collection of short stories, *The Sorcerer's Apprentice* (1986). One of the themes of "Exchange Value" concerns setting in motion forces that one cannot then control. Loftis is shown as an ambitious young man, who sews labels of expensive suit manufacturers into the suits he buys at discount clothing stores. When he finally obtains the material things he longs for, however, he is unable to deal with it.

Many of the stories in *The Sorcerer's Apprentice* deal with magic. In "Exchange Value," the transformational value of money as a universal value system that can put a number and a value on anything is presented as a powerful force, dangerously magical in quality, which spellbinds both Cooter and Loftis. Loftis reasons that the dollar value of the piano they push to their apartment is equal to that of two gold lamé suits, a trip to Tijuana, or twenty-five sexual encounters with a prostitute. Like wizards, Cooter says, they now have the power to transform these things into anything that they wish.

It turns out to be the power itself that entrances Loftis. Remembering a time when, as a child, he traded a piece of family jewelry for a few pieces of candy, he determines not to make such a deal again. Like Elnora, he becomes a miser: After they move Elnora's things into their own apartment, he drags two trash bags of discarded clothing in, because he sees some use for them.

While Cooter watches Elnora being taken away, he has a sense of insight into what moved her to become a hoarder. Having finally and unexpectedly come into wealth, she became worried about loss, and reasoned that every act of spending was a poor deal because it resulted in a loss of buying power, and a loss of life.

When Loftis does not come home for four days, Cooter falls into the same type of behavior that Elnora had exhibited in her life. He stays inside much of the time, refuses to call for help when there is a plumbing problem, and goes out only to beg for food. When Cooter sees that Loftis has attached a note to a penny he found, he deduces that Loftis has been roaming the streets looking for loose change, and wonders if they are doomed to become misers like Elnora.

The story strongly suggests that Cooter was correct when he suspected that Elnora's things were cursed. The money and wealth of material possession that she came into did her no good: She went from being a hard-working maid to a beggar, and now, apparently, something similar is happening to Cooter and Loftis. The general theme is that the greatest power of money is not its power to transform one thing into another (by selling a piano to buy two gold lamé suits, for instance) but its power to captivate the imagination so the power of the exchange value of money, or anything else, becomes itself something to accumulate and hoard.

A more specific theme relates to the importance of values within the African American community. When members of this community accept the accumulation of wealth as itself a value worth pursuing, they risk losing themselves. The wealth that comes first to Elnora Bailey and then to Loftis and Cooter from a wealthy, established white family does not liberate them—instead, it limits and contains them. In accepting this wealth, they are accepting someone else's values as well, and those values inhibit them and virtually enslave their lives.

## Style and Technique

"Exchange Value" is a tightly compressed story. The majority of the story concerns Loftis and Cooter's discovery and removal of Elnora Bailey's wealth. Because Johnson has serious ethical questions to explore, he uses many careful techniques to tip off his deeper meaning. For example, Loftis's transformation into a miser like Elnora is signaled in part by adjectives. When Cooter recalls giving Elnora some change, he describes her walk as "crablike"; several pages later, when he returns from his shopping spree, Loftis is described as "crabby."

Similarly, Johnson uses language to present Cooter as a keenly intuitive young man aware of the magical nature of this money. When he sees Elnora's wealth, he tells Loftis that he is afraid the money is cursed. Later, as they are moving her things to their apartment, he imagines himself and Loftis as two wizards, able to transform one thing into another. Finally, seeing Elnora Bailey's body carried away, he understands that her wealth had a spellbinding quality on her.

The colloquial language of the first-person narrator makes for an entertaining and compelling narration. When Johnson has the narrator suddenly experience deeper insights, the narrative suffers from lack of consistency. The problem any writer faces when trying to use a spoken language as the basis for a written narration is that the true hesitations, digressions, and ellipses of spoken language would be intolerably distracting on the page. Faced with this dilemma, Johnson opts to suggest a spoken language, rather than accurately depict it. Even so, Cooter's sudden realization that Elnora feared depletion because she realized that every purchase was "a poor buy: a lack of life" is not consistent with the narrator that Johnson invented whose own reading is largely confined to comic books, and who calculates the worth of a piano in terms of the sexual favors it could buy from a prostitute. Similarly, the rather abrupt change in Loftis at the end of the story is not carefully enough delineated to be entirely believable. The references to magic begin to sound like an excuse for a lack of character exploration.

Although the artistry in "Exchange Value" is flawed in minor ways, it does make for compelling storytelling. Because the story is told from the point of view of Cooter, who is largely dependent on Loftis for his survival, the helplessness he feels when he sees how Loftis is changing becomes paramount at the end.

*Thomas Cassidy*

# AN EXPERIMENT IN MISERY

*Author:* Stephen Crane (1871-1900)
*Type of plot:* Social realism
*Time of plot:* 1894
*Locale:* The Bowery section of New York
*First published:* 1894

> *Principal characters:*
> A YOUNG MAN, the protagonist
> THE "ASSASSIN," his companion

*The Story*

Late one rainy night, a shabbily dressed young man trudges along a New York street taunted by voices calling him a bum. As he reaches City Hall Park, he seeks companionship but spots only well-dressed people on their way home. Moving on to Chatham Square, where the pedestrians' clothes match his "tatters," he sees a saloon sign that advertises "Free hot soup tonight." Moving through its swinging doors, which snap "to and fro like ravenous lips," the youth is served a schooner of frothy beer and a bowl of watery chicken broth. Turning down a second helping, he returns to the street to search for cheap lodging.

The youth is making inquiries with a seedy-looking man when along comes a bushy-haired drunk who appears "like an assassin steeped in crimes performed awkwardly." His eyes have a guilty slant and his lips look as though they have just consumed "some tender and piteous morsel." When he begins begging for some money, the seedy man tells him to "go t' hell," but the youth agrees to give him a few pennies in exchange for finding them inexpensive accommodations.

The "assassin" leads them to a seven-cent dive, a foul-odored den that reminds the youth of a graveyard "where bodies were merely flung." Inside the gloomy room, the faint flame of a gas jet casts ominous shadows. Putting his derby and shoes in a tall locker resembling a mummy case, the youth lies down on a cold cot next to a man who is so still that he might be taken for a corpse. Across the room, his companion is sprawled on his back, snoring through a bulbous nose that shines "like a red light in a fog." Throughout the night, the youth is kept awake by shrieks and moans, the melancholy dirge of a forgotten underclass. The morning rays of the sun produce a cacophony of curses, snorts, and gruff banter. Naked men parade about casually, looking like "chiefs" until they put on their ragged clothes, which exaggerate their deformities.

Out on the street, the youth offers to buy the assassin something to eat at a run-down basement restaurant whose sign reads "No mystery about our hash!" Six cents purchases two coffees and rolls. While they are eating, the assassin launches into an "intricate, incoherent" personal tale of suffering at the hands of his father and various bosses. Meanwhile, the proprietor prevents an old man from leaving because he is carrying a tiny package of food. "B'Gawd, we've been livin' like kings," the assassin chortles after breakfast. "Look out, or we'll have t' pay for it t'-night," the youth replies.

The two companions make their way to a bench at City Hall Park. Watching people hurrying to their morning destinations reminds the youth of the huge gulf between his present plight and "all that he valued." Guiltily, he pulls down his hat, feeling like a criminal. A babble of tongues roars heedlessly, and behind him multistoried buildings cast their pitiless hues. They seem "emblematic of a nation forcing its regal head into the clouds, throwing no downward glances . . . [at] the wretches who may flounder at its feet."

### Themes and Meanings

The point of the story is that the misery of poverty is so immobilizing that victims do not have the will to overcome their wretchedness. Stephen Crane is elusive on the issue of cause and effect: whether the poor are responsible for their fate or are merely tragic pawns in an immutable world. The experimenter rapidly sinks into a state of "profound dejection," concluding finally that "there no longer could be pleasure in life." Misery loves company, as the saying goes, and the youth feels like an outcast among the well-dressed and purposeful, preferring the company of those who trudge aimlessly, stare dolefully, loiter patiently, get swallowed up by the saloon, and heave on flophouse cots like "stabbed fish."

Misery also breeds passivity, but there are exceptions such as the little pudgy fellow who curses like a fishwife and the enigmatic "assassin" whose gestures are awkward but extravagant. Claiming to be a gentleman "down on his luck," he begs for coppers in a coaxing voice that resembles that of an affectionate puppy. The youth's handout makes his countenance "radiant with joy." On his cot he snores with "incredible vigor," his wet hair and beard glistening and his nose shining "with subdued luster." Liquor clouds his memory and makes him, at times, incoherent, but a warm breakfast puts a red grin on his face and leads him to declare that "we've been livin' like kings." In his limping step is a "suggestion of lamblike gambols." Unmindful of the youth's warning that they have to hustle to survive the next night, the assassin refuses "to turn his gaze toward the future."

During the 1890's, proper society considered the poor to be a criminal element. Ironically, the youth accepts this indictment as he surveys the bustling crowd from his bench and pulls down the rim of his derby. The refuse of a success-oriented society, the poor lacked motivation or ambition. Their crime was resignation. In Crane's concluding line, the young man's eyes take on a "criminal expression that comes from certain convictions."

"An Experiment in Misery" underscores how wide a gulf existed between the rich and the poor. Behind the park are awesome, shadowy skyscrapers. Streetcars rumble along softly "as if going upon carpet stretched in the aisle made by the pillars of the elevated road."

Crane examines the culture of poverty by describing four haunts visited by the youth: the saloon, the flophouse, the hash house, and the park bench. Most alluring is the saloon, with its delectable advertisement, ravenous swinging doors, frothy schooners of beer, and bewhiskered host dispensing soup "like a priest behind the altar." In contrast, the lodging house is a nightmarish morgue, with unholy odors and demoniac wails, causing the sleepless protagonist to "lay carving biographies for these men from his meager experience." The careworn restaurant has coffee bowls "webbed with brown seams" and tin spoons "bent and scarred from the attack of long forgotten teeth." The final resting place is "sanctified by traditions" and leads the youth to see himself inexorably as one with a class of people cut off from the blessings of the world.

*Style and Technique*

Crane has been hailed as America's first modern writer, whose tough-minded realism and symbolic impressionism broadened the parameters of twentieth century fiction. His literary career resembled the passing of a comet, brief but brilliant. His first important work, *Maggie: A Girl of the Streets* (1893), had a motif similar to that of "An Experiment in Misery." Despite its lack of commercial success, Crane began work on *The Red Badge of Courage: An Episode of the American Civil War* (1895), which would bring him international acclaim. The previous year, however, at the time he wrote "An Experiment in Misery," he was a struggling journalist trying to persuade editors to publish his work. The country was in the midst of a depression, and Crane himself was frequently without funds. For the sake of research he even stayed in a flophouse and stood in breadlines; the latter experience inspired an article called "Men in the Storm."

"An Experiment in Misery," like others of Crane's tales of Bowery life, uses an impressionistic style to depict a milieu that is hostile and incomprehensible. The story was first published in the *New York Press* with an explanatory introduction and conclusion that Crane later deleted when it was published in *The Open Boat, and Other Tales of Adventure* (1898). In the original introduction, the youth tells an older friend that he wants to discover the point of view of the tramp by living like one: "Rags and tatters, you know, a couple of dimes, and hungry, too, if possible." At the end, the youth reports that although he did not discover the tramp's point of view, "mine own has undergone a considerable alteration."

By deleting the introduction and coda, Crane heightened the story's gloomy mood and its sense of mystery and dread. The youth becomes virtually an outcast, not merely an extension of the narrator. For Crane, realism went far beyond journalistic accuracy. He left to reporters such as Jacob August Riis the task of depicting the poor in *How the Other Half Lives* (1890). He used imagery, color, and symbolism to evoke the culture of poverty. Sherwood Anderson claimed that the impact of Crane's style was like an explosion and that his Bowery sketches were the outpouring of an individualist who felt with every nerve within him.

The most puzzling aspect of "An Experiment in Misery" is the character of the young man. Is he in the Bowery as an experiment or as a victim of nature's fate? In the story's original form, the narrator deliberately dons the identity of a Bowery denizen. Without the prologue and epilogue, Crane leaves the issue unresolved, and the tone of doom is more palpable, although not totally unrelieved.

The shortened form gives rise to a metaphysical interpretation: the young man as pilgrim passing through baptism (saloon scene), Original Sin (flophouse scene), Holy Communion (breakfast scene), and Judgment Day (park bench). Perhaps Crane intended to suggest a parody of the doctrine of predestination. Whatever the case, the shortened form of the story is more powerful than the original. Its technique better reflects the author's naturalistic underpinnings.

*James B. Lane*

# A FABLE

*Author:* Robert Fox (1943-    )
*Type of plot:* Fable
*Time of plot:* The 1960's
*Locale:* New York City
*First published:* 1972

> *Principal characters:*
> THE YOUNG MAN, a typical lower-middle-class suburbanite who
>     has just started his first full-time job
> THE BLOND, a beautiful but empty-headed young woman
> HER MOTHER, a domineering woman who wants her daughter to
>     make a good match

*The Story*

A neat and clean-shaven young man is taking the subway to Manhattan to begin his first day on the first regular job he has ever had. He feels happy, thanks to his new status as a middle-class office worker, the prospect of being able to buy things that he has always wanted, and the day's invigorating weather. Indeed, he is in love with the whole world because of the optimism and self-confidence infused by his new career. When he spots a beautiful young blond, who is evidently out shopping with her mother, he is so strongly attracted that he cannot help staring.

The blond notices the young man's attention and complains to her mother, who simply explains, "He's in love with you." The young man then seizes an opportunity to sit next to the blond and starts a conversation by saying, "I'm in love with you." Although he has never met her before, he proposes marriage on the spot. Neither woman is surprised by this abrupt proposal. Neither displays any emotion. Both are interested only in learning whether the eager young man is a good catch. The blond asks if he has a job and what his future prospects are, but the naïve suitor has only the vaguest idea of what his work will entail. All he knows is that he will have his own desk and handle a lot of paperwork. However, he says that he is getting a good salary and that he intends to work his way up in the company.

The mother is especially concerned about the young man's ability to be a good provider. She asks him why he wants to marry her daughter. He merely answers that the daughter is pretty and that he is in love with her. "Is that all?" the mother asks. "I guess so," he answers. "Is there supposed to be more?" "Not usually," the mother answers.

When the mother feels satisfied that the young man really is in love—or at least that he has convinced himself that he is—and that he fully intends to provide a good lifestyle for her daughter, she invites him to propose to her daughter again. The young woman, who appears to be entirely dependent on her mother's direction, then accepts his proposal. The other passengers in the subway car have all been listening to this interchange like an audience in a movie theater. When the blond accepts the young man's proposal, everyone smiles and applauds.

The conductor approaches the couple with a Bible in his hand, ready to perform a marriage ceremony on the spot. Like everything else in the story, it must be performed quickly, because the train is nearing the end of the line.

### Themes and Meanings

Robert Fox's "A Fable" illustrates the emptiness, sterility, and anomie of modern existence. Like all fables, it relies heavily on its implicit moral. The most famous writer of fables was Aesop, whose little stories about animals generally show them engaging in foolish behavior in order to teach by implication what intelligent people should do. For example, in one fable a dog loses the bone that he is holding in his mouth when he tries to snatch the bone that he sees in the mouth of his own image reflected in a pond. The moral might be expressed as "a bird in the hand is worth two in the bush." The moral of Fox's short story may be harder to express in a single sentence. It would be too simplistic to express the moral as "marry in haste, repent at leisure." The young man and young woman in the story are certainly marrying in haste, but they may never develop enough insight into their own identities to repent at all. If they go through life without knowing whether they are happy or unhappy, they will be just like almost everybody else.

Fox's story is a modern fable similar to those of the famous American humorist James Thurber, collected in *Fables for Our Time and Famous Poems* (1940). As such, "A Fable" is considerably more complicated than the fables, parables, and myths of classic literature. Life has gotten complicated because of the onslaught of mass media, the frantic pace of life driven by modern transportation and communication, the fragmentation of labor created by modern production methods, the anonymity and alienation created by millions of people being crowded together in dehumanizing urban centers, and the spiritual disillusionment created by modern science. People are turning into robots: They behave, not as they are taught to behave, but as they are conditioned to behave.

The story is presented with a deceptively light touch. It seems much like a film comedy set in New York City—the type of fare that has been served in motion pictures from the time of Ginger Rogers and Fred Astaire up to the latest flimsy variations on the same boy-meets-girl plots. The notion of an intimate love affair being conducted publicly under the scrutiny of dozens of sympathetic urbanites seems to come straight out of a Hollywood film. This similarity is undoubtedly intentional. It is meant to suggest that modern Americans get their opinions, values, and aspirations from films; however, whereas the people on the screen are only shadows who will disappear when the projector goes off, the people who are influenced by their meretricious values and pseudo-sophisticated behavior are made of flesh and blood and will have their lives irrevocably affected.

*Style and Technique*

"A Fable" is a short short story. Such stories are typically not longer than one thousand to fifteen hundred words and take only a few minutes to read. There are many different types of short short stories. What they have in common, besides brevity, is that they start much closer to their climaxes than more conventional short stories, which usually offer more description and background information. Because of the need for brevity, the writer of a short short story devotes few words to describing characters or the settings in which the action takes place. There is usually only one incident occurring in a single setting. "A Fable" is a classic example of a short short story in many respects; its entire action takes place within a few minutes in a section of a subway car.

By not giving characters names, the author emphasizes the fact that they are strangers. The reader is placed among the ranks of the anonymous, voyeuristic subway passengers, who are also strangers to one another. The characters are not intended to represent real people but types of people to be seen in a metropolis every day. The young man is like thousands of other young men rushing to work downtown. The young woman is like thousands of other young women who want to get married to upwardly mobile young men who will provide them with homes and all the standard amenities of modern middle-class life. They will probably be no more or less happy or unhappy than millions of other American couples who get their opinions and emotions from the media, particularly from Hollywood, and who live and die without ever finding out who they really are.

The dominant impression of this story is that things happen much too quickly. A young man should not fall in love with a young woman and propose to her within the space of a few minutes. It is important to note that the effect of speeding everything up is heightened by placing the action on a fast-moving subway car. This setting provides a sense of urgency, a "ticking clock," because the train will soon reach Manhattan, where the young man must get off to go to work and the blond must get off to go shopping with her mother. In a city the size of New York, their chances of ever meeting again are minuscule.

The most important thing about a story, as Edgar Allan Poe pointed out long ago, is its "effect"—not what it says, but the feeling that it evokes in the reader. "A Fable" evokes a complex effect, or feeling, of amusement, pity, melancholy, and perhaps a few other emotions, including the embarrassment that goes with recognizing one's own mistakes in others.

Everything in "A Fable" is unreal. The comedy is not meant to be truly comic but just the opposite. Although the situation depicted seems completely unreal, it is not so much different from what really happens to many young people who think they are falling in love because they are ripe to fall in love and feel that it is expected of them. The action is accelerated and exaggerated to make the point that this is indeed the way too many people live in modern times. They are not only strangers to everyone else but strangers to themselves.

*Bill Delaney*

# THE FACES OF BLOOD KINDRED

*Author:* William Goyen (Charles William Goyen, 1915-1983)
*Type of plot:* Domestic realism
*Time of plot:* About 1920-1950
*Locale:* Houston, Texas, and an unnamed Midwestern city
*First published:* 1952

> *Principal characters:*
> THE COUSIN, a sensitive, compassionate, melancholy member of a
> large Texas family
> JAMES, a wild, mysterious, lonely boy who lives briefly with his
> cousin

*The Story*

"The Faces of Blood Kindred" focuses on the relationship between the protagonist and his cousin James, and on two particular incidents that had a deeply felt and lasting effect on the protagonist. The lives of these two boys are shaped by and characteristic of the larger life of their wandering and suffering extended family. The mystery and profundity of blood ties and the essential sadness of human life are two of William Goyen's primary concerns here and throughout his fiction.

Their story begins as James is coming to stay with the protagonist, who is referred to simply as "the cousin" (both boys are fourteen years old). James's father ran away long ago, and his mother, crippled by arthritis, is hospitalized and unable to care for him. The two boys have little in common other than "their mysterious cousinhood, a bond of nature that they instinctively respected." The cousin is timid, obedient, naïve, and sensitive; James, a "faintly hairlipped" stutterer who had owned and loved fighting cocks, is "wild," "mysterious, wandering," and fiercely independent. In spite of their differences, the boys get along well. James tolerates his cousin's timid and fearful nature with tender disdain; the cousin idolizes James for his daring and experience and pities him for his loneliness and isolation.

One afternoon at James's suggestion, the boys go to a farm at the edge of the city to look at some Cornish fighting cocks raised, trained, bought, and sold (illegally) by a roosterlike man named Chuck. The cousin, drawn by the illicit excitement of the venture, agrees to come, though he is afraid and feels guilty because he "stole away" and "did not tell his mother." The cousin's anxiety and awe increase when James counts out fifteen dollars to purchase a "big blue cock with stars on its breast." He is afraid that they will get into trouble at home, that James will have no place to keep the cock. James assures him that he has a place for the bird, and they hitchhike back to town and go to their grandmother's great, rambling house, where James intends to hide the cock for a night.

The big, old, rotting house of the grandmother is filled with members of the family and appears to be a desolate place full of human misery, chaos, frustration, and waste.

The cries of Aunt Beatrice seem to give voice to the collective pain and need of the whole various clan: "Somebody! Please help me, I am so sick." Behind this old house is a small grove of fig trees that conceals "a secret place, a damp and musky cove" known only to the children of the house. James intends to keep his new cock in the dark security of this grove for the night. The bird escapes from his grasp, however, and springs into a fig tree; James shakes the tree violently in an effort to get the bird back. The cousin, overexcited by the disconcerting events of the day, concerned that James will "ruin Granny's figs," and terrified of being caught or getting home too late, panics and hurls a stone at the cock, the embodiment of his anxiety. To his surprise and horror, his aim is true, and the Cornish cock falls at James's feet. The cousin retreats beyond the deep shadow of the tree and watches in despair as he sees James "fall to the ground and kneel over his Cornish cock" and hears him "sob softly." The cousin walks away from his grandmother's house, leaving James and the dead cock under the fig trees. He is overwhelmed by the grief he has caused and by the suffering in the dark house. He cannot understand how his admiration and affection for James could have yielded such agony, or why there seems to be "a doom of suffering over the house of his kinfolks." In his naïveté, he believes that he will understand one day, and he resolves to try "one day [to] save all his kindred from pain or help them to some hope." He returns home to "the benevolent figure of his mother in the kitchen fixing supper." James does not come back, though; he runs away to St. Louis and seeks out his father, whom he has not seen in seven years.

Years later, the cousins see each other once again. The cousin, having attained a measure of success in life, is in a large Midwestern city where he is being honored for his achievements. James appears in the hall and moves forward through the crowd: "There was something James had to say, it was on his face." The cousin is drawn away momentarily to receive the congratulations of some dignitary, and when he turns with trepidation to face James, "to look back into the face of his own secret sorrow, James was gone; and the cousins never met again." This final, failed encounter forces the cousin to shed whatever illusions he has managed to hold on to about his having "answered any speechless question, atoned for the blind failing, the outrage, and the pain on the face of his blood kindred." Human beings' essential isolation, their inability to communicate, the emptiness of public life, the inadequacies of love, are all borne home on the adult cousin in this moment. He carries from that instant a wound deeper and more painful than the one he opened so many years before on the night he accidently killed the big blue cock.

*Themes and Meanings*

As the title suggests, "The Faces of Blood Kindred" is concerned with the enigmatic nature of blood relationships. Ancestry and family ties are of particular interest to Goyen (and many other southern writers) and form a recurrent motif in his fiction. Other themes that are present here and throughout his work include human isolation, the oxymoronic nature of humankind and experience (spirit and flesh, good and bad, and so on), and the poverty of modern life.

Goyen's interest in blood kindred takes two forms here: In the foreground is the relationship between James and the cousin, and in the background is the large and diverse family that surrounds them. The boys' family, the dark, teeming life of the grandmother's house as well as the various family members in other cities, is a microcosm of the human family; its variety (its pain, fragmentation, and confusion) is representative of the rich complexity of human life. The story of the cousin and James is clearly but one story among the many; the failed effort of the two boys to give voice to their deep and mysterious sense of connection, to manifest the tenderness, loneliness, and hope of their secret lives, is characteristic of the flawed endeavor of all human beings. The depiction of each of the boys is quite touching, and their inability to establish an open and loving relationship is poignant, especially when it becomes clear, as it does in the end, that adults are generally less hopeful, less vulnerable, less atuned to love or mystery than are children. James's rigidity in the presence of his dying mother, his inability to speak without stuttering, and his fierce love for his fighting cocks all suggest that he is a lonely and passionate youth, full of love, confusion, anger, and need. The cousin is acutely sensitive to the suffering around him and has an instinctive desire to help his kinfolk, to make their lives better, yet he is unable to redeem his people from their misery.

The dual nature of experience and humanity is stressed in "The Faces of Blood Kindred." The cousins are clearly representative of the conflicting element in the human composition: James is fair, inarticulate, isolated, wild, and passionate; the cousin is dark, well-spoken, loved, obedient, and timid.

The isolation of people is everywhere apparent in this story, not only in the delineation of the cousins but in the rendering of their family as well. Perhaps the central image of loneliness here is that of the aged grandmother abandoned by her husband, deaf, sitting in her rocking chair alone and ignored in the midst of her family. The impersonal and sterile quality of modern life is also apparent here. Fay, who works in a shop selling ready-to-wear clothing, is married to her third husband, a listless, violent sailor. Suffering family members are relegated to hospitals and nursing homes; the city is alien and unfriendly to James; and the public life of the successful cousin is empty and unrewarding.

This story, like numerous others of Goyen's tales, has a strongly autobiographical flavor; one last characteristic note that it sounds is a longing for the ability to help others, particularly one's family, to make life more beautiful and more loving. The child resolves to "one day save all his kindred from pain or help them to some hope"; the grown man has no illusions about the possibility of success in such a task but is nevertheless committed to it. All of Goyen's fiction seems an effort to restore and redeem the human family.

### Style and Technique

"The Faces of Blood Kindred," in spite of being fairly specifically located in time and space, has a mythic quality. The quiet voice of the omniscient narrator, the namelessness of the "cousin," the phrase "blood kindred," and the "unnamed" city, all serve to give this story a universal dimension. The experiences of the cousin speak to all people who have questioned the unfairness of life and striven to help their fellowmen.

One of Goyen's characteristic techniques is evident in this tale. Although he focuses on particular figures, here James and the cousin, Goyen makes one aware of the rich texture of life around these central figures that both frames and shapes them. It is as if there were a baroque symphony playing quietly in the background and a romantic concerto based on the same basic themes and motifs playing in the foreground. The music is communal, even universal; the symphony never ceases though particular melodies may fade into silence.

Many of Goyen's stories, like "The Faces of Blood Kindred," do not conclude in a conventional sense; they simply end. Like music, they are not quite understandable. One is left with a sense of melancholy, perhaps a sense of longing. Goyen does not believe in simple and complete resolutions. The cousin faces deeper and more perplexing questions at the close of the story than he did as a child.

*Hal Holladay*

# FAITH IN A TREE

*Author:* Grace Paley (1922-    )
*Type of plot:* Satire   ·
*Time of plot:* The late 1960's, during the Vietnam War
*Locale:* A neighborhood playground in New York
*First published:* 1967

> *Principal characters:*
> FAITH ASBURY, the protagonist, who is up in a tree in a
>     playground
> RICHARD and
> ANTHONY (TONTO), her sons, aged nine and six years,
>     respectively
> MRS. JUNIUS FINN, her neighbor
> KITTY SKAZKA, her closest friend, an unmarried woman with
>     several children
> ANNA KRAAT, another friend, a beautiful woman with a bad
>     character
> ALEX O. STEELE, formerly an organizer of tenant strikes, now a
>     businessperson
> RICARDO, Faith's former husband, an explorer and writer
> PHILLIP MAZZANO, an attractive man, formerly Kitty's lover
> DOUGLAS, a police officer

## The Story

Faith Asbury is perched in a tree in a neighborhood playground in New York although she would prefer to be out in the "man-wide" world or with a "brainy companion" who could speak to her "of undying carnal love." Below her, under the tree, are her children, Richard and Anthony. Scores of other neighborhood children, "terrible seedlings," watched over by their mothers, swarm about the playground: "Among the trees, in the arms of statues, toes in the grass, they hopped in and out of dog shit and dug tunnels into mole holes." There are also men in the park, "young Saturday fathers," and older fathers, holding the hands of the young children of "a third intelligent marriage." Several characters stop under Faith's tree to chat with her.

As Faith mulls over her past and tries to think about her future, and as passing characters stop to speak with her, the reader learns that Faith had been married to Ricardo, who is now in an unspecified exotic country, presumably living with a younger woman who "acts on her principles" the way Faith had once done. The reader also learns that Faith was reared in a Jewish, socially conscious family, that she has an unfulfilling job by which she supports her children, and that she really does not know what to do next in her life. Faith is also "up a tree" concerning her beliefs. She notes that

My vocabulary is adequate for writing notes and keeping journals but absolutely useless for an active moral life. If I really knew this language, there would surely be in my head, as there is in Webster's or the *Dictionary of American Slang*, that unreducible verb designed to tell a person like me what to do next.

Faith leaves her perch briefly to flirt with Phillip Mazzano, an attractive man who was once the lover of Kitty Skazka, Faith's best friend. Formerly a teacher and later with the State Department, he now wants to become a comedian. He forms an instant rapport with Richard, Faith's elder son. Faith, however, returns to her tree limb when Phillip appears to be more interested in beautiful Anna Kraat, another friend who is "not interested in anything."

Up to this point in the story, there has been little or no action: Faith, static in her tree, the others playing or lounging below it. A new group now enters the park, a group composed of men, women, and children together. The children are banging pots and pans, and the adults carry three posters. The first poster, showing a picture of a man and a child, poses the question, "WOULD YOU BURN A CHILD?" The next poster depicts the man putting a burning cigarette to the child's arm and gives the answer, "WHEN NECESSARY." The third poster, carrying no words, shows a napalmed Vietnamese baby "seared, scarred, with twisted hands." The group seems to impose an automatic silence on the others in the playground.

Douglas, a police officer, tries to remove the antiwar protesters, who stop, regroup, and continue their march more sedately, discarding the wooden poster handles to which Douglas has objected. When Anthony, Faith's younger child, protests against Douglas's interference with the antiwar group, the police officer answers, "Listen Tonto, there's a war on. You'll be a soldier too someday. I know you're no sissy like some kids around here. You'll fight for your country." Richard angrily rebels against Douglas, as well as against Faith and the other passive onlookers: "I hate you. I hate your stupid friends. Why didn't they just stand up to that stupid cop." He then writes the question and answer on the sidewalk, using bright red chalk: "WOULD YOU BURN A CHILD? WHEN NECESSARY." Richard's pain and anger over such apathy in the face of cruelty bring Faith to a sudden realization of her place and purpose in life. From this point onward, she moves "out of that sexy playground" and into the world again.

*Themes and Meanings*

"Faith in a Tree," like many other Grace Paley stories, has, as principal characters, divorced or unwed mothers who tend their children in parks and playgrounds while waiting to find a man who will deliver them from their stymied lives. Forming a counterpoint to these characters are the more bourgeois, financially successful (usually male) characters who sacrifice emotional honesty in order to achieve respectability.

Early in the story, the reader learns that Faith was reared to believe in a "sensible, socialist, Zionist world of the future," destined, as an American child, to be independent and free. Instead, her "lumpen time" and her "bourgeois feelings" are spent caring for her children. Clearly, Faith, like many middle-class children who came of age in the 1960's, was meant for better things. Now, in every sense, she finds herself "up a tree." The people who find themselves with her in the playground are in no better position, although they try to give her advice: Alex O. Steele tells her to "speak clearly, Faith, you're garbling like you used to"; Mrs. Finn cautions, "You answer too much, Faith Asbury, and it shows"; Kitty worries, "Faith, you'll fall out of the tree, calm yourself"; even nine-year-old Richard cries, "Faith, will you quit with your all-the-time philosophies."

The other characters in the playground also seem to be stymied, going nowhere. Steele had once organized tenant strikes. Now he works in the East Fifties (it is unclear exactly what he now does, but he seems to have exchanged his former principles for financial success); Phillip Mazzano, who had once been a teacher and then worked for the State Department, now claims to "make a living. Here. Chicago. Wherever I am. I'm not in financial trouble." He now has aspirations of becoming a comedian, although he is "not funny." Faith's friend, Kitty, who has several children and many former lovers (Phillip is one, and another is also in the playground, selling marijuana), "has made one mistake after another." Anna, although beautiful, has a bad character and is not interested in anything.

That Faith and the other characters find themselves in a playground is a clear reference to the fact that she, and they, are not living their true lives and have not entered the real world. The adults, like the children, are still playing. They are forming liaisons, they are enjoying music, they are climbing trees. When the small group of protesters enters the playground, it is as though the children, banging on the pots and pans, have startled Faith—and, one would hope, some of the others—into attention. They, like Faith's children, give Faith the impetus to leave her limb and reenter life, to be where she can meet "women and men in different lines of work, whose minds were made up and directed out of that sexy playground." Further, that impetus is offered by Faith's children's "heartfelt brains," the necessary combination of reason and emotion, which leads to action. In this sense, it is the children, the "seedlings," who bring back a feeling of faith to the protagonist and, by extension, the other members of Faith's generation.

*Style and Technique*

Paley uses the first-person point of view in this story, allowing the reader to see the playground and the characters in it from her perspective, which, throughout most of the story, is several feet off the ground. The protagonist is thus "above it all," allowing her to be fairly objective about the other characters but unable to be really part of the life of the playground: She has not yet come down to earth. The reader is brought to epiphany along with Faith, descending, with her, from the branches and back into the world.

Language is an extremely important factor in Paley's stories. The various ethnic idioms of New York City and the rich use of the vernacular add life and texture to her works. Language is also an important metaphor in the story. Faith is looking for the right vocabulary, the "unreducible verb" that will tell her "what to do next." The other characters seem also to believe that she lacks such a language. Richard says, "That's a typical yak yak out of you, Faith"; Steele accuses her of "garbling"; Mrs. Finn cries "Blah blah. . . . Blah to you." Even Faith's attraction to Phillip seems somehow related to his knowledge of languages. Ironically, however, it is a simple question and an even simpler answer that move Faith's children, and thus Faith, to action.

The most evident metaphor in the story is the tree, on whose limb Faith waits to re-enter life. The reference to the children as "seedlings" reinforces this image—it is the children who ultimately bring Faith out of the tree and back into the world.

Finally, it is the pure force of Paley's language that carries this almost static story, entertaining and enlightening the reader. Describing one of the more respectable but less feeling inhabitants of the playground, she writes: "Along the same channel, but near enough now to spatter with spite, tilting delicately like a boy's sailboat, Lynn Ballard floats past my unconcern to drop light anchor, a large mauve handbag, over the green bench slats." Paley, unlike Faith, has no language limitations.

*Rochelle Bogartz*

# THE FAITHFUL WIFE

*Author:* Morley Callaghan (1903-1990)
*Type of plot:* Sketch
*Time of plot:* The late 1920's
*Locale:* A train station restaurant and a nearby boardinghouse
*First published:* 1929

*Principal characters:*
GEORGE, a young lunch counter attendant
STEVE, his boss
LOLA, a shy, pretty woman who frequents George's restaurant

## The Story

George has been working at the lunch counter of a train station restaurant in order to save money for college. It is his last day on the job before he leaves. The restaurant is frequented by young women on their lunch hours. Though these women usually avoid contact with the three other men who work at the restaurant, they occasionally chat with George. Though not a handsome man, George has a polite and generous nature and is well liked by Steve, the restaurant's manager.

George always notices one particular young woman (later identified as Lola) who comes to the lunch counter, yet something in her manner suggests an aloofness that makes him hesitate to speak to her. On this day when she comes in, George again notes how shy and pretty she is, even though she is dressed somewhat shabbily. She does not even have a piece of fur around the collar of her thin blue coat—something that most young women can afford.

After returning from a break that evening, Steve tells George that a young woman has telephoned for him and left a number. Not knowing who might have phoned, George returns the call and learns that it is the shy young woman from the lunch counter. She invites him to visit her at half past ten that evening.

At the woman's boardinghouse room George is somewhat nervous, not knowing what to expect, but the young woman quickly takes charge. Wearing a tight red sweater, she invites him to sit next to her. Soon he is kissing her. She responds excitedly to his embraces, but as George grows overly eager, she breaks away from him and begins pacing the poorly furnished room. When George asks what she is doing, she explains that she is expecting her roommate to return shortly, so he must leave.

George suspects that something strange is going on when he notices the mark from a ring on the woman's finger. He asks her if she is not really waiting for her husband. She breaks down and tearfully confesses that her husband is a war veteran with a serious spinal injury who will soon return from the sanatorium where he has also been recuperating from tuberculosis. Because of his physical limitations they can no longer make love. She insists that she has been a faithful wife, but that when she learned that

George would be leaving the next day, she decided to take advantage of the situation—trusting that he would not complicate her life after their "affair." After she asks George to hold her once more, he leaves. He briefly considers asking for his job back in order to be with Lola but decides not to spoil things for her because she has it "all figured out."

## Themes and Meanings

Morley Callaghan's short stories frequently question conventional morality, and "The Faithful Wife" is an example of this type of interrogation. This purposefully open-ended sketch suggests an examination of calculated pretense, or the idea of consciously hiding one's true nature for the purpose of breaking with traditional codes of moral behavior.

Though the story begins simply, it becomes complicated as young George is invited to the apartment of a young woman about whom he has been dreaming. Although there are reasons to suspect that George is not a total innocent, he is unaccountably nervous at the prospect. For one thing, it is clear that George has a respectful admiration for this woman to whom he has never even spoken. His impression is based on the disposition that she wears at his lunch counter each day. Seeing her as pretty, shy, and aloof, he assumes that she is unapproachable. He empathizes with her somewhat shabby appearance and feels sorry for her. It is not surprising, therefore, that George should be nervous when she boldly invites him to meet her at her apartment. Her behavior seems to conflict with the image that he has built of her. The resulting tension manifests itself in George's awkwardness in her room. However, the idea that Lola is not who she has seemed to be is taken to a further level as she reveals to George that she is married.

Callaghan, seeming at first intent on exploring the morality of a casual affair, leads to a consideration of a more knotty problem. What does one make of Lola's real loneliness and isolation? The aloof mask that she wears at the lunch counter each day hides her true desperation and sorrow. No casual need for idle fulfillment, her use of George is seen as an urgent plea. The reader initially suspects her need is solely for physical contact, yet the implications are deeper. Not only is she denied physical fulfillment with her invalid husband, but she must support them both, pay the hospital costs, and endure a terrible isolation. George's reaction, "That's tough, poor kid," may be a heartfelt reaction to the true details of her life.

The story might be viewed as ironic, sad, mildly tragic, or even affirming—if the reader interprets George's decision not to interfere with Lola any further as altruistic. As Callaghan does so often in his short works, he leaves the interpretations to the reader. He himself makes no moral judgments about Lola's, or George's, behavior, rather forcing the reader to weigh ideas about morality and immorality. Why is Lola given the ironic label of "faithful" wife? What constitutes faithfulness? What is the emotional cost to Lola in breaking with conventional behavior? These questions may have no simple answers, but they reflect the types of questions that Callaghan's stories frequently pose.

*Style and Technique*

"The Faithful Wife" is the first of thirty-nine short stories that Callaghan published in *The New Yorker*. Though his style changed over the years, developing even more of the flat, uninflected, and pared-down quality of modernist American contemporaries such as Sherwood Anderson or Ernest Hemingway, here Callaghan focuses on a moral dilemma by almost meticulously presenting a series of contrasting images.

The oppositions are abundant and are initially suggested by the contrast of coldness and warmth in the first paragraph. George's characterization contrasts with those of the more worldly countermen and "red-capped porters" who work at the train station. Lola contrasts with the other young women who frequent the lunch counter; to some extent this is highlighted by the dissimilarity of their appearances. Lola is shabby and poor, while the other young women are "brightly dressed and highly powdered." Lola has no fur collar on her coat, while most of the others have "a piece of fur of some kind." Further, the other young women smile at George, who knows them by their first names, while Lola remains shy, aloof, and nameless.

Callaghan does not present these oppositions merely to define George and Lola, for both are more than their mere opposition to others first suggests. For example, George is seemingly shy about speaking to Lola, but he may be more experienced than the initial contrasts made between him and the other counter workers make him appear. Steve remarks about George's not being able to keep straight all the phone numbers of his girls. Also, when Lola makes her intentions clear at her apartment, George does not hesitate to embrace and kiss her. Lola is even more unlike what the reader expects her to be after Callaghan first describes her. Her shyness and hesitant manner give way to passion and seeming desperation. Not only does she become aggressive toward George, but she dresses and acts in a manner antithetical to the quiet, poorly clothed girl of the lunch counter who invoked George's initial sympathy.

In a way the reader is led to see Lola and George in opposition, though they may initially appear soul mates. As Lola sits at the lunch counter, George "remain[ed] opposite her." Later, at her apartment, she sits down "opposite him." However, George and Lola are not necessarily opposites at all, and both turn out to be capable of genuine feeling. It is possible that the deliberate contrasts serve to focus attention on each's perception of the other. Ultimately, it becomes apparent that just as Lola is not who George expects her to be, so George may not be what she thinks either. It is probable that she expects him to be like the other counter workers. Instead, George surprises her by genuinely caring about her. His caring, however, undermines her plan, as she wants to have no emotional strings attached. Although Lola does not have things quite so "figured out" as she thinks, George concludes that it is probably best to carry on as if she has.

*George T. Novotny*

# THE FALL

*Author:* Alberto Moravia (1907-1990)
*Type of plot:* Psychological
*Time of plot:* Unspecified
*Locale:* Italy
*First published:* "La caduta," 1940 (English translation, 1954)

> *Principal characters:*
> TANCREDI, a preadolescent Italian boy
> HIS MOTHER
> VERONICA, his mother's maid

*The Story*

Tancredi, a young Italian boy, has been ill for a few months, so his parents get a villa near the ocean for the remainder of his recuperation. During his illness, he has changed from a willful, capricious boy with curly hair to a short-haired, scrawny, and listless youth. He feels obsessed, guilty, and remorseful but does not know about what.

The villa into which he, his mother, and her maid move belongs to an antique dealer who allows them to stay there in return for favors that the family has done for him. The antique dealer has been using the massive, three-story building as a storehouse, and every room is crammed with ugly, unsalable furniture, paintings, tapestries, and knickknacks. Even its windows fail to provide much light, because many are covered with stained glass. Its rooms smell of old wood, mold, and mice, rather than healthful sea air. Tancredi's mother finds the house uncomfortable and worries that one of them might damage something, but for Tancredi, the house is both terrifying and seductive. Although he can play outside on the beach, he increasingly spends his time exploring the house. Particularly attracted to its attic, he thinks of the rooms there as being like cells, whose low, whitewashed ceilings and rough floors he is sure contain the secrets of tragic lost loves. The rooms are filled with large, dark paintings, and Tancredi spends hours lying on his back in them, inventing terrifying stories based on their pictures.

One day in the midst of such a reverie, Tancredi remembers that he has made a slingshot and goes outside to test it in an enclosure adjoining the villa. When his sleeve becomes stuck on brambles through which he has passed often before, he believes that the brambles are consciously trying to stop him but still manages to enter the trash-littered sunken enclosure. Although he is outdoors, it is as oppressive as being inside the house; the day is overcast with dark clouds, and the acrid smell of rubbish fills the still air. He puts tin cans from the trash heap on the wall and shoots stones at them. When a large cat living at the villa strolls across the wall, he aims a stone at it but does not really expect to hit it. He is shocked when his stone puts out one of the cat's eyes, and the cat stands motionless, surprised, staring at him. Rather than fearing the cat will attack him, Tancredi imagines that the cat will gain revenge by loyally attaching itself to him. After a sudden clap of thunder, Tancredi races home, only to find the injured cat waiting there for him; it rubs up against his bare legs, and Tancredi runs away, screaming. The cat follows him through the house, sometimes looking terrified, sometimes hopeful. Tancredi seizes a pistol from a table filled with ancient weapons and throws it at the cat, but instead of hitting the cat, he breaks the glass on the dining room door. Tancredi escapes into a third-floor bedroom, soundlessly closing the door.

The room he has entered is adjacent to the room that he left earlier, and quite like it, except that it is barren of pictures. The door connecting the two rooms is ajar; Tancredi hears two voices coming from the other room but sees no one when he peeks inside. He becomes aware that one voice is a man's, then hears someone leave the room, and someone else drop onto the bed. Tancredi then sees Veronica's naked, white legs on the bed; at first, they seem unable to keep still, moving wearily and voluptuously, then they stop. Although unsure what he has seen, Tancredi is overcome with shame.

Tancredi falls asleep, and awakens to darkness. He hears rats in the ceiling, and then a piece of plaster falls on him. Seeing a rat in the ceiling, he calls frantically for Veronica. She comes in from the next room and knocks the rat out of the hole, but it falls on her and both she and Tancredi become hysterical. His mother then enters the room, and Tancredi wakes up from his dream about the rat.

A thunderstorm has started and caused an electrical fuse to blow out. Tancredi, who is very handy with electrical things, is asked to get his tools and fix the fuse. The cat appears while he is working on the fuse box, and he determines to kill it this time. As he aims a screwdriver at it, there is a blinding flash, and he passes out.

Two days later, Tancredi's mother tells her friends over a game of cards that the cat got caught in electrical wires, causing the flash and electrocuting itself. She adds that she has forbidden Tancredi to go near the electricity again.

### Themes and Meanings

Alberto Moravia was a lonely, sickly, isolated child, suffering for most of his preadolescent and adolescent years from tuberculosis. Between nine and seventeen years of age, he spent five years in bed, including a period in a sanatorium in the Italian Alps when he was sixteen. It was during this confinement that he began writing; his first book of verse was published when he was thirteen. It is likely that "The Fall" reflects his experiences as a sickly adolescent to some extent. It certainly speaks to the burgeoning imaginative powers of a child trapped in hospitals and infirmaries with few diversions other than his imagination.

It has been said that Moravia regards love and sex as indispensable tortures, and that he probably fears women as much as he loves them. According to critic R. W. B. Lewis, everything in Moravia's novels either is an extension of sex or is converted to it. In "The Fall," Tancredi reflects not merely the normal confusion felt by a young boy entering puberty, but the heightened intensity experienced by a child with no normal social outlets. Although Tancredi's exact age is never given, it is stated "that his childhood was over and that he was on the threshold of his turbid and troubled adolescence." The shame, guilt, and confusion he feels over mysterious physical changes in his body leave him vulnerable to greater confusion when he sees Veronica's naked legs in the adjacent room.

In the introduction to *Bitter Honeymoon, and Other Stories* (1954), the collection in which this story first appeared in English, Philip Rahv says the male characters in these stories "are at once fired with desire and filled with fear of the objects of their desire . . . ridden by a sense of the intimate menace of sex" and that they see the women in a way that reduces their humanness. Significantly, Tancredi sees only Veronica's legs—disembodied parts of her, rather than the whole person. It is also interesting that when Tancredi hits the cat, his fear is not that the cat will die or attack him but that it will become attached to him. The responsibility of commitment may seem too intense for a solitary child unused to much human contact.

*Style and Technique*

Many of Moravia's works, particularly his novels, exhibit a documentary style of writing. His short stories and novellas, however, generally are regarded by critics as more successfully dramatizing his recurrent sexual themes. Although reported primarily by a limited omniscient narrator, "The Fall" escapes the boundaries of reportorial writing because of the surrealistic, hallucinatory perspective of the overwrought adolescent protagonist. With the exception of its final few sentences, in which the narrator switches to the mother's point of view, all the story's events are seen from Tancredi's perspective. The closed, airless, dark setting of "The Fall" provides a perfect incubator for Tancredi's fantasies.

In "The Fall," only Tancredi is a fully developed character. Although his mother is broadly sketched, she is seldom mentioned. His father, if he is even at the villa, is never mentioned. This is consistent with Moravia's life and most of his fiction—in both of which the mother is the dominant parent. There is little description of Veronica, and no indication of who the mysterious man visiting her might be; he might be Tancredi's father, a neighbor, or someone employed to work at the villa.

The ending cleverly points out that Tancredi is changing in ways that escape his mother's notice. While playing cards with her friends—her main amusement while her son spends his days alone—she states, "I've strictly forbidden him ever to go near the electricity again. Boys are so reckless." In the final line, "And the game began," the narrator ironically emphasizes what the reader already knows: The woman's reckless little boy undoubtedly will be playing with "electricity" again.

*Irene Struthers Rush*

# THE FALL OF THE HOUSE OF USHER

*Author:* Edgar Allan Poe (1809-1849)
*Type of plot:* Horror
*Time of plot:* 1839
*Locale:* Unspecified
*First published:* 1839

*Principal characters:*
THE NARRATOR
RODERICK USHER, his friend from childhood
MADELINE USHER, Roderick's twin sister

*The Story*

Summoned to the House of Usher by a "wildly importunate letter," which "gave evidence of nervous agitation," the first-person narrator goes to reside for a time with the writer of this letter, Roderick Usher. Although Roderick had been one of his "boon companions in boyhood," the narrator confesses early in the story that "I really knew little of my friend"; yet, by the end of this gothic tale, he has learned more about the occupants of the House of Usher than he is equipped to deal with. Indeed, one of these occupants is Roderick's twin sister, Madeline Usher, who is suffering from an unspecified but fatal illness. One of the symptoms of this illness is catalepsy (muscular rigidity marked by a lack of response to external stimuli); significantly, this symptom is crucial to understanding what happens in the course of the story.

His sister's illness is only one reason for Roderick's agitation, one reason for his desire to have the "solace" of the narrator's companionship; it is not the only—or most significant—reason. Usher himself is suffering from a "mental disorder," which is "a constitutional and . . . family evil, and one for which he despaired to find a remedy." Why "evil"? one wonders, until one recalls that, in the third paragraph of this story, even before Roderick has been seen for the first time, the narrator mentions that the ancient "stem" of the Usher family never "put forth . . . any enduring branch . . . the entire family lay in the direct line of descent, and had always . . . so lain." In other words, Roderick and Madeline Usher are the products and inheritors of an incestuous family lineage—one that has remained predominantly patrilineal, so that the name of the family always remained Usher.

Roderick's dilemma, therefore, is this: Madeline is the only relative he has left on earth, and the dictates of the Usher tradition require that, to perpetuate the race of Ushers and the family name, he marry his twin sister and—through incest—sire future Ushers. (It should be noted that at no place in the story does Roderick say any of this directly; while it is intimated throughout, his dilemma is made clearly apparent only by careful reading of his and the narrator's words on this matter.) Thus, when

Roderick refers to his "family evil," the reader may better understand why the narrator earlier mentions, in the second paragraph of the story, that "of late" the family has received some recognition for "repeated deeds of munificent yet unobtrusive charity." Such alms, it should be understood, have been given penitently, in the hope that they will absolve the "evil" of incest germane to the Usher tradition. Nevertheless, absolution comes to the Ushers in no form other than complete annihilation.

During the term of the narrator's visit with Roderick, they read to each other literature concerning classical myth, penitential rituals, theology, physiology, supernaturalism, and demonism—all of which are meant to indicate to the reader Roderick's preoccupation with anything that might help him understand his and his sister's dilemma. What he comes to feel certain about is that the house itself—because it was built and lived in by his forefathers, and because he believes there is "sentience [in] all vegetable things" (and the house consists of such sentient things)—has a "terrible influence" on him and Madeline, and that it has "made him."

The House of Usher becomes a living, feeling character in Poe's story, and one that, Roderick suggests, may be urging the two remaining Ushers to commit incest; although the narrator attempts to convince the reader that he is too rational and realistic to be taken in by Roderick's hypochondriacal theories, he gradually begins to feel "infected" by his host's condition: "I felt creeping upon me, by slow yet certain degrees, the wild influences of his . . . fantastic yet impressive superstitions." Thus, the stage is set for the story's horrifying climax, beginning one evening when Roderick informs his guest that Madeline is dead.

Rather than burying his sister in the family cemetery some distance from the house, Roderick decides to keep her body for two weeks in one of the many vaults within the house—for, after all, one suffering from catalepsy may seem dead but not, in fact, be dead; it would be horrible to bury Madeline alive. In short, the narrator assists his host in entombing the body temporarily in, first, a coffin with its lid screwed down, and then in a vault behind a massive iron door of profound weight. There she remains for a week, as Roderick roams through his house aimlessly, or sits and stares vacantly at nothing for long hours.

One tempestuously stormy night—a "mad hilarity in his eyes"—Roderick enters the narrator's bedroom, where they sit together, the narrator reading to him and both of them trying to ignore the terrible grating sound they hear coming from below the bedroom (the vault into which they placed Madeline's body is directly below this bedroom, and the heavy door to that vault always makes a loud grating sound when it is being opened). As the sound continues more noticeably, Roderick suddenly informs the narrator that he has been listening to noises downstairs for many days, but— apparently fearful that his sister was still living, and that he would again have to face the evil prospect of perpetuating his family's tradition of incest—he says, "I dared not speak!" Abruptly, the bedroom door swings open and Madeline, her white robes bloodied by her struggle to escape the coffin and vault, falls into the room and on Roderick, who, "a victim to the terrors he had anticipated," hits the floor "a corpse."

The narrator flees the house, and from a short distance away he turns to look back and sees the House of Usher split in two and crumble into the dark waters of the tarn before it.

## Themes and Meanings

Although Edgar Allan Poe claimed in his essays and reviews that he was against any didactic motive in literature, and although "The Fall of the House of Usher" is not a didactic story, Poe does communicate a definite moral message here. Importantly, however, the morality with which he is concerned is not that prescribed by any specific religion; instead, he seems to be suggesting that, despite the incestuously twisted and mentally deranged life of the Ushers, there exists an unwritten but operative universal morality that is ultimately as inescapable as the hereditary forces that determine a person's life.

While one may argue that Roderick's angst, as well as his acute hypochondria and seeming madness, appears to be the consequence of centuries of incest, which biologically diminishes a creature's ability to survive, Poe is nevertheless careful to note the "repeated deeds of munificent . . . charity" offered "of late" by the Ushers (presumably by Roderick himself because the story takes place in the nineteenth century, when men, according to tradition, were in charge of financial affairs). Significant, too, is the pejorative appellation of "evil" that Roderick gives to his family, in itself an indication of his own moral sense. Indeed, it is precisely Roderick's morality that causes the internal conflict he suffers, between his inherited traits and his moral revulsion over them, and it is his morality that prompts him to leave Madeline in the vault even after he discovers that she is still alive. Granted, knowingly allowing his sister to die, when he could save her, is immoral; yet Roderick's sense of right and wrong has transcended concerns for what is good for the Ushers and their perpetuation, and becomes a greater, higher concern for the future of the human race. It is no wonder, then, that when the hereditary forces have succeeded in joining the brother and sister together in the house, itself an emblematic agent of those forces, a greater force prevails as it obliterates the Ushers and their house, truncating the incestuous "stem" of the family for all time.

## Style and Technique

In an 1842 review of Nathaniel Hawthorne's *Twice-Told Tales* (1837), Poe discusses the importance of "effect" in stories, and he suggests that a "wise" writer will not fashion "his thoughts to accommodate his incidents; but having conceived, with deliberate care, a certain unique and single effect to be wrought out, he then . . . combines such events as may best aid him in establishing this preconceived effect." He also asserts that the first sentence of a given story must contribute to the "outbringing of this effect." Essentially, then, according to Poe a good story need not be believable to be successful, so long as the integrity of its effect is not disturbed. Applying Poe's credo to "The Fall of the House of Usher," the reader must admit that, yes, this story is a success for its effect.

The first sentence sets the mood, begins to create the overall effect, as the narrator describes the day as "dull, dark, and soundless," the clouds hanging "oppressively low." When he arrives at the house, he is struck by its "melancholy" appearance, and his spirit is overwhelmed by a sense of "insufferable gloom." Not only is Poe working to create the story's mood in the first paragraph (as he does throughout the story), but he is also intent on personifying the house when he has his narrator describe its windows as "eye-like" and the fungi implicitly as hair-like, "hanging in a fine tangled web-work from the eaves." Symbolically, the web of fungi, the house itself, and the "black and lurid tarn," which lies near the house, are all extensions of the Usher family's heritage and psychology; the atmosphere around this family reeks "a pestilent and mystic vapour, dull, sluggish . . . and leaden-hued."

However, while Poe's story is a success for its overall effect, the problem that exists in his credo extends into the story—that is, reason and probability are treated as unimportant. How, a reader must ask, does Madeline escape her coffin, the lid of which was screwed on, survive in the airless vault for seven or eight days without nourishment, and then escape the vault by forcing open the immensely heavy iron door? What causes the House of Usher to break in half and crumble into the tarn? No doubt Poe would have dispensed with such questions by pointing to the source of his story's lasting success, its gothic and gloomy effect.

*David A. Carpenter*

# THE FALLING GIRL

*Author:* Dino Buzzati (Dino Buzzati Traverso, 1906-1972)
*Type of plot:* Fantasy
*Time of plot:* After World War II
*Locale:* A city on the Italian coast
*First published:* "Ragazza che precipita," 1966 (English translation, 1983)

*Principal characters:*
MARTA, the nineteen-year-old falling girl
UNNAMED RESIDENTS of the skyscraper

*The Story*

A nineteen-year-old girl named Marta falls from the top of a skyscraper that houses apartments and business offices; the story chronicles her slow-motion toppling from the roof toward the street.

Marta lets herself fall from the building after she watches the brilliance of the sunset over the city, which "provokes dreams of greatness and glory," and after she sees that the city she lives in is filled with mansions, diamonds, parties, and affairs. She hopelessly lets herself fall, perhaps because she recognizes that she cannot achieve the greatness and glory others have.

Marta slowly floats past various floors of the skyscraper and interacts with nameless inhabitants. She passes millionaires' balconies, where she is invited in to join the cocktail parties. Marta refuses, however, saying she is in a hurry, and floats onward, feeling enormously satisfied that the rich people notice her; she feels fascinating and stylish because of the attention paid to her by the wealthy.

As the sun plunges into the sea and evening comes on, Marta continues past offices where employees sit in long rows, looking up at the falling girl, and somewhat enviously ask who she is and where she is going. Marta only laughs and falls, saying she is expected down on the street. She notices the street is filled with long black cars and that the rich in their sparkling jewels are entering the building for a party, exactly the kind of event that she had dreamed of ever since she was a child. She imagines that if she arrives on time at the entrance to the building, she will find the true beginning of her life, the romance and wonderful fate for which she has been waiting her entire life.

Unfortunately, Marta notices that she is not alone on her plunge: Other young women also are streaming down the side of the building, head first, waving as they drop. Marta notices that they are more fashionably dressed, some even in minks, and she begins to feel less self-assured and more fearful. She wonders if she has made some kind of error. As she continues her fall, a new day dawns, but Marta is feeling worse because everyone has left the ball by now and the long black cars are gone from the front of the building.

At the story's close, Marta is seen from the perspective of a forty-year-old man, Alberto, and his wife, who live on the twenty-eighth floor. Their dialogue reveals that Marta has aged tremendously and is now an old woman. The couple enjoy their breakfast and discuss the advantages and disadvantages of living on their floor: They only see old women falling past their windows, but they do have the opportunity of hearing the thud when these women hit the ground. Alberto listens for a number of minutes but hears no thud; dissatisfied, he takes another sip of his morning coffee.

*Themes and Meanings*

In "The Falling Girl," Dino Buzzati offers a critique of post-World War II Italy and, by extension, of all industrialized countries in which conspicuous consumption and hierarchies based on class exist. The skyscraper provides a metaphor for the gradations in society based on wealth. On the top floors, luxurious cocktail parties are attended by rich, elegant people who make silly conversation and enjoy the interesting diversion that has become a regular occurrence in the building: the falling girls. Near the bottom of the building, the tenants' diversion is less pleasant because the girls who fall have become old women; the tenants realize that the apartments on higher floors cost more because of the splendid views of the city, the sea, and the falling girls.

No one seems concerned for the girl, Marta, because the society is based on consumption, pleasure, entertainment, and diversion. Other people exist solely for one's pleasure. Marta is no revolutionary hero who dies in protest against this consumer society; she is simply a young girl who wants access to this world of diamonds and minks. She does not want to bring this culture down; she wants to become a member of it.

Those who work in the building either are trapped in their rows with their typewriters, or they run to the windows, view the girls falling, and feel envy for those who, in free-falling, seem somehow to have escaped the constraints of the world of labor, the world of weariness. They envy Marta; she envies the rich who attend the ball; Alberto envies those on the higher floors who have the more pleasant views; and those on the highest floors seem to envy no one, content with their diversions, silly conversations, and stylish clothes.

The culture that Buzzati depicts offers nothing but pleasure and the possibility of pleasure. There is no sense that those values that have been ascribed to women in the past—sacrifice, love, selflessness, or concern—are considered important by this culture; perhaps this is, in part, why it is only women who are toppling from the skyscraper. On the other hand, perhaps women have been so well acculturated that they have accepted the values of the culture completely; they fall to their deaths hoping for fulfillment, for the enjoyments of ravishing couture and pointless pleasures, but they only provide others with visual pleasures until they age. Then they provide those on the lowest floors with the pleasure of hearing the thud when they hit the ground.

*Style and Technique*

Along with Tommao Landolfi and Italo Calvino, Buzzati is considered one of the master fantasists of twentieth century Italian literature. Buzzati, however, does not abandon realism completely in his stories; he combines realistic with fantastic elements to create a world that seems oddly familiar and strange at the same time. Everything in "The Falling Girl" is said so matter-of-factly, in such a controlled tone, that the fantastic element is muted somewhat. The reader does not question how a falling girl can dramatically age as she falls, or how she can engage in conversations at certain balconies. The rather plain, journalistic prose provides some sure footing for the reader, and also works in counterpoint with the bizarre, stranger-than-life plot.

The story achieves its effect by dramatically slowing down the events in the story, freezing the frames, then letting them roll again. Most authors condense time in their stories, abbreviating events and long passages of time; Buzzati, however, slows time down, lets the free-falling girl gradually become aware of her plight, lets her mood swing from elation to despair in slow steps.

Buzzati also implicates the reader in his story because the reader too is put into the position of being a voyeur, a witness of the girl's dramatic flight. Like the characters in the story who watch her fall with a calm akin to callousness, the reader appreciates the pyrotechnics of the plot and receives pleasure from the comic artistry. The reader too is a consumer, an inhabitant of this unnamed city in which pleasure is the central priority. Readers can enjoy the story, turn their backs from the falling Marta, and, like Alberto, return to the realities of their own world—their sips of coffee, their pages turned.

Fiction, however, leaves its mark. Alberto seems not to come to any awareness about his life, his position in the society. Buzzati's fiction, however, allows the reader both to receive pleasure and to achieve some sort of insight into the condition of members of industrialized societies. The reader is not simply a consumer; the reader produces meaning, recognizes himself or herself in the inanities of the fictive world. Because Buzzati never allows Marta to fall completely to the street, she is still in flight in the reader's imagination, still opening up a vision of human culture, which is revealed in its horrible pointlessness, its petty pleasures, its obliviousness to others' pain.

*Kevin Boyle*

# THE FALLS

*Author:* George Saunders (1958-    )
*Type of plot:* Psychological
*Time of plot:* The 1990's
*Locale:* A town on the fictional Taganac River, somewhere in the United States
*First published:* 1996

> *Principal characters:*
> MORSE, a husband and father, and a poorly paid office worker
> RUTH, his wife
> ROBERT, his son
> ANNIE, his daughter
> ALDO CUMMINGS, an unsuccessful writer who lives with his
> mother

*The Story*

"The Falls" moves back and forth between the third-person perspectives of two men—Morse, a self-doubting, apprehensive family man, and Aldo Cummings, a writer who feels sure the world will someday discover him and accord him the acclaim he feels he is due. Most of the story takes place in the minds of the men as they stroll along the Taganac River, until an event unfolds that snaps each of the men from his self-absorption.

The story opens with Morse walking home past the St. Jude Catholic school. The reader is quickly introduced to the state of Morse's mental affairs as he deliberates over whether he should smile at the young girls playing in the St. Jude lawn and playground—and possibly be thought a pervert—or frown and be thought grouchy. Caught in this quandary, Morse tries to maintain an expression between friendliness and impassivity, while trying to always maintain what Morse sees as the most important characteristic a person can have: humility.

As Morse continues on toward his home, his internal speculations reveal more and more of his character. He lives in a small rental house with his wife, Ruth, and his son and daughter. As he worries about not being able to afford a piano for his son who is taking lessons (their piano having lately been repossessed), the reader senses that Morse is a man who feels he has failed on many levels. He has failed to gain financial and professional accomplishments, he has failed to be a successful breadwinner for his family, and he believes he has failed to be a good father and a good husband.

In contrast, Aldo Cummings, who snubs Morse when they pass each other, considers himself a starving artist. He spends each step of his walk constructing writerlike descriptions of the walk itself, even as his mind wanders further and further from the walk and into fantasies. For example, he tells himself that he will have to remember to bring a blank yellow writing pad with him to capture the whimsical literary creations spawned during his walk, and perhaps one day when he becomes a famous writer, his yellow pad will be a collector's item, and thus many women would want to meet him.

As each man continues along his way, the reader sees how their lives are contrasted. In the eyes of society, Morse is at least somewhat successful: He has a job, is married, and has children; however, as he walks, his self-doubt and certainty of failure plague him. His son Robert is not as kind, smart, or talented as their young Pakistani neighbor, Ben; in fact, Robert reminds Morse of the bullies who assaulted him when he was a young man. What if his daughter Annie grows up to bring home horrible boys? How can he keep his wife happy, who once had an infatuation with their son Robert's karate instructor?

Cummings, on the other hand, is a grown man who still lives with his mother and who has not achieved any visible measure of success, yet he is cocksure in his life of the mind. He envisions a time when he will become so successful as a writer that members of the literati will wear T-shirts with his face emblazoned on them, a time when he will be able to buy his mother a Lexus automobile, and a time when he can take trips to Paris with beautiful women. He sees Morse as a representative of corporate society, which Cummings, as an "artist," must necessarily resist. Just like Cummings, Morse also is a success only in his mind, as he daydreams about possibly being a prisoner of war who would refuse to talk or a winner of the lottery who gives all the money away.

Each man is thrust into reality when, on the banks of the Taganac, both realize that the two girls in a canoe they have each seen are in danger of being carried down river to the cataract known as Bryce Falls. Each is paralyzed for a moment by indecision: Morse is sure that in attempting to rescue the girls, he will make a mistake. Cummings stumbles about with no notion of what to do. As Morse thinks more and more about the situation, he realizes that there is nothing he, a weak swimmer, can do to help and that the girls are doomed; nevertheless, as the story ends, Morse kicks off his shoes and launches himself into the river.

## Themes and Meanings

The Taganac River and Bryce Falls in "The Falls" serve, in a sense, as a metaphor for life. The girls in the story have disembarked onto the river in a canoe; it seems that they do not have paddles, and consequently they are swept along the river, powerless, condemned to meet their fate in the falls. Similarly, Morse seems to feel that he has been powerless to effect changes and to make things happen in his life; he has in effect been swept along by strong currents, lacking a paddle to fight them. His son is not kind and sweet but instead resembles the bullies who made his adolescence so painful, and his wife is not supportive and helps to chip away at his self-confidence. Morse has been a weak swimmer all his life, one at the mercy of currents.

At the same time, Morse and Cummings both show the danger of living too much in self-constructed worlds of fantasy and not enough in the real world. Morse and Cummings represent two sides of the same coin. Morse, frozen by doubt and anxiety, only creates fantasies in which he is a hero or enjoys some form of success after he has already envisioned the various horrible things that could happen to him. Cummings, on the other hand, ignores the reality of who he actually is, instead choosing to revel in his supremely self-aggrandizing mental picture of himself. Both fail to fully exist in the actual world of the here and now.

Just as there will always be currents in life that carry people against their will into a variety of experiences, sooner or later there will always be a falls: a moment when a person either acts or fails to act, a moment when a person either succeeds or fails. Actual experience in life perhaps prepares one somewhat to deal with such situations; however, those who never engage life because they are sure of failure or who ignore the facts of life because they do not measure up to the pleasures of their mind are possibly doomed before they start. When Morse finally kicks off his shoes and throws himself into the river despite his anxiety and host of misgivings, the reader sees a victory for him. What is important for Morse is not that he actually succeeds but that he at least tries. Indeed, his heroic act may cost him his life, just as he fears; however, a life lived paralyzed by doubt and without the willingness to take chances is not much of a life at all. In contrast, George Saunders's portrayal of Cummings's internal monologues, showing how everything that happens to the writer immediately becomes fodder for his work, perhaps also reveals to the reader the danger of being an artist who is a voyeur of life but not a participant.

*Style and Technique*

Many of Saunders's other stories, such as "The 400-Pound CEO" and "Bounty," either make use of comically absurdist characters and settings or are dystopian satires of modern American society. "The Falls," by making use of the interior worlds of everyday, realistic characters, offers more of a commentary on individual consciousness. At the same time, the main character of "The Falls" is a character made familiar by other Saunders stories: the man who is seemingly pathetic on the surface, yet capable of acts that surprise even himself. The digressive, flowing language of "The Falls," as best demonstrated during Cummings's internal ramblings, is another staple of Saunders's writing.

Saunders is purposefully operating within a certain literary tradition in "The Falls." The story of men who live in their imaginations being called on to act is an old one, perhaps most famously presented in the short story "The Secret Life of Walter Mitty" (1939) by humor writer James Thurber. Morse is called on to make a more desperate decision than Mitty ever is, however, and in the end, he breaks the paralysis created by his anxiety in order to perform a heroic, if possibly futile, action.

*Scott Yarbrough*

# A FAMILY AFFAIR

*Author:* Guy de Maupassant (1850-1893)
*Type of plot:* Satire
*Time of plot:* About 1880
*Locale:* Paris and its suburbs
*First published:* "En Famille," 1881 (English translation, 1903)

> *Principal characters:*
> ALFRED CARAVAN, a fat, aging chief clerk in the Admiralty
> MADAME CARAVAN, his thin wife
> MADAME CARAVAN, his disgruntled ninety-year-old mother
> MARIE-LOUISE, his twelve-year-old daughter
> PHILIPPE-AUGUSTE, his son
> DR. CHENET, formerly a ship's surgeon, now in private practice
> ROSALIE, the Caravan maid
> MADAME BRAUX, Alfred's sister

## The Story

Monsieur Alfred Caravan is an aged chief clerk in a government office; he has trod the same circuit as commuter and drudge for some thirty years, for which service he is awarded a lapel pin by the bureaucracy. He is fat and officious, with an atrophied mind and a deeply ingrained dread of his superiors. One hot July night, he and his friend Dr. Chenet travel from Paris to their home at Courbevoie on the Neuilly steam-tram, as usual; they pause once more to tipple at the cafe, and part. At home (the story focuses comically and cruelly on the bureaucrat's so-called home life), in a minuscule apartment, Caravan greets his lean wife, a compulsive housekeeper and cleaner, and later encounters his filthy young children, who usually play in the neighborhood gutter. Tedious talk rehearses Caravan's being passed over—again—for a better job at the office. He is henpecked by his wife, while both in turn are domineered by Madame Caravan, Alfred's quarrelsome ninety-year-old mother, who is housed above them.

The narrator has caustically observed earlier that Caravan's ceaseless round of tedious conduct never alters, that nothing has transpired to disrupt his boring existence. However, the story is devoted precisely to relating one very unusual alteration, for, as all are sitting down to dinner, Rosalie the maid hysterically announces that Mama Caravan has collapsed upstairs. Dr. Chenet is summoned, the mother is pronounced dead, and a round of hysteria and lamentation commences—mechanical and sincere on Caravan's part, halfhearted and improvised on the part of his wife—and some species of chaos is come at last. All, including the doctor, brokenly attempt to complete their meal, and, absentmindedly, they eat and (especially) drink too much. Caravan and Chenet wander out into the fresh air for relief. Caravan conjures up sentimental remembrances of things past, and he even visits his cafe to solicit sympathy, but none is forthcoming from the busy customers.

Subsequently, back home and in bed, Caravan submits to his wife's plans. Because Mama has died intestate and because his estranged sister will want the best leftovers for herself, the two must "salvage" and secure any heirlooms at once, in the middle of the night. They tiptoe upstairs and confiscate Mama's monstrous ugly clock, which depicts a girl in gilt bronze playing cup-and-ball, and a heavy chest of drawers with a marble top. Mama's clothes are summarily packed in a wooden crate. Next day, notices are sent everywhere, and all the nosey neighborhood comes to inspect the deceased; even the children's dirty ruffian friends sneak in and take a peek. Finally, Madame and Monsieur Braux, Caravan's sister and her socialist husband, are telegraphed and asked to come from Charenton. Exhausted, the whole family sits down to dinner once again; the lamp runs out of oil; and, only twenty-four hours after her demise, it is discovered that Mama (who often suffered from fainting fits) has revived. Pandemonium ensues as everyone rushes upstairs. Dazed and sulky, Mama is back to normal—and hungry. The entire family is courteous beyond measure. Then, as all descend on the crowded stairs, the rival sister and her husband appear. Fighting ensues; Mama demands her possessions back and arranges a visit with the sister. The men quarrel lustily about politics. Dr. Chenet reappears, delighted to encounter in Mama such a medical recovery; he abruptly resumes eating and drinking. Caravan's wife quarrels with the sister and her husband; the tension increases until the relatives depart. The Caravans at the close are left, briefly, alone. However, they are filled with grief and terror about the renewed presence of Mama, and fearful of Alfred's employers, because Caravan has, in all the hurly-burly, managed to miss a day at the office and now has lost his excuse for the absence.

*Themes and Meanings*

Guy de Maupassant is best known for his brief, realistic tales of Norman peasantry, of Paris life, and of the insignificant bourgeoisie. Often his stories are notable for their speed, drama, climax, and surprise endings. Moreover, he is usually admired for his shrewd deployment of a persistent irony. All these qualities figure prominently in "A Family Affair." Together with several other stories, such as "The Piece of String," "The Necklace," "The False Gems," and "The Umbrella," "A Family Affair" is one of his best-known pieces.

Unlike some, however, this tale does not feature cool authorial detachment. Rather, it is a scathing frontal assault, sketched with roller-coaster rapidity and acid commentary, depicting a typically trite, rapacious, empty-headed suburban family. Indeed, it provides a behind-the-scenes glimpse of terrible mediocrity; the phrase *en famille* usually indicates domestic privacy and bliss, a cozy being "at home." Perhaps a modern translation of the title might coyly be "All in the Family." Clearly, the title is employed, as is virtually all else in this story, with raw sarcasm.

In such a satire, it is difficult to imagine who is not intended as a target. With widening inclusiveness, everyone and anything is indicted: commuters, doctors, bureaucrats, suburban housewives, mothers-in-law, gluttony, avarice, politics, antiques, children, and death. The very breadth and diffuseness of this list renders the story something of a circus, with various dumb animals performing simultaneously in every ring. Just such overcrowding and excess give the story its absurdity, vitality, and grim farcical humor.

## Style and Technique

Maupassant, following in the steps of Gustave Flaubert, is the master of precise detail; he frequently captures with exactitude the minutiae of urban life. In the oppressive July heat, Maupassant observes the city's "white, chalky, opaque, suffocating, and warm dust" in the air, which damply adheres to everything, and he is sensitive to city tenements clustered with small noisome flies. He swiftly caricatures Caravan's restless wife, who compulsively rubs mahogany chairs with a piece of flannel; he sketches dainty family members at table overeating with "a sort of studied inattention"; and he surveys the curious from all over town who file in, "stealthy as an army of mice," to observe the corpse.

Maupassant is similarly the master of exaggeration; his deft overemphasis repeatedly transforms normal actions into melodrama. Thus, Caravan in mourning is portrayed as flinging himself on the body of his supposedly deceased mother and as incessantly moaning and weeping. Caravan's inebriated vision of Mama in the past is overpainted—old memories are laid on, as it were, with a trowel; for now, with his loss, he vows that his life has been sliced in half, that this separation will be eternal, that he will lose all recollections of his past. This hyperbolic emphasis discolors the scene, rendering the reader suspicious and amused. Hence, it is no surprise that Caravan feels sated, relieved, and comfortable shortly afterward, so that he can turn his attentions more efficiently to the acquisition of Mama's possessions.

Last, Maupassant undercuts the whole scene he is presenting by injecting sweeping summaries that diminish and debase. Caravan, for example, at his mother's wake stares at the corpse, and the reader is told that he is "revolving in his brain those apparently profound thoughts, those religious and philosophical commonplaces, which trouble people of mediocre minds in the face of death." In fact, the entire world of middle-class bureaucrats in commuterland is handsomely summed up at the tale's very outset. Females on the train are depicted as "stout women in strange toilettes, shopkeepers' wives from the suburbs, who made up for the distinguished looks that they did not possess by ill-assumed dignity." The males aboard fare no better.

This grotesque painting strikes exactly the right note between comedy and horror; its portrayals are exaggerated, but all too often with just enough of the truth to be bitingly effective. Maupassant's is the brilliant culinary art of heaping on too much and basting it until it is very well done indeed.

*John R. Clark*

# A FAMILY SUPPER

*Author:* Kazuo Ishiguro (1954-    )
*Type of plot:* Psychological
*Time of plot:* The late twentieth century
*Locale:* Tokyo, Japan
*First published:* 1982

*Principal characters:*
> A YOUNG JAPANESE MAN, who has recently returned to Tokyo
> HIS FATHER, formerly a business executive
> KIKUKO, his sister, a student

*The Story*

"A Family Supper" is told alternately from the narrative perspective of a young man joining his father and sister for dinner at their father's home and in the form of a dialogue among the members of the family. The young man has just returned to Tokyo from California, where he has been living for the past several years. His father, a World War II veteran and widower, has been forced to retire because the firm in which he was employed as an executive collapsed. The dinner is being held to reunite the family for the first time since the mother's death, and the father has prepared a special dish for the occasion. In the first paragraph of the story, the narrator mentions that traditional Japanese dishes made from *fugu* (puffer fish or blowfish) have a special significance for him because his mother died in somewhat ambiguous circumstances after eating the fish. The preparation of the fish involves a great deal of skill because some of its glands contain a deadly poison and must be carefully removed.

While the son was living in the United States, he was not in close contact with the other members of his family. At the dinner, he learns that after the firm failed, his father's partner for seventeen years, Watanabe, killed himself as a matter of "principle and honor." His mother had always refused to eat *fugu* but accepted an invitation from an old schoolfriend "whom she was anxious not to offend." His father expresses the hope that the narrator will remain in Japan, but the son tells him that he is not sure about plans for the future. A degree of tension fills the conversation, "punctuated by long pauses," but the father underscores his desire to bring the family closer together.

Kikuko, the narrator's sister, arrives from Osaka University where she is a student, and the strained formality of the conversation changes when their father leaves the room to attend to supper. She and the narrator discuss the ways in which they disappointed their parents by their adherence to the ways of a new generation and by their casual disregard for the patterns of the past that their parents cherished. When they return to the house from the garden, Kikuko somewhat reluctantly accepts her father's invitation to help with the meal, and father and son wander through the house, which the son notices seems dimly lit and "startlingly empty." One room, however, is filled with books and papers, as well as an intricate model of a battleship. In addition to developing his culinary skills, the older man has been carefully assembling the plastic warship that he tells his son is like the craft he served on during the war.

The family then begins the meal in silence, consuming various courses until one large pot remains unopened. Intrigued by its appealing and unusual taste, the son asks what they are eating. "Just fish," his father replies. Then the son wonders what his father thinks of Watanabe's decision to take "his whole family with him." The older man explains that the collapse of the firm had weakened his partner's judgment. His son asks if Watanabe's action was a mistake, to which his father replies, "of course."

The two men sit in silence for a while, the room becoming dark as the daylight ends. Their conversation is more relaxed now, as the father asks whether his son will remain in Japan, inviting him to stay in the family home if he wishes. Neither man seems particularly certain about their future, but they reassure each other that when Kikuko completes her studies, "things will improve." This ambiguous pronouncement is emblematic of the easing of tension that has occurred.

### Themes and Meanings

"A Family Supper" deals with the difficulties that a generation, accustomed to power and confident that an established culture will continue indefinitely, faces when its familiar world is swept away. Kazuo Ishiguro was born in Japan and came to the British Isles at age five when his father, an oceanographer, was invited to participate in a British government research project. Although England was a primal part of the victorious Allied effort in World War II, while Japan experienced defeat, both countries were utterly changed by the conflict. England suffered a stunning decline in power in the aftermath of its empire, and Japan was transformed from a semi-medieval regional power into a modern economic colossus.

"A Family Supper" examines the ways in which both the generation that governed Japan before the war and the next one, which grew up in an entirely different social and political situation, attempt to deal with drastic changes in a nation fully involved in previously scorned foreign patterns of behavior. The father represents the older generation, bitter in the face of defeat and loss. The collapse of his firm is a symbol for the failure of the older Japanese approach to the world. His partner Watanabe's decision to commit suicide is an appropriate response in terms of traditional Japanese culture but somewhat questionable in postwar Japan. His choice to take his family with him is completely outrageous by any but the most primitive codes of behavior. Although he is stunned by the turn of events, the narrator's father shows an unexpected adaptability when he learns to cook—women's work—after the loss of his wife. His wife's decision to risk eating poorly prepared and possibly lethal *fugu* to avoid offending an old friend is as questionable as Watanabe's sacrifice of his family and seems equally pointless in terms of its effects. Both she and Watanabe have been trapped by an outmoded course of action. The father, when he turns his attention to the careful crafting of a model battleship, is choosing to occupy his time with a project of no intrinsic value but the choice is a positive one. He has not just given up in the face of a drastic reversal of fortune and has some hope for a viable if diminished future.

His son's somewhat aimless wandering is typical of a generation with no clear, tangible goals. He has been cut loose from family, country, and culture and has become a kind of international nomad, with no specific goals and no particular responsibilities. Probably about thirty years old, he has begun to wonder whether his generation's total rejection of Japan's past has been an entirely successful venture. His return home is part of a tentative effort to reestablish some connections to his family and to try to get to know his father, a man distant and aloof throughout his childhood.

Ishiguro strongly implies that the main course of the meal that the father prepares is *fugu*. The older man is both honoring the memory of his late wife with her insistence on risking death to avoid giving offense and testing both his ability to serve the fish safely and his children's willingness to trust their father's skill and his judgment. Although it could be argued that the father is following the traditional Japanese custom of salvaging personal honor through the act of suicide—a death with honor that would correspond to his pride in having "pure samurai blood"—this interpretation reduces the hovering mystery that makes the story so compelling.

*Style and Technique*

The aura of silence and shadows that permeates "A Family Supper" is at the crux of Ishiguro's method for evoking and maintaining a mood of uncertainty throughout the story. Amid the narrative flow, small details are crucial in determining the thought and emotion behind each character's utterances. Although the narrator's mother and younger sister play an important part in revealing the central conflict between traditional ways of being and the necessity for change and adaptation brought about by a radical alteration in circumstances, the two men are the primary players in the tableau. Similarly, the references to the ghostly presence in the garden are more of a suggestion of the existence of mysterious, uncontrollable forces rather than a crucial plot element. Subtle nuances of speech and the implications of motive in a careful control of tone are the ways in which Ishiguro explores psychological foundations.

As the narration progresses, the shift toward dialogue from the initial alternation of conversation and exposition moves the focus from the son to his father, whose admission that there "are other things besides work" indicates that the son's expectations about rigid attitudes are not entirely accurate. Paradoxically, the father's somewhat tentative and distant responses are replaced by a direct declaration that Watanabe's decision was a mistake, echoing Kikuko's description of the murder and ritual suicide as "sick." Nevertheless, the father's explanation that he would have preferred service in the air force because a plane, when struck, was "always the ultimate final weapon" seems to support Watanabe's determination to retain his honor. However, the father's hopes for a future with his family indicate a different attitude. This method of incremental adjustment and advance in comprehension gives "A Family Supper" a resonance that reverberates considerably beyond the story's apparent conclusion.

*Leon Lewis*

# THE FANCY WOMAN

*Author:* Peter Taylor (1917-1994)
*Type of plot:* Psychological
*Time of plot:* Probably the late 1930's
*Locale:* A country home in Tennessee
*First published:* 1940

>    *Principal characters:*
>    JOSIE CARLSON, the protagonist, a young, single woman
>    GEORGE, who treats her like a mistress
>    AMELIA, a black servant
>    MR. AND MRS. ROBERTS,
>    MR. AND MRS. JACKSON, and
>    MR. AND MRS. COLTON, friends of George visiting from
>        Memphis
>    JOCK and
>    BUDDY, George's sons, ages seventeen and fourteen

*The Story*

From the opening sentences, the story portrays a mental state as well as narrating a series of events; this emphasis on subjectivity means that the impact of events is at least as important as the events themselves. The story's central consciousness, Miss Josephine Carlson, has been invited by her man George to spend a week at his country place, and the sentence fragments and uncertain grammar of her "voice" hint at both anger and anxiety. In this opening scene, the combination of alcohol and sex with Josie's lack of options in the relationship sets the stage for all that follows. As preposterous as it might seem at the end of the story, this "fancy woman" wonders whether George loves her, whether she might be the social equal of the white Memphis visitors she meets, and whether George is eventually going to marry her. For her, and her only, this is a "love story."

The narrative is divided into twelve sections, and each section makes it clearer that George, even when absent from the scene, controls all that goes on. For him, love and marriage are not the issues. One should, however, also note the contrasts between day and night: The events of three nights and three days make up the story and give a sense of progression.

Sections 2 through 5 narrate the events of the first morning when only George, Josie, and the servants are present. In this isolation, Josie reveals her insecurity and defensiveness about her respectability and her lack of power with George—she seems to have only passivity or the whiskey bottle; when in section 4 she becomes sick to her stomach and falls off her mount, George laughs mockingly and leaves her. In section 5, her vacillations reveal the full measure of her insecurity and ambition: One moment she rejects him but thinks immediately afterward that "he was lonesome. There was, then, a place to be filled." The sequence reveals George as a single-minded bully and Josie as a would-be manipulator; because of the doubtful reliability of both these characters, it leaves many elements of their relationship ambiguous.

The heart of the story, sections 6 and 7, introduces the three Memphis couples and narrates the afternoon and evening of wife-swapping and drinking. In Josie's shock at learning about their organized adulteries, however, there is a positive note of naïveté; her wanting to dance only with George ("because she so liked to dance with him") and her resolve not to care what the others do make her for a time seem the most genuine person present. Again, Peter Taylor's narrative seeks to maintain ambiguity, to forestall taking sides or condemning too quickly.

In the eighth section, when Josie concludes the next morning that Mr. Jackson had come to her bed during the night and derives from this conclusion the satisfaction that "they're none of 'em any better than the niggers. . . . By God, nobody's better than I am," the strong but by no means dominant theme of Josie-as-victim begins to fade. Her desire to get even with George by flirting with his seventeen-year-old son Jock changes her image completely. In declaring a suicidal war against George, she shows the worst in herself, seeing the boys as "smutty" sexual creatures, dreaming that Jock tries to enter her room (another man—and this time, significantly, one does not learn who or even if Josie knows who—has already used her). Josie's confrontation with Buddy, the fourteen-year-old, takes on gothic overtones: This has become a tale of a lone woman in a house of horror, except that the woman has clearly sought the confrontation. Motives even now are not clear, especially Buddy's motives; the only certainty is George's imminent violence against her.

*Themes and Meanings*

Taylor's major theme in this early story is the disintegration of the family and the collapse of the values associated with the genteel South. Allied with that is an investigation, showing Freudian preoccupations, of the effects of this disintegration on a lone woman's psyche ("A Spinster's Tale," written about the same time, focuses for the same purpose on a woman who unlike Josie was reared in the upper-middle class). The results suggest that the social breakdown has revealed sadistic and masochistic elements that appear as twisted versions of the male aggressiveness and female passivity associated with the old, genteel chivalric love tradition.

George, who appears often in the story wearing white, rides horses on his country estate, drinks expensive whiskey in his mint juleps, and is impetuous with his inferiors and sentimental with his children, represents a soulless version of the southern gentleman. His behavior toward his mistress is summarized as follows: "He either laughed at her or cursed her or, of course, at night would pet her. He hadn't hit her." The organized infidelities of his friends are further evidence of social breakdown; his allowing those friends to share his mistress, and his sons to see her, contrasts with his violent defense of those sons from her supposed advances and adds a final grotesque touch to the treatment of "social standards" in the story.

Of at least equal importance, however, is the related theme of the consequences of social and familial disintegration on women. Josie is out of her usual social element here—thus her loneliness and eagerness to please a man she barely knows. Taylor, however, avoids the pitfall of sentimentality by characterizing her as an adventurer who thinks she can rise in the world: She will, it seems, suffer anything for George. Her essentially conservative assumption about the need for a wife in this "family" is ironic, and does not serve her well. George feels no such need. Events make it clear that Josie, to promote her own interests, is willing to become a drunk, to prostitute herself, to commit adultery with strangers, and to seek to take advantage of what she suspects to be the worst impulses of George's adolescent son. She matches and perhaps exceeds George's desire to manipulate people. For both George and Josie, freedom is a concept unconnected with responsibility, and this license makes their final confrontation inevitable. It is significant that after her constant worry about respectability, she should be named "fancy woman" by George's younger boy, whose precocious insight is an indictment of all the adults in the story.

### Style and Technique

Taylor's artistry is subtle but powerful. "The Fancy Woman" communicates the themes of disintegration by its skillful use of the third-person limited point of view, its adaptation of grotesque elements from the gothic tradition, and its ironic portrayal of social nuances.

Limiting the point of view to Josie, an unintelligent and relatively inexperienced woman now out of her social element, Taylor severely restricts the readers' knowledge about other characters' motives. Josie maintains a hopeful view by grossly simplifying everything, especially human nature: "She'd find out what was wrong inside [George], for there's something wrong inside everybody, and somehow she'd get hold of him."

The narrative also reflects her weaknesses by what it omits; for example, no explanations or reflections concerning the strangers in her bed enter the narrative because Josie herself refuses to think about what she has done. The sight of George's boys on the lawn reminds her of "a scene from a color movie, like one of the musicals": She habitually perceives experience in terms of clichés—the only sources of comparison and judgment that she possesses.

The gothic elements are well disguised at first by the dark comedy of Josie's ignorance and George's callousness. Nevertheless, the vaguely dangerous man, the secretive servants, the isolated house, the mysterious guests, the night visitors to Josie's room, the turning doorknob, her strange dreams, the enigmatic young boys, and finally her isolation with the younger son, whose voice "came from one part of the house and then another," firmly imprint the damsel-in-distress motif on the narrative and prepare the reader for George's violence at the end. Like the use of Josie's flawed consciousness, the gothic elements work largely in the service of irony.

Finally, another very important ironic element is the pastoral scene, used to bring into bold relief the leisure habits of the "quality" people of urban Memphis. In this simplified environment, this Tennessee Versailles, in its freedom from artificial social constraints, the "sophisticated" people can show who they really are, and they do. Josie remains unaware of all this, but the arrangement of events in the narrative creates ironic commentary on all notions of "class."

The rituals of conversing, eating, drinking, appreciating nature and the arts (music, poetry, dance, games, and sports)—all communal rituals, in fact—are mocked by these characters. The most dignified persons are the servants. By focusing on a character who is ignorant of these nuances, who misunderstands what is important and concentrates on what is not, the story exposes the hypocrisy and decline of this culture from beneath rather than from above, an approach that places Taylor directly in the tradition of William Faulkner.

*Kerry Ahearn*

# THE FARM

*Author:* Joy Williams (1944-      )
*Type of plot:* Psychological
*Time of plot:* Around 1980
*Locale:* New England
*First published:* 1981

> *Principal characters:*
> SARAH, an upper-middle-class suburban woman
> TOMMY, her husband
> GENEVIEVE BETTENCOURT, a mother whose teenage boy Sarah
>     and Tommy accidentally run over

*The Story*

Sarah and Tommy are an affluent couple leading a comfortable life in suburban New England. On the face of it, nothing is wrong with their lives, but one shadow plagues their happiness: They both have a drinking problem. As Sarah and Tommy go to their third party on a certain night in August, Sarah recounts a story about a young child eaten by an alligator. Tommy does not seem to respond to the story, and Sarah begins to reflect on the troubled state of their marriage.

The party is one of many in the couple's customary routine of drinking and socializing, interspersed with name-dropping and boasts of European travel. After the party concludes, the couple go home. Sarah, who is driving, begins to feel the effects of her heavy alcohol consumption and starts to hallucinate. Her visions are brought to a sharp halt when she runs over a teenage boy standing in the middle of the road, killing him instantly.

The police exonerate the couple in the death of the boy, Steven Bettencourt. No charges are filed, and Sarah is not prosecuted or held legally accountable for the young man's death. Nevertheless, Sarah feels a severe sense of guilt and vows to give up drinking and orient her life in a new, more positive direction. This resolution, however, does not improve her emotional state. Indeed, Sarah feels disoriented by no longer drinking; it is as if her entire identity had previously depended on her alcoholism.

During the next three months, things seem to be returning to normal, but just as Sarah's sense of psychological solidity begins to be restored, her life receives a sudden and disagreeable jolt. Unannounced and unexpected, Genevieve Bettencourt, the mother of the boy Sarah ran over, comes to Sarah's door. She is weirdly amicable, showing no overt resentment. She and Sarah exchange information about their lives and families, in a manner at once intimate and coldly formal.

There is an unreal quality about the meeting. Genevieve reveals that Steven was hardly the perfect son, but still she displays a sense of deep mourning for him. Sarah apologizes to Genevieve, but Genevieve will not accept her apology. Sarah begins to realize that Genevieve's friendliness is a form of calculating revenge. Genevieve is determined not only to make Sarah feel guilty but to ruin her life. Genevieve's actions constitute harassment, even stalking; but they are also a form of retribution, and Sarah cannot help but feel a sympathy for Genevieve that is against her own best interests.

Tommy feels that Sarah is being harassed by Genevieve and wants his wife to stop admitting her to their house. The eerie presence of Genevieve in the couple's home is the subject of a long and increasingly nettlesome tug-of-war between husband and wife. Sarah persists with the acquaintance, noting that Genevieve seems to take a particular interest in their own daughter, Martha. In attempted atonement for her misdeed, Sarah offers to share Martha with Genevieve. Genevieve, though, continues to bring up more memories of her son, until Sarah feels that the intruder has taken over her life. Tommy wants to move the family away to a farm in the country, but Sarah realizes that she cannot escape the psychic burdens symbolized by Genevieve's presence in her life. For her, things can never be as they once were.

*Themes and Meanings*

Although "The Farm" does not carry an explicit thesis about alcoholism, much of the story's emotional resonance derives from the impact of alcoholism on its characters' lives. Alcoholism is examined not merely as a clinical malady but as a metaphor for any syndrome by which alienated characters seek to remedy the lack of meaning in their lives. Tommy and Sarah are complacent, assured members of a privileged social class. They attempt to paper over the emotional gaps in their flawed and unexamined relationship by drinking and by maintaining a false sense of self-satisfaction. Joy Williams analyzes alcoholism as both a medical and sociological phenomenon but stresses primarily its destructive psychological effects. Alcoholism immures Tommy and Sarah within their own neuroses. It heightens the problems they already have and prevents them from finding any solutions to them.

The walls they have built around their own hypocrisies are shattered by the death of Steven Bettencourt. The killing introduces an alien and disturbing element into the couple's lives, and forces them to interrogate all of their previous assumptions. There are also class and religious elements here: Tommy and Sarah are propertied and Protestant, whereas the Bettencourts are working-class Roman Catholics. More compellingly, Steven's death makes Sarah, in particular, cognizant of the disturbing contradictions in her life that she previously repressed.

The nature of the title is significant. "The Farm" does not refer to the farm Tommy wants to buy Sarah at the end of the story but to the colloquialism "to have bought the farm," meaning to have died. This phrase, introduced into the story by Genevieve in conversation with Sarah, implies that death is not just extinction or disappearance but entrance into a new and disturbing realm. Steven has "bought the farm" in figurative terms, but metaphorically, so have Tommy and Sarah. Steven's death has made them aware of their own inadequacies. In order to escape this newfound self-knowledge, Tommy attempts to "buy the farm" in the sense in which one usually employs the word "farm," to move his family to a new, reassuringly agricultural domicile. The serene and placid reference Tommy intends tumbles over into the more threatening and unsettling slang phrase. A conventionally restorative flight to bucolic safety is not feasible. Geographic distance alone will not restore the past. The couple's earlier complacency is gone forever.

## Style and Technique

Like such modern short stories as "The Garden-Party" (1922) by Katherine Mansfield, "The Farm" uses the unexpected death of an outsider to reveal unexpressed problems in the lives of comfortable and self-assured characters. Williams does not use Steven Bettencourt's death manipulatively, however. One reason for this is that Williams makes her characters so ordinary, so everyday, that the presence of the unexpected or the unlikely does not strike the reader as gratuitous or unearned.

Williams's stories are generally agreed by critics to resemble, in structure and in tone, the minimalism pioneered by the late Raymond Carver. Williams, however, imparts to her fiction a surrealistic air all her own. This surrealism can be seen in the telling anecdote of the child being killed by the alligator. At first, this seems to be a pointless interruption of the narrative, but it has a twofold function within the story. It reveals a panoply of incident and example that anchors the story's metaphoric register, foreshadowing Steven's death. In Williams's thick, braided mode of narration, every quote and every detail matter in the tale's ultimate composition.

Williams is a self-conscious artist, eager to advertise the sophistication of her own fictional mode, while also operating on a very human level. The odd interruptions, sudden swerves of voice and narrative, and the sense of fey, winsome, if slightly wry wonder that pervades the story mirror the situations of the characters. Far from being structured, Williams's surrealism reflects the way in which the random tragedies of life rupture the self-assurance of people who thought they had their world under control. The artistic skill with which the story is rendered mirrors the messiness and incoherence of real life.

*Margaret Boe Birns*

# THE FAT GIRL

*Author:* Andre Dubus (1936-1999)
*Type of plot:* Psychological
*Time of plot:* 1955-1975
*Locale:* Louisiana and Massachusetts
*First published:* 1977

> *Principal characters:*
> LOUISE, an overweight, compulsive eater
> CARRIE, her college roommate
> RICHARD, the young lawyer whom Louise marries

### The Story

Louise was kissed for the first time at the age of sixteen, when a drunken young man roughly grabbed her at a barbecue. Her father, a wealthy lawyer in a small city in Louisiana, often kisses her as well, but she can see pity in his eyes along with love. The reason for Louise's lack of affection from young men her own age and for her father's pity is that, since she was nine years old, she has been putting on weight from overeating. Her slim and pretty mother, worried about Louise's attractiveness to boys, feeds her dietetic lunches, but Louise later sneaks into the kitchen and makes peanut butter sandwiches to eat secretly. At school, she makes a show before her friends of refusing fattening foods, emerging from the cafeteria line with only a salad. Later, however, she sneaks sandwiches at home and buys candy bars, storing them in her bedroom closet behind stuffed animals from her earlier childhood. At the movies, she is fascinated by fat actresses, and at home, by fat friends of her mother. Like herself, she rationalizes, they are different, and she believes that she, like them, is fat because God has made her that way. However, she is curious about them. Do they try to lose weight? Do they, too, go around thinking of food all day?

At a women's college in Massachusetts, Louise continues her old ways; however, now she does not need to hide anything from her mother. She stores candy bars in a drawer and eats whatever she wants. She senses her parents' disappointment when she chooses an all-female school, away from boys, and at college she feels out of place, especially in gym class where she must wear shorts. She hates her body. Her only college friend is Carrie, a thin, unhappy girl with thick glasses who becomes Louise's roommate for four years.

In the summer before her senior year, Carrie falls in love with a music student in Boston and experiences both love and sex. Concerned about Louise and wanting her to be loved the way that she feels loved, Carrie offers to help Louise lose weight. She puts her on a strict diet, does all the shopping, serves her small portions of broiled meat, fish, chicken, and lettuce in their room, and nurtures her through each day. Louise suffers enormously, starts to smoke cigarettes, and becomes irritable with Carrie, but sticks to the diet and eventually loses more than seventy pounds. When she goes home, her parents are proud of her, all of her relatives tell her she is beautiful, and for the first time since childhood Louise swims in the country club pool without embarrassment.

After graduation, Louise returns home, takes an inconsequential job just to have something to do, and starts seeing Richard, a young lawyer who has joined her father's firm. He is the first man to kiss her since that first drunken boy. After she gives herself to him, they are married; Carrie flies down from Boston to serve as her maid of honor. With Richard, Louise now seems to have everything: a husband who loves her, a beautiful home by the lake, and vacations in Mexico, Canada, and the Bahamas. While vacationing in Europe during their fifth year of marriage, Louise and Richard conceive a child.

Louise becomes increasingly troubled by her newly found happiness. She thinks that by becoming thin, she has somehow compromised herself, bought into the pleasures of the thin people she has always envied. She believes that she chose her friends merely because they were thin. She believes that even Richard does not see her or love her completely, because he cannot relate to the fat girl who she once was. During her pregnancy, her body is gaining weight, and she starts to develop her earlier craving for sweets. She begins to hide candy bars in the bedroom, waiting for Richard to leave the house. Her mother starts to worry about her again, while Richard becomes increasingly cold and distant after the birth of their son. They quarrel frequently and Richard does not touch Louise anymore because she is letting herself go. At night, Louise eats candy bars in the darkness of the bathroom, she buys loose dresses to hide her body, and she avoids wearing bathing suits and shorts. Richard's anger about her weight seems not to touch her, and Louise remains calm, hidden beneath the layers of her expanding flesh, as she watches his frustration and helplessness.

In the final scene, Richard is raging at Louise, the baby is crying, and Louise is holding the child against the folds of her flesh. Richard offers to help Louise, even to eat the same things that she eats, but she sees in him none of the compassion and love she saw earlier in Carrie, although she remembers nothing of that final college year except the hunger. She is continually hungry now, and when she comes downstairs, after putting her son in his crib, she is eating a candy bar, surprised to see Richard still there, for she is certain that he is about to leave her.

## Themes and Meanings

Andre Dubus's "The Fat Girl" is not so much a story about a young woman's uncontrollable urge to eat to the point of obesity as it is the story of a psychological hunger, not only for love but also for acceptance as a whole person. The protagonist, Louise, clearly does not grow up in a cold and indifferent family environment. On the contrary, her father showers affection on her, indulges her, and never chides her about her weight. Her mother is concerned about her appearance and tries to give her dietetic lunches and motherly advice. What then is Louise's problem?

One might say that the source of her disturbance is her difference, the fact that she is a fat person in an unaccepting world of thin people. In that sense, she is not unlike many other people who are different in some way. Both of Louise's parents are thin, and they expect their daughter to be the same way. In fact, when she does try to fit in by losing weight, she tries to emulate her mother who, like Louise, has long pale blond hair and smokes cigarettes—a habit that Louise takes up during her diet. Louise is not popular with boys not because of who she is, but because of her weight. Even after she marries Richard and has his child, Louise feels that he only loves her because she is now thin and would not have loved the earlier, fat Louise. Both Louises, the fat one and the thin one, are the totality of Louise, and she wants to be loved as a complete person. As it turns out, her suspicions about Richard are correct, for as she gains weight, Richard becomes more distant. At the end of the story, it is clear to Louise that Richard—and most of the world—will not love her for who she is; he will simply respond to what she looks like.

This is not to say that Louise is an admirable character in the story. She is self-indulgent, willful, deceitful, and ultimately self-destructive. She is, nevertheless, uncompromisingly herself, something that everyone is—or wishes to be—and she is not entirely to blame. In a world where thin is beautiful and the different do not fit in, many people like Louise are doomed to loneliness, shame, and pity.

*Style and Technique*

While he does provide glimpses into the mind of Louise, Dubus relates her story with a clinical objectivity similar to a case study of abnormal behavior, as the opening line, "Her name was Louise," suggests. It is an appropriate style, for it keeps the reader emotionally detached from feelings of ridicule or pity. The flat narrative tone is designed to increase the reader's understanding, to give one a series of sketches of Louise from high school, through college, to marriage and childbirth. Everything is narrated, and little, until the end, is dramatized, so the reader will reserve judgment until all the facts are in. It is only when one sees the confrontation between Louise and Richard toward the end of the story that one feels an accumulated pity for and understanding of the protagonist.

The story is told in three sections: Louise's high school years, her college years and loss of weight, and her marriage to Richard. One might say, in fact, that because parts one and three show Louise as a fat girl, with the story of her thin self sandwiched in between, the construction of the story is a perfect illustration of the old adage, "Inside every fat person is a thin person trying to get out."

*Kenneth Seib*

# THE FAT MAN IN HISTORY

*Author:* Peter Carey (1943-      )
*Type of plot:* Absurdist
*Time of plot:* A vague post-revolution future
*Locale:* Unspecified English-speaking country
*First published:* 1974

### Principal characters:

ALEXANDER FINCH, the central consciousness of the story
MILLIGAN, a taxi driver and the only one of the group employed
GLINO, an emotional vegetarian
MAY, the sole married man of the six
FANTONI, a talented thief, and the house leader
THE-MAN-WHO-WON'T-GIVE-HIS-NAME, the original tenant
NANCY BOWLBY, the rent collector called Florence Nightingale

## The Story

Alexander Finch, gross and obese, walks out of a department store with bed sheets he has stolen, as well as with several cans of smoked oysters that fill the large pockets of his floppy trousers. Struggling through the revolving door, he reflects on the irony that, since the revolution, to be fat is to be an oppressor. Before the revolution, "most fat men were either Americans, stooges for the Americans, or wealthy supporters of the Americans." However, with the collapse of the "old Danko regime," everything has changed. Finch had once been a lovable blimp, a political cartoonist known as "Teddy," but gradually after the revolution, the influence of the Central Committee of Seventy-five had turned the word "fat" into "a synonym for greedy, ugly, sleazy, lazy, obscene, evil, dirty, dishonest, untrustworthy." So Finch, once the secretary of the Thirty-second District, has shifted sides to become the secretary of the underground organization "Fat Men Against the Revolution."

Finch's five housemates are an irregular lot. Milligan, who drives a taxi with iridescent blue and yellow stripes, is the only one of the six with a job. Glino is a vegetarian who plants radishes in the front yard. May, the only married man in the group, plays a scratched Sibelius record constantly while moping for "Dear Iris," the wife to whom he writes many letters. Fantoni, at twenty-eight the youngest of the householders and an accomplished thief, is a menacing figure, the "leader and driving force" that holds the conspirators together. The sixth man, first to occupy the house, is known only as "the-man-who-won't-give-his-name," and it was to provide him agreeable company that Florence Nightingale, as they call their rent collector, invited Fantoni to take a room. The others soon followed.

The daily lives of the fat men are banal, as they endure tedious conversations and drink Glino's homemade beer, a routine punctuated only by visits from Florence Nightingale to collect the rent money. She slips into Finch's room early one night, he calls her by her real name, Nancy, and they enjoy a brief "sexual/asexual flirtation" while joking about the military leaders of the revolution. One evening, Glino plays the "Blue Danube" on his mouth organ while Florence Nightingale dances with the-man-who-won't-give-his-name. When Finch comes up short with rent money, Fantoni pays him to dig a pit in the backyard, ostensibly to barbecue Florence Nightingale so that he can eat her. Finch explains that "by bodily consuming a senior member of the revolution," then "the bodies of Fat Men will purify the revolution."

One night Florence Nightingale is discovered in bed with the-man-who-won't-give-his-name, discussing Fantoni's planned cannibalism. The scene jumps to the next evening with the vegetarian Glino vomiting in the backyard after being forced to eat a bit of the human barbecue—not of Florence Nightingale but of Fantoni. The-man-who-won't-give-his-name then assumes Fantoni's name and takes his room. A new nameless man arrives to fill the role of anonymous. These odd events conclude with an epilogue in the form of a memo on "Revolution in a Closed Society—A Study of Leadership Among the Fat" by Nancy Bowlby. It seems that the leader—the "Fantoni"—invariably becomes the subject of a "crisis" that leads to his death in a "revolution" in which the "'Fantoni' was always disposed of effectively and the new 'Fantoni' took control of the group." The experiment has so far produced "twenty-three successive 'Fantonis'" and will continue.

*Themes and Meanings*

Behind the absurd events of "The Fat Man in History" lie the mysterious revolution and the shadowy generals, Kooper and Alvarez, who are alluded to several times. The pre-revolution leader had apparently been a corrupt figure named Danko, who along with the generals is described by Finch as fascists. Other unexplained individuals are Calsen, "an academic, who was kicked out of the university for seducing one of 'the little scrawnies'"; Deirdre and Annie, "fragile girls with the slender arms of children," who had loved Finch "with a total and unreasonable love"; and Miles Cooper, the Cooper with a 'C', who had betrayed the revolution.

Before the revolution, fatness was apparently to be accepted, perhaps even admired, as evidence of one's prosperity, presumably even one's selfishness and willingness to exploit the poorer classes. To be fat, however, came to be seen as the mark of an oppressor, a capitalist running dog of the Americans, who are identified with the vicious Danko regime. Thus, Finch and his fellow fat men, each a mountain of flesh, huddle together as pariahs in a filthy rented house, surviving mainly by shoplifting. As the self-appointed "Fat Men Against the Revolution," they scheme with their leader, Fantoni, to blow up the 16 October Statue. Fat induces their alienation, their bitterness, their susceptibility to exploitation.

Food and eating play a large role in this story, not only in the humiliating bloat of the characters, prisoners in their own corpulence, but also in the cannibalism theme. The barbecue pit that Finch digs in the backyard is—he is told by Fantoni—for cooking Florence Nightingale, but eventually it becomes the site of Fantoni's immolation and consumption. Ironically, the cannibalism is only one instance in a series of twenty-three horrible human feasts cooked up by Nancy Bowlby, also known as Florence Nightingale, as part of a cold-blooded academic experiment.

The sex scenes are anything but erotic. When Florence Nightingale slips into Finch's room one suffocating hot evening and kisses him on the cheek, calling him "Cuddles," her mildly provocative behavior leads to nothing and she departs, leaving Finch "nursing some vague disappointment." In one of their evenings, everyone is a bit drunk and Florence Nightingale dances first with Milligan, then with May and Finch, and finally waltzes with the nameless man as Glino plays the "Blue Danube." Again, the sexuality of the evening fades but later culminates in Florence Nightingale's being found in bed with the-man-who-won't-give-his-name.

*Style and Technique*

There is no resort to the supernatural or to obvious allegory in Peter Carey's third-person narration, but the oblique presentation of events colors the whole story with shadows of the unreal. Contributing to this effect is the division of the story into twenty sections, some very brief, with no transitions between them. Section 17, for instance, ends with Fantoni entering the room where Florence Nightingale has been found in bed with the nameless roomer, and without explanation, section 18 follows with Glino vomiting with vegetarian horror from what becomes clear was the consuming of the barbecued Fantoni. Apparently Fantoni had been strangled with a blue sheet, presumably one of the sheets that Finch steals at the story's outset. This bit of foreshadowing has correlates: At one point Florence Nightingale tells Finch not to be frightened of Fantoni for "he won't eat you."

Carey is adept at description. Finch's plight is poignant when he considers his bulk: "He is Alexander Finch, thirty-five years old, very fat, very tired, and suddenly, hopelessly sad. He has four large rolls of fat descending like a flesh curtain suspended from his navel. His spare tyres. He holds the fat in his hand, clenching it, wishing to tear it away. He clenches it until it hurts, and then clenches harder." When Fantoni eats the omelette Glino prepares for him, "He buries the dainty pieces in the small fleshy orifice beneath his large moustache."

These vivid descriptions are complemented by the way Carey catches the men wrestling with their private demons. Finch's despair is matched by the agony of the sexually frantic May, who writes fruitless letters to his wife and leaves blood all over the front door after battering it for three hours with his head.

Numerous allusions enrich the texture of the prose and deepen the characterizations. Besides the "Blue Danube" played by Glino, May plays his only piece of music, a Sibelius record, "incessantly." Finch reveals considerable feeling for cultural "bric-à-brac," including a Rubens print, postcard reproductions of renaissance paintings, an early Iceland map, and a Botticelli book that he examines "gently, loving the expensive paper as much as the reproductions."

*Frank Day*

# THE FAT OF THE LAND

*Author:* Anzia Yezierska (1880?-1970)
*Type of plot:* Social realism
*Time of plot:* The early 1900's
*Locale:* New York City
*First published:* 1919

> *Principal characters:*
> HANNEH BREINEH, the protagonist, the mother of six children
> FANNY, her only daughter
> MRS. PELZ, her friend and neighbor

*The Story*

In the first section of the story, the narrator introduces two Jewish women who are neighbors in a tenement. Hanneh Breineh, a self-centered and hyperemotional woman, calls out her window to the kind and somewhat philosophical Mrs. Pelz for help. Hanneh's washer-boiler is broken, and she asks to borrow Mrs. Pelz's.

Hanneh engages Mrs. Pelz in a dreary conversation, but as she is doing so, one of her six children falls from his high chair. The mother characteristically overreacts, rushing hysterically to her son, while the more sedate Mrs. Pelz offers up a superstitious solution for avoiding such future occurrences.

Mrs. Pelz also tries to comfort Hanneh with the thought that, although a burden now, six children will eventually provide much more income when they are old enough to work. Then, Hanneh will live off "the fat of the land." Ignoring this prophecy, Hanneh continues to lament the particulars of her awful life. Suddenly realizing, however, that she is behind schedule, Hanneh rushes to the marketplace, returning later only to find one of her children missing. Desperately searching the local streets for her Benny, she is shadowed by a crowd of concerned residents. At the end of this search, while Hanneh is reviving from a fainting spell, a police officer appears with the frightened and tearful Benny. Hanneh's earlier tormented concern quickly turns to anger and resentment. Instead of welcoming her son lovingly, Hanneh tells him to sit down and eat, and while eating to "choke."

In the second section of the story, Mrs. Pelz returns to live in New York City, apparently after some time away. She is on her way to visit the widowed and wealthy Hanneh, who now resides in a brownstone with her daughter, Fanny. The brief absence of the servant on this day allows Hanneh the momentary pleasure of eating in the kitchen. She and Mrs. Pelz do so, in a manner reminiscent of their tenement days.

It is true that she is quite wealthy, Hanneh declares, but she then proclaims through tears how wealth has enslaved her. This once envious woman, now the very object of local envy, secretly longs for her poorer days. Interrupting this poignant moment, the servant returns, and the two former neighbors are forced to end their meal.

The third section of the story begins as all of Hanneh's children gather in the brownstone one day. The conversation centers on Benny and his successful Broadway play and on the family's plans to attend a performance together. Suddenly, however, Hanneh tearfully starts to chide her offspring for not having invited her to go along with them. Fanny, it seems, thought it best to have Hanneh attend on a different night, and because it was her duty to ask Hanneh to accompany them, the mother never received an invitation. According to Fanny, the ill-mannered and uneducated Hanneh would be a social embarrassment. In addition, she would prove detrimental to Fanny's career if the daughter had to introduce her to the influential Mrs. Van Suyden. In further defense of her actions, Fanny accuses her brothers of abandoning Hanneh, while she, the daughter, has had the difficult chore of living with their mother.

As a result of this disclosure and discussion, the children agree among themselves to provide Hanneh with an apartment of her own. This decision makes Hanneh even more unhappy because the new apartment is without a kitchen, that one refuge to which Hanneh could always turn in order to stay busy. The idleness that this creates, along with the humiliation of being stared at in the public dining room, intensifies Hanneh's unhappiness. One day, she finds solace by returning to her old neighborhood to bicker and bargain with the vendors there.

Back at her new apartment building, which has strict regulations concerning food delivery, she defiantly enters the front lobby with her bag of groceries, including a large fish. Confronting there the very staid and proper hallman, Hanneh makes a stand. During the ensuing drama, Fanny enters the lobby with Mrs. Van Suyden. Immediately running to elicit aid from her daughter, Hanneh emotionally explains the situation. Instead of providing support, however, Fanny sides with the hall-man. Dejectedly, Hanneh goes to her room upstairs. Fanny apologizes to the departing Mrs. Van Suyden, who suggests that they meet again at some better time.

Blaming her mother for this lost opportunity, Fanny storms into her mother's apartment to deliver a tirade. An argument erupts, with mother and daughter accusing each other of various past and present abuses. When the fish finally arrives at the door, Hanneh flings it across the room and leaves.

Shortly afterward, at Mrs. Pelz's house, Hanneh seeks consolation and a sense of solidarity from her impoverished friend. Hanneh catalogs the unendurable conditions of her current lifestyle, ending her confession of grief with a request to stay the night with Mrs. Pelz. However, the uncomfortable bed and the vermin combine to drive the former tenement dweller away. She walks back toward her more comfortable apartment with the realization that she can never return to the arduous, simple life. With bitter laughter, she scorns her original enchantment with those magic words, "the fat of the land," and again enters the civilized enslavement of her apartment building.

## Themes and Meanings

Anzia Yezierska's short story deals with the ongoing social phenomenon of impoverished immigrants struggling to become a part of the American success story. In this story, one family from the Jewish ghetto in New York City achieves that dream, only to discover that there is a price to be paid for this success.

On a superficial level, the story depicts the hazards to be found in the extremes of both poverty and wealth. On another level, though, it indicts the hypocrisy of a society in which children grow up to be ashamed of their parents. The price for "Americanization," for success, that Hanneh's children, particularly Fanny, must pay is the denial of their Old World streetwise mother. The price that Hanneh must pay for achieving her desire to live "off the fat of the land" is loneliness and bewilderment. The driving purpose of her life—to survive under difficult circumstances and to ensure the survival of her family—has been removed by wealth, and by a society that places a higher value on social etiquette than it does on familial love and respect. Hanneh's children are Americanized and, in the process, dehumanized.

In particular, Fanny's adoption of the social code of the status-oriented and the success-seeking virtually severs the mother-daughter bond of love and respect. This tragedy leads the mother to recognize that in many ways the affluent are less free than the tenement-dwellers. She is bound by the rules of a rigid social code that she does not understand. The author leaves Hanneh with the dilemma of despising her newly acquired social position and acquaintances while realizing that she cannot return to the degradation of poverty. The reader is also left with a dilemma, or more accurately, an opportunity to draw his or her own conclusion: Does Yezierska simply illustrate one of life's paradoxes, or does the author point out the need for moderation and tolerance?

*Style and Technique*

Much of the force of this story derives from the characters' speech. The richly idiomatic language of the immigrant community establishes both Hanneh's character and her environment. Through the dialogue, the characters paint their self-portraits on a canvas of sound, colored by expressions reflecting their social and ethnic ties. Narration is minimal, and descriptive passages, when they occur, are usually sympathetic to Hanneh's point of view. For example, the hall-man is described as "frigid with dignity," supporting Hanneh's opinion. Thus, through the dialogue and narration, the world that the reader views is Hanneh's world, rendered in her language.

While the author uses diction to establish character, the story's structure contributes to its thematic development. Each section is framed by a character's movement to or from a passageway. The only exception is the section that concentrates on Hanneh's children. This is significant because the children are attached to this new environment, while Hanneh is not. The movement that either initiates or ends a scene symbolizes the mother's sense of abandonment. This device is so essential that Yezierska chose to close the story with Hanneh on the threshold; Hanneh's movement through the doorway is left unfinished, leaving her neither inside nor outside. She remains framed in the reader's mind in a position symbolizing her inner state. The woman who has traveled from poverty to affluence has yet to arrive at any feeling of belonging. She is suspended as it were, between two worlds, at home in neither one.

*Paul Kindlon*

# FATHER AND I

*Author:* Pär Lagerkvist (1891-1974)
*Type of plot:* Sketch
*Time of plot:* 1901
*Locale:* Sweden
*First published:* "Far och jag," 1923 (English translation, 1955)

> *Principal characters:*
> THE NARRATOR, a thirty-year-old man recalling a moment when
> he was nine
> HIS FATHER, a railroad employee

## The Story

The short, recognizably autobiographical sketch appears merely to describe a Sunday walk in the country taken by a nine-year-old boy and his father and to be without complication in plot or narrative. This appearance is qualified, however, by complex perspective and a complexity of reactions detailed by the narrator as he recalls his first awareness of the life that he was to live.

The walk begins in bright afternoon sunshine, as the father takes his son by the hand. They wave good-bye to the mother, who returns to preparing the evening meal, and move off to the woods. There they listen to the singing of the birds and the sounds of nature, to which they are accustomed but for which they have never lost appreciation.

As they make their way along a railway line, they share a sensation of freedom and privilege. The father is free because it is Sunday and he does not have to work; and both are privileged to walk along the railway line, a route forbidden to others, because the father works for the railroad. This privilege is further established as a train passes by and the father signals a familiar greeting to its engineer. The narrator then notes an odd but pleasant combination of scents, those of field flowers and the tar on railroad ties. To this mixture of nature and technology the reader is offered the opportunity to add another: The narrator notes that the telegraph poles "sang"; this picks up the narrator's note of the birdsong and combines the two types of song, one technological and one natural. Up to this point everything is harmonious under a clear sky on a beautiful day.

Mention of the clear sky and the beautiful day is then followed by intimations of discord. Scanning a field of oats, the father understands the perfection of the crop, but the son, whose orientation is town life, does not. As they cross a bridge over a stream pleasantly swollen by the springtime flood, they hold hands to lessen the danger of falling through the railroad ties. Each delight now includes its check of inharmony. A visit to the cottage of a railroad lineman, who provides them with a snack, and the father's subsequent ascertainment of a semaphore's position make it clear that the Sunday afternoon is not entirely free of chores. As they walk along a river, enjoying its beauty, the father is reminded of his own boyhood delight in perch-fishing there, an idyllic pleasure for which he now has no time. After a cheerful contest of throwing pebbles into the water, they grow tired and turn homeward.

Twilight comes on, and the woods become unpleasantly strange. The boy catches sight of a glowworm under the darkening trees, but the father does not respond to his son's reaction. The telegraph poles, which sang in the daylight, now rumble hollowly with a menacing, subterranean voice. Crossing the bridge again, the boy is terrified by the roaring of the stream in the dark abyss below.

In full darkness the discord becomes complete, and the father's calm is in strong contrast with his son's fear and trembling. The boy's complaint about horror in the darkness is brushed off by his father, who is sustained by his unquestioning belief in God. The boy feels lonely and forsaken and considers the invisible God to be part of the horror. This moment of alienation of son from father is dramatically punctuated by the mighty roar of a black train speeding past. The entire train is unlit save for the coal fire of the engine, in the glow of which a strange engineer, unknown to the father, stands immobile and stonelike, intent solely on plunging into the darkness. Choking with dread, the boy realizes the anguish that will be his in his movement out of the secure and real world of his father, who will not always be able to protect him, and into a life that hurtles "blazingly into complete and endless darkness."

## Themes and Meanings

Early in his life, Pär Lagerkvist became aware of his incapacity for upholding and adhering to the stern and uncompromising religion of his forebears and of his consequent exclusion from the security and meaning that their religion provided. His estrangement from religious faith engendered his humanism, and his need for the security and meaning denied him produced his anguish (*ångest*) and his longing (*längtan*). His humanistic inclination and his experience of *ångest* constitute the theme of "Father and I."

The nature of Lagerkvist's humanism, with its development of an emphasis on alienation and authentic individualism, already much in evidence in "Father and I," came to coincide with existentialism, not so much in the character of Jean-Paul Sartre's philosophy as in the intonations of Albert Camus's fiction and lyrical essays. Like Camus, Lagerkvist was tormented by the essential unhappiness of human life and sought, not to escape it through rational philosophy or self-deception but to nurture, as the nucleus of human unhappiness, that longing that—because it cannot be satisfied—becomes its own meaning and, as such, the fulfillment of the life of one who confronts it with the same constancy as Camus would have one confront the absurd. Where wisdom for Socrates consisted in knowing that he did not know, happiness for Lagerkvist, as for Camus, consisted in pursuing it while remaining unflinchingly aware of its untenability. The awareness entails *ångest*, which in turn intensifies life, which is its own value.

The religion of the father in "Father and I" is, like philosophical formulas for the achievement of happiness, a form of self-deception, so far as Lagerkvist is concerned.

The father sees neither the glowworm nor the significance of the baleful glow of the black train's fire, the one representative of life, the other intensified life. The son, who is conscious of both, experiences the anguish (the existentialists' *Angst*) that informs such consciousness.

Lagerkvist presented "anguish" as his inheritance (*arvedel*) in *Ångest*, a work that he published in 1916. His inheritance was not a spiritual tradition but the anguish of life itself. To him, life is not inherently good in the moral sense. In its meaninglessness and in the competitive struggle to survive, it is a form of evil, of original sin without a redeemer. It is like that fiery black train with its diabolical engineer. In *Ångest* he describes his life struggle: "I tear my sore and wounded hands/ against the hill and darkened woods/ against the black iron of the sky." He selected "Father and I" to be the first in his collection of stories entitled *Evil Tales* (*Onda sagor*, 1924; English translation, 1955). Without a god of light or a savior to atone for the evil of life, Lagerkvist saw only endless darkness and the responsibility of an individual to save his own or her own self, not as an immortal soul but as a vitally mortal self. "Father and I" presents a nine-year-old boy's initial awareness of this lonely and fearful struggle.

*Style and Technique*

In his 1952 commentary on "Father and I," Arne Häggqvist says that Lagerkvist has "here composed one of his finest autobiographical sketches, realistically suggestive and, at the same time, acutely symbolical." This observation about Lagerkvist's style applies as well to all of Lagerkvist's later fiction, in which labyrinthine allegory assumes a surface of lyrical but simple narrative. By the early 1920's, Lagerkvist had fully abandoned his early expressionistic style, with its exclamatory color, in favor of a style governed by the subtle multiperspectivity of cubism.

The narration of "Father and I" is in the cubistic mode. Concretions in the first half of the story—such as the passing train, telegraph poles, and the rushing stream—are reconstituted and reconfigured in the second half, in the manner of segments of planes redisposed on a cubist canvas. The combined perspectives of day and night are interspatial with the combined perspectives of the thirty-year-old narrator and the child that he was at nine. The reactions of the child are genuinely those of a nine-year-old, and they are imperceptibly, almost indistinguishably, deepened by the symbolic content of the mature narrator's recollections. For example, after the black train is engorged by the night, the father puzzles over the strange train and the strange engineer, while the son has a presentiment of its significance and a sense that it was for his sake that the train roared past them: Speaking as narrator about his boyhood experience, he interprets that experience retrospectively as an anticipation of the anguish that he would much later articulate in this autobiographical depiction.

*Roy Arthur Swanson*

# A FATHER-TO-BE

*Author:* Saul Bellow (1915-    )
*Type of plot:* Domestic realism
*Time of plot:* The 1950's
*Locale:* New York City
*First published:* 1955

*Principal characters:*
ROGIN, the protagonist, who lives and works in New York City
JOAN, his fiancé

## The Story

Rogin, a research chemist entering middle age, is on his way one Sunday evening to have supper with Joan, his fiancé. When she asked him on the telephone to buy some food, he feebly asked what happened to the money he already gave her. He begins to ponder his relationship with Joan. Although beautiful and aristocratic, she is not working and cannot—or will not—support herself without Rogin's help. As he is paying off her debts, she is buying expensive, frivolous presents for him and her sister, Phyllis. However, Rogin thinks, he loves her too much to complain.

At the delicatessen, Rogin is pleased by the smells of the foods and the general aromas of life itself. He admires the counterman who admonishes a Puerto Rican boy in a cowboy hat about to knock over a display. As he buys the food, Rogin recalls how difficult Joan is but also how beautiful. Descending into the subway, he overhears a brief conversation between two men, one of whom confesses to the other that he is an alcoholic currently on a miracle cure. The conversation prompts Rogin to recall his own desperate need for more money.

Seated on the speeding train, Rogin observes his fellow passengers. He sees two little girls with their mothers, each with the same kind of muff, and he notes the annoyance of the mothers and the little girls' complacency. A strange-looking foreign family next engages his attention. The mother is old and worn out, the son looks like a dishwasher. Between them sits a dwarf, an androgynous creature who at once repels and fascinates Rogin. He thinks of the chemistry of sex determination and recalls his dreams of the previous night involving an undertaker, who was cutting his hair, and a woman he was carrying on his head.

The passenger who most affects him, however, is a middle-aged man who strikes Rogin as a dandy. Dressed in expensive clothes, too ostentatiously dapper for Rogin's taste, the stranger somehow irritates him. The man's features remind Rogin of Joan's father, even of Joan herself. Rogin begins to construct a fantastically hypothetical relationship between the man and himself. This man, so resembling Joan, could be what her son would look like in forty years. If Joan were the mother, then he, Rogin, would be the father of this fourth-rate model of responsibility and dullness.

From such contemplation, Rogin briefly considers the possibility of breaking off his relationship with Joan, but in a few minutes he gets off the train and walks to Joan's apartment. When Joan opens the door, Rogin notices a vague resemblance to the stranger on the train, and he is frightened. In a minute, however, he is inside and Joan is kissing him.

In the final scene, Joan insists on washing Rogin's hair. Still irritated by his contemplation of the stranger, he tells himself that he will rebuke Joan and sever their relationship, but when Joan begins to wash his hair, to pamper him, Rogin submits quietly and lovingly.

## Themes and Meanings

Although creditable as a short story in its own right, Saul Bellow's "A Father-to-Be" can be appreciated also as a kind of working draft for his short novel, *Seize the Day*, which was published in 1956. In that work, Tommy Wilhelm, the protagonist, feels overwhelmed by his financial and emotional debts to his estranged wife and to his father, whom he both loves and despises for his mean-spiritedness. Rogin, like Tommy, feels burdened by what he believes are his obligations to support Joan and his conflicting desire for freedom as a man.

The character of Rogin most engages the reader, for the plot is really a series of contemplative actions that shed light on his personality. His name—related to the Latin *rogo*, to ask—suggests an essential element of his nature, that of the questioner, the seeker. As in many of Bellow's works, much of the action and meaning of the plot depends on a character's attempt to interpret, to seek, to plumb the bottom of the well of experience.

What Rogin seeks is at the crux of the meaning of "A Father-to-Be." He is a research chemist by profession, one who seeks answers in the elemental substances of nature; but he is a researcher into the human heart by inclination, seeking to find sympathy and understanding as a man in a tough, desensitized world. His adventures on his way to Joan's apartment form steps in his contemplation of his own place in that world. The journey Rogin makes is one of discovery about himself.

In his first step—the delicatessen—Rogin sees himself as the harried provider, a financial supporter of Joan's extravagant lifestyle. He also reveals that he is a man in love with life: He appreciates the smells of food and admires the honest toughness of the counterman, a man of the city, a survivor.

By the end of this first stage, Rogin is suffering, in conflict between his feeling of being used and his desire for love; he recognizes Joan's faults but chooses to ignore them. In the second stage of his contemplation, Rogin descends into the subway, a symbolic descent into the underworld in which he learns more about himself and his conflict. He does this by studying his fellow passengers. They provide his personal summary of humanity and their foibles—the alcoholic man, self-deluded by his presumed cure; the two little girls and their mothers, by turns smug and annoyed; the strange foreign family with their androgynous offspring—these help Rogin understand his own need for finding a place in the world, a place secured not by money but by love.

The third and final stage of his contemplative journey begins with his observation of the subway passenger next to him. This stage is introduced by Rogin's recollection of his recent dreams. The significance of these dreams is both symbolic and foreshadowing. The undertaker who wants to cut Rogin's hair is a figure of emasculation, a modern allusion to the biblical story of Samson and Delilah. As Samson's strength was in his hair, so the undertaker's cutting of Rogin's hair is an image of emasculation and the death of his manhood. The woman on Rogin's head, the figure of the second dream, is a clear evocation of Joan, who Rogin is carrying, supporting. Both images ultimately connect with the final scene in which Joan, Delilah-like, washes Rogin's hair while he weakly submits.                                         .

In the third stage, Rogin observes the man who he imagines resembles Joan and her father. Prepared by his previous observations, Rogin invents a clever way of breaking his relationship with Joan. He convinces himself that this future son will be the end result of this relationship, this son who will be a curse to his father.

Rogin's illumination in this last stage seems born out of delusion, out of the preposterous notion of himself as a father-to-be. In a real sense, however, Rogin understands that he is, indeed, a victim, ill-used but ultimately helpless, weak, submissive.

## Style and Technique

"A Father-to-Be" typifies Bellow's colloquial, ironic, humorous style. The language and tone of the story are distinctly casual. Accuracy of observation is heightened by a crisp directness that seems informal. The scene in the delicatessen, for example, is presented with an economy of detail, but those details are precise and rendered in language uncluttered by a literary tone.

Bellow is a realist, but his realism is tempered by irony and understatement. The scene in the subway is richly detailed, but the odd, almost bizarre pictures of the passengers are presented in such matter-of-fact language that their oddity is seen as natural, even ordinary. The humor of the dream sequences, and in the final scene when Rogin submits to Joan's blandishments, is achieved largely by Bellow's careful use of understatement, a technique by which Rogin's conflict is blunted, his anxiety defused, and which emphasizes in the end his role as victim and sufferer.

*Edward Fiorelli*

# FATHERS

*Author:* Robley Wilson (1930-    )
*Type of plot:* Social realism
*Time of plot:* The 1970's or 1980's
*Locale:* A golf course
*First published:* 1984

### Principal characters:
A YOUNG WOMAN
A MAN, her golf-playing companion

## The Story

Opening with a young woman and man on a golf course, the story has five scenes, four on the golf course and one in a clubhouse, with no transitions between the scenes. In the first scene the man is looking for his golf ball. He has made a bad stroke, and neither he nor the young woman knows where the ball landed. She suggests that he take a drop—that is, forget finding the ball and drop another at the spot where the lost ball disappeared. Because this will cost him a penalty stroke as well as his ball, he does not want to do it. The man asks the young woman where she thinks his ball went; she replies that he hooked it so badly she could not follow it. He says that he did not hook it, he sliced it, and she should know the difference by now. Hook or slice, she says, the ball is lost, so there is no difference. She ought to learn the difference, he says. Perhaps he should play with florescent orange balls so that he could find them more easily. Eventually, he comes around to her original suggestion: to take a drop.

On the seventh green the man has already had four strokes and now cannot see the flag. When he asks the young woman what she thinks, she says that if she were the pin, she would be back and to the left of the green. When he explains that he wants to know which club he should use, they begin a new argument, until he prepares to use his seven iron. After going through elaborate preparatory motions, he steps back from the ball and then climbs the hill to see where the hole is. It is exactly where the young woman said it would be, so he decides that it is, after all, an eight-iron shot.

In the third scene, the man becomes discouraged by his score, so the woman reminds him of the game's other benefits—such as fresh air and exercise. The man suggests that she does not really like the game, and he encourages her to try playing herself. If she found that she liked it, he would buy her a set of clubs. Changing the subject, she offers him a four-leaf clover that she has found. He puts it in his shirt pocket, thanks her, and kisses her on the forehead.

The fourth scene opens at the eighth hole, which will be a difficult shot. The green is trapped all the way around, there is very little fairway, and the hill from the tee to the green is steep, sandy, and rocky. From the tee, the green is invisible, so the woman is stationed down the hill to follow the ball's path. After she calls out that she is ready, she hears the man call "fore" and hears the club hit the ball. The ball bounces through the rough, ricochets off a rock or stump, and is propelled toward the green, where it rolls into the hole. A hole in one.

When the man asks where his ball has landed, the woman does not immediately reply. Instead, she lets him wonder, telling him where the ball landed, amidst the rocks, and waits for his next question: "Did it ricochet?" he asks. Yes, she answers, right toward the green. She tells him that he will be surprised. After she finally tells him that the ball is in the hole, she must work to convince him. The man turns away from her and throws the ball, which he has fished out of the hole, at the trees, an expression, she assumes, of happiness.

The final scene starts abruptly. Reminiscing, the man describes his father's old clubs, with which he learned to play: their slightly crooked wooden shafts, heavy twine bindings, varnished look, and the singing feel of a club as it hits the ball. The man muses over his score, forty-six, and tells the woman that yes, in a way his father did teach him the game, but his father was a really poor golfer. The woman tells him that he is a good golfer, in spite of his father. This reply carries much of the story's meaning: "How one generation resists the faults of another."

### Themes and Meanings

Robley Wilson never states explicitly that the man in this story is the young woman's father, but one may assume that the characters are indeed father and daughter. Not only the story's title but also the interaction between the two characters suggests this relationship. Wilson is also speaking about fathers in general terms. That he never names his two characters, thus denying them particularity, takes this story beyond the details of this specific relationship to a more universal statement about relationships between generations.

The beauty of this story lies in its use of a seemingly simple game of golf to reveal much about its characters. In the early scenes it is clear that the young woman is astute and possibly has better judgment than her father, who often disregards her opinion. In the first scene he is slow to realize that he cannot find his lost ball and should take a drop—just as the young woman has recommended. At the seventh hole the young woman correctly guesses where the out-of-sight pin is, as well as which club is best for the shot.

The young woman also teases her father, but he seems not to catch her humor. Despite his insistence that she should learn the difference between a hook and a slice, she quips that there really is no difference if he cannot find his lost ball. In the hole-in-one scene she taunts her father, parsimoniously doling out the news that his ball is already in the hole. He doubts not only his ability to make a hole-in-one but also her word. As soon as he believes her, she gives him another playful dig: Yes, it "actually" made it into the hole, but the shot did not showcase the best form in the world; the father is a pawn in her hand in this scene, extremely vulnerable, and she plays with him.

There is also tenderness between the two. The father expresses his emotion physically, whether this means throwing a ball toward the tops of the trees to express his joy, or kissing his daughter to express affection. The woman, on the other hand, reveals her emotion for her father with symbols, be they lucky four-leaf clovers or encouraging words. Expressing tenderness and kindness, the woman tells her father that he is a good golfer. This may be true—although it is not illustrated in the story—or it may be an innocent, well-meaning lie.

On a more universal level, the story comments on fatherhood and the relationship between generations. The subtle (and sometimes not so subtle) tension between the man and his daughter arises from his desire to shape her and her efforts to resist. Thus, the daughter's bantering is her means of gentle but firm resistance. It may be just a game of golf, Wilson suggests, but in such mundane moments as these, human beings reveal themselves. The story's ultimate irony is that the man has insight into his relationship with his own father but cannot extrapolate beyond that. Thus he understands his own resistance to his preceding generation but not his daughter's resistance to him.

### Style and Technique

"Fathers" deviates from the traditional linear plot. Instead of giving a continuous narrative thread, Wilson offers a series of snapshots. There are no smooth transitions and there is minimal narrative intrusion; the reader must painstakingly sift through these particles of dialogue and action in an attempt to reach conclusions about the story's meaning. Apparently trivial details may be filled with possibility: Every sentence is loaded with possibility.

Perhaps the most interesting and telling aspect of Wilson's technique is his penchant for starting in the middle of things. There is no preamble that provides context of time, place, or significance. The style is rather minimalist, and instances and events appear as independent units. The implication is that the reader infers or creates meaning in order to synthesize and organize these ostensibly distinct sketches.

*Julie Thompson*

# THE FATHER'S DAUGHTERS

*Author:* Muriel Spark (1918-    )
*Type of plot:* Psychological
*Time of plot:* 1957
*Locale:* Nice, France; London and Essex, England
*First published:* 1961

> *Principal characters:*
> HENRY CASTLEMAINE, an eighty-year-old novelist
> DORA CASTLEMAINE, his unmarried forty-six-year-old daughter
> BEN DONADIEU, a thirty-one-year-old teacher at the Basil Street
>    Grammar School in London
> KENNETH HOPE, a celebrated novelist
> CARMELITA HOPE, Hope's twenty-one-year-old daughter

*The Story*

After having spent thirty-five comfortable summers at Nice, the Castlemaines are faced with poverty. Novelist Henry Castlemaine's name has been forgotten; in fact, people believe that he died long ago. His forty-six-year-old daughter, Dora, who has decided to serve her widowed father and attend to "his needs as a public figure," is worried about money. It has been thirty years since her father was recognized everywhere. Henry insists on patronizing an expensive place near the casino in Nice; Dora protests but relents, chided by her father for being "vulgar," that is, concerned about costs and prices.

One March, when Dora and her father are forced to abandon their expensive hotel, she meets Ben Donadieu, who is vacationing with his friend Carmelita Hope, the daughter of the famous novelist Kenneth Hope, "a shy, thin, middle-aged man" whose creative "magic" Dora admires. Carmelita likes Ben for being an "intellectual," but she thinks that Ben loves her chiefly for being the novelist's daughter. Ben is keenly interested in talking to Carmelita's father, whom she praises for not interfering in her life.

Dora accepts a job as an elocution teacher. Her father objects; he sulks and complains that he is a burden to her and that he ought to "go off and die." It is one of their affectionate quarrels: They are "shrewd in their love for each other." In her job, Dora again encounters Ben, who inquires, to her delight, if she is related to Henry Castlemaine.

Meanwhile, Ben's relation with Carmelita is in trouble; he wants to find out if Carmelita still means anything to him without sex. Carmelita wonders if Ben is "practising a form of cruelty to intensify her obsession." Her father does not want to help Ben for her sake. When Ben mentions his acquaintance with Dora, Carmelita thinks that his interest in the Castlemaines would "make everything easier for both of us." It turns out that this friendship spells the end of Ben's engagement with Carmelita. Henry Castlemaine urges Dora to marry Ben, and Dora accepts this as a kind of "destiny." The father-daughter conspiracy manifests a shrewdness capable of absorbing Ben as "a born disciple."

### Themes and Meanings

From the title, one can infer that the narrative will explore the corrupting potential of a quasi-incestuous father-daughter relationship, its unnatural persistence, and its tension with the absent or canceled roles of mother and wife.

Patriarchal power dominates in the Henry-Dora bond: What the father dislikes, the daughter also dislikes. Dora cannot openly tell her father how poor they are. He always uses his formulaic defense against the world: Dora is "vulgar" if she mentions money. She has subordinated her needs to her father in the belief that he stands for a vital interest in life. As he says, "The world is ours. It is our birthright. We take it without payment." He ignores the need for earning money. It is Dora, however, who must solve the problem, even to the point of marrying Ben for his income.

On the other hand, patriarchal authority withdraws in the relationship between Kenneth and Carmelita, even though its effect is registered in Carmelita's personality. Unlike Henry, whose novels deal with "individual consciences" (his vanity, however, seems immune to the claims of others), Kenneth's art opens "bricked-up" windows. Dora is fascinated with Hope's illusory world of adventurous spirits. Unlike Henry, Hope does not visibly interfere with his daughter's life. He refuses to help Ben write an essay about himself; he hates disciples. He thus refuses to help his daughter because he believes that she should be independent and know what she wants.

Although Hope presents a "smiling and boyish . . . party face" to society, he conducts an inner struggle with himself during his creative moods, experiencing (as he confesses to his daughter) "a comedy of errors." His daughter is abandoned by Ben, whose quest for a father would sacrifice the erotic pleasure offered by Carmelita for the "marriage of true minds"—as Henry Castlemaine puts it. Hope's inventiveness fails in grappling with real-life problems or empathizing with suffering kin.

Carmelita's belief that there is more to discover in an intellectual type such as Ben exemplifies a blindness, or inadequacy of perception, explainable by her being Hope's daughter. For Dora, on the other hand, Ben represents money and a revival of her father's works, a recovery of youth, and the value of the immediate present. In her anger and despair, Carmelita has a moment in which she intuits the essence of her father's depression, during which he "miraculously wrote the ache out of his system in prose of harsh merriment." Distanced from her father, the daughter is able to gain this insight.

Separation of kin and respect for individual integrity may be read into the Hope-Carmelita relationship, whereas negation of self and triumph of paternal vanity characterize the Henry-Dora relationship. Dora's liking for Hope's imagination is a symptom of her suppressed life, of her victimization by a puritanical and hypocritical code to which she willingly submits. Her justification of her marriage to Ben as "destiny," or as evidence of a former life, and her gambling in the lottery all testify to her inability to take control of her life.

Muriel Spark satirizes Henry Castlemaine's aristocratic pretense and his phony interest in "individual consciences." She also caricatures the "cultivated type" represented by Ben, whose parasitism of famous authors is a mirror image of Henry's parasitism of his daughter. The main target of Spark's satire, however, appears to be the bohemian foibles of the two fathers: Henry's creed that the true artist's sensibility transcends the world of commodities and money, and Hope's "comedy of errors" resolved by his escapes to Morocco or the Middle East. This self-serving aestheticism is the privileged space for the male psyche guaranteed by the subservience of women.

Where are the mothers in this narrative? The theme of sexual domination through the mind and of psychological bondage—the women's utterances are always being interrupted or sidetracked here—may be conceived as a repression of women's creativity, the stifling of both Dora's and Carmelita's self-fulfilling drives. The fathers can "father" while the daughters minister to their needs. When Dora secures a teaching job, her father is jealous. Carmelita is a sexual object for Ben and is later discarded. The maternal can be discovered in the folds of "vulgarity," in the world of pleasure that the fetishism of art and the mystification of the intellect tend to deny. Perhaps the maternal impulse surfaces and asserts itself in Dora's conception of "destiny," and in Carmelita's admittedly unwilling "liberation" from Ben.

*Style and Technique*

Spark has often been credited for her whimsical wit and her "crotchety originality." What stands out in this polyphonic blending of voices and scenes, the interweaving of the lives of two daughters and the men who control their lives, and the consistently mistaken interpretations of motives and purposes, is a complete mastery of the banal peculiarities of English family relationships and the petty eccentricities of male writers.

The narrative structure consists of the alternation of scenes involving the couples Henry and Dora, Carmelita and Ben, and Carmelita and Kenneth. Each scene comments on the other and unfolds the ironic implications in the limited knowledge of each character. The impoverished Castlemaines want the past restored, while Carmelita looks forward to a vague future. By juxtaposing the last two scenes—Carmelita's dilemma, her problem of how to satisfy Ben's intellectual ambition, and Dora's hesitation to marry Ben—the narrative exposes Carmelita's pathetic blindness, her self-deception induced by her fatal admiration for her father. The third scene functions as a pivotal disclosure of Dora's will to assert herself against her father, suggesting that, while she may not be as free as Carmelita (whose fixation on Ben testifies to her father's predominant influence), she can make practical decisions within the framework of her symbiotic relationship with her father. Her job epitomizes her ethical limit: "a reformer of vowel sounds."

Spark's critical thrusts are both direct and oblique. Henry tells Dora that she is "a chip off the old block." Dora uses her father's all-purpose epithet "vulgar" to signal their moral and aesthetic superiority to the world. She adjusts whatever she wants to say to her father's moods and idiosyncrasies. Her thoughts, however, especially about Hope's magic, betray a repressed dimension of her psyche, which is absent in Carmelita. Only at one point does the narrative enact a dialogue in Carmelita's consciousness symptomatic of the split that women suffer in a patriarchal regime, in which women must keep their private thoughts to themselves and assume predetermined roles. By a sudden turn of dialogue or shift in tone, the two women's voices are always drowned or absorbed by the male voices, which invariably impose male opinions, caprices, and follies.

Given the montage of scenes depicting antithetical but also parallel lives, the comment by the dark-skinned blond at the lottery kiosk in Nice seems apt: "Life is a lottery." The wheel of fortune transfers Ben from Carmelita to Dora; a new disciple for Henry Castlemaine appears. Dora's belief in destiny and in a former existence may be an ideological blinder for her submission to her father's wish for a revival of his fame, for her passivity or adaptability; yet it also intimates the larger, overarching structure of economic, political, and cultural institutions, whose impact on individual lives generates such cross-purposes, misunderstandings, and self-deceptions as the narrative exposes with acute satiric finesse.

*E. San Juan, Jr.*

# A FATHER'S STORY

*Author:* Andre Dubus (1936-1999)
*Type of plot:* Domestic realism
*Time of plot:* The early 1980's
*Locale:* Northeastern Massachusetts
*First published:* 1983

*Principal characters:*
> LUKE RIPLEY, the narrator and protagonist, a divorced, middle-aged man
> JENNIFER, his twenty-year-old daughter
> PAUL LEBOEUF, a Roman Catholic priest in his sixties, his spiritual adviser and friend

*The Story*

Luke Ripley, who narrates his own experience, is fifty-four, a divorced father of four who lives in northeastern Massachusetts, near the New Hampshire line and the Atlantic Ocean. Apparently neither rich nor poor, he runs a stable, boarding and renting out thirty horses and giving riding lessons. Luke still broods over the Wednesday that his wife, Gloria, left with the kids and a trailer, some ten or so years earlier.

Largely a solitary person, Luke is a friend of Father Paul LeBoeuf, the balding, sixty-four-year-old pastor of a nearby Catholic church. Father LeBoeuf, of French-Canadian descent in a church still dominated by the Irish, has been a weekly visitor to Luke's house since before Luke's marriage failed. No longer willing to ride horseback, Father Paul still takes long walks with Luke and finds time occasionally to join him fishing and duck hunting. An earthy man of simple yet profound piety, Father LeBoeuf listens with understanding to Luke's spiritual dilemmas and to his rebellious objections to a church that he loves but does not always respect.

Luke's self-reliant life is generally happy—or at least content. He has nearly gotten over missing his wife, if not watching his three sons and a daughter grow. He accepts church regulations forbidding divorced Catholics to remarry and—more reluctantly—celibacy, confessing that he has had two brief affairs in the intervening years. He has come to grips with his lonesome life through an appreciation of nature and an orderly routine. He does his own cooking, reads an occasional detective story, and follows the baseball season. His business provides him the opportunity for rides through a countryside to which he responds more sympathetically than most contemporary males.

Like many believing Catholics of the late twentieth century, Luke has modified the strictures of his church to suit his particular needs. Some of these modifications are slightly eccentric, for example, his refusal to support his parish church despite his friendship with its pastor. Convinced in a stubborn peasant way, which Father

LeBoeuf tolerantly accepts, that the contributions of the faithful are not always wisely spent, Luke prefers that the money he gives goes into people's stomachs and on their backs.

Furthermore, Luke still resents the effects he believes the Roman Catholic church's teaching on birth control had on his marriage, attributing early tensions and frustrations to the rhythm method he and his wife practiced to avoid conception. Nevertheless, he has made his peace with the church. He rises at 4:45 A.M. for a period of devotion as he prepares his breakfast, offering to God every act of the day before him. During this hour he talks to God, thanking Him for his blessings, not excluding the two women with whom he made love after Gloria left. Afterward, he saddles a horse and rides over for morning mass at Father Paul's church.

During the summer, Luke's daughter, Jennifer, pays her annual visit from Florida, a vestige of his divorce's custody terms. Luke worries more about his daughter than his older sons, who are now settled in various places about the country. He is proud of her athletic abilities, her fully developed womanhood, and her open manner with friends but is vaguely uneasy about the role she must play in a culture so different from the one in which he grew up. He does not exactly disapprove of the fact that twenty-year-old Jennifer is neither a virgin nor a believer, but he misses the certainty of older times, as stifling as they often were.

One windy summer night, Jennifer and two girlfriends take her car to go to a movie, then visit the beach. In the course of the night, each drinks four bottles of beer. On the twenty-minute ride home, after dropping off the others and singing with a cassette, Jennifer crests a dark hill only to get the briefest glance of a moving figure before experiencing a heart-stopping thud. Panicked and only half aware of what has occurred, she takes her foot off the brake she has jammed on and continues home to her father.

Awakened by his sobbing daughter, Luke questions the hysterical girl closely in the kitchen over several calming shots of whiskey before setting out to the accident scene. In the gusty darkness after a hasty search, he discovers in a ditch the body of a young man whom he desperately attempts to examine. At one point, he thinks that he hears sounds in the man's chest. Then there is a silence, and Luke returns home, still without notifying authorities.

He sends his daughter to bed, surveys the damage to the car, and removes the empty beer bottles. For the rest of a sleepless night, he listens to opera records, planning how he can rescue his daughter. Finally, in the early morning, he drives her car in the rain to church and deliberately crashes the front right side of the car into a tree in the parking lot before entering the church to hear mass and receive Holy Communion.

### Themes and Meanings

The novelist Joyce Carol Oates has noted that Andre Dubus's characters perform criminal actions but may be redeemed in the eyes of the reader by "the author's extraordinary sympathy with them." Such a figure is Luke Ripley, whose daughter expects him to call the police after she has struck and killed a man while driving after having been drinking.

In the concluding passage of "A Father's Story," Luke justifies his ethical decision in another one of his dialogues with God, a startling tour de force reminiscent of the biblical Job, to whom he has earlier tacitly compared himself. Just as when he had mentioned the two women with whom he was involved after Gloria in his morning prayer, he reminds God almost blasphemously, "You never had a daughter." God does not concede Luke's point without a retort of His own: He asks if that means that Luke loves his daughter more than him, "a love in weakness." Luke, however, has the last word, reminding God it is similar to his love of humankind.

Luke's witty, nearly testy, defense of his conduct draws God into the conspiracy as another father like himself. Nevertheless, it cannot hide the fact that Luke is again playing fast and loose with church doctrines. In indulging in what the church has condemned as situational ethics, he is reserving once more the right to decide for himself what is right and what is wrong. To readers who hold romantic beliefs in the sacredness of the individual, Luke will seem a sympathetic character. Still, nagging doubts may remain about his decision.

*Style and Technique*

Dubus often writes of parents' love for their vulnerable children, specifically, how the death or injury of a child is nearly unbearable to them. Such a theme emerges clearly in "A Father's Story," where he uses a series of images and allusions to link it with another theme: the debate with God. Both of these strands come together in a host of religious, literary, and folkloric versions, ranging from the story of Abraham and Isaac and the Book of Job in the Bible, to the life of Jesus in John Milton's *Paradise Regained* (1671), to the story of Faust as told by Johann Wolfgang von Goethe. Two of these analogues, the lives of Job and Jesus, are directly mentioned.

In the archetypal version of the myth, Satan challenges God for the soul of a man of faith, a man very like Luke Ripley. Other times God merely decides to test the faith of one of his special servants. Often the death of a child is involved, as when God commands the pious but wily Abraham to sacrifice his son Isaac to him. In that case, Isaac is saved at the last moment when God rewards his father's faith. In other versions, children die, as do Job's or the Son of God himself, Jesus, who died to redeem the world from Satan—although God the Father is often shown as reluctant to allow this sacrifice on the part of his son.

In Dubus's version of the archetype, the father refuses to sacrifice his child—who has become, fittingly for the late twentieth century, a daughter—and argues with God as slyly as Satan does in Johann Wolfgang von Goethe's *Faust* (1808-1832; *The Tragedy of Faust*, 1823-1838), or Abraham in trying to save the City of Sodom from destruction.

*James E. Devlin*

# FAUSTINO

*Author:* Max Martínez (1943-    )
*Type of plot:* Social realism
*Time of plot:* The mid-twentieth century
*Locale:* South Texas
*First published:* 1977

### Principal characters:

FAUSTINO, an uneducated Mexican American farmworker
MARIA, his patient, devoted wife
BUSTER CRANE, his employer
MRS. CRANE, Buster's sex-starved wife

*The Story*

A native-born American citizen of Mexican ancestry, Faustino belongs to a segregated minority within Texas's dominant Anglo American culture. He lives with his wife and children in a shack on land belonging to his employer, Buster Crane. Born on this ranch, he cannot imagine any other world or any other life. This is typical of the feudal relationship that has existed between Anglos and Chicanos for generations.

One day Faustino is sent to get a wrench in the toolshed adjacent to Buster's house. Buster's young wife is outside, hanging clothes to dry. Quite deliberately, she tries to arouse Faustino with exaggerated movements that accentuate her breasts, legs, and buttocks. Faustino understands what Mrs. Crane is doing and is indeed sexually aroused.

At the same time he feels guilty at the thought of committing adultery with his employer's wife, as well as terror at the thought of the possible consequences. He realizes that involvement with such a woman would ultimately lead to exposure and his eviction from the ranch—if not his own death at the hands of an outraged employer. Although an unspoken caste system in South Texas makes it taboo for Chicano men to have sexual relations with Anglo women, Anglo men can freely have sexual relations with Chicanas.

Mrs. Crane lures Faustino to her kitchen by asking him to empty a big can that collects leaking sink water. Once he is inside, she rubs against him, fondles his genitals, and removes all of her clothes. Faustino is torn between desire and fear, but the latter is stronger, so he flees, leaving behind his boss's wrench.

Instead of returning to Buster and his foreman, who are still waiting for the wrench in the field, Faustino goes home intent on having sex with his own wife. Although accustomed to obeying her husband, Maria cannot respond satisfactorily to Faustino's sexual demands and is alarmed and confused by his strange behavior. They argue, and he beats her. Leaving his long-suffering wife in tears, he drives off to meet his employer. Along the way, he stops to masturbate in order to relieve his sexual tension. He is still thinking about Buster's young wife, who simultaneously attracts and revolts him. Unable to remember what happened to the wrench, he decides to say that he could not find it.

Faustino is not surprised at Buster's angry outburst. Buster correctly suspects that Faustino has taken so long on his errand because he stopped to have sex with Maria— but he can hardly imagine the complex circumstances involved. When Faustino lies that he could not find the wrench, Buster shows him the tool and explains that he fetched it himself. His wife told him she had it in the kitchen because she was trying to fix the leaky drainpipe. Buster now orders Faustino to go back and empty the tub of water for Mrs. Crane, explaining, "My wife will show you what to do."

*Themes and Meanings*

Max Martínez's sympathies are with his fellow Chicanos. He resents the way that they have been treated by Anglos, who own most of the land in the Southwest and have historically taken it for granted that the Chicanos are an inferior class to be abused and exploited. "Faustino" is a cry for social justice. The story's patient, humble, hardworking, uneducated protagonist symbolizes the majority of Chicanos in South Texas who do not understand how they are victimized by an unjust social system and who—because of their segregated situation—are essentially unaware of the contempt in which they are held by most Anglos. "Faustino" offers many examples of the crude and subtle ways in which Anglos discriminate against Chicanos in order to maintain a caste distinction for their economic advantage. One such example is Martínez's offhand observation that while Anglo ranch hands feel free to enter the boss's house, Chicanos know without being told that they are expected to wait outside.

Martínez is writing primarily for his fellow Chicanos, urging them to develop self-awareness—awareness of their suppressed condition, and awareness of their potential political strength. Not interested in appealing to Anglos to change their behavior, he appeals to Chicanos to force the changes needed to bring about equality. His attitude toward others is especially evident in his frequent and extensive use of Spanish-language dialogue, which effectively reverses the normal relationship between Anglos and Chicanos by making his non-Spanish-speaking readers feel snubbed and excluded.

In "Faustino," Martínez says, in effect, that although Anglos think they are better than Chicanos, the truth of the matter is that the Chicanos are better than Anglos in many important respects. This idea is not much different from what Mahatma Gandhi devoted his life to teaching fellow Indians, who had developed a national inferiority complex under British rule. Economic and political domination not only do not imply moral superiority, but they also may actually imply just the opposite.

In describing Faustino's abuse of his loving, patient wife, Maria, Martínez dramatizes a truth that he has observed in interrelations between Anglos and Chicanos. Because Chicanos do not fully understand their own resentment of their oppressed condition, they consequently do not direct their hostility against those who have traditionally exploited them. Hostility does exist, however, and must find an outlet some-where. Chicanos tend to direct their aggression against one another instead of unit-ing to demand their rights—a situation that makes it easier for Anglos to maintain their feudal domination. Gandhi, who has been an inspiration to oppressed people around the world, noted the existence of a similar situation in India. He was strongly opposed to the existing caste system and the age-old hostility between Muslims and Hindus because these divisive factors helped the British to retain control of the country.

Martínez is a militant writer with a sense of humor. "Faustino" is included in his collection titled *The Adventures of the Chicano Kid* (1981). A posed photograph on the book's back cover shows the bearded, uninhibited author holding a big revolver.

### Style and Technique

Martínez has very likely been influenced by John Steinbeck and William Faulkner. Although his prose is often as simple as that of Steinbeck, it is sometimes as convo-luted and wordy as that of Faulkner. The plot of "Faustino" is reminiscent of Steinbeck's *Of Mice and Men* (1937). In both works, a young, promiscuous, and fool-hardy married woman causes havoc in a simple man's life. Like Steinbeck and Faulk-ner, Martínez is given to philosophical and sociological reflections on the experiences of his inarticulate characters. Faustino has strong feelings but cannot verbalize them. As a spokesman for Chicanos, Martínez feels free to intrude into dramatic scenes to explain what is going on inside his viewpoint character. For example:

> Faustino had a sense, something as palpable as the callouses on his hands, that he be-longed on the ranch, that he belonged to the ranch; that he must give of himself and of his labor to it; knowing all the while but never thinking that he did not own the land, that he would never own the land; that finally the land was neutral, that what happened on it was something else; that his devotion to it was one-directional.

Another striking feature of "Faustino" is that all the extensive dialogue between Faustino and his wife is in Spanish. This is not simple Spanish, such as the dialogue in some Ernest Hemingway short stories, which any intelligent non-Spanish-speaking reader can figure out through guesswork based on similarities with English and knowledge of a few Spanish words. Martínez's heavy use of Spanish dialogue full of slang, idiom, and Mexican profanity indicates that he knows full well that he is ad-dressing a primarily Chicano audience.

Martínez suggests by implication that Anglos have never shown any concern about Chicanos' feelings, opinions, or experiences. He seems to be deliberately turning his back on the mass market of predominantly Anglo readers and trying to cultivate a small but sympathetic audience among fellow Chicanos. Perhaps paradoxically, this feature makes his stories more interesting to perceptive Anglos, who feel they are learning the inside truth and not looking at the inscrutable facades that Chicanos cus-tomarily present when interrelating with gringos.

Martínez also makes effective use of the invaluable artistic technique of contrast. For example, he contrasts the lewd, adulterous Mrs. Crane with the chaste, loyal Maria. He contrasts the hardworking, respectful, and virile Faustino with his impotent, abusive, and cuckolded employer Buster Crane. In making such contrasts, Martínez highlights some of the worst characteristics of the dominant Anglos in general and some of the best characteristics of the subordinate Chicanos. Faustino's extreme virility, for example, seems to exemplify the vitality of the Chicano people in general, pointing up their unrealized potential. There is obviously a strong implicit message that the existing feudal system in the American Southwest should not be allowed to continue.

*Bill Delaney*

# FEMALE TROUBLE

*Author:* Antonya Nelson (1961-    )
*Type of plot:* Psychological
*Time of plot:* The late twentieth century
*Locale:* Tucson, Arizona
*First published:* 2001

> *Principal characters:*
> McBride, a drifter, sometime bricklayer, in his early thirties
> Daisy, his former girlfriend and county hospital patient
> Martha, his current girlfriend
> Alberta, Martha's transvestite next-door neighbor
> Claire, a patient at the hospital with whom McBride has an
> affair
> Donatella, Daisy's baby

*The Story*

"Female Trouble" is told in the third person in a discursive narrative style. The plot, while straightforward, is relayed in a series of short vignettes that describe the drifter McBride's encounters with the three women with whom he is simultaneously involved: Daisy, Martha, and Claire.

The story opens in February with McBride visiting his former girlfriend, Daisy, a native New Yorker who is now a patient at the Pima County psychiatric hospital in Tucson, Arizona, following a breakdown. Visiting her disturbs both Daisy and McBride, who reflects on their past relationship, especially their sexual encounters and his inability to deal with her and with women in general.

Following his visit, McBride returns to his home, which is the house of his current girlfriend, Martha, who works for the accident victim's report section of the police department and is also a research assistant who interviews rape victims for a university research project. In contrast to Daisy, the thirty-six-year-old Martha is a capable, artistic woman whom McBride believes "lived among the bizarre in order not to feel so bizarre herself, normal by comparison." While they are talking, Martha's neighbor, a transvestite whose name is Alberta, comes out of the house in full dress, and McBride comments on how much work it must take for a man to make himself up like that. Though he lives with Martha, McBride dreams of Daisy and moments of tenderness they shared. He and Martha then begin to talk about Daisy. Though his tender memories fade, he continues to visit Daisy, who reveals to him that she is pregnant, though not with his child.

Martha accompanies McBride on his next visit to see Daisy, and the three of them sit on Adirondack chairs on the hospital grounds and talk. Martha and Daisy discuss Daisy's pregnancy and women's aging. Though Martha does not talk about it, McBride is aware that she would like to have a child.

While Martha and Daisy talk, McBride steals into Daisy's room and inspects her belongings. Another woman patient, Claire, enters the room. She asks McBride if he is also a patient and is relieved to find he is not. They smile, and Claire leaves the room. McBride looks out the window and notices that the Adirondack chairs are empty.

In the next scene, Daisy, at Martha's invitation, is staying with her and McBride. Martha explains to McBride that she has invited Daisy to stay with them because Daisy is his friend and she does not believe that Daisy is crazy, but rather simply abused and in trouble. Martha and McBride have sex, and she declares that acts of rape and love are essentially the same. However, McBride does not want to engage in the discussion. The scene ends with a pun on the word "paradox."

Martha and Daisy develop a friendship that unsettles McBride. In the summer, McBride begins sleeping with Claire, who is still at the hospital. After one sexual encounter, Claire tells McBride that he does not have to think about suicide. McBride, who up until then had not thought about suicide, often begins to think about it.

When McBride returns to Martha's house, he finds Daisy in Martha's sewing room, and they resume the struggle, both emotional and physical, of their relationship, which is one of mutual attraction and repulsion. They fight; Daisy bites McBride, and he tells her to leave. Examining his injury in the bathroom mirror, McBride realizes that his heart is pounding.

Claire, knowing McBride lives with Martha and has had a relationship with Daisy, wants him to have an exclusive relationship with her. They discuss the nature of sexual relationships, and McBride, returning to Martha, finds himself caught between his involvement with the three women and his self-confusion, which he believes to be caused by the disjunction between his sexual desires and Daisy's, Martha's, and Claire's attempts to claim him.

While visiting Claire in the hospital, McBride finds she has been put on a suicide watch. Meanwhile, Daisy, seven months pregnant, has fled Tucson. Martha and McBride search for Daisy, who eventually phones them from Phoenix. The search for Daisy involves Martha and McBride in discussions of their own relationship. Once Daisy resurfaces, Martha again takes her under her wing. McBride finds himself again caught between his own feelings and the relationship between Daisy and Martha.

Claire, who has been released from the hospital in the care of her parents, sits with them and McBride in a motel room. McBride decides to leave her and returns to Martha's house to find Daisy entertaining the transvestite. McBride once again questions the nature of his relationship with Daisy and his relationship with himself.

Daisy gives birth to a child, Donatella, whose father was apparently African American, after being helped through labor by Martha. McBride responds to Donatella's birth coldly, saying, "Reminds me of an eggplant." Martha chides him for his coldness.

After Donatella's birth, McBride learns that Claire has committed suicide. Through her parents, he receives a letter she had written to him. Holding the unopened envelope in his hands, he realizes that what he feels about women is that they are essentially a mystery he cannot explain or understand. Seeking freedom, he gets in his car, and the story ends with McBride driving out of Tucson resolving, ambiguously, not to look back.

## Themes and Meanings

In her fiction, Antonya Nelson writes of relationships among men and women, parents and children, siblings, and members of all manner of extended families. Her recurrent themes are those of loss, loneliness, and disintegration. The title "Female Trouble" plays on the pun of the characters' dual troubles. McBride has his "female trouble" with the women he is involved with just as the women have trouble with their own female nature and all its attendant biological and emotional angst.

The theme of troubles and struggling is foregrounded in the opening paragraph with McBride visiting Daisy in the psychiatric hospital. How she got there is unclear; however, that she, like McBride, has always been somewhat of a drifter is indicated by the narrator, who relates that McBride had discovered her "on the highway near the Triple T truckstop carrying a portable typewriter, trying to hitch a ride" outside Salt Lake City, where McBride had hoped she would stay. However, she has shown up in Tucson, where McBride has somehow managed to increase his female trouble by developing a relationship with Martha.

Though McBride clearly views women primarily as sexual objects, he nevertheless is drawn to their stabilizing power, and so he appears, for the length of the story, to be dependent on Martha, whose placidity and solicitiousness, as well as her willingness to share her bed and her home with him, earns her the role of the most "trouble-free" of McBride's three women.

In a conventional story about alienation and relational difficulty, the reader might expect that McBride would resolve his troubles by making his home with Martha and discarding all other women. However, Nelson's characters and the circumstances in which they find themselves are never conventional. McBride is continually torn between his attraction to women and his masculine insistence that women and their problems are the root of what is wrong with him. In his self-perpetuating confusion, he literally wanders into yet another troubled relationship, with Claire.

The corrective influence of Martha, although it does not completely satisfy McBride, offers hope and compassion to Daisy. However, McBride finds himself baffled by the women's ability to bond with one another in spite of their knowledge of one another's involvement with McBride. Therefore, though the central consciousness of the story is McBride, the primary theme of the story is how women, given their biological nature and its needs as well as its difficult choices, often are faced with the struggle to survive (Daisy) and either thrive (Martha) or do not (Claire).

## Style and Technique

Nelson's style is that of a postmodernist who works within language to find correspondences between it and the outside world and between people's relationship to themselves and the world. Nelson is fascinated with how words play into and out of one another and how the characters, finding themselves enmeshed in a web of words they themselves often do not fully understand, must still fashion meaning for themselves, however temporary the meanings may appear to be. As a result, the story develops out of a series of puns, riddles, jokes, taboo language, pop culture lingo, and vernacular phrases. The third-person narrator delves into the minds of the characters when it is appropriate in order to tell the story, but the narrator never intrudes or makes judgments. The judgments in the story are all made by the characters themselves, and the reader is left to decide which of them, if any, is the most accurate in his or her assessment of their situation.

*Susan M. Rochette-Crawley*

# FERN

*Author:* Jean Toomer (1894-1967)
*Type of plot:* Psychological
*Time of plot:* The early 1920's
*Locale:* Macon, Georgia
*First published:* 1922

*Principal characters:*
FERN, a young African American woman living in Georgia
THE NARRATOR, a Northern businessperson who once visited
Georgia on business

*The Story*

The narrator, a northern white man, recalls an unforgettable black woman named Fern whom he once met in Macon, Georgia. Everything about this young woman is defined by her captivating eyes, which link all of her to the Georgia soil and to universal human needs. "Her face flowed into her eyes." Indeed, "like her face, the whole countryside seemed to flow into her eyes."

Fern's eyes tell men that she is easy. When she was young, a few men took her but got no joy from it. Afterward, they felt bound to her, obligated in ways that they could not explain. As Fern grew up, men kept bringing their bodies to her, but she only grew weary of them, turning them off. Nevertheless, they felt a need to return to do some fine thing for her. She did not deny them, but they nevertheless were somehow denied. She seemed somehow above men.

The narrator happened to pass Fern's house one day while walking with a stranger. When he saw her sitting on her front porch, sad and listless, with her head leaning on a post, slightly tilted to avoid a protruding nail, he asked the stranger who she was. Because local people already regarded the narrator as stuck-up and nosy, her name was all the information he got, so he let the matter go. Nevertheless, he immediately felt bound to Fern.

One evening the narrator went out of his way to walk by Fern's house and stopped to say hello. Her family was there, but they left quickly as if accustomed to giving men room. Not knowing what to say to avoid giving the impression that he wished to seduce Fern, the narrator asked her to walk with him. She seemed to understand his intentions and to want to trust him.

As they walked, they become more comfortable with each other, although people gaped at them, and crossed a cane field to a stream, where they sat under a sweet-gum tree until darkness fell. Growing pensive in the Georgia night, the narrator felt strange, as he always did in Georgia at dusk, and began feeling that unseen things were becoming tangible. He had heard stories of strange happenings at night in Georgia, such as a black woman who saw the mother of Christ and drew her image on a courthouse wall.

Almost unconsciously, the narrator put his arms around Fern. Her eyes, "unusually weird and open," seemed to hold him, and even God, in their gaze. Suddenly she sprang up, ran, then dropped to her knees and swayed back and forth, as if her body were tortured with something that it could not release. Then she began to sing—like a Jewish cantor with a broken voice. She seemed to be pounding her head on the ground in anguish. When the narrator rushed to her, she fainted in his arms.

Afterward, the narrator got ugly looks from men in the town and there was talk about running him out of town. Eventually he returned to the North. As he left the town, he saw Fern: She was again sitting on her porch, with her head tilted to avoid the nail, her eyes on the sunset. Nothing ever really happened, and nothing ever came to Fern—or to him, no fine unnamed thing that he would do for her. "And, friend, you?" he asks the reader. "She is still living. I have reason to know. Her name, against the chance that you might happen down that way, is Fernie May Rosen."

*Themes and Meanings*

The deceptively simple story line of Jean Toomer's "Fern" is developed within a carefully crafted, theologically symbolic description of a young Georgia woman with a Jewish name and a blended cultural heritage. Fern is aloof, masking a deep need for spiritual renewal even as she gives herself to a stream of men who are "everlastingly bringing their bodies to her." From the outset it is clear that she is not merely a prostitute, or just another young black woman trapped in a racially discriminatory southern city. Like the narrator, she is more than she appears, and at times she seems aware that more than their own personal liberation is at stake in their relationship.

The narrator's long exposition on Fern's character, personality, and appearance is essential to the story. Her full name is Fernie May Rosen, a Jewish name in a community in which most African American names are typically Anglo-Saxon. The narrator describes her nose as "aquiline, Semitic." She reminds him of a Jewish cantor whose woeful singing can touch you and make "your own sorrow seem trivial compared with his."

An outgrowth of Toomer's experience as a teacher in Georgia in 1921, "Fern" is a symbolic story with powerful social and theological implications. From the early period of Toomer's writing, "Fern" hints of the half-hidden southern image that men are hopelessly corrupt, and that women are the potential source of salvation who carry inside them the seeds of deliverance. Even as men take Fern's body, they want to find deeper communion with her, to give her something more than their bodies. That Fern herself is a troubled, lost soul intensifies their elusive quest. Southern men, and perhaps men everywhere, want to be viewed as aggressive and protective. However, they also need women for deeper reasons.

Fern is more than a lover to them. She seems to be a modified Mother-of-God figure, surrounded by symbols of Christ's suffering. Fern is no Immaculate Mother but is herself in anguish, seeking a redemptive genuine love. If the narrator thinks at first that he might be her deliverer, he falls short even of the other men. He wonders if any man could do better, even the most sophisticated northerner. "Could men in Washington, Chicago, or New York bring her something left vacant by the bestowal of their bodies?" He knew that he had failed. What if Fern were to move to New York or Chicago or some other Northern urban area totally alien to her? He visualizes her as a "cream-colored solitary girl sitting at a tenement window looking down on the indifferent throngs of Harlem," or as the wife of a successful urban professional, and concludes that none of it would make any difference. What she needs is a special love that most men could not give.

Fern herself changes little in the story, despite her traumatic trance. One might have expected some dramatic metamorphosis at this juncture because she had grown weary of the roles that she and the men were playing. "Something inside of her got tired of them, I guess," the narrator says simply, "for I am certain that for the life of her she could not tell why or how she began to turn them off."

The story ends with Fern again sitting on her porch, her head tilted to elude the apparently symbolic nail. Some critics see in this a cross symbol and a focus of Toomer's theme. Instinctively the narrator identifies with Fern, confessing that he, too, has dreams like hers. However, he has discovered that he, like the other men, failed to "push back the fringe of pines upon new horizons." With that, he raises a gnawing question for all men to ponder: What would a man really do? Would he do it for Fern, or for himself? If he saw her sitting on the porch, would he get off at the next station and walk back to take her away from all this, or simply use her and then leave quickly and forget her? "She is still living," he says. "I have reason to know that. Her name, against the chance that you might happen down that way, is Fernie May Rosen." Significantly, the last word in the story is a Jewish family name.

## Style and Technique

"Fern" is a poetic, symbolic story. Reflection and story line are integrally intertwined, and the reader is integrally involved. Readers, perhaps especially males, can identify with its timeless themes of relationships between men and women, the meaning of sexuality, and the proximity of religious experience to human love. By using universal questions Toomer repeatedly engages the reader in the process of defining the meaning of the story.

Imagery is powerful and effective in "Fern." From the first paragraph, Toomer sets the stage for the climax by creating poignant religious imagery, whose intensity is heightened by Jewish symbols. Ultimately, "Fern" is not a theological statement but sociological and psychological realism that raises fundamental issues of life's most sensitive and exciting bond, human love.

*Thomas R. Peake*

# FEVER

*Author:* John Edgar Wideman (1941-      )
*Type of plot:* Historical, social realism
*Time of plot:* August through November, 1793
*Locale:* Philadelphia, Pennsylvania
*First published:* 1989

*Principal characters:*
RICHARD ALLEN, an African American minister
A DISTANT OMNISCIENT NARRATOR
A SERIES OF LESSER NARRATORS

## The Story

This title story in John Edgar Wideman's second collection of short stories is a horrifying fictional account of a historical event, the 1793 yellow fever epidemic that devastated the city of Philadelphia, Pennsylvania, killing more than four thousand people, an estimated one-tenth of the city's population. The story is told in an episodic montage of narrative voices that demand the reader's close attention, each voice revealing a distinct point of view. Knowledge of the historical event would enhance the reader's appreciation of the story but is not essential to its understanding.

The primary narrative position is that of an actual historical figure, Richard Allen, a former slave who bought his own freedom and that of his wife and educated himself, rising to leadership in the black community as founder of the first African American church. Allen speaks at times in first-person stream of consciousness and also, in one instance, in an actual letter from his memoirs. Central to the story is a narrative voice commenting on the events out of an omniscient view of world history. Among other voices are those of a slave in the hold of a ship, a clinician describing the medical phenomena of the disease, a physician of the time (perhaps Benjamin Rush himself), a Jewish immigrant dying from the fever, and three voices speaking from the 1980's.

The complex interplay of these voices builds a dense layer of episodes that portray the city and its citizens in the throes of disaster. At the time, it was not known that yellow fever is caused by a virus transmitted to humans by infected mosquitoes. After yellow fever breaks out, the citizens of Philadelphia blame the disease on those most despised in the community: slaves transported to the Americas by their masters after the revolution in Santo Domingo and ultimately the entire black population of the city, who they believe are immune to the disease. Free African Americans do indeed die from the fever, but many risk their lives by responding to the demands of city officials that they assist the physicians by treating the afflicted, conveying the dead to the cemetery, and burying the bodies of yellow fever victims.

Richard Allen is assigned to assist Dr. Benjamin Rush, a noted physician of the time, criticized for his practice of bleeding victims of the disease, further weakening them and causing death. Allen, whose black parishioners have been expelled from the white church, forms an African American congregation. He feels both anger and love toward some of his brothers, sorrowful that, having escaped from slavery, they have further enslaved themselves by leading dissolute lives instead of following Christian beliefs. Others, like Allen himself, risk their lives to help the living and bury the dead. Allen sees at firsthand that disease makes no racial distinction; it kills the poorest black people in their hovels as well as the wealthy in their luxurious homes. He could extract payment for his services from the white people who refuse to acknowledge his humanity, but he will not do this. Despite his physical and emotional exhaustion, he is driven by his Christian faith, by compassion for suffering, and at times by desperate force of habit.

Other voices mock Allen, speak for other black Philadelphians, state the prejudices of the people of the time, or give historical details. Three brief narratives close the story but offer no resolution. One voice is that of a young black man speaking in the cynical street language of the late twentieth century. He is a poorly paid nursing home attendant, indifferent to the sufferings of his elderly patients, both black and white. Another speaker is the African American mayor of Philadelphia in 1985, justifying the bombing of the neighborhood of the anarchic African American MOVE group that kills eleven people, five of them children. The final voice describes the autopsy of one of the African Americans healers who died from the fever in 1793, the clinical details contrasted with the surreal vision of a child's hand reaching for the victim's heart.

## Themes and Meanings

"Fever," with its unresolved ending, probes deeply into the philosophical mystery of goodness and evil in human nature. Specifically, the author explores the history of racism in the United States, as it affects not only African Americans but also all immigrants who, themselves initially despised, climb the social ladder to oppress those who follow. Richard Allen is the principal figure giving cohesion to the fragmented narrative. In the midst of his errands of mercy, he questions his own motives. Why does he willingly serve the community that refuses to acknowledge his humanity? One voice, using extreme racial insults, calls him a fool, taunting him with the accusation that he cannot see the futility of his choice and should leave the country. Allen, however, driven to heroism by his firm Christian faith and an inexplicable love of humanity, continues his mission despite his near despair and exhaustion.

Other voices reveal their blind, unreasoning hatred of African Americans. In contrast to the extreme examples of human goodness and evil, the autopsy report shows that the exposed brains of fever victims cannot be identified as black or white. In death, all are equal. In this story, human nature, which is capable of both good and evil, remains a mystery.

A more startling statement comes in the voice of the omniscient narrator, speaking out of history to conflate physical disease with spiritual affliction: "We have bred the affliction within our breasts. . . . Fever grows in the secret places of our hearts, planted when one of us decided to sell one of us to another."

Ultimately Wideman, in juxtaposing the conflicting voices of the various narrators, is questioning the validity of traditional historical accounts that claim to speak truth.

*Style and Technique*

Wideman's stunning command of language and his experimentation with multiple centers of consciousness are characteristic of his work. He has said that the power of language to reveal character absorbs him. In a *New York Times Book Review* interview, he reported that he was fascinated by the story of the historical Richard Allen, a former slave of African descent who could write his memoirs in formal English. Research for "Fever" led to Wideman's full-length work about this event, *Philadelphia Fire* (1990).

Irony is a prominent feature of the story. The distant omniscient narrator, a survivor of history, speaks sometimes ironically, sometimes with compassion for the sufferers of yellow fever. In contrast to the prevailing view that African Americans were responsible for the disease, the clinical voice describing the autopsy of a fever victim notes that the physical remains cannot be identified as black or white. The devoutly Christian white ministers see no conflict in their decision to expel the African Americans from the church. Richard Allen reveals in his letter his love for his family and his devotion to duty. This portrait, as well as the imaginary narratives created by the author, shows a black American, reviled as less than human, as the most humane character in the story.

A series of realistic descriptions of the grotesque ravages of the disease on the human body and the stench and ghastliness of the streets of the stricken city invoke horror and pity of tragic dimensions. Especially gruesome is the explosion of the bloated body of a dead woman that showers the black cartman who takes the bodies to the potter's field. The cartmen themselves, in a ghastly mockery of their duties, race to dump the bodies in the makeshift cemeteries, placing bets on who can get there first and celebrating in a drunken orgy.

Wideman, a scholar of history and literature committed to including an African American view of history, expresses a sweeping view of prejudice and oppression in the United States. The voice of Abraham, a Jewish merchant who emigrated to the United States after his son was killed in a pogrom in Antwerp, recites the history of the suffering of Jews at the hands of Christians but is himself the owner of an indentured servant. The final voices from the late twentieth century, those of the mayor and the nursing home attendant, along with the autopsy report, connect the tragic events of the past and suggest a future of continuing misery if human beings refuse to acknowledge the common bonds of humanity that transcend race.

In his editorial comments in *The Best American Short Stories, 1996*, Wideman defines the art of fiction as subversive, questioning traditional assumptions about the nature of reality and accepting mystery at the heart of human behavior. The technical and emotional force of this story confirms his commitment to this belief.

*Marjorie Podolsky*

# THE FIELD OF BLUE CHILDREN

*Author:* Tennessee Williams (Thomas Lanier Williams, 1911-1983)
*Type of plot:* Psychological
*Time of plot:* The 1930's
*Locale:* A small university town in the United States
*First published:* 1939

> *Principal characters:*
> MYRA, a college student
> KIRK ABBOTT, her boyfriend; later her husband
> HOMER STALLCUP and
> HERTHA, college students

*The Story*

Myra, a university student, is rather typical, a sorority girl pinned to Kirk Abbott, a fraternity man. She still accepts dates from other men, so it is quite clear that the two are fairly casual about their relationship.

No matter how many parties Myra attends, no matter how often she dances until she should be exhausted by the evening's end, she always feels that something is missing in her life. This neurotic sensation makes her feel as though she has lost something, misplaced some unknown item, the exact nature of which eludes her. Sometimes she visits the rooms of other women in her dormitory, exchanging anecdotes until she must return to her own room, where she cries into her pillow or stares out of the window until dawn—always without knowing the cause of her consternation.

Myra has always written verse, and sometimes when the unexplainable emotion grows too great, she finds relief in jotting down some lines, which could range from a couplet to an entire poem. In April, she writes "Words are a net to catch beauty" in the back of a history notebook. From then on, her bewilderment seemed less acute.

She belongs to a poetry club on campus, at which she becomes acquainted with Homer Stallcup. Through the year, she has felt his avoidance of her must mean he dislikes her, but she finally realizes that the contrary is true: He is in love with her.

None of Myra's friends know Homer, because he waits on tables at a campus restaurant, fires furnaces, and does chores for his room and board. His frequent female companion, a strange girl named Hertha, is not a member of the "in" group either, but she belongs to the poetry club. She makes a fool of herself whenever Homer reads his work aloud, insisting that the entire group praise his poems. No one is willing to do this, except Myra, who voices her admiration. This seems only to embarrass Homer, who flushes, looks at the floor, and fidgets with his papers.

After the club's last meeting, Myra approaches the young man and tells him that his work is extraordinary, suggesting that he submit it to some poetry magazines. Still not looking at her directly, Homer digs into his briefcase and brings out a sheaf of poems, thrusts them into her hands, and asks that she critique them.

That night, Myra reads through the poems with a rising sense of excitement, although she does not understand much of what she is reading. Without really thinking about her actions, she dresses hurriedly, goes to the house from which she has seen Homer emerge, and knocks.

Through a glass pane, Myra sees a flight of steps to Homer's basement room. The door is open, and she sees him throwing on a robe before coming up to meet her. She tells him that she felt a need to come and talk to him about his poetry, especially one piece, "The Field of Blue Children." Because she is afraid to accept his invitation to come in, he returns to his room to dress. Myra feels oddly stirred by the sight of his naked chest and full, powerful arms. Almost like sleepwalkers, Myra and Homer walk to the field described in the poem and make passionate love among the waving blue flowers. The next day, Myra sends the poems back with a short, stilted note of explanation. She is going to marry Kirk Abbott that summer; what happened in the field was unfortunate, and any continuation of their relationship is impossible.

A few years after their marriage, Kirk comes home from work one soft spring evening to find a note from Myra, saying that she has driven to Carsville for a few hours. For Myra, it is a visit to the field of her memory, where she sobs and cries for nearly an hour among the blue flowers. Then she brushes herself off and calmly returns to her car, knowing that she will never repeat the journey. She has accepted the reality that her youth is over.

*Themes and Meanings*

"The Field of Blue Children," like much of Tennessee Williams's work, juxtaposes the practical, materialistic world against the more ephemeral arena of the artist. Concomitant with this division, the author places sexual desire, passion, and creativity in the poet's corner, contrasting it with the workaday world in which Myra and Kirk live after their marriage.

The names of the characters are significant in this regard: Myra means "wonderful," Kirk means "church," Hertha means "the earth," and Homer suggests the Greek bard. At the beginning, Myra feels that something significant is missing in her life, although, on the surface, she seems to enjoy all the typical activities of a popular college girl. This sensation is so overwhelming that she might be called a hysteric in the clinical sense. She assuages her pervasive uneasiness to a degree by writing verse, culminating in her recognition that "Words are a net to catch beauty!" Here she comes close to becoming what Williams would think of as wonderful.

After the episode in the field of blue flowers, Myra has an opportunity to come down on the side of passion, to accept the impractical, but thoroughly satisfying, life of art. She lacks the courage, however, to embrace Homer for more than just one night. In the author's view, she has given up her chance to be wonderful when she demurs and chooses to repress her strongest instincts in favor of a practical marriage to Kirk Abbott.

Kirk represents the completely unromantic, steady materialist. He accepts Myra's dating other men after they are pinned. He never becomes her confidant during her time of almost constant angst. After their marriage, he takes a job with the telephone company in a neighboring town, living with Myra in an efficiency apartment, where they are reasonably happy.

Myra does not write poetry anymore, and because she has not seen Homer's work in any literary magazines, she has decided that perhaps his poetry was not very good after all. In short, she has settled for not being the free spirit she might have been had she chosen the poet. The only time she sees Homer after their night of love, he is walking across the campus with Hertha clinging to his arm, perhaps symbolic of all-forgiving Mother Earth, all that is left for him.

The title of the story further validates Williams's feelings about artistic endeavor. The blue flowers in Homer's poem have become blue children, the natural result of the creative life force.

The final episode, Myra's return to the one significant scene in her life, indicates the author's assessment of her. She has equated the field of blue flowers with her troublesome youth, now successfully put away forever. She has forfeited her chance to fulfill the meaning of the name Myra.

## Style and Technique

Writing as though recounting events in the lives of a rather average group of college students, Williams never intimates any underlying meanings. He simply describes occurrences in an orderly fashion, waxing only somewhat poetic in his description of the field of blue flowers itself. Here the wind rustling through the flowers sends up "a soft whispering sound like the infinitely diminished crying of small children at play."

Through its characterizations, however, the story has psychological depths typical of all of this author's work. Homer lives in a basement room and does menial work, but he is able to express great beauty through his poetry. He seems inarticulate, clumsy, and embarrassed much of the time, but when Myra gives him the opportunity, his underlying passion erupts with great force.

Kirk, on the other hand, is given short shrift as a character, perhaps put into the story merely to contrast with Homer. He meekly accepts what he sees of Myra's behavior but fails to recognize what really motivates or troubles her.

Myra, like many of Williams's female characters, is capable of deep emotion but is fearful of living outside what she perceives as the decrees of her society.

As a group, these characters subtly represent the author's view of people. Most are fearful of taking up the really difficult challenges; most prefer to repress their deepest passions; and most settle for a calm, relatively uneventful life, bypassing, without regret, the fields of blue flowers.

*Edythe M. McGovern*

# THE FIELD OF MUSTARD

*Author:* A. E. Coppard (1878-1957)
*Type of plot:* Realism
*Time of plot:* The 1920's
*Locale:* Rural England
*First published:* 1926

*Principal characters:*
> DINAH LOCK, a married woman about forty, vivacious and
> sensual
> ROSE OLLIVER, a woman about the same age, more reserved

*The Story*

On a November afternoon, three "sere disvirgined women" are gathering kindling at the edge of a gloomy forest bordered by a field of mustard plants. Dinah Lock, a "vivacious woman full of shrill laughter, with a bosom as massive as her haunches," teases an old man about a watch that was given to his uncle for "doing his duty"; Dinah says that she "never got no watch for doing that a-much."

Dinah and Rose Olliver, a tall, angular woman, leave the woods while the third, Amy Hardwick, remains behind, slowly bundling up her collection of kindling. While they wait for Amy, a "sour scent" rises from the mustard blooms, and the dark woods lie on the hill "like a dark pall over the outline of a corpse." Oppressed by the pervasive melancholy of the scene, Dinah laments that "cradle and grave is all there is for we"; turning to Rose, she says, "I like you, Rose; I wish you was a man."

The two women go on to discuss the dissatisfactions of their lives. Dinah asserts that she is young at heart, while her husband is "no man at all" since an illness. Rose rather bleakly contrasts her childlessness with Dinah's family of four children. Rose takes a clipping from her purse and reads a passage that envisions the world as a beautiful garden filled with cherubic children; when she finishes reading it, she crushes the paper. Dinah says that, while she is willing to sacrifice for her children, she never really wanted any of them: "Somehow," she says, "I've been duped, and every woman born is duped so."

The recollection of her husband's feebleness leads Dinah to reminisce about Rufus Blackthorn, a gamekeeper and a "fine bold man" who was her lover several years before. She recalls how Rufus passed her house while she was working in her flower garden and took her to a wedding where they celebrated boisterously. Thereafter, she was "mad after Rufus" and met him regularly at night.

Dinah has described Rufus as "a perfect devil," but Rose asserts that he was a kind man, particularly toward women. She then tells Dinah a story that Dinah had not previously heard—of how Rufus once concealed the body of a drowned gentleman in his bed so that he could collect the reward for recovering the body. When Rose says that

Rufus also made her a pair of reed slippers like a pair he made for Dinah, Dinah accurately infers that Rufus was Rose's lover as well as hers. Rose comments, "We was all cheap to him, cheap as old rags; we was like chaff before him." Dinah and Rose again feel the gloom of the day and of the mustard field, but Amy's arrival prevents further discussion of Rufus.

As they trudge home, bearing the heavy burden of the kindling, Rose envisions Dinah's children in a series of sentimental, almost romanticized, vignettes, while Dinah counters with complaints. Rose thinks of the children as waiting eagerly for Dinah and imagines her "setting round your fire with 'em, telling tales and brushing their hair," while Dinah only says, "Ah, they'll want their bellies filling." Rose speculates that the children will "make you a valentine, and give you a ribbon on your birthday." Dinah responds that "they're naught but a racket from cockcrow till the old man snores—and then it's worse!" Then Dinah envisions Rose spending a quiet and pleasant evening playing draughts or dominoes with her kind husband, who will, she says to Rose, "stroke your hand now and again."

As the two women part in the windy, threatening evening, Dinah again says, "I like you, Rose. I wish you was a man." Rose, however, does not reply. As the women return to their homes, clouds are blown rapidly across the heavens and "the lovely earth seemed to sigh in grief at some calamity all unknown to men."

*Themes and Meanings*

As is the case with many stories, the theme of "The Field of Mustard" depends on a series of carefully arranged contrasts and on a revelation that is unexpected, at least by one of the characters. The contrasts begin to become apparent when Rose reads the clipping that describes an idyllic storybook garden, populated with cherubic children. As an image of what the world is like, this garden contrasts sharply with the "actual" world of the story: a dark wood on a gloomy November day and a field of sour-smelling mustard plants. Dinah also mentions that she "loved a good flower" at the time that she met Rufus and wishes "the world was all a garden." This contrast between the world as it is, a sour-smelling mustard field, and the world as the women would like it to be, an idyllic garden, is reinforced by the unfulfilled expectations and the disappointments of the women's lives. Rose is childless; Dinah's husband is "no man at all" since his illness. Although Dinah cares deeply about her children, they are an encumbrance that she never really wanted to have.

Almost certainly, the most fulfilling experience of Dinah's life was her love affair with Rufus, a "fine bold man" whose sensuality and fondness for boisterous fun matched her own. The revelation that Rufus has also been Rose's lover somehow diminishes, for Dinah, her own affair with him: It is evident that she was not as special to Rufus as he was to her. Rose's bitter appraisal—"We was all cheap to him"—is, sadly, more accurate.

The resentment that Dinah apparently feels at this discovery that she was not Rufus's only love expresses itself in her rather irritated responses to Rose on their walk home, but the bleak circumstances of the women's lives impel Dinah to seek the support of Rose's friendship. As "the wind hustled the two women close together, and as they stumbled under their burdens," Dinah reaches out, touches Rose's arm, and repeats that she likes Rose and wishes she were a man. That Rose again fails to respond to this overture of friendship suggests the ultimate isolation of the women, even from each other.

The story's concluding description of the "darkening world" as "windy, dispossessed, and ravaged" and the comment that the "lovely earth seemed to sigh in grief at some calamity all unknown to men" reassert the theme of the desolation of the women's lives. In the context of the story, it seems likely that the final "men" may refer more to the male sex specifically than to humankind in general, for surely the story emphasizes the disappointments that women face because they are women more than the disappointments that are common to all humankind.

*Style and Technique*

Perhaps the most conspicuous aspect of A. E. Coppard's technique is his near-symbolic use of setting and landscape in developing the significance of the story. The melancholy gloom of the November afternoon, the darkness of the wood, and the sour smell of the mustard plants, all mentioned several times in the story, parallel the dismal circumstances of the women's lives. Both Dinah and Rose, at different points in the story, chew on a sprig of mustard flower—Rose, when she contrasts her childlessness with Dinah's family of four, and Dinah, when she begins to contrast her husband's feebleness with Rufus's virility. The mustard flower, while not precisely a symbol, is clearly used to draw attention to the principal disappointment in each woman's life.

Although the "wind hustled the two women close together . . . as they stumbled under their burdens" on their way home, Rose's failure to reply to Dinah's gesture of friendship at the end of the story suggests that even friendship fails as a consolation in the bleak world that is the lot of these women. This view is reinforced by the way Coppard handles point of view, scrupulously avoiding direct revelation of the two women's thoughts. Their thoughts may to some extent be inferred from their words and gestures, but the fact that the thoughts themselves are never directly revealed subtly reinforces the aloneness and isolation of the women's lives.

*Erwin Hester*

# FIESTA, 1980

*Author:* Junot Díaz (1968-        )
*Type of plot:* Domestic realism, coming of age
*Time of plot:* 1980
*Locale:* Northern New Jersey and the Bronx in New York City
*First published:* 1996

> *Principal characters:*
> YUNIOR, the narrator, a Latino adolescent
> PAPI, his father
> MAMI, his mother
> RAFA, his older brother
> MADAI, his younger sister

*The Story*

Told in the first person by an adolescent Latino boy, "Fiesta, 1980" chronicles a family of immigrants from the Dominican Republic driving to a party in the Bronx in New York City and the events of the party itself. Interspersed with the narration of these events are various family memories as recalled by the narrator, Yunior.

The family consists of Papi and Mami; their two sons, fifteen-year-old Rafa and twelve-year-old Yunior; and the youngest child, Madai, a preadolescent girl. The story begins in the family's modest home in northern New Jersey as they dress for a fiesta to be held at Mami's sister's home in the Bronx. At the beginning, Yunior, the narrator, discloses that Papi is carrying on an affair with a Puerto Rican woman and that everyone in the family probably knows about it, though the subject is avoided.

Yunior has a reputation in the family for getting carsick, and Papi scolds Mami for allowing the boy to eat before the car ride to the Bronx. Papi fears food in Yunior's stomach will make him sick. Yunior feels ostracized by his family for this affliction, and his father and brother needle him about it, making him feel worse. Mami sticks up for Yunior, saying it is not his fault that he gets sick. A believer in corporal punishment, Papi threatens Yunior with a beating if he should he get sick in the van.

During the drive to the party, Yunior begins feeling queasy, and Mami offers him hard candy to help him through the spell of nausea. Sucking the candy, Yunior reminisces to himself about the many times he became sick in the Volkswagen van. Sure enough, before the family gets to the Bronx, Yunior vomits in the van, confirming his brother's and father's impression that he is a weakling.

At the party, the hosts and other guests, all of whom seem to be Latinos and many of whom are related, greet Yunior and his family. The food, music, and dancing have a particular Latin flavor. The adults talk loudly in the kitchen while the children watch television in the living room. Rafa joins two adolescent girls on the couch and immediately begins flirting; Yunior is too shy to interact with the girls, but another, younger boy, Wilquins, who is mute, attracts his interest. Papi's domineering voice in the kitchen overpowers the other adults' voices.

Watching television, Yunior reminisces to himself about a time when his father brought him to the house of his mistress, who let him watch television downstairs while she and Yunior's father disappeared upstairs for an hour. Knowledge of his father's secret relationship with the woman troubles Yunior.

When the food is served, Papi forbids Yunior to eat, afraid he will become carsick on the ride home. Yunior's aunt, Tia Yrma, requests his company on a walk to get some ice, and she smuggles him some pastelitos to eat outside the apartment. Away from the party, Yrma questions Yunior about his mother's marriage and her state of mind.

Yrma and Yunior return to the party. Soon the adults begin dancing. Yunior watches his mother and Yrma standing together having an intimate conversation. He tries to imagine his mother before she was married, recalling a photo of her as a young woman that he once had seen. He imagines she was happier then and drifts off to sleep.

Later, Yunior is awakened; it is time to go home. On the long ride, his two siblings fall asleep, but Yunior feels carsick. The nausea increases as he watches his parents riding quietly, seemingly content, in the front seat. Finally, he calls to his mother, and his parents realize he is going to be sick again.

*Themes and Meanings*

Several themes compete in this story, but they are subordinate to the main theme of a young boy, an innocent in many regards, who struggles with the difficult knowledge of his father's extramarital affair. The story can be interpreted as a coming-of-age story or as part of the journey from innocence to experience. However, because the story entails only one evening in time, the transformation from innocence to experience is not complete. In fact, Yunior's knowledge of his father's extramarital affair troubles him but leads, at the end of this story, to confusion rather than resolution.

The father, a loud, domineering man, is a foil to his sensitive son Yunior and exhibits his controlling patriarchal character, if not his misogyny, throughout the story. Papi makes all the decisions. Yunior describes how the decision to have the fiesta was Papi's, even though it takes place at Tia Yrma's house. Dressed and ready to depart, the entire family must wait for Papi, who arrives home at the last minute and must take a shower first, as Yunior suspects, to rinse away the perfume of the Puerto Rican woman.

Another recurring example of the father's controlling patriarchy is his use of corporal punishment to make his family obey him. Yunior states his father "expected your undivided attention when you were getting your ass whupped." The entire family accepts and endures this treatment.

The family alliances in the story divide along gender lines, the masculine types associated with control and coercion and the feminine types with passivity and compassion. For example, big brother Rafa follows Papi's example, demeaning his younger brother verbally and punching him to humiliate him. Papi and Rafa think of themselves as strong men, but their strength is defined mainly as the ability to control others, and it is a particularly misogynistic type of control. They think of women as playthings, and Rafa's constant flirting and boasting of sexual conquests are not unlike his father's having a mistress.

Mami, on the other hand, is passive and compassionate; she sides with her weaker son Yunior, consoling him when Papi or Rafa humiliates him for being carsick. An archetypal long-suffering wife, Mami looks away from the petty, and not so petty, abuses of her husband. The characters align themselves in conflicts polarized by gender, with the shallow masculine characters, Papi and Rafa, oppressing the sensitive feminine characters, Yunior and Mami. For the time being, the young daughter Madai avoids this conflict, most likely because as a preadolescent her sexuality is not fully formed and presents no threat to the polarized stasis of the family.

Whether the conflict among the family is created by the characters or by the Latino culture is debatable. Although Papi and Rafa are cruel in their attitude toward Yunior and women in general, one must also recognize that the Latino culture, as depicted in the story, encourages their actions, or at the least, tolerates them. For example, the girls whom Rafa ogles do nothing to discourage him, and one of them encourages his sexual advances at the party. Moreover, when Papi brings Yunior to his mistress's house, the Puerto Rican woman gladly obliges Papi's sexual advances even while his son waits in the living room downstairs. At the party, it is Tia Yrma who questions Yunior how he feels and how his mother is doing while Tio Miguel simply jokes about how a boy Yunior's age in the Dominican Republic would "be getting laid by now."

These events and relationships seem to demand that the twelve-year-old Yunior position himself as a man in an immigrant Latino American culture. However, he is not sure exactly what that means. The bold, domineering actions of the male role models, particularly his father and brother, seem at odds with Yunior's natural inclinations toward reflection and compassion. Yunior's confusion as to his developing identity is underscored in the final scene, in the van returning from the fiesta, when he becomes nauseated while looking at his parents seemingly content in the seat in front of him. Yunior's nausea is a physical manifestation of his confusion about gender roles in his family and his culture.

## Style and Technique

The most noticeable stylistic features of the story are the narrator's diction and the dialogue, which express the authentic and colorful language of an immigrant Dominican culture. The narration and dialogue contain numerous Spanish words and slang, without italics to set them off, forming a hybrid form of English and Spanish. This unique language suggests that the characters, perhaps especially Yunior, live not solely in a Dominican culture or an American one, but rather one that is a hybrid of the two. Yunior's diction and syntax are sophisticated, containing only infrequent grammatical irregularity, an appropriate expression for a thoughtful, reflective, intelligent youngster.

The dialogue is concise and somewhat idiosyncratic, appropriate features for communication among family members of a distinct culture about practical daily matters. The dialogue of particular characters sharpens their portrayal: For example, Papi's and Rafa's dialogue is antagonistic and declarative, suggesting their physical control over other characters, especially Yunior. In contrast, the dialogue of Mami and Tia Yrma is supplicating and questioning.

The story contains little dramatic action, as it chronicles dressing for a fiesta, the drive to the fiesta, the fiesta itself, and the drive home. However, the movement of these scenes, ending with the family's return to their house, where the story began, suggests a completeness to the story.

*Chris Benson*

# THE FIGHT

*Author:* Dylan Thomas (1914-1953)
*Type of plot:* Autobiographical
*Time of plot:* 1928
*Locale:* Swansea, Wales
*First published:* 1939

> *Principal characters:*
> DYLAN THOMAS, a fifteen-year-old boy
> DAN JENKYN, his friend
> MR. AND MRS. JENKYN, Dan's parents
> THE REVEREND AND MRS. BEVAN, friends of the Jenkyns

*The Story*

In this short story, Dylan Thomas captures the bravado, friendship, and artistic dreams of his youthful days in Swansea. The story opens with the young schoolboy Dylan teasing old Mr. Samuels. The boys from the school keep Mr. Samuels on guard against their throwing apples and balls into his window. While Dylan rudely stares at the old man, suddenly a strange boy pushes Dylan down an embankment. They proceed to fight, the stranger receiving a bloody nose and Dylan a black eye.

Their battle quickly makes them allies as they see Mr. Samuels egging them on. They both throw gravel at the old man and walk off together as comrades. Dylan's newfound friend, Dan Jenkyn, says that Dylan has "the best black eye in Wales," and Dylan admires his friend's bloody nose.

Dylan spends the rest of the day glorying in his battle scar, enjoying the respect of the local girls and the boys at school. The young boys' conversation at school then turns to their dreams of owning expensive automobiles, large houses, and harems with "the girls in the gym," and of smoking fancy cigarettes.

That evening, before he visits his new friend, Dylan describes the small world of his bedroom: It is clearly the room of a young poet, with pictures of William Shakespeare, Walter de la Mare, Robert Browning, Rupert Brooke, and John Greenleaf Whittier (among others) hanging on his walls. He also has a copy of a poem he has published in the newspaper, pasted on his mirror.

As he walks along the street toward Dan's house, Dylan recites aloud his romantic verse. When he sees a young couple approaching, he quickly changes his recitation into a tune and hums his way past them. As he nears the house, he hears music coming from it and expresses his admiration for Dan's accomplishments: "He was a composer and a poet too; he had written seven historical novels before he was twelve."

Dan proceeds to play some musical pieces for Dylan, and the young poet, in turn, reads to him from an exercise-book full of his poems. The two boys seem to enjoy the prospect of an artistic future "spread out beyond the window." While they are waiting for supper to be ready, they imagine that they will edit a magazine together—*The Thunderer*. Then Dan suggests that they look at the bedroom of the family maid. As the call for supper reaches them, Dan promises that one day they will hide under her bed.

Besides Dan's parents, at the dinner table are their friends, the Reverend Bevan and his wife. The two boys enjoy indulging in rather profane thoughts, as when Dylan, struck by the gray-haired and gray-faced Mrs. Bevan, imagines that she might be all gray. He proceeds to undress her in his mind but cannot bring himself to go beyond the navy bloomers to her knees.

When it is revealed that Dylan is a poet, Mr. Bevan asks him to recite one of his poems. Embarrassed by the request, Dylan nevertheless begins to say aloud one of his poems filled with images of lust and violence, until Dan kicks him under the table. Mr. Bevan pretends to content himself with recognizing Alfred, Lord Tennyson, as the influence on the boy's poem, but he and the Jenkyns are obviously shocked.

Back in Dan's room, the boys discuss Mrs. Bevan. Dan tells him that she is mad and once attempted to jump from the upstairs window of his house. At this point, she enters the room and the boys open the window and coax her to jump out, but she merely sits there awaiting her husband. The boys grow tired of watching her, Dan plays one more tune on the piano, and Dylan says his good-byes and walks out of the house with Dan. They look toward the upstairs window and see Mrs. Bevan's face pressed to the glass. Half afraid that she might jump, they run down the street and say their good-byes to each other. Dan says that he needs to finish a string trio tonight, and Dylan announces that he is busy working on a long poem "about the princes of Wales and the wizards and everybody."

*Themes and Meanings*

Thomas's chief aim in writing this autobiographical sketch is to capture the happy hooliganism of his boyhood. His head filled with poetry, pranks, and dreams, Dylan discovers a kindred spirit through his bloody little fight with a strange boy. Although surrounded by straitlaced adults, the two boys create and maintain a wonderful world of their own, filled with immense hope and joyful, profane energy that threatens to crush everything in its path, including a maid's privacy and a minister's sense of propriety.

In all of Thomas's poetry and fiction, he consistently praises the joys of primal energy, the life force that drives the blood, and the juices of the grass and flowers. He takes a special interest in children, following the tradition of the Romantic poets, because children best symbolize a natural oneness with the unchartered life force. Still free from the constraints of civilized society and its debilitating rituals, boys such as Dylan and Dan represent the hopes of the mature artist. If the child is father of the man, as William Wordsworth says, then the fifteen-year-old Dylan in this story is indeed the shaping influence of the mature poet, Dylan Thomas, the irreverent singer of the sacredness of life.

*Style and Technique*

Written from the first-person point of view, this sketch embodies the boisterous and self-assured tone of its fifteen-year-old narrator. Thomas not only captures the headstrong vitality of the boys through his narrator but also manages to maintain an ironic perspective on the boys' untested dreams. Dylan's admiration for Dan's amazing accomplishment of having written seven historical novels before he was twelve reveals not only a youthful mutual admiration society but also a monumental absurdity.

By presenting the adult world through the eyes of a boy, Thomas renders their conversations and attempts to communicate with the youngsters as comic failures. The adults and the boys live in two separate worlds. The adults restrain and repress the vitality of youth, and whenever the boys are alone together, Thomas's language becomes more poetic, unrestrained, and self-indulgent, as if to say here are two boys, artistic prodigies turning their dreams into words and music that the adults cannot fathom or appreciate. The gray Mrs. Bevan, for example, carries in the color of her skin the death of vitality. She is interesting to the boys only insofar as she might be manipulated into a glorious fiction, a madwoman leaping from a tall window. That is excitement, and that is what life and poetry are all about.

*Richard Kelly*

# THE FIGURE IN THE CARPET

*Author:* Henry James (1843-1916)
*Type of plot:* Metafiction
*Time of plot:* The late Victorian period
*Locale:* London
*First published:* 1896

*Principal characters:*
> THE NAMELESS NARRATOR, a minor literary journalist
> HUGH VEREKER, a novelist of some standing, whose works are
>    the subject of curiosity and analysis by several of the
>    characters
> GEORGE CORVICK, a friend of the narrator, the husband to
>    Gwendolen Erme, and the purported discoverer of the secret of
>    Vereker's work
> GWENDOLEN ERME, a minor novelist, the wife of Corvick and
>    later of Drayton Deane
> DRAYTON DEANE, a prolific literary journalist who marries
>    Gwendolen Erme after the death of Corvick

*The Story*

Having reviewed Hugh Vereker's latest fiction in *The Middle*, a literary weekly (this a result of the kind offices of his friend George Corvick), the nameless narrator is invited to a country-house weekend, during which he encounters Vereker. The novelist reads the narrator's notice and comments derisively on it, only to relent when he learns the identity of the author. In a gesture of compensation (one supposes), Vereker confides to the narrator that his fictions are all linked by a single idea or scheme that no critic has ever noticed but that is the very secret of all of his work. This is the famous "figure in the carpet" of the story's title, and it is what Vereker sets the narrator to discover.

On his return to London, the narrator sets about his work of investigation and analysis, to no avail. He confides his secret to Corvick, who in turn (and with the help of Gwendolen Erme, herself a novelist) pursues the same goal of discovering the elusive design in Vereker's writings. Baffled and unsuccessful, Corvick departs for India, ostensibly on a journalistic assignment, but (one learns later) in actuality with the intention of distancing himself from the immediate engagement with Vereker's books, the better to discover their secret. Corvick succeeds, or so he asserts, as a cable from Bombay to Miss Erme informs her that he has discovered the "general intention" in Vereker. Corvick rushes to visit Vereker in Rapallo, Italy, where (once again the news is cabled to London) Vereker confirms that Corvick has indeed stumbled onto the secret of the fiction. Corvick immediately proposes a long, definitive piece on Vereker but not before demanding of Miss Erme that she become his bride as the price for his revealing to her the treasure that he has discovered. She consents, her mother (who has consistently opposed the union) conveniently dies, and the two are wedded, while the narrator is called away to Germany to assist an ailing relative.

Corvick's marriage to Gwendolen proves ill-fated, for on their honeymoon, he is killed in a cart accident in the country. The grieving Mrs. Corvick returns to London, where the narrator inquires of her whether Corvick had written his essay on Vereker. He had merely begun it, she admits, but he had nevertheless confided to her the secret itself. The narrator presses her for it, and when she refuses to reveal its nature or even to hint at it, he expresses doubts that Corvick had in fact ever known. Insulted, Gwendolen departs, thus enforcing a more or less permanent break with the narrator.

Six months later, Vereker publishes *The Right of Way*, which will be his last fiction. In an attempt to ingratiate himself with Gwendolen, the narrator delivers his copy to her, only to discover that she has already read it, having obtained a copy courtesy of Drayton Deane, who is reviewing it for *The Middle*. Deane is, in the narrator's view, more or less a hack, and the review confirms his judgment. However, Deane manages nevertheless to impress Gwendolen so that she consents to make him her second husband. She continues to write novels, and Deane's career as a literary journalist flourishes, while the narrator languishes in his ignorance of the secret of Vereker's work. In the meantime, Vereker dies, as does Gwendolen, as a result of the birth of her second child. Encountering Deane at their club after Gwendolen's death, the narrator inquires whether she had ever shared with her second husband the secret confided to her by her first. Deane, expressing first bemusement, then shock that his wife had possessed so momentous a secret and had kept it from him, is left at the end of the story utterly crestfallen—whether at the loss of the precious knowledge itself or at the sense of having been betrayed by his wife is unclear. The narrator, meanwhile, derives a certain compensatory satisfaction for the permanent loss of Vereker's secret in the distress of Drayton Deane.

## Themes and Meanings

Numerous commentators, from Richard Blackmur to Tzvetan Todorov, Wolfgang Iser, and J. Hillis Miller, have noted that "The Figure in the Carpet" is a fiction about fiction, a story about the formal properties of storytelling and the interpretation of narrative. What remain unsettled, however, are both the meaning of this curious device (what the figure in the carpet signifies) and the connections to be drawn between it and the overall project of Henry James's writing. Nor is it entirely decided among James's readers and critics whether this tale itself is meant as a joke, a tragedy, or something else entirely. In short, "The Figure in the Carpet" has remained as elusive in its ultimate significance as the emblem in Vereker's fiction that gives the story its title.

What does seem incontestable, however, is that James intended to suggest, perhaps no more honestly than Vereker, that fictions do instance a controlling idea or schema. There is ample evidence in James's letters, notebooks, and nonfictional prose to suggest that exactly such a concept of the architectonic structure linking the works of an author one to another was very much the ideal toward which James strove in his own writing and which he thought characterized the most successful novelists of his and previous epochs. His famous criticism of certain British and Russian novels of the nineteenth century for lacking precisely this controlling intention, for being "loose and baggy monsters," testifies to this. Nevertheless, James remained characteristically vague, scarcely more helpful than the fictional Vereker himself in giving any solid clues to what the overarching idea behind his fictional practice might be. Resourceful scholars have labored toward this goal but with scarcely more to show for their pains than the narrator in "The Figure in the Carpet" could boast. One might hazard the judgment that James no more intended that they should succeed than, as seems perfectly plausible, Vereker did in the narrator's case. In a sense, in order to discover the secret of a writer's entire oeuvre, one would have to be that writer oneself.

*Style and Technique*

"The Figure in the Carpet" is somewhat unusual among James's major tales for being written in the first person, rather than in the third-person, partially omniscient mode characteristic of his fiction. This may account in part for the relative directness of the style itself, which, if one compares it to the contemporaneous "The Altar of the Dead" or even to the earlier "The Aspern Papers," seems simple and unproblematic. None of the infamous convolutions associated with the famous "late style" is evident here. Such a stylistic practice does not, however, prevent the story from being an excellent example of that ambiguity and elusiveness that is often remarked in James's most important fiction.

Indeed, the seeming straightforwardness of the tale is a kind of falsely comforting, or purposefully deceptive, device for luring the unsuspecting reader into the labyrinthine difficulties and possibilities presented by the plot and characters. In a world where most of the characters speak comparatively plainly and directly (unlike the later novels and tales, "The Figure in the Carpet" is not clotted with a dense structure of conflicting metaphors and other figures of speech), one is likely to believe that they themselves are, in the end, fairly transparent in motive and straightforward in action. Nothing could be further from the truth. One is never certain whether Vereker is telling the truth when he confides a hint about his secret to the narrator, or whether Corvick did indeed make the discovery he has claimed, or most of all whether he confided his knowledge to his bride. Nor can one be certain of the motive for Gwendolen's silence both in the face of the narrator's importunings and with regard to her second husband—or was she silent with him at all? In a tale so fraught with mysteries and potentially deceptive behavior, one would be foolish to take at face value the narrator's judgment concerning Drayton Deane's ultimate ignorance. It is just such naïveté, which the narrative manifestly defeats in its theme and in its action, that the plainness of James's style invites. It would probably be incorrect to label this disjunction between style and theme a contradiction; it would not be so wrong to discern in it yet another puzzle in this most puzzling of James's major short stories.

*Michael Sprinker*

# THE FINAL PROOF OF FATE AND CIRCUMSTANCE

*Author:* Lee K. Abbott (1947-    )
*Type of plot:* Metafiction
*Time of plot:* The 1960's to 1980's
*Locale:* Texas
*First published:* 1983

> *Principal characters:*
> DADDY, a career army officer
> TYLER, his son, the story's narrator
> NADINE, Tyler's wife

## The Story

Tyler is telling his wife, Nadine, a story that his father has told him many times before. Tyler passes his Daddy's stories on to Nadine, taking on the role of storyteller that Daddy has practiced for many years and that has become the basis of their father-son relationship.

Tyler starts by narrating one of Daddy's most compelling stories, in which Daddy killed a man in a tragic car accident when he was twenty-eight years old. What makes Tyler's rendition of the story so engaging is the quality of detail he occasionally adds to his father's story: "His car, as I now imagine it, must have been a DeSoto or a Chrysler, heavy with chrome and a grill like a ten-thousand-pound smile." As Daddy was meditating on some of the joys and tragedies of his life, he rounded a corner of a county road at high speed and smashed into a car, sending it some fifty yards down a gully. After realizing he was not hurt, he began the grim task of trying to find the driver's body. His anxiety increasing, he came on the body of the ironically named Morris E. Valentine, who, although still warm, was quite dead.

Tyler tells Nadine that Daddy had told him that story again today, as father and son were sipping on a bottle of Oso Negro rum, the best thing to drink while reminiscing, in their opinion. Tyler gradually begins to realize the profound experience he is having with his father on this particular day: "I was in that cozy place few get to these days . . . that place where your own father admits to being a whole hell of a lot like you." Once Daddy is able to acknowledge their emotional and psychological identification, he tells Tyler a story he has told no one, not even Elaine, his present wife and Tyler's mother.

Daddy relates this brand-new story in a third-person narrative, calling the main character "X." Tyler immediately recognizes X as his own father, but he makes no attempt to get his father to admit to that fact. It is Daddy's way of revealing to his son the deepest and darkest secret of his life. Daddy's first wife was a French woman named Annette D'Kopman, whom he had met at an army golf tournament in San Antonio when he was thirty-one. Although not a particularly beautiful person, she had a grace and charm of movement that was irresistible: "a method of getting from oven to freezer with style enough to make you choke or ache in several body parts."

Annette and X married and lived at Fort Sam Houston, where he was a supply officer and she the dutiful and erotically satisfying new bride. Although there was some drinking and fighting, their relationship was fulfilling. She died suddenly, and X, after the initial traumatic shock, felt nothing—neither grief nor heartbreak. X kept waiting for the grieving process to begin but felt only an empty numbness. About halfway to the graveyard, X ordered Munroe, the driver of the limousine, to stop and let him out. Munroe, a quasi-unconscious neurotic, was stunned by the order. The mourners following the funeral coach were even more troubled. X did not know where he was going; he only realized that he had to move away from the sorrow and death that had finally registered in his consciousness: He experienced a massive sadness and found it unbearable. The next thing he knew, he had walked into an ice cream parlor and ordered three vanilla cones, which, he declared, were the best he had ever eaten.

During this threshold experience, X felt neither bleakness nor happiness, shape nor beauty. He simply reveled in the sheer physical ecstasy of consuming the vanilla ice cream. Then X experienced the major epiphany of his life—a visionary experience in which he passed out. He felt light-headed and partially blind and sensed the walls tipping and closing in on him and the floor rising and spinning. He had experienced the moment of death, a moment combining both hope and doom.

Tyler tries to explain to Nadine what effect the revelation of his father's darkest secret has had on him as it coalesces with Tyler's equally important revelation. Nadine asks what the moral of this story is, and Tyler says it shows that everything is fragile. He does not tell Nadine what followed Daddy's revelation, as Tyler is torn between weeping and feeling much older. He had wandered about the house surveying his father's golf trophies, the contents of the medicine chest, and the other personal items that composed his father's life. Tyler decides that he will tell Nadine tomorrow that he entered his father's bedroom, listened to him snore, and beheld his father as a beloved yet fragile human animal who will someday lie in a grave.

*Themes and Meanings*

Lee K. Abbott clearly announces the story's major theme when Nadine asks what is the moral of Daddy's final story, and Tyler answers that everything is fragile. There is more to this lucidly complex story than Tyler's explanation, however. The title of the story, "The Final Proof of Fate and Circumstance," clearly explicates another theme of the story. The story is also about a son becoming aware that he is becoming his father, and few stories have traced that complex procedure better than this one. What unequivocally joins Tyler to his father are the stories that Daddy tells his son, which his son passes on to Nadine. In their crucial function as storytellers, they are identical. More important, however, Tyler begins to understand that life is a brutal process of fate and circumstance unless and until a voice structures it in humanly significant narratives. Tyler consciously comes to realize the lesson his father unconsciously teaches him: that life without imaginative narrative is a meaningless series of discrete happenings that has no point. Only verbal utterance gives life form and, therefore, meaning. Stories create reality. Abbott's stories within stories brilliantly delineate the process of how the chaos of human activity acquires significance through the medium of language; without language, we are mere victims of fate and circumstance. "The Final Proof of Fate and Circumstance" is certainly a profoundly existential narrative.

## Style and Technique

The most compelling technique used throughout this story is the ingenious manner in which Abbott interweaves stories within stories within stories on three narrative levels. These levels also deepen character development and demonstrate the methods that Abbott uses to interconnect narratives. Textually, the story brilliantly illustrates the way the human imagination linguistically interweaves stories within stories, but it also shows that without stories, we cannot comprehend the meaning and significance of life itself. Equally important is the way Daddy's narratives become Tyler's. "The Final Proof of Fate and Circumstance" also illustrates how stories evolve and are passed down, and shows how Tyler adds details of his own to vivify his father's stories and to make them his own. He has, indeed, become his father. Several allusions to the old song "Dry Bones" trace the interconnectedness of bones throughout the human anatomy and act as a chorus reminding us that we are mere flesh and bone without the human imagination. The unspoken allusion to the subject matter and theme of Wallace Stevens's poem "The Emperor of Ice Cream"—that in the brutal face of death we revel in such delicacies as ice cream—becomes an intertextual connection not only to Stevens but also to a kind of poetry that reminds us of our mortality.

Abbott's highly charged language also vivifies various narrative voices because this story is also about the ability of words to engage and reveal the reality of violence, loss, and death itself. Abbott's language reverberates with the gorgeous specificity of Elizabethan playwrights and resonates with biblical rhythms and the masterful styles of such writers as John Cheever and Harold Brodkey. "The Final Proof of Fate and Circumstance" is a compelling story about the crucial connection between narratives and their power to create meaning and significance in an empty, existential cosmos.

*Patrick Meanor*

# FINDING NATASHA

*Author:* Madison Smartt Bell (1957-    )
*Type of plot:* Psychological
*Time of plot:* The 1980's
*Locale:* New York City
*First published:* 1989

> *Principal characters:*
> STUART, a recovering alcoholic and drug addict
> NATASHA, a prostitute and drug addict
> CLIFTON, a drug dealer
> ARTHUR, a bartender

## The Story

Stuart, a recovering alcoholic and drug addict who has been undergoing treatment at Millbrook in upstate New York, returns to his favorite bar, Henry's, in Brooklyn. The place has been renovated; the former owners, Henry and Isabel, have retired; and Arthur is behind the bar. At first, Arthur does not remember Stuart, but eventually he recognizes him, as does Clifton, a former acquaintance who used to supply drugs to Stuart and his friends. All of Stuart's old friends have moved on: Henry and Isabel have moved out of the city, Ricky has moved to Greenpoint, Rita has reportedly moved to Los Angeles, and nobody has seen Natasha.

Stuart returned to the city a week earlier, after having been away for two years. He did not know why he was returning, or what he was seeking to recover, and felt that he should have stayed away forever, but something drew him back to his old haunts. Living in a cheap room in Times Square, Stuart drifts from bar to bar, street corner to street corner, hoping to run into Natasha. Why Natasha? He had closer friends than Natasha, and she had never answered the letters he had written to her from Millbrook. Stuart was not exactly looking for her either. He merely expects to run into her; he believes that she will simply appear.

Rita, Stuart discovers, did not go to Los Angeles after all. She is in Bellevue Hospital recovering from hepatitis A, probably contracted from a dirty needle she used while taking drugs. She is pencil-thin but probably will survive—this time. Stuart asks her about Natasha, who Rita thinks has been working as a prostitute for a pimp called Uncle Bill, who lives on 125th Street. When Stuart goes to the address, a black child sitting on the railing of the tenement informs him that Uncle Bill is in "the trench," a pauper's graveyard. Stuart begins to give up hope of finding Natasha; her image is beginning to fade, and he now doubts that he would recognize her if he did find her. The only thing that is still certain for him is that he recognizes people who are not her.

Stuart continues to prowl the New York streets and starts drinking again, although he stays off drugs. In a restaurant called the Golden Corner, he meets a prostitute and strikes up a conversation. He tells her about Natasha, but when she questions him, he cannot really say why he is looking for her. He says he has survivor's syndrome, feels responsible for her somehow, feels that if he can take hold of her, then she will take hold of someone else, and everybody will be saved through some kind of magical chain of connection. Stuart kills time going to martial arts movies around Times Square, observing that the theme of return is prevalent in them. Sleeping in his grubby hotel room, he dreams uninterpretable bits and pieces but wakes up one night muttering "Clifton."

Back at Henry's, he finds out where Clifton is living, a half-renovated shell of a building on 8th Street. Carrying a rolled-up newspaper with a length of pipe inside, Stuart knocks on Clifton's door, and when Clifton sleepily lets him in, Stuart knocks him across the room, bloodying Clifton's mouth and knocking out a tooth. Clifton still does not know anything about Natasha and vows to kill Stuart if he comes around again. Stuart continues to think about Natasha. Every day he reads the newspaper accounts of missing people—Stuart calls them "gone people"—but there is no Natasha.

One spring day, when the coldness of winter has passed, Stuart sees an old friend named Tombo in Tompkins Square. Tombo has all the characteristics of a junkie but has not aged much and is wearing expensive-looking clothing. Tombo, for the moment, is doing all right but has not seen Natasha in more than a year. Stuart, however, claims that he has quit looking for her: Now he is just waiting to find her. "Interesting strategy," Tombo observes somewhat cynically. Walking the city, Stuart finds that his sense of urgency and expectation of encountering Natasha has become an end in itself, as it used to be when he looked forward to a fix.

On the fifth or sixth day of spring, Stuart finds Natasha. She is sitting on a bench in Washington Square, her head back and her mouth open, "tapped out" on drugs. She is dreaming—he can see her eyes darting back and forth beneath her closed lids—and she is thin, track-marked, and possibly dying. Stuart does not think about these things, however, as he keeps on walking toward her. He has finally found the moment he has believed in for so long.

## Themes and Meanings

Madison Smartt Bell's story is to the 1980's and 1990's what F. Scott Fitzgerald's "Babylon Revisited" was to the 1920's—a lost-generation tale of loss and attempted recovery. In fact, there are many similarities. Both are about men who return to their past in order to put together the broken pieces of their lives. Both begin in a bar—Bell's story in Henry's and Fitzgerald's in the bar of the Ritz Hotel in Paris—with the protagonist asking about old acquaintances. Both are about men whose lives have been shattered by addiction—Stuart by drugs and Fitzgerald's Charlie Wales by alcohol—and both stories end ambiguously, with no indication that the protagonists will survive their past ordeals.

The theme of this story is return, the same theme that Stuart finds in the movies with which he passes time. Bell tells us that the dope smokers and street toughs in the theater look to the screen only when there are fight scenes and violence, while Stuart watches everything, even the love scenes. A metaphor for the society in which Stuart moves, the theater audience is hooked on violence, drugs, and vengeance, while Stuart looks for love, redemption, and personal survival. Natasha becomes a symbol of that love and redemption. If Stuart can find Natasha, she will no longer be a gone person. Someone will have cared enough to seek her out and find her, to touch her life, perhaps even to bring her out of the vast loneliness of herself. As Stuart observes to the hooker in the Golden Corner, humanity is a vast chain of people, "if everybody holds on tight, we all get out of here."

This may be a false hope, as Bell accurately suggests. Natasha needs more than friendship to pull her out of drug addiction and a certain early death. There is a world of Cliftons and Uncle Bills, prostitutes and addicts, hopeless victims and helpless sufferers. Kind words and a couple of dollars are not going to save Natasha. In fact, the woman whom Stuart sees in Washington Square may not be Natasha at all. Throughout the story, there are rumors that she is in Chicago, hints that Stuart would not recognize her if he did see her, and assertions that she has not been around for at least a year. Perhaps it is not Natasha sleeping on the park bench after all. It makes no difference: Stuart believes that it is Natasha, and that is enough. In the vast chain of humanity and our responsibility to link ourselves to others, one has to start somewhere.

*Style and Technique*

Bell narrates "Finding Natasha" from a limited third-person point of view. The reader sees in the story only what Stuart sees, and encounters Natasha in the final scene in the same way that the protagonist does. Bell puts the reader inside the character of a recovering drug addict, so that one can thread one's way through the dark places of his past exactly as he does. The story moves from the shadowy space of Henry's bar in the first scene, with faces that Stuart cannot make out in the darkness, through the coldness of a New York winter, to the final light and breezy springtime scene in Washington Square. In the same way, Stuart moves from darkness, shadow, and emotional coldness, to sunlight and thaw. By finding Natasha, Stuart also finds himself.

On another level, the story is structured as fifteen short scenes, each representing a different level of Stuart's awareness as he tries to recover the past. Friends have moved away or do not remember him; others such as Rita are ill from drugs; pimps such as Uncle Bill are dead; drug dealers such as Clifton are still dealing death; Tombo is pretending he is not addicted. The total picture is one of death, despair, hopelessness, and loss. All of this is told in objective, matter-of-fact prose that avoids both moralizing and condemnation. This is Stuart's world, Bell tells us, the only one Stuart knows. By finding Natasha, he just may learn to live in it, without despair and without false hope.

*Kenneth Seib*

# FINDING THE CHAIN

*Author:* Mary Hood (1946-     )
*Type of plot:* Wit and humor
*Time of plot:* The 1980's
*Locale:* Georgia
*First published:* 1986

> *Principal characters:*
> BEN STEVENSON, a man who takes his family to the mountains
> CLIFFIE STEVENSON, his wife, whose family home they are visiting
> DREW, his stepson
> MARY J, his daughter
> JONDI, his two-year-old son

## The Story

Ben and Cliffie Stevenson and their children live on the Georgia coast, in Ben's native Glynn County, where he is a fisherman. Cliffie hails from the north Georgia mountains and yearns for the farm where she grew up. Drew is Cliffie's son by a previous marriage, and although Ben has legally adopted him, Drew has achieved only an uneasy truce with his stepfather. When the youngest child, Jondi, was born, Ben promised Cliffie he would take them all to the mountains to visit her now empty birthplace at Wildrose.

The story opens on Thanksgiving Day, the morning after the family's arrival at the mountain cabin. They are safe and sound but in considerable disarray. Their dog, Shin, had roused a skunk the moment that they arrived, well after dark, and she now sits, tied and reeking, with a pink flush from a tomato juice scrubdown. Shin has ruined Grandma Gable's Storm-at-Sea quilt by dashing into the house, skunk sodden, and rolling on it as the exhausted travelers were curled up to sleep. The cabin has no running water or electricity; when Ben started a fire on the first night, the house filled with smoke from a choked chimney flue. To clear the blockage, Ben ties snow chains, trace chains, and chains from a swing-set to a flat rock wrapped in a feed sack, which he pulls up and down in the chimney's crooked gullet. All of this goes on in the rain.

The narrative now shifts back two years, when Cliffie was sick and Ben promised to take her home; it then jumps ahead to the beginning of the trip. All of Cliffie's family, the Gables, are now dead, and Cliffie wants one last visit to the old mountain home before selling the place. The trip wears on everyone's nerves. The children fuss, the car slides off the rain-slick mountain road, and Cliffie mixes up the directions. The narrative follows Mary J's thoughts as she steers the car while the others push it back on the road and the bedraggled travelers unpack at the farm. The story then shifts back to the events of the first morning. Ben has now cleaned the chimney and Mary J has broken Grandma Gable's treasured candy jar. The stage is set for a full day's comedy.

The bored Drew casts around for something with which to occupy himself and lights on the chain Ben used to clear the chimney. While Drew is hurling the chain, like a track and field athlete throwing the hammer, Jondi dumps Grandma Gable's button collection down a knothole in the floor and Ben must crawl under the house to retrieve the precious bits of bone and metal. When he hears someone cry "Fire," Drew gives the chain one last heave and heads for the barn, only to learn it is a false alarm. After this crisis subsides, Ben has the sulky Drew, still the classic resentful stepson, help him load a trunkful of red clay into the car. It will be a surprise for Cliffie's Christmas.

While these events play out, Cliffie discovers that the swing chain is missing. It had been a "courting swing" that her father had put up after taking her to the feed store on her sixteenth birthday and buying a good grade of chain. Cliffie wants the chain back and confronts the sullen Drew about it. A snowfall threatens as the whole family searches for the holy relic of the swing chain.

The hunt takes them to a ravine that once served the family as a trash dump. Amid old bedsprings and pickle jars Cliffie unearths another decrepit heirloom—a porcelain doorknob with a special history. When Grandmother Gable's earlier home burned down, she saved the doorknob for the housewarming at the new house, the one the family is now visiting. The doorknob has lost its shaft, and Cliffie tosses it away in a symbolic acceptance that time is irredeemable.

The snow comes down in big flakes—the first that the children and Ben have ever seen—and Cliffie despairs of finding the chain. As they march solemnly across the field, "shoulder by shoulder, like a chorus line," in the fading daylight, Drew stumbles and falls. Floundering around in the mud, Drew discovers the chain in front of him. He shouts, holds it up, and they all gather around to clutch the chain. The soaring finale finds them striding to the lamplit cabin, all holding the chain, all one family, as the snow falls lightly all around and smoke from the cleared chimney drifts over the yard.

*Themes and Meanings*

"Finding the Chain" effectively deploys several popular archetypal themes. There is, first, the journey. Only Cliffie has been in the north Georgia mountains before, so for the others a trip that far becomes an adventure. They deliberately avoid the interstate highway, instead taking another route that goes through towns and offers variety and richness. Moreover, the day after they arrive is Thanksgiving, a true American holy day, and to complete the sacrament they are blessed by softly falling snow—not a terrifying whiteout but just enough to baptize them all as a family after the prodigal son, Drew, redeems himself by finding the sacred relic.

Whereas Ben and the children see the long trip as a venture into the unknown, Cliffie experiences it as a homecoming. However, she suffers much ambivalence about it all: Her joy at seeing the old sights struggles with the pangs stirred in her by warm memories. The quilt goes first, ruined by the hapless dog. The buttons dribble down the knothole, the swing chain gets lost, and the doorknob turns up in the dump. These minor mishaps prove mostly correctable, but they put Cliffie through a swirl of emotions.

Through all these largely comic misadventures, the undercurrent of tension between Ben and Drew flares up repeatedly. Nothing suggests that Drew presents serious problems either in school or at home, but everything indicates that he resents Ben's intrusion into his life with his mother and that he does not accept Ben as his father. Moreover, Ben accuses Cliffie of taking Drew's side in disputes, and his charges all ring true. Drew's sullenness discourages sympathy for him—after all, he is lucky to have Ben as a stepfather—but the revelation that Drew endures great adolescent unhappiness at school sheds new light on him. He has difficulty understanding jokes and fitting in, and this slowness and his large ears lead to his nickname of "Dumbo." He suffers his alienation silently, fantasizing about the day that he will join the army and prove his manhood. No one is surprised when Drew loses the chain; however, this lapse proves to be the means of his salvation.

When Drew finds the chain, the family is already marching in formation across the field but it is transformed by the chain's recovery. Significantly, it is Ben's name that Drew calls out first as he holds up the chain. He has achieved something to please Ben, something that will bond them both literally and figuratively. The scene completes the foreshadowing of an earlier passage in which Ben remarks, "We're all Stevensons now," alluding to his recent adoption of Drew. The story thus ends in a great swell of Walton-family uplift, the family in chains of their own choice.

## Style and Technique

The old convention of beginning a story by jumping into the middle of things draws the reader so far into this story that there is no giving up. Poor Shin immediately stinks up the homecoming, then Ben fills the cabin with smoke and improvises the snake of chains to clean out the chimney. Only then, halfway into the Stevensons' frustrating but ultimately triumphant day, does the narrative turn backward to recount the journey itself. The story's success owes much to Mary Hood's skilled manipulation of the sequence of events.

The story manages an easy, colloquial language with just enough southern slang (such as "reckoned") and geographical landmarks (such as Macon) to achieve a mild feel of local color. Also, the Stevensons live in a "Jim Walter" home, an allusion that many southerners will recognize. Dominating the story, however, is the chain, a powerful symbol that shines in several directions. It is first a synecdoche, a figure that stands for the whole farm, Cliffie's adolescence, and the vanished past. Beyond that, it emerges as the instrument of Drew's reconciliation with his stepfather. Finally, after the ordeal of the journey and the petty calamities of the Thanksgiving Day, it brings the whole family together in a spirit of true thanksgiving that gives every sign of enduring.

*Frank Day*

# THE FIREMAN'S WIFE

*Author:* Richard Bausch (1945-    )
*Type of plot:* Psychological, domestic realism
*Time of plot:* The 1980's
*Locale:* A city in Illinois
*First published:* 1989

> *Principal characters:*
> MARTIN, a firefighter
> JANE, his wife
> TEDDY LYNCH and
> WALLY HARMON, firefighters
> MILLY, Wally's wife

*The Story*

"The Fireman's Wife" unfolds from the point of view of Jane, the firefighter's wife. It is a September evening in an unnamed Illinois city. Jane and her husband, Martin, are at home, entertaining their friends Wally Harmon and Teddy Lynch, also fire-fighters, and Wally's wife, Milly, who is expecting a baby soon. All are old friends and native to the area except Jane, who feels somewhat of an outsider.

After dinner, Martin proposes a game of Risk, which all but Jane have played for years. Jane resists, claiming a headache and concerned about the lateness of the hour. However, Martin insists. As preparations are made for the game, Milly mentions a dream she had the night before about her pregnancy. Milly's dream prompts others to recount particularly vivid recent dreams of their own: Jane of fishing with her father, who had in fact died when she was a baby; Wally of drowning and, paradoxically, hav-ing to be the one to break the news to his wife; and Teddy of being shot and falling on concrete.

Jane and Milly are the first to lose and leave the game. They retire inside the house to converse. Milly talks about her pregnancy and about how uneasy her husband's dream mak.es her and then probes Jane's moodiness. Jane is defensive and claims she just has a headache. However, Milly suggests that perhaps Jane is unhappy in her mar-riage, feeling trapped and angry.

Jane does not commit herself one way or the other. However, there are indications that Milly is correct. The game finally ends, and the others go home, leaving Martin and Jane to prepare for bed. Martin wants to make love, but Jane again claims a head-ache and goes to sleep.

The next morning, Martin is sheepish and Jane is distant as she helps him get off to work, more it seems to speed his departure than to show support or love. She works at a car dealership, and soon after her arrival, Martin calls. He is apologetic and tries un-successfully to prompt some affectionate responses from his wife.

That evening, Jane and her coworker Eveline go to a local café. The night is stormy. While talking with Eveline, Jane daydreams about having a baby. She is surprised to discover that she wants a child and that Martin in her daydream seems different from the Martin she knows and lives with. The storm intensifies; Milly Harmon arrives and joins Jane and Eveline.

Almost immediately Milly tells Jane that she had a troubling dream the night before, as she had suspected she would after hearing Wally's dream. She dreamed that Wally left her soon after the baby was born. As they talk, thunder, lightning, and wailing sirens add to the tense atmosphere. The storm abates, and Jane returns home.

There, in the late evening, the full weight of her unhappiness reveals itself to Jane, and she decides to leave her husband that night. She begins to pack but decides to wait until the morning to make a final decision. She falls asleep.

Sometime later she is awakened by the voices of firefighters who are bringing her husband home. The sirens were from trucks responding to a major fire, in which Martin was injured and Wally was killed. Martin, in great pain from serious burns on his hands, sleeps on the living room sofa.

In the morning, Jane helps Martin with routine personal activities that are now difficult for him, owing to his bandaged hands. He is distraught over Wally's death (he held his dying friend in his arms) and also shocked by the discovery of Jane's partly packed suitcase, intuitively recognizing its meaning. He promises to try to do better for Jane, and she treats him with great gentleness and understanding. Later, she reminisces about their marriage and decides to stay temporarily until Martin recovers. The decision, which she intends to keep to herself until the end, brings her relief and a sense of certainty.

Jane's certainty, however, does not last long. There is so much she has to do and decide, and the extent of Martin's dependency is much greater than she anticipated. Recognizing how much her husband needs the healing effects of sleep, she helps him into bed and lulls him gently, tenderly to sleep, almost as a mother would a child. As she is leaving the room, she realizes with wonder and amazement that such tenderness and solicitude for another can only come from the deepest love.

### Themes and Meanings

"The Fireman's Wife" suggests the depth and complexity of human feeling that lies beneath the most ordinary facades of life. The story is set in a middle-class suburban neighborhood and focuses on the life of people who do not seem unusual or extraordinary. The men are longtime friends, share professions and hobbies, enjoy Sunday dinners together, and in general live day to day in a relatively automatic and unthinking way.

Jane, the firefighter's wife, does not seem unusual either, at least on the surface. She has an ordinary job, a circle of friends with whom she is intimate, and aspirations for love, social acceptance, and her own family that are shared by many. Furthermore, she welcomes the routine aspects of her life, even wanting to reinforce them because they keep her from thinking too much about the elements of her life and marriage that disturb her. However, even these annoyances are common enough: She is bored by her in-laws, feels periodically that her husband is a stranger despite two years of shared physical intimacy, and is less than enthusiastic about the pastimes and hobbies that her husband and their friends enjoy.

However, beneath the calm and apparently superficial surface of these characters' lives, one glimpses profound psychological currents in their dreams, reveries, and unconscious actions. The dreams of Wally and Teddy seem to come from deep wells of uneasiness and are understandable in the light of the dangers to which their jobs periodically expose them. Milly's dream of abandonment is likely a response to her husband's recounting of his dream about dying and captures an understandable sense of her vulnerability at this time. However, the story predominantly belongs to Jane, and the most significant developments involve her deepening awareness of her own reality, her own selfhood.

Jane's dream about fishing with the father she has never known suggests the depth of her need for a stable, male figure in her life. She does not draw this conclusion herself, but it seems likely in the light of the entire story. Later, in a reverie, Jane discovers with genuine surprise that she wants to begin a family of her own. Moreover, in that reverie, she sees a Martin who is different from the man she knows, or thinks she knows, suggesting the possibility of growth in her relationship with her husband. In a series of interior monologues, she uncovers deeper feelings and desires—her frustration, her longing, her love. Significantly, it is not until the very end—after the certainty that comes from her decision to leave Martin—that she discovers the depth of her love for him. As the story suggests, people are mysteries not only to others but also to themselves.

*Style and Technique*

The centered consciousness of this story is that of Jane, a young wife in a midwestern American city who is having difficulty adjusting to her role and her future with her husband. The reader learns only what Jane sees and hears, thinks and feels. The language, dialogue, and description are consistent with her character and point of view, suggesting at one level the mundane reality of her life as well as that of her husband and friends.

Little information is given about the setting. It takes place in an anonymous midwestern American city, which is not described or characterized in any significant way, except for the storm that shatters the evening calm. Scenes unfold in a bedroom, a bathroom, a café, and a fire station, but these also are left largely as blanks. So there is nothing to divert the reader's attention away from the central drama of Jane's interior life and discovery of her love for her husband, a discovery that equally surprises her and the reader.

The success of the story depends on the fact that the author has so thoroughly prepared readers for this discovery. The time involved from beginning to end is quite short, approximately forty-eight hours. However, within that time frame, there are a number of cycles of waking and sleeping, conveying a sense of conscious activity followed by subconscious activity. Also, the characters alternate between talk about the everyday and talk about their dreams, the latter indicating to themselves and to the reader the deep psychological currents in their lives. Then tragedy suddenly interrupts the flow of ordinary events, shocking the mind and heart into a new awareness. In addition, Jane's interior monologues, in which she probes deeper and deeper into herself, lead to her discovery of her profound love for her husband at the end.

The generalized setting, the dialogue shifting between surface experience and dreams, and the series of interior monologues take the reader surely and yet surprisingly to a profoundly moving and convincing resolution. The game of Risk that the characters are playing at the opening, in which pretend armies contest for the world, takes on a metaphorical weight at the end when death, loss, and love are recognized as the stakes involved in these ordinary lives.

*Michael J. Larsen*

# FIRST, BODY

*Author:* Melanie Rae Thon (1957-     )
*Type of plot:* Psychological
*Time of plot:* The 1990's
*Locale:* Seattle, Washington
*First published:* 1995

### Principal characters:

SID ELLIOTT, a war veteran who works first in the emergency
 room then in the morgue of a hospital
ROXANNE, his girlfriend
GLORIA LUBY, a corpse

*The Story*

"First, Body" portrays people for whom the American Dream is merely a phrase. The events are seen through the eyes of Sid Elliott, who, although struggling to find his own way, still reaches out to others.

In a city park, Sid, an emergency-room attendant of eight months, encounters Roxanne, a forty-nine-year-old woman who has stopped using heroin but still abuses alcohol. Sid no longer drinks but smokes marijuana. Roxanne goes with him to his home, a one-room loft in a warehouse, where she remains a number of months.

Both have suffered physically and psychologically. Roxanne started drinking at age nine, acquired a drug habit, and left her daughter because "it got too hard, dragging the kid around." Sid, big and clumsy as a child and as an adult, is psychologically scarred by a war, unnamed but clearly Vietnam. Mostly what he wants from Roxanne is for her to stay. Roxanne, in an expression of support for him, quits drinking but smokes more cigarettes, several packs a day. After two months together and thirty-nine days of abstinence from alcohol, she returns to whiskey and to life on the streets. She comes back beaten up, and Sid is there to offer her comfort, food, and cigarettes, but it is not enough, and she leaves again. He imagines her in the street people he meets: The man who sifts through the trash for food, the fifteen-year-old prostitute, and the woman whose bloated body was retrieved from the river.

After being criticized for dropping a sterilized tray of equipment when he prevented a patient from hitting her head against the wall, Sid is transferred to the morgue. There he knows he cannot think of the bodies as female, a hint that perhaps Sid has a problem with determining what is appropriate behavior toward girls and women. His sister earlier asked that he stay away from her three daughters whose slightness and quickness frightened him; his father asked that he move out of the family home because he "touched his mother too often and in the wrong way."

In the final section Sid wants to recognize the humanity in the deceased Gloria Luby, an obese woman who is brought to the morgue for a postmortem. Gloria, a street person, destroyed her body with alcohol. To receive hospital care while she was alive, she agreed to an autopsy. Even though she outweighs him by almost ninety pounds, Sid decides to lift her instead of rolling her as the doctor suggested. He wants to do it alone because another orderly might ridicule her. He will be "the last person alive who will touch her with tenderness." However, her 326 pounds prove too much. As Sid lifts her to transfer her from the gurney to the table, the tendons in his knee tear, and he collapses underneath her. He crawls away leaving her face down on the floor. His knee is permanently damaged, and the prognosis is that he will spend time in a wheelchair and then with a walker, but he should eventually, with luck, be able to walk with a cane.

In his hospital room, Sid, in a Demerol-induced haze, imagines he sees Roxanne, who laughs at his attempt to give Gloria some dignity, and his father, who thinks what a waste it is for Sid to have survived the war only to be disabled by a fat woman. He sees Gloria, who, offering warmth, lies down next to him, then the young street prostitute who hands him a cigarette, and for a second time, Roxanne, who presses the button that releases the pain-reducing drug. The story concludes with Sid knowing the importance of love and understanding the risks involved.

## Themes and Meanings

Melanie Rae Thon writes about the difficulty of life for the unfortunate and the vulnerable. In her novel *Iona Moon* (1993), the protagonist, a teenage girl, leaves school to care of her dying mother, faces potential abuse from her brothers, and hitchhikes to escape her rural Idaho hometown. In *Sweet Hearts* (2000), a brother and sister, raised by their alcoholic mother, become involved in a series of violent acts. The same darkness is seen in "First, Body." The title comes from emergency-room protocol: First, the body must be stabilized, the bleeding stopped and the heart beating, before the head can be examined.

The story is a critique of a society that allows people to fall through the cracks, a society that has throwaway people, not just the homeless but also Sid's father, who was laid off because his superior determined that he was too old to collect tolls for the ferry. Thon suggests that because of the pervasive harshness in the world, people need to assist and comfort one another. The nurse in Sid's room emphatically tells Sid that he is there if Sid should need him. Even though Sid's desire to respect Gloria results in failure, Sid continues to insist on her humanity. After the accident, he, in an imagined conversation with his father, insists on stating her exact weight rather than the more generalized figure given by his father. Gloria was an individual, and the details matter. The interdependence between people is symbolized in Sid's fantasy about the autopsy. He imagines that Gloria's vastness could engulf a man, that the man could accidently be sewn up in her after the procedure. Gloria's condition is not just hers alone but is part of everyone's.

Running throughout the story is the undercurrent of Sid's experiences in war, an extreme example of an uncaring world. His memories enter into his thoughts about his father and into his lovemaking with Roxanne. After a period of no sexual contact, he and Roxanne make love, but the event merges with his images of Vietnam. He is brought back to the present when Roxanne begs him to stop. He has been traumatized by the war—the randomness of the killing and the banal ways one can die. It is probable that the conflict contributed to his past drinking and has led to his present marijuana use, his frequent job changing, and his difficulties with women.

Thon counters the darkness in her fiction with the compassion her characters have for one another. She suggests that everyone must do what is possible to provide comfort to the needy, otherwise one is responsible for their pain.

*Style and Technique*

Thon's writing suggests a naturalistic bent that recalls Stephen Crane's *Maggie: A Girl of the Streets* (1893). The characters, although well meaning, are fighting against forces over which they have no control and which will ultimately overwhelm them. Sid stops a woman from hitting her head and is demoted because he drops a tray; he wants to show respect to a cadaver and opts to lift her instead of rolling her, and her three-hundred-pound weight destroys his knee. His father dies because no one happens to notice that he has collapsed while watering the yard. In the emergency room, the good are not more likely to survive than the criminal. The apparent randomness of life contributes to the dark atmosphere of the story.

"First, Body" is presented primarily through Sid's thoughts. He recollects the events of the emergency room: the holes, a precaution against hemorrhages, that are drilled in the heads of drunks who have passed out and hit the pavement, and the doctor who places bets on the numbers of motorcyclists who will be brought in. However, there is also the other side: the salvaged body parts that will be placed in others, giving them a chance to live, a process Sid terms a "sacrament." Some of this he would like to tell his mother on his occasional visits, but all she wants to know is that he holds a respectable job.

Sid thinks about his father and wishes that his father had asked him about his experiences in the war and that his father had given him the choice of going to Canada to avoid being drafted. He regrets the conversations that did not happen and the distance that was between them. He thinks about the war and the dead girl he pulled from the river, a girl who might have been a sniper but was still just a young girl. Because Sid is revealed primarily through his disordered thoughts, the reader slowly gathers information about him; the process is one of discovery. The story gradually builds momentum as more and more details are uncovered.

Thon's style tends to be graphic. The reader is given vivid descriptions of street life (the boy who is hustling his body), of the medical condition of Gloria Luby (the diseased liver, the accumulating fluid in the abdominal cavity, and the internal bleeding), and of the war conditions in the jungle (the mud, mosquitoes, and infections). The effect is disturbing but powerful. Thon's work is often described as dark, but she is recognized as an impassioned storyteller.

*Barbara Wiedemann*

# FIRST COMMUNION

*Author:* Tomás Rivera (1935-1984)
*Type of plot:* Domestic realism
*Time of plot:* The 1940's and 1950's
*Locale:* Southwestern United States
*First published:* "Primera comunión," 1971 (English translation, 1971)

*Principal characters:*

THE NARRATOR, who recalls an experience of his youth
HIS PARENTS
HIS GODFATHER
A PRIEST
A NUN
A COUPLE

*The Story*

The narrator recalls the time when, as a young boy, he was excited the night before his first Holy Communion. This was to be a memorable day in his life, not because he would get a godfather and would be able to have all the sweet treats that he could eat after the ceremony but because of what he was to see in the window of the tailor shop next to the church.

He recalls how he could not sleep the night before his first Communion because he was trying to remember all of his sins. He had been taught that it was blasphemous to go to Communion without confessing the exact number of his sins. He also could not sleep because his mother had put "phantasmagorical" pictures, including a depiction of hell, in his room. He also remembers the nun who taught him about confession, various categories of sins—especially sins of the flesh, which bring the punishments of hell. He was frightened of punishment in hell because he had burnt his calf a few months earlier when he fell into a tub of coals used to heat his room, so he knew that an eternity of burning in hell would be horrible. To make sure that he would not attend Communion as a sinner and then burn in hell, he determined that even though he could only recall 150 sins, he would confess 200 of various types and all degrees—just to be safe.

After waiting for his aging mother to finish preparing his clothes, he arrived at church so early that it was still locked. He walked around until he heard laughter and moans emanating from a tailor shop next to the church. Not expecting to find anyone, he peered into the window and saw a man and woman having sex. He could not stop watching. Eventually, they saw him, covered themselves, and yelled at him. He was so scared that he ran back toward the church.

Now knowing what sins of the flesh must be, he could not put the image of what he saw out of his mind. He even began to believe that because he had seen the man and woman lying on the floor, he, too, was guilty of "that sin of the flesh." Thoroughly confused, he wondered whether he should still go to Communion. He had better not confess, he thought, because he was forever ruined by forbidden knowledge. In the midst of these internal debates, however, he considered going back to watch the couple again and became greatly worried about how to deal with this situation.

When he finally reached confession, he told about his 200 sins but not about "his" sin of the flesh. He then attended Communion. On returning home, everything seemed smaller and somehow less significant. When he saw his mother and father, he imagined them naked on the floor together, like the couple in the shop. He also imagined that the people in his house were naked with distorted faces, and he visualized the priest and nun on the floor, as well. Unable to eat the wonderful treats—sweet bread and chocolate drinks—because of what he was thinking, he ran out the door.

His father and godfather thought that he was leaving because of youthful vigor or bad manners, but he was simply disturbed by what he had seen, withheld, and thought of on this day of his first Communion.

After spending time alone up a tree in the midst of a scrub-desert, he again recalled the scene at the tailor shop and realized that he actually derived great pleasure from remembering it. Forgetting that he lied to the priest, he felt the same way he did when he first heard about the Grace of God. For a moment, he felt that he wanted to learn more about life, about everything. However, after this feeling of elation passed, he realized that, perhaps, nothing had changed after all.

*Themes and Meanings*

Tomás Rivera often portrays religion and tradition as powerful and central elements of both Latino culture and American culture in general. He also tends to emphasize their repressive nature, and this short story is no exception. His fiction is founded on an intense love for humanity, and "First Communion" (which has also been published as "First Holy Communion") portrays an anguished human soul that is victimized by the absurdities that develop when tradition and religious dogma collide with the hard, human facts of everyday life. When a person gets caught up into the center of this collision, real human suffering results. "First Communion" is perhaps Rivera's most poignant depiction of such a human struggle.

The title of this narrative is richly suggestive. Not only is it the story of a boy's First Communion at church, it is also a story about his first experience, or communion, with sexuality. The scene in the tailor shop—itself a type of communion—uncovers a vital element of human life that furthers the narrator's progress toward adulthood, in spite of the feelings of guilt imposed on him by his religious training. Furthermore, this is a story about a boy's first self-communion; seeing the couple and keeping his knowledge secret intensifies his awareness of other people and helps to develop his sense of identity. He thus becomes more self-aware by the end of the story. This is a narrative of communion in another sense in that it chronicles the boy's first awareness of, and confrontation with, alienation from a world that seems to be both nightmarish and distorted, yet is also disappointingly familiar. Finally, this narrative captures a moment of disillusionment with what organized religion has to offer. This story, then, tells of a first communion that occurs on many levels of his life.

One of the things that makes this story so powerful is that it incorporates many traditional images into a narrative that undoes and problematizes many traditional elements within the Christian and Latino cultures. This story may be seen as a retelling of the biblical Eden myth, a central element of the Christian religion. As the young boy tells his story, he resembles an innocent Adamic figure who is exposed to the forbidden fruits of sexuality and forbidden knowledge for the first time. He tries to keep his new knowledge a secret but cannot escape the sensual and vibrant reality of his sexual awareness; the subsequent alienation that he feels is reminiscent of a fall from Eden's Paradise.

This narrative does something new, however: It leaves the boy in the wilderness without any desire, much less hope, for renewal or redemption. This is both a despairing and a hopeful ending. Rivera shows the boy's sense of alienation that is almost overwhelming, but there is also a sense that this smart, likable young man might be able to come to an understanding about his place amid the powerful traditions of his family, culture, and society.

## Style and Technique

Rivera's writing style in both his prose and poetry is laconic—he writes in terse, concise sentences. Although he writes very clearly—even plainly—each of his sentences is crafted for maximum effect; one must not mistake his subtlety for lack of skill or craftsmanship. He wants to convey a certain simplicity and frankness that should exist in all lives. For Rivera, the complex codes and dilemmas of modern life obscure the beautiful simplicity of life, and his method of fiction is one way to get past this problem. He tries in his fiction to strive for an authenticity and dignity that are often overshadowed by the cares of the modern world and various cultural hegemonies.

"First Communion" contains powerful images that Rivera employs in the hope that he might cause others to remember their own youth and to search their hearts in order to become more free from the traditions and hatreds that bind them. Perhaps the most powerful images created in the story are those associated with the couple having sex in the tailor shop. He takes pains to describe the window through which the narrator looks, the clothing on which they are lying, how the woman's hair is "all messed up," and how she looks sick after the boy "catches" them. The subsequent images of his own parents and their friends are also powerful devices that help Rivera to convey the simultaneously beautiful and brutal workings of this world.

*James A. Stanger*

# FIRST CONFESSION

*Author:* Frank O'Connor (Michael Francis O'Donovan, 1903-1966)
*Type of plot:* Psychological
*Time of plot:* Probably the late 1930's
*Locale:* Unspecified, but probably Cork, Ireland
*First published:* 1939

>*Principal characters:*
>JACKIE, the narrator, a seven-year-old boy
>NORA, his older sister and primary antagonist
>THEIR MOTHER
>GRAN, their paternal grandmother
>FATHER, the priest who hears Jackie's confession

*The Story*

The tale is narrated by Jackie, a seven-year-old boy who must make his first confession before receiving his first Communion. A precocious boy, Jackie is distressed because his paternal grandmother has moved from the country to live with his family. He is disgusted by the woman's love of porter beer, her inclination to eat potatoes with her hands, and her favoring his sister, Nora, with an allowance denied him. The boy feels that his sister and grandmother side against him and make his life unbearable.

He has been prepared for the sacraments of penance and communion by another elderly woman, Ryan, who impresses on the children the gravity of the rituals by emphasizing the perils of damnation. As Jackie tersely remarks, "Hell had the first place in her heart." She tempts the children with a half-crown if one of them will hold a finger in a flame for five minutes, and she relates a terrifying story of a man who has made a bad confession. The man comes to a priest late at night demanding that he be allowed to confess immediately; as the priest dresses, day dawns, the man disappears, and the only evidence of his presence is a pair of palm prints burned into the priest's bedstead.

Jackie fears that he has broken all the commandments and is forced to go to confession with Nora. Inside the confessional, he plants himself on the armrest and tumbles out of the booth when trying to talk with the priest. An outraged Nora begins beating him, but the priest scolds her and makes a special case of Jackie's confession. When the boy admits that he has contemplated murdering his grandmother and sister, the priest acknowledges that he is indeed a bad case. Jackie's pride swells because the priest appears to take him so seriously and because he appears to have an ally in his growing discontentment with women. They discuss the gruesomeness of hanging for grievous crimes, and, at the end of his confession, the boy who earlier was reluctant to confess is genuinely sorry to part with the priest, whom he regards as the most entertaining character he has ever met "in the religious line."

On their walk home, Nora is shocked at the length of her brother's confession and disgusted that he has not been given a more severe penance. When he tells her that the priest has even given him some candy, she is outraged that there is no advantage to trying to be good.

## Themes and Meanings

Frank O'Connor is regarded as one of twentieth century literature's most unabashed and thoroughgoing realists. His concern is always with the everyday world in which people move and function, and he seeks verisimilitude in characterization, plotting, and setting. In this story, he captures brilliantly the angst that Roman Catholic children often endure when preparing for the early sacraments of penance and Communion. Almost all children, once they learn about the Ten Commandments, feel, like Jackie, that they have violated the lion's share of them.

Despite Jackie's extreme revulsion toward his grandmother, O'Connor renders convincingly the tensions that exist in any family. The sibling rivalry between Jackie and Nora is entirely believable, and the ways in which she lobbies members of the family to her point of view reveal the complex dynamics of family life. The devotion and uncritical love that Jackie feels for his mother is consistent with the relationships among many of O'Connor's fictional sons and mothers. O'Connor himself adored his mother, and sympathetic maternal figures often appear in his stories. Jackie feels that his mother is his only friend and ally, and she is his protector in family squabbles. It is therefore understandable that Jackie is disturbed that she would forgo accompanying him to his confession and send Nora instead.

Jackie's other ally in the story is the young priest in the confessional. Initially, he appears to be another austere authority figure who is censorious of the boy's indiscretions. After he witnesses Nora's self-righteous indignation, however, he becomes a patient, sensitive audience for Jackie's confused emotions. Priests are often central characters in O'Connor's fiction, and his clerics appear under a number of guises. They typically are one of two types: a weathered, sometimes impatient, or even narrow older man, who brings a severe, unforgiving version of religion to his congregation; or a young, sensitive man, some of whom are quite inward and brooding, and others, such as this priest, who offer patient solicitude to their parishioners. O'Connor himself often felt he should have chosen a religious vocation; the priest in his story embodies the kind of cleric O'Connor believes is most influential in the laity's lives.

This confessor understands perfectly the nature of Jackie's relationship with Nora. The boy is chagrined that adults cannot detect her duplicity, especially his grandmother, who lavishes her love on the girl. When he tells the priest that he once swung at Nora with a bread knife, the confessor responds, "someone will go for her with a bread-knife one day, and he won't miss her." The priest is also a major factor in the story's central irony—that the punitive version of religion that the women in his life would enforce on Jackie is far more benign, even kind, in the hands of the man responsible for dispensing the Sacraments.

Just as he was fascinated with priests as central characters, O'Connor centered many of his later stories around the experiences of children and juveniles. Often these are naïve, sensitive figures who struggle with what seem to them the insoluble mysteries of existence. Jackie is a perfect example of such a character, a boy who is making an uneasy passage into the adult responsibilities of his faith. He wrestles with emotions that trouble him—he knows he should love and honor his grandmother, but she embarrasses him. He is shocked that adults in his family cannot discern his sister's obvious hypocrisy, and that her most passionate moments are spent tormenting him.

*Style and Technique*

Much of the story's energy emanates from the subjective narrative point of view. Because the reader learns everything from Jackie's viewpoint, one is naturally sympathetic with his observations, even though many of those are immature and self-serving. One would also expect that the story's prose would be quite immature and unsophisticated; however, the tale reveals sophisticated stylistic effort. To add depth and texture, O'Connor often weaves in language and observations that are not typical of an ordinary child, although a precocious youngster might conceivably express himself in such a manner.

Jackie twice describes himself as "heart-scalded" because of his misfortunes, and, after falling out of the confessional, he despairs, "I knew then I was lost, given up to eternal justice." These are clearly not phrases most seven-year-olds might use, yet they graphically express the emotions of such a child. On the other hand, Jackie's fascination with the details of hanging as punishment and his mortification over his grandmother's rustic ways are certainly the reactions of an immature character.

The tone of the piece is relaxed and conversational; the effect is that of a person sitting before the reader recounting a particularly traumatic event that has made a deep personal impression. O'Connor always was disdainful of modernist writers such as James Joyce and what he regarded as their effete, willfully obscure language. The story's diction is clear and straightforward, language that any moderately educated audience could understand.

The narrative technique and the subtle ironies of situation and observation indicate a refined sensibility. O'Connor begins the story ominously—"All the trouble began when my grandfather died and my grandmother . . . came to live with us"—but as one moves further into the story, what appears threatening becomes comical. Jackie's precociousness is also comical; he imagines himself a man of the world, and those moments when he looks down bemusedly on adults are also humorous. Perched on the elbow rest, looking upside down at the priest in the confessional, he understatedly asserts, "It struck me as a queer way of hearing confessions, but I didn't feel it my place to criticize."

"First Confession" is O'Connor's most widely anthologized story, and its popularity is largely due to the precise, humane depiction of a child undergoing a rite of passage. O'Connor's desire to write genuine literature for those beyond the literati is clearly fulfilled in this story.

*David W. Madden*

# FIRST DARK

*Author:* Elizabeth Spencer (1921-    )
*Type of plot:* Ghost story
*Time of plot:* About 1946
*Locale:* Richton, Mississippi
*First published:* 1959

*Principal characters:*
FRANCES HARVEY, a woman in her early thirties
MRS. HARVEY, her mother, an invalid
REGINA
TOM BEAVERS, a former resident of Richton

*The Story*

Tom Beavers, a native of Richton, Mississippi, recently returned from World War II, lives in Jackson but frequently drives to Richton to check on the elderly aunt who reared him after his mother ran away with a salesperson. He is talking with the pharmacist in the local drugstore about a ghost that is a part of the mythology of the town. For years, people have reported seeing an elderly man waving at them from the Jackson road near Richton at twilight, the time of day referred to as "first dark." A group of men on a chain gang once reported having had a conversation with the man, who asked them to move a bulldozer because he had a sick girl in his wagon and had to get her to the hospital.

During the discussion, Frances Harvey, a woman in her thirties who lives with her invalid mother, enters the store. Overhearing the conversation, she asks Tom why he is inquiring about the ghost. When he relates that he had seen the waving man the night before as he drove into town at first dark, Frances says that she saw the figure at about the same time. Although the two of them have never known each other well, the ghost story draws them into conversation, and the next Saturday at twilight, they are sitting in his car at the spot where the ghost had been sighted. Frances recalls that, as a child, she and her sister, Regina, were terrified by stories of the ghost related by her family's servants.

The couple soon discovers that they are attracted to each other and begin meeting on a regular basis. Eventually Tom is invited up to Mrs. Harvey's bedroom one afternoon for tea. Although she is an invalid, the old woman is still a powerful force, an often bitter and even cruel woman with an acid tongue, who rules the house and her daughter as imperiously as ever. Although Mrs. Harvey approves of Tom as a prospective husband for her daughter, Frances is afraid to marry him and bring him into the house, knowing that her mother will dominate both their lives. As she tells Tom, "She'd make demands, take all my time, laugh at you behind your back—she has to run everything. You'd hate me in a week."

Their courtship continues in a limbo created by Frances's mother's strong hold on her, until Mrs. Harvey unexpectedly dies. In the weeks that follow, Frances suffers from insomnia and recalls a favorite humorous comment of her father: "Let all things proceed in orderly progression to their final confusion." She has always thought the "final confusion" referred to death, but she decides now that chaos can occur at any point. Her mother's many expensive clothes, for example, have created a dilemma for her: There is no room for them in the attic, but she knows that she cannot simply sell them or give them away.

One afternoon, coming out of the cemetery after visiting her mother's grave, Frances encounters an elderly black man who requests that she move her car, which is blocking the road, so that he can carry a sick girl to the hospital in his wagon. That night, Frances is unable to sleep, worried because she did not offer to drive the girl to the hospital herself. She goes to her mother's room for the sedatives that she bought the day before her mother's death. When she finds the box empty, she realizes that her mother, unable to express her love in words, had committed suicide so that she and Tom could be married. The next morning, Frances hurries out to the spot where she saw the old man and finds him plowing. She inquires about the girl and is told that she will be all right.

When Frances tells Tom about her experience, he determines not to reveal to her that the story parallels that reported by members of the chain gang years before, because she already is burdened with "ghosts" enough—her mother and the house itself. He quickly decides that the only way to solve their problems is to take her away from the house. Her immediate response is that she cannot abandon the family home, one of the grandest in town, but he insists, reminding her of all of her mother's clothes. Impulsively, she concedes that he is right and goes to get her coat. As they leave, she locks the door and places the key under the doormat, "a last obsequy to the house."

The story concludes with an enigmatic, somewhat ghostly paragraph in which the house seems to take on a character of its own. The narrator observes that it has become more beautiful than ever, apparently unaware that it has been rejected by Tom, perhaps pleased to have rid itself of an undesirable element, "to be free, at last, to enter with abandon the land of mourning and shadows and memory." Like the two lovers in John Keats's poem "The Eve of St. Agnes," Frances and Tom leave behind them the ghosts of a past that might have continued to haunt them and move toward whatever the future may hold.

### Themes and Meanings

In many of her stories, Elizabeth Spencer examines the social pressures of life in small southern towns, in which all actions are open to public scrutiny; family obligations stifle individuality; class distinctions are strong and even oppressive; and, as William Faulkner observed, "The past is never dead, it's not even past." Tom Beavers grew up on the wrong side of the tracks, the son of a woman who created a scandal, and he was reared by an aunt considered odd by many of the townspeople. Frances Harvey, on the other hand, is from one of the town's best families and lives in one of its grand houses. Tyrannized by a mother who is described as wicked and mean, she seems destined to remain a spinster. The mother, however, is somewhat humanized for the reader when it appears that her suicide was an act of love, a drastic measure taken because she had never learned how to express that love to her daughter. Thus the rigid social pattern of the town stifles emotions, and only through a dramatic, shocking act of locking up the house and fleeing can the couple hope to make a life for themselves.

As in many of her stories, Spencer stresses the significance of place, particularly in the South. Both the town and the house seem to be characters in the story: the town as a composite of public opinion, the house as a distillation of the spirit of the dead mother. The powerful influence of place and the collective memory of the past that adheres to it can, as the narrator points out, deprive characters of their individual identities and make them ghosts. In one telling passage near the conclusion, Spencer writes that "In Richton, the door to the past was always wide open, and what came in through it and went out of it had made people 'different.'" At some unnoticed moments in their lives, fact becomes faith, life turns into legend, and people become bemused custodians of the grave. It is Tom's perception of such a moment that provides salvation from such a fate for Frances.

## Style and Technique

Spencer uses the limited omniscient point of view in "First Dark," entering into the consciousness of Frances, her mother, Tom, various citizens of the town, and even, whimsically, the house. Many short-story writers limit themselves to one point of view, and only an author as skillful as Spencer can convincingly handle multiple viewpoints. There is something of a mythic tone in the story, an appropriate element in what is, to an extent, a ghost story with the classic trappings: graveyard, a mysterious vanishing figure, and a haunted house. There is also an ironic tone: for example, the fact that the mother, a domineering tyrant, seems to have sacrificed her life in order to spare her daughter from spinsterhood. A third tone, somewhat surprising but very effective, is one of humor, especially in the description of various of the characters: the druggist, Frances's hypocritical sister Regina, and Mrs. Harvey, whose methods of controlling those around her are so exaggerated as to be amusing, despite their detrimental nature.

Spencer's symbolism is organic to the story. For example, first dark, the time in which many of the events occur, including the appearance of the ghost, symbolizes a time in Frances's life that is a turning point, when she can slip quietly into the darkness of a lonely spinsterhood or begin a new life for herself.

*W. Kenneth Holditch*

# FIRST LOVE AND OTHER SORROWS

*Author:* Harold Brodkey (1930-1996)
*Type of plot:* Domestic realism
*Time of plot:* The 1950's
*Locale:* St. Louis, Missouri
*First published:* 1957

> *Principal characters:*
>> THE NARRATOR, a bookish sixteen-year-old boy who is easily
>> embarrassed
>> HIS MOTHER, a woman desperate to return to the wealth and
>> status that she enjoyed in her youth
>> DODIE, his older sister, a beautiful young woman obsessed with
>> finding a wealthy husband
>> PRESTON, his friend who wants to be a physicist
>> ELANOR CULLEN, a neighbor girl
>> JOEL BUSH, a handsome, popular boy
>> SONNY BRUSTER, the son of a rich banker whose marriage
>> proposal Dodie accepts

*The Story*

Not a traditionally structured story, "First Love and Other Sorrows" does not confine itself to a strictly focused plot. It is a sentimental education in miniature that captures the feelings of an intelligent but insecure sixteen-year-old boy just beginning to gain insight into the human experience. Rather than plot, the story is constructed out of nuance and discovery.

The story is set in St. Louis, Missouri, during an era when people know their neighbors, listen to radios, send telegrams, go to double features, and know what "zoot-suiters" are. At home, the narrator is almost an outsider. Since his father's death, his family's station in life has fallen, and his mother and sister are coconspirators in a search for a suitable husband for the sister. As the story begins, the narrator cannot understand why his mother is so eager that Dodie accept one of the rich boys who court her. He quietly takes his sister's side when she argues with her mother that she is too young to marry and does not want to stop having a good time. Each time a rich boy is "won," Dodie rejects him. Gradually, the narrator perceives how his mother's own craving for wealth and social standing is seeking an outlet in his sister. The mother becomes increasingly anxious at her daughter's willfulness.

Long enthralled by his sister's beauty, the narrator finds it difficult to imagine her doing anything wrong. After she breaks a necklace, however, he realizes that she does not know what she is doing and that his is "not necessarily a happy family," but one that might make mistakes. Gradually, the narrator grows more able to break out of his self-consciousness. At the beginning of the story, he is very much a little boy when his mother scolds him for getting muddy. Later, he is embarrassed when his mother and sister ask him how often he shaves. He accepts without complaint that he must move his "treasures" (baseball glove, postcard collection, dirty comic books, personal notes) out of the house for spring cleaning. He berates himself for being too gloomy and serious. He agrees with his friend Preston's personal criticism. They envy the beautiful, confident Joel Bush, who gets girls.

As the narrator's self-consciousness turns more toward self-awareness, he admits that more than anything else he wants to be a success because he knows of no other way to be "lovable." By the end of the story, he understands the precariousness of his sister's position and, as a result, the importance of her new clothes (the mother borrows money to buy them), her earrings, and her long conferences with her mother about social nuances.

### Themes and Meanings

Harold Brodkey's story is about growing up. The narrator's sister realizes that she cannot forever play the anxious, callow, and pleasurable game of thinking about whom to choose for a mate. Eventually she not only becomes willing to accept one particular man, but she also even admits to her brother that getting married is "scary." For his part, the narrator discovers that thoughtfulness itself can be a trap, one that can prevent the kind of intimacy—especially intimacy with a young woman—that he craves. Rather than slowly drown in envious admiration for people—such as his sister and Joel Bush—who possess charm, beauty, and admirers of the opposite sex, he learns to seek love for himself.

The narrator's eventual realization that unhappiness is real and that it is "even likely" marks the beginning of the end of his adolescence. His next logical step is to act. Before long, rather than think about abstract matters—such as how a siphon works—the narrator takes steps toward participation in life. He learns to accept the transitory nature of happiness. After his sister announces her engagement, his small family shares hugs and kisses in the kitchen, showing a warmth that has been noticeably absent. The narrator sees this little moment of happiness passing but has the emotional understanding to participate in it before it is gone.

"First Love and Other Sorrows" is also about two symbols of success: money and beauty. The narrator's sister and Joel Bush have beauty; his sister's serious suitors have money—just as his family had before his father died. The narrator envies and admires successful people and sees himself as lacking the traits of success. Elanor Cullen, like the narrator, is insecure. She expresses her misgivings about her looks and her ability to be of much interest to another person. The narrator, managing to step outside his own insecurities, reassures her. In a tender moment, Elanor decides to cook him some eggs; cooking is something she feels good about. With these small, ordinary domestic encounters, the story creates a lasting impression of the narrator's emotional world and his emotional growth. Given the narrator's insecurity—especially in the company of women—it seems unlikely that he would ever kiss a young woman. Nevertheless, by the end of the story he does exactly that when he visits Elanor at her house. He does it suddenly, directly, and without his characteristic reflection.

## Style and Technique

"First Love and Other Sorrows" is told in the first person by an unnamed narrator who implies that he is describing past events. Perhaps wishing to set the record straight, he is fair and generous in his portrayals of these events. Objectivity and clarity are fundamental parts of the story's technique. The reader learns of the characters' thoughts and feelings not through the pronouncements of an omniscient narrator but rather through what the characters say and do. For example, at the beginning of the story, the narrator explains his mother's saying that the family would "have to settle for sandwiches" one night with the observation that "my mother pretended that now all the cooking was done for my masculine benefit." It is up to the reader to notice that the next thing that the mother talks about is a suit for her daughter: "Ninety dollars isn't too much for a good suit, don't you think?" During the 1950's, ninety dollars was in fact a great deal of money to many families.

At the end of the story, the sister comes home after an evening out with the news that she is engaged. The narrator begins to eat some chicken as he discusses the big news with his sister in the kitchen. His sister joins him in eating chicken, saying: "I guess emotion makes people hungry." The mother then enters the room and asks her son: "Are you eating at this time of night?" When his sister says that she is also hungry, the mother decides to heat up some soup. The narrator relates this exchange without comment. Such clarity and objectivity about a brief, telling moment of family interplay permit readers to feel that they are witnessing, rather than reading about, this little gathering in the kitchen. It is up to the reader to infer that the narrator is gratified that his sister is actually joining him in something, treating him as an equal, and taking his side against their mother. The moment makes a nice contrast with the scene opening the story in which the narrator is eating sandwiches that his mother has made for him.

*Eric Howard*

# FIRST LOVE, LAST RITES

*Author:* Ian McEwan (1948-    )
*Type of plot:* Realism
*Time of plot:* The twentieth century
*Locale:* A city in England
*First published:* 1975

*Principal characters:*
THE UNNAMED NARRATOR
SISSEL, his lover
ADRIAN, Sissel's brother
SISSEL'S FATHER

## The Story

"First Love, Last Rites" is told by an unnamed narrator who lives with his girlfriend in a quayside apartment in England. Both are seventeen or eighteen years of age. It is early summer, and the lovers, filled with youthful passion, make love regularly on a mattress-covered table in front of a big, open window. Once, while they are lying on the table, the narrator becomes aware of clawing sounds behind the wall; shortly afterward, Sissel also hears the noise.

Sissel's ten-year-old brother, Adrian, comes to visit them. The narrator becomes acquainted with Sissel's father, and together they plan to catch eels in the river and sell them live in London. The narrator and Sissel's father spend two months making eel traps and placing them in the river.

The narrator and Sissel continue to lie on the mattress-covered table, talking and making love. Sissel develops foot rot, the smell mingling with the smells of mud and seaweed coming in through the window. The narrator hears the creature in the wall and imagines it is his own creature in Sissel's body—one of feathers, claws, and gills. Sissel hears the creature also, and her lover thinks the scratching sound that grows out of their lovemaking is part of her fantasy also.

By mid-July, the lovers touch less, no longer enjoying their room. Adrian comes to visit them every day and wants to fight with Sissel as in former days. He is sincerely disgusted when the lovers touch. No breeze comes through the window—only heat, flies, and odors of dead jellyfish. The food tastes like the river, and the floor is covered with greasy sand. Sissel's foot rot spreads to the other foot and contributes to the stench in the room. Every night the couple is awakened by the scratching behind the wall. The rubbish gathers around them, and the narrator finds himself unable to carry it out. He takes long walks along the river.

Sissel gets a job at a cannery, removing rotten carrots from a conveyor belt. On her second day at work, the narrator waits for her at the factory gates. As the women leave the factory, he tries unsuccessfully to see Sissel, convinced that if he could not, they were both lost and their time together worthless. When he arrives home, Sissel admits that she saw him at the gate but could think of nothing to say after her shift.

Two days later, Sissel and the narrator bait the eel traps and place them on the river bed, marking each with a buoy. The next day, when he and Sissel's father row out to pull the traps in, they have trapped one eel and most of the traps are missing. They return to the hotel where the father is staying and eat breakfast. They do not discuss the lost traps, pretending they would be found. Sissel's father proposes a new scheme to make money on shrimp.

Back at their room, the narrator finds Sissel sitting on the bed staring toward a corner where the creature is crouching behind some books. At that moment, it runs across the floor, a huge gray rat dragging its belly on the floor. Adrian enters the room noisily. Using a coat hanger, he drives the rat from behind the chest of drawers as the narrator attempts to strike it with a poker. The rat charges them, its teeth bared. The narrator throws the poker at it and misses.

Again, Adrian drives the rat out, and the narrator splits it with the poker. A small purple sac containing the rat's unborn young slides onto the floor. Sissel kneels and pushes the sac back inside the mother rat and closes the rat's fur over it.

The lovers deposit the rat carefully in the dust bin outside their room and go for a walk. The narrator returns the trapped eel to the river as Adrian departs for a holiday. Sissel resolves to give up her job at the factory. It is autumn, and the lovers lift the mattress onto the table as they did in early summer. They agree to clean up the room and go for a long walk later that afternoon.

*Themes and Meanings*

"First Love, Last Rites" is one of Ian McEwan's few optimistic stories in which characters succeed in achieving a stable love relationship. Like many of his stories, this one contains characters who are adolescents. To McEwan, adolescents are extraordinary individuals who are close to childhood and, at the same time, are bewildered and frustrated by their initiation into adulthood. The narrator and his girlfriend, Sissel, are adolescents who find themselves in a world that is fundamentally threatening and realize that survival comes from their union to protect themselves from the cruelty and insensitivity of the world.

McEwan typically sees the city or the immediate surroundings as an irritant or hindrance to the lovers' progress. In fact, the environment becomes an antagonistic character in the story. The growing disorder in their room and the acrid odors from outside reflect the collapse of their relationship and the growing distance between them. They lie in the piled-up rubbish, unable to bring themselves to carry it out. No longer interested in cleaning the room or making eel traps, the narrator goes on long walks.

The lovers' environment is further complicated by the frequent visits of Adrian, Sissel's brother, who is desperately trying to escape the unpleasantness at his home. Adrian is at a loss to understand the change in Sissel, wanting to fight with her as they did in former days. The plan of Sissel's father to sell eels exhausts the narrator's resources, necessitating Sissel's taking a job.

The lovers' estrangement is emphasized by the narrator's inability to pick out Sissel in the crowd of women leaving the factory. He realizes they are no different from any other striving couple. Sissel's dreary job and her initiation into the drab workaday world suggests a paralyzing conformity to the narrator that denies the worth of their relationship.

The creature's scratching inside the wall is more insistent, and it is at this point that the narrator attempts to break the bonds of the ensnaring surroundings. They kill the mysterious creature, a rat living in the wall, destroying their own fears and uncertainties. With love and determination, the couple demonstrate their ability to escape the destructive forces around them.

## Style and Technique

McEwan's desire to shock his readers is an integral part of his fiction. He wants readers to be uncomfortable in his depictions of the brutalities of everyday life lest they become immune to them. McEwan suggests that acknowledgment is the first step toward combating the sordidness and filth of the real world.

In "First Love, Last Rites," McEwan's style is intense, and, combined with his disturbing images, is aimed toward portraying the world as a threatening place. The creature heard scratching behind the wall represents the narrator's anxieties about fatherhood and eventually comes to embody both lovers' doubts and apprehensions. The narrator's fantasies about the creature extend to believing that he and Sissel are characters in the slime, overwhelmed by the uncertainty of their future, parenthood, and their relationship.

The narrator's anxiety is exacerbated by his realization that he and Sissel are no different from any other couple. The horror of sliding into a worthless conformity, recognized by him when he was unable to locate Sissel in the crowd of women workers, apparently resolves him to attempt to break free from their situation.

The act that sets the lovers free is the killing of the rat living in the wall of their room. In an act of aggression that startles even him, the narrator kills the charging rat, only to discover a pathetic pregnant creature. The lovers' fears and anxieties are eliminated as they realize they can control their own lives and not be victims of the imaginary restraints imposed on them.

*Mary Hurd*

# FIRSTBORN

*Author:* Larry Woiwode (1941-    )
*Type of plot:* Domestic realism
*Time of plot:* The early to mid-1960's
*Locale:* New York City
*First published:* 1982

> *Principal characters:*
> CHARLES, a father-to-be and a radio advertising executive
> KATHERINE, his wife, a mother-to-be
> NATHANIEL, their firstborn
> HARNER, Katherine's obstetrician

*The Story*

"Firstborn" opens as Charles, the protagonist, is reading from Leo Tolstoy's *War and Peace* (1886) to his wife, Katherine, who is in labor. She has fallen asleep, but he continues to read. He reads the part in which Pierre, realizing his feelings for Natasha, goes out under the Moscow skies and sees the comet of 1812, "a comet that is supposed to portend all sorts of disasters but for him speaks 'his own softened and uplifted soul, now blossoming into a new life.'" This quotation from *War and Peace* foreshadows the course of the story.

As Katherine sleeps, Charles thinks about their marriage four months earlier. She had been pregnant by then, and he had assumed that the child was his. Later, she confessed that there had been a relationship with another man but that the child was Charles's, that she would not have married him if it were not. At first, he considered divorce but could not go through with it. Then followed a period of turmoil in their marriage. Finally, two weeks ago, as they were leaving a party, his anger had risen and he had impulsively kicked her and sent her sprawling on the icy sidewalk.

Now, although she is only seven months along in her pregnancy, Katherine is about to give birth. The contractions become more severe, and they leave for the hospital. The events leading to the birth and subsequent death of Nathaniel, their firstborn, follow. Later, after hearing that the child has died, Charles goes to a bar while Katherine lies alone in her hospital bed. Charles, during a chance meeting with Aggie, an aged prostitute, faces what he had previously avoided: He, too, had been having an affair. He hears "a faint whisper at his ear, Murderer. You'll never quit paying for this."

The final section of the story indicates that this incident is being related from the future, from the vantage point of several years and four children. The marriage has survived, but it is only at this point that Charles is finally released from his guilt and "freed into forgiveness, for himself, first, then for her, the rest falling into place."

*Themes and Meanings*

Although the story is most obviously about the birth of Charles and Katherine's first child, it really focuses more on their marriage. Their relationship calls up the comparison with Tolstoy's *War and Peace* in its movement from peace to turmoil and back again. The marriage's precariousness is most shockingly demonstrated in Charles's assault on his pregnant wife, which sets the stage for the story's two central themes, struggle and redemption. The story's primary theme is struggle—out of which joy may possibly emerge. As Katherine is struggling to give birth to their child, the more fundamental conflict between her and her husband is unfolding.

Charles's struggle with himself is the appropriate culmination of a story that has struggle as its central theme. Originating with Nathaniel's struggle to be born, the story reveals the struggle in the relationship between Charles and Katherine. Perhaps the reference to *War and Peace* overstates the difficulties that the couple experience and their significance, but the author's quotation from the Russian masterpiece is justified by subsequent events, which enact the same unnerving, uncanny, and ultimately redemptive combination of objective menace and personal deliverance. Though Katherine is more able to offer Charles immediate emotional comfort, such a resource has to find its own season in him, has to occur naturally, as peace follows war.

Out of this central theme comes the story's complementary theme, redemption, again evoked by the mention of Tolstoy, who often treated this theme, and by the specific quotation from *War and Peace* at the beginning of the story. However, the most obvious resolution to the theme of struggle is not employed: The birth of the child is no cause for joy but is rather one for grief. At the end of the story, however, at the point at which true understanding is reached by Charles, he realizes "that the child had always been with him, at the edges of his mind and in his everyday thoughts, as much as any of their living children (more, he thought)." By virtue of never having lived, Nathaniel haunts his father until such time as Charles's spirit is assuaged and he can make his peace with his dead firstborn. One of the story's most commanding artistic features is that it neither shuns the metaphysical dimension of its material nor pretentiously exploits it. The dimension arises with persuasive ease out of the material's naturalistic foreground. The story is no more a philosophical speculation than it is an obstetrical case history: It informally declares itself to be an experience lived. The story thus outgrows, though never forgets, the context of the delivery room. More important, Charles perceives in his closing, consummating moment of acceptance the current of energy common to all living things and which all living things experience.

At the end of the story, Charles undergoes a rebirth. In terms that invoke the imagery of light and vision, Charles "began at last to be able to begin again to see." The inference is that, not only in the aftermath of the firstborn's tragic birth but also in all the events leading up to and surrounding it, Charles has experienced a type of blindness. His stumbling, erratic footwork may be cited as confirmation of his condition.

*Style and Technique*

Given its dramatic occasion, it might be expected that "Firstborn" would positively teem with metaphors concerned with birth, breeding, newness, and succession. In particular, events seem primed for meditations on the miracle of paternity, the joy of motherhood, and the like. The events of the story, however, preclude such obviousness.

The style of "Firstborn" is essentially plain and direct. Occasionally, however, sentences become flamboyant and plethoric, infused, so it seems, with a surge of energy greater than that required to complete the fundamental task of narrative. The unpredictable occurrence of the latter type of sentence is an effective enactment of a central feature of the story, its "moral stamp" (Larry Woiwode applies the phrase to Tolstoy). This feature is the capacity for erratic change exemplified both by Charles and by Katherine, their ability to grow and, ultimately, to outgrow.

In a sense, because of the random interplay of differing syntactical tensions (from directly informative simple sentences to more complex units conveying difficult emotional conditions), it might be said that the author does not possess a particularly distinctive style. Although obviously a lover of language, Woiwode does not treat language with very much indulgence. He is ready to use a colloquialism as a verbal gem. One reason for this apparent casualness is that it effectively communicates the sense of improvisation and inconclusiveness that suffuses the central characters. Another reason for the style's comparative lack of polish is that its plainness provides access to the minutiae of daily life, communicating thereby the inescapability of the common lot in its mundane context. The stylistic fluctuations of "Firstborn" accurately dramatize the tissue of conflicting experiences on which the story is premised.

By concentrating on the immediate drama of the birth and the circumstances directly leading up to it, the author imparts a basic momentum to the material. The story's strong sense of pace befits the subject matter. The natural-seeming, though deftly orchestrated, pattern of lurch, stall, rush, and ebb closely engages the reader in the vivid moment at the center of the work. This pattern also reproduces the story's psychology of uncertainty and articulates its problematical idea of consummation.

Complementing the story's variety of styles are its structural features. Through concentrating on a basically simple chronological development, a nominal stability is provided. The taut chronological core, dealing with events directly pertaining to labor and delivery, however, has its narrative integrity offset by the story's larger temporal framework. Nathaniel's case provides "Firstborn" with its dramatic pretext. However, the case is also used to illuminate the quality and trajectory of the energies that went into making it, as well as the burdensome but survivable aftermath. As is true of other aspects of the story, a structural view reveals a mutuality between the intense moment and the accumulation of the years. The long view is latent within the ostensibly discrete episode. Thus, while the conclusion of "Firstborn" may seem somewhat sketchy or condensed, on structural grounds it is crucial to the story's vision. Time's duplicitous but eventually therapeutic duality, which the conclusion tacitly establishes, is the reader's most immediate access to the story's rather generalized but nevertheless genuine philosophical concerns.

*George O'Brien*

# THE FISHERMAN FROM CHIHUAHUA

*Author:* Evan S. Connell, Jr. (1924-      )
*Type of plot:* Character study
*Time of plot:* The 1970's
*Locale:* Santa Cruz, California
*First published:* 1980

*Principal characters:*
> PENDLETON, the owner of a Mexican restaurant in Santa Cruz, California
> "THE TOLTEC," a Mexican mechanic and regular customer, whose face resembles the carvings of Mexico's ancient Toltecs
> DAMASO, the Toltec's mysterious dark Mexican companion

## The Story

"The Fisherman from Chihuahua" takes place during the off-season in a waterfront Mexican restaurant in the resort city of Santa Cruz, California. The restaurant is owned by an American named Pendleton, from whose perspective the narrative unfolds. Pendleton, who does not speak Spanish, has learned to prepare Mexican food from a short, light-skinned Mexican mechanic whom he thinks of as "the Toltec" because he feels his face resembles one of the carvings done by the ancient Toltec people of pre-Columbian Mexico. As his reward for teaching Pendleton to cook, every night the Toltec is given dinner at the restaurant, after which he likes to listen and dance to the restaurant's nickelodeon.

The story depicts a singular episode in the life of Pendleton involving the Toltec and his companion, a man from Chihuahua, Mexico. For a brief period of time, the Toltec is accompanied on successive nights by this tall, dark Mexican, whose good looks are accentuated by his oiled hair and romantic clothes, especially his white silk gaucho shirt, which opens to reveal an enameled crucifix. However, what is most singular about the dark Mexican is his tortured and mystical singing, which for Pendleton suggests not the songs of Mexico but those of the Arabic or Moorish peoples.

The next night, when the dark Mexican once again fills the restaurant with his uncanny shrieks and cries, his audience includes a man and wife from Iowa City, Iowa, who have been shaken by the dark Mexican's performance and, as a result, try to reduce it to manageable terms; the wife suggests that perhaps the dark Mexican has been unlucky in love. Pendleton, although also disturbed by the sound of the singing, finds he is contemptuous of the couple's unimaginative and small-minded response. He turns away from his customers and toward the sound of the rolling night sea outside his restaurant. Even though Pendleton resents the reaction of the Iowa couple, his own ambivalence about the singing leads him to quarrel with the Toltec and to request a cessation of the dark Mexican's performance. However, when the dark Mexican persists in his powerful outpouring of mysterious emotion, Pendleton discovers that the dark Mexican is drawing more customers than he alienates.

One night, however, the dark Mexican fails to appear with the Toltec. Pendleton, disconcerted and curious, pumps the Toltec for information about his companion and learns that the mysterious man is probably actually a Gypsy from Spain. He also informs Pendleton that the dark Mexican, whose name is Damaso, likes to stand by himself on the seawall as if considering suicide and that currently he is on a drunken bender. In addition, the Toltec informs Pendleton that he is certain that, contrary to the opinion of the Iowa housewife, Damaso's tortured emotional life has nothing to do with a lost love.

When Damaso returns a few days later, the restaurant is full of people waiting for him, but he refuses to sing, instead bowing his head down on his arms, which allows his crucifix to drop out of his shirt and to swing to and fro, glittering in the light. The next night, the Toltec returns alone to announce that Damaso is gone. Pendleton's dismay at suddenly realizing how much he had depended on the presence of the mysterious Mexican is indicated only by his sudden awareness of the desolate slap of the waves of the sea and by his going to the door to look and listen for the slim possibility of the man's return. Using the epithet "Jesus Christ" to signify his frustration with Pendleton's inability to let go of Damaso, the Toltec advises him to forget about the mysterious stranger, that he is gone for good.

*Themes and Meanings*

This story contains two major themes, one concerning Pendleton's situation, the other the symbolic meaning of Damaso, the mysterious man from Chihuahua. The meaning of Damaso and his singing is kept deliberately ambiguous throughout the narrative because the reader must understand that his way of being in the world is not really accessible to Pendleton or to the other customers in his restaurant. Damaso appears to be an otherworldly figure whose singing suggests that he is bearing a message from a remote and mystical land far from American shores. Although some characters attempt to attribute Damaso's isolation and strange singing to a broken heart, it eventually becomes clear that his singing is about spiritual longing or spiritual suffering. The crucifix Damaso wears and the mention of Jesus Christ in association with him at the end of the narrative also lead to an interpretation of his singing as expressing a deep and tragic spirituality.

The use of the sea in relation to the almost extraterrestrial Damaso also allows a distinction to be drawn between him and the other characters in the story, who are associated with the land. The fact that the title of the story suggests Damaso is a fisherman not only suggests the wider liberty of the sea but also points symbolically to early Christianity, which had a fish as its symbol, and to the promise of Jesus Christ to make his disciples "fishers of men."

The second theme involves the emotional and spiritual limits of the modern American sensibility. Evan S. Connell, Jr., adds a couple from Iowa to include a more satiric depiction of the stultifying effects on individuals of too much social propriety and conformity—this narrow-minded and naïve couple are contrasted not only with Damaso but also with Pendleton, who forms a bond with Damaso and in the process is able to deepen his emotional and spiritual life. Pendleton comes to understand that Damaso's wild, inspired cries enlarge and extend the borders of reality and validate an expressive and creative consciousness that can explore the side of life associated not only with the sea but also with an inner world of intuitions and feelings that are as powerful and as mysterious as the ocean itself.

### Style and Technique

This story is structured as a series of episodes, each depicting successive evenings in Pendleton's restaurant. With each successive evening, more is revealed about not only Damaso but also the evolving response of Pendleton as he becomes more intrigued with the man. The story does not build to a conventional dramatic turning point but instead turns on the rather anticlimactic disappearance of Damaso. Connell's purpose is not to solve the mystery of the fisherman from Chihuahua but to retain his mystery while at the same time developing in the reader a greater sense of compassion and understanding of Pendleton's situation.

Connell intentionally keeps the character of Damaso at a distance, so that he remains a mystery. Because it is important to maintain a separation between the ordinary world of Pendleton and the extraordinary world of Damaso, Connell uses the figure of the Toltec as a bridge between the two men. He is used structurally as an intermediary because Pendleton never speaks directly to Damaso, and Damaso never speaks to him. If the Toltec is closest to Damaso, the figures who are farthest away are the Iowa couple; their comic presence is a contrast to the uncanny fisherman and ironically deepens the seriousness of Damaso's story.

Yet another significant aspect of this story's narrative is the use of the sea as both image and symbol. Pendleton's growing awareness of the sea suggests possible ways in which the meaning of the fisherman and his singing can be interpreted. In addition to the sea, Connell also introduces premodern references such as his evocation of the marketplaces of the Near East, religious imagery such as that of the crucifix, or imagery associated with the tragic such as the Toltec's stories of murdered women and drowned men. These all suggest possible ways to interpret of Damaso's music but remain in the realm of inference, so that nothing is made transparent or easily assimilated in the ordinary range of experience.

A final interesting creative choice on the part of Connell is the story's title. Because Damaso is associated with the Gypsies or the Moors of Spain, Chihuahua as a literal city fades into insignificance. Damaso's relationship to the Mexican city is ultimately not clear and logical but poetic and musical. It is the sound of the Mexican city that communicates its meaning—its name is deployed by Connell onomatopoetically, to echo the fisherman's cries of pain and longing.

*Margaret Boe Birns*

# FITTING ENDS

*Author:* Dan Chaon (1964-    )
*Type of plot:* Domestic realism
*Time of plot:* The 1980's and the 1990's
*Locale:* Pyramid, a small village in Nebraska
*First published:* 1995

> *Principal characters:*
> STEWART, a man trying to piece together his past
> DEL, his brother
> THEIR FATHER AND MOTHER

*The Story*

Because "Fitting Ends" is about a man trying to fit all the loose ends of his life together into a coherent story, it does not have a chronological plot structure. Instead it revolves around various stories the narrator, Stewart, recalls from his childhood. The first such story, about his brother Del, which appears in a book titled *More Tales of the Weird and Supernatural*, recounts three different appearances of a ghostly figure walking on the railroad tracks near the nearly deserted village of Pyramid, Nebraska, and then falling on his knees in front of a train. A few years after these supposed sightings began, Del, who was seventeen at the time, was killed by a train while walking along the tracks.

About a year before he died, Del saved Stewart's life. The two brothers had gone to the top of the grain elevator to fix a hole. While Stewart was clowning around dancing and singing, he slipped, but Del caught his arm and pulled him back up. However, when the boys' father grabbed Stewart to punish him for his foolishness, Stewart said that Del had pushed him. The boys' father believed the lie because Del had a history of violence against his brother; he had just returned from a special program for juvenile delinquents after trying to strangle Stewart. When they were younger, Del had thrown a can of motor oil at Stewart's head and pushed him out of a moving pickup truck. The boys' parents never find out about Stewart's lie.

In the next section of the story, Stewart, who now has a job at a small private college in upstate New York, is married, and has had his first child, comes to visit his mother, who has gone deaf, just after her sixtieth birthday. During the visit, when Stewart and his father are sitting together one evening, Stewart brings up the time he almost fell off the elevator but does not confess to the lie, saying only the event "seems significant sometimes."

The story then moves back to an account of the strained relationship between Stewart and Del after the incident on the grain elevator. Stewart knew there was no way out of the situation he had created, and after a while Del stopped denying that he had tried to push Stewart, perhaps beginning to believe that he had. Until his death, Del remained a defiant and belligerent young man. The story ends with Stewart watching his deaf mother moving about in the kitchen during his visit, thinking that at such a moment, everything seems clear to him.

## Themes and Meanings

Dan Chaon has said that "Fitting Ends" owes a debt to the self-reflexive story "Death in the Woods" (1926) by Sherwood Anderson. Like that story about a boy who sees a mysterious scene in the woods and tries to understand the meaning of it, Chaon's self-conscious concern here is with how "storytelling" tries to come to terms with the ambiguous relationship between truth and lies by pulling disparate events together into a significant whole.

The theme is announced in the first paragraph when the narrator tells how his brother's death has been transformed into the stuff of story in a book called *More Tales of the Weird and Supernatural*, a book that the author says is based on "true facts." The event the author describes is concerned with one of the basic aspects of fiction—the presentation of events that anticipate events yet to occur. The author's fascination with the story of the sightings of a ghost on the train track results from the fact that the ghost of Del appears two years before he died. As Stewart says, it is the nature of story that the reader can "imagine the ending." This anticipates the ending of "Fitting Ends" when Stewart notes that at certain moments, all the loose ends of his life fit together as easily as a writer can write a ghost story in which all the details add up so the reader knows the end even before the last sentence.

Other references to story in "Fitting Ends" include Stewart's telling young women the story of his brother's ghost as a way to seduce them. Also, in Del's composition story about his experience during the Outward Bound program, he writes that the experience allowed him to reach deep inside and grasp values that would "tell the story" of the rest of his life. This storytelling theme ties in with Stewart's creation of himself as a character in stories. When Stewart reads about Del's repelling down a mountain while the smallest fellow in his group held his safety rope, he imagines that he is the little guy holding Del's safety rope. When Stewart recalls a childhood event in which Del must clean his father's boots after he stepped in dog feces on the lawn, Stewart makes himself the one cleaning the boots rather than Del.

The central event that troubles Stewart is his lie that his brother tried to push him off the grain elevator. Stewart, always the storyteller, justifies this lie by placing it in the realm of subjunctive reality, insisting that even if Del did not do it, it was something he could have done. All the themes of the story revolve around Stewart's using storytelling devices to try to pull together loose ends to make sense of the past. At the end, although Stewart does not articulate what final realization he has come to, it is sufficient for him as a storyteller to be content with the mystery, just as the boy in Anderson's "Death in the Woods" must be content with the mystery of the dead woman he sees lying in the snow.

## Style and Technique

The self-reflexive nature of "Fitting Ends" is suggested most strongly in the last paragraph when the narrator/protagonist says that at certain moments, everything seems clear to him, as if he could take all the loose ends of his life and fit them together as easily as a writer could write a ghost story in which all the details added up so that the reader knew the end even before the last sentence. At such moments, even though people know they will go on living, everything is summed up with "clarity and closure."

The basic technique of the story reflects its theme, for Stewart recounts various anecdotes about his childhood in an effort to make them fit into a coherent story. In his contributor's notes to *The Best American Short Stories, 1996*, in which "Fitting Ends" appeared, Chaon says that writing a story for him is like putting together a jigsaw puzzle in which he writes hundreds of pages of fragments and puts them in a folder hoping they will "mate." He says that he had a folder three inches thick full of jottings about the brothers Del and Stewart, and in other folders, he had notes about the grain elevator in the town of Pyramid, a mock ghost story of the *True Ghost Stories* type he loved as a child, and impressions of an essay about the Outward Bound program that one of his students wrote. When it came to putting these fragments together, he says he found it helpful to find inspiration in the works of others, such as Anderson's "Death in the Woods" and Alice Munro's stories about time and loss.

What the reader encounters in "Fitting Ends" is a reflection of the process by which Chaon writes stories, as Stewart recalls events that become connected only when the writer finds some way to fit them together. The moments that serve as epiphanies for his understanding occur when he wakes from a dream while in college to the wail of a train that he can see out of his window and when he sees a child who looks like Del coming out of a bar. However, the final image that crystallizes the various fragments for him is the view of his deaf mother sitting at the kitchen table, watching the snow come down, and exhaling her cigarette smoke in a long thoughtful sigh that makes him realize she was remembering something. Chaon has said that one of the things that made this story come together for him was a quotation from Wright Morris: "It is the writer's nature and his talent to restore to the present much assumed to be lost."

*Charles E. May*

# THE FIVE-FORTY-EIGHT

*Author:* John Cheever (1912-1982)
*Type of plot:* Psychological
*Time of plot:* The 1950's
*Locale:* New York City and its suburbs
*First published:* 1954

> *Principal characters:*
> BLAKE, a businessperson and womanizer
> MISS DENT, his erstwhile secretary and onetime "conquest," also
> a former psychiatric patient

*The Story*

Among the more successful of John Cheever's urban tales, extending into suburbia, "The Five-Forty-Eight" recounts the brief but harrowing ordeal of a selfish, thoughtless male executive whose recent past comes back to haunt him in the person of a deeply disturbed young woman lately employed—and dismissed—as his secretary.

When Blake first spots the young woman apparently waiting for him to emerge from his office building at the end of the day, he readily recalls her face but not her name. Only gradually does he come to suspect that she might be following him, yet when her "contorted" face pops into view directly behind his own in the reflection of a store window, Blake suddenly wonders if she might be planning to kill him. In any case, Blake chooses not to recognize her and continues on his way, telling himself that she will be "easy to shake."

Stepping into a bar that caters exclusively to men, Blake locates a well-hidden seat and proceeds to order a Gibson cocktail; as he drinks it, he recalls the few facts that he has ever known concerning Miss Dent, or Bent, or Lent, whom he had dismissed from his service several months earlier after a single night of lovemaking—presumably because of her strangely "undisciplined" handwriting glimpsed by chance during their brief assignation. Crucially and doubtless typically, Blake has failed then as now to draw the obvious inferences: In a person as shy and restrained as "Miss Dent," such disorderly handwriting might well indicate a similarly disordered and even unbalanced personality; Blake has also failed to spot the potential significance of Miss Dent's expressed gratitude for giving her "a chance" after eight months in the hospital. Even now, in the bar, Blake does not seem to wonder in what sort of hospital she might have been.

On finishing a second cocktail, Blake observes that he has missed his usual train to the suburbs, the express, and will instead have to take the local, the five-forty-eight of the story's title. On his way to the station, Blake notes with some relief that the woman seems to have stopped following him; once aboard the train, however, he nervously seeks familiar faces, noting with some dismay that the two acquaintances present are no longer his friends. Mrs. Compton, his next-door neighbor, is both a busybody and a confidante of the beleaguered Mrs. Blake. Mr. Watkins, an object of Blake's disdain both because he is an artist and because he rents his home instead of owning it, has long since stopped speaking to Blake thanks to Blake's disruption of a growing friendship between their adolescent sons.

As the train emerges from underground into the fading daylight, Blake hears a female voice addressing him and finally recalls the young woman's name as Miss Dent. In response to Blake's reluctant, perfunctory questions, Miss Dent replies that she has again been "sick" and has been unable to find other work because Blake has "poisoned their minds." When Blake nervously prepares to move toward another car, Miss Dent informs him that she is armed with a pistol and quite capable of killing him, albeit reluctantly; all she really wants, she claims, is his attention to what she has to say.

Pulling an unmailed letter from her purse, Miss Dent forces Blake to read it as she rambles on about her sense of persecution and her need for love. On arriving at the Shady Hill station, where Blake normally dismounts, the woman forces him, at gunpoint, to precede her off the train. Marching him north of the station, toward a freight house and coal yard, Miss Dent finally forces Blake to kneel down and put his face in the dirt. Repeating her earlier declarations that she knows more about love and life than Blake does, she continues, "Oh, I'm better than you, I'm better than you, and I shouldn't waste my time or spoil my life like this. Put your face in the dirt. Put your face in the dirt! Do what I say."

Taking the woman at least at her word, Blake stretches flat on the ground, weeping as he does so. "Now I can wash my hands of you," declares his unlikely captor, and before long she is gone, the sound of her retreating footsteps resounding in Blake's disbelieving ears. Hesitantly, Blake at last raises his face to discover that Miss Dent is indeed gone, having apparently "forgotten" him, having "completed what she wanted to do." Picking up his hat from the ground, he proceeds on his way home.

*Themes and Meanings*

Anticipating by at least a decade the developing current of feminist literature, "The Five-Forty-Eight" presents in credible and memorable terms the compelling evidence, and possible means of redress, against the "institution" of male chauvinism as exemplified in the prototypical relationship of "boss" and secretary. The author was himself male, and one potential weakness of the story is that Miss Dent might be dismissed by the reader as merely "crazy." Cheever, nevertheless, has taken care to present her in accessibly human terms, even as his characterization might tend toward Freudian stereotype. Blake, in contrast, remains dehumanized, even in his own mind, by the self-perpetuating masculine stereotype that, according to Cheever and others, tends to prevail, at least in the commercial world. Until the present moment of confrontation, Blake has had little reason to question either the principles or the conduct of his life, even under the continued censure of such individuals as Mrs. Compton and Mr. Watkins. Presumably reared and advanced according to the entrepreneurial conventions of his generation, Blake, to his eventual peril, equates success with domination, even with exploitation.

Faced with the immediate prospect of death, Blake recalls "in a rush" his battlefield experiences during World War II and the frequent sight of unburied corpses. In counterpoint to Miss Dent's complaints as he believes that she is preparing to shoot him, Blake briefly recalls pleasant memories from his childhood. Cheever, whether deliberately or not, rehearses through Blake's experience the "moment of truth" common to the work of the French existentialists and to that of Ernest Hemingway as well; it is doubtful, however, that Blake will ever learn the lessons implied in his experience: Just as he had forgotten "Miss Dent," whose name is drawn solely from his admittedly defective memory and is never confirmed—and as "Miss Dent" appears to have forgotten him, Blake in all likelihood will forget what happened to him that evening on the local train.

## Style and Technique

Narrated throughout in the "affectless" third person, "The Five-Forty-Eight" is notable for the reader's implied identification with "Miss Dent," no doubt certifiably insane, and not with the supposed viewpoint character, similarly identified only by his family name: Apart from Blake's son Charlie, the immediate cause of his quarrel with Mr. Watkins, only Mrs. Compton is identified by her given name, Louise, and then only in passing. Mr. Blake, it seems, is most pleased when so addressed, and when keeping the rest of the world at a similar distance of conventional formality. Louise Compton, apparently, has been mentioned to Blake so often by his unhappy wife that he cannot help but recall her first name. From the unexpected slant of the narration, it soon becomes apparent that Blake, and not the unfortunate Miss Dent (who may, or may not, have made a "dent" on Blake's consciousness), is truly the more estranged and alienated of the two.

*David B. Parsell*

# FIVE-TWENTY

*Author:* Patrick White (1912-1990)
*Type of plot:* Psychological
*Time of plot:* The 1960's
*Locale:* Sydney, Australia
*First published:* 1973

> *Principal characters:*
> ELLA NATWICK, the protagonist, an elderly widow
> ROYAL NATWICK, the antagonist, her invalid husband
> AN UNNAMED OLDER MAN, the driver of a car that the Natwicks
> watch daily

*The Story*

Ella and Royal Natwick, having retired to a small bungalow along Parramatta Road, a decaying suburb of Sydney, are spectators of the modern, industrial world that passes by them. Their chief summer activity is watching the traffic each day from their porch. Royal, a belligerent, insensitive invalid, is confined to a wheelchair; Ella, his lifelong devoted mate, dotes on him, suppressing any display of emotion that might upset him. As they watch one of the frequent traffic jams, Royal singles out for ridicule a man driving a pink-and-brown Holden: The car's color betrays masculinity, and the man's head appears deformed. Ella, without directly challenging Royal, suggests that the man may have a domineering wife and notes that the man passes each day at five-twenty, suggesting that he may be a business executive. That comment brings further slander from Royal, who complains ironically about the lack of achievement by white-collar workers: His own life has been a failure to achieve the status that he now belittles.

One evening, Ella assists the victim of a traffic accident in front of their house. Royal, indifferent to the tragedy of others, worries only about how Ella will wash the blood out of blankets that she has provided; in response, she kisses him on the forehead, immediately regretting her public display of affection for underscoring his powerlessness in the chair. Royal's only concerns are what he is to eat, his illusion of superiority over Ella, her proper care for him, and the habitual flow of traffic, in which Ella always notes "that gentleman . . . in the Holden."

Amid their evening recollections, the omniscient narrator provides fragmented flashbacks over the course of the Natwicks' lives. Royal's family settled in Australia from Kent, and the young Ella McWhirter liked to think that there was a hint of English royalty in those Natwicks who came to New South Wales. Royal's ambitions surpassed those of his bookkeeper father, but he never made them fruitful despite a series of moves from one town to another, until finally settling in Sydney. Ella has always been subservient to Royal, and, at Fulbrook, she worked as a waitress, nurturing both their savings account and Royal's deluded self-image as a successful business-man. In Sarsaparilla, an outer suburb of Sydney where Royal opened a grocery store, she postponed having a child at Royal's admonition that starting a new business would not be compatible with starting a new family. Throughout those years Ella de-fended Royal from customers' complaints and continued her devotion to him. Ig-noring a doctor's implicit suggestion that Royal might be impotent, Ella accepted the failure to conceive as her own shortcoming, quietly brooding over "her secret grief."

On the Natwicks' retirement, Ella turns her energies to caring for the garden, the house, and Royal's increasingly deteriorating health. With a hernia, heart trouble, and arthritis, Royal becomes incontinent and confined to the wheelchair. The traffic jams, the air pollution, and the man in the pink-and-brown Holden become their only mu-tual diversions from drab routine. Indeed, when the man does not drive by for a few days, there is almost a crisis for the Natwicks: "Nothing would halt the traffic, not sickness, not death even." Before he resumes his five-twenty schedule in a new, cream-colored Holden, Ella dreams that she meets the man in her garden, a dream that she does not share fully with Royal. Having repressed her sensuality and her desire for affection for a lifetime, Ella is hardly conscious of her increasing obsession with see-ing the man pass by. In a second dream, she drops a double-yoked egg, breaking it on the path in her tunnel of cinerarias in the garden. Only these dreams disrupt the mo-notony of Ella's life.

Royal's death in early autumn deprives Ella of an object for her devotion. She with-draws into herself; Royal had been all-consuming of her emotions: the "feeling part of her had been removed." She remains compulsive about seeing the man in the Holden pass each evening, but she becomes indifferent to the care of her garden and her house, spending much of the autumn and winter sorting reflectively through a box of keepsakes and changing daily the water in a tumbler that holds Royal's dentures. The traffic and the cinerarias—head-high blossoms of purple, blue, and wine spires—oc-cupy her most devoted attention.

One late winter evening, Ella is walking among the cinerarias when the man in the Holden appears in her garden, asking to use the telephone because of car trouble. She notices that he has a harelip, a deformity that earlier had repulsed her, and that "his eyes, she dared to think, were filled with kindness." Waiting for the tow truck, Ella be-comes suddenly exuberant, bragging about her garden, laughing and showing off her cinerarias. As she begins to tell him about them, she "switched to another language," seemingly inarticulate in an "almost formless agonized sound." In response, the man seeks to comfort her, and as they embrace, Ella kisses him, "as though she might never succeed in healing all the wounds they had ever suffered." Before he departs, Ella has invited him for coffee the next evening.

Ella's preparations for her meeting occupy her entire day. She learns how to brew coffee from Mrs. Dolan, her neighbor. She spends a considerable part of the day shop-ping for cosmetics and applying them, but she removes them when she appears to her-self to be mirroring a purple cineraria. She considers hiding Royal's teeth but decides against it. Having made the coffee early, she waits on the porch. When a traffic accident occurs, she remembers helping once before but decides to "save herself up" on this evening. She chats with Mrs. Dolan, but she cannot repress her "lust" for kindness, intensified by the man's late arrival. She realizes that the man does not know that she has measured her life in the passing of his car, and she retires to the garden to walk among the cinerarias. Then she hears him coming into the garden.

Immediately Ella senses that he is sick; his voice fades, and he falters. When she reaches him, she begins mumbling pet names, supporting him in the throes of a heart attack. In her frantic desperation, she tells him that she loves him, even as he slips from her arms to the ground. She covers the dying man with her kisses. Without knowing him or even his name, Ella concludes that "she must have killed him by loving too deeply, and too adulterously."

*Themes and Meanings*

Just as "Five-Twenty" marks the end of the day, it also marks symbolically the end of Ella's routine of meaningless suffering, yet Ella is left with only an ambivalent redemption at the end of the story. Ella possesses an inherent goodness, embodying Patrick White's belief, expressed in his autobiographical *Flaws in the Glass: A Self-Portrait* (1982), that "only love redeems. . . . I mean the love shared with an individual. . . . [I]t is making do . . . whatever our age, in a world falling apart." There is little apparent reason for Ella's goodness, for her devotion as mate to a brutally insensitive Royal, but her capacity for sharing love is beyond doubt. With the man in the Holden, sharing love becomes a possibility.

Ella's goodness, however, has suffered at the cost of her desire; she has repressed her desire for expressing affection, or receiving it, just as she has given up hope for a child. Royal's frustration of Ella's affections does not, however, succeed entirely: Her obsession with the man in the Holden becomes the blossoming of her desire just as her devotion to the phallic cinerarias signals the coming opportunity for love, for kindness. With the rise of her desire in the wake of her lost object of devotion, Ella becomes a whole person with a last hope for love. The man's own implicit suffering because of his deformities echoes Ella's suffering in her subservience to Royal. In her unconscious fantasy of loving the man in the Holden, Ella achieves wholeness by balancing her devotion with her desire.

As Ella's dream of the meeting gives way to her dream of the double-yoked egg, both become realities: Ella has the chance for new life but loses it (as in "losing" the child) in the man's heart attack, itself an ironic situation of mutual pain, his physical and hers emotional. She has become a whole person, redeemed in love, only to lose the confidence of that love in her presumed guilt that she has "loved too deeply, and too adulterously." Ella, then, is one of "the poor unfortunates" in the epigraph of an early collection of short stories, *The Burnt Ones* (1964). She redeems herself in the free expression of her love only to suffer the greater pain of condemning her own just desire to love and to be loved. Ella's devotion, her very goodness, is the self-constructed prison from which she cannot escape, for it destroys the very balance on which her wholeness depends.

*Style and Technique*

White's ability to explore a profound theme underneath the surface imagery of a decaying, superficial urban world rests largely on his use of irony and symbolism. The chief irony is that while Ella is far more deserving of devoted love than Royal, it is Royal rather than Ella or her friend who enjoys the devotion, and he demands it instead of appreciating it. Doubly ironic is the turn of plot that introduces a deformed man to serve as Ella's liberating object of desire when she herself has been emotionally deformed by her lifelong repression of desire, particularly in the recent care of her invalid husband (an emotional invalid far more than a physical one). The crowning irony of the conclusion is that Ella believes she has been adulterous in the explosion of her sensuality, despite her status as widow and Royal's callous indifference to her affection. Instead of recognizing the redemption of love, Ella, in typically self-deprecating fashion, assumes responsibility for her would-be lover's death. The unifying irony of the entire story is that Ella's very goodness is the source of her own undoing.

Through a precise use of images, White further complicates the story by his use of symbols. The traffic jams reverberate with Ella's repressed desire just as the accidents foreshadow both the chance encounter and the man's death. The cinerarias are pointedly phallic in shape and in Ella's perception of them, just as the garden itself becomes her object of desire while she cares for Royal. The garden tunnel, where the cinerarias are located, seems strikingly vaginal as Ella dreams of meeting the man within it. With the use of obvious sexual symbolism, White can suggest something far more important to Ella than sexual fulfillment: the desire for love and the desire to express love freely, not mere sensual gratification. The symbolism, then, becomes a mask for the quest of love. Even Ella's kisses in the mock mouth-to-mouth resuscitation of the final scene symbolize her attempt to love both of them back to life. Ella's attempt to save the dying man is a last attempt to save her own momentary wholeness on which her goodness rests, and gasps.

*Michael Loudon*

# FLESH AND THE MIRROR

*Author:* Angela Carter (Angela Olive Stalker, 1940-1992)
*Type of plot:* Autobiographical
*Time of plot:* Summer, probably early 1970's
*Locale:* Tokyo, Japan
*First published:* 1974

> *Principal characters:*
> AN ENGLISH WOMAN, the narrator
> HER LOVER, probably Japanese, who ends his relationship with her
> A YOUNG MAN, probably Japanese, who has sex with her

*The Story*

"Flesh and the Mirror" is narrated by an English woman, who recalls a day-and-a-half period in which she wanders the streets of Tokyo, weeping, searching for her lover. She turns herself into a character in a melodrama, she later realizes, living her life as a performance, relishing her anguish and hysteria. She observes her own life from outside, as if it were taking place on stage. She has always lived as if she were a actor in a romantic play and now she eagerly throws herself into the age-old role of abandoned lover, loving the opportunity to indulge in self-dramatization.

The narrator returns to Japan from an emergency trip home to England, expecting her Japanese lover to meet her. He is not there, and she wanders the rainy, crowded streets of Tokyo's pleasure quarter, relishing her showy unhappiness, weeping, observing her own performance as if she were the heroine in a soap opera. The narrator switches, briefly, from first to third person, underscoring her later realization that she had turned herself into a puppet moving through life as if it were a stage production.

A stranger—a young man, presumably Japanese—falls into step beside her and asks why she is crying. They go to a hotel that caters to sexual trysts and take a room that has a mirror on the ceiling above the bed. As they make love, the mirror reflects the narrator back to herself as an "I" stripped of all the social constructions that has made her who she is, allowing her to experience herself shorn of history and context. The mirror assaults the narrator with her own flesh, a reflection seemingly more real than the drama she had made of her life. Japan had confronted her with a land beyond her ability to imagine; now the mirror assails her with a self—herself—she had never envisioned.

Disturbed, she dresses and leaves her anonymous young companion. She goes out into the hot, gritty city and resumes her search for her lover. She wanders, weeping, admiring her own romantic self-spectacle. She has not yet absorbed the lesson that the mirror offered.

She locates her lover. They immediately quarrel. She realizes that she wants the love affair to end in a tragic and passionate scene, like it might in a romantic storybook. She has constructed her lover in the guise of a ghost-self that lives only in her mind, ignoring anything about him that does not fit that image. In a rage to love, she has created her own love-object and has turned herself into a mawkish version of a heroine in love. The mirror has scrambled her world, confronting her with a gap between her constructed self and her real self.

She and her lover go to a hotel. They make love passionately, as lovers in romantic dramas are supposed to do, although their flesh tells them a more mundane story, that of a moribund love affair. She and her lover soon part. Tokyo ceases to be a magical and strange place, and she learns to laugh at her own histrionics. The mirror has transformed her reality.

## Themes and Meanings

Angela Carter said that all writing is political. She was a feminist but refused to confine her dazzling imagination and corrosive intellect to any ideological category. Her work dissects the thought patterns and social and political institutions that limit and warp the lives of women and other marginalized people. She exposes the mechanisms by which supposedly free societies shackle people's minds, showing readers the gears and levers of control, potentially transforming the way they see the world, just as the narrator in "Flesh and the Mirror" comes to see her lover, herself, and the city through transformed eyes.

Carter said that living in Japan radicalized her and taught her to be a woman. In the 1960's she established herself as one of the most promising young writers in England, but then she won the W. Somerset Maugham Award and used the prize money to go to Japan, partly to flee a disintegrating marriage. Carter lived at first with a Japanese lover and later alone. She remained in Japan from 1969 to 1972 and, while there, wrote "Flesh and the Mirror."

Carter's friend, novelist Salman Rushdie, has said the dark eroticism of Japan challenged Carter and deflected her writing into an exploration of female sexuality. Carter said her writing project was to investigate the social fictions that regulate people's lives. The foreignness of the Japanese culture helped her understand how people, including women, are the products of social construction, not artifacts of forces outside human control. Humans create society through their own decisions, which then shape their roles as women and men or members of particular ethnic groups and social classes. Social roles are not handed down by a god or by nature but are constructed by humans. For example, patriarchy is the product of human decisions and, therefore, subject to change by people's actions. The foreign customs of Japan helped her see the artificiality of habits and institutions that had once seemed natural and inevitable. Sexuality especially seems to most people to be a universal, a part of inherited human nature. Not so, said Carter. Flesh, or human sexuality, comes to people out of history, a lesson the mirror forces the narrator to acknowledge.

The mirror reveals the games people play in their relationships. It leaves the narrator confronting reality itself. The knowledge is so disconcerting that she dresses and flees, but she is unable to escape what the mirror revealed.

When Carter died at age fifty-one, many admirers wanted to portray her as a mischievous good witch, as a fairy godmother, or as an earth mother. Carter would have none of that in her own life. She regarded all mythical versions of women from the virgin to the healing mother as, she said, consolatory nonsense. In "Flesh and the Mirror" she examines and laughs at the woman as victim, the woman blinded by romantic love, hysterical with showy passion. That is a traditional character, one that Carter deconstructs by turning her raucous laughter on herself, in the person of the narrator. Carter has been called a cultural saboteur, which is an accurate description of the role she plays in this story.

*Style and Technique*

Carter turned out an immense body of work in her fifty-one years: short stories; novels; radio, screen, and stage plays; poetry; children's stories; essays; and an opera libretto. She wrote history and painted and taught. She was well read in Western and world literature. She was influenced by French Symbolists and Dadaists and social theorists such as Michel Foucault. She wrote realistic fiction, speculative fantasy, and gothic short stories, and she famously deconstructed folktales. In her work one might encounter ordinary people, flamboyant hippies, sociopathic killers, cowboys, vampire descendants of Vlad the Impaler, and many versions of Cinderella, Red Riding Hood, and both Beauty and the Beast.

Salman Rushdie has described Carter's writing style, with its verbal pyrotechnics, as that of a tightrope walker, often swaying but seldom falling. Her prose can be stark and precise or lush and baroque. It is always clear and compelling. Even in the midst of the most dazzling of her verbal fireworks, she never forgets the reader and always remembers that she is first of all a storyteller. Her imagery is powerful, and her writing has a visual, often sensual, intensity.

One often hears the echoes of other writers and genres in Carter's work. In "Flesh and the Mirror" she positions her writing in relation to the "I-novel" tradition in Japan, the intense first-person narratives often dealing with sexual obsession. In this literature, women often serve as one-dimensional objects, important only as they disturb the dense inner world of the self-absorbed male narrator. Carter shows her mastery of that mode and then deconstructs it. The narrator laughs at her own self-obsession.

Carter uses a chatty style that establishes a confiding tone with the readers, but the autobiographical tenor of this and her other Japanese stories can be misleading. She herself said they were true but not strictly accurate.

*William E. Pemberton*

# FLEUR

*Author:* Louise Erdrich (1954-      )
*Type of plot:* Sketch
*Time of plot:* 1920
*Locale:* Argus, North Dakota
*First published:* 1986

> *Principal characters:*
> FLEUR PILLAGER, the protagonist, a young Chippewa woman
> PAULINE, the narrator, the stepdaughter of Dutch James, of mixed blood
> PETE KOZKA, the owner of a butcher shop
> LILY VEDDAR,
> DUTCH JAMES, and
> TOR GRUNEWALD, men employed at Kozka's butcher shop

## The Story

Pauline recalls an earlier time when a young Chippewa woman named Fleur survived a drowning. Pauline also remembers about Fleur's association with Misshepeshu, the devil-like waterman monster of Chippewa myth. Pauline calls Fleur a woman who "messed with evil," who laughed at the women of the tribe, wore men's clothing, and hunted. Fleur was feared and mistrusted by her tribe.

In 1920 Fleur lived in Argus, a small town in North Dakota, where she worked at Pete Kozka's butcher shop—a place that was part slaughterhouse and part store. Kozka hired her because of her strength. At that time the narrator also worked for Kozka. Unlike Fleur, who worked with the men, the narrator cleaned floors and stoked fires in the smokehouses. Existing only on the fringes of activities there, Pauline describes herself as invisible.

After the death of Pauline's mother, Pauline's stepfather, Dutch, took her out of school so that she could take her mother's place in the home. She then had to spend half her time working at the butcher shop and the other half doing housework. Seemingly the only person aware of Pauline's existence, Fleur treated her kindly as Pauline watched the interminable card games—the primary recreational activity of Fleur and the men.

Lily, Dutch, and Tor grew increasingly irritated with Fleur because she beat them at their own game. She never bluffed and always ended the evening with exactly one dollar until one night, when she won a huge pot and then refused to play any more. Afterward the men drank heavily and—with Pete away—raped Fleur. Pauline recalls hearing Fleur cry for help and call her name.

The next morning a tornado struck and the men disappeared. Days later, after the storm subsided, Fleur's three attackers were found frozen to death inside the shop's meat locker. They were hunched around a barrel on which their cards were still laid out. Pauline reveals that it was she who slammed down the great iron bar that locked the men in the ice locker. Her motives were not simple; they were probably a combination of her desire for revenge against the treatment her stepfather gave her and her desire to avenge Fleur—especially because she had failed to respond to her cries for help.

In the months following the incident, Pauline helped Fleur through the winter, when she gave birth to a child with green eyes and skin the color of an old penny. No one can decide if the child was fathered by Misshepeshu, the water god, or by one of the men who raped Fleur in the smokehouse.

*Themes and Meanings*

Louise Erdrich's novel *Tracks* (1988), from which "Fleur" is taken, has two principal narrators: Nanapush and Pauline. The latter, also known as Sister Leopolda, is established as an unreliable narrator by Nanapush, who points out several times that she does not always tell the truth. The events that Pauline relates in "Fleur" are therefore not necessarily what really happened to Fleur Pillager.

Two themes in this story are quite evident. The more important theme—as in Erdrich's longer fiction—concerns the ways in which Native Americans must struggle to survive and maintain their own cultures. Erdrich as author links destruction, survival, and continuity in the characters of both Fleur and Pauline. The second important theme is the merging of myth and reality through conflicts between traditional Native American and modern Western cultures.

Both Pauline and Fleur are survivors. Fleur is tied closely to both her Chippewa heritage and her white immigrant heritage. In her essay "Where I Ought to Be," Erdrich says that Native American writers "must tell the stories of contemporary survivors while protecting and celebrating the cores of cultures left in the wake of the catastrophe," that is, the destruction of Native American cultures by European Americans.

According to Pauline, Fleur has survived two drownings, estrangement from her tribe, and rape. Pauline describes her as being both physically and spiritually strong. "Fleur" concludes with Fleur giving birth—an act that establishes both a literal and a symbolic continuity. For her part, Pauline has survived her mother's death and the cruelty of her stepfather; her murder of Fleur's three attackers further demonstrates her strength. Erdrich continues Pauline's story in *Tracks*, in which Pauline describes herself as ready to join the convent and become Sister Leopolda; thus Erdrich again presents survival and continuity.

The second theme, that of clashing cultures, also is presented through both women. Pauline explains that Fleur survived her drownings because the waterman Misshepeshu wanted her for himself. Fleur ignored the warnings and traditional advice of the old women of her tribe by dressing as a man does, but at the same time she used half-forgotten tribal medicine. When she went hunting, her tracks turned into bear tracks: Pauline recalls that "we followed the tracks of her bare feet and saw where they changed, where the claws sprang out, the pad broadened and pressed into the dirt." When Fleur went to Argus, she worked in the white settlers' milieu, in which she was again mistrusted and punished for being different.

Pauline presents the cultural clash through her blurring of tribal religion and Roman Catholicism. Mixing American Indian and Judeo-Christian religious traditions, she sees herself as a visionary savior. In her mind, Misshepeshu, the Chippewa spirit of Lake Matchimanito, is the same as the Christian devil who is to be chained and thrown into a lake of fire.

*Style and Technique*

Some scholars of Native American writings believe that "mixed blood" writers such as Erdrich—the daughter of a Chippewa Indian and a German—approach writing as a means of linking not only their own cultures but also the worlds of spirits and human beings. Erdrich had such difficulty in writing *Tracks* that she put her original manuscript aside for ten years. Only after she had worked backward in time by writing *Love Medicine* (1984) and *The Beet Queen* (1986) did she return to *Tracks* and begin to link it to her completed novels about more recent generations of Chippewa and white settlers in North Dakota.

Within Erdrich's long fiction, points of view often change, with the narrative voices shifting among both characters and occasional omniscient narrators. In shifting points of view, the reliability and truthfulness of narrators is always in doubt—as is the case with Pauline and Nanapush in *Tracks*. Nanapush, an old man who has lost his family and becomes a father figure to Fleur, repeatedly insists that Pauline does not always tell the truth. Readers must therefore remember that only Pauline's narration reports on Fleur's rape.

Erdrich's technique of changing narrators and publishing chapters as individual stories breaks down the traditional form of the novel. Each appearance of an individual narrator suggests a separate "storytelling" experience, perhaps a return to a time when the line between history and myth was not clearly defined. This technique seems to be common to Native American writers. As a result of these separate storytelling experiences, separate chapters such as "Fleur" also stand alone as short stories.

Erdrich's style and language also reflect and present blurring of cultures and boundaries between myth and reality. Although her language is concrete and specific, her allusions are subtle, often leaving the reader not knowing exactly what has occurred. For example, the Chippewa language uses the same word for both flirting and hunting game—a coincidence that subtly connects Fleur's sensuality with her hunting in a man's domain. Another Chippewa word suggests both using force in intercourse and killing a bear with one's bare hands. These connotations merge in Pauline's narration. Thus, Erdrich presents her major themes through style and language as well as through her use of double narrators and shifting point of view.

*Betty Alldredge*

# FLIGHT

*Author:* John Steinbeck (1902-1968)
*Type of plot:* Realism
*Time of plot:* The early 1900's
*Locale:* Monterey, California
*First published:* 1938

### Principal characters:

PEPE TORRES, a nineteen-year-old farmboy
MAMA TORRES, his mother, a middle-aged widow

*The Story*

Pepe Torres is a "gentle, affectionate boy" whose only fault is his laziness. Reared by his protective and loving widowed mother, Mama Torres, who struggles to provide her children with a stable emotional environment and a meager material existence on the family farm, Pepe would rather not work. Hour after hour, he plays with his dead father's switchblade, throwing the knife at a post until his aim is extremely accurate.

One day, Mama Torres sends Pepe to town for some salt and medicine. Pepe has never been trusted with such a mission, and he feels proud when his mother gives him his father's round black hat with the tooled leather band and his green silk handkerchief to wear on the journey. After he has left, Pepe's younger brother asks if Pepe has become a man today; his mother answers, "A boy gets to be a man when a man is needed. Remember this thing. I have known boys forty years old because there was no need for a man." Mama Torres's wisdom is sound, but she does not foresee the tragic events that are about to unfold.

Pepe returns home in the middle of the night, stopping only briefly in his flight to the mountains. He tells his mother that in town he was called names he "could not allow" as a man, and that in the subsequent fight, he killed with his knife the person who called him such names. The definition of manhood in his society required such action. The mother understands, declaring, "Yes, thou art a man, my poor little Pepe. Thou art a man." She gives Pepe the father's rifle and his black coat, and when the other children ask where Pepe is going, she states that "Pepe is a man now. He has a man's thing to do." As soon as he leaves, she begins "the high, whining keen of the death wail," for she intuits that he will not be able to survive in the mountains.

The second, longer part of the story follows Pepe into the high mountains, where he attempts to elude the posse. He has no real choice in his actions now: He meets the ordeal that he must endure with "a man's face." His initiation into manhood, which began with his journey into the city, is complete, and he struggles against the forces of society and nature with the status of manhood. Occasionally, he sees dark figures in the landscape watching him: forms of men who are always faceless, suggesting the formless figures of death.

Although Pepe successfully evades the posse for a few days, one morning his horse is shot out from under him without warning, and in the ensuing gun battle, he is wounded in the hand by a sliver of granite, chipped off a rock by a bullet. Although he does escape into the high barren peaks, he is without water, and soon his hand and arm begin to swell with the wound.

During the course of these events, he loses his father's possessions piece by piece: the hat, the horse, the coat. When his hand and arm become gangrenous, he is almost crazed from pain and lack of water. At last he finds a dry streambed in the bottom of a ravine, digs down into it for a few drops of water, and falls asleep. When he awakes in the afternoon, a mountain lion is watching him from twenty feet away. The beast has no fear of Pepe, for in his present condition, Pepe no longer presents a threat. Pepe is himself a "hurt beast." The lion watches Pepe until evening; it appears that the lion is about to fall asleep, and then suddenly it leaves. A few moments later, Pepe hears the dogs of the posse looking for his trail. He struggles to his feet and once more eludes the posse. Weak from his ordeal, he falls asleep again, near the top of a high, barren ridge. When he awakes and goes on, he realizes that he has forgotten his rifle; he returns but cannot find it. The last item once belonging to his father is now gone.

In the final scene, Pepe crawls up the slope of the ridge, and as the dawn breaks, he stands up on the top of a big rock on the ridge peak. He cannot actually see the members of the posse, but he knows they are nearby. There he is shot, standing upright to take the bullet. His body tumbles down the slope, starting a small avalanche. "And when at last he stopped against a bush, the avalanche slid slowly down and covered his head." The forces of society have overwhelmed him, but he has died with dignity, achieving a tragic stature in his struggle.

## Themes and Meanings

Beneath the surface, realistic detail of this story, John Steinbeck develops the moral allegory of a boy growing into manhood. The opening events resemble the simple plot of a fairy tale: A boy leaves home on a journey of initiation, he undergoes a trial, he returns a man. Steinbeck, however, brings the tale to a new conclusion: In this society, the achievement of manhood can demand the life of the protagonist. Built within the framework of society is a code by which the individual must act—but the individual may well die as a result of this action. Thus, to choose to be a man by society's definition of manhood can have tragic consequences.

That Steinbeck has chosen a *paisano* for his hero is significant. Steinbeck defined the *paisano* as a mixture of Spanish, Indian, Mexican, and assorted European bloods—someone whose ancestors have lived in California for a hundred or more years. These people are poor by the Anglo's materialistic standards, for, by and large, they do not subscribe to the Anglo work ethic but live in a different moral structure, one in which a man's behavior is much more important than his possessions. The focus in this story is on the nature of that behavior: To be a man can require action that society must condemn, and the paradoxical nature of this requirement is what makes for the possibility of the tragic figure. When that figure struggles against society with honor, he achieves an individual dignity that elevates him to a tragic status. Thus, in his final days in the mountains, Pepe becomes the symbolic tragic hero of his society.

The concept of a powerful society overwhelming the individual—the guiding idea of the literary movement known as naturalism—works its way through this story. Steinbeck viewed society as a huge organism that operated by natural laws, unmindful of the individual's wishes and desires, yet he also viewed the individual as being capable of acts that bring him human dignity. Pepe's story is the result of Steinbeck's artistic exploration of these contradictory truths.

*Style and Technique*

Steinbeck explores the story's themes using a third-person point of view that focuses on the consciousness of Pepe during his ordeal in the mountains. The author achieves a poetic grace with plain language that is appropriate to the thought processes of his protagonist. Contained in that language is the sharp detail of the physical landscape, which has a beauty of its own. Steinbeck also uses the detail of the physical landscape to suggest Pepe's inner emotions. For example, in the scene before his death, Pepe sees that "strewn over the hill there were giant outcroppings, and on the top the granite teeth stood out against the sky." The stark image of the "granite teeth" works to reflect the emotion that Pepe feels; trapped in his fate, he senses powers that will overwhelm and "devour" him. The images of the landscape provide a backdrop for his final act of defiance, of standing up to be shot down.

The dialogue early in the story between Pepe and members of his family is filled with short, declarative statements and the use of "thy" and "thou," which gives it a stilted quality. By such devices, Steinbeck—rather like Ernest Hemingway in *For Whom the Bell Tolls* (1940)—was attempting, unsuccessfully, to convey the archaic dignity of his characters' speech.

Steinbeck's technique and style are appropriate to his subject: Pepe's direct, uncomplicated emotions are presented without authorial comment, being placed directly before the reader with a simple honesty that gives this story both power and poignancy.

*Ronald L. Johnson*

# FLOATING BRIDGE

*Author:* Alice Munro (1931-      )
*Type of plot:* Domestic realism
*Time of plot:* The 1990's
*Locale:* Ontario, Canada
*First published:* 2000

*Principal characters:*
JINNY LOCKYER, a forty-two-year-old woman dying of cancer
NEAL, her fifty-eight-year-old husband
HELEN, a girl who is going to help care for her
MATT and
JUNE BERGSON, foster parents of Helen's sister
RICKY, June's son

*The Story*

"Floating Bridge," a story about learning to accept the tentative nature of human life, begins with an account about a time when Jinny left her husband, Neal, briefly to sit in a bus shelter near her home, reading graffiti on the wall and identifying with people who feel they have to write things down. When she returns home, she asks Neal if he would ever have come after her, and he says, "Of course. Given time." Neal's detached attitude toward Jinny and his cavalier treatment of her despite her life-threatening illness is an undercurrent that runs throughout the story.

The present time of the story begins with Jinny, who is terminally ill with cancer, leaving an appointment with her oncologist to meet Neal. He has hired a young woman named Helen who works at the Correctional Institute for Young Offenders where he teaches to help them during Jinny's illness.

Helen, who comes from an abusive family, has been brought up by foster parents. When Neal and Jinny meet her, she must go pick up her good shoes from the home of June and Matt Bergson, where her sister lives. When they arrive at the trailer park, they are invited in, but Jinny wants to stay outside. Neal says if they do not accept the invitation, it will seem as if they think they are too good for them, so he goes inside while Jinny waits in the car. She goes down to a nearby cornfield, wanting to lie down in the shade of the tall stalks until Neal comes out and calls for her. However, the rows are too close together and she gets lost. When she comes out, Matt comes out of the house and tells her a bawdy joke, which is intermingled with her recollections of her meeting with her doctor. The oncologist has told her that her tumor has shrunk and that they have cause to be cautiously optimistic.

After Matt goes back in the house, a young man named Ricky, June's son, arrives and offers to drive Jinny home. He takes a shortcut through an area where they drive on narrow bridges over shallow water. When the boy says he is going to show her something she has never seen before, she thinks that if this had happened back in her old normal life she would be frightened. When they walk out over a floating bridge, she realizes she does not have her hat on and that the boy does not mind her bald head. He slips his arm around her and kisses her mouth. As they walk back to the car, he asks her if that was the first time she had ever been on a floating bridge. She says yes and asks him if it was the first time he had ever kissed a married woman. He says yes and agrees with her that he will probably kiss a lot more of them in the years to come.

The story ends with Jinny thinking of Neal having his fortune told by June and feeling a lighthearted sort of compassion, a "swish of tender hilarity, getting the better of all her sores and hollows . . ."

## Themes and Meanings

The floating bridge, providing an uneasy security above dark mysterious water, is a spatial metaphor for Jinny's situation that holds together the thematic elements of this story. Related to this spatial metaphor is the motif of Jinny's uneasy position in time. On this particular day, the doctor has told her that there is reason for cautious optimism, but this does not make Jinny feel better. Before, she was relatively sure of her future, knowing that she had little time. This new information forces her to go back and start the year all over again, removing a certain "low-grade freedom" from her life. The new knowledge has removed a "dull, protecting membrane" she did not even know was there and leaves her feeling raw and vulnerable. Since learning of her illness, she has felt a kind of "unspeakable excitement" that results when a disaster releases one from responsibility for her life. Now that is gone and a numb ennui remains.

Part of Jinny's emotional turmoil at the time of the story stems from Neal's excited reaction to Helen; he becomes more animated, enthusiastic, and ingratiating around her, as he often does around other people. Helen has a "fresh out-of-the-egg" look, and Jinny thinks that everything about her is right on the surface, which gives her an innocent and disagreeable power. Neal teases Helen, his whole being "invaded" with silly bliss. It is not that Neal desires Helen; rather, it is just that her innocence and simplicity seem a welcome relief from the complexity of Jinny's situation.

The seventeen-year-old Ricky creates a similar reaction in Jinny. There is an innocent simplicity in his desire to show her the floating bridge where he takes his girlfriends. His kiss provides an innocent acceptance of her, regardless of her baldness and her illness. When Jinny is on the floating bridge, she imagines that the road is a floating ribbon of earth, underneath which is all water. After the kiss, Jinny thinks of Neal getting his fortune told, "rocking on the edge of his future," and accepts the tentative nature of her own future, feeling a lighthearted compassion for Neal.

## Style and Technique

Alice Munro is perhaps the most accomplished short-story writer of her time practicing that often underrated art. The style of "Floating Bridge," typical of Munro's technique, is an example of the classic realistic short-story style that originated with

Anton Chekhov. The understated and restrained language and rhythm of the prose, suggesting Jinny's resigned acceptance of her illness and her impending death, is sustained throughout, even though at the very beginning of the story, Jinny has learned that her cancer has entered a stage of remission. Because she has already accepted the relative freedom from responsibility that knowledge of her incurable disease gave her, she shows no exuberance at this new knowledge that she has more time than she thought she did.

Jinny's inability to accept the new information of her cancer's remission also justifies the fact that the reader does not learn of her reprieve until late in the story. Even then, Jinny's memory of the interview with the doctor is intercut by an obscene, but actually harmless, joke that Matt tells her. The irony of this scene, in which the sacred gift of life forms a counterpoint with bawdy humor, is indicative of Munro's technique of setting up thematic parallels that echo throughout the story.

Munro's use of the final metaphor of the floating bridge is also typical of her art, as well as a tendency of the short story in general to reconcile complex moral issues aesthetically because they seem to be impervious to reconciliation any other way. The story's structure plays a balancing act similar to that required of walking on a floating bridge. The firmness of solid ground is only an illusion; all around lies the danger of loss of self. However, even though the bridge seems to be shifting and tentative, it is sufficient if one is content to live in the realm of the unsure. Munro's story reflects this tentative and delicate balancing.

The most problematic stylistic problem of the story is Neal's treatment of Jinny, which seems, if not cruel, at least unfeeling. The reader may feel he is much too excited by the presence of the young girl Helen and much too indifferent to Jinny's plight. However, there is nothing to suggest that he does not love Jinny or that he has sexual designs on Helen. He, too, is on a shifting floating bridge, trying to find something to cling to, even if it is of such little substance as an innocent young girl who is healthy and sound. Similarly, there is nothing to suggest that the young man, Ricky, at the end of the story has any sexual desire for Jinny. In contrast to the messy complexity of her life, his kiss is the epitome of innocent acceptance, instilling in her a tenderhearted sort of compassion.

*Charles E. May*

# THE FLOOD

*Author:* Joy Harjo (1951-    )
*Type of plot:* Magical Realism
*Time of plot:* 1971
*Locale:* An Oklahoma Indian reservation
*First published:* 1990

> *Principal characters:*
> THE NARRATOR, a Creek Indian
> AN UNNAMED SIXTEEN-YEAR-OLD CREEK GIRL
> HER PARENTS
> THE MAN WHO LIVES BY THE LAKE
> THE FEMALE ELDER OF THE CREEK TRIBE
> THE CRAZY WOMAN

*The Story*

In the first of two first-person narratives, a Creek tribal member recalls the events leading to the death of a sixteen-year-old Creek girl. In connecting these events with the Native Indian myth of the watersnake, the narrator emphasizes the importance of old myths to the survival of the Native American people. The narrative voice then switches to the girl herself, who underscores how the myths of her people have "soaked into my blood since infancy like deer gravy so how could I resist the watersnake, who appeared as the most handsome man in the tribe."

In paralleling the incidents of the girl's life, the myth of the watersnake is a central influence on her perception of reality. One version of the legend recounts the tale of a young girl who is seduced by the water monster, who has transformed himself into a handsome warrior. The girl leaves her family to become the watersnake's bride and then lives with him at the bottom of a lake. In "The Flood," the sixteen-year-old girl also meets a man by the edge of a lake and allows herself to be seduced by him. From her point of view, the man who seduces her "was not a man, but a myth" and is an incarnation of the watersnake. Because of the mythic nature of the incident, the girl believes that she has participated in a sacred event. On the other hand, her parents simply regard her premarital sexual experience as shameful. By arranging a quick marriage to an "important" older man of the tribe, her parents attempt to erase the dishonor brought on their family by her misconduct. The daughter persists in believing that the man she met by the lake is the embodiment of the water monster who unleashes his power in violent rain and wind storms. The girl rejects the marriage arranged by her parents because she no longer feels comfortable in the "real world" that her family and future husband inhabit.

The girl disappears during a tornado that destroys her family's home. However, she dies not as a result of the force of the storm but from drowning. The oldest woman of her tribe regards the girl's behavior as a bad example to other young girls and believes that the water monster has punished her for disobeying her parents when she gave herself to a man before marriage. Other tribal members believe that the girl, in a drunken fog after consuming a six-pack of beer, has accidently driven her car into the lake and drowned.

The narrator offers a third point of view concerning the girl's death. She maintains that the impact of the tribal oral tradition had such a strong influence on the girl's imagination that her perception of reality could not be contained within the limits of day-to-day experience. The narrator implies that the contrast between the girl's futile life on the reservation and her belief in the rich heritage of her people has led her to despair and suicide. The influence of the mythic tradition on the girl at first appears anomalous to the narrator. The influence of modern life on the narrator is just as strong as the power of tradition has been on the dead girl. As a result, the narrator admits that she no longer considers the old stories important. Interpreting the events of one's life from a mythic point of view is out of place in modern society, just as the crazy woman who appears in the convenience store at the end of the story is out of place. The appearance of the crazy woman causes the narrator to remember the death of the teenage girl as well as the influence that the old stories had on her. As if in response to the evocation of the memory, it begins to rain. The water monster, in his role as a storm god, makes his presence known. He demonstrates his displeasure at being forgotten by the people by sending rain "that would flood the world."

## Themes and Meanings

The central theme of Joy Harjo's "The Flood" is that the power of imagination and the importance of the Native American oral tradition are essential to the survival of the Native Indian culture. The storyteller is responsible for the transmission of myths that shape Native American identity. In her role as a traditional storyteller, Harjo uses "The Flood" to warn Native Americans to keep their legends alive and preserve the meanings of their stories, otherwise their culture will die and their identities will be threatened.

Like Harjo herself, her fictional teenage girl steeps herself in the myths of her Indian heritage. The influence of the legends on the girl is so profound that "there were no words describing the imprint of images larger than the language she's received from her mother's mouth, her father's admonishments." The sacred power of the myths, coupled with the girl's imagination, allows her to perceive a reality that goes deeper than the surface reality of reservation life. Her mind and spirit are shaped by the legends that she heard as a child.

Ironically, the girl's parents—the very people who have told her the stories—regard the myths as little more than fairy tales that have no relevance to daily life. Their daughter's preoccupation with these tales, especially with the story of the water monster, seems unhealthy to them. They believe that her imagination must be controlled and brought into line with what is considered normal in their society. They alienate her by refusing to acknowledge the importance of the watersnake myth and by trying to force on their daughter an arranged marriage. From their point of view, belief in the oral tradition is anachronistic in the context of modern life. The girl's death symbolizes the death of the importance of imagination and the oral tradition in American Indian society. Unless imagination and the oral tradition are allowed to thrive, the cultural landscape will suffer a "drought" and American Indian culture will erode.

The attitude of the narrator toward the appearance of the crazy woman at the end of the story is a symptom of this cultural erosion. The narrator, influenced by contact with white culture, is discomforted by the presence of the crazy woman. She draws a parallel between the insanity of the woman and the supposed madness of the girl who foolishly believed the old tales. The narrator's view matches the general perception of the rest of the tribe. The old stories, including the watersnake legend, are no longer told. Instead the people have compromised their cultural roots and grown accustomed to the ways of dominant white society, which is symbolized by the convenience store. By allowing the old myths to die, Native Americans endanger their cultural survival.

The title of the story is linked to physical as well as cultural survival. Because of their adoption of white culture, Native Americans have not only lost touch with their myths but have also lost contact with the natural forces represented by the ancient stories. The intimate connection with the natural world that tribal peoples of the past enjoyed is no longer recognized as important by the people in "The Flood." However, the power of nature personified in the watersnake, a storm deity, nonetheless continues to affect the lives of the people. As the title and the impending storm at the end of the story imply, the spiritual power that informs the natural world must be recognized and respected by humanity. If the respect is not offered, then cultural ruin and physical disaster will be the result.

*Style and Technique*

Harjo's interest in poetry is strongly reflected in the prose of her story. Her goal is to achieve "shimmering language" that conveys an ethereal and otherworldly mood. Harjo is also a musician, and her musical training, combined with her skill as poet, lends a songlike quality to her prose.

Music and poetry both have their roots in oral tradition. The influence of the Native American oral tradition is central to Harjo's work. She uses Indian myths to dramatize modern concerns of Native American people. She comments that "the older stories are like shadows dancing right behind" the contemporary stories that she tells. Thus the power of the watersnake myth is connected with the contemporary problems of teenage sex, alcoholism, and the encroachment of the dominant white culture on American Indian identity. Her skillful weaving of past and present, old and new, serves to enhance her central theme of survival.

*Pegge Bochynski*

# FLOWERING JUDAS

*Author:* Katherine Anne Porter (1890-1980)
*Type of plot:* Psychological
*Time of plot:* About 1920
*Locale:* Mexico
*First published:* 1930

### Principal characters:

LAURA, a twenty-two-year-old American who teaches school and participates in the revolution in Mexico

BRAGGIONI, the leader of the revolution and suitor of Laura

MRS. BRAGGIONI, his wife, who works hard for the revolution and weeps for her husband

EUGENIO, a political prisoner who takes an overdose of narcotics, which he has obtained from Laura

*The Story*

In "Flowering Judas," Laura, after teaching school and visiting Eugenio in prison, comes home to be warned by Lupe, the maid, that Braggioni is waiting for her. Although she detests his presence, Laura, a young American, allows the Mexican revolutionary leader to sing to her. She is afraid of him, as he is known for his cruelty and vanity. As she "owes her comfortable situation and her salary to him," however, she does her best to tolerate him. For the past month he has been spending the evenings with her. Laura is in the precarious predicament of attempting to resist his advances without seeming to do so. His "gluttonous bulk . . . has become a symbol of her disillusions" with revolution and leaders. Braggioni has come to represent the disunion between her idealistic view of life and the life she is actually living.

Born a Roman Catholic, Laura still slips into a church now and then but can no longer find comfort in it. She instead tries to embrace revolutionary theories but without much success. Her private heresy is not to wear lace made by machines, even though the machine is "sacred" to the revolutionary forces with which she is working. She fears that she may become as corrupt as Braggioni, who sits before her in his expensive clothes and his great self-love. As he sings his love songs and lectures on his philosophy, Laura wonders why she stays in Mexico. She teaches the Indian children, attends union meetings, visits political prisoners, smuggles letters and drugs, and delivers messages. However, her motives are unclear.

To the Mexicans who know her and see her in the street, Laura is an erotic mystery. Although she remains aloof she is admired for her green eyes, sensual lips, beautiful walk, large breasts, and long legs. The legendary virginity of the gringita spurs Braggioni and other potential lovers into constant courtship—but Laura says no to everyone. Not even the children are able to penetrate her remoteness, and they, too, remain strangers to her. The word "no" becomes symbolic of Laura's entire existence, as she denies to all people and things the chance to affect her emotions. Braggioni, however, believes that he has all the time in the world to break down her resistance. As a teenager, Braggioni was rejected by his first sweetheart, and now he makes every woman pay for the anguish he suffered. His wife is included in this vengeance, despite her devotion to him and to the revolution. She works hard organizing unions for the cigarette factory girls but spends much of her time weeping for Braggioni because this is what he prefers. Currently, he is observing a month of separation from her for what he describes as higher principles. Laura, though, envies Mrs. Braggioni's loneliness because she feels trapped by Braggioni's persistent presence. As he sings on, she reflects on her visit to the prison that day and on Eugenio's condition.

Braggioni interrupts her thoughts by telling of the May Day disturbances he is planning for Morelia, where the Catholics and the Socialists will be having celebrations. He asks Laura to oil and load his pistols, while he speaks of revolution and sings of love. He wraps his fingers around the throat of the guitar as he sings, and he strokes the pistol in Laura's hands as he expounds on Marxist philosophy and his faith in dynamite. Laura finally hands back his gunbelt and tells him to make himself happy by killing someone in Morelia. When he leaves, Laura feels a sense of relief, but she does not flee, as she knows she should.

Braggioni goes home, ending the month long separation from his wife. She continues her weeping at his appearance and even offers to wash his feet. As she performs the task, she begs for his forgiveness. Braggioni happily consents because her endless tears and humility refresh him.

Laura, meanwhile, prepares for bed. Before she falls asleep, she is concerned about her confusion with love and revolution: her inability to understand what her life is all about. Haunted by the thought of Eugenio, who may be dead by now as a result of taking the drugs she delivered to him, Laura has a nightmare in which Eugenio asks her to follow him. He calls her "Murderer" and offers her flowers from the Judas tree. She accepts them from his fleshless hand and eats them greedily. He calls her "Cannibal" for eating his body and blood. Laura cries "No." She awakes and is afraid to sleep again.

*Themes and Meanings*

Laura and Braggioni obviously live by different sets of values. The latter, who masquerades as a professional philanthropist, loves himself most of all and will exploit the revolution and the people whenever it is to his advantage. He will never die for his principles or his love for humanity. He is an egomaniac who uses people and things for his own benefit. Laura, in contrast, is filled with guilt to the point that she suffers from moral paralysis. She merely goes through the motions of being a teacher and rebel without understanding the reasons behind them. While Braggioni will betray anyone, Laura betrays herself. She is unable to compromise between her concept of life as it should be and life as it is. The chaotic world of revolutionary Mexico overwhelms her.

Braggioni is the primary problem for Laura, who has a romantic view of what a revolutionary leader should be. He does not have the gauntness, the heroic faith, the abstract virtues associated with the ideal leader; his bulk, Jockey Club clothes, selfishness, and indifference to political prisoners offend her. She is also worried by his courtship. The threat of violence is always in the background. He is fascinated by his power, which includes the right to own things and people. He indulges in his love of small luxuries, and Laura fears that she is being placed in that category; he eventually may demand more from her than delivering messages and cleaning his guns. She may be only an interlude for Braggioni, like the revolution itself, but that does not reduce the threat. Braggioni's main concern is to be comfortable, to be flexible in his principles so that he can take care of himself as profitably as possible. He is at perpetual peace with himself, but Laura is lost.

Katherine Anne Porter began her writing career in the 1920's, when the wasteland motif was popular. Stemming from T. S. Eliot's poem *The Waste Land* (1922), and a recurring theme in the work of writers such as E. E. Cummings, Edwin Arlington Robinson, Edgar Lee Masters, Sinclair Lewis, Ernest Hemingway, F. Scott Fitzgerald, and William Faulkner, this concept emphasizes the lack of morality in society. Economic values are more important than moral values. Money and social position are depicted as being the prime goals in life. In "Flowering Judas," Braggioni is an example of a character who prospers in this kind of environment. Laura is an easy victim of those who play by rules that are foreign to her. She cannot come to accept the ugly reality of Braggioni. She is full of romantic error, according to the rebels, who have, in comparison, a strong sense of reality. Thus, Laura is not at home in the world. Like Prufrock, in Eliot's poem "The Love Song of J. Alfred Prufrock" (1917), she suffers from moral ennui. She acts without thinking, or, when she does think, she is incapable of meaningful action. Indeed, she aids the corrupt Braggioni and helps Eugenio commit suicide; because the values of her former life do not apply, she denies the value of everything. She gives in to her environment and tries to convince herself that things are beyond her control.

This resignation to her fate is a form of self-betrayal. She rejects her old value system but fails to replace it with a viable philosophy. She disclaims the principles of the revolution, the propositions of her suitors, and the love of her schoolchildren. Laura no longer makes moral decisions, and the wasteland claims her.

*Style and Technique*

In a story noted for its symbolism, the major symbolic patterns involve sex and religion. The sexual emphasis is used primarily to show how Laura is victimized by Braggioni. Under his domination, she yields to a fatalistic view of life in which events are beyond her control. The religious symbolism reveals the self-betrayal of this surrender.

Braggioni represents the potential of sexual violation. His fat body, encased in expensive clothes, calls attention to the power he has over Laura. As he strokes the guitar and the pistol and sings his love songs, his amorous intentions are made clear to

Laura. His name, resembling "braggadocio," further suggests his boasting, macho behavior. Laura's aloofness and her attempt to hide her body in heavy material merely add to the challenge that she represents to the rebel leader. His great bulk threatens her physically just as his corruption destroys her romantic illusions. In resisting him physically, however, she yields to him intellectually and morally.

The title of the story suggests its religious symbolism. Judas, the betrayer, supposedly hanged himself from a redbud tree. In Laura's dream, Eugenio offers the flowers of the Judas tree, which she readily devours. The dream indicates the guilt she feels as a result of her amoral activity. The guilt, suppressed during her conscious hours, comes forth in a parody of religious ritual, much like the washing of Braggioni's feet by his wife. Laura's dream thus embodies the story's themes in a highly charged symbolic language.

*Noel Schraufnagel*

# FLOWERS FOR ALGERNON

*Author:* Daniel Keyes (1927-    )
*Type of plot:* Science fiction
*Time of plot:* March 5 to July 28, 1965
*Locale:* New York
*First published:* 1959

*Principal characters:*
   CHARLIE GORDON, a janitor who is mentally limited
   MISS KINNIAN, a teacher of slow adults
   DR. STRAUSS and
   DR. NEMUR, scientists experimenting with an intelligence-
      enhancing surgical procedure
   ALGERNON, a white mouse

*The Story*

Charlie Gordon, thirty-seven years old and with an IQ of 68, dreams of being smart. Intelligence, he imagines, lies somewhere in the domain of reading and writing—a belief that has made him the hardest-working pupil in Miss Kinnian's class for slow adults. Charlie is so "motor-vated" that Miss Kinnian recommends him as a test subject for an experimental surgical procedure that promises a threefold increase in intelligence. Excited by the prospect of having his dream come true, Charlie begins his diary at the request of Dr. Strauss. Each "progris riport" reveals Charlie's thoughts, feelings, and fears as his intelligence rises dramatically, then plummets.

With a childlike eagerness to please, Charlie faces psychologists who attempt to administer personality and intelligence tests. Try as he may, he can see neither pictures in the "raw shok" inkblots nor stories in the scenes of the Thematic Apperception Test. Charlie fares no better in his contests with a white mouse named Algernon. Algernon runs through a maze box as Charlie attempts the same maze with pencil and paper. Algernon always wins.

Charlie is troubled by preoperative fears, but his rabbit's foot and a gift of candy see him through. The operation entails little discomfort and recovery is rapid, but Charlie is disappointed when he notices little immediate rise in his intelligence. Dr. Strauss advises patience, pointing out that Algernon's progress was slow after he underwent the same procedure. Now the reason for the animal's superior maze-running is revealed: "Algernon beats me all the time because he had that operashun too. That makes me feel better. . . . Maybe someday I'll beat Algernon. Boy that would be something."

Charlie returns to his job as a janitor at Donnegan's Plastic Box Company. He is happy to be back with his friends, oblivious to the mockery and practical jokes that his coworkers enjoy at his expense.

Dr. Strauss introduces a subliminal learning machine that teaches while Charlie sleeps. The breakthrough comes only a month after the journal entries begin, when Charlie beats Algernon. After that, his intellect expands at an ever-increasing rate. He reads widely; masters grammar and punctuation; learns foreign languages, mathematics, and music; and even conquers the Rorschach inkblot test that so baffled him before his operation.

As knowledge enters Charlie's world, so too does the recognition of evil. His most bitter lesson about people comes at a factory party. As he dances, his coworkers repeatedly trip him, laughing at his falls. The ridicule of those he once counted as friends devastates him: "I didn't know what to do or where to turn. Everyone was looking at me and laughing and I felt naked. I wanted to hide myself. I ran out into the street and I threw up. . . . I never knew that Joe and Frank and the others liked to have me around all the time to make fun of me. . . . I'm ashamed."

He suggests a highly profitable improvement in procedure at the factory and earns a meager bonus, but his coworkers fear the new Charlie so much they sign a petition demanding his dismissal. He realizes that he loves Miss Kinnian, but his superior intellect poses a new barrier between them. He now can no longer communicate with her.

A shift in Algernon's behavior augurs Charlie's fate. The mouse turns vicious, and his intelligence diminishes. Realizing that his own intellectual prowess is also temporary, Charlie throws himself into research, attempting to develop a calculus of intelligence. He concludes that artificially increased intelligence deteriorates at a speed proportional to the quantity of the increase.

After Algernon dies, Charlie puts the mouse's body in a cheese box and buries it in his backyard. He places flowers on the grave regularly in the weeks that follow.

Charlie's own intellectual decline accelerates, and he mourns his losses one by one as memories and skills disappear. Once again mentally handicapped, Charlie decides that his best hopes lie in a new beginning somewhere outside New York. He harbors no malice, bears no regrets: "dont be sorry for me Im glad I got a second chanse to be smart becaus I lerned a lot of things that I never new were in this world and Im grateful that I saw it all for a little bit." Proud of his accomplishment, however transitory, Charlie congratulates himself for being "the first dumb person in the world who ever found out something importent for sience." He asks nothing from his teacher, his doctors, or his readers but that flowers be placed on Algernon's grave.

*Themes and Meanings*

In this story, which was the basis for the film *Charly* (1968), Charlie travels from ignorance to great intelligence and back again. Ironically, that same journey takes him from innocence to disillusionment to innocence recaptured. Charlie's fleeting intellectual prowess carries an exorbitant price: an excruciating awareness of the cruelty that he has suffered at the hands of his coworkers. Charlie also finds pain in self-knowledge. He hides a picture of "the old Charlie Gordon" from himself in the hope of escaping the specter of his former illiteracy and childish naïveté, but he is haunted by the suspicion that he always saw—even through the veil of his dullness—his own isolating inferiority. He writes, "A child may not know how to feed itself, or what to eat, yet it knows of hunger."

Charlie's expanded intelligence fails to deliver the expected benefits. Although he delights in his newfound capacities for reading, memory, and logic, Charlie finds himself in a lose-lose situation with people. He writes on April 30: "The intelligence has driven a wedge between me and all the people I once knew and loved. Before, they laughed at me and despised me for my ignorance and dullness; now, they hate me for my knowledge and understanding."

Fanny Girden, one of Charlie's coworkers, invokes the Garden of Eden story from the Bible to explain the fear that Charlie's intellect provokes: "It was evil when Eve listened to the snake and ate from the tree of knowledge. It was evil when she saw that she was naked. If not for that none of us would ever have to grow old and sick and die." Charlie understands her message. His recognition of his coworkers' attitudes toward him has made him feel naked and ashamed.

Through Charlie, Daniel Keyes probes societal attitudes toward the mentally handicapped. Charlie's darkest hour comes at the peak of his intelligence, when he finds himself laughing along with everyone else at the clumsiness of a mentally handicapped boy. Charlie, unlike the others, becomes furious with himself for laughing and defends the boy: "He can't help what he is! But for God's sake . . . he's still a human being."

Keyes also questions the nature of friendship. As Charlie's intelligence declines to its preoperative level, he concludes that because letting people laugh is a good way to make friends, he should have lots of friends in his new home.

The only true love demonstrated in the story is Charlie's devotion to Algernon. He hates the mouse at first for winning all the races, but soon he develops an affection for the animal so intense that Algernon's death evokes profound grief. Charlie's friendship with Algernon grows from shared experience. He and the mouse face the same trials and endure the same painful outcomes. Keyes implies that the victories and defeats of life might link human beings in a similar way if only we could learn mutual trust and respect despite our differences.

### Style and Technique

"Flowers for Algernon" is a classic "what if?" story. Keyes explores the proposition, "What if an operation could increase human intelligence?" from the point of view of an experimental subject, using the intimacy of a diary to immerse readers in Charlie Gordon's reality. Keyes uses a bittersweet, but always respectful, humor to illuminate Charlie's interpretations of events. For example, when one coworker accuses another of "pulling a Charlie Gordon" when he loses a package, Charlie reflects, "I dont understand why he said that. I never lost any packiges."

Charlie's spelling, grammar, and syntax mirror his changing intellectual and emotional states. His first "progris riport" on "martch 5" establishes Charlie as uncomplicated, guileless, and eager to please. His elation as his intelligence grows is reflected in later entries when he uses punctuation marks with exuberant abandon. In the ensuing weeks, his writing becomes flawless, and his subject matter grows increasingly complex. As his intelligence declines, his grammar, spelling, and punctuation revert to substandard forms.

"Flowers for Algernon" is a science-fiction story because it is set in a future time and involves a speculative technology. Keyes needs no distant, alien civilization to expose the failings of contemporary human interactions. Instead, he probes the inadequacies of a society uncomfortable with human diversity through the eyes of an unforgettable character.

*Faith Hickman Brynie*

# THE FLY

*Author:* Katherine Mansfield (Katherine Mansfield Beauchamp, 1888-1923)
*Type of plot:* Psychological
*Time of plot:* After World War I
*Locale:* England
*First published:* 1922

*Principal characters:*
THE BOSS, the protagonist
MR. WOODIFIELD, a visitor
MACEY, the office messenger

## The Story

"The Fly" is a story told primarily through the eyes of "the boss," the protagonist, who is described not by name but by function. The story has two parts. In the first part, Mr. Woodifield (whom the boss thinks of as "old Woodifield"), retired since his stroke and woman-dominated, visits his friend the boss, who though, five years older than Woodifield, is still in charge of the firm. Woodifield and the boss have one experience in common: Both lost sons in World War I.

The boss enjoys showing Woodifield his redecorated office and benevolently offering him some whiskey. Then Woodifield, who has momentarily forgotten what he meant to tell the boss, remembers. His daughters have been in Belgium to see the grave of their brother, Woodifield's son, and they have also seen that of the boss's son. After Woodifield reports that the cemetery is well kept, he leaves, and the first part of the story is concluded.

Feeling that he must weep, the boss tells the cowed messenger, Macey, to give him a half hour alone. He feels as if he can see his son in the grave. However, although he muses that his life has been meaningless since the death of his promising only son, whom he was grooming to take over the business, the boss cannot weep.

At this point, the boss sees a fly in the inkpot, pulls it out, and puts it on a blotter, where he proceeds to torture it, placing one drop of ink on it at a time and repeating the operation every time the fly seems to have extricated itself and gained hope. Even though he admires the fly and cheers it on, the boss continues to drop ink on it until at last the fly dies. He feels miserable, but he cannot remember what he was thinking about before he began his experiment with the fly.

## Themes and Meanings

"The Fly" is a story of death. It begins with a meeting of two men who have lost sons in the war, and it ends with the death of a fly. In a deeper sense, however, there are six deaths indicated in the story.

When the boss first looks at old Woodifield, he sees a man who appears to be totally different from him. Woodifield is retired. He is dominated by his wife and daughters, who keep him in the house every day except Tuesday, when they dress him up and send him out to visit his friends. His passive, infantile life causes the boss to think of him as a baby. He is useful as someone to impress and to patronize. The boss enjoys offering him whiskey, which Woodifield's women deny him; thus, the boss can assert his own power, which elevates him above the rules of Woodifield's own bosses. Even Woodifield's forgetfulness suggests the decline he has suffered since his stroke. Clearly Woodifield is on the downhill road toward death; yet the fact that he could not remember the girls' visit to his son's grave suggests a second death, the death of his son's memory in his own mind.

On the surface, the boss is very different from Woodifield. He is healthy and active. He dominates Macey, his messenger, as a master would a dog. However, he thinks that his life ended six years ago, when the son for whom he intended the business was killed in the war. In response to his son's death, the boss himself has died, or so he thinks.

However, now, six years later, he finds himself staring at an unfamiliar photograph, which does not seem to look like his son; worse, he finds himself tormenting a fly rather than grieving; and finally, he forgets why he feels so miserable. If his son has been alive in his memory, he is now unfamiliar and unremembered, and in a sense, dead. Furthermore, if the boss loved only the son who always agreed with him, both father and son died a long time ago. All that is left is the boss's self-pity. His inability to feel for the son, hard as he may try, is like his inability to feel for the fly. Healthy, prosperous, domineering, the boss is, however, dead to feeling, and perhaps he has always been too self-centered to feel anything for others.

A fifth death is the death-in-life to which the boss has reduced his messenger, Macey, who is referred to throughout the story as a dog rather than a man. Macey, too, is old. His boss's attitude toward him is reflected in the thought that everyone, even Macey, liked the son. If Macey has learned to survive by doglike obedience, perhaps, Mansfield implies, Macey and the boss's other subordinates were counterfeiting their admiration of the son, whom the boss remembers as always having been pleasant, but who evidently looks like quite another person in his photograph. At any rate, Macey must have died as a human being at some time in the past, when he became the boss's faithful dog.

Finally, there is the death that gives the title to the story, that of the fly. Godlike, the boss first rescues the fly, then tests it repeatedly, cheering it on, sadistically applying a fresh ink drop just when the fly has survived the last, and finally deliberately putting what he knows will be the killing drop on the fly.

In "The Fly," perhaps the most pessimistic of Katherine Mansfield's stories, death conquers all. It may be death to feeling or death to memory; it may be death-in-life through self-love or through self-abnegation; it may be the death of will; finally, it will certainly be literal death, as it has been experienced by the two sons and by the fly.

## Style and Technique

In "The Fly," Mansfield typically uses a minimal amount of action in order to reveal human emotions. The real drama of the story involves a dialogue between two men, a direction to a messenger, a soliloquy, the torture and death of a fly, and another direction to the messenger. Throughout the story, the point of view is that of the boss, as he moves from self-satisfaction to inability to feel to preoccupied torture to misery. Because the boss, in contrast to Mansfield's sensitive protagonists, is essentially self-centered, however, the revelation in the story must come to the observant reader, rather than to the protagonist himself.

It is the reader, not the protagonist, who will notice the various parallels that are carefully built into the design of the story. The boss does not notice that he and Woodifield are alike in managing to forget the deaths of their sons. Nor does he realize that Woodifield's stroke and his own life's end, when his son died, have both been followed by a rebirth, by the capacity for pleasure, whether in a day out or in showing off the new furniture.

It is also the reader, not the protagonist, who sees that the fly itself has symbolic significance. Much as the boss may pity himself, in that he has lost the son whom he was shaping to follow him, he does not admit any feelings of identity with anyone or anything—not with Macey, not with Woodifield, certainly not with the fly he kills. However, the fly can be interpreted to represent every human being, including the insensitive boss. Just as the boss puts drop after drop on the fly, whatever powers there be put burden after burden on humanity, whether through nature, through war, through a hierarchical social and economic structure, or through the human need to dominate another creature. The pattern of human life is like the brief ordeal of the fly, which staggers, hopes, and rises, growing weaker each time, until at last it is conquered by death.

If Mansfield's symbolism in this story is directed toward the observant reader, rather than toward the insensitive protagonist, her language reflects the nature of the boss. There are no incomplete sentences, no fragments of thought, such as are found in Mansfield's indecisive characters. In his conversation with Woodifield, the boss observes himself bending to his inferior: winking, joking, and generously offering the whiskey. Even in his thoughts, the boss moves logically, as if he were arguing a case with the gods. It is only when he begins to torture the fly that he becomes oblivious to himself, so involved is he in the kind of action that has made and kept him "the boss." Even after the fly's death, when he feels miserable, he does not drift into half-sentences but gives Macey an order. Only three sentences before the end of the story is there a momentary hesitation in the style, when the boss realizes that he has forgotten something. Even then, though, he acts, he wipes his neck, and the final ironic line—"For the life of him he could not remember"—is in a style as self-assured as his whole life.

*Rosemary M. Canfield Reisman*

# FLYING HOME

*Author:* Ralph Ellison (1914-1994)
*Type of plot:* Psychological
*Time of plot:* World War II
*Locale:* Macon County, Alabama
*First published:* 1944

*Principal characters:*
> TODD, a black candidate in the army's Flight Training School
> JEFFERSON, an old, black tenant farmer
> TEDDY, his young son
> DABNEY GRAVES, a white man, the owner of the land that
> Jefferson farms

*The Story*

Todd, a young black man, a candidate in Flight Training School in Macon County, Alabama, during World War II, is just returning to consciousness after an accident. The narrative soon reveals, in one of several flashbacks, that Todd's "exultation" in flight had carried him away. He had flown "too high and too fast"; the plane had entered a tailspin, and before he could react a buzzard had smashed into his windshield. Panic caused him to lose control. A crash landing has thrown him from the plane and has broken his ankle. Over him stand an old, black farmer, Jefferson, and his son, Teddy. What immediately preoccupies Todd even more than the physical pain in his ankle is the anxiety over his failure as a pilot. His white officers will see the accident as confirmation that blacks are not capable of flying or of aerial combat. Because for Todd, earning his wings and fighting overseas are his escape from social inferiority—and from the stereotypical black traditions that he sees epitomized in Jefferson—the accident is a crisis in his young life. Jefferson instinctively understands much of what Todd is experiencing.

Jefferson sends his son to Dabney Graves, the symbol of white civil authority in the region and the owner of the land that Jefferson works, in order to get help, and then tries to take Todd's mind off the pain. He first tells him a brief anecdote about once finding two buzzards inside the remains of a dead horse and comments that Teddy's name for a buzzard is jimcrow. To Jefferson, this identification is both comical and meaningful. He then tells a more lengthy tale about his past life, when he was in Heaven. Though he was a black angel and required to wear a harness, he violated the rule and showed off his extraordinary powers of flight. His daring, however, became dangerous and offensive to God. As punishment, God took away his wings and sent him to Macon County, Alabama. This myth of origins again prompts Jefferson to laugh hilariously, but Todd, interpreting the two stories according to his own egotistical fears, accuses him of mockery. Todd takes the buzzards and the flying black angel to be satiric representations of himself. Jefferson had no such intentions and can only express his regret and empathy for Todd's painful situation.

Somehow, Jefferson's attempts to distract him, the empathy, and the physical pain succeed in taking Todd outside himself and releasing memories from his childhood. He recalls in detail his early obsession with airplanes and his attempt once, when he was getting a fever, to grab from the sky a real plane, which he mistook for a toy. In his feverous state during the next few days, he dreamed of capturing planes just beyond his grasp and of hearing his grandmother warn him about his arms being "too short/ To box with God." After a brief conversation with Jefferson about the plight of black people in a white society and after Jefferson's warning about the fickleness of Dabney Graves, Todd in painful delirium recalls another childhood moment. He was walking down a street on election day. Black faces peered fearfully from the houses, and one person seemed to be begging for his aid or perhaps warning him of danger. He saw a shower of leaflets descend from a plane high against the sun. When he picked up one of them, his mother took it and read a warning from the Klan: "Niggers Stay Away From The Polls."

Todd awakens from the dream to see three men approaching. Dabney Graves and two hospital attendants put him in a straitjacket, intended for Dabney's crazy cousin Rudolph but placed on Todd by Dabney as a joke. When Todd comes to full consciousness of what is happening, that the men have also laid him on a stretcher and are about to carry him away, he rebels. He steps out of the role of the inferior "nigger" and demands that they not touch him. Incensed by such independence in a black man, Dabney kicks him in the chest. The physical violence suddenly transforms Todd. It causes him to observe the entire situation with objectivity. He now sees his salvation in Jefferson. As Jefferson and Teddy, at Graves's command, carry him off to the "nigguh airfield," he loses his sense of isolation. Jefferson's care and the confrontation with the white bigoted world have transformed his confused and frustrated sense of identity into peace and harmony.

## Themes and Meanings

"Flying Home" is a story about racism. The main characters represent essential elements in the racial conflict in America: Jefferson is the traditional figure from the days of slavery; Todd is the young, modern black trying to escape from racial distinctions; Dabney Graves is the white landowner still governed by the bigoted assumptions of his ancestors; the white army officers, though not actually present in the story, still carry on in a nonagrarian context the old prejudices. Ralph Ellison uses the anecdotes told by Jefferson and the memories of Todd to insist on the same racial theme: Blacks are jimcrow buzzards feeding on a dead horse; they are angels who even in Heaven are ruled by a white god and subject to special restrictions; they are taught by their parents not to aim too high and are threatened by the Klan not to participate in the nation's political life. The end of the story offers no resolution to this social conflict. Todd returns to the airfield knowing that the white officers will regard his accident as a further sign of racial ineptitude. Dabney Graves would still eject any black from his

land who showed signs of disrespect for the old standards. So long as the white attitude remains, the conflict will remain.

The story is not, however, primarily about racism in society; it is about racism and
the effects of racism within Todd. He is experiencing an identity crisis that takes at
least four forms. First, he wants to be an individual totally dissociated from his race:
The burden of his every action being a partial definition of his race (a Sartrean theme
in Ellison's story) is more than he wants to bear. Second, he is ashamed of his past: He
wants to dissociate himself entirely from Jefferson, who fits Todd's Uncle Tom image
of the black man. This is a sign that Todd has internalized the whites' perception of the
black race. Third, he unconsciously wants to be white: Flying toward the sun makes
him white; falling toward the earth makes him black. Fourth, he measures his own
worth by another's standards. Though he has found that the judgments of the traditional black (slave) culture and of the white American authority figures are inadequate
(that is, he has rejected these judgments consciously, if not unconsciously), his goal as
a military pilot is to prove himself in battle so that the enemy will sanction his worthi-
ness. Although the story offers no solution to the social conflict, it does resolve the inner conflict. It is possible for the black man in American society to live at peace with
himself.

The solution that Ellison finds, on the purely thematic level, is a common one in
black American literature. At the root of racism and other prejudices is ignorance, not
only of others but also of the self. What Jefferson teaches and what Todd learns during the experience is a way of achieving first self-knowledge and then a knowledge of
others.

At the beginning of the story, Jefferson already possesses wisdom but only on an instinctual level. It is a part of his heritage. It is present in the stories that he tells Todd.
They are peculiarly appropriate to Todd's situation. They represent the state from
which he needs to escape, the black man as a buzzard feeding on a dead horse, and the
state that he needs to achieve, the free-flying angel who paradoxically must acknowledge human limitation and failure without denying his essential humanity. The tales
initiate Todd into awareness. Todd is not free because racism has distorted his understanding of his identity, his heritage, his home—that is, his human reality. Jefferson
would appear to be not fully conscious of how appropriate his anecdotes are, but they,
as repositories of traditional wisdom (Todd has heard a variation of the angel "myth"
as a child), speak directly to his need. Todd's initial refusal to accept the meaning of
the tales is reflected in his angry reaction. He cannot accept the truth about himself.

For some unstated reason, however, the truth hidden in the tales provokes repressed
memories about Todd's childhood fascination with airplanes and their associations
with racial oppression. Though again unstated, what Todd seems to learn is that the
airplane, instead of being a legitimate means of escape and of finding identity, represents an attempt to become white, to be what the white man is, to get his power. What
Ellison does state clearly is that the airplane is for Todd an escape from the "world of
men." At the end of the story, he finds in Jefferson, not the old Uncle Tom, but a human being who understands him. "A new current of communication flowed between

the man and boy and himself." Nor should one leave unstated the obvious. In finally yielding himself to Jefferson and Teddy and accepting the earth as his home, he is also declaring an allegiance to American soil in spite of those who would reject him.

Todd has returned to his roots. However, even this is not the special theme that recurs in black literature. Jefferson's tales are significant as much for their tone as for their meaning. After telling both, he laughs hilariously. He knows that they are jokes. They are his way of coping with racism, with what Todd comes to view as "an insane world of outrage and humiliation." Further, and more important, they are a sign of, and they encourage, objectivity. They allow one to get outside oneself and view the self and the world from another perspective. Jefferson is the two-headed juju man. Ellison emphasizes the crucial nature of this act of stepping outside the self several times during the story.

The tales themselves offer projected presentations of Todd. However, more directly, before Todd's first childhood recollection, "a part of him was lying calmly behind the screen of pain." At the beginning of the second recollection, Todd, in his delirium, sees two Jeffersons, one "that shook with fits of belly-laughter while the other Jefferson looked on with detachment." By the end of the story, Todd has emitted his own "blasts of hot, hysterical laughter," while "a part of him stood behind it all, watching the surprise in Graves's red face and his own hysteria." No longer bound by his own ego, he can see himself and others in perspective and, hence, can follow a reunion with society and an inner peace.

## Style and Technique

Ellison primarily uses the third-person point of view in "Flying Home," yet very early he alerts the reader that he will play some tricks with it. While in a state of semiconsciousness, Todd hears voices, not placed in quotation marks, which are both inside his head and outside. Where the voices are coming from, who is speaking, what one intends or perceives, and what biases govern thought and speech—these questions that Ellison raises involve an interrelationship between theme and point of view. When Jefferson speaks of buzzards and black angels, Todd perceives himself as the actor in those roles. When Todd enters the world of his past for the first time, Ellison almost without warning shifts to the first-person point of view and thus places the reader intimately within the mind of his protagonist. It is as though, along with Todd, the reader has difficulty distinguishing between external and inner reality. Todd's second memory is, on the other hand, clearly noted as his own thoughts. The progression in the story, in fact, is a gradual clearing of Todd's mind so that by the end he sees clearly both himself and the outer world. Both technically and thematically, point of view comes into focus.

This manipulation of point of view, however, is not nearly as interesting in itself as are its implications in another facet of Ellison's technique. Typically, Ellison likes his stories to operate on a mythical level. While maintaining a high degree of realism, including psychological realism, Ellison controls characters and events to fit into mythical patterns that universalize them. The story about a young man coming to awareness, for example, is clearly a vision of the initiation motif. His fall from the sky, like the black angel's condemnation to the hell of Alabama, follows the pattern of death and rebirth. The buzzard that feeds on death is in the final statement of the story "a bird of flaming gold," perhaps a reference to the phoenix, and certainly a reinforcement of the death-rebirth motif. The identification of Todd with Icarus and Jefferson with Daedalus is unmistakable. Flying too close to the sun Ellison interprets in his own way as part of the black man's dilemma in American society. Elements of Christian myth, Heaven and Hell, and especially the question of knowledge and how much man has a right to, and the pride of the original Fall lie behind Todd's experience. One must not forget the folk tradition that Ellison includes, Jefferson's creation and re-creation of myth. Indeed, this last is especially important because of the relation of myth in the story to theme and point of view. Myths are useless if not understood and reinterpreted in the light of immediate experience, and Todd's education is, in part, a coming to terms with his heritage.

Ellison's mythical ventures operate in the Jungian manner. The myths are not only outside Todd but also within his racial unconscious. The events in the story are his acting out the patterns that already exist in his mind. If he is not to play out the roles blindly and chaotically, he must raise them to consciousness, and choose and reinterpret those that he needs in the modern world. The story does not show Todd reaching such a level of sophistication, but it does show Ellison's own preoccupation with the task. The reader does, however, observe Todd acting out some changes in his conceptions. At the end, for example, he no longer views Heaven and Hell as whiteness and blackness, or as flying in the sky and living on the earth. Earth becomes the human community rather than Hell. Flying home is flying back to Earth.

It is also a return to the true self. A part of Carl Gustav Jung's theories about the unconscious mind suggests the presence of archetypal images of the self—persona, anima, shadow—and of various other figures, such as the wise old man. Until late in the story, however, Todd rejects the promptings of the anima, still projects the evil and prejudice in himself outwardly on such figures as Graves and the white officers, and perceives Jefferson as ignorant rather than wise. By the end of the story, his soul lives in harmony. He has internalized Jefferson's wisdom (the mythical father resides within him); he has accepted his girl's advice that he not continually prove his intelligence to the white man (that he not feed on that dead horse); he has, by accepting Jefferson as his savior, admitted a prejudice in his own psyche, and no longer blindly projects such evil on the Dabney Graveses of the world. His perspective has cleared. His inner voice is in harmony with outer voices: "Like a song within his head he heard the boy's soft humming."

Without at all denying the black heritage, Ellison insists on the presence of all cultures within the human psyche. As he says elsewhere, it is possible for a black to be a Renaissance man, one who incorporates all experiences.

*Thomas Banks*

# FOOTFALLS

*Author:* Wilbur Daniel Steele (1886-1970)
*Type of plot:* Fable
*Time of plot:* The 1920's
*Locale:* An unnamed New England coastal town
*First published:* 1920

*Principal characters:*
BOAZ NEGRO, a hardworking, happy, blind cobbler
MANUEL, his shiftless son
CAMPBELL WALKER, his lodger, a bank clerk

*The Story*

Boaz Negro, a blind Portuguese immigrant cobbler living in a small New England fishing village, has faced his disability and other hardships, such as the death of his wife, unflinchingly and with a cheerful equanimity that flows from his ineradicable joy in life. He loves his fellow townspeople, whom he recognizes by their footsteps, but he especially dotes on his son, Manuel. He is always ready to supply the young man with pocket money, unable to see that his spoiling has made Manuel too lazy to set on a definite career path. Manuel contrasts sharply with Campbell Walker, Boaz's lodger, who has moved to the town to take an important position at the local bank, and who gives every sign of being destined for prominence.

The story's pivotal events occur one evening when Campbell tries to make Boaz aware of his son's slothfulness. Their conversation is inconclusive because Boaz resolutely maintains that his son is too sickly to hold a steady job. In the course of the talk, Campbell drops a concealed money bag. Taking the cobbler into his confidence, he explains he must hide some bank gold in his room overnight. Campbell does not realize that Manuel is eavesdropping from the other room. Later, Boaz hears Campbell invite Manuel to a game of cards and then hears one man leave the building. Boaz broods over these occurrences, finding out almost too late that his house is on fire.

Once the fire is doused, a charred body, apparently that of the young clerk, is discovered on the bed. His skull has been bashed in and his money is missing. Rather than comment on his son's apparent viciousness, Boaz withdraws into himself, not speaking except to swear that he will repay that *cachorra*, referring to the murderer with the Portuguese word for dog.

Many years pass and Boaz works on stubbornly, having become cold and taciturn where he was once jolly and lively. He refuses to rebuild his dwelling, residing in the largely burned-out hulk of the original structure. The only time that Boaz arouses himself is when he hears an unfamiliar footstep.

One evening a man enters the shop and startles Boaz, who remembers the sound of the man's steps from long ago. After extinguishing the lights to hinder his opponent, he wrestles him to the ground and strangles him to death. Feeling his victim's face, Boaz is upset by the roughness of a beard. When townspeople force their way into the shop, having been alerted to trouble by the sounds of a violent struggle, they meet the fantastic sight of Boaz kneeling beside and shaving the man he has slain. The second shocker for them is that the corpse is Campbell, who had faked his death in order to cover the tracks of his escape.

Boaz now states that on the night of his son's murder he recognized the fleeing man by the way he walked but had been afraid, given the stereotyped views most people held of his son and the clerk, that no one would believe his story. Thus, he had nursed his knowledge in secret.

Because of the extraordinary nature of the provocation, Boaz is not brought to trial and now, although chastened, he returns to his better spirits and sets to work to rebuild his house and renew his life.

*Themes and Meanings*

A resonant theme in American short stories written after World War I, such as Ernest Hemingway's "My Old Man" (1923), is that of the betrayal of the father. In such stories, a son typically grows up to learn his father is much less capable and ethical than he had supposed. In Wilbur Daniel Steele's own "For Where Is Your Fortune Now?" (1918), a son who follows his footloose but disarmingly charming father quickly finds the man is a bum and a womanizer. One can conjecture that stories on such themes were provoked by the disillusionment that the young felt over the pointless carnage of the war, which many thought had been precipitated recklessly by their elders.

When a theme becomes suggestive for a period, it does not mean that every writer follows the same line in treating the subject. Rather, the theme provides grist for different fiction writers to mill. In "Footfalls," Steele takes up the relations of fathers and sons as well as the loss of innocence but reverses the normal weighing of the terms. In place of a son who finds his father wanting, he creates a father who appears brokenhearted by his son's deeds. Boaz did not doubt his son, but the townspeople and the reader assume he does through much of the tale because of the cobbler's ambiguous use of *cachorra*. Moreover, rather than the story gradually leading up to a disillusionment, here the father's seeming misgivings are dispelled at the conclusion.

Steele thus ends by affirming a positive continuity between generations, while still acknowledging the possibility that bad blood can contaminate the relations between a father and son. This latter point is emphasized through the fact that, for most of the story, readers believe that Boaz is shattered by his discovery that his son is a blackguard. The story's final twist confirms what might seem to be a normal state of affairs but what, in the 1920's, was a minority view: that a member of one generation in a family can accurately read the heart of the member of another generation and be justified in judging that member kindly although appearances are against him or her. The fact that Steele endorses this view in a surprise ending can be interpreted as an attempt to move his audience to accept the truth of his then-unpopular contentions by way of the provocative force exerted by the readers' astonishment at the concluding turn of events.

## Style and Technique

Although Steele's story is realistic and plausible, a host of features indicate that it should be read as a fable. A fable is a brief tale that uses stylized characters and, often, fantastic elements to present a simple moral lesson. Steele's tale qualifies for such a categorization through its use of narrow plot, simplified characters, fairy-tale motifs, and a somewhat didactic ending.

The plot is reduced to the minimum. Only the three central personages are named and described, and only two scenes—the events surrounding the two murders—are painted in any detail. What happens between these key incidents is sketched lightly, with the reader being told, rather than shown, what occurs in the intervals.

The characters are two-dimensional. The son is identified as shiftless, and little else is said about him. Boaz, the one character who is portrayed in some depth, is accorded a few exaggerated traits, such as the possession of super-acute hearing, and these are drawn in a stylized way. In describing how Boaz has brooded about the murder and fire while working steadily at his bench, for example, his arms are depicted in expressionist terms. "One could imagine those arms growing paler, also growing thicker and more formidable with that unceasing labor; the muscles feeding themselves omnivorously on their own waste, the cords toughening, the bone tissues revitalizing themselves without end."

Fantasy elements are deftly added to the story with clever touches, as in the way that the bank clerk brings home a bag of gold to hide. Carrying such a bag would seem to be a highly unlikely way to transport wealth in that time, but the use of this method slyly suggests fairy-tale motifs.

Finally, there seems to be a firm set of moral messages delivered by the story. The first is that a father is the best judge of his child's character; the second, that one should never accept society's prejudices unless one has tested them on reality.

If one accepts the classification of "Footfalls" as a fable, then certain possible criticisms of the story, such as that its characters are flat, do not apply. Flat characterizations and other simplifications are part of the nature of a fable, for it is the purpose of this type of literature to minimize color and detail so as to maximize the impact of selectively highlighted images and statements. The story's messages and the late image of Boaz shaving his victim gain force by their being set within a fable's simple surfaces and arguments.

*James Feast*

# FOR ESMÉ—WITH LOVE AND SQUALOR

*Author:* J. D. Salinger (1919-    )
*Type of plot:* Psychological
*Time of plot:* April, 1944, to May, 1945
*Locale:* Dover, England, and Gaufurt, Bavaria
*First published:* 1950

*Principal characters:*
>STAFF SERGEANT X, a young American stationed in Europe in the
>last year of World War II
>ESMÉ, a thirteen-year-old English girl whom X meets
>CLAY (CORPORAL Z), X's insensitive jeepmate during this year

*The Story*

The story opens in 1950, immediately after the narrator has received an invitation to Esmé's wedding. He and his "breathtakingly levelheaded" wife have decided that he cannot go, so, instead, he writes these "few revealing notes on the bride as I knew her almost six years ago."

The story proper (still in the first person) begins in April of 1944. The narrator is one of sixty enlisted men stationed in rural England, undergoing pre-Invasion Intelligence training. On the afternoon of his last day in Devon, he walks through the rain to the small town and wanders into choir rehearsal in a church. There he notices a girl with "the sweetest-sounding" voice, "an exquisite forehead, and blasé eyes." Later the girl, her five-year-old brother, Charles, and their governess come into the tearoom, where the narrator has gone to escape the rain. The girl gives him an "oddly radiant" smile and then comes over to talk with him because he looks "extremely lonely." Esmé is precious and precocious, her conversation peppered with large words and delightful misinformation about the United States ("I thought Americans despised tea").

The narrator learns that Esmé is titled, that both her parents are dead (she wears her father's oversized military wristwatch), and that she is being reared by an aunt. When Esmé finds out that the narrator is a writer, she asks if he would write a story for her and suggests that he "make it extremely squalid and moving." When she leaves, Esmé asks if he would like her to write to him. "It was a strangely emotional moment for me," the narrator relates. Esmé says good-bye and adds, "I hope you return from the war with all your faculties intact."

The second half of the story—"the squalid, or moving part," as the narrator says in its first line—takes place in Gaufurt, Bavaria, and is narrated in the third person. The protagonist (now "cunningly" disguised as "Staff Sergeant X") is sitting at a table in his second-floor room in an occupied German house several weeks after V-E Day (in other words, more than a year after the first scene). He has returned that day from a two-week stay in a Frankfurt hospital, where he was sent after an apparent nervous breakdown, but he does not look much improved. His hands shake, he has a facial tic, and his gums bleed at the touch of his tongue. In an attempt to hold on to something, he opens a book by Joseph Goebbels that was once owned by the thirty-eight-year-old woman who lived in this house and whom X arrested as a minor Nazi functionary. On the flyleaf, the woman has written, "Dear God, life is hell," Beneath that inscription, X now writes, "Fathers and teachers, I ponder 'What is Hell?' I maintain that it is the suffering of being unable to love," but when he finishes, he discovers that what he has written is "almost entirely illegible."

After a painful scene with his jeepmate, Clay, whose insensitivity to X's real situation keeps him from being very helpful, it is clear that X is near collapse. Suddenly, in the pile of unopened mail in front of him, he spots a package, opens it, and finds a letter from Esmé written almost a year earlier, with her father's wristwatch, sent to X "as a lucky talisman." The crystal to the watch is broken, and X does not have the courage to see if the watch still works. After holding it in his hand "for another long period," X realizes that "suddenly, almost ecstatically, he felt sleepy." The gift has somehow saved him, for, as he writes in the last line, a really sleepy man "always stands a chance of again becoming" a man with all his faculties "intact."

*Themes and Meanings*

"For Esmé—with Love and Squalor" is one of J. D. Salinger's most romantic and popular stories. In fact, when Salinger's first collection of short stories, *Nine Stories* (1953), was published in England, it was retitled *For Esmé—with Love and Squalor* (1953). Like so many works in the limited Salinger library, this is a story of redemption by love, and, as in most of these works—from *The Catcher in the Rye* (1951) through "A Perfect Day for Bananafish" (also in *Nine Stories*) to *Franny and Zooey* (1961)—the saving gesture is made by a child. Children are special in Salinger's work, for they alone are capable of making the sacrifice of love.

The contrast in "For Esmé—with Love and Squalor" is clear, for all the other characters want something from the narrator; only Esmé gives. The uncommunicative soldiers with whom he is first stationed in Devon talk to one another only when they want to borrow something; the letter from his mother-in-law that he reads in the tearoom asks him "to please send her some cashmere yarn." Clay wants X to make his letters to his girlfriend more interesting; a letter from X's brother asks him to send "the kids a couple of bayonets or swastikas," now that the war is over. The protagonist at the end of the story has just gone through five campaigns, he is barely holding himself together—and people are still making selfish demands on him. Only Esmé gives—and gives the thing most precious to her, the watch from her father, who was "s-l-a-i-n in North Africa," as she spells it out in the tearoom so her younger brother will not understand. It is true that Esmé asks for something too, a story, but that is a creative offering the narrator gives gladly, for he has been saved from collapse by her love.

As in other Salinger stories, there is a philosophical component to this theme. The German woman quoted Goebbels when she wrote, "Dear God, life is hell," and Sergeant X quotes Father Zossima (the elderly monk who preaches love in Fyodor Dostoevski's *Bratya Karamazovy*, 1879-1880; *The Brothers Karamazov*, 1912) when he adds that Hell "is the suffering of being unable to love." All around X are examples of this lack of love—not only in characters but also in the war itself. Esmé herself is trying to become less "cold" and training herself to be "more compassionate," as she tells the narrator in the tearoom, but her gift demonstrates that she alone is capable of pure and unselfish love. Salinger is debating the nature of life, love, and suffering through the actions and characters of his story. He posits Dostoevski against Goebbels (and ultimately Hitler), and the simple, almost childish gestures of Esmé against the selfishness of other characters and the horrors of the war. However, what X writes on the flyleaf is "almost entirely illegible." It only becomes legible, or real, through the gift of Esmé. Only Esmé is truly "sincere."

### Style and Technique

Salinger's style in this story (as in much of his work) is marked by humor, irony, and romantic lyricism. The humor is partly one of situation, particularly in the early scene in the English tearoom. There, the narrator is confronted by Esmé's little brother, the ingenuous Charles (who asks questions such as, "Why do people in films kiss sideways?"), and by Esmé, whose poise and vocabulary are in sharp contrast to her innocence and ignorance ("when I'm thirty, I shall retire and live on a ranch in Ohio"). Even the scene with Clay, in which X is barely holding himself together in the face of his companion's crude insensitivity, holds moments of kidding.

A subtler kind of humor derives from Salinger's tone; the pervasive irony of the story (aided by irony's companion, understatement) helps to deflect its implicit sentimentality. "Are you at all acquainted with squalor?" Esmé asks about the story that the narrator has promised to write for her. "I said not exactly but that I was getting better acquainted with it, in one form or another, all the time"—which is an ironic and understated way to talk about the "squalor" of war that the protagonist experiences.

Finally, Salinger's style is characterized by romantic lyricism. This is, after all, a story of orphans in wartime, a sensitive hero surrounded by vulgarity, a man on the edge saved by a child. It is also a love story, even a story of thwarted love (because it opens with the announcement of Esmé's marriage to another). While with one hand Salinger muffles the romantic dimension with irony and understatement, with the other he pulls out stops on the stylistic organ, especially in the voice of Esmé. His shift from first person to third in the last half of the story is undoubtedly an attempt to gain distance from the melodramatic action, but even here Esmé's language, in her letter to Sergeant X, breaks through:

> Charles and I are both quite concerned about you; we hope you were not among those who made the first assault upon the Cotentin Peninsula. Were you? Please write as speedily as possible.

Esmé has been known to make grown readers cry.

*David Peck*

# FORGIVENESS

*Author:* Edna O'Brien (1930-    )
*Type of plot:* Psychological
*Time of plot:* The 1980's
*Locale:* The coast of southern Italy
*First published:* 1984

*Principal characters:*
EILEEN
MARK, her adult son
PENNY, Mark's girlfriend

*The Story*

Only a few days into her vacation at a villa on Italy's southern coast, Eileen is becoming tired of her companions—her grown son, Mark, and his girlfriend, Penny. Weary of their small "irksome" habits, she is lost without the props of her work and her own friends and she wants to go home. By the third day, she cannot even sleep but cannot decide whether or not to leave.

The next day the three companions are together on the beach. After they return to their villa, Penny cuts her bangs as Mark holds a mirror for her. Afterward, she leaves her hair cuttings on a table, which Eileen soon finds herself cleaning. The incident contributes to Eileen's growing desire to leave the couple.

As the three companions return from dinner that evening, Eileen complains about Penny's driving, the cost of the villa, the hair trimmings, the cost of their rental car—about virtually everything that concerns their holiday. "We can't go on like this," she tells Mark, who reacts strongly in order to protect Penny from his mother's attack. Eileen feels that in that moment she is losing her son forever in a most violent way.

The next day Eileen encourages Mark and Penny to go sailing together, as she wishes to be alone. After the young couple leave to follow her suggestion, Eileen ventures into town alone with an Italian dictionary in order to shop. There she is surrounded by chattering children and is harassed by a simple-minded man on the beach. After youths on motorcycles chase her through a glade, she makes her way back to the villa and the weather suddenly turns ugly. With a violent storm threatening, Eileen reaches the villa worried that Mark and Penny may be in danger on the open sea.

Just as Eileen is imagining every possible disaster that might have befallen her son and Penny, the couple return. Filled with high spirits, they tell Eileen that they abandoned their plan to go sailing because of the weather and instead went to a restaurant, where they want to take Eileen that evening. So contagious is the young couple's enthusiasm, that by the end of the story they have "forgiven" her—"she who could never find it in her heart to forgive herself, or another."

*Themes and Meanings*

Edna O'Brien's story revolves around the tensions that build when a mother, her grown son, and his girlfriend holiday together in a foreign land. Its foremost theme is the process through which forgiveness—which gives the story its title—comes about, especially for the young, who seem to find forgiveness a more spontaneous, if not easier, response to hurt and sorrow. While the tensions between Eileen and Penny seem "natural" in the sense that Penny represents for Eileen a kind of "replacement" of the mother figure in Mark's life, Eileen's outburst in the car and the resulting emotional damage it causes are inexcusable. However, after a day of separation and mutual exploration, Mark and Penny discover the means to reestablish the triangle while Eileen discovers that without Mark and Penny's company, her visit to Italy means little. It is not until Mark and Penny return that Eileen can see that her sense of emptiness is linked to her inability to forgive even herself. The theme of forgiveness, then, follows on the heels of violence and emptiness.

This underlying theme of the relationship between violence and forgiveness is expressed through Eileen's emotional outburst and is mirrored in the violence of the next day's weather. Alone during the storm, Eileen has ample time to reflect on the disagreement and work herself into a state of anxiety over the safety of the couple. She goes so far, in fact, as to imagine that the car door signaling the couple's return is actually that of the authorities coming to tell her of a tragedy. It is not until she finally sees the young couple and experiences the overwhelming relief that she feels at their safe return that she begins to understand the meaning of what they have all been undergoing. In this way, the reader can see how the themes of forgiveness, of violence, and of struggle between the young and the old are intertwined.

That there is a "generation gap" between Eileen and her son is clear enough. The figure of Penny simply becomes a catalyst whereby Eileen comes to see that her own youth and sense of extravagance are waning. By the end of the story, however, Eileen sees that it is not that Penny usurps her role as mother but that Mark, as the grown man he now is, realizes his need for Penny and his mother. By the end of the story, then, each character reaches a point of maturity that makes it possible to express remorse, joy, and a restored sense of adventure and unity.

*Style and Technique*

The anonymous third-person narrator of this story is not omniscient; the only character whose mind the narrator enters is Eileen. As readers see the story through her eyes, they sense her struggles with her own jumbled emotions and ineptness at dealing fairly with Mark and Penny. O'Brien's use of a third-person narrator with limited omniscience is ideally suited to her revealing the mind of a character who cannot see her own inability to forgive. It is through Mark and Penny that Eileen achieves a better understanding of herself. Through them, she has an epiphany, or moment of self-awareness, at the end of the story in which she views her place in the world with greater clarity than she ever has before.

O'Brien's use of the epiphany in this way typifies twentieth century short stories, in which such moments of self-awareness often come swiftly, incisively, and usually at the close of the story. In this way, O'Brien uses several narrative devices—suspense among them—to build the story in several different stages.

The use of suspense in this story is not meant to be a sensational technique designed to deal out a clear "moral." Suspense is created through the building of tension between the characters and the mirroring of that tension through the long day of absence and stormy weather. Although the reader is taken directly into the thought process of Eileen as she frets about Mark and Penny's safety, the suspense that builds is always founded on sound psychological reaction to circumstances. Thus, while the safety of the couple remains in doubt, the reader can participate, along with Eileen, in the creation of a suspense that does not require an inevitably negative resolution. The building of this psychological suspense is further enhanced by the fact that the use of omniscience is limited only to Eileen's train of thought. A wider use of omniscience might give the reader knowledge of the couple's safety and thus play ironically on Eileen's worries, but such an omniscience would detract from the sense of genuine remorse that Eileen feels and the complete authenticity of the couple's enthusiasm at the end of the story.

O'Brien's ability to create three believable and fully rounded characters within the limited confines of a relatively short story reveals the extent to which she has mastered the form. Unity of action and place are always preserved and, given the short span of the story, the character of Eileen is presented in as many dimensions as are necessary for the reader to identify with her, feel compassion for her, and, at the same time, recognize her shortcoming at the story's end.

A final technique that helps O'Brien's story to work is its use of ironic contrast between its characters and its setting. Although the story takes place in a classically romantic setting—southern Italy—the story itself is a romance in only the most muted and subtle of ways. It is the need to forgive, which is essential to all forms of romance—Oedipal or otherwise—that ensures that the story's romantic locale is recaptured and given deeper meaning.

*Susan M. Rochette-Crawley*

# THE FORKS

*Author:* J. F. Powers (1917-1999)
*Type of plot:* Social realism
*Time of plot:* The 1940's
*Locale:* An American city
*First published:* 1947

> *Principal characters:*
> FATHER EUDEX, an unassuming and diligent Roman Catholic
>    priest with genuine scruples
> WILLIAM FRANCIS XAVIER, his tormentor, the Monsignor
> JOE WHALEN, the janitor at the rectory
> MRS. KLEIN, a widowed parishioner

*The Story*

Decent and selfless Father Eudex returns from morning Mass at the orphanage, driving a car that belongs to his more worldly superior, the Monsignor. At the rectory, Monsignor waits for Father Eudex, eager for assurance that his big new car is unharmed. Hoping for Monsignor's approval, the unassuming priest seizes the moment to announce nervously that he has a chance to buy his own car. Under Monsignor's patronizing questions, the priest reveals that the bargain he has in mind is not a sparkling new Ford V-8 but merely a used Model A. Monsignor laughs at his request for permission to buy the car, dismissing the topic with the reminder that "You know the class of people we get here."

Turning to his morning paper, Monsignor spots a story about his archenemy, a local bishop who is admired by the press for his support of left-wing labor causes. As Monsignor fumes about communism and fellow-traveling priests, it becomes clear that his main concern is to keep the good will of a Mr. Memmers of the First National Bank, a prominent parishioner. As Father Eudex well knows, Monsignor's ongoing complaining stems from his desire to become a bishop.

To ease his suffering over communists in the church, Monsignor takes his car for a spin. Meanwhile, Father Eudex pores through his mail—which today includes a check for one hundred dollars, "Compliments of the Rival Tractor Company." Father Eudex knows that an identical envelope addressed to Monsignor contains a check for two hundred dollars—the going rate for pastors. Although Rival Tractor contributes to ministers and "even rabbis," the spiritual leaders of the company's Catholic work force get the best checks in these strike-troubled times.

As the scrupulous curate muses over his check, he encounters Joe Whalen, the janitor, muttering about Monsignor's plan for a large garden featuring a fleur-de-lis pattern surrounded by Maltese crosses. The obliging priest strips down to his undershirt and helps Whalen turn the soil, only to have Monsignor reprove him for his lapse in dignity when he returns. Monsignor regards Father Eudex's stripping to his undershirt and wielding of a shovel as foreign to "the mind of the Church" and indicative of his lack of taste.

At lunch, Monsignor grumbles that his tutti-frutti salad has green olives in it, apparently a breach of culinary good taste. Father Eudex's admission that he likes olives in his salad again demonstrates his vulgarity to Monsignor, who abruptly announces that the priest would benefit from a year's study leave. The remark about the olive is the last of many offenses that Father Eudex has committed. Others include Father Eudex's offering to shake hands, emerging from his bedroom in pajama bottoms without a robe, and eating an entire meal with only a single knife, fork, and spoon. The thought of this last breach of etiquette drives Monsignor to a vernacular explosion about Father Eudex's ignorance of forks.

After Monsignor recovers from the olive incident, he suggests that Father Eudex might use his Rival Company money to buy a "decent" car. The curate, however, confesses that he intends to donate the money to the strikers' relief fund. Monsignor huffs that all the company had in mind in donating the money was traditional good works, then departs for his afternoon nap with an irritated and contemptuous laugh.

As Monsignor dozes, a parishioner named Mrs. Klein—who explains that she is German, not Jewish—arrives, asking for advice about how to handle the considerable bank account that her late husband has left her. Assuming that the woman has charitable causes in mind, Father Eudex recommends using the money to help the poor. When Mrs. Klein angrily tells him that he is not much of a priest, he realizes that she has come seeking only investment tips. Soured by this final blow to his priestly ideals, Father Eudex tears his Rival Company check into small pieces that he donates to the sewage system.

*Themes and Meanings*

The paramount theme running through "The Forks" is the contrast between Monsignor's materialism and pharisaism and Father Eudex's natural kindness and spirituality. Monsignor's pride in his car approaches blasphemy, his concern for outward show disgraces his position, and his cozy relationship with Rival Tractor Company reveals a blatant disregard for honor. These attributes contrast sharply with Father Eudex's natural modesty and probity: He would be happy with a used Model A, he knows instinctively that helping Joe Whalen dig the garden overrides any offense implicit in working in his undershirt, and he destroys the insulting check without a trace of regret.

In one wonderfully conceived passage, Father Eudex imagines what kind of bishop Monsignor might make. He envisions the perfect Pharisee: that man of righteousness whose devotion to outward and visible forms of conduct—down to using the right forks—conceals an inner emptiness. To observe feast days and speak beautiful, flawless Latin are accomplishments subject to care and practice; to love your neighbor as yourself—even when he is in his undershirt—demands innate qualities that cannot be summoned up by the will. Father Eudex thinks, "His reign would be a wise one, excessively so. His mind was made up on everything, excessively so."

Monsignor's venality afflicts so many men of the cloth that the widow Mrs. Klein just naturally assumes that the rectory functions as a kind of high-class bookie joint. Her late husband had always told her that if she had a problem, see the priest; when she wants to know how to invest her money, she naturally assumes that the curate will know where the smart money is going. When Father Eudex suggests she give her money to someone who needs it, she responds irately, "You ain't much of priest! What time's your boss come in?"

A large theme opens up in the question of the church's role in politics. Monsignor's conservative ideology shows up clearly in his hatred for the left-wing bishop and anything reeking of communism—attitudes that complement his readiness to accept checks from a capitalist tractor company that will pay him to preach against the unions. That the church tolerates, at least to a degree, both activists and supporters of the status quo seems clear in its accommodation of both Monsignor and the bishop whom he loathes. Father Eudex aspires to a position untainted by ideology; he clearly agonizes over what is right, and his decision to destroy the check perhaps argues that ideally the church speaks for no ideology, left or right. Perhaps it should seek only to heal the sick, raise the dead, cleanse the lepers, and cast out devils.

*Style and Technique*

Although an omniscient voice narrates "The Forks," it is clearly Father Eudex's story that is being told. J. F. Powers immediately establishes the reader's sympathy with the curate and follows his thoughts as Monsignor comes and goes. "The Forks" then ends happily insofar as Father Eudex tears up his check in a victory for honesty and goodness.

Nothing fixes Monsignor's character more vividly than his loving courtship of his sleek car, which is always described with feminine pronouns. Monsignor is "helpless before her beauty"; he cannot "leave her alone"; "he had her out every morning and afternoon and evening"; he devotes "daily rubdowns" to her. On one occasion, as he prepares to drive off, he gives a fender "an amorous chuck" before departing "to see the world, to explore each other further on the honeymoon."

Low-key dramas in a rectory hardly lead to broad humor, but Powers always spices his stories with wit and irony. As Monsignor pulls away down Clover Boulevard on his "honeymoon," a respectful cop clears a way for him, "for it was evidently inconceivable to him that Monsignor should ever venture abroad unless to bear the Holy Viaticum, always racing with death." Again, when he learns of the garden with the fleur-de-lis and the Maltese crosses, "the whole scheme struck Father Eudex as expensive and, in this country, Presbyterian." One last example, an observation that occurs after Monsignor has lectured Father Eudex on vulgarity and evangelical zeal: "The air of the rectory was often heavy with The Mind of the Church and Taste." Although these are small jokes and narrow ones at that, they are excellent examples of their type.

*Frank Day*

# FRAZER AVENUE

*Author:* Guy García (1955-    )
*Type of plot:* Social realism
*Time of plot:* The 1960's
*Locale:* East Los Angeles, California
*First published:* 1992

*Principal characters:*

THE NARRATOR, a Mexican American college student
AL, his childhood friend
JOHN VELASCO, his high school friend
GRANDMA, his grandmother
TÍO, his uncle
THE GIRLFRIEND, a college student and Chicana activist

## The Story

The narrator, a Mexican American college student, recalls his life ten years earlier on Frazer Street—a lower-class barrio of East Los Angeles, where on Sunday mornings one could see drunks leaving Millie's bar after all-night revelries. He remembers one particular Sunday, when the neighborhood's most responsible citizens gathered on the lawn of his parents' house to discuss the neighborhood's deterioration. On that day, his parents announced their intention to move away out of concern for his future. He had recently befriended youths who passed their evenings shooting out streetlights. Their leader was a boy named Al, a cynical and bitter orphan whose mother died from illness and whose father was a victim of violence. Although the narrator refused to participate in the group's vandalism, he realized with regret that the barrio would always remain a part of his life as his family was moving away.

The protagonist returns to his old barrio—a place now inundated by police cars, broken glass, boarded-up buildings, and burned-out storefronts. He recalls having once been a part of this neighborhood—a fact that he denies in his new neighborhood. He expresses his loathing for the "typical Mexican" and regards himself as vastly superior.

The protagonist next recalls a college demonstration in which he participated in which the police clashed with Chicano activists marching in a civil rights protest. Although he was involved in the movement, he was skeptical of it and considered himself an outsider.

Going even further back in his memory, the narrator remembers an incident involving himself and his friend, John Velasco. One day, after their school won an athletic event, he and John were walking home when they noticed an automobile stalking them. After the car's unknown passengers followed them, a chase on foot began. The narrator jumped to safety over a wire fence, but his friend was caught and beaten by their pursuers. Seeing his friend savagely beaten and not being able to do anything greatly affected the narrator, who had to flee for his own safety.

The protagonist now finds himself in front of his grandmother's residence. Nothing has visibly changed in the ten years since he left the neighborhood. He feels uneasy being around these people; although they share his heritage and bloodlines, he does not consider himself like them. He has returned for his grandmother's birthday, and she is overjoyed to see him—especially as he is the last person whom she expected to come. When his uncle greets him, he confesses to himself that he dislikes the man because he is so typically Latino: loud and boorish. His college education allows him to feel superior to everyone present at the party.

The protagonist then recalls breaking up with the girlfriend who had drawn him into Chicano activism. Eventually he realized that his reasons for supporting the cause were as contrived as his love for the girlfriend. His rejection of her has left him feeling alone and numb to all passions in the world.

Meanwhile, the birthday party is filled with music, singing, dancing, eating, and drinking. The narrator remains distant from the other guests and is embarrassed by his grandmother's strained singing and her drunkenness. When he approaches her to say good-bye, she asks him to sit next to her and he notices that she is in some kind of physical discomfort. Unexpectedly, however, she suddenly forces him onto the floor to dance. As they stumble about awkwardly, the narrator begins imagining his grandmother as a beautiful young girl whom he loves deeply, when she suddenly collapses into his arms. Shortly afterward she dies, stunning the people attending her party.

The narrator remains at his grandmother's house for some time afterward. Suddenly, and with great determination, he rises to leave. When his uncle calls out, "Where are you going?" he simply replies, "South."

*Themes and Meanings*

The central theme of "Frazer Avenue" is cultural survival. From its opening passage, the narrator's disdain for his former neighborhood and its inhabitants is evident. He and his family belong to the class of "good Mexicans" who have moved away. He now considers himself "different" from the others and admittedly avoids "anything that links me to these people and this place."

In a new class in his predominantly middle-class neighborhood, he once dreaded hearing his name being read aloud during roll call because it exposed his heritage. Since then, evidently, he has made every effort to avoid being labeled a Mexican. Not surprisingly, he acknowledges that he does not know who he really is: "My cultural identity had been broken into little pieces." He senses that he may not belong anywhere, that he fits into neither the middle-class neighborhood nor the barrio. He wishes the Latinos well in their political struggle, but he cannot identify with them.

The narrator's dislike for his own people is evident. They are beings that he has "scraped off his skin." Success in college gives him the luxury to feel superior to them. He even admits to being ashamed of his own parents, claiming that "the forefathers that mattered were from England." At his grandmother's birthday party, he mingles as little as possible with his relatives and detests "their gawky stares."

Throughout the narrative, it is clear that the central character is always fleeing or hiding from something. He first runs from his childhood friends when they taunt him for not breaking streetlights. He then flees from the barrio. In his new neighborhood, he runs away when his friend, John Velasco, is caught and beaten. Later still, he runs from his girlfriend. In reality, however, he is running from himself—a flight that has left him "weary and exhausted."

Nevertheless, the narrator remembers stories that his grandmother told him about her childhood village in Mexico. It was a place where young men hung around street corners, not committing acts of vandalism but playing checkers. Immediately after she dies, the stories that she once told him about Mexico flood his memory. Realizing that he saw something positive in her just before she died, he now misses the unconditional love that she had for him. The village of her youth calls out to him; when he answers "South" to his uncle's query about where he is going, it appears to be the first time in his life that, instead of running away from himself, he is prepared to search for his true identity.

*Style and Technique*

In order to convey the disdain that his central character feels for other Mexicans, Guy García begins "Frazer Avenue" by applying the simile of "dazed cockroaches" to the customers of Millie's bar who pour on to the street after a wild night. The undesirable Mexicans whom the narrator remembers moving into the neighborhood are called *marranos* (pigs). Throughout the story the narrator views Mexicans from a high perch. However, in order to provide balance, García offers brief glimpses of moments when the protagonist seems envious of these people who are secure in their identities even though they will leave no mark on the world.

All this is achieved through an interior monologue in which the central character recalls his life up to the moment of his grandmother's death, which is also the moment of his awakening and of his self-discovery. The manner in which the story is structured—the telling of the present with recollections of the past inserted throughout—intensifies the feelings of alienation, frustration, and confusion that the narrator experiences. The single word that concludes the story, "South," has the impact of allowing the reader to share in the moment in which the character reclaims his culture and begins to discover his identity.

*Silvio Sirias*

# THE FRESHEST BOY

*Author:* F. Scott Fitzgerald (1896-1940)
*Type of plot:* Psychological
*Time of plot:* The 1920's
*Locale:* A train from the Midwest to St. Regis, the St. Regis school for boys in Eastchester, and New York City
*First published:* 1935

> *Principal characters:*
> BASIL T. LEE, a middle-class boy in a rich boys' school who begins as a smart aleck
> DR. BACON, the not very tactful headmaster of St. Regis
> LEWIS CRUM, a fellow Midwesterner who attends St. Regis
> BUGS BROWN, a slightly insane classmate
> FAT GASPAR, an amiable but easily influenced classmate
> TREADWAY, Basil's short-term roommate
> MR. ROONEY, the football coach and Basil's chaperon into New York City

*The Story*

Basil T. Lee, the fifteen-year-old protagonist of "The Freshest Boy," is first introduced to the reader as the swashbuckling hero in the scenario of his escape into fantasy from the lonely, hostile reality of the prestigious St. Regis school for very rich boys. This scene is contrasted with an account of Basil's train ride from the Midwest to St. Regis and his anticipation of what his life at the school will be like. He has been so steeped in the tradition of attending an Eastern boys' school that "he had a glad feeling of recognition and familiarity. Indeed, it was with some sense of doing the appropriate thing, having the traditional rough-house, that he had thrown Lewis's comb off the train at Milwaukee last night for no reason at all." On this trip, Lewis, a fellow student from the Midwest, reminds Basil that his reputation at his former school was that of being "a little fresh," and Basil resolves to make a new start, fantasizing about being a football hero.

At school, Basil is embarrassed that he is not from a wealthy family and writes his mother, stating, "All the boys have a bigger allowance than me." Basil feels humiliated when Dr. Bacon, the headmaster, confronts him with his poor grades and emphasizes the Lees' financial sacrifice in sending him to St. Regis. These humiliations are made more difficult to bear by the fact that Basil is aware that he is the least popular boy in school. Within the first few weeks he has gained the nickname of "Bossy" and has been involved in several fights. Consequently, it is November before the headmaster agrees to let Basil go into New York City for the weekend, and then only on the condition that he find two other boys to accompany him, which proves an impossible task. Basil sneaks off the grounds to find the only three boys who might even consider going with him. He finds Bugs Brown, who is so strange that he can associate only with "boys younger than himself, who were without the prejudices of their elders." An appointment with his psychiatrist prevents Bugs from accepting. Fat Gaspar, a generally amiable boy, gives in to peer pressure, and rather than tell Basil that he cannot go to New York City, he laughs at him and tells him that he does not want to go. Basil finally locates Treadway, his new roommate, who also rejects Basil's offer: "Like Fat Gaspar, rather than acknowledge himself eligible to such an intimate request, he preferred to cut their friendly relations short." Emphasizing Basil's isolation, Treadway packs up and moves out, leaving Basil utterly alone. In the midst of flagrant hostility, Basil again escapes into fantasy, focusing on the poster girls and identifying with Babette, crying, "Poor little Babette!" His tears are really for himself.

Mr. Rooney, the football coach, finally agrees to take Basil into New York City, not out of the goodness of his heart but because he also wants to get away from the stifling environment of the school. Mr. Rooney chides Basil, saying, "You oughtn't to get so fresh all the time," and continues by accusing him of being a coward while playing football. He lectures Basil mercilessly, but on remembering that he is going to have to trust Basil to keep quiet about his activities in New York City, he relents. When they arrive in New York City, Mr. Rooney goes off and gets drunk while Basil attends a Broadway play. Before the play, Basil discovers a way out of his misery by reading his mother's letter, in which she presents the opportunity for him to go to school abroad. Basil is tempted by this offer of escape and fantasizes about what he will say and how he will act toward his schoolmates, concluding that "he need no longer hate them, for they were impotent shadows in the stationary world that he was sliding away from, sliding past, waving his hand."

The play that Basil attends has a typical plot: Boy and girl meet, fall in love, face a few minor problems, resolve them, and live happily ever after. Basil imagines that life is like that and believes that he, too, has reached a happy ending to his school problem. Reality forces itself on him, however, as after the play he follows the beautiful actress and her lover, the Yale football captain, and overhears their conversation. Her decision to marry her benefactor because he has done so much for her career shatters Basil's belief in easy answers in life; he realizes that "life for everybody was a struggle, sometimes magnificent from a distance, but always difficult and surprisingly simple and a little sad."

Basil finally locates Mr. Rooney, who is very drunk, and manages to get him on the train and back to school. These instances of others' problems and reactions illustrate to Basil that one cannot escape from life. "Suddenly Basil realized that he wasn't going to Europe. He could not forgo the molding of his own destiny just to alleviate a few months of pain." He starts over at St. Regis, continuing to make some errors, but the other boys sense his new attitude, his willingness to accept responsibility for his actions, and with his new maturity he gradually becomes accepted; his new status is confirmed when Brick Wales, a former enemy, assigns him a nickname (Lee-y) during a basketball game.

*Themes and Meanings*

Two dominant themes in F. Scott Fitzgerald's works are the arrogance of the rich and the rite of passage from adolescence to adulthood. Both these themes are reflections of Fitzgerald's own experiences as a young man whose social position exposed him to the manners and expectations of the very rich without providing the means to participate directly and effectively in their way of life. Of particular importance is the positive outcome of the story. Basil, the middle-class protagonist, matures and accepts responsibility, a resolution that contrasts with Fitzgerald's stories in which the protagonists are reared in wealth and fail to mature. It was Fitzgerald's belief that the wealthy fail because of their sense of superiority to all others.

Basil has been indoctrinated about and had idealized life among the rich, specifically life at an elite boys' school. He knows that he is not really one of them and hence mimics their arrogance, creating a protective facade for his insecurity. Sensing his vulnerability, the other boys see that he does not really believe in his own superiority as those who have been reared in wealthy families do. They perceive him as a fraud, and with the cruelty typical of children they ridicule and ostracize him.

Basil cannot understand why there is such a contrast between his life, in which everything goes wrong, and the play and his fantasies, in which everything turns out right. This confusion reflects naïveté rather than arrogance; he is unaware, until he witnesses the scene between the actress and the football star, that everyone has problems. Once he realizes that he is not alone in his misery, he is able to become more objective, to face and analyze reality and accept responsibility. In short, he matures because of his experiences, and through his subsequent refusal to escape, he develops a self-respect that cannot be destroyed by his classmates. Once they recognize that he is no longer vulnerable, they begin to accept him. His facade of arrogance is replaced by a real strength of character that makes him actually superior to the rich boys around him.

*Style and Technique*

To develop the psychological realism of "The Freshest Boy," Fitzgerald employs a third-person omniscient point of view to delve into the minds of his characters, particularly focusing on the turmoil of the adolescent boy as he struggles to establish his identity in a hostile environment.

The use of fantasy elements does not remove this story from the realm of psychological realism, for Basil's fantasies are ones common to adolescence. Basil alternately sees himself as hero and victim, but the fantasies do allow him to escape, and they thereby emphasize for the reader the real trauma of Basil's life at school, where he feels that he has no control over his life.

Fitzgerald further emphasizes his theme of the difficulties of growing up by his use of Lewis as a foil to Basil. Basil's innocent idealization of life at a rich boys' school is contrasted to Lewis's more experienced and realistic view of the regimentation that actually exists.

Another contrast between the real and the idealized is developed when Basil visits New York City. The happy ending of the play represents Basil's naïve belief in easy solutions, while the real-life scene between the actress and her lover illustrates to Basil that in reality life consists of difficult and sometimes painful situations that are not easily resolved.

Fitzgerald effectively uses letters to illustrate Basil's dilemma and to forward the plot. Basil's letter to his mother provides a concise summation of his psychological state, while his mother's letter in return prompts his evaluation of his circumstances and, by offering him an alternative, makes his decision to stay at St. Regis a matter of mature choice rather than mere necessity.

*Jane B. Weedman*

# A FRIEND OF KAFKA

*Author:* Isaac Bashevis Singer (1904-1991)
*Type of plot:* Sketch
*Time of plot:* The early 1930's
*Locale:* Warsaw
*First published:* 1968

### Principal characters:

THE NARRATOR, a fledgling writer
JACQES (JANKEL) KOHN, a former Yiddish actor and onetime friend of Kafka
THE COUNTESS, a widowed aristocrat
BAMBERG, a decayed writer

*The Story*

Jacques Kohn repeatedly borrows money from the narrator, who willingly lends it to him because he wants Kohn's friendship. Although Kohn was once an important actor, the narrator values him more for his literary and cultural associations. Supposedly, Kohn was the first to recognize Franz Kafka's talent, and he has corresponded with other important figures: Marc Chagall, Stefan Zweig, and Martin Buber. As the narrator's cultural guide, Kohn shows him his letters and photographs, and he even arranges for him to meet Madam Tschissik, with whom Kohn performed and whom Kafka allegedly loved.

For the narrator, then, Kohn is an important link to European art and literature. For Kohn, the narrator is not only a source of money but also an audience, to whom he recounts the adventures of his younger days, such as taking Kafka to a brothel or attending an orgy with a number of writers, including the decayed writer Bamberg. As these examples indicate, Kohn's stories often are sexual, even though he is now impotent and claims that he does not find women attractive.

He does, however, have another encounter with a woman. One winter night he hears a banging at his door and the sound of a woman crying. The woman, a widowed countess, pleads with Kohn to let her hide in his apartment until morning; she has been visiting her lover in Kohn's building, but the man attempted to kill her in a fit of jealousy. Kohn points out that his apartment is unheated and that he can offer scant protection should her lover follow her and find them together.

Waving aside all objections, she insists on remaining with Kohn and even on sleeping with him. To his surprise, he is able to make love to her; the next morning, before she leaves, she kisses him and urges him to call her. Their relationship has continued, but Kohn has never tried to sleep with her again. He agrees with the Talmudic saying, "A miracle doesn't happen every day."

*Themes and Meanings*

Kohn does not regard this recent amatory adventure as the work of some benevolent Cupid. Instead, he views it as merely another move by the "tough angel" who is playing chess with him for his life. Kohn knows that this opponent will win finally, but Kohn seeks to prolong the game. Fate, as Kohn elsewhere names his adversary, also enjoys playing; he does not want to kill Kohn too quickly. "Break the keg, but don't let the wine run out" is the aim of Fate.

Fate tortures Kohn with poverty, sickness, despair, and cold. He brings the countess to Kohn's door not to give Kohn pleasure but to torment and threaten him: As Kohn had feared, the countess's lover does come after her. He pounds and kicks on the door, which barely holds. Kohn considers saying the prayer of the dying and is restrained only by his refusal to give his "mocking opponent" further pleasure from the situation.

However, if man is pitted against an opponent he cannot beat, he remains a player rather than a pawn; he is not totally powerless. Thus, one bitterly cold night Kohn loses the key to his apartment. The janitor has no spare, so it appears that Kohn will have to spend the night outside. His opponent has made a shrewd move. Kohn, though, has the perfect response. If Fate wants to kill him with pneumonia, Kohn will not object. Then the game will end. Almost immediately Kohn finds his key, for his "partner wants to play a slow game."

One of the traditional proofs for the existence of God is the orderliness of the world. Isaac Bashevis Singer points out that man lives in the midst of chaos. Kohn refers to *The Entropy of Reason* by a Dr. Mitzkin and suggests that the author might have written a sequel as well, *The Entropy of Passion*. Chaos, not order, is the law of nature. However, that chaos may be a proof of God's existence. As Kohn says, if there is no God, "Who is playing all these games?"

Kohn's life is only one illustration of the entropy that rules the world, of the tendency of all things to lose their energy and disintegrate. Another is Bamberg, "a corpse refusing to rest in its grave." Even when he dances, he appears to be asleep. The orgy that Bamberg attends with Kohn disintegrates into a pseudointellectual discussion and breaks up when Bamberg becomes ill. Kafka's visit to the brothel also remains unconsummated as he, like Bamberg, gets sick. Dr. Mitzkin claims that "true wisdom can only be reached through passion," but he himself is incapable of passion.

For Singer, sex is a powerful positive force. The impotence of his characters—their inability to procreate—becomes a symbol of their inability to create and highlights the chaos in the world of the story.

However, as this world is uncreated, it does not return to nothingness. Kohn's story remains, as does the narrator's retelling of that story. Dr. Mitzkin had predicted that in the end "man will . . . eat words, drink words, marry words, poison himself with words," yet that end is also a beginning, as Kohn observes in quoting the first words of the Gospel of John: "In the beginning was the Logos."

Whatever else man loses, he retains his language, the language that can turn "a piece of clay into a living thing," the language that can "create a world." The old writers have lost their abilities, but the numerous literary references in the story show that their medium remains powerful. Kafka has died, but his work endures and even lends importance to a faded actress. "A Friend of Kafka" suggests that in an absurd world, the word may be a person's only weapon against entropy.

## Style and Technique

This is one of Singer's autobiographical stories. The first-person narrator is a struggling young writer who frequents a Warsaw literary club, as Singer did before he left Poland. At the same time, Singer does alter his character for artistic ends. The narrator is shy around women, which Singer never was, because Singer wants to stress the lack of sexual energy in the story.

Singer uses the first-person narrative as a frame for a story-within-a-story, the account of Kohn's various adventures. Like Kohn's life, his account is chaotic: In four paragraphs he rambles from the countess to Kafka to Bamberg to a request for the loan of a zloty. When the narrator asks, "Did the countess ever call you?" Kohn outlines Dr. Mitzkin's philosophy before responding.

This lack of organization, this inability to focus one's efforts for creative ends, is highlighted at the conclusion of the story. Kohn is eager to introduce the narrator to Madame Tschissik—she is even waiting in the next room—yet the meeting never takes place. Instead, Kohn borrows money to go home and ends his tale with a question that has no answer. Entropy has conquered.

*Joseph Rosenblum*

# FROG DANCES

*Author:* Stephen Dixon (1936-     )
*Type of plot:* Psychological
*Time of plot:* The 1960's to 1980's
*Locale:* New York City
*First published:* 1986

### Principal characters:

HOWARD TETCH, a fiction writer and college teacher in search of
the perfect wife

DENISE, his eventual wife

FLORA SELENIKA, a college student with whom he has a short
affair

FRANCINE, a lawyer whom he dates

## The Story

Howard Tetch, a writer and college teacher of writing, is walking down a street in New York City when he accidentally looks in a window and sees a man about his age dancing around the room holding in his arms a two- or three-month-old baby. The music to which he is dancing is the slow movement of a Gustav Mahler symphony. The scene's depiction of a father's perfect moment with his child and the beauty of the paternal dance of love stirs Howard so profoundly that he feels impelled to reproduce it in his own life. Determined to reify that edenic moment in his own life, Howard sets off on a quest to make himself into a happily married husband and father.

He immediately calls three of his friends and boldly asks them to keep an eye out for any available women and, if possible, to invite him to events where he can meet them. The first woman he meets confesses that she knows that he saw a man dancing with his baby and decided that he wanted to be that man. He never calls her again. He meets a second woman at a party; they go to dinner, have sex, and decide not to see each other again because she is dating several men and does not want to tie herself down to any one man. Howard next sees a woman in line for a movie, engages her in conversation, and begins an affair with her. His irksome little habits, such as hanging his underpants to dry out in her bathroom and his refusal to shave before they go to bed, finally make the relationship an impossible one.

Howard next meets an attractive woman at an art show. They spend considerable time together, but she is hesitant to engage in sex with him. He explains that he cares deeply for her but for him love and sex are synonymous. When she refuses to go to bed with him, he finally ends the relationship. After he is invited to another university to read a colleague's students' creative work, he meets and becomes obsessed with a sexually attractive young woman, Flora Selenika, a student he was specifically advised to avoid by his host. After a drunken affair that he barely remembers, he thinks he has fallen in love with her. She insists that their relationship can never work: "No, every-thing's too split apart. Not only where we live but the age and cultural differences. You're as nice as they come—sweet, smart and silly—but what you want for us is un-attainable."

Crestfallen, Howard decides to look for a woman more his own age and meets Denise at a picnic. Although he finds her intelligent and sensitive, he worries that her hips are too wide and will widen with age, and her teeth are not perfect. After dating Francine, a yuppie lawyer who has poor taste in art, furniture, and just about every-thing else, he calls Denise after having had too many drinks. She firmly suggests that he call her when he is sober. He then considers visiting a whorehouse, but the recur-ring image of the happy father dancing with his baby persists in his memory to remind him of his quest for the perfect mate. He rejects the idea of paying for sex and calls Denise again. He sees her anew—her hips are fine and her teeth are straight enough. He also begins to see how intelligent she is—almost too intelligent, but he rejects such self-defeating, perfectionist thoughts. After a normal courting process, they marry and she has a baby. The story concludes happily with Howard dancing around a room with his baby to the last movement of Jean Sibelius's Fifth Symphony. He realizes that he has reified that luminous scene from two years earlier that set him on his adventure to find a mate and become that happy, contented father.

*Themes and Meanings*

Stephen Dixon has taken one of the oldest plot ideas in Western literature and given it a refreshingly urbanized setting and treatment: a young man's call to adventure after he has experienced a spiritual vision that lucidly articulates what he needs to find to make him happy and fulfilled. In "Frog Dances," Dixon takes a middle-aged man em-barking on his spiritual journey almost too late in life. Dixon, who habitually uses the elements of chance to structure his narratives, shows Howard Tetch accidentally look-ing through a window as he casually walks down a street in Manhattan. The scene of a father holding a tiny infant in his arms and dancing around the room to the slow move-ment of a Gustav Mahler symphony bespeaks a blissful, edenic contentment that is so compelling that it constitutes a vision of the ideal that Howard must pursue. That vi-sion becomes for Howard an ideal that he must realize in a literal way or he will never become a fully integrated human being. Howard finally understands what is missing in his life—love, a wife, and a family. The image of the dance as a ritual celebrating the unity of all of life's activities and expectations drives him to find a mate who can fill in the emptiness of his life.

The story is a case study of the overly analytical professor who has virtually lost any feeling for the simpler and more profound yearnings of the human soul. Howard's academic mind, like that of T. S. Eliot's neurasthenic J. Alfred Prufrock, another vic-tim of a similar kind of paralysis of analysis, carries him further into the abstract pro-cesses of his own mind and separates him from the simple but fulfilling joys of mar-ried life. Once he is reengaged with his feelings by the image of the dancing father, he is able to enter the human race, meet Denise, and fulfill the ideal that his quest had proposed for him. Dixon's story suggests that the imagination knows what it needs to grow and flourish, and if one follows it and the authentic feelings surrounding those compelling, visionary images, one will find those necessary ingredients that will make one's life whole and happy.

## Style and Technique

Dixon's stories often use the postmodernist technique of demonstrating what is absent as a method of motivating his protagonists to go in search of something to fill in the emptiness. The desperate need to become that dancing father he accidentally has seen sets Howard in motion so that all of his actions conform to the demands of that imperative. Both the humor and the pathos of the story, although primarily a comic quest, come from how absolutely Howard adheres to his search for a woman who can produce that child.

Another comic technique used in this story, and Dixon's stories generally, is the way in which Howard's overworked mind creates complications where previously there were none. A simple matter of attempting to find the perfect mate becomes, for Howard, a complex process of judging hip width, skin quality, and his future wife's capacity to breed healthy babies. Much of the humor of the story evolves from the almost slapstick desperation of Howard's relentless quest for the future mother of his children. Once the child is born, it enables Howard to generate his own personal Eden and becomes the central image that generated his initial journey.

Dixon's works do not rigidly adhere to linear plots; rather, they follow circles that become cycles that move his characters into periods of both psychological and emotional growth or decline. Dixon's open imagination enables him to take virtually any narrative and move it in any direction, because his stories are process parables that demonstrate the infinitely varied paths the active imagination may take in finding or creating meaning in any human activity.

*Patrick Meanor*

# FUNES, THE MEMORIOUS

*Author:* Jorge Luis Borges (1899-1986)
*Type of plot:* Fantasy
*Time of plot:* The 1880's
*Locale:* The eastern shore of the Uruguay River, in Uruguay
*First published:* "Funes el memorioso," 1944 (English translation, 1962)

> *Principal characters:*
> IRENEO FUNES, the man cursed with perfect memory
> THE NARRATOR

*The Story*

The history of the unfortunate Ireneo Funes is told by an unnamed narrator who, hearing of Funes's death, determines to put something into print about a very remarkable and, in one sense, disquieting man. Although he encountered Funes not more than three times, each meeting stamped itself on the narrator's memory.

The first, he tells the reader, was in February or March of 1884: He and his cousin were riding on horseback to his family's farm. As they rode along, hurrying to outpace a storm, they rode in a lane between high walls. On the top of one of the brick walls appeared an Indian boy. The narrator's cousin asked the boy what the time was, and the boy replied, "In ten minutes it will be eight o'clock." The cousin later explained, with some pride in a local curiosity, that the boy, Ireneo Funes, had the peculiar talent of always knowing the exact time without a watch.

Several times in the years that follow, the narrator asks about "the chronometer Funes," whenever he is in the area. In 1887, he hears that Funes has been thrown from a horse and crippled; unable to walk, he has become a recluse. The narrator glimpses him several times, but there is something strange about each occasion. He sees Funes behind a grilled window in the boy's house, unmoving each time, once with his eyes closed, once simply absorbed in smelling a blossom of lavender.

On a subsequent visit to the farm, the narrator brings along several books of Latin, the study of which he is beginning. During his visit, he receives a letter from Funes, asking if he might borrow one of the Latin texts and a dictionary. The narrator sends the books with some amusement that the small-town youth would think he could teach himself Latin with no more help than a dictionary. He forgets about the loan until he receives a telegram from Buenos Aires informing him that he must return immediately. He goes to the small ranch of Funes's mother to retrieve his books.

When he arrives, the woman tells him that Funes is in his room and cautions him not to be surprised to find him in the dark. Making his way to the room, the narrator overhears Funes reading—in Latin—from the book he has lent him. He enters Funes's room, and they begin a conversation that lasts until dawn.

Much to his surprise, the narrator discovers that Funes has indeed mastered even conversational Latin. They discuss the borrowed book, the Roman author Pliny's *Historian naturalis* (77 C.E.; *The Historie of the World*, 1601; better known as *Natural History*), which tells in one section of amazing feats of memory: Cyrus, the king of Persia, knowing each of his soldiers' names, and the like. Funes is astonished that anyone should think that such things were remarkable. He offers his own experience as an argument.

Funes says that until he was thrown from horseback, he was "blind, deaf-mute, somnambulistic, memoryless." The narrator disagrees, pointing out Funes's earlier talent with the time, but Funes's prior life now seems dreamlike to him. Now he finds that he has the ability to remember in every detail everything that he has ever experienced: every sound, every sight, every smell, as intensely and clearly as normal people do on only the most vivid of occasions. He thinks that his crippling was a small price to pay for an infallible memory. However, there are hints that even Funes does not think of his new mental powers as a complete blessing: Although he boasts that he has in himself more memories than all men have had through history, he also compares his memory to a garbage disposal. The narrator, writing the account years later, thinks of film and the phonograph, two recording devices that did not exist when Funes lived, yet which even in their exact preserving of history are not superior to this one individual.

The mental state of Funes is almost incomprehensible to the narrator as he tries to understand what it would be like to remember every leaf on every tree, not only each time he saw it but also each time he imagined it as well. So oppressive is the power of his memory that Funes finds it hard to sleep; the darkened room, the reader comes to understand, helps him relax because it limits the amount of perception available to him.

At the climax of the story, dawn comes, and the narrator first sees Funes's face, "more ancient than Egypt," although Funes is only nineteen years old. With alarm, the narrator realizes that his every word and gesture will live indelibly in the youth's memory, and he begins to fear. What would the man's memory carry at the end of a long life? The narrator never finds out: In 1889, at the age of twenty-one, Funes dies.

### Themes and Meanings

In a foreword to the publication of *Ficciones* in 1944, Jorge Luis Borges remarked of "Funes, the Memorious" only that it was "a long metaphor for insomnia." As such, it is certainly a strikingly apt metaphor, for often when trying unsuccessfully to sleep, one's memories press insistently to the front of consciousness, and Borges did suffer from insomnia. A poem he wrote around the year 1936 speaks of his mind as "an incessant mirror" which multiplies the remembered details of life around him as he waits for sleep. Critics, however, have been reluctant to consider the story only a "metaphor for insomnia"; some have seen in the work a reflection of Borges's life at a particularly difficult time when his work as a writer seemed unappreciated, when he may well have considered himself a solitary observer of the world.

There is a second theme in the story, a much more general one whose irony may have appealed to Borges: the nature of thought. For all of Funes's accomplishments—he had learned English, French, Portuguese, and Latin in addition to his native Spanish—the narrator doubts that he was capable of much thought. As the narrator points out, thought depends on a paradox: The ability to generalize and to abstract requires that one forget the differences between things and concentrate on the similarities. Funes, however, never forgets. Because his memory forces details on him so violently, Funes finds it almost impossible to overlook the differences between things. His memory of the individual moment is so vivid, he is unable to generalize. The narrator states that Funes not only found it hard to understand how a word such as "dog" could represent any member of the species but also was bothered that the same name could be used for the same dog seen from different perspectives or at different times during the day. As the narrator says, "His own face in the mirror, his own hands, surprised him on every occasion."

In a short story, it is neither possible nor desirable to present a theory of intellection, yet the theme of "Funes, the Memorious" argues that abstract thought may be hampered by a retentive memory. That generalization, the basis of reasoning, requires that a person step away from the particular and the concrete details of experience.

*Style and Technique*

From the very beginning of the story, the memories of the narrator and Funes are contrasted in a cleverly understated way. The narrator is using his memory of the past to write the memoir, but unlike Funes, he can only approximate forgotten details: no exact dates here—"sometime in March or February of the year '84." This was the date of their first meeting. Unlike the narrator, however, when Funes writes to borrow the Latin book, he refers to their encounter "on the seventh day of February of the year '84." A little later in the story, just before he describes the final conversation with Funes, the narrator apologizes for what is to follow: He says that he will not attempt to reproduce the exact words because almost fifty years have passed. Although he regards his summary as "remote and weak," he can only hope the readers can imagine the original sentences themselves.

Borges followed very faithfully Edgar Allan Poe's maxim that a short story must aim at a single effect, and his stories frequently build slowly to a revelation at the climax that forces the reader to reassess all that has occurred to that point. "Funes, the Memorious" is a fine example of that technique. The whole story leads to the rising of the sun and the sight of Funes's ancient face. The story also illustrates that when the climax has been adequately prepared for, the details of the revelation can speak for themselves: The narrator draws no conclusion about this astonishingly old face on a nineteen-year-old; readers can draw their own conclusions about the burden of being unable to forget.

*Walter E. Meyers*

# THE FUR COAT

*Author:* Seán O'Faoláin (John Francis Whelan, 1900-1991)
*Type of plot:* Social realism
*Time of plot:* 1940
*Locale:* Dublin, Ireland
*First published:* 1948

> *Principal characters:*
> PADDY MAGUIRE, a new parliamentary secretary
> MOLLY MAGUIRE, his wife

*The Story*

Paddy Maguire has just been appointed the parliamentary secretary to the minister for roads and railways, and his wife, Molly, is very proud. Paddy and Molly are in the autumn of their sometimes difficult lives, and they believe it is time to have a bit of comfort in their old age. Their early lives appear to have been difficult. Paddy was in and out of prison during the 1920's because of Irish politics and the revolution, while Molly was left alone to raise the children. Money had been tight, so she needed help from Prisoners' Dependents' funds. Now they have the money and position to enjoy life.

The first thing Molly asks for is a fur coat. Desiring the coat but not wishing to seem extravagant, she wants Paddy to understand that she deserves it because of who she is, rather than his buying her the coat because he attained a position of importance. The distinction between these two points is important to Molly, yet Paddy is oblivious to the potential for conflict.

Molly spends a long time trying to convince Paddy that a fur coat would be practical because she has neither the time nor the clothes to dress appropriately for the parties and receptions that they will now have to attend. With a fur coat, she could look respectable despite whatever dress or suit she wears underneath; in her own mind, Molly believes that she can justify the fur coat because she would not spend money on new clothes, and she would not take time away from the house or the family to get ready for events. At first Paddy thinks that a fur coat is a grand idea and is excited about the possibility of Molly parading around with something special on her shoulders for people to see. He has achieved a distinguished position and can afford to give his wife a luxurious token. Now, however, he believes that a fur coat is not grand, but useful, and is no longer interested in the conversation. He tells Molly to buy the coat because it will keep her warm. This is not good enough for Molly, because she believes that Paddy still does not understand that she deserves the coat, and she still detects "a touch of the bravo, as if he was still feeling himself a great fellow" for offering to buy the coat. Molly is unable to drop the discussion of the fur coat. She wants the coat more than anything but is powerless to accept it. Because Molly appears to have an elaborate understanding of the different types of furs, Paddy questions how long she has desired such a coat. This flusters Molly; whenever he gets close to the truth, she gets angry.

Paddy finally insists it is time for Molly to decide if she is going to get the fur coat. She jumps up, throws a basket at him, and screams, "Stop it! I told you I don't want a fur coat! And you don't want me to get a fur coat! You're too mean, that's what it is!" The conversation about the coat finally ends: Molly is in her room sobbing, and Paddy is sitting at his table cold with anger. Paddy has remained calm throughout the many discussions about the coat but being called mean is more than he can tolerate.

Paddy and Molly do not speak for three days; on the morning of the fourth day, Molly finds a check for 150 pounds, which makes her heart leap. Unfortunately, the good feeling leaves immediately, but it makes her realize that the problem is not with Paddy as much as with herself. The story ends with Molly knowing that she wants a coat more than anything but also knowing that she will never have it. The reason for the internal conflict within Molly is not obvious to either Paddy or Molly.

*Themes and Meanings*

Seán O'Faoláin provides limited detail and description about Paddy and Molly's lives. The only thing that he reveals about their earlier lives is that "the years had polished her hard—politics, revolution, husband in and out of prison, children reared with the help of relatives and Prisoners' Dependents' funds. You could see the years on her fingertips, too, too pink, too coarse, and in her diamond-bright eyes." In these two sentences O'Faoláin presents an image of the many young couples who spent time apart while the husbands fought for an independent Ireland. O'Faoláin relies on their conversation and their actions to reveal the characteristics they both now possess. They are complex, contradictory, and realistic.

The author's disappointment with the politics of Ireland and the inflexibility of the Roman Catholic Church is also subtly woven throughout the story by the actions of Paddy and Molly. Rather than explicitly discussing the rigidity of the church or the pain and suffering of Irish politics, he relies on the sophistication of the reader to understand the root of Molly's guilt about accepting the fur coat and Paddy's reaction to being called mean.

O'Faoláin tries to appeal to a complex mass of emotion, sensory experience, and acceptable ideas that he presumes are clear in the reader's mind. He tries to manipulate the reader so that a little will do a lot in his or her imagination, and he assumes that the reader is able to connect and understand what he is doing. Paddy and Molly know each other about as well as two people can know each other, but Paddy does not realize that Molly needs to be told that she deserves the coat. On the other hand, Molly, herself, is not sure why she cannot accept the coat. O'Faoláin implies or suggests situations and relies on the reader's experiences with life and human nature to understand what is not said.

*Style and Technique*

O'Faoláin uses the fur coat as a symbol, a tool to portray many subtleties, while apparently discussing only one subject. He looks at the differences between the sexes, he looks at politics and religion, but what he actually focuses on is human nature. He believes that human nature is "so various, so complex, so contradictory, so subtle, so amusing and so unexpected." The symbol represents more than Paddy's being an inconsiderate male or Molly's being an undeserving female. For Paddy, the fur coat symbolizes his achievement: He now can give his wife luxuries. For Molly, the coat symbolizes her expectations from life: She is a lady who deserves respectable things. The problem with their conversations is that Molly never actually says what she really means, and Paddy never actually listens to what she tries to say. Paddy continuously tells Molly to buy the coat, never realizing that she is constantly feeling the need to defend her request. Molly never actually tells Paddy that she deserves the coat but tries to get him to reach that conclusion on his own.

O'Faoláin introduces Irish politics without saying what that means to Paddy, who was jailed, and Molly, who was alone raising the children. He introduces religion without explaining what that means to Paddy, who wants Molly to parade down Grafton Street in front of the "painted jades" who never lifted a hand for God or man or Ireland. He also depicts Molly as not being able to accept luxury without guilt or an explanation. "The Fur Coat" is uniquely Irish, filled with O'Faoláin's perception of the Irish temperament.

*Rosanne Fraine Donahue*

# THE FURNISHED ROOM

*Author:* O. Henry (William Sydney Porter, 1862-1910)
*Type of plot:* Psychological
*Time of plot:* 1904
*Locale:* New York City
*First published:* 1904

> *Principal characters:*
> AN UNNAMED YOUNG MAN in search of his missing sweetheart
> MISS ELOISE VASHNER, the missing young lady
> MRS. PURDY, the landlady of a boardinghouse

*The Story*

An ordinary young man moves among the proliferation of boardinghouses on the West Side, determinedly on the prowl for a vacant room. Again and again, he tries each of the clustered homes on the brownstone street. On his twelfth attempt, one Mrs. Purdy, an unwholesome appearing housekeeper, answers. She invites this prospective tenant into her home to inspect a recently vacated room. Happy after so many disappointments, the young man follows the woman into an ambience of foul and tainted air, a house reinforcing the hovering gloom he had experienced on the streets. Mrs. Purdy chatters constantly in praise of the furnished room that he is about to see, shrewdly emphasizing its positive attributes: a useful dresser, chairs and tables, plenty of closet space, and a convenient gas connection. She also stresses the class of her operation by telling the young man about the elegant tenants who had recently occupied this room. An upstanding husband and wife vaudeville team—Sprowls and Mooney—recently lodged there, and a framed wedding certificate over the dresser attests the house's respectability. This is important, as Purdy's house is situated alongside the theater district and most theater people, unreliable and unpredictable, come and go, even apparently stable ones. Thus, a vacant furnished room is luckily available at this moment in this eminently respectable boardinghouse. Swayed by the landlady's persuasive presentation but exhibiting no great joy, the young man takes the room and carefully counts out his payment money.

As the satisfied Mrs. Purdy is about to leave, the young man haltingly asks a question, one he has apparently put forth many times in preceding days to other landladies: Has Mrs. Purdy ever rented a room to a Miss Eloise Vashner, a would-be singer looking for a stage career? Eloise is a slim, fair girl with a distinctive dark mole near her left eyebrow. The answer is a quiet but positive no. Mrs. Purdy leaves her guest alone in his furnished quarters to reflect on his strange surroundings and the fruitless, ceaseless, five-month search he has conducted to find his love, Eloise, who had been attracted by the call of glamorous Broadway and its dazzling opportunities. Following the footsteps of many another small-town woman intent on fame and fortune in the theater, she had vanished into the city's "monstrous quicksand." He must now be on her trail; there is an ineffable sense that she is nearby, perhaps even waiting.

The sad young man sits inert on a chair surrounded by ragged upholstery; trifling, sentimental pictures; stray playing cards; and soiled throw rugs. The room exudes noxious fumes. He tries to extract some information and meaning from this threadbare ambience. The furniture is chipped and bruised, dull and broken. The mirror is nicked and scratched. The couch is distorted by bulging springs. The mantel is cracked. A sense of malice and injury is reflected in the room. There is even a threatening quality, ominously suggested by smudged fingerprints on the wall, ugly stains on the scraped wallpaper, and the complete tawdriness of his furnished room, further exacerbated by sounds impinging on his sensibilities from the outside: doors banging, voices raucously raised, dice rattling, cats yowling, elevated trains roaring, a fugitive banjo strumming discordant ragtime. All is cold, dank, musty. Wearily he regards the essence of mildew and listens to the sounds of dissonance.

Suddenly and unaccountably, the furnished room seems to fill with the sensuous, sweet, pungent fragrance of mignonette. The aroma apparently is familiar to the tenant, for he speaks to the emptiness about him: "What, dear?" He believes he has been called to action by an invisible presence. Confused and startled, he reaches out his arms as if to feel or grasp the reality of his missing beloved. She is, he dreamily feels, in this very room. Momentarily, he is jolted from his pleasing vision; aroused from lethargy, he frenziedly bolts around the room frantically looking, inspecting, ransacking. Like a madman, he darts about as if driven by a demon. He cries out. He is certain that of all the furnished rooms on the West Side of New York, Eloise Vashner has been in this one. He tears about, convinced that he is on the verge of a vital discovery, a moonstruck detective about to pounce on the final clue he knows is at hand. "Yes, dear!" he calls as he roots about, coming up with a torn handkerchief, an old theater program, a few odd buttons, a pawnbroker's card—all paraphernalia suggestive but inconclusive. Nevertheless, he knows that his love is nearby.

He dashes from the haunted room to accost his landlady, trying hard to contain his excitement. He quizzes her pointedly on the identities and appearances of all recent female tenants of the furnished room. She responds easily and calmly: Miss Sprowls was short and stout, and her real name was Missis Mooney; Missis Crowder had two children. Other tenants for the past year had been, sad to say, men. Deflated and discouraged, the young man creeps back to the fragrant room, but its atmosphere has changed. The aroma of mignonette has left; all is dead. With hope gone, the disappointed young man methodically cuts up his bedsheets, stuffs the material tightly into all crevices and window sills, extinguishes the gaslight, then turns the gas jet fully on again and lays himself peacefully on the bed to welcome imminent death.

Ironically, while he is upstairs preparing his suicide, Mrs. Purdy and her friend Mrs. McCool are downstairs relaxing in confidential conversation. Mrs. Purdy boasts of her achievement in renting the third-floor room where last week that pretty "slip of a colleen" had killed herself. Both landladies agree on the wisdom of keeping such an event secret, for prospective tenants would be discouraged from renting. It was a sad event, Mrs. Purdy confesses, particularly because that poor girl was so pretty, except for the mole growing by her left eyebrow.

*Themes and Meanings*

O. Henry once said "I would like to live a lifetime on each street of New York. Every house has a drama in it." "The Furnished Room" derives from such a human-interest focus and embodies material of that era when the American city was first beginning to attract significant numbers of adventurous spirits from towns across the country. Thus, the pain of separation, the mystery involved in the quest, and the nervous possibility of misadventure or failure were all thematic subtexts in this tale. The romantic theme of lost love accompanied by a failed, desperate search is intertwined here with the ironic role fate plays in people's fortunes. Here were illustrations and preachments of caution for anyone about to embark on a great urban quest. Glamorous and accessible as the big city might seem, life there is dotted with dangers and pitfalls.

While no profound philosophical underpinnings support the tale's meaning, O. Henry has caught the simple, moving human passions exemplifying the small encounters of everyday life: the missed connections, the inevitable disappointments, the little deceptions. Alongside these considerations, too, is the drama of obsession and its often gloomy results. The young man, propelled by romantic love and driven by the need to find his missing sweetheart, is himself pulled into the quicksand, the melancholia of his persona and the unfounded wildness of his hope ultimately contributing to hallucination and self-destruction. In general, though, O. Henry concentrates on the so-called human comedy: Life is filled with strange twists and turns, its uncharted convolutions driving humanity to strange destinies. One's aspirations, the author suggests, must be tempered by acknowledgment of reality; one's behavior must be governed by common sense. Although the events in the tale seem to emanate from accident and coincidence, the characters might have survived their urban trials had they made rational rather than passionate choices. The dangers of the harsh, unfeeling city and its canny, hardened citizens, therefore, pose a threat to the simple uninitiate that should be heeded.

*Style and Technique*

Heavily descriptive opening paragraphs set a bleak and depressive atmosphere surrounding this tale of life among the ordinary, struggling urban dwellers of New York's seedy lower West Side. A typical O. Henry story, "The Furnished Room" manifests the devices and strategies associated with all his popular tales. Dealing in literary deception and trick endings, he deliberately withholds crucial information in this tale until the very end. Thus, the story depends entirely on event, not at all on character. All pivots and turns on the elements of coincidence and surprise. The author shrewdly parcels out his information to create the unlikely scenario. In lieu of characterization, however, is the inventive trick of creating the furnished room itself as a character, revealing an ability to breathe, to influence, to suggest, to precipitate conversation and reaction. This room manifests a human personality and helps establish an aura of mystery and supernaturalism alongside the young man's psychological disintegration. As he deteriorates and degenerates into the suicidal, the room appears an active participant in the regression. O. Henry's technical skill works to evoke sympathy for the tortured young man caught in the throes of a villainous room whose foreboding pressure appears intent on destroying him.

O. Henry, alternately praised and condemned for employing the artificial over the artistic, artifice over art, infused "The Furnished Room" with familiar journalistic techniques easily recognized and understood in his time as plausible anecdotes of human behavior trapped and controlled by sometimes impassive, often cruel, fate. This story of lost love and thwarted hopes, sentimental and ironic, is directed solely at the reader's heartstrings, requesting simply that one respond with sympathetic passion rather than rational disbelief.

*Abe C. Ravitz*

# GAMES AT TWILIGHT

*Author:* Anita Desai (1937-    )
*Type of plot:* Psychological
*Time of plot:* The 1970's
*Locale:* A large city in India
*First published:* 1978

> *Principal characters:*
> RAVI, a small, sensitive boy, the central character
> RAGHU, his older brother

*The Story*

This title story in Anita Desai's acclaimed collection *Games at Twilight, and Other Stories* (1978) deals with a universal theme of children at play and their fantasies and disillusionment. Desai begins the story objectively from the third-person vantage, but as the action progresses and the tension mounts, she skillfully shifts the narrative focus to the consciousness of the central character, Ravi. The story is remarkable for its insights into child psychology, powerful evocation of atmosphere, vivid imagery, and symbolic use of setting.

The story opens on a hot summer afternoon in an urban house in India. The children who have been kept indoors all day to escape the oppressive heat of the sun feel confined and suffocated, and when they are finally unleashed, they thrill with joy and excitement and decide to play a game of hide-and-seek.

Raghu, being the eldest, is chosen to be "it"—the seeker. All the other children run helter-skelter to find a suitable hiding place. Ravi hides behind the locked garage. When he hears his little brother crying because he has been caught by Raghu, he panics. As Raghu's whistling and the thumping sound of his feet grow louder, in a moment of fright Ravi suddenly slips through a small gap into an abandoned shed next to the garage. From this moment on, the narrative filters through Ravi's consciousness and the reader is brought into the deepest reaches of his psyche.

Though the shed is dark, damp, and spooky, littered with discarded pieces of junk and infested with moths and crawling insects, Ravi finds it a welcome haven. His initial fear of darkness disappears the moment he entertains the thought that no one can possibly find him there. Raghu whistles and whacks his stick in vain around the garage and then moves away. Ravi feels exultant at the thought of not being discovered. In his imagination, he begins to savor the new sensation of his victory over Raghu and the thought of being recognized as a champion in a group of older, bigger children.

He becomes so absorbed in his fantasy that he loses track of time. At twilight, as darkness engulfs the shed, he suddenly realizes that, according to the rules of the game, he has to clinch his victory by dashing to the veranda and touching the "den." To rectify his mistake, he darts out of the shed and rushes toward the house to proclaim his victory. To his great anguish, however, he discovers that the game of hide-and-seek has long been over, that no one has even cared to remember that he was missing, and that now the children are engaged in another game, totally oblivious of his existence. With tears in his eyes, he cries out at the top of his voice to assert his existence and his victory, but no one pays attention to him.

In the last climactic scene, Ravi decides to withdraw from the children's game completely, and in a quick flash of intuitive understanding, he accepts the reality of his situation. Hurt and humiliated, he suddenly becomes aware of his strong sense of alienation, powerlessness, and unimportance.

## Themes and Meanings

Because "Games at Twilight" deals primarily with children at play, its main theme is fantasy versus reality. This theme is symbolically reflected in the title, as the word "twilight" suggests an interplay of light and shadow, blurring the distinction between reality and fantasy. Dealing with a crucial stage in the psychological development of a self-conscious young boy, the story derives its strength from an imaginative application of two postulates of Sigmund Freud's well-known theory that a child's play is motivated by a single wish to be "big and grown up" and that every dream or fantasy is a wish-fulfillment, generated essentially by the desire to correct unsatisfying reality.

Ravi is clearly unsatisfied with the reality of his present circumstances. A sensitive and imaginative child, he feels acutely the inferiority of his status as reflected in the rude and aggressive behavior of his older siblings. On more than one occasion, they remind him that he is nothing but a baby. At the onset of the game, when he proposes that Raghu, being the eldest, become the seeker, a scuffle ensues between them, and Raghu tears his shirt sleeve. He is tired of being kicked and shoved around by his big brother. When he cannot reach the garage key hanging on the nail, he wishes he were big and tall, but he is helplessly aware of the reality that it will be years before he can reach that stage. Similarly, when he thinks of running around the garage if pursued by Raghu, he painfully realizes that his short legs are no match for Raghu's "long, hefty, footballer legs." It is with this frame of mind that he crawls into the shed.

Ravi's retreat into the dark shed is symbolic of his entry into the dark recesses of his unconscious self. As he ventures into this unknown territory, he is surprised at his own audacity. Released from the oppressive fear of being captured by Raghu, he begins to indulge in a fantasy of self-victory, power, and recognition. He clings to his fantasy so long that he overlooks the ultimate requirement for victory.

The clash between fantasy and reality is dramatized at the end of the story. Ravi's ironic correction of his unpleasant situation results in his disgrace and disillusionment. In an archetypal sense, his final resignation, his mood of quiet rebellion, and his decision to withdraw from children's play altogether suggest his awakening into reality and perhaps some kind of realization that he has acted irresponsibly and that to grow up he must pay the price for his daydreaming.

Another theme in the story, as in many of Desai's other fictional works, is alienation of the individual. This theme stems from Ravi's feelings of insecurity and inferiority. He believes that no one takes him seriously or treats him with respect. What hurts him the most is his painful discovery that he has been completely forgotten and left out by his own family. At the end of the story, he feels as if the children are singing his requiem in their mournful chant at the funeral game. His final decision to withdraw completely from children's games is strongly indicative of his acute sense of alienation.

Just as Ravi's fantasizing is an act of unconscious rebellion against the unpleasant reality of his situation, his acceptance of alienation as the human condition is a first step toward the process of individuation, which will eventually lead him to maturity.

### Style and Technique

Desai is a consummate artist known for her distinctive style and rich, sensuous imagery. Her diction is highly formalized and sophisticated. In her own account, though writing comes to her naturally, she works consciously, laboriously, and meticulously to impose a design on the chaotic raw material of life. She regards writing as a process of discovering the truth, which is, for the most part, hidden beneath the surfaces of what people see, say, and do. Because her professed interest in fiction has always been a psychological exploration of the human mind, she does not give much importance to the plot. Instead, she reveals the interior landscapes of her characters' minds.

In "Games at Twilight," Desai provides a psychological exploration of the protagonist's mind by delving into his childhood fears, emotions, perceptions, desires, and thought processes. Her narrative strategy of shifting the omniscient point of view to the limited third-person vantage allows the reader to gain leisurely insights into the inner workings of Ravi's mind.

A distinctive aspect of Desai's style is her use of graphic description and vivid imagery. The story contains a number of memorable descriptions. The opening paragraph describes the oppressive and suffocating environment in the house. The second and the third paragraphs dramatize the impact of searing heat outside by painting a verbal picture of listless life in the garden through a series of visual images and vivid similes. Her microscopic description of the dark shed is meticulous in concrete details. Finally, her evocative and poetic description of twilight is characterized by soft and sensuous imagery appealing to all the bodily senses.

The setting of the story is not only descriptive but also evocative and symbolic. Desai uses many details of the setting to evoke an atmosphere of intense and oppressive heat, which serves as a symbolic background to rising human conflict. The setting also forms an integral part of the action. The garden, the shed, the veranda, and the lawn, all play an important part in shaping the action of the story.

*Chaman L. Sahni*

# THE GARDEN OF FORKING PATHS

*Author:* Jorge Luis Borges (1899-1986)
*Type of plot:* Mystery and detective
*Time of plot:* 1916
*Locale:* Staffordshire, England
*First published:* "El jardín de senderos que se bifurcan," 1941 (English translation, 1946)

> *Principal characters:*
> CAPTAIN RICHARD MADDEN, a British officer
> DR. YU TSUN, an agent for German Intelligence
> DR. STEPHEN ALBERT, a missionary and sinologist

*The Story*

In the prologue to the original edition of *El jardín de senderos que se bifurcan* (1941), the work in which the short story of the same title was published, Jorge Luis Borges classifies the tale as "a detective story" and says that "its readers will assist at the execution, and all the preliminaries, of a crime, a crime whose purpose will not be unknown to them but which they will not understand—it seems to me—until the last paragraph." The other pieces, he says, are all fantasies. Whether "The Garden of Forking Paths" is a detective story, a fantasy, or a combination of the two is a question that, ultimately, each reader must decide for him or herself.

The story begins with a reference to a history of World War I, in which it is stated that an Allied offensive planned for July 24, 1916, was postponed until July 29 because of "torrential rains." Calling the story that follows a deposition, the narrator says that it was dictated by Dr. Yu Tsun, a teacher of English, and the deposition casts light on the postponing of that attack.

The deposition begins in mid-sentence (readers are told that the first two pages are missing), with Dr. Yu Tsun, a spy for Imperial Germany although Chinese by nationality, just learning that he has been discovered. A telephone call to his confederate has been answered by a voice he recognizes, the voice of Richard Madden, a captain in the British counterintelligence service. Yu Tsun immediately concludes that his comrade is now dead and that Captain Madden knows of Yu Tsun's activity. To be discovered at this moment is especially alarming to the spy, because he has just found out the exact site in Belgium of a new concentration of British artillery. Although he knows this vital name, he has no way of getting the information to his superiors in Berlin. After some indecision, Yu Tsun acts to save himself from Captain Madden's pursuit. He takes a train to a nearby village, just ahead of the English officer.

At the village of Ashgrove, he heads for the house of Dr. Stephen Albert, an authority on Chinese culture. As he walks, Yu Tsun thinks of his great-grandfather, Ts'ui Pen, who was governor of Yunnan province. That powerful man resigned his political office to write a novel and to make a maze "in which all men would lose themselves." As he approaches the door of Albert's house, Yu Tsun reflects that the novel made no sense and the labyrinth was never found.

At the house, Yu Tsun is mistaken for a Chinese consul, and is asked by Albert if he has come to see the garden of forking paths. When Yu Tsun enters the house, their talk turns to the novel of Ts'ui Pen. Yu Tsun states that his family wishes it had never been published, calling it "a shapeless mass of contradictory rough drafts." As an example of the nonsensical nature of the work, he points out that the hero dies in chapter 3 but in chapter 4 is alive. However, when Yu Tsun remarks on the labyrinth of Ts'ui Pen, Albert tells him that he has found it and presents a small lacquered box. To a puzzled Yu Tsun, Albert explains that the labyrinth was not a physical maze but was, in fact, the novel itself; those who looked for the maze on Ts'ui Pen's extensive estates were bound to fail. As proof, Albert produces the original manuscript of the book, where Ts'ui Pen wrote: "I leave to various future times, but not to all, my garden of forking paths."

Albert explains that he wondered for a long time how a book could be an infinite maze until he saw the manuscript. He explains that in all fiction, a character facing a decision chooses one alternative to the exclusion of all others. In Ts'ui Pen's work, however, all choices are made. In one part, an army comes to feel that life is cheap, and they therefore win a subsequent battle. In the next part, the army sees a rich banquet in progress; with the possible splendors of life in their minds, they fight hard and win the battle. Then, though, Albert's argument becomes more subtle.

Albert points out that the word "time" never occurs in the novel. Ts'ui Pen apparently believed that time was not absolute and uniform but was rather a series of times that forked apart at some places and converged at others. That great structure includes every possible event: In most of them, Albert notes, he and Yu Tsun do not exist; in other times, one of them but not the other exists. Yu Tsun remarks that in all those possible universes, he is grateful to Albert for "the restoration of Ts'ui Pen's garden." No, Albert corrects him, not in all those many futures: In one of them, he is Yu Tsun's enemy. At that instant, Yu Tsun sees Captain Madden coming toward the house. Yu Tsun rises, fires his revolver, and kills Albert.

The final paragraph is written from Yu Tsun's prison cell. Captain Madden arrested him, and the courts tried him for Albert's murder, found him guilty, and sentenced him to hang. However, he says, he has triumphed: The news of the murder is in all the newspapers, newspapers that will be read in Berlin, where the name of their agent will be connected with the name of Albert—and Albert will be correctly identified as the name of the Belgian town where the English artillery is massed.

*Themes and Meanings*

"The Garden of Forking Paths" is a neat and clever detective story, but it also includes a theme of which Borges was very fond: the notion of multiple possibilities of an action. In science fiction, a whole subgenre of stories has been written to speculate on multiple universes arising from different choices in crucial situations: What would the present be like, for example, if the South had won the Civil War? This is the sort of story that Ts'ui Pen wrote, yet his story included not only an unexpected outcome but also multiple possible outcomes of various actions. The idea so fascinated Borges that he wrote another short piece, "Examen de la obra de Herbert Quain" ("An Examination of the Work of Herbert Quain"); the mythical Quain wrote novels like Ts'ui Pen's. A single first chapter is followed by three second chapters, among which the reader may choose. Each of those second chapters is followed by three possible third chapters, and so on.

As Albert says in the story, people, with their attention fixed on their memory of the past and their limited perception of the future, tend to think of time as a single strand of reality, with all the unrealized events and all the unchosen alternatives only possibilities. This fascination with the theme of multiple universes marks many of Borges's works.

## Style and Technique

Borges was a great admirer of the detective genre and of its leading writers, from Edgar Allan Poe to Arthur Conan Doyle and G. K. Chesterton to Graham Greene. For him, a detective story required certain characteristics: a complex plot, a small number of characters, a satisfying solution that proceeds from clues the reader has seen all along. For all these characteristics, a labyrinth is a satisfying metaphor; it is no coincidence that Yu Tsun reflects on a labyrinth, or that the idea of a maze appears in so many of Borges's works. In few of them, however, does the labyrinth figure so prominently as in "The Garden of Forking Paths."

The labyrinth—a maze of hedges, for example, in a formal garden—is a physical puzzle. Although it appears to contain many pathways, there is only one right solution. In the same way, the detective story is the literary counterpart of the labyrinth.

There are many mazes in the story, yet the conclusion provides a path through all of them: Yu Tsun's great-grandfather was killed by an unknown assassin; to many people who read about the murder of Albert, Yu Tsun is a virtually unknown assassin. Only those with the key to the mystery—the German espionage service in Berlin, waiting for a message—know why Albert has been killed. Captain Madden is tracking Yu Tsun through the labyrinth of England; Yu Tsun is entangling the unsuspecting Albert in the labyrinth of espionage; Borges is leading the reader through the labyrinth of the story. Not until the very end do readers realize why Yu Tsun, fleeing just minutes ahead of Captain Madden, should go to Albert's house and spend an hour discussing Chinese culture with him. Not until the very end do readers find their own way through the labyrinth.

*Walter E. Meyers*

# THE GARDEN-PARTY

*Author:* Katherine Mansfield (Katherine Mansfield Beauchamp, 1888-1923)
*Type of plot:* Psychological
*Time of plot:* The early twentieth century
*Locale:* Unnamed city in New Zealand
*First published:* 1922

> *Principal characters:*
> MRS. SHERIDAN, a well-to-do matron
> LAURA SHERIDAN, her youngest daughter
> MEG SHERIDAN, her oldest daughter
> JOSE SHERIDAN, her second daughter
> LAURIE SHERIDAN, her older son
> WORKMEN

*The Story*

A busy, happy mood prevails in the morning. The day, the lawns, and the gardens—particularly the roses—are perfect. During breakfast, Mrs. Sheridan asks her youngest daughter, Laura, to go outside and give directions to the men who will erect a canvas shelter for a garden party. Although Laura's little mission is successful, she questions herself several times. After rushing out, she feels awkward holding her bread-and-butter, and her formal "good morning" to the men sounds inappropriate. One of the men bluntly questions the location that Laura suggests for the marquee. Then she feels embarrassed for having mentioned that a band will play at the party. Happily, the assured manner of the tallest workman relaxes Laura; he speaks for the group and decides where the marquee should go. When he pinches a sprig of lavender and sniffs it, any concerns that Laura might have about her behavior vanish. In fact, she wishes that men of her own class were as nice as this man.

Laura understands that the awkwardness of this little encounter has resulted from "absurd class distinctions." As she watches the men work, she momentarily feels that she herself is "just like a work-girl." After she runs back into the house for a phone call, however, she forgets about the workmen as she savors all that she sees and hears. This time a florist interrupts her reverie; the frighteningly alive pink canna lilies that he delivers make Laura ecstatic. No sooner has she kissed her mother in gratitude than her sisters and little brother command her and her mother to come to the piano that they have just moved to listen to Laura's sister Meg sing "This Life Is Weary." Although the song laments life's burdens and the imminence of death, Meg wears a "brilliant, dreadfully unsympathetic smile."

Preparations for the party continue throughout the household. The cook requests flags to identify the kinds of sandwiches that she is readying. Another delivery man arrives with irresistible cream puffs—which Sadie, the family maid, insists that the children sample. As the children lick their sticky fingers, unpleasant news arrives: A man named Scott from a nearby poor neighborhood has just died in an accident. Like the Sheridans, his family has five children.

When Laura hears this news, she insists that the garden party should be canceled. However, her sister Jose argues with her. Laura appeals to their mother, but Mrs. Sheridan's first reaction to the tragedy is simply relief that the man did not die on their property. Mrs. Sheridan overcomes Laura's objections to continuing with the party by giving her a beautiful hat. Laura remains unsure about what she should do, but when she sees herself in her new hat, her astonishment quiets her objections about the party. By the time lunch is over and the guests arrive, Laura is content to be praised for her beauty, and she no longer mentions the accident.

The party is successful. Afterward, when Mr. Sheridan mentions Scott's fatal accident, his wife decides to send the leftover sandwiches to the man's grieving family. Laura delivers the basket, feeling painfully out of place in the poor neighborhood. She wants simply to leave the basket at the Scotts' house but instead is taken before the grieving widow. Confused and awkward, Laura tries to leave but accidentally walks into the room where the dead man lies.

The resulting encounter with the dead man confuses Laura even more. She finds the poor man's unmarred face to be "wonderful, beautiful" and "happy." Feeling compelled to cry, she asks him to forgive her hat. After departing unseen, she meets her older brother Laurie, who comforts her. She starts to say, "Isn't life . . ." but cannot finish.

### Themes and Meanings

Of the many people who appear in Katherine Mansfield's "The Garden-Party," the central character is clearly Laura Sheridan—who begins the day in excited anticipation of the party and ends it moved and baffled by death. Through the day she grows increasingly conscious of the consequences of her social position. As she admires the men erecting the marquee, she regards herself as a "work-girl"; however, one senses that something is wrong. The moment that she goes back inside the house, she becomes absorbed in a conversation about party dresses and forgets the workmen. Later, when she carries sandwiches to the Scotts' house, her party dress marks her as an outsider in the working-class neighborhood, and her discomfort in the company of the widow and her sister is extreme.

Laura's "artistic" nature allows her to sympathize with the working class, but her "practical" sister Jose calls such feelings "extravagant," and her mother finds them amusing. Just as the Sheridan children believe that entering the working-class streets would expose them to disease and foul language, the family steers the maturing Laura toward views that they consider proper. The hat that Mrs. Sheridan gives Laura is part of this training. Initially, when Mrs. Sheridan tells Laura that the hat is "made for you," Laura cannot imagine herself in it. Black, with gold daisies and a black ribbon, the hat probably seems too adult to Laura. However, her own beauty and maturity startle her when she sees herself wearing it in a mirror. Although this moment might be regarded as a coming-of-age, in Laura's case social conditioning is also important. For, in giving her daughter the hat, Mrs. Sheridan has distracted Laura from her conscience, teaching her—without words—that one's appearance should take precedence. When Laura comes face-to-face with the dead man, it is significant that she asks him to "forgive my hat."

Laura is still affected by all that has happened; she realizes that the hat represents the upper-class indifference that she has been taught, and which poorer persons—like the workmen erecting the marquee—would find objectionable. When she leaves the Scott house, these same class values—which she tries to dismiss as "absurd"—greet her in the person of her brother Laurie. Laurie tries to shield her from the pain of her experience by calling it "awful." Laura, however, cannot even complete a sentence; she begins, "Isn't life . . . " Whether she will become contained by the views of her class remains to be seen. At the least, she realizes that her concerns about the party have been self-centered.

*Style and Technique*

One can appreciate Mansfield's craft by noting the various ways in which she balances the "class distinctions" with which Laura grapples. The perfectly maintained garden provides escape from the less appealing working-class neighborhood, but it is working people who provide its necessary labor. The family diverts itself with canna lilies, finger sandwiches, party dresses, and cream puffs, but their pleasures are repeatedly interrupted. Laura's mind entertains the perspective of both classes. Although some writers would present ideas about class distinctions in the form of satire, Mansfield fashions "The Garden-Party" to suggest—rather than to state—themes. There is such a fluid movement to the story—and such an upbeat mood—that a reader, like Laura herself, may almost be distracted from serious matters such as poverty and death.

Managing point of view is one of the techniques that Mansfield uses to plant her ironies. The happiness in the opening paragraph turns out to be part of the complacency of the upper class. Note the breathless wording: "Hundreds, yes, literally hundreds [of roses], have come out in a single night." Such language has no place in the Scott house, where Mrs. Scott's swollen red face cows Laura. The reader, therefore, learns to doubt some of the statements, and to consider from which character's perspective they originate. One senses Jose's practicality when she uses the word "extravagant" to dismiss Laura's enthusiasm; likewise, one senses Mrs. Scott's grief in the questions going through her mind as Laura faces her.

The technique known as "stream-of-consciousness" developed in the early twentieth century as a result of the influential psychological theories of such persons as Sigmund Freud and William James. Writers such as Mansfield use it to make words show the workings of the mind, rather than merely summarize a character's thoughts. In "The Garden-Party," Mansfield mainly presents Laura's mind at work, but one must be careful to notice shifts to other characters' minds, as well as to the "mind" at work in passages such as the first paragraph, in which the Sheridan family—or the upper class—outlook appears. Finally, one admires Mansfield's handling of detail. When Laura says that the marquee belongs on the lily-lawn, one workman "thrust[s] out his under-lip" and another frowns. These actions characterize the men and reveal what Laura notices. They are also part of the comic moment that culminates as a workman suggests a location that would be more "conspicuous"—that is, in keeping with the values of her class.

*Jay Paul*

# THE GARDENER

*Author:* Rudyard Kipling (1865-1936)
*Type of plot:* Fable
*Time of plot:* The 1890's to 1920
*Locale:* Hampshire, England, and France
*First published:* 1926

> *Principal characters:*
> HELEN TURRELL, an English spinster
> MICHAEL TURRELL, supposedly her nephew
> GEORGE TURRELL, her late brother
> MRS. SCARSWORTH, an English visitor to military cemeteries in
> Flanders

## The Story

Helen Turrell, "thirty-five and independent," takes charge of the rearing of the supposed child of her brother, George, who dies from a fall from a horse a few weeks before the boy's birth. George, serving as a police officer in India, "had entangled himself" with the daughter of a noncommissioned officer. Helen, in the South of France because of lung trouble, has the infant brought to her and takes him home to Hampshire, England.

Helen explains all the details involving her nephew, Michael, to her friends in the village because "scandals are only increased by hushing them up." As for Michael's mother, she does not insist on her right to the child: "Luckily, it seemed that people of that class would do almost anything for money." Because George has always sought his sister's help when he got into "scrapes," Helen feels justified in "cutting the whole non-commissioned officer connection" and rearing the boy by herself even though she is not, as "far as she knew herself," a lover of children.

When Michael is six, Helen refuses to allow him to call her "Mummy" at any time but bedtime. When he discovers that she has told her friends of this practice, he feels betrayed and swears to hurt her for her disloyalty. He promises as well to die "quite soon" and to continue hurting her after his death.

When he goes away to school at ten, Michael endures taunts for being a bastard but learns to take defiant pride in his irregular "civil status" because William the Conqueror and others born illegitimately "got on first-rate." However, two years later, in delirium from a fever, he speaks of nothing but the disgrace of his birth.

Michael wins a scholarship to Oxford but enlists in the army instead when the Great War breaks out. After some time in France, Michael writes that "there was nothing special doing and therefore no need to worry," only to have a splinter of a shell kill him soon afterward.

After the war, Helen is notified of the location of Michael's grave in Flanders and goes to visit it. On the way to Hagenzeele, she meets an English woman making her ninth such trip. Mrs. Scarsworth claims not to have lost anyone but simply visits the graves of the loved ones of friends, sometimes taking photographs. Later, Mrs. Scarsworth reveals the truth to Helen, that she has lost someone, her lover.

At the military cemetery, with its twenty-one thousand graves, Helen does not know how to begin looking for Michael, and a man she takes to be a gardener offers his help. The gardener says, "Come with me, and I will show you where your son lies."

### Themes and Meanings

Rudyard Kipling employs two autobiographical elements as the basis of "The Gardener." He grew up in England while his parents lived in India, and his only son was killed in World War I. A third inspiration is the story told in John 20:14-15 in which Mary Magdalene fails to recognize the resurrected Jesus, supposing him to be a gardener. Kipling makes the connection to this biblical story clear by writing a companion piece about it, "The Burden," a poem from which "The Gardener" takes its epigraph.

Helen's failure to recognize the gardener at Hagenzeele as the Christ is less important as a supernatural or religious occurrence than a fitting conclusion to Kipling's ironic presentation of identity, responsibility, and guilt. This irony appears in the story's opening sentence: "Every one in the village knew that Helen Turrell did her duty by all her world, and by none more honourably than by her only brother's unfortunate child." However, if the gardener is not speaking metaphorically, and Helen is Michael's mother, she has not done her duty at all. By assuming the role of self-sacrificing, noble aunt devoted to her brother's illegitimate offspring, she has made a lie of both their lives.

Michael gets revenge on his "aunt" by dying, but she does not suffer as much as she might. Her greatest sin is her coldness. Her emotional distance from Michael, from life in general, allows her to avoid the pain that others feel when they lose someone. On the way to Hagenzeele, Helen finds repugnant the emotionalism of a woman from Lancashire who is desperate to find her son's grave. Kipling underscores Helen's insensitivity by having the woman faint on her unfeeling breast. Mrs. Scarsworth asks whether Helen thinks that the dead know anything after death and is told, "I haven't dared to think much about that sort of thing." Helen can control her grief by keeping it as abstract as possible.

She begins to recognize the truth about herself, however, when Mrs. Scarsworth confesses about her lover: "He was everything to me that he oughtn't to have been— the one real thing—the only thing that ever happened to me in all my life; and I've had to pretend he wasn't." This confession, so like the one that Helen is unable to make, almost causes Helen's impersonal facade finally to crumble. Kipling seems to be using Helen to criticize the passionless side of the English character and the almost obsessive concern with appearances and public opinion.

After Michael's death, Helen recalls his taking her to a munitions factory to see the steps in the production of a shell and realizes that with all the rituals that society expects her to observe she is like the shell: "I'm being manufactured into a bereaved next of kin." Because she is expected to play this role, she goes along with the charade, sitting on relief committees and holding "strong views—she heard herself delivering them—about the site of the proposed village War Memorial." One of several interlocking ironies is Helen's lack of awareness of how this role-playing is an outgrowth of her larger lie.

*Style and Technique*

"The Gardener" is notable for those elements typical of Kipling's late style: brevity, subtlety, and irony. Unfortunately, these qualities of the mature artist are occasionally interrupted by the sentimentality so characteristic of Kipling. The telegram notifying Helen that Michael is missing is delivered by the postmistress's seven-year-old daughter, who arrives weeping loudly "because Master Michael had often given her sweets."

More admirable is Kipling's economic style of storytelling as he quickly gets Michael born and killed so that he can proceed with the real story: Helen's response to this death. The ironic tone and relative subtlety of the story can be seen in Kipling's description of the event immediately following Michael's death: "The next shell uprooted and laid down over the body what had been the foundation of a barn wall, so neatly that none but an expert would have guessed that anything unpleasant had happened." Best of all is the description of the military cemetery, where order has ostensibly been imposed on death: "All she saw was a merciless sea of black crosses, bearing little strips of stamped tin at all angles across their faces. She could distinguish no order or arrangement in their mass; nothing but a waist-high wilderness as of weeds stricken dead, rushing at her." This masterly conjoining of death, war, and the chaos of Helen's emotional state helps refute H. E. Bates's claim that Kipling was not an artist but a journalist.

*Michael Adams*

# THE GARDENS OF MONT-SAINT-MICHEL

*Author:* William Maxwell (1908-2000)
*Type of plot:* Autobiographical, character study
*Time of plot:* 1966
*Locale:* Pontorson and Mont-Saint-Michel, Normandy, France
*First published:* 1969

> *Principal characters:*
> JOHN REYNOLDS, an American tourist
> DOROTHY, his wife
> ALLISON, their older daughter
> TRIP, their younger daughter
> LINDA PORTER, their teenage niece

*The Story*

The character of John Reynolds forms the core of "The Gardens of Mont-Saint-Michel," in which he and his family travel to France and visit the famed abbey. During this trip, Reynolds feels disappointment at the commercialism that now detracts from the area where he and his wife had earlier experienced an idyllic honeymoon. As in so much of William Maxwell's work, the story centers on character development, with little emphasis on plot.

In a humorous opening scene, Reynolds strains to drive a rented Volkswagen bus on unfamiliar streets, fearing an accident and suffering from a cramped leg. His charming wife, Dorothy, eccentric daughters Allison and Trip, and niece Linda Porter are unaware of his distress.

The story alternates between positive and negative events. On the way to Mont-Saint-Michel, the travelers pass through Pontorson, where the couple had stayed briefly on their honeymoon. Reynolds fondly recalls the kindness and friendly assistance of the hotel staff. However, increased traffic and widened streets have now rendered their once quaint hotel nearly unrecognizable.

As the family proceeds, they see that nondescript new houses have replaced the beautiful old farmhouses that once lined the French roadside. Rows of tourist buses indicate crowded conditions at their destination. The first view of the abbey is breathtaking, but it soon disappears behind the facade of a new hotel. On arrival at Mont-Saint-Michel, Reynolds is not allowed access to the parking lot he had been instructed to use. The family is forced to hike a long way up to their hotel, only to discover the rooms are overheated. When Reynolds returns to his car to move it to the correct lot, he is inexplicably waved on in. After this, the hotel porter cheerfully and single-handedly carries the whole family's luggage up many flights of stairs.

Settling in, Reynolds finds his mood improving as he recalls the timelessness of the ancient private gardens that the couple had discovered on their first trip. He also recalls the sound of the whisks as the restaurant cooks prepared omelets. However, his warm reverie is soon replaced by dismay. When the family orders omelets for lunch, the waiter claims they have no herbs—a staple of French cooking! Later, on a tour of the abbey, Reynolds is offended that uncaring French tourists slip away without tipping a young tour guide dependent on gratuities for his education. In addition, the sight of a dejected young girl in a nearby hotel room troubles Reynolds and his wife. At dinner, the restaurant service worsens.

The evening improves as the family walks down to the shoreline to watch the incoming tide fill the vast sand flats surrounding the abbey. Surprisingly, they are the only ones there, and the family is free to enjoy the experience. However, when returning to their rooms, they overhear a horrifying scream. Unable to ascertain its source in the dense buildings, Reynolds gloomily concludes that he can do nothing to provide assistance and so strives to reassure his badly shaken family.

In the morning the family enjoys a new discovery—an excellent historical exhibit—and visit a small garden. As they prepare to leave, Reynolds finally realizes that new hotel rooms and enlarged souvenir stores have replaced the gardens he loved. In a rage of disappointment, hurrying to get away, he leaves his travelers checks at the cashier's desk and the family's airline tickets at the concierge's desk. Both employees pleasantly return his property. Reynolds suddenly appreciates these examples of good service. He realizes that to the French, he must seem strange and incomprehensible.

*Themes and Meanings*

"The Gardens of Mont-Saint-Michel," one of only a few of Maxwell's stories set abroad, illustrates some of the difficulties Americans may experience in forming cultural relations with non-Americans. John Reynolds is a conventional American male whose admirable manners control his responses to a series of disappointments. He is middle-class, moral, and literate. His difficulties with circumstances initially appear to be the fault of the French, but these difficulties are in fact a result of his own wavering innocence. Reynolds hopes, in a dreamy sort of way, that after eighteen years he will return to a France as unspoiled as the one he witnessed eighteen years before.

Although Reynolds is sure that he recalls the events and setting of his honeymoon clearly, he is equally sure that he has forgotten experiences that did not serve his emotional needs. He imagines that time has glossed over any unsettling aspects of the earlier trip. Now he misses seeing women in shapeless black cotton dresses, as well as cows, chickens, geese, and bicycles. However, he still thrills to the ethereal vision of the abbey and its spire pointing upward toward a heaven that he doubts many people still believe in. He is both repelled by the size of the new hotel obscuring the abbey and pleased that his family's rooms are new and attractive. He anticipates that when night comes and the bus passengers have departed, he will once again sense the fifteenth century purity of the abbey, its grounds, and the ocean setting.

In spite of his disappointments over the changes he perceives, Reynolds remains eager to relate to the local people. He attempts speaking French several times, even though he realizes that the French dislike hearing the language spoken poorly. On the abbey tour, he is disappointed that they have an English-speaking guide because to him it makes the abbey itself less interesting. Still he tips the guide extravagantly and thanks him in French. As Reynolds describes himself, he is a person whose greatest involvement occurs when making connections with all sorts of people he knows he will never see again.

Reynolds ends the evening at Mont-Saint-Michel in an entirely disenchanted state, certain that he should never have returned to France. Although he recognizes that his disappointments are a sign of his own aging process, he laments that change seems invariably to be for the worse. He expects never to forgive the French for sacrificing historic quality for cash. In the morning, however, he recovers enough to decide that his anger was unjust, a fulfillment of the story's main theme that relations between members of different cultures can be difficult even at best.

*Style and Technique*

Maxwell's considerable skills as a novelist and short-story writer may be less well known than his many years of work as an editor for *The New Yorker* magazine. Although few of his own works appeared in that magazine, he brings his editing ability to bear on his own polished prose. In "The Gardens of Mont-Saint-Michel," the language is translucent, allowing the reader to see and feel the main character's experiences without stylistic disruption. Maxwell portrays a man who is difficult to appreciate, one who experiences chafing dissatisfactions that conflict with his sympathetic instincts. His family acts as a backdrop against which Reynolds appears as a caring and responsible husband and father.

Maxwell's novel *The Château* (1961) begins with a chapter in which a different young American couple arrives in postwar France in 1948. The two couples also travel the same route, visiting first Pontorson and then Mont-Saint-Michel. Commenting on his novel, Maxwell expressed concerns that *The Château* was too much of an autobiographical travel diary. Although the action of "The Gardens of Mont-Saint-Michel" covers a single twenty-four-hour period, it is filled with flashbacks of an earlier trip, one much like that of the couple in the novel. The descriptions of Reynolds as a more mature character add depth to the story, revealing a man suffering from a careworn daily life, one that a mere holiday could hardly relieve.

Through Maxwell's characterization, Reynolds frequently experiences pointedly ambiguous thoughts. For example, the abbey is airy and visionary, a heavenly site, but one reminiscent of a vaudeville act. The full parking lot near the abbey presages a World's Fair crowd, and Reynolds fears the family may have to stand in line to see the tide come in. The tide itself is like an emotion, but a disastrous one like the joy of a man falling in love at the wrong time in life. Maxwell concludes the story by showing a somewhat penitent tourist. In a final reversal, Reynolds generalizes that it is the French who choose not to belittle the memories and emotions of others.

*Margaret A. Dodson*

# GENEROUS WINE

*Author:* Italo Svevo (Ettore Schmitz, 1861-1928)
*Type of plot:* Psychological
*Time of plot:* The early twentieth century
*Locale:* Northern Italy
*First published:* "Vino generoso," 1927 (English translation, 1930)

> *Principal characters:*
> THE NARRATOR, a sick old man
> HIS WIFE, a proper matron
> EMMA, their daughter
> THE BRIDE, their niece
> GIOVANNI, a capitalist

*The Story*

On the eve of his niece's wedding, the narrator and his family attend a dinner party given in her honor. The bride, who is marrying relatively late in life, originally vowed to spend her years in a convent. The narrator wonders why she has changed her mind; he muses ironically that she more likely was seduced than converted.

During dinner, the narrator is in a jolly mood because his wife has convinced Dr. Paoli to allow him to eat and drink whatever he wants on this occasion. Normally, he is on a severe diet but, free to indulge himself now, he feels like "running and jumping like a dog slipped from his chain." This rebellious feeling makes him drink an inordinate amount of a dry Istrian wine, which he hopes will make him forget the cares of life. The wine does not bring him gaiety and forgetfulness, however, but merely makes him even more angry and depressed.

In the midst of the festivities, the narrator—who is a socialist—argues with Giovanni, a capitalist, about the value of money. Their debate becomes heated and vicious; finally the narrator shouts at Giovanni: "We will hang you, a rope round your neck and weights on your feet." Almost immediately, he feels astonished and guilty for having made such a remark. After his sister intervenes to comment on how well he looks, his wife asks him to stop drinking and tells a neighbor to take away his wine. Soon, everyone present begins rebuking him; this makes him even more irate. He is increasingly angry with his wife for humiliating him in such a fashion. When even his daughter, Emma, feels the need to berate him, he scolds her and causes her to cry, creating yet another occasion for guilt and recrimination. Not even when the bride bestows on him a good night kiss does the narrator's anger abate.

At the moment of departure, someone mentions the name of Anna, an old friend whom the narrator courted until the day that he married his present wife. The narrator is suddenly struck by pangs of conscience as he remembers his "offence against love." That night he goes to bed severely depressed. Once in bed, he cannot sleep as he wrestles with the physical discomfort of drinking too much and the psychological pain of his depression. Feeling a burning sensation in his stomach, he tosses and turns in an uncontrollable rage, until he must call for help. After his wife gives him some drops recommended by the doctor, he closes his eyes, thinks of all of the women whom he knew in his youth, especially of Anna, and he falls asleep.

In a horrible dream, the narrator finds himself in a dark cave, sitting on a stool next to a glass chest. Instinctively, he understands that he has been chosen to be asphyxiated in the chest in order to atone for the sins of others. The cave was built by men as a cure for themselves, even though it is fatal to those imprisoned in it. His wife and the guests at the dinner party are with him in the darkness of the cave; all of them exhort him to climb into the glass chest. The bride is also present; she confirms that the chest is indeed meant for him and urges him to comply. In his despair, the narrator shouts that he is willing to give up his daughter Emma in return for his own safety. When he awakens with a start, he realizes that he was about to sacrifice his own daughter in order to save himself (even though his wife thinks that he is calling his daughter's name out of love). He concludes that he must never return to that horrible cave.

The narrator is now ready to obey the doctor's orders and become submissive until the "last fever" when he will definitively confront the glass chest and leap into it willingly.

## Themes and Meanings

A theme that permeates all the works of Italo Svevo is that of mental and physical weakness, which Svevo defines as "senility." It is present in the novel *Senilità* (1898; *As a Man Grows Older*, 1932) as well as in his masterpiece, *La coscienza di Zeno* (1923; *The Confessions of Zeno*, 1930).

In a metaphysical sense, senility entails a withdrawal from reality into the world of dreams or wishful thinking. A typical Svevian protagonist has no grasp of reality; consequently, he cannot make any real decisions, although he maintains the illusion of doing so. As a consequence, other people's actions—and even his own, occasionally—take him by surprise.

All of these elements are present in "Generous Wine." From the beginning, its protagonist characterizes himself "a licentious old fellow." This assertion, however, must be considered in the context of Svevian philosophy. The "senile" character represents humanity itself. Thus the sickness from which the protagonist suffers in "Generous Wine" is the quintessence of the bourgeois disease, against which he is incapable of rebelling, although he is skeptical of his doctor's diagnosis. Living is itself a disease, for as he tells the bride: "One regrets past joy, and this is a pain, but a pain that numbs the fundamental one, the real pain in life." Only at the beginning of life can one escape this terrible truth. Thus, he tells his wife that their children are happy to be alive "because they don't know anything yet." This condition, however, is only provisional, and the illusion lasts a very short time. With age comes a recognition of the banality of life and the realization that one's search for true sentiments and deep feelings is fruitless.

The human intellect, then, is useless in combating this disease, and the body becomes a living museum of the protagonist's humiliation and moral crimes. In "Generous Wine," the protagonist becomes physically ill when he feels that the other wedding guests are mocking him and, later, when he recalls an old love. His punishment is to endure a horribly restless night and to dream of a cowardly and humiliating death. Not even in wine or in dreams can one escape the human predicament. The search for the unconscious to supplement a defect of the intellect is also unable to procure a healthy environment. The author's conclusion seems to be that only by living in solitude and mindlessly conforming to society's rules can one hope to acquire a measure of peace and freedom from guilt.

*Style and Technique*

Svevo wrote "Generous Wine" at the time of the rise of the modern novel, and it employs many of the novel's techniques. Typical is the technique, borrowed from the naturalist writers, of utilizing a single thing or event to portray the whole of human experience concisely. Svevo takes one evening in the protagonist's life and makes the reader understand his existential predicament. His style is deliberately subdued, yet small, seemingly insignificant details become very important. For example, a passing reference by a dinner guest to a name in the protagonist's past evokes a sense of guilt and impotence in him that characterizes his entire life.

Although at times fringing on the ironic, Svevo's style is controlled and depicts a lighthearted resignation to life's vicissitudes and contradictions. The theme of the breakdown of communication is subtly introduced by simple contrast. In his dream, the author calls for his daughter Emma in a cowardly attempt to save his own life, but his wife interprets his crying out of Emma's name as a sign of love. Although the protagonist tries to rebel, he ultimately accepts his situation and vows to conform to what his wife and doctor say is best for him. The banality of life actually becomes a haven; by accepting his situation the protagonist will, at the least, avoid more painful consequences. In the end, it is when daylight arrives that he ceases to feel his shame. In stating that the "dream-world was not my world," he realizes that the wine that brought him to it was not generous.

*Victor A. Santi*

# GENT

*Author:* Rick DeMarinis (1934-    )
*Type of plot:* Psychological
*Time of plot:* The early 1950's
*Locale:* Far Cry, a town somewhere in the United States
*First published:* 1983

> *Principal characters:*
> JACK, the narrator, a twelve-year-old boy
> JADE, his mother
> LADONNA, his eleven-year-old sister
> GENT MUNDY, the man his mother marries, her third husband

*The Story*

"Gent" is told from the point of view of Jack, a twelve-year-old boy, from the time his mother marries Gent Mundy through the next two years. Jackie, as his mother calls him, realizes that his mother has married Gent to provide for her two children. Jack describes events dispassionately and accepts whatever happens in his new family.

The story opens with Jack giving a brief family history. His father, whom Jack remembers as a large and powerful man who was a hero in World War II, committed suicide by shooting himself. A year later, Jack's mother, Jade, married a salesperson named Roger Trewly, who not long afterward also committed suicide by jumping off a bridge into the heavy rapids of Far City River. Neither husband left the family with any money. At the time of her second husband's death, Jade was thirty-two and Jack eleven.

A year later, Jack and his sister LaDonna find their mother dressed up, looking like a little princess. Jade says she is going on a date. A few weeks later, she takes the children to dinner at Gent Mundy's house, where he proudly shows them the redecorated rooms that are to be their bedrooms. Gent is a forty-eight-year-old bachelor, bald and spindly legged. He is enamored of Jade, whom he calls his little jewel, and he assures her his creamery business is doing well. It is LaDonna who speaks up and tells Gent that her mother would be happy to marry him. Jack thinks of his sister as someone who sees things as they are.

The children like Gent well enough, though he is excessively neat and overly concerned with cleanliness. On the day of the wedding, Jack wears a new suit and tie Gent has given to him, with a ten-dollar bill in the pocket. The ceremony takes place in a minister's back office. Jack finds it hot and stuffy inside, and he goes outside and down the street where he buys his first pack of cigarettes and practices learning how to inhale. After the wedding, Gent takes his new family for a drive in the country in his Buick Roadmaster, and they stop by an old abandoned railway depot. Jack smokes his new cigarettes and watches Gent and Jade kissing awkwardly, Jade dropping her purse in the process.

Jack feels older now that he is smoking, and he secretly looks at some of Gent's magazines with pictures of women in skimpy bathing suits. One night he puts on his new suit and walks into the big bedroom. Although Gent and Jade are embroiled in activity in the bed, he calmly lights up a cigarette and starts telling them about an article he is reading. His mother tells him he is old enough to know not to barge into someone's bedroom. Later Jade gives birth to a baby boy, whom she and Gent name Spencer Ted. Gent is exceedingly proud to have a son, though he tells Jack and LaDonna he loves them too and continues to give them presents.

The story ends with a Fourth of July trip to a local lake. While Jack and LaDonna build sand castles and destroy them by pretending to bomb them, Gent stays with the baby, and Jade swims out to a diving platform about fifty yards from the shore. Later Jack starts to swim to join her, but he sees a big and heavily muscled man near his mother. Jade swims again, and the man swims behind her. They return to the diving platform. Jade shakes water from her glossy hair. The man does a handstand and then walks around on his hands. Gent looks across the water to Jade and lifts the baby's arm to point. It is nearly evening and time for the fireworks show.

*Themes and Meanings*

A major theme of "Gent" concerns dealing with uncertainty. Fathers come and go, housing and financial status change, and a new baby or a new man may create further anxieties. How is a young boy to react? One way, the story shows, is to observe rather than to judge or to hope. Whether this is a realistic and admirable coping strategy or a sad commentary on life is left up to the reader. LaDonna, Jack's slightly younger sister, copes by having plans. She wants to be a scientist. For the present, she asks for things she knows she can get: a stepfather who has money and a new microscope he will buy for her.

Jade has lost two husbands to suicide and copes with poverty and depression by marrying a physically unattractive man fifteen years her senior who has money and loves to show her off in public. She produces his son, "the Mundy heir." However, before the baby is a year old, a muscular young man appears very interested in her. What will happen next?

Related to uncertainty is the focus on past versus present versus future. Jack remembers his father as a war hero, but no one ever talks about him, and Jack seldom dwells on the past beyond reciting his set little history of the two husbands, and he does not have plans for the future. He likes feeling older and tries to create a sophisticated style, looking at himself in the mirror while he smokes or imitating a tough film character. However, when the chance encounter occurs between his mother and the new man, he avoids any possibly disturbing anxieties by thinking of the fireworks show about to start.

Intertwined with these issues is the largely unconscious anxiety of a boy his age in relation to his mother and his own growing sexuality. Now thirteen or fourteen, Jack has been looking at swimsuit magazines, and as he watches his petite and beautiful mother swim like a young girl, he admires the arch of her ribs and her nicely muscled legs. When Jade went on her first date with Gent, Jack knew that she could fly away anytime and had wanted somehow to protect her. Now he starts to swim to the diving platform to join her but gives up when he sees her with a muscular man.

Rick DeMarinis neatly ties all this individual anxiety with that of the unpredictable and dangerous world at large, especially in the scene at the end of the story when Jack and LaDonna build sand castles on the beach. Sand castles are by nature ephemeral, indeed they are often used as a synonym for dreams that can never come true. These particular sand castles are not elaborate, and Jack and his sister do not mind wrecking them. In fact, they erect city after city of sloppy skyscrapers for the express purpose of demolishing them. Jack pretends he is a World War II-era B-29 airplane bombing them with an atomic bomb named Fat Boy, the name of the first atomic bomb used by the United States against Japan in 1945, and LaDonna supplies the sound effects. These children of the early 1950's have heard about atomic bombs and incorporate this information into their casual play. What they do not know is the future, when even immensely more powerful bombs will be built, creating an on-going anxiety about the future—or lack of it—of all humanity.

*Style and Technique*

In his numerous short stories and novels, DeMarinis often uses the spare, objective, and unemotional writing style that characterizes "Gent." This postmodern technique is related to minimalism, though not as flat or as totally disconnected from feeling. "Gent" has a few metaphorical passages, such as Jack's description of his mother as a little butterfly emerging from its cocoon and about to fly away, but for the most part, the writing style is a statement of fact, without subjective commentary. The reader is left to supply meaning and connections.

The ambiguous setting, given only as small town Far Cry, implies that similar situations could be happening anywhere. Likewise, using Jack as the first-person narrator not only reveals that he has learned to be unemotional about changes but also suggests that this is a position anyone could take toward an uncertain world. Jack often describes a scene or a person but seldom comments on what this might mean to him. There is very little dialogue, as though talking does little to change anything. The tone of the story is neither upbeat nor tragic, but more a simple and nonreflective report of what happens.

The plot of the story accords well with the style. Jack's only stability has been his connection with his mother, a smoker who has had two marriages end with the suicides of her husbands and who turns to an older man for financial support. Jack reacts to this stoically, except for trying to feel older by wearing his new suit and taking up smoking. He observes his mother being wooed by a younger man clearly more like Jack's father, but rather than think about that, he tells himself the Fourth of July fireworks display will begin soon.

*Lois A. Marchino*

# THE GENTLEMAN FROM CRACOW

*Author:* Isaac Bashevis Singer (1904-1991)
*Type of plot:* Allegory
*Time of plot:* Unspecified
*Locale:* Frampol, a fictitious village near Cracow, Poland
*First published:* 1957

### Principal characters:

THE GENTLEMAN FROM CRACOW, a doctor and a widower, the
incarnation of Ketev Mriri, chief of the devils
HODLE, the daughter of Lipa the Ragpicker—Lilith, a female
demon from Talmudic legend, Adam's first wife
RABBI OZER, a man of God whose warnings go unheeded

*The Story*

Isaac Bashevis Singer develops his narrative carefully in five parts. Part 1 introduces the fictitious little Polish village of Frampol, whose peasants are poor and
whose Jewish villagers struggle against extreme impoverishment. Frampol's only as-
set is its children: boys who grow tall and strong and girls who bloom handsomely.
Suddenly the whole area is stricken by a devastating drought that ends in a climactic
hailstorm accompanied by supernatural events: "Locusts huge as birds came in the
wake of the storm; human voices were said to issue from their throats."

Then an unexpected miracle occurs. A handsome young man in his twenties,
dressed in gorgeous clothes, arrives in a carriage pulled by eight horses and explains
that he is a doctor and a widower from Cracow, come to Frampol to choose a new
wife. He immediately provides lavish amounts of food, and the town is soon basking
in its new prosperity. Only a few protest when he soon has the townspeople playing
cards and gambling in violation of the accepted religious sanctions. Before long, the
women and their daughters are in a frenzy of activity, all hoping to be chosen by the
mysterious suitor.

In part 2, the seduction of the villagers is completed by their approval of a great ball
to which all the eligible young women are to be invited. Despite protests from some of
the elders that such elaborate festivities are not in keeping with Jewish tradition, the
young gentleman has his way, and many lush fabrics are procured by him for the girls'
ball dresses. The stranger goes on merrily eating Sabbath puddings on weekdays and
playing cards, never attending prayer. Rabbi Ozer warns the villagers that they are being tricked by the Evil One, but all are possessed by their plans for the ball.

Part 3 introduces Lipa the Ragpicker and his daughter Hodle. Lipa has taken to
drink after the death of his first wife and now lives with Hodle, his seventeen-year-old
daughter by his second wife, a beggar who left him for nonsupport. Hodle is a village
scandal. She roams the village in rags, stealing chickens and ducks and creating a leg-

end by her lasciviousness. It is said of her that she eats cats and dogs, as well as other stray creatures who have died. She is a tall beauty, with red hair and green eyes, but when the fine fabrics are distributed, she is left with only odds and ends from which to make her gown. Her fury entertains the villagers. When all is ready for the ball, only Rabbi Ozer stays at home, locked in his study. When the dances begin, the gentleman from Cracow arrives on a white mare and watches the girls swaying to the music in the marketplace. All are dancing except Hodle.

In part 4, when the ball is in full swing, the gentleman from Cracow announces that all virgins must marry that night and that he will provide a dowry of ten thousand ducats for each. Brides and bridegrooms will be matched up by drawing lots. Despite the ritual demand that a girl must wait seven days after the announcement of her forthcoming marriage, mass excitement prevails and the only protester, an old man, is gagged. At this point, a virtual orgy breaks out, but at its peak a lightning bolt destroys the synagogue, the study house, and the ritual bath. With this event, the villagers learn the truth: The gentleman from Cracow reveals himself as a grotesque creature covered with scales, having a tail of live serpents. He is Ketev Mriri, chief of the devils. Hodle takes off her dress, appearing in her true identity as Lilith, the Talmudic demon who was supposed to have been Adam's first wife. She is repulsive: "Her breasts hung down to her navel and her feet were webbed. Her hair was a wilderness of worms and caterpillars."

Rabbi Ozer restores reason and order in part 5. The people have learned their lesson. An eternal light burns over Rabbi Ozer's grave, and a white pigeon often appears on the roof of the memorial chapel: "the sainted spirit of Rabbi Ozer."

## Themes and Meanings

Singer was born in a little village near Warsaw, the son of a very poor rabbi. Most of his fiction is drawn from life in Poland's Jewish communities, a life that in his childhood was rife with tales of the supernatural and mysterious. His stories often suggest a belief in a spiritual dimension to existence that science cannot explain, and his imaginative tales often exploit the folklore and superstition on which his childhood fantasies fed. All these aspects of his work are well exemplified in "The Gentleman from Cracow."

The moral of the allegory is clear: To ignore the laws and traditions is to open oneself up to calamity. Easy riches are a delusion. Nevertheless, the gentleman is so glamorous, the people so miserable in their poverty, that the temptation is hard to resist. The good Rabbi Ozer laments after the catastrophe that he should have had more foresight: "And when the shepherd is blind, the flock goes astray."

However, there is more to the allegory than simply the story of the people's weakness, for at the end the villagers are truly regenerated. Their neighbors in the nearby town of Yanev send food, clothing, and dishes. Timber merchants send logs to rebuild the homes and public buildings. The people, including the scholars and town leaders, work diligently, so that a new town is soon created, one wiser and more truly pious. Never again do the townspeople lust for gold and fine things.

The story also expresses a political moral of a sort. Jewish communities in Eastern Europe often were threatened with extinction, and close conformity to laws and accepted practices was vital in unifying a besieged people against external pressures. When life became somewhat easier for these Jewish communities, many of the younger people would feel the pull toward assimilation, regarding the old rituals and mores as outmoded and burdensome. Then it was natural for the elders to lament the temptations of the secular Gentile life to which they saw their youths attracted, and they voiced their fears in warnings of the dangers of the Evil One. Singer must have observed this conflict as a young man in Poland, and "The Gentleman from Cracow" dramatizes not only the moral problems involved in expecting something for nothing but also the strain of conflict between two generations.

*Style and Technique*

Singer wrote his stories in Yiddish and then watched over their translation into English. The Yiddish language is basically German, with many Hebrew words, as well as vocabulary picked up from Polish and Russian during its thousand-year history. It is therefore rich in diction and imagery that grew out of the Jews' long existence in Eastern Europe.

"The Gentleman from Cracow" opens with an exposition of the legends surrounding Frampol's history. The community house contains a parchment that chronicles Frampol's story, but the first page is missing. It is not clear at first that the story that follows is recounted in the pages of the old history, but the conclusion reveals that "the story, signed by trustworthy witnesses, can be read in the parchment chronicle." "The Gentleman from Cracow," then, is cast in a very old narrative framework: the fictitious manuscript.

The story is notable for the wealth of supernatural imagery that it presents. Part 4 opens with a gorgeous pathetic fallacy in which the setting sun stares angrily at the doings in the marketplace. The order of the natural universe has been violated by the villagers' wantonness. "Like rivers of burning sulphur, fiery clouds streamed across the heavens, assuming the shapes of elephants, lions, snakes, and monsters. They seemed to be waging a battle in the sky, devouring one another, spitting, breathing fire." This poetic evocation of God's wrath is followed by a vivid description of the behavior of the satiated humans and animals and of a weird glowing light that appears in the sky as an apparent omen.

Singer's direct style is a graceful medium for depicting his world of folklore, superstition, and the commonplace village life of Eastern European Jews before World War II. He is the foremost expounder of a way of life that has for the most part passed away, but that he knows intimately and re-creates compulsively.

*Frank Day*

# THE GENTLEMAN FROM SAN FRANCISCO

*Author:* Ivan Bunin (1870-1953)
*Type of plot:* Social realism
*Time of plot:* The early 1910's
*Locale:* Italy
*First published:* "Gospodin iz San Frantsisko," 1915 (English translation, 1922)

### Principal characters:

THE GENTLEMAN, a businessperson from San Francisco
THE GENTLEMAN'S WIFE
THE GENTLEMAN'S DAUGHTER

## The Story

This short work has a deceptively simple plot: A rich American businessperson travels with his family to Europe for a vacation and dies suddenly of a heart attack on the island of Capri. He then returns home in a coffin on the same ship on which he went to Europe. However, over the sparse frame of this plot, Ivan Bunin weaves an elaborate narrative fabric richly textured with subtle counterpoint and evocative detail. Some critics have interpreted the tale as an indictment of Western capitalism, but such an evaluation is inadequate. Through his title character, Bunin illustrates a pervasive problem afflicting all of modern society: a fatal preoccupation with the self that leaves one coldly indifferent to other people, to nature, and to God.

Bunin's narrative exposes the shallowness and insensitivity of the gentleman and his fellow travelers through a variety of details. Describing the gentleman's shipboard passage to the Old World, he unveils a lifestyle in which everything is devoted to the passengers' comfort. Unmindful of the turbulent realm of nature outside, the passengers pursue one idle distraction after another. For them, eating is a major pastime, and the crown of their existence is dinner. However, beneath this veneer of civility one finds a core of avarice and hypocrisy. An apparently romantic couple admired by all the passengers is revealed to have been hired by the shipping company to act out the role of being in love. Even the most basic and profound of human emotions—love—becomes a hollow travesty in this banal society.

Once in Europe, the gentleman embarks on a numbing routine of sightseeing. The majestic churches of Italy soon become repetitious and boring, and the sightseers discover that "the same thing is found everywhere: . . . vast emptiness, silence . . . slippery gravestones under the feet and someone's Deposition from the Cross, invariably famous." The images of death here foreshadow the gentleman's own impending fate, but he remains as unmoved by them as he is by the religious objects themselves. Even the image of Christ's crucifixion, one of the central mysteries of Christianity, appears only as a museum piece whose fame is noted and nothing more.

The gentleman's insensitivity continues until the very moment of his death. The narrator asks rhetorically what the gentleman was thinking on the night of his heart attack. The answer is ironic: He was thinking only of his supper. He never arrives at the hotel dinner table, however; his heart attack strikes swiftly, causing consternation among the other hotel guests, who selfishly care more about their ruined evening than about the mystery of death itself. The gentleman's family now discovers the extent of the hypocrisy that runs through their social world. Before the gentleman's death, the hotel management had fawned over them. Now, though, the family is treated with cool disdain: The gentleman's body is put in the poorest room in the hotel and later conveyed to the ship in a cheap soda-water crate.

Despite the dark images dominating his portrait of the gentleman and the gentleman's milieu, Bunin does not provide an unrelievedly gloomy vision of human nature in "The Gentleman from San Francisco." In an important scene that occurs after the gentleman's death, Bunin introduces two characters who display an attitude toward the world that differs radically from that of the gentleman. These two are simple peasants descending the side of Monte Solaro. Unlike the gentleman, the peasants see the natural world around them as a resplendent realm of beauty. When they stop to pray at a statue of the Madonna perched amid the rocks, they offer "naïve and humbly joyful" praises to the Madonna, to God and to the world of nature. For these men, attuned as they are to the ineffable beauty of the universe, the realms of God and nature are one. The simplicity and humility manifest in their joyful reverence stand in sharp contrast to the indifference and selfishness apparent in the lifestyle and worldview of the gentleman's group.

Bunin returns to the world of the gentleman's society at the end of his narrative, depicting the ship carrying the gentleman's body back to the United States. Again, one notes the self-centered pursuit of idle pleasure on the ship, but now Bunin's description contains an ominous new element. In the very bowels of the ship he portrays the coffin holding the gentleman's corpse, and he concludes his tale with this image, a vivid emblem of the rank corruption lying at the core of the selfish modern world. Bunin thus suggests in "The Gentleman from San Francisco" that modern society's frantic pursuit of pleasure and satisfaction is really a macabre dance of death, leading ultimately to ruin and perdition.

*Themes and Meanings*

As Bunin himself commented later, this story can be read as a sober warning to a world poised on the brink of World War I. Modern society, his story implies, has fallen prey to the forces of egocentricity, arrogance, and avarice. Wealth and rank seem to be its only measure of human worth. Thus the gentleman's daughter finds herself spellbound with excitement in the presence of the crown prince of a certain Asian nation. Although the prince is described as unattractive, even corpselike, the thought that he has ancient royal blood coursing through his veins causes her heart to beat with silent ecstasy. As for the gentleman himself, he vainly believes that everyone on Capri, from the cabmen to the hotel staff, lives only to serve him. The fallacy of his perception becomes glaringly obvious after his death, when the hotel staff treats his family with undisguised disrespect. Because the source of their income has departed, they have little use for such unprofitable emotions as pity and compassion.

Although Bunin devotes the major portion of his narrative to the gentleman and his fellow travelers, he does offer a modest counter to this group with the scene involving the two peasants. Their humble spirituality and their evident love both for God and for the natural world offer an alternative to the self-absorption of the gentleman's company, and in this scene the reader discovers Bunin's solution to the perils he saw threatening modern society. Individuals should not act as if the universe were centered on them, but rather they must recognize that they are only a small element in a vast and wondrous cosmos that should be approached with reverence and love, not arrogance and cynicism. Egocentric desire must yield to self-effacing acceptance of the natural order, or the result will be death, decay, and dissolution.

## Style and Technique

To convey his vision of a society riddled with self-indulgence and hypocrisy, Bunin marshaled all of his gifts as a prose artist. The result is a masterpiece of expressive technique. Each word and image contributes to the work's total impact, and hardly any superfluous or insignificant detail can be identified. From the outset, Bunin creates a special narrative style whose very diction carries subtle overtones of irony to expose the folly and vanity of the gentleman's worldview. Writing of the reasons for the gentleman's trip, Bunin states: "He was firmly convinced that he was fully entitled to a rest, to pleasure, and to a journey excellent in all respects." This is not Bunin's normal style. The solemn pomposity of its formulations belongs to the gentleman himself, creating a satiric echo of his own arrogance. It is truly ironic, however, that this self-impressed character remains anonymous throughout the story. Despite his own belief in his personal significance, no one could even remember the man's name after his death.

Bunin also relies heavily on symbolic detail to evoke the shallowness of the gentleman's lifestyle and the dangers inherent in the narrow-minded self-absorption of his society. The relationship between the ship on which the gentleman travels and the sea through which this ship moves provides a good illustration of the writer's symbolic technique. Opposed to the power and majesty of the human-made ship is the churning realm of the gale-swept sea. Bunin's descriptions of the ship and the sea suggest that a profound struggle is being waged between the elemental forces of nature and the artificial constructs of modern civilization. This struggle even takes on spiritual or religious dimensions. Bunin notes that the ship is ruled by the captain, a mysterious figure compared to an idol or pagan god, while the devil himself watches the struggle of ship against sea from the shoreline. It seems as though modern society has created its own gods and its own Hell, next to which the Old World devil seems almost irrelevant. Similar examples of evocative detail can be found in Bunin's descriptions of the gentleman's itinerary, clothing, and pastimes. Bunin's narrative serves as a frank mirror for the gentleman and his milieu, disclosing the severe wrinkles under his makeup and the cheap trappings in which a vain world wraps itself.

*Julian W. Connolly*

# GERALDO NO LAST NAME

*Author:* Sandra Cisneros (1954-    )
*Type of plot:* Sketch
*Time of plot:* The late 1960's to early 1970's
*Locale:* A large American city
*First published:* 1983

*Principal characters:*
    MARIN, a young Puerto Rican woman
    GERALDO, a young Mexican working in the United States illegally
    THE NARRATOR, a young adolescent girl

*The Story*

Marin, a young Puerto Rican woman who enjoys dancing, frequents dance halls in different parts of the city. One night at such a place she meets Geraldo, a young, attractive, and neatly dressed Mexican wearing green pants and a shiny shirt. He tells her his name and adds that he works in a restaurant. That is all the information Marin learns about him.

Later that night Geraldo is the victim of a hit-and-run accident and is taken to an emergency room in a hospital. After he dies, Marin is repeatedly questioned by hospital personnel and the police because Geraldo has no identification on him. In fact, his pockets are empty. Marin can provide only minimal information, for that is all she knows. She cannot understand why there is such intense interest in Geraldo. She thinks of him as a person whom "she didn't even know," yet she feels pity toward him. She thinks if only the surgeon had come, if only there had been more personnel in the emergency room than just one intern, perhaps Geraldo would not have died, or at least someone may have learned from him whom to inform about his death.

Nevertheless, the narrator states that Geraldo's death does not make any difference, anyway. He was not someone whom Marin knew well, like a boyfriend or someone close. In fact, he was "just another brazer," "a wetback"—a person who does not speak English and often acts embarrassed. The narrative then focuses on Marin, raising the question of how she will explain why she has stayed out so late.

The story's last two paragraphs briefly describe how illegal workers live in the United States. Because Geraldo was an illegal worker, his fate will remain unknown to his friends and relatives who live where he came from. His family will wonder why he never contacts them again.

*Themes and Meanings*

"Geraldo No Last Name" is one of forty-four sketches in Sandra Cisneros's *The House on Mango Street* (1984). The voice of a narrator identified as Esperanza in another vignette helps to unify her entire book. As Esperanza tells the stories, such as that of Geraldo, she assesses the situations and expresses her opinions—which seem to reflect the point of view of a preadolescent girl or one in her early adolescence.

Although each of Cisneros's vignettes can stand alone as a story, it is helpful to read all of *The House on Mango Street* for a more thorough understanding of the themes that she develops. A vignette entitled "Marin," for example, presents the background of the young woman who enjoys going dancing. Marin is a beautiful Puerto Rican girl, whose family has sent her to the United States in the care of an aunt.

The main theme of "Geraldo No Last Name" centers on the human tragedy of the illegal worker, who must remain as anonymous as possible in order to survive. Marin's and Geraldo's lives touch only by chance because they happen to be in the same dance hall and they dance together. It is evident that Geraldo wants to reveal little about himself beyond his first name. He tells her that he works in a restaurant, but after his death Marin cannot even remember the name of his restaurant—a fact suggesting that Geraldo told her little about his place of employment.

In addition to Geraldo's death and his total anonymity, other tragedies are implied in the story. The fact that living in fear prevents people from communicating with each other and from forming lasting friendships is an unfortunate situation. All barriers between people are tragedies because they breed misunderstandings and unhappiness that touch many lives.

The narrator thinks that Geraldo's lack of identity and the entire situation are a shame. Moreover, she suggests that people will never know how Geraldo managed to live in his "two-room flats" or in the rooms he rented. He probably acted very discreetly with other people, in the same way that he acted with Marin. Consequently, how could people know anything about him or find out whom to notify about his tragic death? Thus, Geraldo's life does not matter, for it is as if he had never existed. Furthermore, Geraldo's tragedy will extend to his homeland, because his people will continue to wonder about his whereabouts for the rest of their lives.

"Geraldo No Last Name" emerges as an indictment of the uncomfortable situations of illegal workers. In addition, it points out how humanly degrading these situations are. Undocumented workers, states the narrator, "always look ashamed," which means that they make their feelings of guilt evident in their behavior, and hence they feel that their worth as human beings is not the same as other people's.

*Style and Technique*

The writing style of "Geraldo No Last Name" is simple, as is Cisneros's style in her other *House on Mango Street* vignettes. Simulating the speech patterns of the story's young narrator, the language is economical, as if the narrator wishes to express as many ideas as possible in the fewest possible words. In this respect, Cisneros's prose resembles poetry by compressing ideas. Moreover, there are no superfluous embellishments in her prose, so that the reader easily accepts the presence of a young narrator telling Geraldo's story in her own words. In addition to the reader, there is evidence that the narrator is relating the story to someone else whom she addresses as "you" in the fifth paragraph of the story.

The encounter of Marin and Geraldo is presented immediately in the opening sentences: "She met him at a dance. Pretty too, and young." The narrator clarifies rather quickly the idea that the young man is "pretty" or looks pretty when she mentions that he is wearing his "Saturday shirt." This is equivalent to stating that he is wearing his Sunday clothes—those that he reserves for when he is not working.

The hit-and-run accident that kills Geraldo is also mentioned early in the story, for this tragedy is an integral part of the major theme of the story, Geraldo's anonymity. Marin's fondness for dancing, which provides the reason for her being in the dance hall that night, is amply explained by simply mentioning the Latin dances that she knows how to do.

The narrator makes no pretense at objectivity. She expresses her own feelings about Geraldo's situation. She believes that his anonymity is a shameful thing. Marin's feelings are also made evident in the story. Although she cannot explain why the death of a nearly complete stranger should matter to her, she stays in the hospital for hours. She leaves only when they send her home "with her coat and some aspirin." Moreover, the narrator worries about Marin's having to explain why she has been out so late. Hence, through her narrator's subjectivity, Cisneros makes the reader aware that she cares about social issues of this nature.

The narrator never tells the reader how she knows that Geraldo is an undocumented worker. Therefore, the reader surmises that Geraldo's appearance and behavior probably match those of many illegal workers. For example, he does not reveal much information about himself, not even his last name. In addition, the fact that he works in a restaurant that he will not identify, probably as a dishwasher or a busboy, reinforces the idea that he is indeed an illegal worker.

Cisneros's writing technique lies chiefly in the economy of words and in the portrayal of her sincerity through the use of a young narrator's speech. The reader believes the story because Cisneros does not leave any loose ends.

*Cida S. Chase*

# GHOST AND FLESH, WATER AND DIRT

*Author:* William Goyen (Charles William Goyen, 1915-1983)
*Type of plot:* Ghost story
*Time of plot:* About 1930 to 1950
*Locale:* A small town in East Texas
*First published:* 1952

*Principal characters:*

MARGY EMMONS, the narrator and protagonist, a resigned older
woman
FURSTA EVANS, a friend of Margy
AN UNNAMED YOUNG WOMAN, to whom Margy is speaking

## The Story

"Ghost and Flesh, Water and Dirt" is the story of Margy Emmons's life as told by her; it is a sad but evocative and mysterious tale that centers on her relationships with two men: Raymon Emmons, the "ghost" of the title, whom Margy "lost" to "dirt," and Nick Natowski, the "flesh," whom she "lost" to "water." Throughout the story, Margy sits in the Pass Time Club drinking beer, talking to a young woman, recalling the "fire" of her life, and sifting through the "ashes" of her memories. Margy is in her "time a tellin," and she warns her companion to "run fast if you don wanna hear what I tell, cause I'm goin ta tell." Margy speaks very briefly of the present, which for her is inextricably linked to the past and dominated by the ghost of Raymon Emmons, who comes to visit her virtually every night. She begins her story with an account of the first time she ever saw Raymon Emmons. Emmons was a thirty-year-old railroad man whom she met, fell in love with, pursued, and married when she was seventeen. Margy says almost nothing about their life together, but she talks at length about how she was devastated by his death. She did not feel that she could face life alone: "I cain't stand a life of just me and our furniture in a room, who's gonna be with me?" Margy went to the preacher for advice and counsel, but "he uz no earthly help." She went to her friend, Fursta Evans, but Fursta's wisdom did not satisfy her either, and so Margy dedicated herself to mourning the dead (her daughter, Chitta, died two weeks before her husband) and avoiding the life around her. She went from her house to the graveyard and back.

After a year, Margy's miserable routine was interrupted by a visit from Fursta. Fursta came knocking on her door to assail Margy for her hypocrisy and self-pity: "Why are you so glued to Raymon Emmonses memry when you never cared a hoot bout him while he was on earth . . . ?" According to Fursta, Margy's marriage was not a happy one; she was endlessly critical of Emmons and ultimately drove him to suicide by blaming him for the death of their child. Fursta argued that Margy should forget the past and begin to make the most of the days she had left: "honey, we got to greet life not grieve life." Margy responded that Raymon Emmons had "fastened" her to her house, but Fursta convinced her to turn her face toward the future and to give life another chance. Margy reluctantly closed up her house and boarded a train bound for California. There, she found that "the sun was out, wide . . . the world was still there." Margy arrived in California during World War II and promptly took a job in an airplane factory and fell in love with a sailor, Nick Natowski. After a brief period of joy during which Nick and Margy "lived like a king and queen," Natowski sailed away to war and his death, and Margy returned to Texas defeated and feeling like she had "been pastured on a rope in California."

Margy opened her house, got a job in Richardson's Shoe Shop, and resigned herself to the life she has been living since her return to Texas: days of menial labor and nights "full of talkin" with Raymon Emmons's ghost. Margy asserts that she has gained some measure of freedom in these last years by learning to accept Raymon Emmon's power over her: "I set real still and let it all be, claimed by that ghost until he unclaims me—and then I get up and go roun, free, and that's why I'm here, settin with you here in the Pass Time Club."

Once she has told her story, Margy goes on to try to impart some of what she has learned from life to her young companion. She believes that "all life is just a sharin of ghosts and flesh," which is to say that the past and the present are intimately linked to each other, that the ghosts of lost days, of lost friends and family and lovers, are very much a part of the everyday world. Margy even goes so far as to say that she believes that the spirits of the past, the ashes of past experiences, are the dominant elements in human life: "Maybe the ghost part is the longest lastin, the fire blazes but the ashes last forever." Margy encourages her young companion to be open and receptive to the various realms of life and twists of fate: "I believe the real right way is to take our worlds, of ghosts or of flesh, take each one as they come and take what comes in em: . . . even run out to meet what worlds come in to our lives."

*Themes and Meanings*

Several of the themes that pervade William Goyen's fiction are to be found in this early story: the isolation and loneliness of human beings; the uneasy relationship between the past and the present; the melancholy quality of people's lives; and the profoundly important, poignant, and loving nature of storytelling.

Everyone in "Ghost and Flesh, Water and Dirt" is essentially alone. Raymon Emmons never attained more than a brief connection with any other human being; the isolation of Nick Natowski, the young sailor from Chicago on his way to a cold death in the Pacific, was only briefly interrupted by his affair with Margy. Even Fursta Evans, for all her efforts, never makes a lasting connection with anyone. The listener in the bar is remote and only vaguely interested in Margy's tale; Margy lives a lonely and resigned existence, punctuated by periods of sadness so intense that she could not leave the seclusion of her house if her "life depended on it." This story and Goyen's fiction in general seem to confirm Margy's assertions that "the fire blazes but the ashes last forever," that the joys of life are fragile, evanescent, and too often unrecognized or unacknowledged ("it's true that you never miss water till the well runs dry, tiz truly true"), and that a sense of loss, of opportunities missed and promises unrealized, is an inevitable part of human life.

Margy Emmons is clearly haunted by the past, and she speaks movingly and convincingly of the interpenetration of past and present, ghost and flesh, and even of the dominance of the past. Her melancholy example and her unsettling bondage to ghosts, to failure and isolation, are, however, opposed quite forcefully by the words and actions of Fursta Evans. Fursta argues for the primacy of the present. She believes that the world is new every minute, always "as fresh as ever," and that people should forget the past and go forward "fresh and empty handed" into the future: "cause listen honey the sun comes up and the sun crosses over and goes down—and while the sun's up we got to get on that fence and crow. Cause night muss fall—and then thas all. Come on, les go roun." Through Fursta, Goyen creates a counterpoint to Margy, a contrary theme, not sounded so frequently or so loudly as Margy's refrain, but possessing a clear and pure chord nevertheless.

It is evident, however, in this story, as in most of Goyen's fiction, that Fursta, not Margy, is the exception, is the true eccentric. Most human beings do live like Margy, looking over their shoulders, unable to forget the past, and struggling endlessly to forge a positive link between the yesterdays and today. Most readers will accept Margy's notion that "there's a time for live things and a time for dead, for ghosts and for flesh'n bones: all life is just a sharin of ghosts and flesh." However, Margy is in many ways an objectionable person, an unfit model, and an imperfect thinker; she is shrewish, self-pitying, unloving, and self-indulgent; her solutions to the problems of how to establish a positive relationship with the past and of how to live do not satisfy. Somehow, though, it does not matter that Margy's answers will not do for everyone; she has been redeemed through her struggle; she has been made more human, more loving, and more vulnerable through her torment and her submission to a ghost, to the spirit. Goyen's stories frequently manifest the duality that he saw in life: spirit and flesh in a single image; male and female in a single body; beauty and ugliness in a single instant; or, as here, past and present, failure and redemption inseparable one from another.

Goyen's story does not provide a solution to the problems of human loneliness or of how to integrate the past and the present successfully, unless the solution is the telling of the story, the sharing of the problem, the interchange of human experience. Goyen believes that all people have stories to tell and that they should tell those stories, that the quality of life is dependent on a constant interchange of personal experience and personal knowledge. The stories always arise out of trouble and through the telling and the listening a redemption becomes possible; humankind is given hope and the ability to endure, to go forward in peace and with love.

## Style and Technique

Goyen's style and technique are unique and highly personal. His stories typically are told by the narrator and are best understood when read aloud. They do not have plots in the conventional sense but are concerned rather with the creation of a mood or the evocation of a mysterious feeling of kinship with the teller. "Ghost and Flesh, Water and Dirt" consists entirely of a monologue by Margy Emmons with two brief italicized passages in the beginning when she speaks only to herself. Margy begins and ends with a vision of "pore Raymon Emmons," and she will no doubt tell this same story when her "time a tellin" comes again. The listener and the reader cannot help being riveted by this strange tale of lovers and ghosts and are left, if not convinced by Margy's ideas, at least moved by and sympathetic to her humanity.

The lyric quality of Goyen's prose, the recurrence of certain key phrases, and the circular movement of the story call to mind the folk ballad. Indeed, many of his stories are similar in content and quality to folk song; they come from and are about common folk, and they are told in the words of ordinary people. Goyen is a master storyteller with a rare gift for turning everyday language into poetry.

*Hal Holladay*

# THE GHOST SOLDIERS

*Author:* Tim O'Brien (1946-      )
*Type of plot:* War, ghost story, psychological
*Time of plot:* The late 1960's
*Locale:* A jungle and an American firebase in Vietnam
*First published:* 1981

*Principal characters:*
  HERB, an American soldier who is seeking revenge
  LEMON and
  AZAR, soldiers in his company
  TEDDY THATCHER and
  JORGENSON, American medics

*The Story*

"The Ghost Soldiers" is told in the first person through the narrator's memories of his twelve months as a soldier fighting in the Vietnam War. The action of the story occurs at two distinct moments in time: when Herb, the narrator, is shot for the second time, and when he later tries to get revenge on Jorgenson, the brand-new medic who froze instead of immediately treating Herb. Like many of Tim O'Brien's war stories, "The Ghost Soldiers" is equally concerned with the environment of Vietnam and with what it was like psychologically for an American to be a soldier in such a strange, unfamiliar place.

The story begins with Herb's recollections about the two times he was shot. He compares the two incidents by focusing on how he was treated by the medic who was present at each firefight. When he was wounded the first time, medic Teddy Thatcher had kept Herb from becoming scared because of his wound, treated him properly, and made sure he was evacuated by helicopter as soon as was possible. However, the second time Herb is shot, medic Jorgenson, who is new to the platoon, freezes as the battle rages around him, allowing Herb to go into shock and seriously threatening his life. Jorgenson's delayed reaction makes the wound worse, and his mishandling of the treatment results in necrosis, which increases Herb's recovery time.

Once Herb recovers from his second wound, he begins to plot revenge on Jorgenson. He first turns to his friend Lemon for help, but Lemon rebuffs him by telling him that Jorgenson has since become a good field medic and that Herb's plan for revenge is unwarranted. Undaunted, Herb turns to another soldier, Azar, for help. Azar agrees, and the two set up a series of aural and visual deceptions to irritate and torment Jorgenson when he is on perimeter patrol later that night.

The twist of the story comes when the games being played on Jorgenson spook Herb as much as they do Jorgenson. As in many of O'Brien's stories, the landscape begins to come alive, and the ghosts of the dead who have fought and been slain in the jungles seem to come out as each of the ruses goes into effect. Herb starts to imagine what Jorgenson is going through, and he ends up working the revenge on himself. He comes to feel Jorgenson's distress and wants the plot to stop, but Azar will not let him. Azar is a sadist and insists that the scheme run its course. Azar ends up attacking and beating Herb while the latter curls up into a ball from the psychological agony he has unintentionally brought on himself.

The night finally ends, and Herb and Jorgenson later meet. They shake hands, and a sense of mutual understanding arises between them. Jorgenson had been scared by the harassments set up by Herb and Azar, and he ultimately feels that Herb has paid him back for his mistake during the battle. The story ends with a discussion of how they can both get back at Azar for what he had done during the night's events.

*Themes and Meanings*

"The Ghost Soldiers" is one of a series republished by O'Brien in the collection *The Things They Carried* (1990). In each of that volume's tales, the environment and what is unseen but felt in the surrounding environs is key to the story. In the case of "The Ghost Soldiers," the ghosts are not real. The landscape scares the American soldiers who are in it. The revenge plot hinges on this. By putting in front of Jorgenson a number of sounds and movements, Herb and Azar plan to make the medic confront the ghosts that are all around him, hopefully punishing him for his mental lapse the day Herb was injured and reminding him of how vulnerable all the American soldiers are in Vietnam. The plan backfires for Herb because the ghosts are so powerful. No one can control them, and so he, too, becomes affected by the series of games they play on Jorgenson.

What is equally important is the status of men like Herb who once were out in the fields of Vietnam but no longer have to enter the jungles. At the time of his injury, Herb was a seasoned soldier, and Jorgenson was inexperienced. The time Herb must spend recovering, in the safety behind the lines of the firebase's fencing, reverses this relationship. When Herb and Jorgenson next meet, it is the latter who is now accepted by the others in the platoon. Herb is an outsider because he no longer has to experience what it is like to be out with the ghosts where there is no space for hiding or pretending. Out on patrol, real lives are at stake, and a real enemy seems to haunt the men at all times. Because Herb no longer experiences this, his plan is seen by Lemon as unnecessary and unfair. It no longer matters to Lemon that Herb also once faced the unknown demons of the night; what matters to him is that Jorgenson has done so and continues to do so. The unreal ghosts help to create a sense of who is a real soldier in O'Brien's story.

*Style and Technique*

O'Brien likes to bring into question the status of stories as stories. The blending of fact and fiction is one of his stylistic trademarks. This can be seen, for example, in the two different versions of "The Ghost Soldiers." The main protagonist in the original version is named Herb, and the first page of the story in *Esquire* magazine clearly states that the story is a work of fiction. However, when the story was reprinted in *The Things They Carried*, the narrator had been renamed Tim in alignment with the other stories of that collection. O'Brien's style is to not resolve this apparent contradiction, for the key issue is still the power of stories to tell truthful things about people, their lives, and their emotions. It matters little if Herb is really a stand-in for the author; what matters is what the story says about men in combat. It can be hard enough to try to express the feelings and emotions of battle-induced stress to those who have never experienced them. For O'Brien, it is more important to go beyond surface-level veracity to try to give the reader a sense of the core truths of combat.

O'Brien is also known for the psychological rendering of soldiers' lives in the Vietnam War. "The Ghost Soldiers" does not try to be universal. It and many other of O'Brien's stories stand in marked contrast to many other war stories. By giving the reader insight into what was going on in Herb's mind, the reader can see what one person experienced as a soldier in Vietnam. The reader comes to identify with Herb because he experiences through the particularity of his story many emotions that are quite understandable to a broad range of people. The desire for revenge is well known, as is a sense of a plan gone awry. Most people can also find a sense of connection with the feeling of having taken something too far, which is what finally allows Herb to make peace with Jorgenson. The sense of mutually experienced emotions bonds the two of them despite their history. O'Brien's style is most impressive in this moment of bonding because ultimately his story becomes less about war or ghosts than about human connections in times of great stress. His ability to carefully explain the psychology of his narrator allows the reader to feel a connection with both him and the other soldiers trying to survive amid the ghosts of the Vietnamese countryside and the Vietnam War.

*Joshua Stein*

# THE GHOSTS

*Author:* Lord Dunsany (Edward John Moreton Drax Plunkett, 1878-1957)
*Type of plot:* Horror
*Time of plot:* About 1900
*Locale:* Rural England
*First published:* 1908

*Principal characters:*
THE NARRATOR, an intellectual who believes in scientific facts
HIS BROTHER, the owner of a mansion he claims is haunted

*The Story*

The narrator recalls his experience with ghosts on a winter night in a decaying English mansion that was built in the seventeenth century. He has been arguing with his brother over the existence of such supernatural creatures and defiantly offers to stay up all night to confront the ghosts that his brother claims haunt the house. The narrator drinks several cups of strong tea to stay awake and smokes cigars to stimulate his senses. He fully expects to see ghostly figures but firmly believes they will be figments of his own imagination.

At midnight a group of male and female ghosts appear dressed in the costumes of Jacobean aristocrats. Evidently they are former owners of this mansion and their relatives. The ghosts sit down, ignoring the narrator. Then a pack of "black creatures" bursts into the chamber. Although hideous monsters, they behave like devoted hounds. The narrator realizes that these creatures are "the filthy, immortal sins of those courtly men and women." Each beast goes up to its master, who is forced to acknowledge the secret sin symbolized by the face-licking animal ghost. Several human ghosts have more than one nightmarish creatures competing for attention.

The narrator suggests that one of the female ghosts is guilty of murder and that two others, a lady and a courtier, may be guilty of adultery. Otherwise he does not name any specific sins but suggests through his descriptions of the monsters that the sins they represent are of the most vile deeds of which human beings can be guilty.

Suddenly one of the creatures scents the narrator's presence and leads its companions in search of him. A number of the horrible creatures swarm over the narrator and begin clawing him. As their claws touch his body, he is overwhelmed by fiendish desires, such as the idea that he should murder his own brother. He sees how easy this would be. He could pretend that he thought his brother was a ghost and thus fire his revolver in self-defense. Afterward he would dress the body in a sheet and put flour on its face to make it appear his brother had been trying to frighten him.

As the narrator is about to succumb to this temptation, he tries to shut out his wicked thoughts by working out geometry problems in his head. He succeeds in proving the validity of a Euclidian theorem. At this point, logic and reason re-establish themselves and the monsters disappear. It seems inconceivable to the narrator that he has actually contemplated murdering his own brother.

## Themes and Meanings

Lord Dunsany uses the framework of a traditional ghost story to illustrate his thesis that all human beings are capable of the most fiendish sins. He suggests that people hide their true thoughts and emotions behind masks of decorum. His story implies that every human being is capable of committing, or at least contemplating, any of the crimes for which only a few are ever exposed and convicted. Dunsany suggests that reason and logic are tools by which humans have learned to cope with their animal natures, that civilization is built by men and women who systematically occupy their minds with constructive thoughts in order to avoid succumbing to bestial impulses. His story further suggests that civilization is in peril from the wicked impulses of the very citizens who have worked with minds and hands to build it.

Though short, "The Ghosts" is full of implications. The story resembles Oscar Wilde's well-known novel *The Picture of Dorian Gray* (1890) and Robert Louis Stevenson's famous short novel *The Strange Case of Dr. Jekyll and Mr. Hyde* (1886). Both works imply that people's hearts cannot be read through their faces. The world is full of wickedness, but wicked people do not go about wearing signs revealing their true characters. The civilized world is a masquerade in which people take pains to appear to be something other than what they are. Readers are left to judge, by examining their own secret thoughts and impulses, whether Dunsany is speaking the truth.

Like Wilde and Stevenson, Dunsany only hints at the sins that his characters have committed because of the prudery and hypocrisy of the era in which he lived. The Victorian and Edwardian ages were notorious for hiding secret vices behind refined manners and external respectability. Dunsany's story attributes the sins to aristocratic ghosts from the seventeenth century but undoubtedly has gentlemen and ladies of his own time foremost in his thoughts.

"The Ghosts" portrays an older world that was about to be subjected to violent changes with the advent of airplanes, automobiles, wireless communication, and all the modern weapons of war. Whether consciously or unconsciously, Dunsany seems to be portraying the decaying older world that was based on land ownership, aristocracy, and imperialism. His characters seem helpless and passive, haunted with depressing thoughts. They are representatives of the old order that would eventually be displaced by the aggressive, pragmatic, democratic, internationalist spirit of the modern era. The fear elicited by stories such as "The Ghosts" may be a fear of the uncertain future, felt especially by aristocrats such as Dunsany himself.

## Style and Technique

A gifted writer who used many different styles and techniques, Dunsany had a writing career that spanned more than half of the revolutionary twentieth century, during which time literary fashions underwent many changes. His early short stories, of which "The Ghosts" is a good example, are written in an ornate, poetic style reminiscent of the florid writing and romantic literary conventions of Edgar Allan Poe, with considerable emphasis on description of landscapes, costumes, and interior furnishings. Readers had more patience with lengthy passages of such description before modern photography made pictures commonplace. Dunsany's later stories, such as "The Two Bottles of Relish" (1932), published after Europe had been through the devastating World War I and was entering the Great Depression, are far more realistic, more democratic, less descriptive, and even "minimalistic" by comparison.

Dunsany's collected works show great technical virtuosity. His short story "The Two Bottles of Relish," for example, uses the persona of a *faux naïf* Cockney narrator who is obviously poorly educated and has little experience in putting his thoughts into words. "The Ghosts" presents a striking contrast. The narrator is obviously intelligent, sensitive, and well educated. He has a good knowledge of history and an excellent vocabulary. The reader is reminded of the highly articulate and sometimes poetic fictitious narrators of some of Edgar Allan Poe's horror stories, such as "The Fall of the House of Usher" (1839). In fact, Dunsany seems heavily indebted to Poe for many of his inspirations.

"The Ghosts" begins like an old-fashioned ghost story of the type that have elicited fear and trembling since time immemorial. Tellers of such stories enjoy terrifying people by employing a somber tone and presenting lurid descriptions of decay—gloomy old mansions with rats in the walls, eerie noises, cloudy winter skies shattered by bolts of lightning—and their audiences enjoy being terrified. Dunsany begins his story very much in the manner of a conventional ghost story in order to lull the reader into a false sense of security. He even gives his story the title "The Ghosts" in order to make it appear that he is planning to narrate a stereotypical ghost story. The reader expects the skeptical protagonist to see a ghost or two, become badly frightened, and believe in ghosts forever after. As novelist Vladimir Nabokov once noted, "The 'I' in the story cannot die in the story." The fact that the protagonist is telling of his own experience offers the reader assurance that he did not die of fright or go into a catatonic state of psychosis.

The reader is intentionally lulled into a false sense of security; then Dunsany injects a note of true horror by introducing a pack of hideous animal-ghosts. This is not part of the conventional ghost story. It is more than the reader bargained for, but the reader by now is too involved to be able to shut the book. Like the narrator, the reader expects to see only one or two transparent figures dressed in sheets and perhaps to hear a few moans or some rattling chains; now, like the narrator, the reader finds him- or herself trapped in a hellish, life-threatening, perhaps even soul-threatening situation.

Now that Dunsany has managed to capture the reader in the web of his narrative, he goes further, step by step, by using these affectionate monsters from hell to suggest that all human beings have secret impulses that they cannot escape in life or in death. When the narrator acknowledges that he himself is capable of murdering his own innocent brother and concocting an elaborate lie to escape punishment, it is but one step further to accuse the reader of being capable of such unspeakable thoughts.

*Bill Delaney*

# THE GIFT

*Author:* John Steinbeck (1902-1968)
*Type of plot:* Domestic realism
*Time of plot:* The early twentieth century
*Locale:* Salinas Valley, California
*First published:* 1933

### Principal characters:

JODY TIFLIN, a ten-year-old farm boy, the point-of-view character
BILLY BUCK, a ranch hand
CARL TIFLIN, Jody's father

### The Story

Jody Tiflin is a shy, polite, ten-year-old boy, the only child of the Tiflins, who own a small ranch in the Salinas Valley. Billy Buck, the ranch hand, is almost a part of the family and has Jody's highest respect.

One late summer day, Carl Tiflin and Billy drive six old milk cows to Salinas to the butcher. Jody would like to go along, but school has resumed. Before setting out on the mile walk to school, Jody walks up to the sagebrush tine to the spring, and then to the cypress tree where pigs are butchered. On the verge of adolescence, Jody is beginning to lose his childish pleasure in smashing muskmelons or killing mice. He yearns for greater excitement and responsibility.

The two men return late that evening with a gift for Jody, a red colt. However, rather than present the gift immediately, Jody's father only tells Jody to go to bed, that he will need Jody in the morning.

After breakfast the men take Jody to the barn to show him the pony. The insensitive Carl Tiflin abhors any weakness or sentimentality and seems cross and embarrassed about giving his son the gift, but Billy Buck comprehends the boy's elation. Jody names his pony Gabilan, after the mountains next to which they live.

Jody's life now so revolves around Gabilan that he sometimes forgets his chores, but with this new responsibility, he begins to develop greater maturity. Under Billy's guidance, Jody takes good care of the pony and begins to train him. Billy seemingly knows all there is to know about horses, and in the evenings he even braids a tail-hair rope for Jody. The pony produces a strong bond between Jody and Billy.

Carl says that by Thanksgiving Gabilan will be big enough to ride, so in eager anticipation of the great day Jody begins to saddle him daily. Winter is approaching, and Jody leaves Gabilan out in the sunny corral as much as possible. On a day when Billy assures Jody that it will not rain, Jody leaves the pony out in the corral when he goes to school. It does rain, however, and when Jody gets home, Gabilan has taken cold.

For the first time, Billy has failed Jody. However, he assures the boy that Gabilan will get well, and he nurses the pony skillfully. The next day, however, Gabilan is worse, and by the second day Billy admits that Gabilan has "strangles" and is a very sick pony. Billy and Jody take turns sleeping in the barn and nursing Gabilan, but the pony does not get better. Billy lances the pony's throat to drain the pus, and for a few hours the pony is more spirited. However, congestion returns, and later Billy must open a hole in Gabilan's windpipe so he can breathe. Gabilan seems better again, but while Jody naps in the hay that night, the barn door blows open and the red pony runs out into the winter wind.

By the next morning, hope has faded. Jody is sent to breakfast but instead goes to the dark cypress tree—a place associated in his mind with death—to think. He returns to the barn and waits all day with Gabilan, but while he sleeps that night, the barn door again blows open. When he awakes at dawn Gabilan is gone. Jody rushes from the barn and follows the pony's tracks up the ridge; in the sky he sees buzzards beginning to circle. He runs up the hill into the brush, and in a clearing he finds his pony in the throes of death, buzzards awaiting their moment.

Just as the first buzzard alights on the pony's head and sinks its beak into Gabilan's eye, Jody plunges into the circle of birds and grabs the buzzard by the throat. With a rock he smashes the bird's head; he is still beating the bloody bird when Carl and Billy come over the hill. Jody's father is cool and distant as always, reminding Jody that the buzzard did not kill Gabilan. Billy Buck, however, lifts Jody into his arms to carry him home. Only Billy understands how Jody feels.

*Themes and Meanings*

"The Gift" is about a young boy's passage from innocence to experience. The "gift" is more than a pony; it is also maturity. Jody grows up through taking responsibility, through facing death, and through accepting the fallibility of his hero.

Harsh father that he is, Carl Tiflin does help his son grow up by the way in which he gives Jody gifts. He gives Jody a rifle, but no bullets, because he knows that the boy is not ready for the power to kill until he comprehends the meaning of death. Similarly, the pony is given on the condition that Jody take full responsibility for its care.

Steinbeck sends Jody to the spring or to the cypress tree, places that Jody vaguely associates with life and death, respectively, when he needs to think things out. It is from the cypress tree that Jody first sees buzzards circling; he hates them because they eat carrion and are associated with death, but he recognizes that they are a necessary part of the natural cycle. His irrational but understandable attack on the buzzard at the end of the story purges his rage, and Billy understands that this cathartic attack on "death" is not necessarily a childish reaction.

Perhaps most important to Jody's maturation is his recognition, and then acceptance, of Billy's fallibility. He is angry at Billy for being wrong about the rain, and Jody's faith in his hero is shaken by Billy's failure to save Gabilan. However, his final acceptance of Billy's love and his knowledge that, though he failed, Billy gave his best, are adult attitudes.

Especially in the 1930's Steinbeck's stories celebrated the interrelatedness of love and work. In almost every story, one figure of wisdom, authority, and love seems to represent the author's point of view. Invariably, this character is a person of compassion and sensitivity, and is also a worker who is skilled and competent but unpresumptuous and sharing. In "The Gift" this character is Billy Buck; it is he who guides Jody through the traumatic transition to manhood.

*Style and Technique*

"The Gift" was the first of three stories published in 1937 as the novella *The Red Pony*. (The other two stories are "The Great Mountains" and "The Promise"; a fourth story, "The Leader of the People" involves the same characters.)

It was in the 1930's, the decade when Steinbeck's fiction grew out of what he knew best—the *paisanos* of Monterey, the inhabitants, such as the Tiflns, of the small towns and rural valleys of California, and the dispossessed migrant farm laborers of *In Dubious Battle* (1936) and *The Grapes of Wrath* (1938)—that Steinbeck produced his greatest work. He mastered the colloquial language of the people about whom he wrote, and his broad experience among the townsmen, farmers, and farmworkers enabled him to describe these people, their lives and their work, authentically and with intricate detail. Not especially innovative in style and technique, Steinbeck wrote "The Gift" like most of his fiction, in the third person and from the omniscient point of view. The plot is straightforward and readily comprehensible. What is masterful about Steinbeck's style is his rendition of detail.

Having worked as a horse trainer for the United States Army, Steinbeck, like his character Billy Buck, knew horses. From Billy the reader learns that horses are "afraid for their feet," that a horse that puts its whole nose and mouth in the water to drink is spirited, and that the moods of horses are expressed by their ears. Steinbeck was an equally keen observer of human action and motivation. When Carl and Billy come in for breakfast, Jody habitually listens to their steps to hear if they are wearing flat shoes or boots because boots mean that they will be riding somewhere. Though the sounds are implanted in his memory, he always looks under the table anyway, to make sure. In the glow of first possession of the red pony, Jody tortures himself by imagining that the pony has disappeared, or that rats have gnawed holes in the saddle; in his good fortune, the possibility of loss seems so threatening that the possibility must be entertained to soften the loss should it occur. As such passages suggest, Steinbeck's "gift" to the reader is a sensitive, moving depiction of the end of childhood.

*Jerry W. Wilson*

# THE GIFT OF THE MAGI

*Author:* O. Henry (William Sydney Porter, 1862-1910)
*Type of plot:* Domestic realism
*Time of plot:* 1902
*Locale:* New York City
*First published:* 1905

Principal characters:
DELLA YOUNG, a young married woman
JIM YOUNG, her husband

*The Story*

Della Young is a devoted young married woman. Christmas Eve finds her in possession of a meager one dollar and eighty-seven cents, the sum total of her savings, with which she wants to buy a gift for her husband, Jim. A recent cut in the family income, from an ample thirty dollars a week to a stingy twenty dollars a week, has turned Della's frugality into parsimony. Although she lives in an eight-dollar-a-week flat and her general surroundings, even by the greatest stretch of the imagination, do not meet the standards of genteel poverty, Della determines that she cannot live through Christmas without giving Jim a tangible reminder of the season.

Distraught, she clutches the one dollar and eighty-seven cents in her hand as she moves discontentedly about her tiny home. Suddenly, catching a glance of herself in the cheap pier glass mirror, a maneuver possible only for the slender and agile viewer, the perfect solution suggests itself. Whirling about with happiness, she lets down her long, beautiful hair. It is like brown sable and falls in caressing folds to below her knees. After a moment's self-admiration, and another half-moment's reservation, during which time a tear streaks down her face, she resolutely puts on her old hat and jacket and leaves the flat.

Della's quick steps take her to the shop of Madame Sofronie, an establishment that trades in hair goods of all kinds. Entering quickly, lest her nerve desert her, she offers to sell her hair. Madame Sofronie surveys the luxuriant tresses, unceremoniously slices them off, and hands Della twenty dollars. For the next two hours, Della feels herself in paradise, temporarily luxuriating in the knowledge that she can buy anything she wants. She decides on a watch fob for Jim's beautiful old watch. If there are two treasures in the world of which James and Della Dillingham Young are inordinately and justly proud, they are her hair (lately and gladly sacrificed) and Jim's revered gold watch, handed down to him by his grandfather.

She finally sees exactly what she wants, a platinum watch fob that costs twenty-one dollars. She excitedly anticipates Jim's reaction when he sees a proper chain for his watch. Until now, he has been using an old leather strap, which, despite the watch's elegance, has forced him to look at the time surreptitiously.

Arriving back at the flat, breathless but triumphant, Della remembers her newly bobbed appearance. She reaches for the curling irons and soon a mass of close-cropped curls adorns her shorn head. She stares at herself anxiously in the mirror, hoping that her husband will still love her. As is her usual custom, she prepares dinner for the always punctual Jim and sits down to await his arrival. The precious gift is tightly clutched in her hand. She mutters an imprecation to God so that Jim will think she is still pretty.

At precisely seven o'clock, she hears Jim's familiar step on the stairs, his key in the door. He is a careworn young man, only twenty-two and already burdened with many responsibilities. He opens the door, sees Della, and an indiscernible look, neither sorrow nor surprise, overtakes him. His face can only be described as bearing a mask of melancholy disbelief. Even though Della rushes to assure him that her hair grows fast and that she will soon be back to normal, Jim cannot seem to be persuaded that her beautiful hair is really gone. Della implores him to understand that she simply could not have lived through Christmas without buying him a gift; she begs him, for her sake, as well as the season's, to be happy.

Jim, as if waking from a trance, embraces her and readily tells her that there is nothing a shampoo or haircut could do to Della that would alter his love for her. In the excitement he has forgotten to give her gift, and now he offers her a paper-wrapped package. Tearing at it eagerly, Della finds a set of combs, tortoise shell, bejewelled combs that she has so often admired in a shop on Broadway, combs whose color combines perfectly with her own vanished tresses. Her immense joy turns to tears but quickly returns when she remembers just how fast her hair grows.

Jim has not yet seen his beautiful present. She holds it out to him, and the precious metal catches all the nuances of light in the room. It is indeed a beautiful specimen of a watch chain, and Della insists on attaching it to Jim's watch. Jim looks at her with infinite love and patience and suggests that they both put away their presents—for a while. Jim has sold his watch in order to buy the combs for Della even as she has sold her hair to buy the watch chain for Jim.

Like the Magi, those wise men who invented the tradition of Christmas giving, both Della and Jim have unwisely sacrificed the greatest treasures of their house for each other. However, of all those who give gifts, these two are inevitably the wisest.

### Themes and Meanings

O. Henry often chose to translate tragedy or misfortune into an emphasized regard and tenderness for the unlucky or the underdog. He never cared for the so-called higher classes but preferred to cull his characters, and his sympathies, from watching ordinary people on the streets and in the shops and cafés. This perspective on the world around him is highly visible in "The Gift of the Magi," where, to enforce his quasi-religious message, he counterpoints the elements of love and caring with those of poverty and sacrifice.

The extreme devotion manifested on the part of the young married couple becomes almost incongruous when contrasted against the dreariness and bleakness of their material surroundings. Each arrives at the conclusion that it is impossible to live through Christmas without granting the other's supreme wish. It is not "selfish magnanimity"—a desire to revel in the sacrifice of giving—that motivates them. They truly embrace the noble sentiment of selflessness.

Thus, despite the specter of poverty, the story is animated by an unexpressed hope for the future. (This is a variation on the old theme that love conquers all, particularly material setbacks.) By setting the story at Christmastime, the author suggests that simple, unselfish human love is the basis of such hope for humankind.

*Style and Technique*

O. Henry's humor and imagination conquer any journalistic tendencies he may have transferred to fiction. His penchant for dramatic irony, a trademark in many of his short stories, gives his style its distinctive flavor. Gentle and ingenious, his writing is pervaded by that eminently salable quality known as "human interest." This quality is best exemplified in his quest for sincerity: his desire to write about real people in real situations.

Della and Jim are not the products of an overly sentimental imagination. The author strives to create circumstances as well as physical surroundings that ring true to life. Both the protagonists accept life as they find it without giving in to the negative emotions of hopelessness or despair. Della's only moment of doubt still revolves around her husband's well-being, when she seeks divine intervention so that she may remain pretty in Jim's eyes. Jim covers his fear of Della's disappointment with an almost affected nonchalance when he requests that they merely put their Christmas gifts away and keep them for an unspecified future. Only then does he reveal that he has sacrificed his treasure to secure Della's desire. His certainty that they will both use these items in the future provides the unspoken thought that life is bound to improve for them.

The protagonists do not react to each other out of saintliness, duty, or love of self-imposed sacrifice: They simply embody the twin spirits of love and Christmas. For the less-than-devout O. Henry, these essences are one and the same. The author suggests that sentiment does not have to be sacrificed to the cause of realism.

*Rhona E. Zaid*

# THE GILDED SIX-BITS

*Author:* Zora Neale Hurston (1891-1960)
*Type of plot:* Realism, psychological
*Time of plot:* The late nineteenth century
*Locale:* Eatonville, Florida
*First published:* 1933

*Principal characters:*

MISSIE MAY BANKS, a young African American housewife

JOE BANKS, her devoted and hardworking African American husband

OTIS D. SLEMMONS, her lover, a traveling African American dandy

*The Story*

Newlyweds Joe and Missie May Banks frolic in their newfound marital bliss. Their Saturday afternoon routine is especially playful, as Joe comes home from his job at the local fertilizer plant lovingly to toss fifty-cent pieces at his young wife who has been busy preparing for his arrival. She has cleaned and scoured the house, its surroundings, and herself and has prepared Joe's bath water for him to do the same before they settle down to a long afternoon of pleasure.

This particular Saturday afternoon, after the usual tossing of the money and Missie May's playful rifling of Joe's pockets to retrieve the candy kisses he always brings her, Joe has a surprise for Missie May. In addition their usual routine, Joe announces that he is taking his wife to town to the recently opened ice cream parlor to enjoy a treat. This visit will also give Joe an opportunity to show off his wife to the townspeople, especially to the proprietor of the ice cream parlor, Otis D. Slemmons, a recent arrival to the town and a showoff and braggart.

As they return home, Joe is excited over Slemmons's apparent success and is clearly taken with the way that Slemmons shows off his gold pieces, how he wears fine clothes, and how he talks in a citified manner. Missie May, however, is more reflective about the encounter with Slemmons and begins to devise a plan by which she can get some of the gold pieces for Joe.

Some nights later, Joe comes home early from work because of a shutdown at the plant. As he steps into his kitchen door, he accidentally knocks some dishes to the floor and hears a quick movement in the bedroom. Thinking perhaps that he has frightened an intruder intent on harming his wife, Joe springs into action. However, he is immediately stopped in his tracks as he steps into the bedroom and finds that the intruder is none other than Otis D. Slemmons, whom he catches in a compromising position without his pants. After Joe soundly whips and dispatches Slemmons, he turns in sorrow and disbelief to his wife, who pleads that she was doing it all for him. Compounding the absurdity of this betrayal and Missie May's shame, is Joe's discovery that the gold money that Slemmons is so fond of showing off is nothing more than a gilded six-bit coin.

The aftermath of the betrayal finds husband and wife trying to regain lost ground— Joe behaving aloofly as if nothing has happened, and Missie May working overtime to try to win back Joe's love. Eventually, physical desire gives way to a reunion of sorts, but the next morning, Missie May finds the gilded six-bit as payment from Joe, an act that sends her further into despair.

Soon, however, Missie May is pregnant, a condition that fuels speculation as to who the father is. She confirms simply that it is Joe. When the boy is born, he looks just like Joe. Thus the reconciliation begins, as love and family overcome a single act of foolishness. As the story closes, Joe Banks has resumed his routine—marketing in Orlando and purchasing candy kisses for his wife and son with the gilded six-bit left by Otis D. Slemmons. When Joe arrives at home, he tosses the familiar fifty-cent pieces at his wife's door, a signal that they have come full circle. Fortunately, for Joe and Missie May, all is forgiven and all is forgotten.

*Themes and Meanings*

Zora Neale Hurston's intention in "The Gilded Six-Bits" is to counter the lingering "happy darky" stereotype by which African Americans were regarded in her time. Specifically, she refutes the clearly condescending attitude of the white store clerk at the end of the story who wants to be like the African Americans, apparently worry-free and always laughing. Such a perception is rendered ridiculous and absurd by Hurston's story of the internal turmoil caused by an act of marital infidelity and the extraordinary efforts of Joe and Missie May to rekindle their love and save their marriage.

In addition, Hurston's positioning Joe and Missie May in an edenic setting in the opening of the story, complete with bowers of blooms and glistening cleanliness, only to have Eden invaded and defiled by the serpentlike Otis D. Slemmons makes her message abundantly clear: If it can happen to Adam and Eve in the Garden of Eden, why not to ordinary black people in Eatonville? Hurston advances this idea numerous times by insisting on human sameness even in the face of cultural differences.

Moreover, to make her point, Hurston wants there to be no mistake about the racial identity of her characters or the fact that her black characters' day-to-day lives are affected only peripherally by whites. Because of this separateness, whites have little real knowledge about black lives that, on a human level, are little different from their own. Hurston would further explore this idea of human sameness in her last novel, *Seraph on the Suwanee* (1948).

In "The Gilded Six-Bits," Hurston argues that love has the power to heal all wounds if it is given the opportunity. In the beginning of the story, Joe and Missie May's love is a strong, youthful one. There is naïveté on both parts, but because their love is real, it is able to withstand the challenge of the defilement by Slemmons. That Joe can laugh at the matter and resume his routine and that Missie May can respond in kind suggests that love does have the power to heal itself if those who express it do so in a genuine manner. Although the earlier innocence is not restored, clearly Joe and Missie May have learned and grown as a result of this ordeal. Also, the baby boy functions as an agent of healing. The baby is something both Joe and Missie May wanted, and he arrives just in time to save a marriage that might have been doomed otherwise.

## Style and Technique

By the time Hurston wrote and published "The Gilded Six-Bits," she had clearly mastered the short-story genre. This story was her last published short work before she turned to the novel as her preferred genre. Its length, greater than many of her other stories, suggests she was ready to tackle a longer narrative. In this story, Hurston provides an adequate exposition of the facts and then spends most of her time examining the complex realities of the aftermath of the marital betrayal. As usual, she is adept at portraying the emotional responses of both the male and female protagonists, a skill not often recognized by her critics.

As with all of her works, Hurston approaches "The Gilded Six-Bits" with much regard for her setting, her characters, and her subject matter. Therefore, while she foregrounds the black folk, she does so with care and compassion that underscores her ability to portray them in a realistic fashion. Dialect and colorful turns of phrase are used to illuminate character and culture but are never used to condescend to or condemn. Although the events in the story run the gamut from comic to tragic, Hurston uses this range of emotions to further her argument that such responses are human and common, even in the lives of black folk. On another level, the reader can readily ascertain Hurston's fascination with the culture of black folk, as seen, for example, in Missie May's adornment of her kitchen and her garden in a way that becomes an important aspect of Hurston's cultural theory of the African American's desire to adorn.

*Warren J. Carson*

# THE GILGUL OF PARK AVENUE

*Author:* Nathan Englander (1970-    )
*Type of plot:* Magical Realism, domestic realism
*Time of plot:* Between 1949 and 1953
*Locale:* Manhattan, New York City
*First published:* 1999

> *Principal characters:*
> CHARLES MORTON LUGER, a fifty-five-year-old financial analyst
> SUE LUGER, his wife
> DR. BIRNBAUM, his psychologist
> RABBI ZALMAN MEINTZ, the spiritual leader of the Royal Hills
>     Mystical Jewish Reclamation Center

*The Story*

In a taxicab in Manhattan as Charles, a middle-aged, nominally Christian financial analyst, discovers that he has been transformed into an Orthodox Jew during the ride. Charles is so shocked that he tells the cabdriver. His next step is to tell Sue, his wife, but he is nervous about telling her and needs help to approach her about his newfound religion. Charles is depicted as being level-headed and Sue as an ideal wife who has a top-notch job. They have no children.

Charles plans to seek guidance from his psychologist, Dr. Birnbaum, regarding his newly discovered Jewish soul, but he also seeks help from religious individuals. By hunting through the huge Manhattan yellow pages, where he knows he can find anything, Charles locates the Royal Hills Mystical Jewish Reclamation Center (R-HMJRC), a type of clearinghouse for the Judeo-supernatural that deals in messianic issues, dream interpretation, numerology, retreats, and recovered memory.

After traveling to the R-HMJRC, housed in a beautifully renovated Gothic brownstone, he ascends the stairs to the cluttered, dusty attic where Rabbi Zalman Meintz, spiritual leader of the R-HMJRC, has his office. Like Charles's home, much of the furniture is covered in chintz, but unlike the chintz-covered furniture in Charles's newly decorated foyer, living room, and dining room, the rabbi's office couches are old and worn. The rabbi is described as being around thirty years old, wearing a black suit and black hat, and having a long black beard and a large caricaturelike nose. Charles confesses that he is Jewish. The rabbi proceeds to tell him that his statement is quite believable and that he accepts Charles as a fellow Jew.

The rabbi encourages Charles to go home and tell his wife, Sue, an art director for a glamorous magazine. She maintains their home with a decorator's skill, displaying a preference for chintz and elegant table settings. When Charles states that he is Jewish, she thinks he is having a nervous breakdown. His epiphany affects his workplace as he receives numerous telephone calls from Dr. Birnbaum and personal visits from Rabbi Zalman and has confrontations with his chief executive officer, Walter.

At home Sue ignores Charles and serves foods that do not involve kosher issues. Sue and Charles have been married twenty-seven years and argue frequently. She views Charles's behavior as a midlife crisis. One incident that reinforces her opinion occurs when Charles takes a mezuzah from a neighbor's doorpost and nails it to his apartment doorpost. This is inappropriate behavior, and Sue becomes upset. She suggests that he and the rabbi should be committed for their antisocial behavior.

Charles arranges a dinner for Dr. Birnbaum, Rabbi Zalman, Sue, and himself. Sue orders kosher food from a nearby restaurant for the dinner. The elegant service and presentation to which Sue is accustomed are replaced with paper goods and plastic dinnerware that enable the meal to be served in a kosher manner. Sue goes to great efforts to accommodate her husband's newly acquired need. The only kosher wine she finds in the store is a screw-top kosher wine.

At dinner, Zalman makes rude remarks to the psychologist, and Sue is rendered helpless. She kneels on the floor to pray. She plans to pray for God to remove the newfound Jewishness from Charles so that he will be as he was before his Jewish soul overtook him. Charles joins her on the floor, and they have a frank discussion. Sue likens Charles's newfound religion to a new lover. Charles wants to keep his marriage with Sue and hopes that she will accept him and love him as he now is.

*Themes and Meanings*

A "gilgul" is the phenomenological occurrence of souls shifting from person to person. In the back of a taxicab, a transitory vehicle, Charles experiences his transformation into a Jewish man. In several of Nathan Englander's stories, alienated characters seek to be part of a larger group yet remain isolated. Rather than the isolation associated with alienation, Charles—the protagonist in "The Gilgul of Park Avenue"—experiences a disconnection from his earlier life. With this disruption, he experiences a dynamic fear of becoming alienated from his Christian wife, Sue.

Charles has always been forthright with Sue, even when he was trying to tease her about his fidelity. Sue tolerated his teasing about running off with his secretary; this reflected the openness of their relationship. The theme of male/female relationships is strongly explored through the interaction of Charles, who has lived for fifty-five years as a nonpracticing Christian, and his wife of twenty-seven years, Sue. Even though Charles experiences a miraculous change and tries to share his newly discovered reality with others, including the cabdriver, his psychologist, and a rabbi from the R-HMJRC, he does not feel comfortable discussing his new experience.

Situational humor is threaded throughout the story. First, Charles's transformation in a taxicab into a believer of a completely different religion is inexplicable. Second, Sue has just had a root canal and is unable to control her facial features when she tries to respond to Charles's epiphany. Third, Sue's rigid fabric- and color-coordinated decorating techniques foreshadow her enormous distaste for the paper and plastic used at the kosher dinner she serves for Charles, the psychologist, and the rabbi. Fourth, Charles tries to adhere to Jewish laws such as placing a mezuzah containing special blessings on his doorpost. Because he does not know where to buy one, he pries one from his Jewish neighbors' door because the neighbor does not follow the Jewish laws, and therefore, he thinks the neighbor will not miss the mezuzah.

Although Charles experiences no difference in his sensory perceptions, he understands that being Jewish comes with specific guidelines. However, Sue becomes more frustrated with each new rule that Charles tries to add: His new religion requires eating kosher food, praying with a skullcap, and using a prayer shawl. At one point, Charles notices that Sue sounds more Jewish than he does, meaning that she is complaining and nagging in a stereotypical Jewish way. Their relationship is based on teasing and banter, but when Charles explains that he is Jewish, she initially is at a loss for a retort.

In the final scene, Charles and Sue face each other openly. His hope is that Sue recognizes the change in his soul and loves him in his transformed existence.

*Style and Technique*

"The Gilgul of Park Avenue," like much of Englander's fiction, seemingly ends weakly. It concludes with Charles's passively expressed hope that Sue, his wife, will find some way to accept him with his newly discovered Jewish soul. Englander has been identified as the heir apparent to Bernard Malamud, who has been called the king of the American Jewish story. His works also reveal direct roots in the classic Yiddish literature of the nineteenth century writers and in writers such as Shmuel Yosef Agnon and Isaac Bashevis Singer.

Englander includes humorous dialogue to develop each of the characters. Charles plays the straight man to each of the characters. For example, the interchange between Charles and the rabbi is humorous because Charles finds someone who seems to understand his peculiar revelation. In another scene, Charles refuses to take calls from the psychologist who seems to be the most logical person to help him.

The rabbi is a partially comic character. Although he dresses in traditional black garb to look scholarly, he reveals that he has recently experienced a calling from his soul to transform himself and give up a life of addiction to sorrow and drugs. The rabbi explains that the soul Charles possesses is Jewish. He gives Charles books that range from Jewish modern fiction to works on Jewish family purity to rabbinical tomes of law so that Charles will develop a better understanding of his newly discovered soul.

Sue is developed as a dynamic character whose physical pain from the root canal is measured against her emotional pain from losing her Christian husband. The symbolism of the root canal, in which a tooth root is lost, reflects Charles's loss of his roots of fifty-five years. With proper care, the tooth whose root has been extracted will still function after the root canal is filled with another substance. Likewise, after his Christianity has been extracted, Charles will still function once his root (or soul) is filled with the guidelines of Judaism.

*Annette M. Magid*

# GIMPEL THE FOOL

*Author:* Isaac Bashevis Singer (1904-1991)
*Type of plot:* Fable
*Time of plot:* The early twentieth century
*Locale:* Frampol, Poland
*First published:* "Gimpel Tam," 1945 (English translation, 1953)

> *Principal characters:*
> GIMPEL, the narrator and protagonist, who questions whether he
>   is a fool
> ELKA, his promiscuous wife
> THE SPIRIT OF EVIL, who tempts Gimpel

*The Story*

Gimpel, who has had the reputation of being a fool since his school days, is the narrator of his own story. He relates how the other children used to tease and play tricks on him, and how, because he did not want to endure their taunts when he expressed disbelief in what they said, he made the decision to believe them—in the hope, as he says, that it would do them some good.

An orphan, Gimpel was apprenticed to a baker, and all of his customers continued to tease him by telling him outlandish things that had supposedly happened. Gimpel says that he knew the unlikelihood of these tales, but again, rather than argue with his customers, he took the attitude that anything is possible and was again taunted for his gullibility. When Gimpel asked the rabbi's advice, the rabbi told him that the others were the fools, not he, and that it is better to act like a fool for all of one's life than to be evil for a single hour.

Gimpel next describes an event that takes place when he is an adult. Everyone plays matchmaker in his marriage to Elka, a promiscuous girl who has already borne one child out of wedlock. Elka, contrary to tradition, demands a dowry from Gimpel, and he acquiesces and reluctantly goes through with the marriage. She refuses to let Gimpel sleep with her, yet when she has a child in four months, she insists that the child is his. Gimpel does not believe her, but all the townspeople argue him "dumb," as he says. He soon discovers that he loves the child and that the child loves him, so he goes along with Elka's unlikely tale. Although Elka swears and curses at him, he finds that he loves her, too.

One night when an oven bursts and almost starts a fire at the bakery, where Elka makes him sleep, Gimpel returns home unexpectedly and finds Elka in bed with another man. When Gimpel brings charges against her to the rabbi, she boldly denies everything. The rabbi advises Gimpel to divorce her, but as he lies awake at night, Gimpel discovers that he longs for her and the child and that he cannot be angry, so he rationalizes his change of heart: He may have had a hallucination; he tells the rabbi that he was mistaken. The rabbi advises Gimpel to stay away from his wife until the matter is adjudicated.

Nine months later, Elka gives birth to another child, and this time Gimpel decides no good will come from doubting, so he resolves to believe everything that he is told. In the next twenty years, Gimpel becomes a successful baker, and Elka bears four daughters and two sons. He says that many things happened that he "neither saw nor heard"; he simply believed. Finally, Elka becomes ill, and on her deathbed she confesses to Gimpel that she has deceived him all those years and that not one of the children is his. Gimpel admits to being shocked at her confession.

After the proper period of mourning, Gimpel is visited by the Spirit of Evil, who advises him to urinate in the bread dough to revenge himself on the community, and he does so. However, in a dream he sees his deceased wife in a shroud, her face black. She berates him, saying that she had deceived only herself, and that she is now paying for her transgressions. Feeling that his immortal soul is in jeopardy, Gimpel buries the dough in the frozen ground, divides his possessions among his children, and goes wandering through the world telling tales to children and depending on the goodness of people for his sustenance.

As an old, respected man, Gimpel says that he has learned that if something does not really happen, it is dreamed at night. In his dreams Gimpel sees Elka, who now looks as radiant as a saint to him. She tells him that the time is near when he shall be with her again. Gimpel ends his tale by saying that the world is imaginary and that when his death comes he will go joyfully, for the afterlife will be real and he will not be deceived there.

*Themes and Meanings*

Isaac Bashevis Singer is known for stories that re-create the lost world of Jewish life in the Polish ghetto. This is the setting of "Gimpel the Fool," but the story also presents a gently humorous psychological study as well as a thematic analysis of the nature of reality. From the very beginning, Gimpel the narrator cannot quite understand why he is treated as a fool. That he is narrating his own story makes it unlikely that one should consider him foolish in the ordinary sense. He is only partially a naïve narrator; although he is constantly tricked and deceived by others, Gimpel does show an awareness of what they are doing. His apparent "foolishness" consists in his taking the line of least resistance to avoid their teasing: He simply decides that it is easier to believe what he is told than to make an issue of it. In addition, his faith in God makes him believe that many things are possible, so he convinces himself of the improbable. In a sense, his simplicity and naïveté protect him from harm; his narration shows him to be largely oblivious of the viciousness of others' pranks, and this apparent gullibility leads to relative contentment in his life.

The rabbi's comment to Gimpel that the others are the real fools, combined with Gimpel's epiphany on hearing Elka's words in the dream, show that he may not be the complete fool that others have made him out to be. After his temptation by the Spirit of Evil and Elka's advice to him, his decision to go out into the world as a beggar, depending on God to provide for him, shows that he has emerged from his temptation with greater faith. His final comments on the illusory nature of life, that it is "only once removed from the true world," sound profound rather than foolish.

Throughout the story, the narrator shows some understanding of what others are doing to him. Although he does not always realize exactly how terrible things are or might be for him, his attitude of acceptance makes his life bearable. In the final analysis, Gimpel himself has made the decision to believe what he is told, and this decision has led to a life of peace and contentment. The story thus presents an insight into the reality of life, as Gimpel realizes that life is what the individual makes of it.

## Style and Technique

By having the protagonist narrate his own story, Singer achieves a mixture of humor, realism, and fantasy; what Gimpel narrates is unquestionably happening, but the interpretation of the events is that of a simple, naïve commentator (although Gimpel is not really very naïve when he tells the story, because it may be assumed he is speaking after the events, with his newfound wisdom and understanding). From Gimpel's own words, the reader comes to understand the kind of person that Gimpel is, as well as the events in his life, in a way that the narrator himself does not completely comprehend. The reader is able to infer that Gimpel is not as intelligent as others; as Gimpel says, "they argued me dumb." His realization of what others are doing to him is apparent as he comments, "I realized I was going to be rooked'" and "To tell the plain truth, I didn't believe her." His eventual compromise—"But then, who really knows how such things are?"—is a mixture of his attempt to avoid strenuous intellectual debating and his simple faith.

The strong faith, the essential goodness, of the narrator is childlike in its simplicity: He is like a child who does not know how to interpret the incomprehensible things that are told to him by adults. Singer maintains this tone of childlike simplicity by his choice of words and by the unaffected language with which Gimpel expresses his perception of reality.

*Roger Geimer*

# THE GIOCONDA SMILE

*Author:* Aldous Huxley (1894-1963)
*Type of plot:* Social realism
*Time of plot:* The early 1920's
*Locale:* England and Florence, Italy
*First published:* 1922

> *Principal characters:*
>> MR. HENRY HUTTON, a wealthy, philandering English landowner
>> MRS. HUTTON, his invalid wife
>> DORIS, his young mistress
>> DR. LIBBARD, his family physician
>> JANET SPENCE, an unmarried woman in her late thirties who is
>> infatuated with Hutton

*The Story*

Henry Hutton, a prosperous English landowner, flirts with Miss Janet Spence, an unmarried woman in her late thirties. After toying with her affections, Hutton hurriedly departs to take home his young Cockney mistress, Doris, and then to return to his wife, who is an almost complete invalid. Mr. and Mrs. Hutton have reached an impasse in their marriage: He is terminally bored with the relationship, while she approaches life with the querulous disapproval of the chronically ill. In an effort to change the routine, and to provide some secret spice to daily events, Hutton invites Miss Spence to dine with them.

Although Mrs. Hutton begins the meal in fine spirits, saying "I do really feel rather better today," she unwisely eats a plate of stewed currants that the doctor has forbidden. Soon after, Hutton brings his wife her medicine, and Mrs. Hutton, now feeling ill, retires to her bed. After Miss Spence leaves, Hutton tells his wife that he is going to see a neighbor about a war memorial but actually slips away with Doris, his mistress. He returns home to find that his wife has died during his absence.

After his wife's death, Hutton vows that he will control his lusts and desires, including his foolish affair with Doris. Within a week, however, he and Doris are again together. In an impetuous moment, he proposes marriage to Doris—a marriage that must be kept secret for a "decent interval."

During a visit to Miss Spence, Hutton is shocked when she openly declares her love for him, claiming that "I think everyone has a right to a certain amount of happiness, don't you?" Unable to reply, Hutton flees into the night. Soon he and Doris are in Florence, where he continues to find himself unable to resist the lure of female flesh.

Meanwhile, Miss Spence, angered at Hutton's marriage to Doris, is spreading the rumor in England that Hutton murdered his wife in order to marry Doris. After his wife is exhumed, an autopsy finds lethal amounts of arsenic in her body. Extradited to England, Hutton is tried, found guilty, and executed for the murder of his wife.

The story ends with an exhausted Miss Spence admitting to Dr. Libbard that she herself poisoned Mrs. Hutton. The bemused doctor writes her a prescription for a sleeping draught.

## Themes and Meanings

"The Gioconda Smile" is an ironic, even cynical, presentation of human life as a concatenation of events that are ruled by passions rather than reason and that are ultimately at the disposal of a capricious and indifferent fate. Hutton, who begins the story in a fortunate, even enviable position of wealth and ease, loses his good name and ultimately his life because of his overindulgence in sexual escapades that he admits are not even really pleasurable. He is sped to his fall by Miss Spence, whose narrow but intense passions, fueled by Hutton's own indiscreet flirtations, overflow their bounds and shift from love to hatred. She poisons Hutton's wife in order to take her place. Once she is denied her reward, she places the blame for the murder on Hutton, preferring to see him dead rather than in the arms of another woman. It is the revenge of the woman scorned. In a sense, the relationship has a classic form of desire, disappointment, and destruction.

Classic though it may be, Hutton's fall has nothing of true tragedy in it. He is certainly far from a great man in Aristotle's sense, for there is nothing truly noble or even fundamentally decent about him. He refrains from worse crimes than adultery mainly through a kind of moral sloth, which deters him from undertaking anything more serious than casual affairs, indulged through whim and physical desire. Ironically, neither his whims nor his desires are satiated through his actions; his fundamental mental and spiritual state in the story is boredom. Hutton's character, well delineated by Aldous Huxley in a deft series of descriptions of the man's intensely banal interior monologues and thoughts, is shallow and self-centered. He is one of English literature's intriguing but uninteresting characters.

His wife, who significantly is never called anything but "Mrs. Hutton" in the story, is even less of a fully realized character. She is the stock invalid wife who has never understood her husband, whom she now bores. From her whining complaints to her cheating in a card game, she exhibits traits that prevent the reader, or the story's other characters, from feeling any true sympathy or even serious concern for her. This makes her death little more than a plot device; even the revelation that the woman has been murdered brings forth little terror and less pity.

These interlocking themes of passion and indifferent fate are most fully realized by Doris, Hutton's young mistress, and Miss Spence, the woman who craves happiness so much that she is willing to murder Hutton's wife in order to possess him. The first, who is certainly badly educated and unsophisticated, calls Hutton "Teddy Bear" as a term of endearment and continually wonders, rightly, what qualities she can possess to make a man such as Hutton love her. In truth, Hutton is incapable of understanding or appreciating the virtues that Doris possesses, especially her devotion and unselfishness, which are truly, if undeservedly, bestowed. Once again, however, Huxley injects a note of cynical irony, for Doris's fidelity—one of the rare true emotions in the story—brings happiness neither to her nor to Hutton.

Miss Spence, whose very name subtly emphasizes her role as a spinster, indulges in her own excessive passion, which ultimately brings down fate on the small cast of fools. In the story's central episode, she confesses her love to Hutton while a melodramatic thunderstorm rages about them. "Passion makes one the equal of the elements," she intones to Hutton, who mistakenly believes that she refers to him. "I am without passion," he replies, unaware of the intense desire this deceptive woman has for him. In keeping with the tone of the work, Miss Spence's passion can bring only unhappiness and destruction; she is capable of murdering the wife but not of possessing the husband.

*Style and Technique*

Aldous Huxley is one of the most gifted stylists in English literature, producing a clear prose that has subtle modulations in biting, even savage, satire that spares none of his characters or their illusions. "The Gioconda Smile" is a supreme example of that style, which is careful to maintain a cool, even indifferent distance between the characters and the readers. As with the figures in the works of William Makepeace Thackeray (a suave author with whom Huxley has many similarities), Hutton, his wife, Miss Spence, and Doris are clearly puppets to be manipulated by the author through their predetermined downfalls.

Irony and distance dominate the story. The title refers to the famous painting by Leonardo da Vinci that is known, alternately, as the "Mona Lisa" and "La Gioconda." Traditionally, a good part of the fascination viewers have for that painting is the mysterious half-smile that the woman wears. The meaning and cause of that smile have occupied the minds of critics and scholars for centuries. That Hutton graces Miss Spence's pout as "her Gioconda smile" is ironic, and doubly ironic is her adoption of it, for in her spinsterly earnestness she renders it grotesque. As Huxley describes it, "a little snout with a round hole in the middle as though for whistling—it was like a penholder seen from the front." So is one of the great works of Western art rendered ridiculous and trivial, just as the story takes themes of love and death into the territory of the mundane and banal.

To emphasize this triviality, the characters speak and behave as figures in a fiction. Hutton, vain and self-centered, preens himself in a mirror as the story begins, and semi-blasphemously denotes himself the "Christ of Ladies." Doris, the naïve Cockney mistress, can summon up nothing better than "Teddy Bear" for her lover, while Miss Spence falls on her knees during a thunderstorm to declare her love for Hutton. These are familiar characters, yet through Huxley's skillful prose and his unrelenting and unsparing presentation, he has made them and their tawdry interaction a memorable and enduring story of a pitiful, pitiable human tragedy.

*Michael Witkoski*

# GIRL

*Author:* Jamaica Kincaid (Elaine Potter Richardson, 1949-        )
*Type of plot:* Coming of age
*Time of plot:* The early 1960's
*Locale:* Antigua, West Indies
*First published:* 1983

> *Principal characters:*
> THE MOTHER, a West Indian obsessed with notions of middle-class respectability
> HER DAUGHTER, the adolescent protagonist

*The Story*

A West Indian mother orders her daughter to learn how to perform mundane domestic chores (such as washing white clothes and putting them on the stone heap on Monday and washing the colored clothes and putting them on a clothesline to dry on Tuesday). She also offers her daughter advice ranging from commonsensical health precautions about walking bareheaded in the hot sun and practical tips on cooking pumpkin fritters and soaking salt fish overnight to more intimate advice on personal hygiene.

From what appears to be relaxed lessons on blouse making and cooking, the girl's initiation to "womanhood" escalates to more serious matters of etiquette and female respectability ("you mustn't speak to wharf-rat boys"). These matters include practical abortion instructions ("to throw away a child before it even becomes a child") and ominous chants.

The mother soberly hands down the baton of womanly attributes and duties, tested and sanctified for generations, to her daughter, arguably in the very same way her own mother had received and handed them down to her. The mother accomplishes a generational and gender mandate, as it were, in the wake of the inevitable mother-daughter separation and distancing usually marked by creeping adolescence.

In the absence of conventional dialogue, only two lines in the story reveal the daughter's response to her mother's sometimes gentle, sometimes harsh, sometimes distant, sometimes accusatory, "do's," "don't's" and "how to's." However, there is nothing against which the daughter can protest in the female initiation process circumscribed by her mother's list—particularly not its prohibitions. False assumptions that all-knowing adults make too quickly about youthful behavior and blatant accusations by one's own (domineering), too often suspicious mother are difficult to accept or even comprehend. To an earlier interrogation ("is it true that you sing benna at Sunday school?") and its accompanying admonition ("don't sing benna at Sunday school"), the daughter intimates inaudibly, as she only can ("but I don't sing benna on Sundays at all and never in Sunday school"). To the mother's overwhelming, brow-beating warnings against becoming a slut, the daughter's exasperated, again inaudible, "but what if the baker won't let me feel the bread?" speaks her confusion at her predetermined destiny.

*Themes and Meanings*

Jamaica Kincaid's unconventional one-sentence, bare-bones narrative is an initiation story about a girl's coming-of-age set at the moment of separation between the age of innocence and the confusing, transforming entrance into adult experience. It is the story of a mother's attempt to train her adolescent daughter to learn appropriate cultural customs and more important, the rules of social behavior, especially that of proper sexual conduct befitting a well-reared girl.

Although the story is specifically about a West Indian mother's "gender grooming" her adolescent daughter for her impending female domestic role, it could be about any family, about any culture, and about any adolescent daughter's relationship with her mother. Its imperatives, prohibitions, directives, interrogation, "how to's" and accusation suggest the universality of mother-daughter relationships and the inevitability of tension. The girl's age is not specified but appears to be between ten and fifteen because of the nature of the values that the mother is attempting to inculcate in her. By the end of the sketch, there is nothing but a series of imperatives, "how to's" and accusation, prohibitions on doing the laundry, personal hygiene, sewing, proper table manners, setting the table, Sunday school conduct, gardening, house cleaning, entertainment, superstition, fishing, homeopathic medicine, abortion, love, and budgeting.

The first of ten sister stories in Kincaid's first collection of short stories, *At the Bottom of the River* (1983), "Girl" focuses on the theme that pervades all of her fiction: growing up female. It is through this general theme of feminine sensibility that Kincaid inquires into the feminine role in her novels. Strongly autobiographical, *At the Bottom of the River* complements Kincaid's first novel, *Annie John* (1985), much of which is a full development of the sketches in the former. The themes of female initiation, separation, and distancing—which characterize mother-daughter relationships—are juxtaposed with the theme of the experienced voice of womanhood perpetuating the traditional female gender roles that are circumscribed by patriarchy. More important, underlying these themes is the inquiry into the very existence of sexual difference and structure. For example, the very structure of "Girl" bespeaks its protest against the predetermined destiny of the daughter, a destiny that, unfortunately, the mother nurtures with single-minded purpose.

Although the relationship between the mother and daughter is not fully explicated because of the absence of narrative details, it suggests an all-consuming relationship. It is one in which a domineering and strict mother commands complete control, leaving no room for negotiating the terms of female respectability or middle-class "culturedness." The fragmentary nature of the mother's monologue also suggests tension, the forced and implicit announcement of separation that marks a hastening of the distancing often inevitable in mother-adolescent daughter relationships. More important, the tension is exacerbated by the seeming ambivalence of the mother's own value system, which consists of Caribbean/creole and European cultural norms. Paradoxically, in this conflicting bicultural value system, the mother underplays the value of her Caribbean culture in favor of European cultural norms because the latter embody middle-class values that will guarantee a rise in social status. Thus, the mother's seeming groundedness in Caribbean folk wisdom, myths, superstition, and traditional herbal medicine and systems of healing yields to Christian training and good conduct in Sunday school, appropriate ladylike etiquette, and proper sexual conduct. As the ultimate terms for respectability and acceptability, these strictures are carried to the point of sanitizing sexuality to avoid "sluttishness."

## Style and Technique

Without the typical formal structure of setting, characterization, or color that are hallmarks of Kincaid's writing, "Girl" is only slightly more than two pages in length. It is, however, the economy of structure that is compelling. In order to capture speech patterns, Kincaid makes unique use of the narrative voice of a nameless girl recalling her mother's distant and at times sharp remonstrances about things to do and not do lest she become the slut her mother fears she is bent on becoming. The Old Testament, litany-style series of imperatives from mother to daughter are strung together with semicolons, punctuated by occasional commas. The incantatory language is stern and distant ("and this way they won't recognize immediately the slut I have warned you against becoming"), reflecting tension between mother and daughter. The style is haunting, particularly the disjointedness that vividly and characteristically captures the experience of adolescence and growing up. For example, the pattern of the mother's remonstrances is markedly disorderly and fragmentary, most certainly because it reflects the way the daughter recalls and restructures the way she heard them. Or perhaps, fragmentization could be read as daughter parodying mother's well-ordered sense of decorum and sanctimonious respectability.

The tone is one of cold isolation and detachment from emotion and intimacy, ominous at times, yet Kincaid manages to infuse some humor into the remonstrances ("this is how to spit in the air if you feel like it, and this is how to move quick so that it doesn't fall on you"). This "how to" contradicts the very core of the middle-class values of respectability and decorum that the mother so persistently attempts to inculcate in the daughter. One could perhaps read this contradictory, ill-placed instruction as a reflection of the fluidity of an otherwise stern mother's value system or as an ambivalence, a weakness, an inconsistency of the mother's erstwhile correct, strong, dominant, "cultured" posture. The very nature of Kincaid's stance on the idea of structures, strictures, and her resistance to canons points to the latter. The structure of "Girl" is but one small example of Kincaid breaking through the linearity of the canon, the strictures of traditional culture and forms.

*Pamela J. Olubunmi Smith*

# THE GIRL IN THE FLAMMABLE SKIRT

*Author:* Aimee Bender (1969-　　)
*Type of plot:* Psychological
*Time of plot:* The 1990's
*Locale:* A high-rise apartment in an unnamed city
*First published:* 1998

> *Principal characters:*
> THE NARRATOR, a teenage girl
> HER FATHER
> PAUL, her boyfriend
> A GIRL IN A FLAMMABLE SKIRT

*The Story*

"The Girl in the Flammable Skirt" is a series of loosely connected, often symbolic, vignettes narrated by a teenage girl.

In the first section, the girl comes home from school to find her father wearing a backpack made of stone. She tells him to take it off, and he responds by giving it to her. She puts it on her own back and stands bent over in a corner, leaving her father free to move around the house. She asks him what is in the backpack, which is very heavy. He is watching television and replies simply that it is something he owns. She asks if she can put it down, but he says no, it has to be worn. The girl returns to school wearing the heavy backpack. The teacher sits down beside her while the other students do math exercises. The teacher brings her a tissue, even though the girl is not crying. The teacher says she just wanted to bring the girl something light.

In the second section, the girl relates a joke she has heard about two rats, in which one rat is in reality a dog.

The third section returns to the girl and her father. She tells him she loves him more than salt. He is touched by this remark. He had a heart attack two years ago, and because he has weak legs, he must use a wheelchair. Once he asked her to sit in a chair for a day to see what it was like. She sat in it for an entire afternoon and spent an hour of that time knocking against the wooden chair leg with her hands, for luck and protection. This annoyed her father.

She then visited the bathroom and gazed out of the window. The family lives in a high-rise apartment, and the girl often wonders what would happen if there was a fire and they had to evacuate. Who would carry her father? She has a dark fantasy about what might happen in such a situation. The fantasy involves the death of both her father and her mother.

The fourth section is about the girl's relationship with her boyfriend Paul, whose parents are alcoholics. She keeps him in her closet, bringing him food. He loves sitting in the dark and also the fact that her house is so quiet and sober. She says that it is quiet because her father feels bad and is resting in the bedroom. She also reveals that her home is a humorless one, and she imagines a much more relaxed atmosphere in Paul's disorderly home. Paul takes hold of her hand and holds it for at least half an hour, then kisses it. He pulls her inside the closet and kisses her some more. However, he lets her out because she begins to cry.

In the fifth section, the girl's father is on his deathbed in the hospital, but he does not die. The scene has happened several times before, which makes it hard for the girl to take it seriously. She prays for him, but her prayers are strained. When she leaves the hospital, she passes a janitorial supply closet, where two rats poke their noses out of a hole in the bottom. It is late afternoon and she is alone. She does not know what to do with herself and sits down near the closet. She feels free and light but wants her father to come and give her his heavy backpack again; her back is breaking without it.

In the final section, the teenager thinks of a girl in a flammable skirt whom she read about in a newspaper. The girl wore the skirt to a party but danced too close to some candles, causing the skirt to catch fire. Her dance partner rolled her up in a carpet but she received third-degree burns. The narrator wonders whether in the first moments of the fire, the girl believed she had caused it herself in the sheer heat of her passion for the music and the dance.

## Themes and Meanings

The theme of the story is the troubled relationship between a sick father and his teenage daughter and the problems of growing up in a dysfunctional family. The stone backpack the father carries represents the burden of life that he must endure. The girl willingly tries to take it from him, which suggests that she is doing her best to understand what life is like for her father and to make it easier for him. However, the experiment does not work. The backpack weighs her down so she cannot stand upright. This suggests the difficulty, inadvisability, and even impossibility of one person taking on the burdens of another, especially when the individuals concerned come from different generations. Each must carry his or her own load.

At the literal level of the story, the girl's father does not give her much assistance in what she is trying to do. He is distant, more interested in watching television than in trying to understand his daughter. He is also irritable, expressing annoyance at her when she knocks on the chair leg or taps the night stand in the hospital. On the one occasion when she breaks free of her father's baleful influence and feels young and free and full of life, she feels guilty about it, as if she has no right to these emotions. This occurs when she leaves the hospital, and it shows that the girl has not yet learned how to live her own life, not her father's. She longs for the backpack to weigh her down again.

The girl's relationship with Paul is a sign of the difficulty she has in expressing herself and forming a positive friendship with someone her own age. It appears that she is not used to experiencing her emotions fully or receiving physical affection. When he kisses her she begins to cry. So restricted is she at home that she does not feel able to express her sense of humor. The fact that she has a recurring fantasy about a situation in which her mother and father end up splattered dead at the bottom of the stairwell tells its own story.

In the last section, the story of the girl whose skirt caught fire is given a symbolic meaning. The narrator interprets it in this way because she, too, longs for a transcendent moment when all her desires burst forth in a moment of passion, igniting her soul and giving her freedom. Because her own joyless life is so removed from such a condition, she can conceptualize it only in terms of a story about someone else.

*Style and Technique*

The story is told in a nonlinear fashion, more like a series of snapshots of moments in the girl's life than a story in which one event leads to another. However, all the vignettes are connected, even the joke about the rats, which at first seems like a digression. The point of the joke is that a dog and rat, two very dissimilar animals, have come to resemble each other. This alludes to the fact that the girl, in carrying the stone backpack, has come to resemble her father. Just as there is something unnatural about a dog that looks like a rat, it is equally unnatural (although not equally amusing) for a teenage girl to have to carry the burdens of her father.

The language of the story is strongly metaphorical. The use of metaphorical language in what is otherwise a normal everyday situation gives the story its unusual flavor. The first section, for example, cannot be understood on a literal level because it does not make sense for the father to have a backpack made of solid rock. However, it establishes heaviness as one of the three governing images of the story. Heaviness has to be understood in all its ramifications, including the psychic heaviness of the existence of both girl and father. A second image, that of the tissue the teacher brings her, is the opposite of the stone image. It conveys lightness and weightlessness and serves as an image of the ideal psychic condition that the girl attains only once, briefly and precariously. The third governing image is that of the burning skirt, which is an image of neither heaviness nor lightness but of life on fire with itself, burning with its own passion. Thus in the images of stone, tissue, and burning skirt, Aimee Bender conveys three completely different states of the human mind and heart.

*Bryan Aubrey*

# THE GIRL ON THE PLANE

*Author:* Mary Gaitskill (1954-      )
*Type of plot:* Psychological
*Time of plot:* The 1970's and the early 1990's
*Locale:* A jet plane; Choate, Minnesota
*First published:* 1992

> *Principal characters:*
> JOHN MORTON, a salesperson
> LORAINE, a woman he meets on the plane
> PATTY LAFORGE, a woman John knew in college

## The Story

"The Girl on the Plane" concerns a chance meeting between John Morton and a woman seated next to him on the airplane. Their conversation and the memories it brings up for Morton raise issues of responsibility and complicity and reveal their shared lack of empathy.

The story opens with Morton taking his seat on the plane. He is still angry over his interaction with the airline clerk from whom he collected his ticket. Soon a woman whom Morton finds attractive sits down next to him. As he studies her appearance while she leafs through a magazine, he tries to recall the person of whom she reminds him. Soon she strikes up a conversation with Morton, and after a moment, he realizes that this woman, named Loraine, reminds him of a woman he knew back in college, Patty LaForge.

Patty, an attractive woman, was beginning community college as Morton was finishing, and they worked together in the cafeteria. Morton recalls college as the best time of his life. As Morton talks to Loraine, he is surprised to learn that she, too, had gone to a nearby community college in Minnesota. As they speak, he thinks back to his college days and Patty, who had had a crush on him.

Loraine tells Morton that her own college experience was a bad time in her life. She tells him she was an alcoholic then, a piece of self-revelation that also reminds Morton of the early Patty. He recalls a pair of sexual passes Patty had made toward him, particularly one in which she had noticeably had too much to drink and had staggered away as Morton's male friends laughed.

Morton asks Loraine why she is revealing such personal information to a stranger. He is repelled by the large numbers of people who reveal personal problems on television talk shows and recalls how Patty used to brag about her sexual skills.

Morton thinks back to a conversation he once had with his wife about how he had participated in group sex back in college, assuring her that the woman was a willing participant and was not being raped. Then he recalls the particular event, a party, in which a friend called him to a bedroom. There he found Patty on the bed, having sex.

Though he worried as he watched her with a second man, he decided that she had agreed to this, even after the second man poured his beer all over her face. Morton watched her having sex and talked with other men in the room, but when one man decided to pour maple syrup over Patty, Morton stopped him and climbed onto the bed himself. They had sex, which he saw as a tender moment, but she did not appear to really know what was happening.

On the plane, Morton continues to flirt with Loraine. He asks her about why she felt her college experience was so bad. She explains that she was doing what other people expected of her. Loraine tells of a time her father asked her what she felt were her worst mistakes in life. To connect with her, Morton tells her he has made mistakes too, and he tells her he has raped someone. She immediately recoils from him. Though he tries to explain, saying she does not understand, she refuses to speak to him.

Finally, as they disembark from the plane, Morton once again tries to explain himself. Loraine turns and walks away from him. He follows and tries to apologize, but she is gone.

*Themes and Meanings*

"The Girl on the Plane" raises questions of complicity and responsibility, especially when another person is in trouble and might be acting in a self-destructive way. Early in their relationship, Patty tried to start a sexual relationship with Morton, but he did not accept, explaining that he was not as attracted to her. While Patty has sex with different men in the backroom at a party, Morton listens to see if she is fighting against her partners or complaining. He sees nothing wrong when a man pours a beer on her; Morton believes that Patty has gotten drunk and should understand that trouble comes with a choice like that.

As in many of her other stories, Mary Gaitskill paints a picture of sexual encounters in terms of power relationships. People do not connect in tender moments and in healthy relationships; they connect in manipulative, destructive fashions. Relationships are not described in terms of romantic images; they are physical, primal relations between animals. Men are described as working in packs. People circle each other, sniffing the air for fear.

Another theme within this story is the inability of people to connect empathically. The characters lack insight into their own behavior and also fail to connect with or understand each other. At the opening of the story, Morton is angry with a clerk and fantasizing about hitting him, but the problem was caused by Morton being late to the airport. Morton knows he is late everywhere, but he dismisses his wife's explanation that he might be depressed as pop psychology from magazines. Morton sees the clerk as having an attitude problem, placing the blame outside himself and his behavior.

Morton also complains about how confession has changed from something good for the soul into something everyone does as a form of entertainment. He sees both Loraine and Patty as sharing a flaw, a need to share their deepest emotional secrets. Loraine says she revealed to Morton that she was an alcoholic because it is important for people to be honest with themselves and with other people. She argues that her unhappiness was caused by trying to be who she was not, by trying to fulfill the expectations of other people. Morton thinks the explanation is just pop psychology. He does not understand how his desire to impress Loraine leads him to exaggerate the importance of his current job. In the end, in an attempt to share personal revelations and connect with her, Morton says something that frightens her. When she refuses to speak to him, he can only say she does not understand and then futilely apologize.

## Style and Technique

"The Girl on the Plane" uses a third-person limited point of view to relate its story. Morton's thoughts and impressions are the only ones to which the reader has immediate access. Other characters' attitudes and beliefs are given indirectly, through occasional dialogue. Both Loraine and Patty try to talk to John about their lives, but they both acknowledge that they do not really understand why they are doing what they are doing. Mainly, the reader has to study Morton's viewpoint and what Morton sees according to his set of values and decide whether to infer different meaning for the events from the explanation that suits him.

When Morton watches Patty having sex with a series of men, he perceives her as enjoying the experience. Although he recognizes that she appears restless and disturbed, and he realizes she does not quite seem to inhabit her body while he has sex with her, he is unable to recognize that she must be too drunk or drugged to be a fully willing participant. Despite perceiving that Patty's body feels as if it might come apart, he still sees their sex as the tender moment Patty had earlier wanted. Gaitskill refuses to paint this scene in a clear, easy-to-decide fashion either: Morton sees Patty one time after this rape, and she is holding hands at a concert with the first man Morton had watched having sex with her, back at the party.

The story is also structured in a fashion that comments on the problem of understanding another person's experience. The story line first follows Morton as he argues with an airline clerk and then as he talks to Loraine, sitting next to him on the airplane. As their conversation triggers memories, the story uses Morton's thoughts to flashback to his earlier relationship with Patty. However, when Morton tries to tell his story to Loraine, he is stopped by her immediate negative reaction. He tries to explain that her quick evaluation does not consider how complicated the event really was. However, Morton himself does not understand his life well. In the story, he recalls that he has needed more than ten years to admit to himself how awful one of his earlier relationships was. Finally, the reader must decide how to evaluate an event that has been related through the point of view of a person who does not understand the event himself.

*Brian L. Olson*

# THE GIRL WHO LEFT HER SOCK ON THE FLOOR

*Author:* Deborah Eisenberg (1945-    )
Type of plot: Coming of age, psychological
*Time of plot:* The 1990's
*Locale:* New York state and Albany
*First published:* 1994

> *Principal characters:*
> FRANCIE MCINTYRE, an untidy girl who struggles to meet life's demands
> JESSICA, her school roommate who nags her about being untidy
> MRS. PECK, the school principal
> MISS HEALY, Francie's mother's nurse
> MR. ADE, a funeral home director
> IRIS ACKERMAN, a disturbed woman whom Francie meets on the bus
> ALEX, the man who answers the door at Kevin McIntyre's apartment

## The Story

Francie McIntyre is a slob, and Jessica, her roommate at their expensive boarding school, nags her about leaving her socks on the floor. In the middle of their bickering, Cynthia, the secretary, arrives to summon Francie to the office, where the principal, Mrs. Peck, informs Francie that her mother has died of an embolism while being treated for a broken hip in the hospital at Albany. Francie panics, having no family to rely on, and on the bus to Albany reviews in her mind her relationship with her mother, who was a "proud" woman: "Proud of her poverty. Proud of her poor education. Proud of her unfashionable size. Proud of bringing up her Difficult Daughter. Without an Iota of Help." Francie remembers how in her interview at the prestigious private school she attends, she had imagined how stylish the other girls' mothers must be. Thoughts of her "poor mother!" bring a few "companionable tears" to her cheeks.

In Albany, Francie visits her home, now empty following her mother's death, finding in the sink a dirty coffee cup she had left there three weeks earlier. As she sits, pensive, at the kitchen table, her mind goes back to the day in her childhood when her mother had explained to her that her father had died when hit by a bus. Before that, his disappearance before she was born had been a mystery to her.

At the hospital, Francie is bewildered by the need to make decisions, and she tells Miss Healy, the nurse, "I just don't know what to *do*." She is finally directed to the funeral home: "*Owned and operated by Luther and Theodore T. Ade. When you're in need, call for Ade.*" She is astonished at being told by one of the Ades that her mother had named Kevin McIntyre, presumably Francie's father, as her next of kin, and she faints. When she awakens, she is given a cardboard box holding her mother's ashes.

The next day, Francie calls the Ades and gets Kevin McIntyre's address on West Tenth Street in New York City. On the bus she meets a sympathetic woman, Iris Ackerman, who imparts the dumfounding news that her mother had once been in an accident involving a blimp crashing into a building. Francie's annoyed response to this revelation elicits the answer that there are things we cannot understand and, "You see, people tend to settle for the first explanation. People tend to take things at face value." Iris Ackerman turns out to be severely disturbed with paranoid fantasies. Francie, though, admires her because she tries "To *really* figure things out."

Francie finds the apartment of Kevin McIntyre, but another man opens the door and tells her that McIntyre is out. He identifies himself as Alex and offers Francie coffee or a drink. When Francie rejects his offer to take her box with the ashes, Alex remarks on her diffidence: "You're not a very demanding guest, you know." He then comments on what a strange day it has been, "Starting with the blimp." This mystifying dialogue concludes with Francie taking note of the room, which she terms "Pretty and pleasantly messy, with interesting stuff all over the place." As she imagines Kevin McIntyre walking back to the apartment, Francie thinks that "he was going to have to deal with her soon enough."

*Themes and Meanings*

The dirty sock and the "dust-festooned sweatshirt" that Jessica retrieves from under Francie's bed characterize Francie's disorganized life and her helplessness in the face of life's challenges. However, Francie's defense is rather spirited, as she tells Jessica that "There are people in the world who are not afraid to face reality, to face the fact that the floor is the natural place for a sock, that the floor is where a sock just naturally goes when it's off." This attitude contrasts with the temperament of the world's efficient people, such as the severe Mrs. Peck, Jessica and her "tall, chestnut-haired mother," and the hard-working Miss Healy, her mother's nurse. The remark about facing reality foreshadows the courage she will show in dealing with her mother's death and the discovery of her still-living father.

Jessica arrives at the hospital wearing a "short, filmy dress and motorcycle jacket and electric-green socks," and as she stands in Kevin McIntyre's doorway, she remembers that "She'd been wearing the same dress, the same socks, for days." However, despite Francie's slovenly ways and her indifferent manner of dress, her determination to deal with Kevin McIntyre reveals a capable woman under stress, and her story is partly a coming-of-age narrative.

The befuddlement of the pleasant Iris Ackerman emphasizes the strangeness of life, with its crashing blimps and newly discovered fathers. Most important of all for Francie is Iris's toughness, for despite her gruesome visions of bloated skies, dirty rain, and bloody assaults, she soldiers on trying to make sense of her life. Francie thinks, "You had to give her credit, though—she was brave," and her example is clearly an inspiration to Francie. Alex's small talk reinforces the absurd universe created by Iris, for his own remark about the blimp echoes alarmingly and connects to nothing rational.

Social class tensions emerge in Francie's ill ease during her interview with Mrs. Peck, as well as in her relationship with Jessica, whose complaints about Francie's messiness may be interpreted as a function of their social origins. That Francie feels alienated from her fashionable school shows through in several ways. Her occasional coarse language, her cutting lacrosse (a snooty, upper-class sport), and her forbidden smoking all bespeak someone who sees herself as a rebel trapped among the Philistines and Pharisees. When her mother takes her for her interview, Francie is annoyed to find her mother wearing gloves, sheer pretentiousness to Francie, whose own habits of dress express her defiance of the conventions so dear to Mrs. Peck. Francie feels comfortable enough, though, with the unbalanced Iris, whose vision of things only supports Francie and Jessica's sense of the weirdness of life.

What happened to Kevin McIntyre and why he left Francie's mother are left to the reader's imagination. One credible explanation is that he is gay and is living on West Tenth Street with his same-sex partner. Her husband's having left her for a man would explain Mrs. McIntyre's extraordinary bitterness, her long silence, and the lie about the bus accident that she was driven to contrive. The apartment's "nice stuff" and the paintings and drawings on its walls suggest the kind of clichéd interior decoration commonly expected of a gay lifestyle.

*Style and Technique*

Deborah Eisenberg tells her story from an omniscient point of view but with everything perceived through Francie's sensibility, and she reverses narrative time as Francie looks back on events in her life. These are common, unremarkable techniques, but in her many arresting turns of phrase, more poetry than prose, Eisenberg exhibits real originality. For example, in Francie's initial interview, Mrs. Peck is "gluttonous" for Francie's test scores. When Francie sees the secretary, Cynthia, approaching outdoors, she seems oddly out of context, "as if something were leaking somewhere," and her fellow passengers on the bus seem "like a committee assigned to the bus aeons earlier to puzzle out just this sort of thing—part of a rotating team whose members were picked up and dropped off at stations looping the planet."

The night before she leaves for Albany on the bus, Francie talks "feverishly" with Jessica about the terrifying contingencies of existence (the mysterious crashing blimp becomes a prime example), and when Jessica asserts that "Anything can just *happen*," Francie answers, "It's much, much worse." At this response, "Jessica had burst into noisy sobs, as if she knew exactly what Francie meant, as if it were she who had brushed against the burning cable of her life." This vivid metaphor lights up the theme of a young woman's struggle to make sense of her life, a struggle in which "no one had ever said one little thing that would get her through any five given minutes of her life."

*Frank Day*

# THE GIRLS IN THEIR SUMMER DRESSES

*Author:* Irwin Shaw (1913-1984)
*Type of plot:* Psychological
*Time of plot:* The 1930's
*Locale:* New York City
*First published:* 1939

*Principal characters:*
MICHAEL LOOMIS, a man approaching middle age
FRANCES LOOMIS, his wife

*The Story*

"The Girls in their Summer Dresses" chronicles the origin and conclusion of a married couple's quarrel as they walk through lower Manhattan on a Sunday morning in November. Michael and Frances Loomis have left their apartment and are proceeding along Fifth Avenue toward Washington Square. As they are walking along the crowded thoroughfare, Frances observes that Michael has turned to look at a pretty girl and remarks good-humoredly about it. Michael, who seems unaware that she has previously noticed his habitual girl-watching, also makes light of the incident. He explains that the girl's complexion drew his attention to her, a country girl's complexion seldom seen in New York.

The conversation, sprinkled with jokes and patter, suggests that so far they have had an enjoyable weekend. Frances expresses a need for more time with Michael and urges that they call off a previously planned country outing with friends so that the two of them can spend the day in the city together. After Michael readily agrees, she begins making plans aloud for his approval, while they continue their walk. They will attend a Giants' football game, have a steak dinner at a famous restaurant, and go to a film.

As Frances is making her plans, selecting the activities that she knows her husband will enjoy, Michael's eyes stray to another attractive girl, and this time Frances is unable to conceal her frustration and dismay. She intimates that because he is so interested in the girls, he might prefer to spend the day walking along the avenue. Michael's point of view is that he takes only an occasional glance. Further, he tells Frances, there are few really attractive girls to be seen in the city. Frances dismisses this conclusion, making it clear that she considers Michael's behavior habitual and ingrained. Indeed, she can describe not only the frequency of his girl-watching but also his manner of looking and the time he spends on each. The effect of the episodes on Frances is to increase her insecurity, and, as the story progresses, she reveals deepening anxiety and resentment. She takes no comfort from his insistence that he is happily married, for she believes that he looks at every woman who passes with the kind of look he once gave her. In reality, Michael takes pride in his wife but enjoys watching other women. To Frances this seems both contradictory and threatening.

Sensing the beginning of a quarrel that will ruin their day, Michael suggests that they have a drink, even though it is not much past breakfast. Frances rejects the idea and changes the subject temporarily. When they reach Washington Square Park, they decide to walk among the people there, but soon Frances's insecure mood returns and she begins talking about Michael's annoying habit. In an effort to reassure her, he claims that his habit is harmless and that he has always been faithful, but Frances remains troubled and gloomy. After a brief time, she agrees that they should go for a drink.

At a bar on Eighth Street the couple order brandy from a Japanese waiter, having decided that brandy is the proper drink to have after breakfast. As they drink, the conversation returns to the troublesome subject, and Michael now admits that he enjoys girl-watching. After ordering a second brandy, he becomes expansive and loses all restraint. He talks of the countless beautiful girls in New York, classifying them as to places they are found, professional types, racial and national types, and girls who belong to different seasons, among them, "the girls in their summer dresses." Frances believes that he wants the women, and Michael, now no longer caring, acknowledges that he does. When she pathetically declares that she, too, is attractive, he agrees that it is true. When she suggests that he would like to be free, he hesitates and then admits that at times he would. Now weeping, she presses him further, believing that someday he will "make a move," and Michael replies, after further hesitation, that he will. Regaining some of her composure, Frances asks that he not talk to her about the attractiveness of other women and Michael acquiesces.

They call the waiter and, to his astonishment, order a third round of drinks. No longer intent on spending the day alone with her husband, Frances suggests that they telephone their friends, who will take them for a drive into the country. After Michael agrees, she walks to the telephone, and he watches her, thinking, "What a pretty girl, what nice legs."

*Themes and Meanings*

The story employs a dramatic point of view that emphasizes the fragility of human relationships. It shows understanding and agreements to be temporary and tentative, likely to decay under a threat of differences and opposition, to be reestablished only with difficulty. An anatomy of a marriage quarrel, the story centers on Michael's compulsive girl-watching. Michael is visually oriented and essentially superficial; to him women are primarily sex objects.

Frances grasps the underlying problem when she says that his habit is that of a boy. Michael has an eye for other details as well. As he leads Frances to the bar on Eighth Street, the narrator explains, he is "looking thoughtfully at his neatly shined heavy brown shoes." A careful observer himself, he does not suspect that his wife notices his attention to the girls. At first, he tries to be evasive and indirect with Frances; he then tries to minimize the importance of his pastime. In response to her goading, however, he turns to exaggeration and masculine bravado. When his admission finally occurs and he acknowledges his feelings, the reader does not know whether to take him seriously—whether he really means what he is saying or is caddish enough to think that Frances should share his fantasies.

Despite her own attractiveness, Frances is basically insecure, and this leads her to moodiness and a kind of nagging repetition. She apparently has no other role, identity, or interest in life than being Mrs. Michael Loomis. She desperately wants his attention, approval, and reassurance. Her anguish and his ungentlemanliness arise from their superficial characters.

As with other stories by Irwin Shaw, this one touches on the theme of lost or disappearing youth. Both Michael and Frances feel the approach of middle age and seek to fend it off. The title emphasizes this theme. Although the plot occurs in November, Michael recalls, among many other groups, "the girls in their summer dresses" who represent freshness, youth, and vitality as he himself is losing these qualities without being fully aware of what is happening. Frances appears to have no defense against the ravages of time except her marriage, and she finds the prospect of losing this security difficult to bear.

## Style and Technique

The narrative achieves compression within a tightly unified framework. The story works through subtle shifts of mood and tone in the dialogue; the narrative is presented primarily from a dramatic point of view that creates tension and suspense, for the reader can never be sure of each character's actual mental state or interior thoughts. The author allows the story to develop through their conversation. The authorial voice intervenes to describe the characters' reactions, tone of voice, and emotional states as these change during the conversations. The dialogue achieves a realistic colloquial tone and reflects the economy one finds in dramatic dialogue.

The characters themselves are too commonplace to be very interesting. Their interests and conversation are shallow, the remarks on mundane topics sprinkled with joking and exaggerations. They have forsaken their roots in the Midwest and appear to have no ties with the past. They live in Manhattan, in comfort if not affluence; yet their main interests appear to be partying, drinking Scotch, attending films and football games, and, with Michael, girl-watching. Although Frances reveals some emotional depth and intensity, she shares her husband's essentially superficial pleasures. Nothing they say or do indicates that they possess even a casual acquaintance with their environment's cultural wealth—its libraries, concerts, art galleries, or live theater.

Intimacy and distance between the two characters are marked by recurring motifs of hands and touching, a skillful imagistic technique used by Shaw. Michael holds Frances's arm as they walk along Fifth Avenue, and she pats his after the encounter with the first girl. He presses her arm as he is trying to reassure her following the second incident with a girl, but shortly thereafter she withdraws her hand as she complains about his habit. They join hands to go to Washington Square Park. At the bar,

Michael puts out his hand to her after she has poignantly reminded him how good a wife she has been. She withdraws her hand to press him with additional questions, arising from her state of insecurity. By this time, the opportunity for understanding and intimacy has vanished.

As with other Shaw stories, the conclusion circles back to the beginning. Early in the story, Frances mentions their planned outing with their friends, the Stevensons. Preferring to spend the day with Michael, she begins making other plans, only to return to their original purpose after she has been upset by his insensitive behavior. As the narrative concludes, she is walking to the telephone to call the Stevensons and accept their invitation.

*Stanley Archer*

# GLADIUS DEI

*Author:* Thomas Mann (1875-1955)
*Type of plot:* Allegory
*Time of plot:* The late nineteenth or the early twentieth century
*Locale:* Munich, Germany
*First published:* 1902 (English translation, 1936)

> *Principal characters:*
> HIERONYMUS, a disturbed young man
> M. BLUTHENZWEIG, an art dealer

## The Story

Munich is alive and radiant with life and art, energy, and enthusiasm. Young and old, Germans and foreigners, all feel at home in the city. Indolence and leisure—the basis of all culture and civilization—are the characteristics of the lifestyle of the citizens of Munich, especially in the streets of the northern quarter. Handsome men and beautiful women saunter by; both the rich and the poor patronize art and literature.

This pleasant atmosphere is nowhere more evident than on the Odeonsplatz, in front of the large windows and glass showcases of the big art shop owned by Herr Bluthenzweig. There are antiques, modern art, art books, bronze nudes, original paintings, and especially reproductions of masterpieces on display. One large picture, a fine sepia photograph of a sensuous Madonna in a wide old-gold frame, displayed in the first window, is the center of attraction to the art lovers of Munich; the original of this picture was the sensation of the year's great international exhibition, an event well advertised all over town by means of effective and artistic posters.

A young man with hollowed cheeks, wrapped in his own thoughts, covered in a black cloak, with the hood drawn over his head, walks hurriedly. Oblivious of the sun-drenched, fun-loving city, he arrives at a dark church, which is empty except for an old woman on crutches. After genuflecting, the frail young man looks straight at the crucifix on the high altar. He seems to be seeking answers, strength, and reassurance from his God.

After praying and meditating for a little while, the young man leaves the church to go to the Odeonsplatz. Studying the faces of the people staring at the pictures displayed in the showcases in the windows of Herr Bluthenzweig, he concentrates his gaze on the picture of the Madonna. He can hear two university students admiring the sensuous beauty both of the photograph and of the model. Though offended and scandalized, Hieronymus stands staring at the picture for a quarter of an hour, fascination and repulsion revealed in his distraught face.

In fear and trembling, Hieronymus leaves the spot. He cannot understand why the picture of the sensuous Madonna goes wherever he goes. His soul is outraged; no amount of prayer and fasting can exorcise it.

On the third night after his visit to the art shop, Hieronymus receives a command from Heaven: "Speak out against frivolity, blasphemy, and the arrogance of beauty that flaunts itself naked; sacrifice yourself amid the jeers of your foes; you are My martyr and prophet; be not fainthearted; I am giving you the gift of tongues."

Obedient to the unshakable will of God, Hieronymus retraces his steps to the art shop and demands to see Herr Bluthenzweig. No one pays any attention to the poor young man as all the shop attendants are busy waiting on their wealthy clientele. Finally, as Herr Bluthenzweig approaches Hieronymus, the young man demands that the photograph of the Madonna be removed from the showcase in the window and never be displayed again. The picture is a scandal—it ridicules the doctrine of the Immaculate Conception. The world, Hieronymus says, is a valley of tears, corrupt and contemptible, sinful and miserable. This real world cannot and should not be camouflaged by the unreality of art and passing beauty. Art that extols the temporal mocks the eternal God. Genuine art does not lead humankind to sin; genuine art teaches humankind to hate the world and love God. Hieronymus charges the dealer to burn the picture and throw the ashes to the four winds. His voice reaches the crescendo of a scream: "Burn, burn, burn everything—all these antiques, statues, busts, and volumes of erotic verse; these are remnants of accursed paganism."

Herr Bluthenzweig loses his patience. When he asks Hieronymus to leave, the young man does not budge; peremptorily, Bluthenzweig orders his servant Krauthuber, a big, burly human hulk, to throw Hieronymus out.

The next minute, Hieronymus finds himself in the street—exhausted, weak, and powerless. He does not see the jeering, amused people around him. He sees in the mosaic square in front of him the vision of an *auto-da-fe*—vases, busts, erotic books, pictures of famous beauties, and nude statues, all heaped in a pyramid and going up in flames as a result of his burning words and to the exultation of his followers. He sees the sword of God (*gladius Dei*) rising in splendor, quick and fast (*cito et velociter*), above the doomed city. In peace and serenity, Hieronymus lowers his eyes and covers his head.

*Themes and Meanings*

"Gladius Dei" dramatizes the perennial tension between Christ and Apollo, the sacred and the secular, Christianity and paganism, God and the world, the city of God and the city of humankind. It is another echo of the famous rhetorical question of the Christian apologist Tertullian in the second century—What has Athens to do with Jerusalem?—and of the question of Alcuin in the eighth century—Is there anything in common between Ingeld and Christ?

For the radical believer, art and religion are antithetical unless art is employed explicitly in the service of religion: One cannot serve two masters. In contrast, the ordinary believer does not see an absolute dichotomy: For him, art and religion are two complementary realities; there is no necessary opposition between the two, and he believes that he can have the best of both worlds.

Thomas Mann dwells on this dialectical nature of the subject of art in a number of works, especially in his play *Fiorenza* (1906), his most important work of the years 1904-1907. "Gladius Dei" is an offshoot of *Fiorenza*, and Hieronymus is a descendant of Brother Girolamo.

*Style and Technique*

The principal characters in "Gladius Dei" are not well-rounded, nor are they intended to be; instead, they are clearly identifiable types. Hieronymus represents the extreme view that art that is not unequivocally in the service of religion is an affront to God. Bluthenzweig, the spokesperson for the common person's liberal faith, manages to win this battle, but the war between Christ and Apollo goes on forever. Indeed, even in defeat, Hieronymus thinks that he has triumphed: It is a personal victory to stand up for one's beliefs.

The meaning of the story and the character of Hieronymus are evocative of the famous dream of Saint Jerome (Hieronymus, in Latin), in which the classicist writer Jerome is confronted by the Supreme Judge Jesus Christ, who accuses him: "You are a Ciceronian, not a Christian." Interestingly, though Jerome promised his Master and Judge to give up classical studies and avoid pagan ideals in his writing, he continued to use pagan myths and classical images in his Christian writings. Like Jerome's dream, "Gladius Dei" exposes the dialectical elements found in the nature of art and in the life of the artist.

*Zacharias P. Thundy*

# THE GLASS MOUNTAIN

*Author:* Donald Barthelme (1931-1989)
*Type of plot:* Metafiction
*Time of plot:* 1970
*Locale:* Manhattan
*First published:* 1970

> *Principal characters:*
> THE NARRATOR, a mountain climber
> THE ENCHANTED SYMBOL, the reason for the narrator's climb
> THE EAGLE, the guardian of castle tower

## The Story

Above a mob of acquaintances, the narrator climbs against a bitter wind, inching up the glass mountain toward a castle of pure gold that is guarded by an eagle. In it sits the beautiful enchanted symbol of happily-ever-after fairy tales. The narrator is two hundred feet above the street. Below him, his rapine acquaintances pillage among groaning knights and horses—who are apparently failed climbers of the mountain.

These acquaintances pass around a brown bottle, speak inanities, and jeer crudely at the climber. As he climbs six feet higher, it becomes evident that he is new to the neighborhood; that the people below have disturbed eyes. He tells readers, "Look for yourselves." Hundreds of young people shoot up drugs and older people walk dogs.

Climbing the mountain requires a good reason; the narrator's reason is to "disenchant a symbol." Contemporary egos still need symbols; he considers conventional literature's arbitrary distinction between its "symbols" (nightingales) and mere contemporary "signs" (traffic lights); he sees a nightingale fly past with traffic lights affixed to its legs. From a surreal, slightly unconventional but nevertheless happily-ever-after Americanized fairy tale, he learns the conventional means of gaining the castle: that "means" is an eagle. The tale makes him afraid, but recalling a literary quotation that celebrates humankind's imagination, he bravely follows its conventions. The eagle appears, and he uses it to reach the castle, where he claims the beautiful enchanted symbol. Unlike the aforementioned tale, the climber's story continues: At his touch, the symbol changes into a beautiful princess, whom he promptly throws down the mountain where his acquaintances will deal with her. A final paragraph deconstructs any conventional theme or meaning that the story's prior content may suggest.

## Themes and Meanings

If paragraph 100 disrupts—without remedy—any conventional themes and meanings, what does Donald Barthelme, perhaps the leading postmodernist writer in the United States, mean by this "story"? What theme threads through it, what label defines this work? Barthelme himself resisted using conventional labels for his texts, preferring to call them "whatchacallits," or "an Itself." Critics who examine the work of the postmodernists say, aptly enough, that the theme of their fiction is fiction itself.

In only four and a half pages of one hundred numbered paragraphs, "The Glass Mountain" presents a fiction that examines the need for rejuvenated literary conventions. In doing this, Barthelme engages readers in linguistic play, baiting them to try proving that his text "can-too" be labeled with conventional terms, that it "does-too" express conventional themes and meanings. Takers of the bait lose. Deliberately, Barthelme designs slippery surface themes and meanings for his fictions so that they will avoid producing traditional forms, teasing traditionalists with layered text that suggests, but will not fulfill, multiple conventional themes.

In "The Glass Mountain" the fairy-tale theme works for ninety of the one hundred paragraphs before it falls apart. The climber's observations of the streets below suggest social realism as a possible theme for the story; however, it, too, fails. In both cases, it is paragraph 100 that completely disrupts and denies the plausibility of either conventional theme because Barthelme makes the eagle central to any reading of "meaning" in the story. Paragraphs 58-60 provide that meaning, stating that the narrator risks climbing the glass mountain in order to "disenchant [a literary] symbol," but that the late twentieth century's "stronger egos still need symbols." To accomplish this theme, the climber must reach the castle, and the tale-within-the-tale establishes an eagle as his means of access. Without an eagle, no conventional meaning exists: The story fractures its own internal conventions. The text's last words, "Nor are eagles plausible, not at all, not for a moment," leave for analysis the actual meaning of this whatchacallit: the standard fiction-about-fiction theme of postmodern texts.

Barthelme builds this theme on a writer new to the neighborhood and bent on climbing the mountain of conventional literature to disenchant the dictates of literary tradition. He hints that traditional literature has a dearth of symbols for the "stronger egos" of postmodern society (in the story, his "acquaintances"). The story views these vulgar, mean, waspish people sympathetically, treating them to just over a quarter of his text, while disdaining other people who come, seemingly to laud the mountain, giving them but an eighth of the paragraphs. In back-to-back paragraphs, two ambiguous—and possibly slanderous—references to those people demonstrate the trickiness of finding meaning in this story: In two short paragraphs the narrator (having said, "Everyone in the city knows about the glass mountain,") says, "People who live here tell stories about it. It is pointed out to visitors."

The meaning of both paragraphs seems crystal clear, but in juxtaposition, because the climber plans to "disenchant" canonical literature at its source, they raise questions: Does the first mean that people who promote the canon (canon makers) tell its stories, or does it mean they tell lies to protect it? Does the second mean tours to the canon are given to "tourists" (students), or does it mean tourists/students are given warning about the lies canon makers/protectors tell? Such is the slippery nature of theme and meaning in "The Glass Mountain."

Read as a theme about fiction-making, all one hundred paragraphs fit comfortably together. Perhaps the theme means, as Barthelme seems to make clear, that no rules should be placed on how humanity uses imagination to produce fiction. In paragraph

87, he quotes English writer and critic John Masefield: "In some centuries, his [humankind's] imagination has made life an intense practice of all the lovelier energies." To Barthelme, creativity (companion of imagination) comes from the unconscious and provides any "magic" found in fiction. Ruled by conventions, fiction is, of necessity, produced and framed by conscious acts. By Barthelme's definition, then, it can have no magic. The fact that the narrator's thoughts turn, specifically, on literature and its conventions in a third of the text supports the validity of this theme.

If disenchantment with authoritative canonical control is the theme, problematic paragraph 100 makes sense, as the narrator uses the conventions of canonical form to enable himself to reach and liberate its enchanted symbol (paragraphs 97-99). In paragraph 100, a shift in narrative voice distances readers from the story to present its moral: Literature must be rejuvenated, allowed new realities, and made accessible to postmodern people who still need symbols that literature best provides. To convey a moral, Barthelme borrows and erases the most authoritative symbol available—the eagle—depicting it as lean-headed (bald) and ruby-eyed. As the story's single designated escort to the archives of canonical literature and sole guardian of its captive symbol, these adjectives suggest that the eagle has been invested with excessive power, both political (guard duty) and economic. It thus appears safe to suggest that this story's theme is liberation of literature from the cumulative authority of convention that controls access to the high tower of literary aspiration. It is that eagle as symbol of authoritative control, not a fairy-tale princess, Barthelme's story disenchants.

*Style and Technique*

If a conventional label need be applied to "The Glass Mountain," "fable" works best. Actually, the text merges fable, fantasy, and grotesque fairy tale—which is unsurprising, as collage was Barthelme's favorite creative principle. He said, "The point of collage is that unlike things are stuck together to make, in the best case, a new reality." The writer demonstrates this principle in the story, defiantly tying the mere "signs" of today's society to "sacred" symbols of literature and watching them fly together as a new reality.

Presented in numbered paragraphs composed of simple sentences, the clarity of the prose draws readers in. So clear are its statements that some time passes before readers realize that although such events might happen, they cannot happen on a glass mountainside. Likewise, the story's events can be clearly plotted in a conventional pattern, almost to the end, but those events, themselves, remain unconventional.

Like collage, these unconventional aspects typify Barthelme's postmodern style. In merging "new realities," this fiction about itself comments on the plight and promise of literature. It helps to examine sophisticated fiction as an effective sample of postmodern work. "The Glass Mountain" appears to be a somewhat odd but fairly ordinary, story until the moment a climbing iron clangs. Then glass shatters and a plunger comes unstuck and it is clear that the story is anything but conventional.

*Jo Culbertson Davis*

# THE GLEANER

*Author:* H. E. Bates (1905-1974)
*Type of plot:* Lyric
*Time of plot:* Probably the early 1930's
*Locale:* Probably rural England
*First published:* 1934

*Principal character:*
THE GLEANER, an old woman

## The Story

An old woman toils slowly up a hill from her village to the harvested field where she will glean scraps of stalks and rubble after the plowing, which has been a right traditionally reserved for the rural poor for many centuries in England. She reaches the gate of the field, passes through, and, sack in hand, bends to her gleaning. It is noon on an early autumn day, and the sun beats down mercilessly on the gleaner. She works quickly and anxiously; it is a race against time because her occupation is confined to the daylight hours, and she fears the arrival of other gleaners, competitors for these leavings that are essential to her survival.

As she labors alone in the center of the field, memories return of her childhood many years before, in an earlier century. Then, as a little girl, she did exactly the same work, made the same gestures as she does now, taught originally and prodded on by her mother, in a long generational line of gleaners. The old woman is the last survivor of this ancient calling.

It is late in the afternoon. The gleaner continues to work but more slowly now, bowed down by fatigue and by the success of her endeavor, the half-filled, heavy sack. A thistle wounds her hand, drawing blood. She continues her gathering, oblivious of the multicolored flowers through which she makes her way, but deeply content in her vocation.

Now she can do no more; it is dusk. The sack is almost completely filled and very heavy. She has reached the climax of her task: She must somehow get the burdensome prize, for which she has toiled so long, up on to her shoulder. She makes one great hoisting effort—but it fails, and the sack falls to the ground nearly upended. Righting the sack, she tries again, and with a last, stupendous attempt, brings her winnings up on to her shoulder, and tears of pain and weariness to her eyes. Slowly she turns, moves out of the field and down the road on which she came, disdaining to wipe her tear-stained face. As she moves homeward, the evening breezes dry her tears.

## Themes and Meanings

In this story and in many others, H. E. Bates attempts to communicate his love and reverence for the rural working people among whom he grew up in the Midlands of

England. The solitary character in "The Gleaner" is simultaneously a literal, clearly visualized, individual person and a mythic heroine whose trip up and back from the hill is a quest for both survival and meaning. Bates depicts it as a successful, triumphant quest; ranged against the gleaner are various elements of nature, as well as the weakness of her sex and advanced age. She works against time, the heat of the sun, and the denuded land, which does not yield up its substance without her strenuous effort, wounding her in the process. However, the gleaner never questions her role or her function in life. Working almost by reflex, she is part of nature even as she opposes nature and it opposes her efforts. A tiny figure as she bends in the center of the vast field, she nevertheless dominates her world as the only human presence in it.

Four cycles are interwoven in the story. The individual cycle of the gleaner's life is limned from childhood memory to present old age; the cycle of her vocation, many generations of gleaners, spans the centuries, although with the present avatar's death, this race will become extinct. Part of Bates's sorrowful early life experience was to see the countryside that he loved increasingly ravaged by the factory-slum complex of the Industrial Revolution. In this story, however, nature is unchallenged; the gleaner moves through portions of two nature cycles: the daily one, from noon to dusk, superimposed on the seasonal shift from summer to autumn. Perhaps the most basic meaning of the story is its insistence on conflict and harmony in almost perfect balance in the natural world. The sun causes the old woman her deepest suffering through the heat of its rays, yet the light of the sun is absolutely necessary for the successful completion of her task.

*Style and Technique*

One of the central meanings of Bates's story is his assertion of the close, organic connection between the gleaner and her natural environment; throughout the narrative, striking metaphors urge this connection. At the very beginning of the story, she is introduced in terms of plant imagery, as a very ancient, bare branch of a gnarled, little tree. Her face is the hue and texture of wood that has been etched and planed down by the centuries. Her gestures as well as her appearance link her to the animal kingdom. She is compared to a bird, relentlessly foraging for each minute speck of grain. Separate aspects of the gleaner take on a life of their own; at times, Bates creates the illusion that she is an army of allied organisms, not simply one frail person: Thus, her hands move almost independently over the rough ground, like a pair of scouring mice, as she gleans. Her fingers are similarly animated, like the young ends of ancient trees.

From these and other examples, it can be seen that Bates is a very visual writer, and dynamically so: From beginning to end, the gleaner is presented in action, confronting her environment rather than a passive victim of it. This incessant activity contributes to the image of a heroic, mythic figure who transcends time and place. Some of the images, therefore, emphasize her great age; others, paradoxically, describe her as a very young person. As the gleaner's day wears on, her accumulating fatigue slows down her movements to the pace of a little girl who has been playing in the sun too long. By not specifically naming his heroine or her locale, Bates emphasizes her timeless, mythic dimension. The archetypal aspect of this woman is made explicit in a passage near the end of the story in which she is referred to as an earth mother, whose origin merges with that of the grain she bears.

Bates writes in the tradition of the modern, streamlined story of Sherwood Anderson and Ernest Hemingway, in which, more often than not, plot is subordinated to character. "The Gleaner," however, is by no means a plotless story; in it, the earth-figure protagonist undertakes and completes a mythic journey that is both trial and quest. This journey is framed by the gleaner's trip up the hill to the field at noon, followed by her return down to the village at dusk. The trial is of her skill and resourcefulness—almost no speck of grain eludes her by the end of the day—as well as of her strength and endurance. In her trial she is aided, not by individual helpers but by her own instinctive, unconscious nature. Complementing passages in the story that metaphorically link the gleaner to aspects of her environment are others personifying often gigantic figures that heighten her trial and obstruct her quest, such as the great trees rimming the field that throw out balls of shadow on it in the waning day.

The elixir, the object of great value that shapes the journey as quest, is literally the filled bag of gleanings, perhaps the central symbol of this story. There are two aspects to the meaning of this symbol: life as process (the bag as the gleaner fills it during the course of the narrative) and life as attained goal (the heavy, brimful burden, which she successfully hoists over her shoulder in the climax of the journey).

Bates was a dynamically visual writer, and here his handling of point of view is similar to that of a modern filmmaker, who follows his subject with a variety of panoramic, angled, and close-up shots. For contrast, the print medium enables Bates to move inside his heroine's consciousness for brief, flashlike moments of memory and perception. Perhaps no single aspect of short-story technique is more difficult to bring off successfully than the ending; here, Bates's visual technique triumphs. The gleaner recedes down the hill on her way home. The tears of exertion and earlier frustration have now been dried by the evening air, leaving salt, which she can taste on her lips—her own salt, which the author, in his last line, urges the reader to see as merging with the salt of the earth she treads: Character and setting, kept separate though organically linked from the beginning, finally become one.

*Sanford Radner*

# GLIMPSE INTO ANOTHER COUNTRY

*Author:* Wright Morris (1910-1998)
*Type of plot:* Wit and humor
*Time of plot:* 1983
*Locale:* San Francisco and New York
*First published:* 1983

> *Principal characters:*
> HAZLITT, an elderly San Francisco academic
> MRS. HAZLITT, his wife
> MRS. THAYER, a visitor to New York
> DR. THAYER, her husband

*The Story*

Hazlitt, an elderly San Francisco academic, goes to New York to see a specialist about a matter of "life assurance." On the plane, he is bemused by the behavior of the woman seated next to him as she completely ignores him. Hazlitt is not offended because he is "guarded even with his colleagues at the university," and he is attracted by the woman's intelligent profile and "appealing intactness."

Hazlitt considers it rude, however, when she does not share *The New York Times* with him and is "flabbergasted" when he observes her beginning to read D. M. Thomas's *The White Hotel* (1981) on its last page and continuing to read the final chapter in reverse. Shifting to a news magazine, she finally speaks to Hazlitt, declaiming about the dangers of travel. The ice broken, he finds himself telling her that he knows the author of *The White Hotel* (in fact, they have never met), who "would consider it a personal favor if you read his book as it was printed, from the front to the back."

Shocked, the woman complains about this apparent madman to her husband, whom Hazlitt deduces is a fellow academic. Hazlitt apologizes, and Dr. Thayer introduces himself. The neurotic Mrs. Thayer responds by thrusting the "filthy book" at Hazlitt: "Read it any way you like!" She then returns to maintaining "to the last his nonexistence."

Arriving in New York and checking into the Plaza Hotel, Hazlitt remembers his wife's caution to carry a hundred dollars in twenties "so that when the muggers looked for money they would find it." He takes a horse-drawn carriage to Bloomingdale's and on his arrival is surprised to find Mrs. Thayer purchasing something from a street peddler, so surprised that he topples out of the carriage and into the peddler's arms. The peddler is amused and gives Hazlitt "the smile of a collaborator."

In Bloomingdale's, Hazlitt impulsively buys what he considers expensive bracelets for his wife, but while the clerk takes his driver's license away to have his check approved, the store is suddenly closed because of a bomb scare. He calls his wife to tell her about his day but leaves out the bomb scare because it would disturb her, and "for some reason," he does not mention Mrs. Thayer either.

The next day Hazlitt receives the assurance he wants from the specialist and feels that he is now "free of a nameless burden." He returns to Bloomingdale's to regain his driver's licence, and with his new sense of freedom, he impulsively exchanges the bracelets for an expensive strand of pearls. He cannot afford them, but "writing the numbers, spelling the sum out gave him a tingling sense of exhilaration." He imagines his wife's "wide-eyed astonishment, her look of disbelief."

Hazlitt proceeds to the Metropolitan Museum of Art, where he, as a graduate student, had enjoyed watching people contemplate the works of art. In the gift shop, he sees another browser, the omnipresent Mrs. Thayer, read the last in a collection of Vincent Van Gogh's letters, then the next-to-last, then the next. He goes to the Fountain Court lunchroom, which he remembers so fondly from his youth, but it has been renovated, eliminating the dusky pool and sculptured figures he recalls so vividly.

In the basement rest room, he finds a group of boys, apparently under the influence of drugs, making a toilet overflow to flood the room and smearing themselves with shaving cream. They demand that he give them something but knock the handful of coins he offers into the water. He gives them the pearls and leaves them fighting over their booty.

He returns to the gift shop to buy an Etruscan pin "that he felt his wife would consider a sensible value." Outside, he passes a bus and hears tapping on a window. Mrs. Thayer waves to him, her eyes giving him "all the assurance he needed."

*Themes and Meanings*

Hazlitt is one in a long line of elderly or aging characters in Wright Morris's fiction who feel somewhat displaced in the modern world. They encounter change, however, with more confusion than bitterness. Hazlitt, who does not fly very often, has the stewardess explain how to pull the dining tray from the seat in front of him and pry the lid from his salad dressing, but he recognizes such new—to him—things as inevitable, as is the change in the Fountain Court. Instead of experiencing nostalgia, Hazlitt simply makes connections between the present and the past, as when street sounds remind him of radio plays of the 1940's. Still, things are not as they should be, as the bomb scare indicates. The porter at the Plaza explains that the bathroom faucets turn opposite the usual directions: "A sign of the times, Hazlitt thought."

Other dilemmas facing the modern human are touched on in "Glimpse into Another Country." Hazlitt has difficulty communicating with the Thayers on the plane and does not understand why he criticizes her reading the novel backward. When Dr. Thayer explains that, though "there is something in what you say," his wife is free to read as she pleases, Hazlitt is nonplussed: "It was usually he who was the cool one, the voice of reason in the tempest, the low-keyed soother of the savage breast. Worse yet, this fellow was about half his age." In the taxi from the airport, Hazlitt wants "to chat a bit with the driver, but the Plexiglas barrier between them seemed intimidating."

However, Morris's world is not one of stereotypes, cliches, and simplistic alienation. When Hazlitt becomes separated from his driver's license, he has not lost his identity but gained a peculiar sense of freedom, "an obscure elation." His wife fears for him in New York, but the porter at the Plaza, the street peddler, and the clerks at Bloomingdale's go out of their way to be friendly and helpful. Hazlitt almost brings the rest room incident on himself by refusing to recognize a potential danger.

Like many Morris characters, Hazlitt journeys through life with an amused detachment, never taking anything truly seriously because there are plenty of others—such as his wife and Mrs. Thayer—willing to assume that burden for him. For Hazlitt, past and present, the strange and the everyday seem to merge; he moves about as in a dream. In Bloomingdale's, he watches a television picture of a milling crowd in India indifferently passing by dead or sleeping bodies: "The film gave Hazlitt a glimpse into a strange country where the quick and the dormant were accustomed to mingle. Perhaps . . . it was not the walkers but the sleepers who would range the farthest in their travels." Because everything becomes part of the inexplicable interrelatedness of life, Hazlitt is not surprised at finding Mrs. Thayer everywhere he goes.

*Style and Technique*

Morris mixes whimsical and poetic fictional styles to reflect the alternately matter-of-fact and bewildered points of view of his characters. Appropriately for a dreamlike story, "Glimpse into Another Country" uses water imagery for poetic effect; Hazlitt observes events as if they were beyond the limitations of normal time and space, as if they were happening underwater.

The most significant use of water imagery occurs in the museum scenes. Hazlitt expects to encounter water at the Fountain Court; instead, he finds a pool in the rest room. When the boys fight over the pearls, "They thrashed about violently at Hazlitt's feet like one writhing, many-limbed monster." It is as if he has returned the pearls to the sea, where they belong. When he leaves the museum in the rain, he sees Mrs. Thayer's face "only dimly through the rain-streaked window" of the bus. Their relationship, as always, is out of focus, as in a dream, as if underwater: "What appeared to be tears might have been drops of water."

Sensory imagery is used to reinforce Hazlitt's sensitivity, because of his awareness of mortality, to the nuances of everything around him. Hazlitt is particularly alert to sounds. When he calls his wife, he asks if she can hear the car horns in the street below his hotel window, and he imagines the sights and sounds of their kitchen: "Hazlitt knew so exactly just how it all was that he could hear the sound of the wall clock—stuffed with a towel to mute the ticking." After visiting the specialist, freed of anxiety about the approaching muting of his own ticking, he walks through the lobby of the Waldorf-Astoria hotel "for the pleasure of its carpet and the creak of expensive Texas luggage"—yet more assurance, the sound of life.

*Michael Adams*

# GOBSECK

*Author:* Honoré de Balzac (1799-1850)
*Type of plot:* Psychological
*Time of plot:* The early nineteenth century
*Locale:* Paris
*First published:* 1830 as "Les Dangers de l'inconduite," revised 1835 (English translation, 1896)

### Principal characters:

JEAN-ESTHER VAN GOBSECK, a powerful moneylender
COUNTESS ANASTASIE DE RESTAUD, a faithless wife
COUNT ERNEST DE RESTAUD, Anastasie's husband
COUNT MAXIME DE TRAILLES, Anastasie's lover
ERNEST DE RESTAUD, Anastasie's only legitimate child
MR. DERVILLE, the narrator of the story and one of its agonists

### The Story

"At one o'clock one morning, during the winter of 1829-1830, two persons not members of the Vicomtesse de Grandlieu's family were still in her salon. A handsome young man left the room as he heard the clock strike." Thus casually begins a story in which another story will be told—a detailed recounting of social and moral evils.

Madame de Grandlieu, the viscountess, has noticed in her daughter Camille a romantic inclination toward the young Count Ernest de Restaud, who has just left, and warns the seventeen-year-old girl that he has a mother capable of squandering away millions; as long as the mother lives, no family would approve the marriage of a young daughter with Ernest de Restaud. The other visitor that night, Mr. Derville, a lawyer and friend of the family, overhears Madame de Grandlieu's words to Camille and announces a story that will modify the viscountess's opinion about Ernest de Restaud's fortunes.

More than a decade earlier, relates Derville, he sublet a room from a usurer, then a man in his late seventies. The moneylender occupied another room in the same damp and dark building. The only person with whom the miser had any neighborly communication was the narrator, at the time a law student of very limited means. There follows a description of the gaunt, strong old man, a striking personality notwithstanding his negative traits. Jean-Esther Van Gobseck was born about 1740 in the city of Anvers (Antwerp), of a Dutch father and a Jewish mother. When he was ten years old, his mother sent him away to the Dutch colonies in the East Indies. During the ensuing half-century, he knew the feeling of life imperiled and then saved, of fortune lost and found again; he did business with historic figures in remote lands; he became acquainted with all the particulars of the American Revolution. His religion was uncertain.

The old man spent most of his time either sitting in his dark room by a fireplace with more ashes than embers, or running about Paris hounding his debtors. He expressed his philosophy to Derville: "You believe in everything; I believe in nothing. Keep your illusions if you can"' and "Gold represents all the human forces." Gobseck related his encounters with two persons exemplifying extremes of behavior: a young working woman striving against all odds to support herself and a countess living in luxury but unable to satisfy a note signed to pay for the gambling losses of her lover. Gobseck boasted: He was rich enough to purchase the consciences of those who pulled the strings within the government; was that not power? He could have the loveliest women's caresses; was that not pleasure? Did not power and pleasure sum up the whole social order? In the eyes of Derville, the gaunt, little old man grew into a grotesque figure personifying the power of money; life, especially humankind, horrified the young man. There is a ray of light in this spectacle of vice: The narrator, now the successful lawyer Derville, lets Madame de Grandlieu know that his wife is that same humble working girl long ago mentioned by Gobseck.

The narration returns to the point where Derville finishes his studies and is able to acquire an independent office owing to a significant sum of money that Gobseck lends him at a high though not usurious rate of interest. A year later, Derville is present at a visit from Count Maxime de Trailles to the already octogenarian Gobseck; this count is the same well-known dandy—a supremely elegant, high-class gambler, and an unprincipled adventurer and exploiter of women—who several years before had played a role in the episode of the spendthrift countess. The beautiful noblewoman, Anastasie, appears at the moneylender's quarters and shows him her diamonds—really those of her family—the value of which amounts to a fortune. Derville instructs the parties with his unfailing honesty while trying to hold out a hand to the distraught woman: It is not likely that the diamonds could be validly pawned without the consent of the countess's husband. Gobseck reacts at once: He will only buy the diamonds.

Derville still whispers in the woman's ear that she ought to appeal to her husband's mercy rather than sacrifice a fortune belonging to her family. However, the money evidently is needed for her lover, who then uses emotional coercion, and Anastasie accepts the usurer's low offer of eighty thousand francs. Now Gobseck gives the screw another turn: He delivers fifty thousand francs to the countess and, completing the price, some notes signed by Maxime de Trailles and already due and protested, which Gobseck has discounted far below their face value from his fellow moneylenders. The young Trailles roars an insult; the old man coldly produces a pair of pistols and observes that, being the insulted party, he will fire first. Trailles stammers an apology. Anastasie bows and disappears, undoubtedly terrified, and Trailles follows her. The act unravels with the excited appearance of Anastasie's husband. Derville intervenes in the resulting dispute, advising Gobseck and the count to compromise, and a document is signed allowing the latter to recover his diamonds at a sacrifice.

Some days later the count walks into Derville's office. A conversation follows in which new light is thrown on the moneylender's personality. Derville reveals that he is convinced that aside from Gobseck's financial doings and cynical observations about human nature, he can be the most scrupulous and upright of men. There are two men in him, a miser and a philosopher; should Derville die leaving children behind, Gobseck would be their guardian. The count has health problems and is afraid of what may happen to his properties in case of his death; therefore, he asks Derville to prepare documents transferring his properties to Gobseck, as well as a defeasance to be signed by Gobseck and kept by Derville, by virtue of which his principal estates are left to his only legitimate child and heir to his title.

At this point in the narration, sleepy Camille goes to bed; consequently the viscountess indicates that Derville can call the count by his name, Restaud—the reader recalls the family name of the young visitor who attracted Camille's attentions. The story is resumed and climaxes in a series of highly dramatic scenes. The count is taken to his bed gravely ill and, unable to send the defeasance to Derville, hides it from his wife, who, accompanied by her children, keeps a permanent vigil in the adjoining room. Derville tries in vain to convince the countess that it is also in her interest that he should see her husband. When the count finally dies, Derville and Gobseck arrive and force their way into the death chamber only to find the count's body lying on the floor like another piece of litter, and the Countess Anastasie, disheveled and bewildered, who in her blind distrust of her husband and Derville has just found and burned the defeasance.

Gobseck, faithful to his nature and ideas, keeps Restaud's estates as long as he lives, taking very good care of everything; the principal heir and very young count will benefit from growing up in adversity, the greatest teacher. Derville ends his narration with the news of Gobseck's recent death at the age of eighty-nine, in a revolting scene of ruinous hoarding and miserliness. Now Ernest de Restaud, already a young man of good character, will come into possession of his estates and be able to marry Camille. The story concludes with Madame de Grandflieu still voicing some reservations, which can be surmounted.

## Themes and Meanings

The succession of versions, titles, and labelings of this novella, or rather long short story, reveals a shifting of thematic focus. In the definitive text, the figure of the moneylender has reached its fully rounded size and is central as the portrayal of a remarkable individual as well as a social phenomenon, and the conflict between the Comtesse de Restaud and her ill-treated husband—or the consequences of misconduct—remains as an important secondary theme.

Honoré de Balzac's art grew in parallel with the growth of "Gobseck," in which its salient topics and motifs are already found in full bloom: the interplay of polar principles—a moral polarization also working within the characters' psyches—the dramatic situations and outspoken, confrontational dialogues, the characters grandiloquently describing and justifying themselves with regard to the opposing characters and society—not only the usurer Gobseck but also the dandy Count Maxime de Trailles. There is also the keen attention directed both toward moral conflicts deep in the individual consciousness and toward the conflicting forces and affairs observed in society.

In trying to transport the Parisian milieu of 1830 to his own distinct social conditions and mentality, the American reader may find correspondences between some of Balzac's incidents and, for example, those in the popular soap opera "Dallas." Balzac was accused of succeeding better in the portrayal of evil than in the presentation of virtue. Repeatedly and from several angles he answered this charge. Commenting on Samuel Richardson's *Clarissa* (1747-1748), he replied to one of the editors of *La Semaine:* "Do you think that such work would be readable if it were necessary to have the decent people whose lives lack drama occupy in it the extent of space they occupy in social reality?"

*Style and Technique*

Balzac's style is easily translatable; in other words, the reader of a good translation does not miss much of the enjoyment that the original text ought to produce. It should be remembered that many of the very greatest novelists—Stendhal, Herman Melville, Fyodor Dostoevski, Leo Tolstoy, and Italo Svevo—although vigorous and also stylistically effective in rendering their fictional worlds, have not excelled in poetic expression or beautiful language; to this assertion in all its parts Balzac is no exception.

The important characters of this story appear again, sometimes with leading roles, in many of Balzac's novels, beginning with *Le Père Goriot* (1835; *Père Goriot*, 1860). Considering chronologically the development of "Gobseck" and the gestation of *Père Goriot*—whose protagonist, Anastasie's father, is also mentioned in "Gobseck"—it is plausible that the strong types of Gobseck and Maxime de Trailles as well as the social state of affairs represented by Goriot's daughters and their aristocratic husbands and lovers inspired Balzac's vision of a great cycle of novels to be entitled *La Comedie humaine* (1829-1848; *The Human Comedy*, 1885-1893) in an analogy with Dante's *The Divine Comedy* (c. 1320; English translation, 1802). In this aspect as well as in those pointed out in the previous section, "Gobseck" occupies a central position in Balzac's oeuvre.

*A. M. Vazquez-Bigi*

# GOGOL'S WIFE

*Author:* Tommaso Landolfi (1908-1979)
*Type of plot:* Surrealist
*Time of plot:* The mid-nineteenth century
*Locale:* Unspecified
*First published:* "La moglie di Gogol," 1954 (English translation, 1963)

> *Principal characters:*
> NIKOLAI VASSILEVITCH GOGOL, a Russian writer
> CARACAS, his "wife," a balloon doll
> FOMA PASKALOVITCH, the narrator, his biographer

*The Story*

The story is purportedly a chapter of a biography of the great nineteenth century Russian writer, Nikolai Vassilevitch Gogol. The supposed biographer, Foma Paskalovitch, begins suspensefully by pointing out that he is about to relate something about Gogol's wife that is so scandalous as to cause him to hesitate revealing it. After this suspenseful beginning, the narrator reveals that Gogol's "wife" was actually a life-size balloon in the form of a woman. The plot's exposition consists of a description of the inflatable doll and two incidents in which the biographer, who was apparently close to Gogol, observed the "wife."

What distinguishes the inflatable doll is that with each inflation it takes on a different form, depending on the amount of air pressure that is filling out its anatomy. It can never be made to look the same way again once it is deflated. To give even greater variety to the appearances of the doll, Gogol has a number of different wigs and shades of makeup with which he ornaments it. Thus, the doll can be made to conform, more or less, to the desires and tastes of Gogol with each inflation. From time to time, when the doll has taken on a form especially pleasing to Gogol, he falls in love with that form "exclusively," and maintains it in that form until he falls out of love. After a few years of living with the doll, Gogol bestows a name on it, Caracas.

It is to demonstrate the relationship between Gogol and his balloon woman, and the decline of that relationship, that the biographer recounts two incidents in which he observed Gogol and Caracas together in Gogol's home. In the first incident, Paskalovitch hears Caracas speak. He is sitting with Gogol in the room where Caracas is always kept—a room where no one is normally allowed to enter—and the two writers are discussing a Russian novel. Caracas is sitting on a pile of cushions against a wall and is made up as a beautiful blond. Suddenly, and surprisingly, she utters in a husky voice, "I want to go poo poo." Gogol, horrified, jumps at the doll and, ramming two fingers down its throat where an air valve is located, he deflates it. He makes apologies to Paskalovitch and attempts to resume their talk, but it is impossible. Gogol explains that he loved that form of Caracas, and now he feels despondent having lost her. It is impossible to reconstruct that exact form.

Before relating the next incident, Paskalovitch comments on a specific tension that developed between Gogol and Caracas. He notes that over time the doll seemed to acquire a distinct personality that unified all its various manifestations. Through all its changes—from blond to redhead to brunette, from plump to slim—some unnameable quality seemed to pervade that gave Caracas a sort of identity, something that gave it distinction as an individual independent of Gogol's control. Moreover, to Gogol this identity appears hostile. What expresses this hostility most dramatically for Gogol is his contraction of syphilis. Gogol claims to have had no contact with any woman other than his balloon-wife, yet he contracts the disease and undergoes the painful treatment of it. He says to Paskalovitch, "You see what lay at the heart of Caracas; it was the spirit of syphilis."

The second incident makes up the plot's climax, recounting the tragic end of Gogol's "marriage" to Caracas. Gogol, tortured by feelings of "aversion and attachment" to Caracas, has begun to speak more fantastically about her, complaining that she is aging, that she pursues pleasures he forbids, even that she has betrayed him. On the night of the silver anniversary of their "wedding," Paskalovitch is with Gogol and Caracas in their home. Gogol's behavior is inconsistent, vacillating between affection for Caracas and repugnance. At one point, he exclaims, "That's enough! We can't have any more of this. This is an unheard of thing. How can such a thing be happening to me? How can a man be expected to put up with this?" Gogol then grabs his air pump, inserts it in the tube at the doll's anus, and inflates her persistently, weeping and shouting all the while, "Oh, how I love her . . . my poor, poor darling! . . . most pitiable of God's creatures. But die she must!" The doll swells to distorted proportions, her face running through various expressions, of amazement, supplication, disdain. Finally it bursts violently, scattering small fragments of rubber around the room. Gogol gathers these pieces and puts them in the fire, crossing himself with his left hand. With Gogol's wife thus "murdered," Gogol surprises Paskalovitch with yet another dramatic act. Charging Paskalovitch to hide his face against a wall and not to look, Gogol rushes to another room. He reenters bearing a small bundle that he also hurls into the fire. Paskalovitch has peeked, and he perceives that the bundle is a baby—a rubber doll that might, by its appearance, be regarded as Caracas's son.

The denouement of the story consists of Paskalovitch looking ahead to the next chapters of the biography of Nikolai Vassilevitch Gogol, and his reflections on the purpose of this chapter treating Gogol's wife. He has at least, as he puts it, "given the lie to the insensate accusation that he ill-treated or even beat his wife, as well as other like absurdities."

*Themes and Meanings*

"Gogol's Wife" contains many qualities typical of Tommaso Landolfi's writing, including criticism of intolerance, especially intolerance of any disinclination to accept the extraordinary. Here, Landolfi dramatizes this in a story that is Kafkaesque in its representation of a monstrosity that does not yield itself easily to reason. In its sensational combination of the prosaic (as a biography of a famous writer) and the absurd (Gogol's regarding his inflatable doll as his wife) the story is surrealistic: Otherwise mundane, everyday elements become monstrously distorted.

Within this surreal framework, themes are developed regarding identity and the struggle between reality and fantasy. The question of identity arises in Landolfi's treatment of Gogol's balloon-wife. The first qualities of Caracas that are described are her mutability: Gogol can change her at will into vastly different forms of woman; in fact, he has no choice because the doll can never be made the same way twice. Diversity, change, mutability, are all elementary characteristics of Caracas. However, as the story unfolds, Gogol and Paskalovitch become increasingly more aware of unifying traits in the doll, which are apparently not so much the result of physical similarities from one manifestation to another as they are the result of a developing personality. Gogol refers to the doll's acting out independently, first in relatively trivial ways, as when it embarrasses him with its utterance, "I want to go poo poo." Gogol explains at this point that "she only does it for a joke, or to annoy me, because as a matter of fact she does not have such needs." As Paskalovitch suggests at one point, Gogol likely bestowed a name on the doll because of such indications of individuality. Ultimately, however, this independence manifests itself more cruelly with Gogol's contraction of syphilis, which he attributes to his contact with Caracas, and finally to behavior in the doll that causes him to accuse it of betraying him. The specific behavior that leads to this and other complaints of Gogol is never revealed. The important question is, what is it that Gogol loves? What attracts him in this love-hate relationship? If, on the one hand, the meticulous description of the doll underscores its unreality (as a "wife," in any case) and instability (never being the same twice), on the other hand, Gogol's devotion to the doll as Caracas and his emotional involvement, which is emphasized rather than diminished by his destroying it, attest the existence of something very real. Furthermore, Gogol's and Paskalovitch's perception of the unifying traits of the doll cannot be denied. This treatment of identity, then, is paradoxical: Caracas is at once unreal and real, both created by Gogol and creating him, inasmuch as she alters his behavior.

This enigmatic treatment of the evasiveness and rich ambiguity of identity serves to point out the coexistence of reality and fantasy. In Landolfi's story these do not cancel each other, but work to re-create each other. In a rather distasteful pun, Paskalovitch suggests that the unifying attributes of Caracas are "no less than the creative afflatus of Nikolai Vassilevitch himself." Caracas is, by this interpretation, Gogol's "inspiration," in a literal as well as a figurative sense, the product both of his air and of his imagination. Caracas is in this sense no less real than Gogol's body of literature that supported him and made him famous.

Gogol's destruction of Caracas and the doll baby expresses his acknowledgment that he no longer has control of his creation, which presents him mysteriously with unwanted results: embarrassment, anxiety, syphilis, and a doll son.

*Style and Technique*

While giving serious treatment to the relationship between reality and fantasy, "Gogol's Wife" also bitterly parodies literary biography. Through use of the first-person point of view, in the persona of Foma Paskalovitch, the biographer of Nikolai Gogol, Landolfi mimics and exaggerates what he regarded as the sensationalism inherent in biographical studies. From the outset, Paskalovitch dons an exaggerated fastidiousness that interferes with more than it assists in the "biography." There is the regular intrusion of such phrases as "I should specify," "perhaps I should say at once," "let us not mince matters," and "as my readers will already have understood." With this fastidiousness is also suggested a fawning admiration of his subject, expressed by means of ill-timed references to Gogol's genius, usually juxtaposed with lurid or sensational details about the balloon-wife.

The biographer's interest in the lurid details of the balloon-wife maintain the atmosphere of sensationalism at a high pitch. Thus, much detail is offered in the treatment of the doll's genitalia, in the valves at the back of its throat and anal sphincter, in Caracas's private room, with its Oriental decor. When the biographer notes that he was eyewitness to the dramatic end of the affair, he is quick to exclaim, "Would that I had not been!"

Landolfi pokes fun at the sensationalism most pointedly, however, through the biographer's use of suspense. In the opening sentence the biographer states that he hesitates to relate the story about Gogol's wife. He indicates then that what he is about to disclose will probably be offensive to many, and that in fact he himself recoils at the thought of it. Arguing the responsibility of a biographer to tell the whole truth, he then promises a detailed account of the affair. This hesitation and then determination to be truthful bring up a serious question about biographies, and especially those literary biographies that have revealed damning details of their subjects' lives. Landolfi himself, in his own time, refused interviews and discouraged curiosity about his personal life, denying the value of such details for use in literary studies. The serious question is here mocked, however, for Paskalovitch's hesitations, drawn out over several pages and renewed before every new sensational revelation, only create suspense and arouse prurient interest. When he states, after a string of disclaimers and hesitations, that he will continue "without more ado," he only draws attention to the unnecessary ado he has already squandered; and when he curbs himself with "but let us not anticipate," he only emphasizes how much has already been anticipated, and encourages more premature guesswork about Gogol's relations with his wife.

In a final tone of mockery and as an indictment perhaps of literary biography in general, Landolfi ends with the acerbic irony, "And what else can be the goal of a humble biographer such as the present writer but to serve the memory of that lofty genius who is the object of his study?"

*Dennis C. Chowenhill*

# GOING

*Author:* Amy Hempel (1951-    )
*Type of plot:* Domestic realism
*Time of plot:* The 1970's or 1980's
*Locale:* Southwestern United States
*First published:* 1985

*Principal character:*
THE NARRATOR, an unnamed college-age man

*The Story*

The narrator is in the hospital following an accident in which he was the only victim, having flipped his car twice while going sixty miles an hour on a straight, flat road and landed in a ditch. He takes some offense at a typo on the hospital menu, "the pot roast will be severed with buttered noodles" because some part of himself could have been severed during the accident; instead, he only has twenty stitches on his chin and a two-day memory loss.

He reports several dual experiences: experiencing things as far away and close at the same time, while he was still in the same place; in the ditch, feeling that the air was unbelievably hot while his skin was unbelievably cold; thinking the accident happened fast and slowly at the same time; and having a memory loss that encompasses two days. "Maybe those days will come back and maybe they will not. In the meantime, how's this: I can't even remember all I've forgotten," he says. He also comments on the dual presence, of someone's being someplace physically at first, with only the idea of their remaining after they are gone.

Because the narrator hit his head during the accident, the doctor has kept him in the hospital for several days of observation. It does not matter to him that he will miss a few days of school because the accident was a learning experience—at least, that is what everyone thinks it should be. He recalls that one of his teachers had related to the class that once while he was drinking a glass of orange juice, he had realized some day he would die. The narrator compares the teacher's observations with certain of his own, which seem equally obvious and therefore of little use as learning experiences.

He remembers being in a bar near the Bonneville flats two days before the accident and watching the bartender demonstrate how putting a drop of tequila on a scorpion's tail makes it sting itself to death. He also can remember the accident—just nothing in between.

He likes the night nurse especially because she "makes every other woman look like a sex-change" and because he likes having a woman in his room at night. When he cannot sleep, she returns to his room with a telephone book and they look up funny names such as Calliope Ziss and Maurice Pancake.

Embedded in his story of the car accident and of the stay in the hospital are two incidents from his past, which correspond with certain olfactory hallucinations that he has experienced. Once, he smelled smoke when his parents' house was burning down three states away; another time, he smelled his mother's face powder in his room the night she died three states away. Now in the hospital room he has a third—he smells a worm.

*Themes and Meanings*

The major theme of Amy Hempel's story is duality—duality of experience and memory, and the more universal knowledge, but a very singular experience, that everyone is going to die. The motif of duality is introduced in the narrator's statement, "things are two ways at once," and are underscored by his several descriptions of experiencing events in two—usually opposite—ways simultaneously: near and far, fast and slow, hot and cold, not being there but being there. These same descriptions reflect the duality of memory: Memory brings things from the past (far away) into the present (closer)—a kind of binocular-vision of one's life. Memory also brings things that are absent into presence, such as the nurse: "After she leaves the room, for a short time the room is like when she was here. She is not here, but the idea of her is." Memory is stimulated by smells: a Christmas candle, smoke, face powder; any one of these odors recalls into the present a person, an event, or both.

The concept of life is a dual one, for it must include the notion of death. Living is not just a movement through space and time, but also a movement toward death. From the moment of birth, each person begins to die, and living is that time in between. Death is quietly present throughout, although it is mentioned indirectly only once, in the teacher's observation, and directly once, when the narrator mentions the night his mother died. The narrator himself could have died in the accident, but just as accidentally did not. The hospital room smells like worms, an olfactory symbol for death. The image of the scorpion stinging itself to death suggests a form of suicide. Because the narrator can remember nothing that happened between that image and the image of his accident, one must consider the connection. Although the scorpion kills itself, it is not a voluntary suicide because the stimulus for its action is an outside source. The scorpion does not so much kill itself as it strikes out at something outside itself only to find out that the victim is itself after all. Using this scenario as the key to assessing the narrator's brush with death—and keeping in mind his noncommittal answer to the bartender's question as to where he was going, "I said I was just going"—one could determine that the narrator's near-death experience was his own fault: not a conscious attempt to die, but like the scorpion, the way he chose to deal with the moment could have killed him. It was just that he did not care where he was going, that is, if he died.

The reader does not get the impression that the narrator has learned anything from the car accident. Although he says that it was a learning experience, he indicates that it is not he, but "You" who "know—pain teaches." Nothing he relates as an example of personal epiphany—that is, a sudden insight into the essential nature of something, or an intuitive grasp of reality in a flash of recognition—appears to be anything more than an observation of the obvious. However, is it not the obvious that often escapes people? If so, then his observations are astute indeed.

## Style and Technique

The term most applied to Hempel's short fiction is minimalism, a technique that creates fiction that appears deceptively simple and realistic. At its best, minimalism creates a concentrated and uncluttered narrative. It also is a style that reflects the characteristics of the short story, and it is the short story that houses minimalism most often and best. Both minimalism and the short story rely heavily on figures of speech. Minimalist stories often use heavy symbolism; in this story, the odor of worms, one aspect of rotting bodies, is used to stand for the entire concept of death.

Memory, issuing from a split second of actual experience, is partly myth-making because it contains the element of desire or wishing. So it must be a dual experience to remember an event as what it was as well as what one wants to remember it as. One corrects experience according to expectation or desire. Experience occurs in three phases of time: There is only a split second of "present" in each event, the greater part is "past," and a small part is "future" (expectation)—so what one already experiences is mostly memory even as each event occurs. The single experience is the microcosm. Life is the macrocosm of this whole thing called experience.

This same characteristic of life, experience—and this narrator's story—all reflect the technique of minimalist fiction and the technique that is the short story, that is, the focus on the moment and the moment as past and present.

*Cynthia Whitney Hallett*

# GOING AFTER CACCIATO

*Author:* Tim O'Brien (1946-    )
*Type of plot:* Psychological
*Time of plot:* October, 1968
*Locale:* Vietnam, near its Laotian border
*First published:* 1976

> *Principal characters:*
> CACCIATO, a seventeen-year-old U.S. Army deserter
> LIEUTENANT CORSON, the officer leading the squad pursuing
>   Cacciato
> PAUL BERLIN, the narrator, an enlisted man sympathetic to
>   Cacciato
> DOC PERET, a squad medic
> STINK HARRIS, a bitter and violent enlisted man

*The Story*

The title alludes to a character who only exists as an off-stage presence throughout this story, which opens as two soldiers tell their weary lieutenant that Cacciato (an Italian word meaning "hunted") has left and plans to walk from Vietnam to Paris. Although the officer is almost immobilized by dysentery, age, alcohol, and disbelieving incomprehension of Cacciato's plan, military discipline triumphs over his inertia. He orders Cacciato's squad to pursue the deserter. The seven men set off in the ceaseless rain toward the Laotian border to the west.

As the group crosses the flat rice paddies and begins its ascent into the mountains, Paul Berlin, the narrator, becomes fixed on the object of their pursuit. The squad consensus is that Cacciato is outstandingly dumb: childish, immature, stupid, and unrealistic. As Cacciato's presence continues to hang just out of reach—a figure glimpsed on the trail above, a chocolate wrapper found on the trail, traces of a camping place—Berlin begins to feel pity and affection for him, and eventually a kind of wonder at Cacciato's simple-minded and single-minded plan of escape.

Doc Peret, the nurturing member of the squad, reasonably and compassionately counsels his ill officer to let Cacciato go, to declare him missing in action and let his plan fall flat under the weight of its own foolishness. The lieutenant orders the men to persist, in spite of his weakness and distaste for the hunt. Stink Harris, a member of the squad, is maliciously delighted by the decision.

The men climb mountain after mountain, and Cacciato walks before them, making no attempt to hide or evade his pursuers. He waves at them from the trail. Although they cannot hear him because of the thunder of the monsoon storm, he shouts cheerfully at them, apparently unaware of the seriousness of his actions. His pursuers marvel at his stupidity. Berlin begins to hope for their quarry's escape but has a frightening vision of Cacciato being murdered. He hopes for a miracle but knows that the realities of war are likely to strike Cacciato down.

As they near the border, that magical line beyond which the squad will not go, Cacciato begins to jettison the trappings that both made him a soldier and protected him. The followers find his dogtags, armored vest, helmet, entrenching tool, and ammunition. Disarmed, he offers himself to their view.

In his eager rush to catch Cacciato, now tantalizingly close, Stink triggers a booby-trap set by Cacciato. The entire squad endures the humiliation of terror as the trip-wire turns out to be connected only to a harmless smoke grenade—a practical joke. The lieutenant understands the prank to be a message from Cacciato meaning that he could have killed them all but chose not to.

The lieutenant sends Oscar Johnson to parley, but Cacciato refuses to come back. Doc Peret once again suggests letting him go. Berlin fantasizes about the improbable possibility that Cacciato might actually escape on foot to Paris. As the rains end and the sun comes up, the lieutenant orders the men to deploy to capture Cacciato. Berlin complies, reluctantly, but the story ends as he first whispers, then says, then shouts the ambiguous exclamation, "Go." It is not clear whether he is speaking to Cacciato, or to himself.

*Themes and Meanings*

Tim O'Brien's story was selected for inclusion in *The Best American Short Stories, 1977,* won the Pushcart Prize, and grew into the novel *Going After Cacciato* (1978), a National Book Award winner. It illustrates the Vietnam draftee's terrible ambivalence about the war—the passionate desire to be someplace else, balanced against the impossibility of leaving. O'Brien writes about this conflict in several of his works. In "On the Rainy River," the protagonist of *The Things They Carried* (1990) debates whether to report for induction or to flee to Canada. The draftee in *The Nuclear Age* (1985) actually does flee. In *If I Die in a Combat Zone, Box Me Up and Send Me Home* (1973), the main character complies with the draft but then considers deserting from advanced infantry training. In "Going After Cacciato," one side of the issue is embodied in the deserter Cacciato, and the other in the obedient soldiers.

Cacciato is a fool. His simplemindedness frees him to think simple, direct thoughts and take simple, direct actions. His foolishness liberates him from the weight of duty, propriety, inertia, and expectation that chains the more mature soldiers to the war. When he wants to be elsewhere, he simply goes. His going is a radical act that threatens the whole conceptual structure of the war, because he enacts the possibility of saying "no." The entire war mentality, as seen by O'Brien, depends on individual men finding it unthinkable to say "no" in such a way. So Cacciato, always seen in the distance (like a wishing-star or a mirage), becomes the image of possibilities for Paul Berlin, the obedient soldier.

Although O'Brien has discussed in other writings what exactly it is that holds an individual to military service in a war that person believes is wrong, the obedient soldiers in "Going After Cacciato" are largely silent about their motivations. It is through the lieutenant's long hesitations before acting that readers understand that he, too, is in conflict. It is through the men's continuing to follow Cacciato up the long trail in the rain that readers understand which side in the conflict masters them. As Stink puts it, "Can't hump away from a war, isn't that right sir? The dummy has got to learn you can't just hump your way out of a war."

*Style and Technique*

O'Brien's craft is often compared to that of Ernest Hemingway and Joseph Heller, other twentieth century American writers who shared the project of telling a true war story. Like them, O'Brien creates a carefully controlled net of unstated meaning. Through understatement, oddities of style, and the juxtaposition of superficially unrelated information, O'Brien shows and does not tell. Much is implied. By cooperatively reconstructing the implicit material, the reader actively participates in co-creating the story. Because of this, readers may find themselves more engaged with O'Brien's work than with other, more explicit, texts.

For example, at the beginning of the story, Doc Peret must say three times that Cacciato has gone AWOL before he gets any response from his lieutenant. The unexplained repetition requires the reader to hypothesize a reason and, through this process, information about the lieutenant's mental state is conveyed. Perhaps he is emotionally exhausted. Perhaps he does not want to hear the news: It will require action on his part, and it foretells a tragedy for one of his men.

Readers can never know for sure that they have decoded the implied material correctly, so the understanding of implicit texts is always more uncertain than the understanding of explicit ones. O'Brien has written elsewhere that chronic uncertainty was one of the defining characteristics of the Vietnam soldier's experience and must be created for the reader in any story that purports to be faithful to the reality of the war. In this way, his highly implicit style not only serves to invite active engagement on the reader's part but also mimics the confusion and uncertainty of the soldiers whose story he is trying to tell.

Another way in which O'Brien strives to tell a true war story is in his attention to the physical details that make up the life of a soldier. The rain, the mud, the fungus that grows in the socks, the jungle-rot that attacks the skin, the exact sound of a booby-trap wire being tripped, the precise physical sensation of bowel-loosening terror—these are the facts of a Vietnam foot soldier's life, and these are the details that enrich the texture and reality of "Going After Cacciato." Through careful sensory detail, O'Brien attempts the impossible task of telling the true story of Vietnam so clearly that even those who were not there may stand in witness.

*Donna Glee Williams*

# GOING ASHORE

*Author:* Mavis Gallant (1922-    )
*Type of plot:* Social realism
*Time of plot:* The 1950's
*Locale:* Tangier
*First published:* 1956

*Principal characters:*
    MRS. ELLENGER, a rich and neurotic young widow
    EMMA, her dutiful but independent teenage daughter

*The Story*

Mrs. Ellenger and her thirteen-year-old daughter, Emma, are enjoying a winter cruise on the Mediterranean. A widow, Mrs. Ellenger is rich, attractive, and bored. Emma is a quiet but observant child who is disturbed by her mother's depression: Mrs. Ellenger is rude to other people, she smokes and drinks too much, and she constantly reminds Emma of what a lucky girl she is, while bragging to others about how Emma lacks for nothing. What Emma lacks is the magic that should suffuse a trip to exotic places. Instead, she is forced to see things through her mother's jaundiced eyes.

When they arrive at Tangier, the Ellengers are the last to disembark for the mainland, even though Emma can hardly wait to get there. She has even made a tentative date with Eddy, a fatherly bartender on holiday, for lunch in the square. When Eddy shows up, however, Mrs. Ellenger brushes him off and then sits for hours in a sidewalk café drinking, smoking, and reading cheap magazines. Emma is waiting patiently to explore this fabulous town all around them. Mrs. Ellenger finally agrees to look around a bit, and they enter a shop in which she buys Emma an enamel bracelet that is both too expensive and too small. The owner then gives Emma a tiny toy tiger, which, he says, was made by people in the hills and contains magic that can grant her every wish.

Back on the ship, Emma clutches the tiger and makes wishes while her mother converses with a new passenger, Mr. Boyd Oliver. Mrs. Ellenger sends Emma back to the cabin, and she spends the evening with Boyd. When she returns to the cabin, she confesses to Emma that Boyd is married and makes Emma promise never to have anything to do with men. Even so, Mrs. Ellenger plans to see Boyd the next day and requests that Emma address him as "Uncle Boyd," the way she has been trained to address all her mother's male friends. Meanwhile, Emma has been clutching the toy tiger to the point where its paint begins to flake, exposing the "Made in Japan" imprint on its bottom.

Emma is saddened but also emboldened by the events of the afternoon. She senses her mother's pathetic ignorance and resolves not to be victimized by it. First, she decides not to call Mr. Oliver "Uncle Boyd." Then she puts aside the toy tiger. She has loved it for an afternoon but knows there is no magic in it. She makes up her mind to place her hopes in Europe instead. As the ship approaches Gibraltar and Mrs. Ellenger sleeps, Emma watches the shoreline of Europe grow clearer. She feels a tide of newness come in with the salty air and senses the beginning of a new life, totally unlike her mother's.

### Themes and Meanings

Mavis Gallant, a Canadian writer, often writes of displaced wanderers who are not quite certain of what to do with their lives. In "Going Ashore," she portrays a familiar type, the affluent widow accustomed to depending on men and not smart enough to cope with ordinary life. Mrs. Ellenger is not an entirely unsympathetic character. She may not be the perfect mother, but it is clear that she values the companionship of her daughter and probably even realizes how dependent she is on the child. It is this dependence that makes her act the way she does, for she reveals time and again, in her ill-fated relationships with men, that she would rather be more independent. She knows that leaning on Emma is not good for either of them, yet she is at a loss to know what else to do.

Mrs. Ellenger is less a victim of circumstances than a product of her age and background. She apparently was a shallow but attractive young woman who married well, had a child, and expected to be taken care of the rest of her life. Instead, she is now a widow who enjoys being taken for her daughter's sister but is painfully aware that she is fooling no one. She quite simply does not know what to do with herself. So she goes on a cruise, taking her daughter along for protection. She hopes to meet eligible men, but when she has the chance to befriend Eddy, a genial widower with two children, she rejects him out of obvious embarrassment. Her refusal to be civil to her table companions, another mother and daughter, is a rejection of the reality of her own situation.

Emma is a dutiful daughter, but she is also a wise one. She is smart enough to feel sorry for her mother rather than simply despise her. When she tries to set her mother up with Eddy, she understands at some level why her mother backs away. The enamel bracelet is symbolic of the damaging hold that her mother has on her, but when Emma takes it off and puts it away, along with the toy tiger, she is making her first gestures of resistance. She is not quite ready to make a break with her mother, but she is beginning to know her own mind and to value, even at thirteen, an independence that her mother will never know.

### Style and Technique

Gallant's writing style is transparent, a straightforward style that ultimately has the power of journalism. What she says rings true, and the direct way in which she says it reflects the seemingly uncomplicated course of her characters' lives. A closer look reveals artful manipulation of the reader's responses and a clever use of simple language to reveal complex and conflicting emotions.

Gallant uses limited third-person narration to interesting effect. The story is told through the eyes of Emma, the teenaged daughter, whose powers of observation have been sharpened during long spells of living exclusively in her mother's company. Seeing things from her point of view allows the reader to see Mrs. Ellenger as the shallow person she is, as if there would be no point in going inside her head anyway. It also allows one to appreciate the subtle, compassionate, maturing sensibilities of Emma herself, whose head is clearly worth going inside.

Through Emma's eyes, readers see, or so it seems, all they need to see, and come to appreciate the fact that Mrs. Ellenger is not an evil person, or even a particularly mean one. She is simply self-absorbed and thoughtless; the pain that she causes others is unintentional. It is still pain, however, and that is what Emma cringes in the face of.

Gallant uses symbolism so skillfully that it never intrudes. The chief symbols in this story are the enamel bracelet and the toy tiger. The bracelet reveals much about Mrs. Ellenger. For example, it is clear that she knows it is of no value because the store she finds it in is described as a junk shop. As a gesture of generosity it falls short, but she is trying her best to salvage something of the afternoon for the sake of Emma, and this is the least troublesome way to do it. When the owner sees that the mother is about to purchase it, he offers the toy tiger to the daughter as a gift. It is clear to all concerned that its price is more than covered by the overpriced bracelet, but nobody mentions it. Later, when the bracelet pinches and nearly poisons Emma, she does not take it as an insult but as another failed attempt on the part of her mother to do something right. She feels sorry for her mother and is relieved that evening when, after a nap, her mother is feeling herself again. She knows the whole Tangier experience has been painful to her mother, who could find no good reason to bother with the place.

Gallant does not present the toy tiger in a way that requires elaborate interpretation. It comes as no surprise that it was made in Japan and does not have magic powers. For a few hours, however, it allows Emma to hold dearly to something of her own and think of it as a good omen, a sign that one should take what one is offered for what it is worth. Afterward, she is ready to put it aside and place her trust in the new life that is about to welcome them, a life that she will embrace wholeheartedly, while her mother wonders what in the world it is all about.

*Thomas Whissen*

# GOING HOME

*Author:* William Trevor (William Trevor Cox, 1928-    )
*Type of plot:* Domestic realism
*Time of plot:* Probably the 1960's
*Locale:* The South of England
*First published:* 1972

*Principal characters:*
> CARRUTHERS, a thirteen-year-old boy who attends boarding school
> MISS FANSHAWE, a thirty-eight-year-old undermatron at the school
> ATKINS, a waiter in the dining car of a train

*The Story*

At the end of each term, Carruthers and Miss Fanshawe travel together by train from the Ashleigh Court school to their separate destinations. The journey has become a ritual, and in this no-man's-land on the train an unusual relationship has developed. Although Miss Fanshawe has a certain supervisory responsibility for Carruthers, he seems to have taken advantage of the freedom on the train to act out his aggression, and she appears to indulge more than restrain him. He smokes, drinks alcohol, lies, and embarrasses her with outspoken comments and questions. The verbal aggression is directed against her and the waiter, but it is evident that his mother and the headmaster of the school are his real targets, and Miss Fanshawe's indulgence is the result of her tacit approval of his anger.

In the first part of the story, they are alone in the dining car, and because the story is almost all dialogue, the reader must slowly piece together the information about the characters. The waiter has a part only insofar as he becomes the butt of Carruther's aggression; because the waiter is new, the boy forces him to listen to his story. His father and mother divorced when he was three, and he spends his summers with his mother, mostly at fashionable Continental resorts. His mother "has men all over the place. . . . She snaps her fingers and people come to comfort her with lust." Adolescent disgust heightens this account, and it is clear that he likes to invent salacious fantasies about other people's lives, but what is most evident is that Carruthers does not feel that he is going to a real home. School is an equally loveless and unpleasant place, where he has joined in the communal games of sadism and victimization.

His conversation explains his aggressive behavior, but on this occasion, he is especially vindictive and seems to exceed the rules of the ritual. He tells the waiter about Miss Fanshawe's life of service at the school, where she is constantly put on and unappreciated. In general, he sketches Miss Fanshawe as a purposeless person who is "watching her life go by," and he demands to know whether it is fair that his mother, "the female," should have so many lovers and Miss Fanshawe none at all. In a frenzy, Carruthers tears the waiter's sleeve, and the furious waiter shouts, "That child is a raving lunatic."

When they return to their compartment, Carruthers reveals to Miss Fanshawe that this is their last time together because he has been expelled for attempting to steal from the headmaster's office. He apologizes to her and confesses that when she comforted him once, he had been crying because he had "thought [the school] would be heaven, a place without Mrs. Carruthers"—in other words, that school would provide him with a real home. Now he seems to break down, admitting that Miss Fanshawe was the only one there who was kind to him and that he does not know why he acts so aggressively.

Suddenly, the quiet Miss Fanshawe begins to tell him about her home life, prompted by her recognition that she has been drawn to him because of his need for care and love. She tells him about her concealed despair and her desperate craving for love, "to be desired, to be desired in any way at all." She tells of her unhappy and dull life with her aging parents, who treat her as a failure and have "sucked everything out of her." She begins to implore him to understand when he tells her that he does not, and her frenzied account of her dream that she could take him and provide him with a real home life terrifies him. When he tries to cut short her account of her life, she refuses to stop and, finally, withdrawing from the role in which she has placed him, he tells her that she "doesn't make any sense." She is forced to admit to him that she may be mad "beneath the surface . . . out of loneliness and locked up love."

By the end of the story, the boy is overwhelmed by the intensity of her revelations, resentful of her confession, and sick of alcohol. At his journey's end, he walks away from her onto the railway platform, and she watches him meet his mother.

## Themes and Meanings

This story challenges the reader with a question: How much honesty can human relationships bear? Beginning with the rather clichéd situation of the English schoolboy in revolt against the restraints of middle-class codes of behavior, the story quickly deepens to explore what may be revealed in a situation of total honesty. What the boy sees as hypocrisy and dishonesty are "appearances" that ought to be dropped while they are in the no-man's-land of the train, but the anarchy of individual impulse that replaces the accepted rules is so frightening to others that it is labeled "lunatic" and "criminal." More important, perhaps, the fragile relationship that has existed between him and Miss Fanshawe cannot sustain total self-revelation; Carruthers fails to "understand" Miss Fanshawe and wishes for the train journey to end as usual so that he can escape from her confession.

In an ironic twist, the title takes on another meaning: These characters are striking home to the core of each other, and when they get there, they seem to discover that there is a limit to the degree of confession and aggression that other people can tolerate. When everything about another person, all the dirty linen, is revealed in public, the story seems to ask, what then? Which is preferable, the later phase, in which everything that Miss Fanshawe has felt ashamed to express is put into words, or the earlier phase, when Miss Fanshawe and the waiter practiced the technique of indulgence ("Take no notice"; "He couldn't help himself") and restraint ("Lies like that, she explained, could get a waiter into trouble"; "She didn't answer")?

The story reveals a conflict that is without resolution because of the unchangeable nature of certain elements of individual experience. For example, Carruthers and Miss Fanshawe have a similar wish for a different home, but children do not choose their parents, any more than Miss Fanshawe can undo the fate of being "untouched by beauty." Carruthers responds to emotional deprivation with a fearless form of self-assertion, which may be a criminal impulse, whereas Miss Fanshawe's response is to withdraw into passivity and fantasy. There may be a suggestion here of a gender difference. In addition, there is a wide age difference, but, most of all, there is the fact that love is what one needs, and yet love cannot simply be given when requested. What is learned from total honesty, then, is the basic unfairness of life, which assigns advantages and opportunities to individuals by some perverse logic. Total honesty does not change this recognition or the facts of life by making them more explicit.

Because the story does not include any suggestion that either Miss Fanshawe or Carruthers has been changed by this episode, the setting on the train and the time frame should be considered. Their relationship is destined to end anyway, so it is fitting, perhaps, to see this kind of self-revelation as a safety valve. A no-man's-land of this kind provides the necessary opportunity for self-expression, which is therapeutic because it is occasional and outside the characters' ordinary routine.

*Style and Technique*

"Going Home" engages the reader in the tensions that are central to the meaning of the story, "the longing to speak, the longing above all things in the world to fill the compartment with the words that had begun." First conceived as a radio play, it has very little narrative comment. Indeed, the story resembles the plays of Harold Pinter, the bizarre tensions in the dialogue paralleling the conflicting desires of the characters, who both yearn to be intimate and are frightened of intimacy. At first, the reader has to work hard to piece together from implications in the dialogue the factual basis of the relationship, and then, perhaps, compassion for the characters grows, but the reader is finally alienated by the rawness and the hopelessness of these revelations.

Because the characters are so enclosed spatially, and because they become so intimately involved in private matters, the reader is put in the situation of a voyeur. The atmosphere of the story is one of impending violence and scandal. Simple expressions bear such an extraordinary cargo of implied violence and pain that the story borders on the horrific; it almost becomes a bad dream. At first the boy's voice dominates, but when the dam bursts and Miss Fanshawe begins to talk, her simple narrative is shocking in its pain and explicitness.

*Denis Sampson*

# GOING TO MEET THE MAN

*Author:* James Baldwin (1924-1987)
*Type of plot:* Psychological
*Time of plot:* The early 1960's
*Locale:* A town in the American South
*First published:* 1965

> *Principal characters:*
> JESSE, a white deputy sheriff
> GRACE, his wife
> JESSE'S FATHER AND MOTHER, who teach him to be a racist
> A BLACK CIVIL RIGHTS LEADER, who challenges racism in the
> South

*The Story*

"Going to Meet the Man" divides clearly and purposefully into two parts. In the first half, the main character, Jesse, a white deputy sheriff in a southern town, lies in bed with his wife, Grace, for the first time in memory suffering from insomnia and impotence. James Baldwin catches Jesse on this night at a moment of crisis, which he shares with other white males: The Old South is now history, the blacks are protesting en masse by registering to vote, and a new South that Jesse cannot conceive is about to be born. That he cannot accept what is happening is clear from hints about what he, as deputy sheriff, will be doing the next day to break up the registration. However, his resistance is much more evident in his paranoid reflections about African Americans; what he would like to do is escape from the black world altogether.

Jesse describes to Grace (who is, however, probably sleeping) an incident that took place earlier in the day at the courthouse. To stop the blacks from singing, the sheriff arrested "the ring-leader" and began to beat him senseless. Jesse continued the brutality at the jail, but before falling unconscious, the young black leader reminded him of an incident in their past when he, as a little boy, had defied this white man for showing disrespect toward his grandmother. The memory raises Jesse's antagonism to an even higher pitch; he wishes to exterminate the black race. He and his fellow whites in the South are "soldiers," "out-numbered, fighting to save the civilized world." However, as Baldwin comments, they cannot succeed in organizing because they are, in fact, "accomplices in a crime." This note of guilt, which actually lies behind Jesse's paranoia, ushers in the second half of the story.

One of the black spirituals, like those that have haunted him all day, comes "flying up at him" from "out of the darkness . . . out of nowhere." It brings with it both fear and pleasure, and a memory out of his childhood. This flashback, which continues until the last paragraph of the story, is the pivotal event in Jesse's life. It begins on another evening when he is unable to sleep. A black man accused of raping a white woman is fleeing the vengeance of the white community and by morning has been caught. The child has no awareness of the situation; he only senses the excitement. His parents tell him that they are going on a picnic. What he actually witnesses is the castration, burning, and mutilation of the captured black man. As Jesse observes the festive occasion, the sensual fascination, and the strange beauty on his mother's face, he himself experiences the greatest joy of his life and an uncommon love for this father who had "carried him through a mighty test, had revealed to him a great secret which would be the key to his life forever."

Indeed, it is. His psychic life is henceforth warped. the sadistic memory transforms him, as well as his wife: "the moonlight covered her like glory," and "his nature again returned to him." His sexual potency, his identity as a man, is inextricably linked to brutality, to the projection of his own guilt on the black man as a scapegoat. However, curiously, and symbolically, he becomes the "nigger" raping his own wife. The last sounds that he hears as the story ends, the cock, the dogs, and "tires on the gravel road," only suggest that he may at last realize his guilt and suffering.

*Themes and Meanings*

Baldwin's story operates on a political level. The setting in the American South during the early 1960's, and the depiction of events that were probably taking place at the very time that Baldwin was writing (voter registration among the blacks began in earnest in 1964; the story was published in 1965) suggest composition in the heat of the moment, unlike Baldwin's more youthful works, which tend to be reflective, balanced, and objective. It is even, perhaps, a political satire, the protagonist being its object—a warped white mentality in the South that contentedly and periodically sacrifices a black to the gods as a deterrent against the eruption of savagery. Still, the main interest in the story is not political, and Baldwin's expose of the white mentality is hardly a simple projection of evil onto the enemy. Instead, what one gets is a psychological and spiritual study that argues against such projections: There is a cautionary identification of the white protagonist with the human race, a call for empathy and introspection that raises the experience above a moment in history.

The story traces the experience of a man in torment. At first he does not even know that he, like the society to which he belongs, is on the verge of a crisis. He is a man damned by his inheritance, by his past, and in need of salvation. As he lies in bed, he senses that something is wrong, but his sleeplessness and impotence are merely the tangible signs of his malaise. He would like to turn to his wife for relief, but he thinks that she cannot give it because she is too pure. He cannot ask her to perform sexual acts that would cure his impotence and hence his insomnia. At this stage, Jesse's only solution is sexual release. That his wife's name is "Grace and that he regards her as a sanctuary" suggest to the reader, but not to Jesse, that the real solution is on a spiritual rather than a physical level.

His recollections of the day's events offer a second avenue of escape for Jesse, the projection of his own guilt onto someone else, for it is guilt, after all, that is causing his crisis. As he beats the civil rights leader, he begins to shake even more violently than his victim—beating is an exorcism misdirected. The experience does, however, begin to work on his memory. He recalls an earlier experience with that black man as a boy. The solution to his present crisis, readers begin to discover, is in the past, in memory, but Jesse does not reach the crucial experience until the flashback.

The story is a journey backward in time. Each memory brings Jesse closer to the truth and at the same time elicits rationalizations to protect his moral being. Against his will, however, a song out of the past forces the crucial memory on him; "the key to his life" was the lesson that the community had taught him. It had demonstrated vividly the way to purification, projection of guilt onto the black race. He had wished then to be the man holding the knife that castrated the "rapist." The experience justified his subsequent behavior, emasculating the black male and substituting himself in his place: He shouts at the black man in jail, "You lucky we pump some white blood into you every once in a while—your women!" This repressed event out of Jesse's past has continued to operate on an unconscious level. It inextricably connected his instinctual sexual life with society's racial bigotry. Now that this memory has become conscious, Jesse, at the end of the story, says aloud to his wife that he is the "nigger" performing the sexual act. Through this empathetic ritual, instead of projecting his guilt, Jesse becomes the guilty man. This is a violation of the code, a betrayal of the tacit conspiracy among whites.

This Freudian accounting for racial bigotry in Jesse would suggest that he is on the way to being cured of his illness. All one knows for sure, however, is that Baldwin leaves him as a vulnerable man, defenseless because he has lost his mask, alone because he has betrayed his race, and susceptible to the fear rather than to a black victim. A recurring theme in Baldwin is once again clear: Color is deceit, reality is within. If freedom is an escape from one's inheritance, the story offers on assurance that such escape is possible.

## Style and Technique

What makes the story effective is a tension between the naturalism of the subject and much of the language, and the artistry that so clearly controls them. Baldwin is hardly prudish about the details or the realities of humanity's animalism, yet he responds to them with a refined sensibility. The artistic intelligence is evident even in the density of the text. As he explores Jesse's typical white attitudes, Baldwin is able to include every conceivable motif in the history of racial conflict in the United States: the sexual provocativeness of the black race to the white mind; the instinctive fear of reprisal by the repressed race; the aesthetic provincialism in whites toward black features; typical assumptions about black inferiority; bafflement before the Uncle Tom image; naïve reactions to black music; use of the Bible to sanction prejudice against the accursed race; whites as protectors and guardians not only of these primitive peoples but also of the civilized world. The list could continue. Baldwin makes Jesse's story a microcosm of the white role in the racial struggle. Jesse's mental journey, his memory, is not only personal but also racial.

Baldwin's artistry, however, lies not merely in the density of the text, in its universalizing effect. What is even more fascinating to watch is the multitude of parallels that Baldwin works into the fabric. To emphasize the effect of the pasts, Baldwin presents both Jesse and the civil rights leader as boy and man; he also sets up the little black boy, Otis, against the black "rapist." He divides the story neatly into halves to show present and past; in both parts the man and the boy begin their experiences in bed. In the past the boy wishes he had held the knife; in the present he actually holds a cattle prod and strikes the black man in the genitals. While in bed, Jesse is touching himself, protecting himself, as he remembers the castration scene. The act of recollection, in fact, is a castration ritual as Jesse deprives himself of his identity as a man. Baldwin carefully works in the sound of gravel three times during the story: at the beginning, when Jesse fears the arrival of black avengers; in the middle, as cars leave for the castration ritual; and at the end, as Jesse once again awaits the avengers. What all these parallels have in common is the suggested identification of Jesse with the black man who is his enemy. This is especially evident in the empathetic identification at crucial moments in the story; not only does Jesse await violation as the two black males in the story had, but he also shudders along with his victim in the jail and becomes the "nigger" in raping his wife. Although the presence of such artistry in a naturalistic story may seem self-conscious and illogical, the parallels themselves are appropriate to a theme that announces the essential identity of all human beings.

The most fascinating parallel of all, however, places the racial struggle of the American South in a larger context. In this case the parallel is ironic. The several Christian symbols in the story suggest that Baldwin's choice of his protagonist's name was not arbitrary. Jesse believes that is a Christian man, living according to the Bible. For him the black race is of the tribe of Ham. It is accursed. The sacrifices of the "rapist" and the civil rights leader are repetitions of the Crucifixion—though Jesse is blind to the parallel. The cock that crows at the identifies Jesse with Peter, yet Jesse is hardly one to found a church. Nor is Jesse able to fulfill the role of his namesake, the father of David, the ancestor of Jesus. Baldwin's Jesse will have no such place in history. The only branch that will grow from his root will be his own phallus, or a knife, or a cattle prod. He has not, like David or Jesus, created a world where "the wolf shall dwell with the lamb," nor does he "decide with equity for the meek of the earth" or possess "the spirit of wisdom and understanding." Jesse's children shall not inherit the earth; he is childless—unless Baldwin's irony turns back on itself, as is often the case in the works of he and other black writers who understand the ironies of life. The tragic truth is that Jesse is all of us, human beings trapped by a past from which there may be no escape. Baldwin himself had to leave his father's home, and even America, to find freedom from a Puritan consciousness; the haunting past appears as much like Original Sin as like Freudian repression. The artistry in Baldwin's story is not, after all, inconsistent with the naturalistic theme; though the past has its inevitable hold, the conscious mind makes its effort to give order and to transcend. The tension is in Baldwin, and in his story; it may be in Jesse once he raises his past to consciousness.

*Thomas Banks*

# THE GOLD-BUG

*Author:* Edgar Allan Poe (1809-1849)
*Type of plot:* Mystery and detective
*Time of plot:* The 1800's
*Locale:* Sullivan's Island, South Carolina
*First published:* 1843

> *Principal characters:*
> WILLIAM LEGRAND, a recluse
> THE NARRATOR, a physician and friend

*The Story*

Many years before the story's present, the unnamed narrator of "The Gold-Bug" made friends with William Legrand, a descendant of an old Huguenot family of New Orleans, who now lives in a hut on Sullivan's Island, nine miles from Charleston, South Carolina. Once wealthy, Legrand lost his fortune and now lives a simple life with his Newfoundland dog and one servant, an old black man named Jupiter, a former slave. Well educated, misanthropic, subject to mood swings between enthusiasm and melancholy, Legrand spends his time fishing, exploring the island, and collecting shells and entomological specimens, of which he has many.

One unusually cold day in October, the narrator visits Legrand after an absence of several weeks. As the narrator warms himself by the fire, Legrand enthusiastically tells him about a strange bug he has found, one of a brilliant gold color with three black spots and long antennae. Because he has lent the bug to a soldier from nearby Fort Moultrie, Legrand cannot show the insect itself; instead, he draws a picture of it on a piece of paper he takes from his pocket. As the narrator holds the paper, the dog jumps on him, causing his hand to move close to the fire. When he looks at the drawing, he sees a representation of a skull rather than a bug. Legrand is visibly upset by his friend's reaction, examines the drawing by candle, and then locks it in his desk, saying nothing more. The narrator thinks it prudent not to upset Legrand further and takes his leave.

About a month later, Jupiter delivers a note from Legrand to the narrator in Charleston begging him to come at once. The urgent tone of the note and Jupiter's comments that Legrand is acting strangely and must be ill alarm the narrator. Jupiter insists that Legrand has been bitten by the gold bug. The narrator fears that his friend's mind has become unhinged, especially when he sees the spades and scythe that Jupiter has been told to buy. On returning to Legrand, the narrator is even more fearful. Legrand says that the bug will make his fortune, as though the insect were real gold. He promises that the narrator will understand his excitement if the narrator will accompany him and Jupiter to the mainland on an all-night expedition. The narrator's assistance is needed and he is the only person in whom Legrand can confide. The narrator fears that Legrand has indeed gone mad, but he agrees to Legrand's request.

The party is led by Legrand to an area of densely wooded hills and crags. Using the scythe, Jupiter clears a path as directed to a tall tulip tree. Legrand instructs him to climb the tree, taking the gold bug with him. The narrator is now convinced that Legrand has lost his mind. Jupiter, however, follows instructions, climbs out on the seventh limb, and there finds a skull. Legrand directs him to drop the bug (which is unusually heavy) through the left eye socket of the skull.

After Legrand makes calculations on the ground, the party begins digging but finds nothing. Remembering Jupiter's confusion concerning left and right, Legrand rightly concludes that Jupiter made a mistake. The error is corrected, and digging proceeds in another spot. By now the narrator is beginning to guess that there is method in Legrand's apparent madness. The digging uncovers some human bones and a large chest; inside is a wealth of gold and jewels. After some difficulty in removing the treasure to Legrand's hut, the men examine their wealth, estimating it to be worth a million and a half dollars, an estimate that the narrator says later proved to be much too low.

Once the men's excitement has subsided, Legrand explains how he was able to solve the riddles that led to finding the treasure. The paper on which Legrand had drawn the bug proved to be parchment and therefore nearly indestructible; it was found half-buried near the wreck of a longboat and near the place where the bug was captured. Legrand had wrapped the bug in the parchment in order to carry it home and had put the parchment in his pocket when he lent the bug to the soldier. When the narrator held the parchment near the fire, the heat made visible the drawing of a skull. By using heat, Legrand uncovered additional markings, including the picture of a kid, which he took to stand for the pirate Captain Kidd.

Knowing the persistent rumors in the area concerning Kidd's buried treasure, Legrand was sure he was on to something. Further heating revealed lines of numerals and other notations, forming a cipher. Legrand describes in detail how he broke the code, enabling him to locate the tulip tree and measure to the correct spot for digging. At the end, Legrand admits that dropping the bug through the skull, instead of dropping a bullet as the code directed, was designed to mystify the narrator further. Legrand had been annoyed that his friend doubted his sanity and enjoyed puzzling him. The skeletons found with the treasure, Legrand speculates, were those of Kidd's helpers, whom he did not want to live to tell the secret of the burial place. Thus, by the end of the story, Legrand has explained all the mysteries attending the discovery of the treasure.

*Themes and Meanings*

A mystery story need not necessarily involve an intellectual theme in the ordinary sense of the term. The gradual unraveling of the mystery and the suspense created are usually sufficient to hold the reader's interest. The reader receives pleasure from matching his wits with the character attempting to solve the mystery and the character who created the mystery. In Edgar Allan Poe's detective and mystery stories such as "The Purloined Letter" and "The Gold-Bug," the main characters themselves, such as Dupin and Legrand, receive this kind of pleasure, as well as expectations of monetary reward. At the same time, in their explanations of their procedures, they often make comments on human nature that serve as themes.

One such theme is expressed by Legrand as he tells the narrator how he decoded Kidd's cipher. Legrand has the skills in logic and the past experiences with such codes to succeed at the task. Yet more fundamentally, he bases his attempt on the conviction, he says, that any mystery that one human intelligence can construct, another human can solve if the person applies his or her intellect properly and persistently. Thus armed, Legrand cracks the code with little difficulty, to the amazement of the narrator.

The experience of the narrator in trying to understand what motivates Legrand early in the story supplies a second theme. Because of Legrand's reputation for being mentally unbalanced, at least at times, the narrator jumps to conclusions about his friend's condition, despite the fact that the narrator is a physician. Some of Legrand's actions are puzzling, and he takes no one into his confidence until after the discovery of the treasure. At times he seems to mystify the narrator purposely, as though he were playing a game. As a result, the narrator throughout the first half of the story has growing doubts about Legrand's sanity. Not until the treasure is virtually in their hands does the narrator realize that Legrand has had rational purposes all along. The narrator then comments on the narrow line between sanity and insanity and how easily one can misjudge a person's mental condition.

*Style and Technique*

Legrand, the hero, is similar to other Poe characters; he is well educated, possessed of excellent reasoning powers, somewhat reclusive, formerly wealthy, and known for his mental instability. Like Dupin, the hero of Poe's later detective stories, Legrand's actions puzzle other characters, especially the narrator friend, with whom the reader tends to identify. Combining two such characters with a puzzling situation became a formula for Poe in creating suspenseful stories.

The structuring of "The Gold-Bug" in two parts is also typical of Poe. Suspense builds in the first part because neither the narrator nor the reader understands Legrand's actions. The quotation used as a head note implies that Legrand may indeed be mad. When his actions lead to the discovery of the treasure, one mystery is solved. A major question remains: How did Legrand know where to look? In the second half of the story, Legrand explains the reasoning that led to such success. Again, suspense builds as he gives his detailed explanation, which by the end of the story ties up all loose ends. Regardless of whether he guesses the answers, the reader is treated to mystery and suspense in a well-wrought tale in which the hero accomplishes his goal.

In addition to suspense, "The Gold-Bug" includes a touch of humor, principally achieved by the incongruity between the elevated language (used by many Poe characters) of Legrand and the narrator and the dialect of Jupiter. Blacks in Poe's tales are often comic stereotypes; their powers of understanding and intellect are limited, and their language contrasts sharply with that of other characters. In Jupiter's case, Poe gives him the black dialect of Virginia rather than that of South Carolina, no doubt because Poe was more familiar with Virginia blacks.

"The Gold-Bug" immediately became popular after winning the *Dollar Newspaper* story contest (and a prize of one hundred dollars) in 1843; it has also inspired much critical comment. It has been praised for its original plot and for the realism of the description of Sullivan's Island. The story is one of a relatively small number in which Poe used a real place as a setting. In many incidental details, it reflects Poe's experiences during his tour of army duty at Fort Moultrie, between 1827 and 1828.

Whatever the source of the popularity of "The Gold-Bug," it remains one of Poe's best-known stories. It appeals to readers who love a mystery, a cryptograph, and sustained suspense, and who enjoy a happy ending with well-deserved rewards.

*Louise S. Bailey*

# GOLD COAST

*Author:* James Alan McPherson (1943-    )
*Type of plot:* Social realism
*Time of plot:* The late 1960's
*Locale:* Cambridge, Massachusetts
*First published:* 1968

*Principal characters:*
> ROBERT, a young black man, an aspiring writer working as a janitor
> JAMES SULLIVAN, his supervisor and friend
> MEG SULLIVAN, his wife
> JEAN, his rich, white girlfriend
> MISS O'HARA, a tenant in Robert's building and Sullivan's enemy

## The Story

Robert, a young, black aspiring writer, supports himself by working as a janitor in a Cambridge, Massachusetts, apartment building. In "the days of the Gold Coast," the old building near Harvard Square had been a haven for the rich; later, poet-novelist Conrad Aiken lived there; now, it is rather run-down. Even seedier is Robert's predecessor, James Sullivan, an elderly Irishman who has been forced to retire. Sullivan lives in the building with Meg, his half-mad wife, and their smelly, barking dog. He is technically Robert's supervisor, and most of the story concerns their relationship.

Robert likes being a janitor because he is confident of a bright future as a writer, and he also enjoys making the white liberals he meets at parties uncomfortable by talking enthusiastically about his duties, which include, he insists, being able "to spot Jews and Negroes who are passing." His youth and confidence make him pity Sullivan: "He had been in that building thirty years and had its whole history recorded in the little folds of his mind, as his own life was recorded in the wrinkles of his face." Sullivan acts the role of an all-knowing mentor forever dispensing advice to his young "assistant." Excessively proud of his Irish heritage, he repeats stories of sitting in bars with James Michael Curley, the longtime boss of Democratic politics in Boston, and of knowing Frank O'Connor when the Irish writer taught at Harvard.

Robert considers one of the pleasures of his job the opportunity to find material, assuming "that behind each of the fifty or so doors in our building lived a story which could, if I chose to grace it with the magic of my pen, become immortal." However, the tenants prove too ordinary to supply what he needs; even going through their garbage reveals little of interest. Sullivan tries to help by surveying the evidence but can conclude only that "Jews are the biggest eaters in the world." Robert thinks that Sullivan does not really hate Jews but simply resents "anyone better off than himself." Ironically, Sullivan's antagonist is Irish. Miss O'Hara hates the Sullivans for reasons

Robert never discovers. She accuses the former janitor of never being sober and has been trying to get him fired for twenty-five years. She also conducts a campaign to have the couple's dog removed from the building.

In addition to his writing, Robert's main interest is his relationship with Jean, "a very lovely girl who was not first of all a black." He likes being with her because she does not expect him to play a role, as so many in the turmoil of the late 1960's are doing. She wants him only to be himself and to write: "Like many of the artistically inclined rich, she wanted to own in someone else what she could not own in herself. But this I did not mind, and I forgave her for it because she forgave me moods and the constant smell of garbage and a great deal of latent hostility." She resents, however, his wasting his time with Sullivan, who, chased by Meg to a filthy sofa in the basement, calls Robert at two o'clock in the morning to drink with him. Robert admires Sullivan for being well-read and able to spew out his diatribes against hippies and the medical profession in well-constructed sentences.

Chaos enters the lives of Robert and Sullivan at about the same time. When Robert's affair with Jean ends, he writes little and no longer enjoys his other work, because he is "really a janitor for the first time." When Miss O'Hara finally succeeds in having the Sullivans' dog taken away, Meg's madness and her husband's sad loneliness increase. To appease Meg, Robert writes a letter from a New Hampshire farmer telling the Sullivans how happy their dog is living with him. After carrying it about for days searching for someone with New Hampshire license plates to ask to mail the letter, Sullivan tears it up.

Deciding that he can no longer be a janitor "because there is no job more demeaning," Robert moves out. He later sees Sullivan in a crowd in Harvard Square but decides not to speak to him. This episode in his life is over.

*Themes and Meanings*

The main themes of "Gold Coast" deal with racial and age differences and with loneliness. James Alan McPherson captures many of the surface details of American life in the late 1960's with hippies, drug dealers, and lonely middle-aged men driven wild by young women wearing miniskirts. More important, Robert's confidence about his writing career reflects the growing optimism of many American blacks resulting from the decade's progress in civil rights. The relationship of Robert and Jean is a testing of the generally more liberal social atmosphere but fails the test. Sullivan is uneasy about their affair because "it is in the nature of things that liberal people will tolerate two interracial hippies more than they will an intelligent, serious-minded mixed couple." The latter poses a more substantial threat to the prevailing social order. Their seriousness makes them feel estranged from both white and black worlds, as when they ride in the subway and find themselves in a car with whites on one side, blacks on the other, tension and hatred all around. With no room on either side for both to sit, they stand, holding a steel post, in the middle, "feeling all the eyes, [trapped] between the two sides of the car and the two sides of the world." Leaving the subway, "we looked at each other . . . and there was nothing left to say."

The age difference, more than the racial difference, creates tension in Robert and Sullivan's friendship. Although the old man enjoys talking to Robert because he thinks his "assistant" needs the wisdom he imparts to get along in the world, the young black man understands the complexities of their changing society much better. Sullivan's Boston, with its colorful Irish politicos, is no more. The Sullivans' being out of step with their times is emphasized when a hippie insults them in Harvard Square: "Don't break any track records, Mr. and Mrs. Speedy Molasses."

Robert respects Sullivan but occasionally has difficulty doing so. When Jean is around, Robert, perceiving the old man through her eyes, sees him as dirty and uncomfortable. Robert hates passing the Sullivans' apartment because of the "smell of dogs and cats and age and death about their door." He does not want to be confronted by James Sullivan's mortality, because he does not want to think about his own. Sullivan reminds Robert that "nothing really matters except not being old and being alive and having potential to dream about, and not being alone." Listening to one of Sullivan's drunken late-night harangues, Robert is distracted by the laugh of a girl on the street outside, by the sound of youth and the promise of the future, and he resents Sullivan, hating himself for doing so: "I was young and now I did not want to be bothered." This barrier of age, tinged with the contrast between the failure of one and the potential success of the other, is what keeps Robert from speaking to the old man at the end of the story. The demons of loneliness and rejection plague characters of all ages and races throughout McPherson's short stories.

*Style and Technique*

As with many writers of his generation, McPherson employs brand names and the titles of songs and television programs to establish time and place and to reveal character. Robert draws conclusions about a married couple in his building based on their garbage: S. S. Pierce cans, Chivas Regal bottles, back issues of *Evergreen* and *The Realist*.

Close attention to detail defines McPherson's style throughout "Gold Coast." Because Meg Sullivan loves animals more than people, she keeps "little pans of meat posted at strategic points about the building." McPherson uses many such details to establish Meg's character: "She was never really clean, her teeth were bad, and the first most pathetic thing in the world was to see her sitting on the steps in the morning watching the world pass, in a stained smock and a fresh summer blue hat she kept just to wear downstairs, with no place in the world to go." Miss O'Hara is fanatical about cleanliness and puts out "her little bit of garbage wrapped very neatly in yesterday's *Christian Science Monitor* and tied in a bow with a fresh piece of string." Robert wonders where she gets the string and imagines "her at night picking meat-market locks with a hairpin and hobbling off with yards and yards of white cord concealed under the gray sweater she always wore." This use of details to create both pathos and humor while maintaining a skillful balance between the two keeps "Gold Coast" from being annoyingly sentimental.

*Michael Adams*

# THE GOLDEN APPLE OF ETERNAL DESIRE

*Author:* Milan Kundera (1929-        )
*Type of plot:* Social realism
*Time of plot:* 1963
*Locale:* Prague, Czechoslovakia
*First published:* "Zlaté jablko vecné touhy," 1963 (English translation, 1974)

*Principal characters:*
THE UNNAMED NARRATOR
MARTIN, his friend, a notable womanizer

*The Story*

The story opens with a quotation from the French author Blaise Pascal: "They do not know that they seek only the chase and not the quarry." The quotation is an ironic commentary on the game of womanizing played by the story's two middle-aged male protagonists. The unnamed narrator is in a café, reading a book obtained with great difficulty from a library. His friend Martin, a seasoned veteran of the game of womanizing, joins him and draws his attention to a woman sitting at another table. When she gets up to leave and collects her shopping bag from the cloakroom, Martin drops the narrator's precious book in her bag. He explains that it is uncomfortable to carry by hand, and suggests to the narrator that he carry the bag for her. The two men accompany the bemused woman to her bus terminal. They learn that she is a nurse, and arrange a meeting on the following Saturday. When the woman's streetcar arrives, she goes to take the book out of her bag, but Martin prevents her, saying they will come for it on Saturday.

Martin does not "arrest" every woman who attracts his attention. There are countless more whom he merely registers without following up with a contact. He considers this a worthwhile achievement because it is easier (and, by implication, less heroic) to seduce a woman than to know enough women whom he chooses not to seduce. The narrator comments that he who likes to look back boastfully will emphasize the women to whom he has made love, but he who looks toward the future must ensure that he has plenty of registered and contacted women.

On Saturday, the two men arrive at the hospital and arrange to meet the nurse and her friend at seven. Martin wants to check out the friend, but the narrator, much to Martin's annoyance, betrays his less-than-devoted attitude to the game by demanding that he first retrieve his book. The narrator confesses that he is a dilettante, merely playing at something that Martin lives.

As they leave the hospital, Martin mentions that he must be home by nine because his wife, whom he loves, expects him to play cards with her on Saturdays. The exasperated narrator remarks that because they must leave for home at eight, they will only have an hour to spend with their new dates. This ludicrous anticlimax is the first concrete sign that Martin is more interested in the pursuit than the catch.

While they are walking in the park, Martin notices an attractive young woman. He approaches her with the concocted story that he and his friend are a famous film director and his assistant, looking for locations to make a film. They ask her to show them a certain castle, and she volunteers to go with them after visiting her mother.

They wait for the young woman to arrive, passing up another contact in doing so. When she fails to turn up, Martin is amazed because she evidently believed in them absolutely. The narrator abstracts the philosophical point that a genuine adherent to a faith never takes its sophistries seriously, but only the practical aims underlying those sophistries. Foolish people, on the other hand, who take the sophistries in earnest, eventually find inconsistencies in them, protest, and finish as heretics and apostates. The woman believed their stories so completely that she told her mother, who apparently pointed out the absurdities, until she became as disenchanted as she previously had been enchanted.

The two men arrive at the hospital to meet the nurse and her friend, but the women do not turn up on time. The narrator states that it is a matter of indifference to him whether they come at all because at the moment when Martin limited their available time to one hour, he shifted the affair to nothing but a self-deluding game. Martin's games are no longer able to cross the line into real life, although he is unaware of this fact.

The narrator observes that although Martin is a captive of his self-deception, he himself sees the delusion for what it is. He therefore has no excuse for assisting his friend in his ridiculous game. He has no illusion that an amorous adventure lies before them, only a single aimless hour with indifferent women. At that moment, the narrator looks in his rear-view mirror and sees the women approaching. He announces to Martin, who has not seen them, that they should give them up for lost, and drives away.

The narrator is struck by guilt. He has betrayed Martin because he stopped believing in him. Will he stop playing the game just because it is futile? He knows he will not; the game will continue. The story ends with a conversation between the two men about an imaginary medical student whom the narrator invented to satisfy Martin's insistence that he is a consummate womanizer. Martin suggests that the narrator pass her on to him, and they decide that Martin will pose as an athlete in order to impress her. As the plan becomes concrete, the narrator sees it dangling before them like a ripe, shining apple: "The Golden Apple of Eternal Desire."

## Themes and Meanings

The theme of "The Golden Apple of Eternal Desire"—the womanizer's unbounded appetite for the chase—is one to which Milan Kundera often returns, most notably in his novel *L'Insoutenable Légèreté de l'être* (1984; *The Unbearable Lightness of Being*, 1984). In this short story, the pursuit of the object of desire, rather than its possession, becomes the driving force behind the action. In the novel, the protagonist's womanizing was potent in its destructiveness of innocence in relationships; in this story, the libidinous episodes always run out of steam before fulfillment. They are rendered impotent, harmless, and more than a little ridiculous.

Martin, happily married and more than forty years of age, maintains the illusion of living a wild and free life. At the same time, he ensures, through such subconscious ruses as making a date with the nurse for seven and having to leave for home at eight, that nothing ever happens. It is the eternal possibility of illicit sex that drives him on, not its achievement. The narrator, too, is a lothario only in his head, inventing an attractive medical student in order to satisfy his friend's expectations.

Whenever there is a possibility of a fruitful encounter, the two men sabotage it. They stand up a contact to wait for the young woman in white, but have already ruined their chances with her by concocting a tissue of wild lies about film directors that is bound to be blown apart by the first rational mind to enter the scene. At the end of the story, when the narrator and Martin seem to be in line for a real date, the narrator has lost faith in Martin's ability ever to translate the game into reality, and simply drives away from the women.

The two men end up planning an encounter with the narrator's fictitious woman in which Martin will play-act as an athlete. The result will be a fake athlete in insincere pursuit of an imaginary woman—the ultimate delusion. The game is futile, but its beauty and integrity lie in that very futility. The quarry is never captured and therefore remains eternally alluring. The Golden Apple of Eternal Desire is best left perfect, whole, and untasted.

*Style and Technique*

As befits a story in which the narrator is divided between the self that acts and the self that stands apart and comments, the action is interspersed with his ironic observations and philosophical abstractions on the game. His attitude toward it is ambivalent. The game is a self-deluding farce, but it is also a vocation to which he has subjugated all personal interests and desires. He remains divided, a combination of the biblical betrayer Judas Iscariot and Doubting Thomas. Martin, the foil to the narrator, is like a character from mythology, an integrated being unhindered by doubts or a sense of irony, fighting the great interminable battle against the narrow confines of time and space.

This religious and heroic imagery, along with the heroic quest-type structure of the story and the elevated terminology used to describe the elements of the quest, combine to create a style that is at once self-mocking and reverential, in line with the narrator's ambivalent stance. In contrast, the image used to describe men who bypass the levels of registration and contact to go straight for the last level—bedding the woman—is positively anti-heroic. These wretched, primitive types are likened to football players who press thoughtlessly toward the goal, forgetting that this rash desire to score will not necessarily lead to a goal, whereas a competent game on the field will.

*Claire J. Robinson*

# THE GOLDEN HONEYMOON

*Author:* Ring Lardner (1885-1933)
*Type of plot:* Satire
*Time of plot:* 1920
*Locale:* St. Petersburg, Florida
*First published:* 1922

### Principal characters:

CHARLEY, the narrator and protagonist, the insensitive, garrulous, and naïve husband of Lucy

LUCY, his tolerant wife of fifty years

FRANK HARTSELL, an old suitor of Lucy, now a veterinarian and married to a female version of Charley

MRS. HARTSELL, a talkative and boring woman

## The Story

At first glance, the title simply reveals the occasion for the story's events, the celebration of a marriage that has endured for fifty years. It is only after reading the story that the readers understand the irony in the celebration of a union more brass than gold. Charley, the ingenuous first-person narrator, recounts his adventures in St. Petersburg, but in doing so reveals himself as shallow, insensitive, and boring. As the plot unravels, so does Charley, yet he remains blissfully unaware of and not bored by a life composed of unrelenting trivia.

The structure of the story is the recollection in detail of a trip to St. Petersburg, Florida. The story begins with the most important word and person in Charley's life, "Mother," as he calls his wife, Lucy. His refrain, "You can't get ahead of Mother," is evidence of his pride in all things connected with himself, whether it be the state of New Jersey or his prosperous son-in-law, John H. Kramer, a real-estate man and member of the Rotary Club, an important status symbol in Charley's eyes. After a tedious and typical explanation of how and why he and Lucy went to Florida for their "golden honeymoon," including prices, detailing to the penny the differences between a sleeper and a compartment on a train and a complete timetable for all stops made between Trenton and St. Petersburg, Charley is ready to begin his real story.

The real story, however, is actually the revelation of Charley's character and his marriage to Lucy, both of which are tested by the vicissitudes of travel and encounters with new and old acquaintances. On the train, Charley unconsciously reveals that appearance and status are extremely important values for him. He notes and admires anyone he meets who is a Rotarian, rides backward on the train, facing his wife, and insists on sleeping in the top berth to protect his image, even though neither he nor his wife sleeps well when he is in that precarious position. During the trip, Charley is nearly left behind in Washington, D.C., an occurrence that entails the admission that it is Mother who manages and carries the money.

It is, however, in describing St. Petersburg and the people that they encounter there that Charley reaches the peak of his powers. Ungrammatical, inelegant, clichéd details concerning the "Tin-Can Tourists," their new president, the "Royal Tin-Can Opener," and their official song, which Charley does not remember exactly, are followed by a complete account of their first night at the meeting of the New York-New Jersey society. No tidbit is too trivial for Charley to recite. After Mother's birthday celebration, marred because the Poinsettia Hotel charged seventy-five cents for a small, tough sirloin steak, Charley and Lucy plunge into social activities at the park: band concerts, checkers, chess, horseshoes, dominoes, and roque. Charley quickly establishes himself as a champion checker player, while Lucy enjoys the concerts.

While listening to a concert, Lucy makes the acquaintance of a Mrs. Hartsell, the woman who married Lucy's cast-off fiancé, Frank. Lucy tells Mrs. Hartsell only that she and Frank had been good friends before he moved to Michigan and became a veterinarian. To Charley's chagrin, the Hartsells join them at every opportunity; they dine together, attend the Michigan Society meeting, which Charley finds far inferior to the New York-New Jersey meeting, and play cards. Although Lucy and Frank enjoy renewing their old friendship, Charley cannot abide Mrs. Hartsell. Because she is presented through Charley's eyes with many of the same characteristics noted in Charley, the feeling is mutual. Threatened, Charley disparages Frank's beard, his former occupation, and his checker-playing ability. Although he easily defeats Frank at checkers, the card games are another matter. Frank and Lucy continually trounce Charley and Mrs. Hartsell, a phenomenon that Charley attributes solely to the constant talking, inattention, and poor skills of Mrs. Hartsell.

To his delight, Mrs. Hartsell receives her comeuppance while playing roque with Lucy. After Lucy withdraws, claiming an inability to play longer because of a lame back, Mrs. Hartsell makes a wild long shot and drops her teeth on the court. Charley laughs long and heartily at both women. The unspoken competition between the two couples intensifies when Frank challenges Charley to a game of horseshoes, a game that Charlie claims not to have played in twenty years. From the beginning, it is obvious that Frank Hartsell is the better player, but he cannot beat Charley when it comes to making excuses. Charley complains of a lack of practice, old horseshoes with points that immediately make his thumb raw and sore, and finally Frank's awkward style and unbeatable luck. Facing certain defeat, Charley quits, but his anger continues.

That night while playing cards and, as usual, being defeated, he blurts out the truth about Lucy's former relationship with Frank. This results not only in an uncomfortable split with the Hartsells but also in a quarrel between Lucy and Charley. In a fit of pique, Lucy says that she wishes she had married Frank Hartsell instead of Charley, and Charley retaliates by agreeing with her. The result of this spat is two days of silence from Lucy. Finally she relents, for the sake of their "golden honeymoon," and they kiss and make up. The Hartsells depart in a huff for Orlando, leaving Mother and Charley to enjoy the remaining days of their vacation.

The remainder of the story recounts their departure from St. Petersburg and their return home; Charley concludes with the observation, "Here comes Mother, so I guess I better shut up."

## Themes and Meanings

The meaning in this story is not in what happens but in how it happens and to whom it happens. The revelation is of character, not plot. Insight is granted to the reader, not to the characters: Charley learns very little, if anything, about himself or about human nature; he and Lucy remain blissfully unaware of their prejudices, their narrowness, their sentimentality, and the banality of their lives. Although this story has been read as a condemnation of middle-class values and marriage, Ring Lardner does not totally condemn Charley and his "golden honeymoon." The meaning of the story lies in the reader's understanding of Charley; perhaps to understand all is indeed to forgive all. Certainly both Lardner and the reader see Charley clearly, much more clearly than he sees himself.

## Style and Technique

Lardner's ear for American dialect and his ability to reproduce its syntax, grammar, and cadence are as important in this story as characterization and plot. The character of Charley is revealed not only through what he says but also through the way he says it. His ungrammatical sentences, awkward diction, and malapropisms are essential to understanding his worldview. In addition, the first-person point of view is a perfect vehicle for a character such as Charley, a naïve narrator who reveals considerably more about himself than he intends.

Thus, the irony promised in the title continues throughout the story. Charley says what he does not mean; he reveals what he himself does not know. This irony softens the story's condemnation of middle-class complacency. Through humor, Lardner suggests that although the "golden honeymoon" may not be solid gold, it is neither futile nor bitter.

*Linda Humphrey*

# THE GONZAGA MANUSCRIPTS

*Author:* Saul Bellow (1915-    )
*Type of plot:* Realism
*Time of plot:* About 1950
*Locale:* Madrid
*First published:* 1954

### Principal characters:

CLARENCE FEILER, a young scholar, unemployed but with a small income, who comes to Madrid looking for the Gonzaga manuscripts

FAITH UNGAR, an art student in Madrid who befriends Feiler

GUZMAN DEL NIDO, Gonzaga's friend and literary executor, who Feiler thinks has the manuscripts

## The Story

For the purposes of this story, Saul Bellow invents a famous modern Spanish poet, Manuel Gonzaga, whose elusive manuscripts set the plot in motion. Clarence Feiler is a naïve young man from California who hears from a Spanish Republican refugee that there are more than one hundred poems by Gonzaga somewhere in Madrid. Feiler wrote his graduate thesis on Gonzaga's *Los Huesos Secos*, an experience that, he felt, put him "in touch with a poet who could show me how to go on, and what attitude to take toward life." Feiler has been leading an aimless fife; he realizes that he is "becoming an eccentric" and is "too timid to say he believed in God," and so his quest for the Gonzaga manuscripts evolves into a quest for his own identity. Finding the manuscripts and presenting them to the world matters to him, and "what mattered might save him."

Feiler's first act on arriving in Madrid is to find Miss Faith Ungar, an art student whose fiancé is an airline pilot regularly engaged in bringing in blackmarket *pesetas* from Tangiers. Miss Ungar is sympathetic to his ambitions, but he frets that "the kind of woman who became engaged to an airline pilot might look down on him." Her friendship with Feiler does seem sincere, though, and perhaps would have developed into something deeper had he had the courage to pursue it. At one time he even reflects, "He should have a woman like that. It passed dimly over his mind that a live woman would make a better quest than a dead poet." The moment passes, however, leaving a faint after-sense of an opportunity wasted.

Feiler takes a room at a pension and immediately involves himself in a verbal exchange with a Miss Walsh, a querulous Englishwoman who baits him about his country's testing of atomic bombs. When she calls him "some sort of fanatic," Feiler responds by identifying her as "a nasty old bag." His discomfiture as an American in Europe thus begins soon and unexpectedly.

The baiting of Feiler the American naif continues when he visits Guzman del Nido, the friend and literary executor of Manuel Gonzaga. Caught in a terrible rainstorm on his way to Guizman's home, Feiler arrives sodden and at a considerable disadvantage among the other guests—an Italian monsignor, an Egyptian woman from New York, and a German insurance executive. When Feiler tells a humorous story, he is mortified by the blank response, and he soon realizes that he is being patronized by Guzman. Feiler discusses Gonzaga's poetry with Guzman, who seems to think that he cannot appreciate the Spaniard's sensibility, and his frustration is complete when Guzman tells him that he gave the poems to a Countess del Camino, now dead. Guzman thinks the poems may have passed on to the countess's secretary, also dead, but whose nephews may know something of the whereabouts of the poems. To conclude his exasperating day, when Feiler returns to his pension he is sure—for no apparent reason—that the police have searched his room.

He resolves to track down the nephews in Alcala de Henares, but when he finds them they can only taunt him with silly anti-American jokes about "*la bomba atomica*" and send him on another quest to Segovia to see Pedro Alvarez-Polvo, who had been a great friend of the countess. Alvarez-Polvo gives Feiler a pompous lecture on Segovian architecture, and in a comedy of misunderstandings reveals that he thinks Feiler is interested in the rights to a pitchblende mine formerly owned by the countess's secretary. The uranium content of pitchblende brings Feiler face-to-face once more with the motif of "*la bomba atomica*," and he finally cries out in fury, "What do I care about atom bombs! To hell with atom bombs!"

So much for the quest for the poems and for Feiler's sense of his mission in life. On his return to his hotel room in Segovia, he is convinced that his valise has been searched. When he berates the manager in a great rage, a man in the lobby mistakes Feiler for an Englishman and harangues him for criticizing Spain: "The whole world knows you have a huge jail in Liverpool, filled with Masons. Five thousands Masons are *encarcelados* in Liverpool alone." Feiler packs up and heads back to Madrid, defeated in spirit and dreading the next meal with Miss Walsh.

## Themes and Meanings

The misadventures of Americans in Europe make up an old theme in American literature. Usually, as best illustrated in the many treatments of the topic by Henry James, the Americans are ingenuous and in danger of coming to grief at the hands of the more worldly Europeans who are eager to exploit them. The story of Clarence Feiler becomes, then, a special version of the initiation rite of the young naif: the innocent abroad and all that happens to him. The naïveté of his desire to "bring the testimony of a great man before the world" appears comic in the light of what befalls Feiler, but there is no real evidence at the story's end that he is yet aware of how ludicrous he must have appeared to the Spaniards. His obvious bitterness, as well as the fact that on the train ride back to Madrid "he sat numb and motionless" suggest, however, that self-knowledge may not be far off for Feiler.

A special aspect of the theme is the hostility toward Americans that shows up in the motif of "*la bomba atomica*." Miss Walsh picks up this theme first, when in a lament about the excessive rain she grumbles to Feiler that "You people may be to blame for that." Feiler is astonished to find himself a member of any group suspected of subverting the average mean rainfall in Spain, and his ensuing dialogue with Miss Walsh is truly comic. He can only protest "I am not all Americans. You are not all the English. . . . You are not Winston Churchill, I am not the Pentagon." At this point they exchange contemptuous epithets and Feiler stalks out in rage.

Equally comic is Feiler's visit to the nephews of the countess's dead secretary. They prove to be "a family of laughers." One of them had lived in England for a few months many years before, and the family rejoices in addressing him as "My Lord." On Feiler's arrival, "My Lord" is encouraged to speak English, and he responds with "Jolly country, eh?" and "Charing Cross," signing off with "Piccadilly. And that's all I can remember."

Dealing with these madcaps and eccentrics unhinges Feiler's nervous system and certainly contributes to the paranoia he exhibits in his conviction that his room and luggage have been searched. His distaste for the people he meets, his disabling frustration in his quest, and the mild sense of rue he retains from his brief friendship with Miss Faith Ungar—all these elements make Feiler a wiser man and give him a kind of self-knowledge that he had not anticipated.

*Style and Technique*

Bellow attempts no razzle-dazzle effects but tells his story in a conventional alternation of dialogue with passages of description and summary from the third-person omniscient point of view. He is economical but effective with figurative language (for example, "The gaunt horse-like Spanish locomotives screamed off their steam" and "Trolley sparks scratched green within the locust trees"). Bellow catches in a few lines the misery of Miss Walsh, whose admitted commitment to life's satisfactions contrasts so effectively with Feiler's aimlessness and timidity. Bellow says of her, "she thought she was a person of charm, and she did have a certain charm, but her eyes were burning." Later, Feiler notes her "busted-up face" and he feels sorry for her "and yet lucky to have met her." She hints at a life wasted for passion when she admits, "You see, I used to read widely once. I was a cultivated person. But the reason for it was sex, and that went." She is a minor character but a memorable one, created by a few quick lines of description.

One of Bellow's most effective narrative devices is his use of descriptions of the weather. It is the relentless rain that precipitates Miss Walsh's tirade against the American scientists' meddling with the laws of nature, and it is the rain that soaks and humiliates the egregious Feiler even before he has to stand up against the condescension of the smirking Guzman. Finally, when Feiler leaves Segovia to return to Madrid and the bitter Miss Walsh at his pension's dinner table, it is the rain that participates in a grand pathetic fallacy to mock the hapless Feiler: "As the train left the mountains, the heavens seemed to split; the rain began to fall, heavy and sodden, boiling on the wide plain."

*Frank Day*

# GOOD ADVICE IS RARER THAN RUBIES

*Author:* Salman Rushdie (1947-     )
*Type of plot:* Realism, postcolonial
*Time of plot:* The late twentieth century
*Locale:* Outside a British consulate in Pakistan
*First published:* 1987

*Principal characters:*

> MISS REHANA, a young woman from Lahore, Pakistan, who is
> applying for a visa
> MUHAMMAD ALI, a crooked professional advice giver

## The Story

The story begins on the last Tuesday of a month when a colorfully painted bus brings Miss Rehana to the gates of a British consulate. This is the day when women, referred to as "Tuesday women," go to the consulate to get visas to join fiancés who are working in England. Muhammad Ali, identified as an "advice expert" watches Miss Rehana descend from the bus and go to the consulate gates, where a guard tells her that the English officials are still eating breakfast. Muhammad Ali is immediately taken in by her beauty. Although he normally is paid for his advice and seeks to cheat women seeking visas, he decides to advise Miss Rehana even though she tells him she has no money.

The aging confidence man leads the young woman to his desk in a corner of the shanty-town near the British consulate. There, she tells him that she is seeking permission to go to Bradford, England, to be with her fiancé, Mustafa Dar. Muhammad Ali warns her that the sahibs, or British officials, are suspicious of the women seeking to go to England and that the sahibs will interrogate her in detail, asking private and sometimes embarrassing questions. If she fails to answer correctly, they will conclude that she is not really the fiancé of a British resident and will refuse her request. These are the claims that Muhammad Ali usually makes to his victims before asking them for money to obtain the proper papers from an acquaintance of his who works in the consulate. However, the old man is so taken with Miss Rehana that he offers to provide her with a British passport.

Muhammad Ali is surprised by his own generosity and feels that, against his better judgement, he is about to give her the valuable passport for free. Miss Rehana, though, is shocked that he is urging her to do something illegal. She protests that such an action would justify the suspicions of the British sahibs, and she walks away from him.

The con man spends the day waiting for Miss Rehana outside the consulate. When she appears, smiling contentedly, he assumes that she has been given the visa. She tells him, though, that he was right. The British officials did ask her detailed questions about her fiancé. The engagement, she explains, was arranged by her parents when she was nine years old and Mustafa Dar was thirty. Because she had not seen Mustafa Dar for many years, she was unable to answer most of the questions about him and permission to enter England was denied.

Muhammad Ali exclaims that the outcome is tragic and that Miss Rehana should have taken his advice. However, the young woman is not at all sad not to be leaving her home for marriage to a virtual stranger in a foreign country. She returns on the bus to her job as an ayah, or nanny, for three boys in Lahore. Muhammad Ali is struck by the happiness in her smile.

*Themes and Meanings*

Beneath its simple surface, "Good Advice Is Rarer than Rubies" deals with complex issues of international relations, cultural differences, and the many-sided nature of human desires and goals. At one level, the story deals with the unequal relationship between Great Britain and its former colony, Pakistan. Muhammad Ali's meager, dishonest living depends on a steady stream of women seeking permission to join husbands or fiancés working in England. When Miss Rehana appears at the gates of the consulate, she is turned away because the sahibs have not yet finished their breakfast. The British officials have complete power to decide whether she will be allowed to enter their country.

It is clear that the British do not understand Pakistan or customs such as arranged marriages. Miss Rehana and the other young women, in turn, do not understand British ways of doing things. Muhammad Ali is able to act as a go-between and to defraud the young women, because he can claim to have some insight into how things are done by the sahibs.

At a deeper level, the story treats the mystery of motivation. Even Muhammad Ali, a greedy and selfish cheat, finds himself motivated to help the young woman without completely understanding why. Miss Rehana herself appears to be motivated to go to England, but in the end she really seems to want to stay home. The difficulty of knowing what people really want makes it hard to say just what good advice is. Muhammad Ali turns out to be right in everything that he tells Miss Rehana. The British do interrogate her, and she is refused permission to go to England when she cannot answer their questions. However, Muhammad Ali is also wrong in assuming that going abroad is what Miss Rehana really wants. In the end, failure has made her happy, and her happiness seems to bring light into the dark life of the old con man, even though he has failed both in his original plan to cheat her and in his efforts to help her.

*Style and Technique*

"Good Advice Is Rarer than Rubies" is told in the third person, but it presents events from the point of view of Muhammad Ali. It is a short and deceptively simple tale that has only two main characters. Nevertheless, in a few pages and a sparse style, Salman Rushdie manages to present an ironic view of life in contemporary Pakistan.

Rushdie's work is often characterized by the style known as Magical Realism, in which fantastic and wildly imaginative events occur within a realistic setting. Much of the effectiveness of this style lies in its ability to draw readers into accepting unlikely or impossible events as occurring in the normal course of daily affairs and in the surprises made possible by unexpected twists of plot. "Good Advice Is Rarer than Rubies" owes its impact to the fact that its characters and its events stay on the level of realistic fiction, presenting nothing impossible or even out of the ordinary, while disrupting the ordinary world in a way that seems magical.

Muhammad Ali's corrupt, sordid life is interrupted by the radiant young woman, and he finds himself unexpectedly changed. The advice that he gives her is good advice, based on the point of view that creates his reality. This point of view suddenly appears to be an illusion, though, along with much else in the story. Evil intentions are transformed into efforts to help. His efforts to help, seen from another angle, are rejected as illegal actions. In the end, the misfortunate results of rejecting well-meant but illegal suggestions are transformed into a fortunate outcome. As Miss Rehana leaves on the bus, the reader is left standing with Muhammad Ali, feeling that there was something magical about her intrusion into the old man's routine.

Rushdie's writing style is simple, ornamented only by the dialogue between the two main characters. This dialogue uses the quaint but oddly poetic dialect of Pakistani English, giving a sense of place and drawing attention to the old man and the young woman. The description of the setting is minimal. Only the brightly painted bus at the beginning is depicted in any detail. After Miss Rehana descends from the bus, the whole story takes place at the gates of the consulate or at Muhammad Ali's desk. This sparseness of description of surroundings, like the dialogue, focuses concentration on the relationship between the two people and on Muhammad Ali's growing sense of wonder as Miss Rehana surprises him and as he surprises himself.

*Carl L. Bankston III*

# GOOD COUNTRY PEOPLE

*Author:* Flannery O'Connor (1925-1964)
*Type of plot:* Realism
*Time of plot:* The late 1950's
*Locale:* A small southern town
*First published:* 1955

> *Principal characters:*
> MRS. HOPEWELL, a farm owner and the scandalized mother of Hulga
> HULGA HOPEWELL, a lonely, sullen young woman with a Ph.D. in philosophy
> MANLEY POINTER, an itinerant Bible salesperson who calls on the Hopewells
> MRS. FREEMAN, a tenant farmer hired by Mrs. Hopewell

*The Story*

Mrs. Hopewell, a widowed farm owner, is in the practice of hiring tenant farm families to assist her in maintaining the farm. Her current helpers, the Freemans, are busybodies, but they are reliable and serve her better than the previous tenants. Mrs. Hopewell regards Mrs. Freeman and her family as "good country people" and is fond of uttering homespun maxims such as "Nothing is perfect" or "That is life!" and being reassured by Mrs. Freeman's frequent rejoinder, "I always said so myself."

The backward, unsophisticated ways of the Freemans, however, only perturb Mrs. Hopewell's daughter, Hulga, who changed her name from Joy when she left home to attend college. Having earned a Ph.D. in philosophy, Hulga is a troubled, introverted young woman; she lost her leg in a childhood hunting accident and has not been "normal" since. She is a source of embarrassment to her mother, who "was at a complete loss" in explaining her daughter's ambitions. One could say "my daughter is a nurse or a school teacher or a chemical engineer," but she could not say "my daughter is a philosopher." That was something that "ended with the Greeks and Romans." With an artificial leg and a heart condition, Hulga seems destined for a quiet life spent irritating her mother and the workers surrounding her.

One afternoon, however, something upsets the ecology of the household. Manley Pointer, who announces himself as an itinerant Bible salesperson interested in "Chrustian" (sic) service, arrives at the door and engages Mrs. Hopewell in a discussion of salvation and Bible truth. At first merely polite to the young man, Mrs. Hopewell is quickly charmed by his "salt of the earth," simple country ways, and invites him for supper. Hulga is appalled by Pointer but sees his visit as an opportunity to enlighten a woefully naïve country boy about the ways of the world. After supper he walks her to the front gate and convinces her to meet him for a walk at ten o'clock the next morning.

Hulga lies awake the night before imagining that she will seduce this innocent, redeeming him from both his religious convictions and his moral inhibitions. When she sneaks off to meet him the next day, she is startled by his unusually aggressive temperament when he asks how her wooden leg is joined to the rest of her torso. Initially disturbed but strangely attracted to Pointer's naïveté, she allows him to kiss her. She suggests that they head toward the barn, imagining herself as the aggressor and seducer. Here she turns their conversation to her philosophical opinions about life and eternal destinies, announcing that she is one of those people who have "taken off their blindfolds and see that there is nothing to see."

After a series of passionate kisses, Pointer begs Hulga to tell him that she loves him. At first she balks, with an elaborate discussion of what she means by the word "love," but finally relents. He asks her to prove her love by letting him remove her wooden leg. Suddenly aware that she is not with the naïve, unsophisticated rube she imagined, she is fearful, crying out "aren't you just good country people?" Opening the briefcase that he had been carrying through their escapade, he reveals an assortment of odd objects, including a flask of whiskey, a deck of cards with pornographic pictures, and a prophylactic. Placing her wooden leg in the briefcase, Pointer declares to Hulga, "One time I got a woman's glass eye this way. . . . You ain't so smart. I been believing in nothing ever since I was born!"

The story ends with the helpless Hulga watching the serpentine figure of Pointer "struggling over the green speckled lake"; Mrs. Hopewell, watching the same scene with Mrs. Freeman and remarking on the sincerity of the young man, muses "I guess the world would be better off if we were all that simple." "Some can't be that simple," Mrs. Freeman replies, "I know I never could."

## Themes and Meanings

Flannery O'Connor clearly designed "Good Country People" as a shockingly ironic story. Hulga is the prototypical O'Connor character whose pride and selfishness come to her only in the midst of a violent or shocking revelation. Hulga regards herself as aloof from the "good country people" among whom she lives; imbibing of philosophy and its contemplation of "deeper questions," Hulga sees herself as liberating people from their illusions, believing she has none of her own.

Manley Pointer serves as the agent for her self-discovery. Pointer at first appears to be a crude, otherworldly Fundamentalist and Hulga's mission is to strip away his Christian principles by seducing him in the hayloft. She is, however, completely fooled by his impersonation; it is she who is "taken in" and in the end, it is she who wants to be reassured that Pointer is "just good country people." Instead, Pointer reveals himself as a country existentialist, living for the moment, unaffected by the pretensions that govern Hulga's private illusions.

Meanwhile, Mrs. Freeman stands out as the only character in the story who "sees through" the illusions of the Hopewell household. She knows her place in the economy of the household and hers is the final comment in the story. When she says "some can't be as simple" as Pointer, she means that she herself could never fall prey to the flimflam antics to which Mrs. Hopewell and Hulga have succumbed.

*Style and Technique*

O'Connor was well-known for her use of the grotesque and the bizarre to rivet a reader to her tales. Here the sudden revelation of Manley Pointer's malevolence is both dramatic and shocking but a fitting climax to a story whose protagonist, Hulga, made a profession of dispelling illusions. The reader expects the confrontation between Hulga and Pointer to occur but is surprised by the role each ends up playing.

O'Connor had an unmatched ability to capture the cadences of country speech and the banalities of everyday conversation. Her depiction of Mrs. Hopewell and Mrs. Freeman's frequent kitchen conversations helps to underscore the role-playing and insincerity lurking behind the southern landscapes that served as the setting of most of her stories. In like manner, O'Connor uses two minor characters in the story, Mrs. Freeman's daughters, Glynese and Carramae, as effective foils for the character of Hulga. Neither Glynese nor Carramae has any illusions about her lot in life, and the homey details of their lives that O'Connor presents—Carramae's bout with morning sickness, for example—serve as a vivid contrast to the airy, philosophical notions with which Hulga has insulated herself.

*Bruce L. Edwards, Jr.*

# A GOOD MAN IS HARD TO FIND

*Author:* Flannery O'Connor (1925-1964)
*Type of plot:* Horror
*Time of plot:* The 1950's
*Locale:* Georgia
*First published:* 1953

*Principal characters:*
THE GRANDMOTHER, Bailey's mother and the protagonist
BAILEY, her son
BAILEY'S WIFE
JUNE STAR, Bailey's daughter
JOHN WESLEY, Bailey's son
RED SAMMY, owner and proprietor of a roadside eatery
THE MISFIT, a psychopathic killer

*The Story*

This grotesque tale of sudden violence in the rural South opens quietly, with a family planning a vacation. The husband, Bailey, his wife, and their children, John Wesley and June Star, all want to go to Florida. The grandmother, Bailey's mother, however, wants to go to east Tennessee, where she has relatives, and she determinedly attempts to persuade them to go there instead. Unable to convince them that the trip to Tennessee will be novel and broadening for the children, the grandmother offers as a final argument a newspaper article that states that a psychopathic killer who calls himself The Misfit is heading toward Florida.

Ignoring the grandmother's wishes and warnings, the family sets out the next morning for Florida. The grandmother settles herself in the car ahead of the others so that her son will not know that she has brought along her cat, Pitty Sing, hidden in a basket under her seat. As the trip proceeds, she chatters away, pointing out interesting details of scenery, admonishing her son not to drive too fast, telling stories to the children. Throughout the drive, the children squabble, the baby cries, the father grows irritable. In short, the trip is both awful and ordinary, filled with the trivia, boredom, and petty rancors of daily life, from which the family cannot escape, even on vacation.

At lunchtime, they stop at Red Sammy's, a barbecue eatery, where the grandmother laments that "people are certainly not nice like they used to be," and Red Sammy agrees: "A good man is hard to find." In this conversation, the grandmother, narrow-minded and opinionated, repeatedly assures herself that she is a lady, a good Christian, and a good judge of character: She maintains that Red Sammy, a bossy loud-mouth, is a "good man" and that Europe "was entirely to blame for the way things were now."

After they leave the roadhouse, the grandmother manipulates her son into making a detour to see an old plantation she once visited as a girl. Suddenly, she remembers that the plantation is not in Georgia but in Tennessee. She is so upset at this realization that she jumps up and upsets her valise, whereupon the cat jumps out onto her son's shoulder, her son loses control of the car, the car overturns, and they all land in a ditch.

As they emerge, an old, "hearse-like" automobile comes over the hill and stops for them. Three men step out, one of whom the grandmother instantly identifies as The Misfit. The grandmother, realizing that he intends to kill them, tries to talk him out of it by appealing to his chivalry, urging him not to shoot a lady. Then she tries flattery, asserting that she can tell that he is a "good man." She tries to tempt him by suggesting that he stop being an outlaw and settle down to a comfortable life. She urges him to pray to Jesus for help and forgiveness. Finally she tries to bribe him with money. All these tactics fail. As she talks with him, he has his henchmen take the other members of the family to the woods and shoot them.

Although The Misfit rejects all the grandmother's arguments, he listens to them closely; he pays particular attention when the grandmother refers to Jesus. Indeed, The Misfit declares, "Jesus was the only One that ever raised the dead. . . . He thrown everything off balance. If He did what He said, then it's nothing for you to do but throw away everything and follow him." In his intense pride, however, The Misfit maintains that he is unable to believe without having been a witness; therefore, "it's nothing for you to do but enjoy the few minutes you got left the best way you can—by killing somebody or burning down his house or doing some other meanness to him. No pleasure but meanness."

When the grandmother is at last alone with The Misfit, she abandons all of her tactics. Her head clears for an instant, in which she sees the murderer as thin, frail, and pathetic. Declaring "Why you're one of my babies. You're one of my own children!" she reaches out and touches him. He recoils in revulsion and shoots her. Having been witness to the grandmother's moment of grace, The Misfit admits that "meanness" has lost its kick: "It's no real pleasure in life."

### Themes and Meanings

This intensely ironic story investigates with horrifying effect what happens when one of the worst anxieties of modern life, the threat of sudden violence at the hands of an unknown assailant, becomes a reality. Because such occurrences are relatively rare, the characters and the reader are lulled into a false security that such a thing will never happen to them. In addition, by voicing anxiety about encountering a psychopathic killer, the grandmother makes such an encounter seem all the more unlikely.

From Flannery O'Connor's point of view, the grandmother's encounter with The Misfit presents her with the supreme test and the supreme opportunity that every human being must face: the moment of death. Her death, moreover, comes through the agency of an apparently gratuitous and incomprehensible evil. Her ability to accept such a death is therefore the supreme test of her faith. That the grandmother at the moment of death truly embraces the Christian mystery is her great triumph. Although, in Christian terms, such a moment is always a gift, it is one for which the recipient has prepared throughout her life. The grandmother's most essential attribute is therefore not her meddlesomeness or her smugness, of which there has been considerable evidence throughout the story, but her maternal compassion and concern, and it is through this maternal love that she has her moment of revelation. As O'Connor once described it, "she realizes . . . that she is responsible for the man before her and joined to him by ties of kinship which have their roots deep in the mystery she has been merely prattling about so far." The action of grace is not confined altogether to the grandmother but begins to undermine The Misfit's own egotism and sadism. Insisting on the possibility of redemption for even this most evil of her characters, O'Connor expressed the hope that "the old lady's gesture, like the mustard-seed, will grow to be a great crow-filled tree in the Misfit's heart, and will be enough of a pain to him there to turn him into the prophet he was meant to become." In O'Connor's own words, this story, like all of her fiction, "takes its character from a reasonable use of the unreasonable, though the reasonableness of my use of it may not always be apparent. . . . Belief, in my own case anyway, is the engine that makes perception operate."

## Style and Technique

In remarks prefatory to a public reading of this story, O'Connor stated that "what makes a story work . . . is probably some action, some gesture of a character that is unlike any other in the story, one which indicates where the real heart of the story lies." This action, which is "both totally right and totally unexpected," must operate "on the anagogical level, that is, the level which has to do with the Divine life and our participation in it." O'Connor, anticipating a non-Catholic audience essentially hostile to her religious and philosophical position, manages to dramatize her views within the story: She shows a human being change and creates an effective scene in which God's grace intervenes in the natural world. Thus, O'Connor makes it possible for the reader to focus on what she sees as crucial: "In this story you should be on the lookout for such things as the action of grace in the Grandmother's soul, and not for the dead bodies."

A balance for the seriousness, even sublimity, of this moment of grace is the black humor of the dialogue between The Misfit and the grandmother, which precedes the grandmother's gesture. Much of this humor derives from the regional particularities of southern speech, which O'Connor's sharp ear accurately registers. When the grandmother urges The Misfit to seek God's help, he replies, "I don't want no hep, I'm doing all right by myself." Another source of humor is the bizarre logic of The Misfit's outlook on the world: "I call myself The Misfit . . . because I can't make what all I done wrong fit what all I gone through in punishment." Finally, there is the sardonic understatement of The Misfit himself, who declines the grandmother's offer of money, noting, "Lady, . . . there never was a body that give the undertaker a tip."

A brilliant mixture of horror and humor, compassion and tough-mindedness, this story epitomizes O'Connor's greatest powers as a writer. Her bedrock of belief in the Roman Catholic faith made it possible for O'Connor to view that most horrifying representative of humankind, the serial killer, with sympathy and hope. Her tough, critical intelligence made her sensitive to the petty hypocrisy and smugness that sometimes accompany religious faith, but she was also able to see that these are at worst venial sins. It was this clear perspective that enabled O'Connor to note "that the old lady lacked comprehension, but that she had a good heart." Thus, the reader may observe about O'Connor what O'Connor observed about the southerner: She "is usually tolerant of those weaknesses that proceed from innocence, and . . . knows that a taste for self-preservation can be readily combined with the missionary spirit."

*Carola M. Kaplan*

# A GOOD SCENT FROM A STRANGE MOUNTAIN

*Author:* Robert Olen Butler (1945-   )
*Type of plot:* Political, allegory
*Time of plot:* The 1980's, with flashbacks to 1917 and 1918
*Locale:* New Orleans, London, Paris
*First published:* 1992

> *Principal characters:*
> DAO, the narrator, a Vietnamese man nearly one hundred years old
> THANG, his son-in-law, a former colonel in the army of the Republic of Vietnam
> LOI, his grandson
> HO CHI MINH, the former leader of Vietnam

## The Story

Dao, a very old Vietnamese man who lives in New Orleans with his family, begins by recounting his most recent dream, in which he is visited by the ghost of former Vietnamese leader Ho Chi Minh, whom he had known in Europe as a young man. The Vietnamese leader, then known as Nguyen Ai Quoc ("Nguyen the Patriot"), lived in London from 1915 to 1917 and in France from 1917 to 1923. Dao was a dishwasher at the London hotel where Ho was a pastry cook. Dao alludes to the work Ho did retouching photos in France.

Dao, who has three dream conversations with Ho, alternates between narrating details of his dreams and describing recent developments in his extended family. He realizes that they are keeping a secret from him but is unable to guess what it concerns. He suspects, however, that the mystery is connected with a recent murder. Nguyen Bich Le, publisher of a Vietnamese newspaper in New Orleans, was shot the week before because he wrote an article arguing that it was time for Vietnamese expatriates to accept the reality of the communist government in Vietnam and to begin to work with the people who control their home country. A nameless representative of a Vietnamese anticommunist group telephoned the paper to claim credit for the murder.

In Dao's three dream conversations with Ho, they recall their past and debate the divergent paths they chose: Dao became a Buddhist and Ho led a political revolution and then a war. Dao finally comes to realize that his son-in-law, Thang, and grandson, Loi, were directly involved in the recent political murder.

## Themes and Meanings

Robert Olen Butler wrote "A Good Scent from a Strange Mountain" as one of a series of fifteen linked stories, each narrated by a different Vietnamese character. Most of them had emigrated to Louisiana as part of the Vietnamese diaspora after the war.

Both the title piece and the final story of the collection, *A Good Scent from a Strange Mountain* (1992), carry more thematic weight and complexity within that context than if read independently. For example, those reading the final story in isolation would recognize that Ho's visit to Versailles invokes the historical event of Ho's efforts to gain an audience with Woodrow Wilson to lobby for Vietnamese representatives in the French parliament. They could not, however, recognize that the reference simultaneously invokes the setting of the first story in the collection, "Open Arms," which is narrated by a resident of another Versailles, a modern community outside New Orleans with a large North Vietnamese population. "Open Arms" also analyzes a discussion between a Buddhist narrator and a communist leader, among other parallels. However, the story may also be read on its own; indeed, fourteen of the fifteen stories appeared separately before Butler published them in the collection.

The three subplots of historical narrative, fantasy encounter, and contemporary violence intertwine to make the thematic point that the causes and effects of the Vietnam War extend deep into the past, involve spiritual as well as political issues, and perhaps most significantly, persist today, not just in Vietnam but in the United States. Ho's decision to follow the Western teachings of Karl Marx and Dao's decision to follow the Eastern spiritual teachings of the Buddha represent a split within the national character that is simultaneously political and psychological, fragmenting both the nation and its individuals. Ho tells Dao, "You have never done the political thing," correctly predicting that Dao will do nothing with his knowledge that his son-in-law and grandson are murderers. However, Dao counters with the provocative question, "Are there politics where you are now, my friend?" The story's final words might summarize this thematic aspect: "I wanted to understand everything . . . you knew you had to understand everything or you would be incomplete forever."

Whether this political and psychic fragmentation can ever be brought together again is left ambiguous at the end. Dao peacefully awaits sleep—and presumably death—at the end of the story in the conviction that he and Ho "will be together again and perhaps we can help each other. I know now what it is that he has forgotten." However, this optimism is undercut by its exclusive focus on the afterlife rather than the real world of political murder: Does Dao's final vision of unity and redemption constitute a higher level that subsumes history and violence or only a continuation of the passivity that leaves action in the hands of the violent?

*Style and Technique*

Dao's three main stories are tightly interlaced, reflecting the aging narrator's inability to separate reality and fantasy, past and present. This intertwining of the three strands is reinforced with multiple patterns of imagery. The title of both the story and the book, "a good scent from a strange mountain," demonstrates Butler's method. The phrase is a translation of *bao son ky huong*, the saying of the Hoa Haos, the Buddhist sect to which Dao belongs. The story uses a variety of scents as vehicles for exploring the story's main themes.

The narration begins and ends with fantasy sequences during which Dao is struck by the sweet smell of sugar on Ho's hands. The smell presumably is related to the two men's experience working in the kitchen of Monsieur Escoffier, the chef at the Carlton Hotel in London. The menial work in the European kitchen foreshadows the dismissive treatment Ho will receive from the diplomats at Versailles and, more broadly, that Vietnam will receive from the United States. As Ho remarks to Dao regarding the Americans' treatment of the Vietnamese, "They had been repressed by colonialists themselves. Did they not know their own history?" The chef's name, which contains the word "scoff," extends both this theme and the extensive use of emblematic names in the story.

One of the threads of the conversation Dao fantasizes is Ho's effort to remember the precise recipe for the glaze fondant. Butler works this sugar motif into the story in several ways. The sugar functions to blur the distinctions between fantasy and reality when Dao's daughter finds the doorknob slightly sticky after Ho, his hands covered with sugar, has left the narrator's room after one of their conversations. Just as the sweet smell of the sugar invokes shared history and positive connotations to complicate the antagonism between Ho and Dao, smells characterize and lend depth to Dao's relation to other characters. At the moment of revealing to Ho that his son-in-law and grandson are involved in a political killing, he can no longer smell the sugar on Ho's hands but only recall the sour smell of milk on his grandson's breath, saying, "and I turned my face away from the smell of him."

Ho's forgetting the recipe for the glaze symbolizes the political revolutionary's forgetting the idealism that had led him to initiate his revolutionary activity, further emphasizing the split between the Marxist Ho and Buddhist Dao. By the end of the story, Dao has recalled the missing element, and this completed glaze recipe is what Dao is presumably referring to in his final claim that he knows what Ho forgot. By this point in the story, the simple recipe has come to serve not only as a symbol of personal, familial, national, and international disharmony but also as the demonstration that Dao and Ho may have succeeded where their descendants have failed; they have engaged one another in conversation and accepted their fundamental differences.

*William Nelles*

# GOODBYE, MY BROTHER

*Author:* John Cheever (1912-1982)
*Type of plot:* Realism
*Time of plot:* The late 1940's
*Locale:* An island off Massachusetts
*First published:* 1951

> *Principal characters:*
> POMMEROY, the narrator
> HELEN, his wife
> LAWRENCE (TIFTY) POMMEROY, his brother
> RUTH, Tifty's wife
> CHADDY POMMEROY, the narrator's brother
> ODETTE, Chaddy's wife
> DIANA POMMEROY, the narrator's sister
> MRS. POMMEROY, mother to the three boys and their sister

*The Story*

The narrator begins the story by announcing that he is a Pommeroy, that his father drowned when he was quite young, and that his mother told her children that their family relationships had a kind of permanence they would not likely find in life again. The Pommeroys enjoy the illusion that they are unique. The narrator then introduces the four children, their places of residence, and their spouses. The narrator relates that, as a family, the Pommeroys used to spend summers on Laud's Head, an island off the Massachusetts coast, where, during the 1920's, their father replaced the family cottage with a big house. It is the narrator's favorite place in the world.

One afternoon late in the summer, all the family members have assembled on Laud's Head, except Lawrence and his wife and children, who finally cross over from the mainland on the four o'clock boat. Although brother Chaddy and the narrator welcome Lawrence, the narrator remarks that family dislikes are deeply ingrained, and he remembers that twenty-five years before he hit Lawrence on the head with a rock. During the cocktail time after the new arrivals have settled in, it becomes obvious that Lawrence is not like the others, as he is critical of his sister, indifferent to what he drinks, and quarrelsome about being called "Tifty," a nickname dating from his youth when his slippers used to make a "tifty, tifty" sound as he walked. His father coined the name. Lawrence has something of the Puritan cleric in his makeup, the narrator remarks, a nature reminiscent of the family's precolonial ancestry. After dinner, the mother becomes drunk and quarrels with Lawrence about the repairs to the old house, which he insists is sliding slowly into the sea and is a waste of money to maintain. The narrator recalls the time when Lawrence, away at boarding school, decided to separate himself from his mother by not returning home for the Christmas holidays. The mother remarks, as she goes off to bed, that in her afterlife she is going to have a very different kind of family, one with "fabulously rich, witty, and enchanting children."

The next morning, the narrator awakes to the sound of someone working on the tennis court. He meets Lawrence's simpering children downstairs and asks Lawrence for a game but is turned down. Later in the morning, he finds his brother examining the house's shingles; Lawrence observes that, though the house is relatively new, their father installed the two-hundred-year-old shingles to make it look venerable. The narrator remembers how in the past Lawrence upbraided the family for their refusal to join the modern world and for their retreat into what they supposed was a calmer and happier time, implying that such an attitude was a measure of an irremediable failure. The appearance of Mrs. Pommeroy, their mother, demonstrates to the narrator that there is little hope of any rapport between the matriarch and the changeling: Their mother suggests that they all go swimming, have martinis on the beach, and "have a fabulous morning."

Lawrence's rebukes to the family force them into a more strenuous physical regime and they swim more often. His comment to the Polish cook that she is sad and ought to get paid more angers her, and she tells the narrator to keep Lawrence out of her kitchen. One evening while playing backgammon after dinner, Lawrence becomes angered by his sister-in-law Odette's flirting with the narrator. Lawrence reads significance and finality into every game; he "felt that in watching our backgammon he was observing the progress of a mordant tragedy in which the money we won and lost served as a symbol for more vital forfeits," says the narrator. Chaddy and the narrator play each other, their mother plays Chaddy, and Lawrence, as usual, gets in the parting shot by remarking that he thinks they would all "go crazy cooped up with one another . . . night after night"; he goes to bed.

That night the narrator dreams about Lawrence and remarks that he should not let him upset the restful vacation that he needs after working so hard during the year. The family prepares to go to a costume ball at a local club during which they are told to come as they wish they were. The narrator and his wife go as a bride and a football player, and the narrator notes that, with the transition wrought by the costumes, they feel as they had in the years before the war. They discover that many people have come to the dance as brides and football players. Lawrence and his wife arrive but are not in costume, and he refuses to dance with her and is appalled in general by the party and the behavior of its guests. The family does not get home until morning.

The next day Mrs. Pommeroy, the narrator's wife, Helen, and Odette all enter their work in the flower show. Ruth, Lawrence's wife, stays home and does her laundry. The narrator observes that Ruth "seems to scrub . . . with a penitential fervor"; he wonders what she thinks she has done wrong. Alone on the beach, he encounters Lawrence and notes his gloomy expression; he reassures him that it is only a summer day. Lawrence responds by confessing that he does not like it on the island, that he wants to sell his equity in the house, that he came back only to say good-bye. However, Lawrence has been saying good-bye to the family and to life as long as the narrator can remember. The narrator suggests that Lawrence fails to grasp the realities of life; Lawrence snaps back that the realities of life are that their mother is an alcoholic, Diana and Odette are promiscuous women, Chaddy is dishonest, and the narrator is a fool. As Lawrence walks away, his brother swings a water-sodden root from behind and hits him in the head. With the sudden strength of two men, the narrator rescues Lawrence from the undertow that was dragging the dazed man down. The narrator returns to the house and joins the others, back from the flower show. Lawrence shows up with a bloody bandage in his hand and confronts the family with the evil deed of his brother. He announces, "I don't have any more time to waste here . . . I have important things to do," and goes upstairs to pack.

The next morning, as Lawrence and Ruth leave for the mainland, only the mother gets up to say good-bye. The matriarch and the changeling look at each other "with a dismay that would seem like the powers of love reversed." As the ferry blows its whistle in the distance, the narrator muses on the beautiful day and laments his brother's fearsome outlook. "Oh, what can you do with a man like that?" he asks, one who will think only of the dark bottom of the sea where their father lies, rather than of the iridescent beauty of the surface, "the harsh surface beauty of life." Later, on the beach, he sees his wife and sister, Helen and Diana, emerge "naked, unshy, beautiful, and full of grace," from out of the sea.

## Themes and Meanings

Like other examples of John Cheever's fiction, this story contains a mixture of sadness and joy. The Pommeroys are a family given over at times to the illusions of their uniqueness, and they do avoid the hard realities of life, as Lawrence suggests. As the narrator cautions at the story's end, however, such illusions are necessary, because they are human, and they provide at least a temporary stay against the "full fathom five" where they all will eventually lie with their father. Helen dyes her hair to hide the years, Odette flirts to restore her youth, Chaddy wins at games, the mother drinks to forget, the narrator overworks and is, perhaps, a fool, but their failures endear them to the reader in ways that Lawrence's harshness, for all of its truth, does not. Cheever does not let the reader off the hook, though, and he forces the narrator to confess his desire to kill his brother and presumably his brother's ability to get at the hard truth. The narrator chooses to observe the harsh beauty of the surface of life and not to plunge to the icy depths below.

Besides the theme of illusion and reality, which he treats with unresolved ambiguity, Cheever also struggles through an examination of the family and its past, to reintegrate his fallen or expelled protagonists into the world as they find it. The narrator is trying to restore the family's sense of identity through description of a nourishing past and using his love to distort truths, and yet to permit the occasional insight that goes beyond the powers of Lawrence, whose omission of love makes existence unendurable. Unable to accept his brother's vision of doom when Lawrence announces that the house will fall into the sea and, by extension, prophesies the downfall of the family, the narrator ends the story with a life-sustaining image that depicts the sea not as a destructor but as life-giving. The names of the two women, Helen and Diana, rich with mythic associations, add a dimension of tradition to his vision and reinforce Cheever's need to explore the past, even into antiquity.

### Style and Technique

The most characteristic element of style in this story is the presence of the unnamed narrator, who characteristically reflects Cheever's comments on the events of the narrative in the wry, compassionate, and detached way of a sympathetic observer; much of the appeal of Cheever's stories derives from his perceived relationship with his readers, available through such a fictional presence.

The story is divided between the rather flat, dour pronouncements delivered by Lawrence and the rich, sensuous counterpassages of the narrator. As Lawrence, for example, calls Odette a promiscuous woman, the narrator describes her in sensual detail, noting the roundness of her shoulders and the whiteness of her skin. Similarly, at the conclusion of the costume party, the guests rescue the floating white balloons from the sea while Lawrence laments the partygoers' foolishness. The lushness of the prose that Cheever employs when describing the smells, the sounds, and the contentment of the narrator's life among his family strikingly contrasts not only with Lawrence's gloom but also with his matter-of-fact language. The sense of possibility of the former overshadows the finality of the latter.

*Charles L. P. Silet*

# THE GOOPHERED GRAPEVINE

*Author:* Charles Waddell Chesnutt (1858-1932)
*Type of plot:* Folktale
*Time of plot:* The American Civil War era
*Locale:* Patesville, North Carolina
*First published:* 1888

*Principal characters:*
THE UNNAMED NARRATOR, a grape grower
ANNIE, his wife
UNCLE JULIUS MCADOO, a former slave
HENRY, a slave

*The Story*

"The Goophered Grapevine" is a story within a story in which each story is told by a different narrator. The first story has a nameless narrator, a vintner who lives in the Great Lakes area during the post-Civil War era. His wife's ill health forces him to move to a warmer climate, so he selects Patesville, North Carolina, as the place to continue his career. He purchases a plantation that formerly belonged to a wealthy planter named McAdoo. One day he takes his wife to see the plantation, and it is at this point that the second story commences.

At the plantation, they encounter an old former slave, who introduces himself as Uncle Julius and informs them, in a strong dialect, that the vineyard on the plantation is "goophered," that is, bewitched. He tells them how the vineyard was goophered during the days of slavery, when old Mr. McAdoo's grapes were being eaten constantly by the slaves from miles around. Despite the best efforts of Mr. McAdoo and his overseer, no one was ever caught. In his desperation, McAdoo appealed to a free black conjure woman, Aunt Peggy, to help him out. Aunt Peggy was renowned far and wide for her ability to conjure, that is, to work magic. After she went into the grapevines and goophered them, she let all the slaves know that any slave who ate grapes from that vineyard would be dead within twelve months.

Shortly after this took place, a new slave by the name of Henry was bought to work on the plantation. No one told him about the goophered vineyard until he had eaten some of its grapes. The overseer took Henry to Aunt Peggy to see if she could do some conjuring to keep him from dying. She told Henry he would be saved if every spring, when Mr. McAdoo began to prune the grapevine, he would scrape the sap from the vine and anoint his bald head with it. Because Henry brought Aunt Peggy a ham on his visit, she told him that he could eat as many grapes as he wished without suffering ill effects as long as he anointed his head as she instructed.

When Henry rubbed the sap on his head, he became young and spry, but by the end of the summer, when the sap began to go down on the grapevines, he got old and stiff once again. This transformation took place regularly over the next few years. Each spring McAdoo sold the youthful Henry for a high price to an unsuspecting buyer and each fall he bought the old Henry back for a song. Henry never revealed the secret of his temporary youthfulness, because he knew that he would be bought back and be well taken care of by McAdoo until his next sale.

McAdoo might have been able to enjoy his game longer had his greed not won out over his good judgement. One year, he followed the advice of a quack on how to improve the productivity of his vineyards and ruined the soil in the process; the vineyard withered and died and so did Henry.

Uncle Julius concluded his story by advising the narrator against buying a goophered vineyard, suggesting that because the old vines were still goophered, death would surely come to anyone who ate from them. The narrator ignores this advice, however. After making his purchase, he learns that Uncle Julius occupied a cabin on the plantation for many years and made a good income from the products of the vine-yard—a fact that he believes accounts for the tale of the goophered grapevines.

### Themes and Meanings

The ostensible purpose of Charles Waddell Chesnutt's story is to entertain its read-ers, providing no serious or profound message about the complexities of life. Ches-nutt wrote the story at a time when local-color literature had gained popularity and af-ter Joel Chandler Harris began publishing his "Uncle Remus" stories. At that time the white reading public was in the mood to read folksy, humorous tales about African Americans, and Chesnutt's short stories satisfied that mood.

On the surface, the tale told is in the tradition of the black folk hero putting one over on an old master. Brer Rabbit, High John the Conqueror, and Stagolee were all Afri-can American folk heroes known for fooling the rich and powerful. When McAdoo cannot stop the slaves from eating his grapes, he tries to control them by playing up to their fears of the unknown and their respect for the powers of the conjurer. He almost succeeds, but Aunt Peggy and Henry outsmart him. Aunt Peggy conjures the grape-vines in such a way that Henry can eat all the grapes that he wants without suffering any ill consequences.

This first work published by Chesnutt reveals hints of the racial themes and topics that were to permeate his later works and make him increasingly unpopular with white critics and readers alike, causing him to cut short his writing career in 1905.

Chesnutt's works comment about the hardships of slave life so subtly that they might easily be overlooked by those reading the story in order to laugh at the expense of foolish and ignorant African Americans. Early in the story, Chesnutt, in describing Uncle Julius, tells us "he was not entirely black" and definitely has "a slight strain of other than negro blood." Because marriage between blacks and whites was illegal in all slave states in the pre-Civil War period, it was clear that Uncle Julius's ancestry re-flects the sexual exploitation of slave women. Chesnutt also hints at the physical hard-ships endured by slaves. For example, Uncle Julius tells how the slaves were willing to walk five or ten miles to get something good to eat. Clearly this tells of the lack of availability of good food for the slaves. When the slaves succeed in eating McAdoo's grapes, he sets spring guns and steel traps to catch them. Uncle Julius also describes how a runaway slave was hunted by McAdoo and his neighbors with guns and dogs. Although Uncle Julius recites his descriptions of McAdoo's brutalities in black dialect and with a touch of humor, the events themselves are anything but humorous. Based on Chesnutt's later works, we can be sure that he did not consider these inclusions irrelevant asides.

The story also shows how the white slaveowner's greed is his ruination. McAdoo not only has no scruples about how he treats his slaves but also cheats his peers with his repeated sales of Henry. Although his grape business does well, he always wants more until he ruins his own vineyard through overcultivation.

A careful reader can examine the harsh realities of slave life while being amused by a well-told, well-narrated folktale.

### Style and Technique

The most obvious stylistic technique used by Chesnutt is the pronounced dialect speech of his African American characters. Critics of his day, William Dean Howells in particular, praised Chesnutt highly for his use of dialect, which they hailed as accurately reflecting the speech of blacks. In his later works, Chesnutt used dialect far more sparingly. No doubt this was in large part because the use of this dialect often aroused condescending laughter at the black characters, enabling the readers to feel a sense of superiority over those whom they considered poor, ignorant blacks. Uncle Julius, in the language he uses, the tales he tells, and the mannerisms he possesses, plays the role of the clown, the buffoon, a role Chesnutt and other black writers hesitated to assign their characters for the purpose of entertaining white readers. Thus, Chesnutt did not use this folksy style of writing in his later works.

*Rennie Simson*

# GOOSEBERRIES

*Author:* Anton Chekhov (1860-1904)
*Type of plot:* Parody
*First published:* "Kryzhovnik," 1898 (English translation, 1916)
*Locale:* The countryside in provincial Russia
*Time of plot:* The 1890's

### Principal characters:

IVAN IVANICH CHIMSHA-HIMALAISKY, a veterinary surgeon
NIKOLAI IVANICH CHIMSHA-HIMALAISKY, his brother, a retired
    landowner
BURKIN, a high school teacher
PAVEL KONSTANTINOVICH ALEKHIN, a landowner

*The Story*

Ivan Ivanich Chimsha-Himalaisky and Burkin are hunting in the countryside when a heavy rain begins; they decide to seek shelter at the home of a local landowner, Pavel Konstantinovich Alekhin. Alekhin is young, unmarried, and a hard worker; he is also inclined to neglect his appearance in the absence of guests. In preparation for dinner and an evening of conversation, Alekhin and his guests bathe in the river; the guests notice that the water around their host turns brown as the dirt cascades off his body. The narrator, who is presumably the author, looks on Alekhin with favor, however, as he accentuates the young landowner's love of hard work and energetic interest in everything around him.

After their ablutions, the three gentlemen settle down with tea as Ivan Ivanich tells Burkin and Alekhin the curious story of his brother's life. Nikolai Ivanich Chimsha-Himalaisky went to work as a clerk in a large city at the age of nineteen. Both of the brothers grew up in the countryside, but their family estate was sold to settle debts. Nikolai Ivanich has never reconciled himself to life in the city and makes plans to acquire enough money to buy a small estate where he can grow gooseberries, which become a symbol in his mind of gracious living in the countryside. He spends his days dreaming of the future estate: where the main building will be located, ducks swimming in a pond, how he will eat soup made from cabbages that he has grown himself, and where the gooseberry bushes will be planted. Ivan Ivanich does not sympathize with his brother's dream, viewing it as an escape from reality and an unnecessary limitation on one's field of action. Instead of retreating to a country estate, a person should see the world and be active in society, he thinks.

After this aside, Ivan Ivanich returns to his story. Nikolai Ivanich becomes very stingy as he pinches pennies in order to buy his estate. In his forties, he marries an ugly, elderly, but rich widow in order to acquire more money for his estate. This poor woman, who was accustomed to good living with her former husband, loses control of her finances and is put on a Spartan regimen by Nikolai Ivanich. Within three years she dies; Nikolai Ivanich buys three hundred acres, and he sets about making his dream come true. There are a few drawbacks, however; there is neither a pond nor gooseberry bushes. There is a river, but it is polluted by a factory on one side and a kiln on the other, making the water coffee-brown. Undaunted, Nikolai Ivanich plants gooseberry bushes and settles into the life of a country squire.

Ivan Ivanich decides to pay his brother a visit in order to see how he is doing. The estate is cluttered with ditches, fences, and hedges, with the resulting impression of complete disorder. A dog that looks like a pig barks at the visitor, bringing out a bare-foot cook who also looks like a pig. The cook directs Ivan Ivanich to his brother, who has grown stout and also resembles a pig. The reader realizes how removed this estate is from the dream that Nikolai Ivanich had envisioned as a youth.

Ivan Ivanich now describes Nikolai Ivanich's life as a landed proprietor. The formerly timid clerk now pontificates on all sorts of issues and demands to be addressed with respect by the peasants, whom he alternately treats with severity and generosity, as the mood becomes him. He opines that education is necessary for the masses, but that they are not yet ready for it; corporal punishment is evil but in certain cases still necessary for the peasants, and so forth.

One evening, the two brothers are drinking tea as the cook brings in a full plate of gooseberries grown by Nikolai Ivanich, the first fruits of his bushes. After five minutes of silent contemplation, Nikolai Ivanich puts one in his mouth and pronounces it to be very tasty. In fact, Ivan Ivanich tells Burkin and Alekhin, the gooseberries were sour and hard. A terrible depression overcomes Ivan Ivanich as he realizes how deluded his brother is and how happy he is with so little.

At this point the story of Nikolai ends as Ivan Ivanich begins a monologue condemning the way of life that his brother is leading. His main complaint is that such a life shuts the person off from the sufferings of people around him as he pursues the goal of personal happiness and leads that person even to espouse opinions, such as Nikolai Ivanich's concerning education and corporal punishment, that prolong the suffering of other people. In an impassioned outburst Ivan Ivanich implores Alekhin never to become such a landowner and not to seek his own happiness as much as to seek to do good.

Burkin and Alekhin are somewhat disappointed at this story, hoping to hear something a bit more exciting and adventurous. They keep their opinions to themselves, however, and go to bed, exhausted. On this note the story concludes, the reader perhaps as perplexed as Burkin and Alekhin.

*Themes and Meanings*

"Gooseberries" is one of a number of stories in which Anton Chekhov views the human penchant for voluntarily limiting one's life. In some cases the reason is fear, in others an inclination toward laziness. The author contrasts the two landowners, Alekhin and Nikolai Ivanich; the former is energetic, while the latter is almost inert. Although it is presumed that Alekhin labors to improve his estate, Nikolai Ivanich is content to leave things as they are and pretend that he has found the ideal for his youthful dreams. In a sense, life has become static for Nikolai Ivanich, who apparently sees no need for change in his life or in the lives of others. He is satisfied but has not fulfilled his potential, and the reader comes to view Nikolai Ivanich's happiness as pathetic.

Nikolai Ivanich's brother, Ivan Ivanich, is particularly incensed at his insensitivity as Nikolai pursues his own level of happiness and cares naught about the happiness of others. This story is one of the very few occasions on which Chekhov takes a stand on social questions of the time, such as education of the peasants and the brutality of the upper classes toward the lower. Chekhov was criticized for his lack of social consciousness and, in this story, six years before his death, he declares himself to be on the liberal side of issues, at least within a Russian context.

In the early 1890's, Chekhov came under the influence of Leo Tolstoy, the famed Russian novelist and religious thinker. Tolstoy advocated retreating from corrupt society to the healthy atmosphere of a simple life in the country. Tolstoy's theory proposed that individuals should perfect themselves, not worry about society, and that through these people finding happiness and peace, society would gradually improve. When Chekhov wrote this story, he had come to the conclusion that Tolstoy's theories were unrealistic. In "Gooseberries," the author satirizes what some people consider their happiness; Nikolai Ivanich's happiness certainly does not lead to the betterment of society. In place of Tolstoy's emphasis on "being good," Chekhov prefers the person who "does good," a much more active approach to social change.

A minor theme in this story is the power of obsession. Nikolai Ivanich's dream so overpowers him that he no longer sees reality and believes that the sour and hard gooseberries are delicious. As a physician, Chekhov saw the benefits of moderation not only in matters of physical health but also in matters of the spirit; obsession will lead the individual to ruin. In this story, it causes Nikolai Ivanich to delude himself, lose contact with reality, and, in Chekhov's view, resign from an active role in the human process.

## Style and Technique

Chekhov is renowned for his economy of words and ability to portray a mood or a person with a single, well-chosen word. In "Gooseberries," he utilizes this technique as usual until Ivan Ivanich gives his speech on the evils of the world. At this point, Chekhov launches into a very uncharacteristic authorial sermon that catches the immediate attention of the reader but that, at times, seems redundant.

Another Chekhovian technique, however, is carefully adhered to: the use of exaggeration of a human characteristic to prove a point. Chekhov wishes to portray the human ability to delude oneself and to settle for less than what one can achieve. In his portrayal of Nikolai Ivanich, Chekhov presents the reader with an absurd example of such a person but not so absurd that the point is lost. Chekhov's immense talent permits him to exaggerate but not go so far that the reader views the work as fantasy or comedy.

*Philip Maloney*

# GORILLA, MY LOVE

*Author:* Toni Cade Bambara (Miltona Mirkin Cade, 1939-1995)
*Type of plot:* Social realism
*Time of plot:* The 1960's
*Locale:* New York City
*First published:* 1971

*Principal characters:*
HAZEL, the narrator and protagonist, a young girl
HUNCA BUBBA (JEFFERSON WINSTON VALE), her uncle
BIG BROOD and
BABY JASON, her brothers
GRANDDADDY VALE, her grandfather

*The Story*

Hazel, a young African American girl living in a black neighborhood of New York City, describes riding in a car with her Granddaddy Vale, her little brother, and her uncle—whom she has called "Hunca Bubba" since she was very little. As she sits in the front seat, she listens to Hunca Bubba describe the woman he loves. As he talks, Hazel recalls an incident that occurred the previous Easter when she and her brothers, Big Brood and Baby Jason, went to see a film that the theater billed as *Gorilla, My Love.*

As Hazel and her brothers settled down in their theater seats with potato chips and jawbreakers, a tattered, brown old film called *The King of Kings* (1927) came on the screen. The children yelled, booed, and stomped their feet until "Thunderbuns," the matron, settled them down. Despite their protests, they never got to see the gorilla film. Hazel demanded that the manager give them back their money, expressing her outrage at adults who are "messin over kids just cause they little and can't take em to court." When the manager refused, Hazel set a fire under the candy stand that caused the theater to close down for a week. She later defended her action by saying that a person should keep his word, "If you say Gorilla, My Love, you suppose to mean it."

Hazel now asks her uncle if he plans to marry the woman he has been telling her about. When he says yes, she asks him if he remembers that when she was little he promised to marry her when she grew up. Hunca Bubba explains that she was just a little girl then and that he was merely teasing. Realizing that what she took seriously was just a joke to her uncle, Hazel cries. She feels betrayed by grownups who do not keep their word. She finds Hunca Bubba's betrayal much more painful to accept than the false advertising of the film.

*Themes and Meanings*

Toni Cade Bambara first published this story in *Redbook* as "I Ain't Playin, I'm Hurtin"—a title that aptly conveys the pain and disillusionment that a sensitive, spunky young girl experiences as she grows up. Bright and sassy, Hazel is proud of her own accomplishments; she even boasts, "I am the smartest kid P.S. 186 ever had in its whole lifetime and you can ax anybody." She is also tough—a girl who will "jump on they back and fight awhile" when boys pick on her or her brothers in the park. She stands up to the big boys in the neighborhood who try to steal money from the younger children or "take Big Brood's Spaudeen way from him." She is an outspoken, determined person with a strong sense of right and wrong. We learn that she "won't back off" when the teachers tell her that her "questions are out of order." She also has a strong conviction that people should stand by what they say. As she puts it: "Even gangsters in the movies say 'My word is my bond.'"

From a child's point of view, Bambara describes a neighborhood filled with colorful characters. Critical of many of the people in her neighborhood, Hazel makes fun of the "chunky" matron who charges down the aisle with her flashlight to keep order in the theater, and she regards with contempt the "oily and pasty" manager who looks at her as if she has lost her mittens or is "somebody's retarded child."

In contrast to the unsavory characters whom she encounters, Hazel praises the strong family members who offer love and protection. When she confronts the theater manager, she compares herself to how her mother speaks to her teachers: "like a stone on that spot and ain't backin up." Her Aunt Jo is "the hardest head in the family," even worse than Aunt Daisy. Throughout the story we see the importance of the family where members of all ages interact and stick together. Hazel believes that her family will protect her. She says that her Mama would be at school "in a minute when them teachers start playin the dozens behind colored folks." Mama is an imposing presence with "her hat pulled down bad" and her fist planted on her hip. She can "talk that talk which gets us all hypnotized." Hazel says that she has grown up in a house where her parents have encouraged her to speak her mind. Her mother says that if "anybody don't like it, tell em to come see your mama." Her father reinforces this advice by adding "tell em to come see me first." Bambara provides a positive view of family life, filled with strong ties and believable characters.

Because of her own strong convictions and her belief in her family, Hazel feels betrayed when Hunca Bubba does not keep his word. When her pain and disillusionment cause her to cry, Baby Jason joins in and cries too. Even though he is too young to understand what is happening, Hazel believes that he "is my blood brother and understands that we must stick together or be forever lost" because grownups do not keep their word. Hazel has learned to protect herself from the outside world, but she is not prepared for her uncle's betrayal because it comes from within the safety of the family circle. Bambara deals with universal themes of disillusionment, and initiation, but she also displays a warm sense of humor as she explores the pain and confusion of growing up.

*Style and Technique*

Bambara employs several techniques to portray Hazel's neighborhood realistically. By using the names of real New York theaters and streets, such as the RKO Hamilton and Amsterdam Avenue, she creates a realistic setting. Adding to the realism, she captures the unique speech patterns of the people who make up this neighborhood. Her characters speak in the rich black dialect of the street with all its vitality and humor. It is their powerful speech patterns that make Bambara's characters come to life in expressions such as "If you scary like me" and "they dusty sometime." She uses "ax" for "ask" and uses verb forms that are formally incorrect, such as "it do get me in trouble." When Hazel says that the film is "not about no gorilla," the double negative sounds typical of a child's language. Hazel's speech contains such slang expressions as "give her some lip" and "no lie." She describes the matron in the theater as getting "too salty."

The imagery that Hazel employs is fresh and believable as the expressions of a child. Hazel describes her uncle's looking at her "real strange . . . like he lost in some weird town in the middle of night and lookin for directions and there's no one to ask." At one moment in his past, Hunca Bubba adopted an African name, which to Hazel sounded "very geographical weatherlike . . . like somethin you'd find in a almanac." The pecans in the truck make a rattling noise "like a rat in the buckets."

Several devices help convey the importance of family in Bambara's story. For example, she uses nicknames to show how closely knit Hazel's family is. Granddaddy calls Hazel "Scout" and "Precious"; Mama calls her "Badbird." She is "Miss Muffin" to Aunt Jo and "Peaches" to Hunca Bubba. Bambara also combines humor and religion to show the strength of the family. In one of the most humorous passages in the story, Bambara uses Hazel's literal view of Jesus on the cross to show that Hazel believes in the Bible story but feels that her family would not have allowed a family member to suffer such a fate. Hazel believes in God and the stories from the Bible but interprets these stories literally. She applies the story of Jesus on the cross to the world that she knows, saying her parents would not stand for anyone treating their children that way. "I can just see it now, big Brood up there on the cross . . . and my Mama say Get down from there you big fool . . . and my Daddy yellin to Granddaddy to get him a ladder cause Big Brood actin the fool . . . and my mama and her sister Daisy jumpin on them Romans beatin them with they pocketbooks."

In "Gorilla, My Love" Bambara has created a world full of humor, love, and laughter, and a family that will surely help Hazel overcome her sense of loss.

*Judith Barton Williamson*

# THE GOSPEL ACCORDING TO MARK

*Author:* Jorge Luis Borges (1899-1986)
*Type of plot:* Mythological
*Time of plot:* March, 1928
*Locale:* The district of Junin, Argentina
*First published:* "El Evangetio según Marcos," 1970 (English translation, 1970)

### Principal characters:

BALTASAR ESPINOSA, the protagonist, a medical student
THE GUTRE FAMILY, consisting of the father, a son, and a girl, caretakers of La Colorada ranch

## The Story

Baltasar Espinosa, a medical student in Buenos Aires, is invited by his cousin Daniel to vacation at a ranch in the district of Junin in the final days of March, 1928. Gutre, who is the overseer of the premises, lives there with his son and a girl of questionable paternity. All three are notably primitive in appearance and in their ability to express themselves verbally. In that environment, Baltasar is to learn lessons about life that he has never before suspected.

A few days after arriving, Daniel must leave for the capital, but Baltasar chooses to stay behind with his textbooks. No sooner is Daniel gone than the stifling heat gives way to a cold rain and the river overflows its banks. Many animals are drowned, and when the overseer's quarters are threatened, Baltasar lodges him and his family in the main house. It is thus that the four come into close contact with one another. They eat together, but because communication is strained, Baltasar reads to them, first from Ricardo Guiraldes's work *Don Segundo Sombra* (1926; *Don Segundo Sombra: Shadows on the Pampas,* 1935) and the document of the Gutre family history, both of which they receive rather unenthusiastically, and later from the Bible, specifically the Gospel of Mark, which conversely sparks an unexplained interest.

In the meantime, Baltasar has become cognizant of certain changes in his own physiognomy and attitude that have taken place during his stay at the ranch. Matters that he would formerly have considered trivial have come to acquire significance. Furthermore, he grows nostalgic for Buenos Aires and his family, from which he feels increasingly separated.

One day, the girl brings to Baltasar an injured lamb that he cures using medicine rather than the spiderwebs she had intended to apply to the wound. Mysteriously, the family thereafter begins to follow Baltasar, both figuratively (they follow his orders) and literally (from room to room). They clean away his crumbs at the table, speak of him with respect, and provide him with coffee. When they ask him to reread the Gospel, he reflects that they have asked him to do so because they are like children who prefer repetition to variation and novelty.

On Tuesday, Baltasar dreams of the Flood, and on Thursday, the girl comes to him and loses her innocence. She says nothing to him nor does she kiss him. For some reason, he knows that he will not relate this episode to anyone in Buenos Aires. The following day, Friday, the father asks questions about Christ that Baltasar answers, albeit with uncertainty. After a final rereading of the Gospel and a sleep interrupted by hammering and vague premonitions, Baltasar is crucified by the three Gutres.

*Themes and Meanings*

In "The Gospel According to Mark'" the passage of two thousand years is eradicated when a twentieth century man who travels to the country finds himself in the first century C.E. Baltasar Espinosa enters the world of the Gutre family, a primitive stage of human consciousness where reality takes place in the physical, literal dimension. There, he becomes the victim in an ancient ritual: human sacrifice.

Baltasar is a contemporary Christ figure: At thirty-three he faces the most important test of his life; through his medical studies, he has acquired the power to heal as demonstrated by the cure of the lamb; he possesses superior oratorical skills that he practices when reading parables to the Gutres; he is a courageous man whose goodness is nearly unlimited. At the same time, Baltasar, like his father, is a man of his times who knows too much to be able to believe wholeheartedly. His nightly prayers are more a matter of honor (keeping his promise to his mother) than faith. Furthermore, his attitude is not informed by the revolutionary's enlightened determination but rather by a complacency and an ambiguity of one who reconciles.

The Journey to La Colorada signifies a return to the inception of humankind, an age of innocence in the history of civilization. That place or time holds lessons for Baltasar about life and therefore death, its attraction for him being the eternal and the transcendent (versus the temporal sorts of interests of his cousin). The experience awaiting him at La Colorada is beyond doctrine, either scientific or religious; it is a return to an original source. As the floodwaters encroach on the ranch, the protagonist moves farther and farther away from Buenos Aires society but closer to that mythological island somewhere in the Mediterranean.

The history of the Gutres traces a regression toward that source or beginning, paradoxically concurrent with the progress of time. Over the course of about a century in the New World, they forget how to write and how to speak languages; the species undergoes reversion instead of evolution. As he comes into closer proximity with the members of that family, Baltasar becomes aware of a correspondence between their almost savage appearance and their behavior described as a difficulty in verbalizing their experiences as well as an inability to remember, yet it is they who will lead him toward the goal of his quest. In a few days' time, contact with them and their environment produces a visible transformation in Baltasar, an outward sign of inner modifications: He is coming into the ultimate knowledge he seeks.

Indeed, the Gutres not only change Baltasar; they create him, or rather a god whose role he is to act out, from the words of the Evangelist Mark. Although the writings themselves are ancient, they propose a new, mystical sort of concept to the Gutres: salvation from eternal damnation through a redeemer. In contrast to the other two texts read, which are merely different versions of their own actuality, the Gospel explains the stranger in their midst and directs their course of action: Baltasar is the healer, the shepherd, the teacher who is to be crucified as the Gutres re-create the Passion of Christ.

### Style and Technique

In "The Gospel According to Mark'" the author rewrites the myth of the return to the origin and, as is often the case with Jorge Luis Borges, constructs his tale drawing on a literary model, here the Bible. At one point in the text, the narrator refers to the climax of St. Mark's account of the life of Christ—the Passion—as one of the two stories that men have repeated down through time. In fact, many structural and thematic elements found in "The Gospel According to Mark'" especially those associated with the ranch, are of an archetypal nature: the eternal way of life at La Colorada; Baltasar's dreams about the Flood; the representation of the ranch as an island; the fanaticism and superstitions that the Gutres have in their blood; their identification with a primitive race of human beings; the circle of men strumming the guitar. Through these primordial references, Borges evokes the dark, forgotten beginnings of existence.

Another set of symbols in "The Gospel According to Mark" issues from Christian mythology and is related to Baltasar and his influence on the Gutre family. Curiously, he is not a confirmed believer and it is ironic not only that he should introduce to them the concept of faith in a savior but also that he himself should be the victim in the crucifixion. The chain of events leading up to that finish is seen to be no more than a series of accidents (how he arrives at La Colorada, Daniel's sudden departure, the rains that lead him to explore the house and find the Bible, his decision to practice translation by reading the Gospel, the cure of the lamb, even his casual answers to the father's questions). Thus, his experience becomes a nightmare based on mistaken interpretation, more akin to a trip to hell than a return to paradise.

*Krista Ratkowski Carmona*

# GOSPEL SINGERS

*Author:* Langston Hughes (1902-1967)
*Type of plot:* Social realism
*Time of plot:* The 1960's
*Locale:* Harlem
*First published:* 1965

> *Principal characters:*
> JESSE B. SEMPLE, nicknamed Simple, the protagonist, a black
> Everyman
> BOYD, the narrator, a college-educated friend and companion in
> the bar

*The Story*

"Gospel Singers" is not really a short story in the usual sense, nor a chapter in a novel, although Langston Hughes's books featuring the character called Simple are listed in bibliographies as novels. The story is found in *Simple's Uncle Sam* (1965), the last of several books devoted to a presumably average, relatively uneducated black man who speaks with a certain folk wisdom about Harlem and its denizens. His relationship to the black community seems somewhat analogous to that of Will Rogers to Midwestern rural and small-town white people of limited means. Simple's social commentary is more confined, perhaps, to strictly local conditions, those that beset urban blacks, late immigrants from the South.

Sketches about Jesse B. Semple, barroom philosopher, first appeared in 1943 in the Chicago *Defender*, perhaps the most widely read weekly newspaper among urban blacks. Semple, or Simple, as he was dubbed, became a kind of folk hero, speaking directly to the relatively unlettered people he commemorated in language that they could understand. Each short piece is a dialogue between Simple and the narrator, a college-educated friend named Boyd, whose somewhat stilted language contrasts effectively with Simple's colloquial dialect and direct approach. "Gospel Singers" is a typical piece of approximately five pages that might appear in the newspaper as a half-comic, half-serious commentary on contemporary life.

Though it has no plot in the sense of a causally connected set of actions, it has a plan that broaches a topic of conversation in the opening lines, explores the topic in the course of its five pages, and signs off with a minor rhetorical flourish. In this case, the opener is an observation about how many theaters are closing down in Harlem, to be reopened as churches with the names of ministers up in lights like those of film stars. There used to be storefront churches in Harlem; now there are theater-front churches. As Simple points out, "the box office has turned into a collection plate, and the choir is swinging gospel songs."

What follows is a discussion of the relative merits of gospel singing as well-paid entertainment. Simple points out sagely that the gospel singers are doing better than many a nightclub act. Boyd expresses the conventional objections to making religion a means for profit. With his usual sly humor, Simple describes gospel "shows" he has attended and, in effect, defends the pursuit of God and Mammon simultaneously, concluding that "good singers deserve their just rewards both in this world and the other."

The talk moves on to the subject of opera, which Simple's wife, Joyce, appreciates but he does not. Boyd defends opera. Simple went with Joyce to one black opera at Carnegie Hall. The program said it was sung in English, but Simple says, "it sounded to me like it were sung in Yiddish," and he asks Joyce, "did she reckon all them colored singers had Jewish singing teachers?"

The conversation ends with a discussion of Marion Anderson at the Metropolitan Opera, and Boyd points out that Simple was sitting right there in the bar and cheering the loudest for Marion. Simple agrees heartily but adds that now that she has retired from opera, Marion ought to take up gospel singing.

## Themes and Meanings

"Gospel Singers" plays ironically with a number of commonly held assumptions about the proper role of religion. One of the distinctive capacities of Simple, which is presumably a strong tendency in urban black experience, is the ability to live comfortably amid contradictions and ambiguities. Hughes is not the only writer who deals with this ambivalence—witness Ralph Ellison's strange character, Rinehart, in the novel *Invisible Man* (1952), who is both a preacher and a procurer.

In one sense, the story is a defense of promoting happiness through religion, and a sly blow at the overly solemn view that religious worship should be steeped in the consciousness of sin and suffering. Black experience is no doubt adequately familiar with this world as a veil of tears without harping on that aspect of existence unnecessarily. Gospel singing, like jazz, that other quintessentially black contribution to American music, is a way to transcend the gloomier realities of ordinary life.

Simple also indirectly attacks the attitude, often given lip service by the pious, that religious people should despise money and prefer poverty as somehow good for the soul. The truly poverty-stricken are seldom aware of any great improvement in their souls attributable to their financial situation. They are more likely to suspect that goodness is a luxury for people who have enough to eat and shelter from the fierce extremes of Harlem weather.

The observations about opera are a comfortable reflection of unsophisticated tastes, directed to an audience of non-opera goers. However, they are offered in such a way as to admit the possible virtues of that medium and suggest that black singers are also gaining recognition there. Even Simple, as unschooled as he is in highbrow music, knows a good voice when he hears one and applauds Marion Anderson.

## Style and Technique

Hughes avoided the more illiterate dialect associated with so many literary black characters, sprinkled with "dis" and "dat" and "ain't no mo'." He tried to retain, however, the distinctive dialect of urban blacks, especially the characteristic "jive" talk and slang of Harlem, as evidenced in this exchange between Simple and Boyd:

> "I seed a poster outside a church last night. Sister Mamie Lightfoot and Her Gospel Show, and they were charging one dollar to come in, also programs cost a quarter, and you had to buy one to pass the door."
>     "Did you go in?"
>     "I did and it were fine! Four large ladies in sky-blue robes sung 'On My Journey Now,' sung it and swung it, real gone, with a jazz piano behind them that sounded like a cross between Dorothy Donegan and Count Basie. Them four sisters started slow, then worked it up, and worked it up, and worked it up until they came on like gang busters, led by Sister Lightfoot."

This example illustrates the role of Boyd, primarily as straight man to keep the attention on Simple's monologues. Occasionally, he functions as a somewhat pedantic repeater of platitudes, in order to emphasize his companion's greater vitality, as in this dull rejoinder to Simple's opinionated view of opera: "Just because you don't understand a thing, do not make fun of it too harshly, or be too critical of others for liking it. Tastes differ." The relationship between the two speakers seems to suggest that the process of indoctrinating the black into the standard speech patterns of white society results in a serious loss of rhetorical vigor.

Hughes has a characteristic way of closing these conversations—a witty twist that reinforces the impression of rather impudent common sense in the barroom orator who asserts his opinions with such gusto. He has just proclaimed that Marion Anderson could make a million dollars as a gospel singer. Boyd says, "Don't be ridiculous," to which Simple glibly returns, "When was money ever ridiculous?"

The main achievement of these dialogues is not so much the isolated opinions expressed through conversation but in the creation of a literary character who achieved the status of folk hero for urban blacks. Critic Saul Maloff describes Simple as

> the wry, ironic, crafty, folkloristic, garrulous, beer-swilling, homegrown barfly philosopher . . . a man who once he got his hands on your lapels, never let go, a hilarious black Socrates of the neighborhood saloons who would at the drop of his hat discourse on anything from marital relations to international relations, lynching to lexicography, the foibles of mankind and follies of womankind. Whatever it was, Simple had the shrewd and loony answer.

*Katherine Snipes*

# GRACE

*Author:* James Joyce (1882-1941)
*Type of plot:* Social realism
*Time of plot:* The early 1900's
*Locale:* Dublin, Ireland
*First published:* 1914

*Principal characters:*

TOM KERNAN, a tea taster with a drinking problem
MRS. KERNAN, his wife
MARTIN CUNNINGHAM,
MR. POWER, and
MR. M'COY, his friends
MR. FOGARTY, a grocer
FATHER PURDON, a Jesuit priest

*The Story*

An unconscious man is found in the lavatory of a Dublin bar. He has hurt himself in a fall and will discover that he has bitten off the tip of his tongue. After being helped to his feet by strangers, the man—who is named Tom Kernan—is assisted home by a friend, Mr. Power, and put straight to bed. Later, as Power and Kernan's wife discuss Kernan's condition, they decide to enlist his friends in an effort to reform him. "We'll make a new man of him," Power assures Mrs. Kernan.

Two days later, the plan is set in motion, when Mr. M'Coy, Mr. Cunningham, and Power visit Kernan, who is still recovering in bed. After some wandering discussion regarding Kernan's accident, the ill effects of drinking, and the state of the Dublin constabulary, Kernan's friends casually mention that they are going on a retreat sponsored by the Jesuit order of the Roman Catholic church. "Yes, that's it," Cunningham reveals. "Jack and I and M'Coy here—we're all going to wash the pot." As if suddenly inspired, they invite Kernan to join them. He hesitates but agrees to go after they assure him that the retreat "is for business men."

Kernan, a former Protestant who converted to Catholicism when he married, cannot resist making pointed jabs at the Church and its doctrines. His three visitors, all practicing Catholics, take great pains to explain the doctrines to him, especially a relatively new one concerning papal infallibility. Their explanations silence Kernan but do not entirely convince him.

The final section of the story is a brief report, in flat, stolid style, of the retreat held at the Jesuit Church in Gardiner Street, and the priest's sermon. From the story's presentation, the event is, indeed, very "businesslike."

*Themes and Meanings*

"Grace" is the penultimate story in *Dubliners* (1914), a collection that James Joyce called "a chapter of the moral history of my country" that would reveal Dublin as "the center of paralysis." The collection's stories proceed through four changing stages of life: childhood, adolescence, maturity, and public life. "Grace" concerns itself with public life—specifically the relationship between the business and the religious worlds.

All the *Dubliners* stories are relatively brief and ostensibly direct presentations of everyday events in the Irish capital. "Grace" is an unremarkable story about ordinary events. Although there is some trauma involved with Tom Kernan's initial crisis (for example, he bites off the tip of his tongue and must remain bedridden for several days), the damage that he experiences is more to his dignity than to his physical health. There may be greater danger to his marital or spiritual well-being, but these possibilities are evaded rather than discussed in the story. The events in "Grace" are simple: A businessperson who drinks too much is taken by his friends to a retreat so that he can reform. It is the underlying theme of irony, expressed through indirection and Joyce's careful use of specific words, that give the story its real meaning, that of the essential hollowness of "religion" in early twentieth century Dublin life.

The Christian concept of "grace" has to do with an unmerited gift from God; that is, a blessing bestowed for which the recipient should be spiritually grateful. In Joyce's story, however, "grace" is viewed primarily as a means for rising in the secular world, for becoming a successful businessperson. Joyce signals this subtle but telling redefinition early in the story, when he states that Kernan has "never been seen in the city without a silk hat of some decency and a pair of gaiters. By grace of these two articles of clothing, he said, a man could always pass muster." The story's characters seem content to aspire to just such a relatively low level of "grace."

In this pursuit, they are aided by the Roman Catholic church, particularly its Jesuit order. Kernan and his friends greatly respect the Jesuits as practical, sensible, and eminently successful. "If you want a thing well done and no flies about it you go to a Jesuit," M'Coy assures them. "They're the boys with influence." This approach is echoed with evident approval by Father Purdon, the priest conducting the retreat, who describes himself as "a man of the world speaking to his fellow-men," and who uses the metaphor of himself as a "spiritual accountant."

The underlying meaning of "Grace," then, is that there is no true "grace" in the story at all. Even well-meaning and thoughtful men such as Martin Cunningham, who is considered by his friends to be "a thoroughly sensible man, influential and intelligent" and with a face "like Shakespeare's," cannot overcome the paralysis that grips life in Dublin—morally, intellectually, and spiritually.

*Style and Technique*

Joyce once affirmed that he wrote *Dubliners* "for the most part in a style of scrupulous meanness." The style of "Grace" certainly fits that description, as it has no poetic flourishes, no elaborate descriptions, and no heavy use of symbolism or other literary devices. Its style is simple, flat, and direct. Conversations are re-created to express the repetitive, rambling nature of real dialogue, and Joyce deliberately lends a banality to them that underscores their "ordinary" nature. This presentation of the commonplace, often through deliberately flat and purposefully prosaic writing, was Joyce's deliberate approach throughout *Dubliners*. He intended to have the moment of realization, the famous Joycean "epiphany," emerge from this deliberate flatness through irony and indirection. "Grace" is an outstanding example of that strategy successfully at work.

Nevertheless, the style of "Grace" reveals meanings beyond what is on the page. The prevalent technique is irony: Words and situations carry double meanings, allowing the reader to translate a subtext that is different and even hostile to the story supposedly being told. This irony begins with the title itself, for there is little actual "grace" displayed here, of either the spiritual or the moral sort. Kernan displays few of the social graces, and neither the retreat nor its sermon seems to have gifted him with spiritual grace. In fact, the title underscores that a lack of grace is at the heart of these lives.

"Gentlemen" is another word that weaves traces of irony through the story. The "two gentlemen" in the lavatory who try to lift Kernan up after his drunken fall are later revealed as heavy drinkers themselves. A bartender affirms that he had indeed served Kernan drinks; as he puts it, "he had served the gentleman with a small rum." Irony returns during the bedside conversation regarding the Catholic church. Its participants see themselves as seriously discussing important theological issues, but they continually trip over the names of cardinals and titles of papal writings, missing the larger points in their wrangling over unimportant details.

Another thrust of irony comes at the story's conclusion, in which Father Purdon's sermon is flatly and briefly described in the third person, instead of being presented by the priest himself. This technique sharply contrasts with the powerful recreation of the hellfire and damnation sermon that so powerfully affects Stephen Dedalus in Joyce's *A Portrait of the Artist As a Young Man* (1914-1915). Joyce's method of presentation purposefully and completely undercuts the supposed meaning and effect of the sermon, revealing it as a drab compromise made by a worldly church to an indifferent secular world.

The overall pattern of "Grace" is, finally, an ironic re-creation of the three-part division used by Dante in his *La divina commedia* (c. 1320; *The Divine Comedy*, 1802): hell, purgatory, and heaven. Kernan's fall in the saloon's lavatory is his descent into hell; his lingering recuperation at home in bed is a sort of purgatory; the retreat in the Jesuit church represents his final ascension into heaven. In place of the wonders of Dante's poem, Joyce provides his characters with a cheap, nasty hell, a nondescript purgatory, and a distinctly non-spiritual heaven. All of the elements are in place, but they are presented with ironic, unsparing realism. In a city of total paralysis, such irony is the only effective strategy for an artist such as Joyce.

*Michael Witkoski*

# LA GRANDE BRETÈCHE

*Author:* Honoré de Balzac (1799-1850)
*Type of plot:* Psychological
*Time of plot:* The early nineteenth century
*Locale:* Vendôme, France
*First published:* 1832 (English translation, 1893)

Principal characters:

DR. HORACE BIANCHON, the frame narrator
MR. REGNAULT, the attorney for La Grande Bretèche
MR. DE MERRET, the late owner of the estate
MRS. DE MERRET, his wife
MR. FÉRÉDIA, her Spanish lover
ROSALIE, her servant
MR. LEPAS and
MRS. LEPAS, the innkeepers

*The Story*

The frame narrator, Dr. Horace Bianchon, begins his story with a lengthy description of a dilapidated residence called La Grande Bretèche, which he discovered while practicing medicine in Vendôme. Although the residence is not ancient, Bianchon speaks of it as if it were an archaeological ruin—one whose mysterious power of attraction is so strong that he regularly scales its garden walls to contemplate the unknown catastrophe that caused it to collapse into such ruins. Bianchon continues to visit its garden in secret until, one day, he receives a call from Mr. Regnault, an attorney and executor of the estate, who forbids him to trespass on its grounds. Bianchon agrees to stop his clandestine visits but implores Regnault to tell him what he knows about the place's catastrophic decline.

Regnault explains how Mrs. de Merret, the owner of the estate, called him late one night to make him the legal custodian of her estate. Curiously, the principal task that she assigned him was to ensure that the place would remain uninhabited and untouched for fifty years after her death. Regnault also passes along other facts about Mr. and Mrs. de Merret's "catastrophic" separation; Mr. Merret's subsequent fall into decadence in Paris; and Mrs. de Merret's return to her native Chateau de Merret, where she withered away to a ghostlike existence. She eventually died clutching an ebony crucifix and uttering these cryptic last words: "Oh! my God!"

Mrs. Lepas, the nosy owner of the Vendôme inn in which Bianchon is staying, picks up the story where Regnault leaves off. She takes Bianchon back to the days before the separation of Mr. and Mrs. de Merret, to a time when Mrs. de Merret received romantic visits from a Spanish prisoner of war named Férédia. Férédia was a deeply religious man who read his Bible like a preacher and attended mass regularly. One day

Férédia mysteriously disappeared, and his clothes were found near a river. Mr. Lepas concludes from this that Férédia either escaped or drowned; but, Mrs. Lepas, who knows that Mrs. de Merret died with Férédia's ebony crucifix in her hand, suspects that Férédia's disappearance was linked to the separation (and subsequent demise) of Mr. and Mrs. de Merret. Because Mrs. Lepas lacks direct evidence to support her theory, she sends Bianchon to see Rosalie, Mrs. de Merret's former servant and the only surviving witness to these events.

The story that Bianchon persuades Rosalie to tell him is a chilling one. Mr. de Merret, who returned home later than usual one night, decided to check in on his wife. As he reached for her bedroom door, he heard another door close inside her room and immediately suspected that his wife was hiding a lover. Mrs. de Merret adamantly denied her husband's accusation and warned him that if he were to look and find nobody in her antechamber, their marriage would be destroyed. Mr. de Merret did not look; instead, he had Rosalie send for her fiancé, a bricklayer, whom he had build a brick wall to seal off the antechamber so that he could observe his wife's reaction. After she did not flinch, Mr. de Merret pretended to go to town to verify her story about purchasing her ebony crucifix at a pawnshop; he immediately doubled back to see what his wife would do next. When he returned, his wife was trying to knock a hole in the brick wall; the moment she saw her husband, she fell ill from agony. Her agony grew more severe, especially during Férédia's final days. Each time that the Spaniard made a noise from behind the wall, Mr. de Merret would chide his wife: "But you swore on your cross that nobody was there."

## Themes and Meanings

The themes of Honoré de Balzac's surface-level narrative are obvious enough: an adulterous woman, a husband's jealous rage, and his horrible act of revenge on his wife and her lover. Though Balzac's story "La Grande Bretèche" is engaging on its own terms, one might uncover a deeper level of cultural meaning in it by interpreting it allegorically. The catastrophic rupture of the union between Mr. and Mrs. de Merret, for example, can be interpreted as an allegory of the catastrophic rupture in the union between France's people and the absolute monarchy of its Old Regime brought on by the French Revolution in 1789 and reinforced in 1830. The ruined condition of La Grande Bretèche visually symbolizes the cultural disintegration that resulted from France's chaotic and often violent process of replacing a society grounded in Christian metaphysics with a society grounded in secular law.

The idea that the estate is associated with an ideal, prelapsarian existence before its catastrophic fall is found in Bianchon's idealization of its "garden"—an obvious archetypal reference to the biblical garden of Eden—to which he is unusually attracted but from which he is excluded by Régnault and the power of law. Moreover, the narrator asks himself a series of questions about the estate's ruined condition that suggest a more universal and allegorical catastrophic event: "What celestial fire swept through here? Did somebody insult God there? Did somebody betray France? That is what we are wondering." These questions, of course, are never directly answered; they serve as an interpretive context through which the reader must filter the text's symbolic evidence.

At the surface level, it is Mrs. de Merret who appears adulterous and thus unfaithful to her cultural heritage; at the allegorical level, however, one can see that her undying love for the Spaniard actually signals her unwillingness to renounce her devotion to the Old Regime ideals. It is significant that the Spaniard is described as a devout Christian and that he gives Mrs. de Merret the crucifix that is found in her hands at her death. It is also significant that Mrs. de Merret's room was decorated in the Old Regime style, that on her nightstand lay a book entitled *The Imitation of Jesus Christ*, and that her dying words make direct reference to God. These symbolic details suggest that Mrs. de Merret could not shift her emotional allegiance from the old society to the new. Ironically, it is Mr. de Merret who is unfaithful from an allegorical point of view because he cannot tolerate his wife's continued devotion to the ideals of the Old Regime and Christianity. To break his wife's will to believe, he must physically separate her from the object of her faith and love by encrypting him behind bricks. He then mocks his wife's contradictory behavior by reminding her that her agony is useless since, by her own testimony, the object she mourns never really existed.

### Style and Technique

The most unusual stylistic aspect of this tale is its narrative structure—the fact that the principal narrator does not pretend to be in control of his story before he tells it but allows the reader to discover it as he himself discovers it through partial stories told by a series of secondary narrators. A common criticism of Balzac's fiction is that his narrators are implausibly omniscient and highly manipulative. By contrast, what arouses the reader's desire to read and interpret this tale is his narrator's very lack of knowledge and his desire to correct this lack.

The narrator's ignorance is, in a sense, ultimately feigned because the reader knows that he has learned the end of his story before he puts the totality down on paper. Because one does not realize this until finishing the story, the enticing archaeological secret successfully encourages one actively to participate in the narrator's conceit of reconstructing a lost story as one reads it.

That is not all; one detects a further twist of narrative sophistication when one learns that the surface-level narrative the narrator offers to unravel the archaeological mystery does not fully unravel it. It is at this point that one confirms one's suspicion that the tale is allegorical—a fact that forces the curious reader to reread and actively look for the solution to the mystery. This ultimately leads the reader beyond a simple understanding of the local, historical events of the decaying estate to an understanding of the broader cultural and historical events of early nineteenth century France.

*Scott M. Sprenger*

# GRAPHOMANIACS
## (A Story from My Life)

*Author:* Abram Tertz (Andrei Sinyavsky, 1925-1997)
*Type of plot:* Parody
*Time of plot:* 1959
*Locale:* Moscow
*First published:* "Grafomany," 1961 (English translation, 1963)

*Principal characters:*
>PAUL IVANOVICH STRAUSTIN, the narrator and protagonist, an unsuccessful writer
>ZINAIDA, his wife
>PAUL, their six-year-old son
>SEMYON GALKIN, another unsuccessful writer, an acquaintance of Straustin

*The Story*

The naïve, cliched subtitle of this story suggests that its first-person narrator is rather inept, hardly a skilled writer. This impression is confirmed within the first page of the story when Paul Ivanovich Straustin, the narrator and protagonist, determines to memorize a phrase that has come to his mind: "the breath of an approaching thunderstorm could be sensed in the air." Oblivious to its excruciating banality, Straustin vows that he will use this phrase as the last sentence of his novel *In Search of Joy*, adding it "if necessary even at the proof stage." As the reader soon learns, however, this novel has been rejected for publication—the fate of all the other books that Straustin has written in twenty years of utter failure.

In the story's opening scene, Straustin meets another writer, Semyon Galkin, a poet translator rather than, like Straustin, a writer of fiction, but equally unsuccessful. However, while they are both failures, Galkin's attitude toward his work and toward writing in general contrasts sharply with Straustin's, and this contrast is pivotal to the story.

In the common view, Galkin says, those who write year after year without so much as achieving publication, let alone the perquisites of the successful author, are simply sick. "Graphomania—it's a disease, the psychiatrists tell us, an incurable vicious urge to produce verses, plays and novels in defiance of the world." Yes, Galkin admits, writers such as he (and Straustin) are sick—but so also were William Shakespeare and Alexander Pushkin. They, too, were graphomaniacs, "graphomaniacs of genius." Straustin, however, rejects this appellation; it does not agree with his fanciful image of himself as a writer, and, worse, it emphasizes his kinship with Galkin and other unpublished scribblers.

After a futile visit to the offices of a publisher, an unpleasant surprise from his six-year-old son (whose first story, consisting of a few lines penciled in a drawing book, Straustin regards as competition), and an argument with his wife (who, sobbing, calls him a "maniac" and says that he needs treatment), Straustin goes to Galkin's apartment, where he stays for three days. Here, the contrast in their attitudes toward writing is further developed. Writing, Galkin says, is not a matter of "expressing one's personality"—quite the contrary: "we labor in the sweat of our brow and cover wagonloads of paper with writing—in the hope of stepping aside, overcoming ourselves and granting access to thoughts from the air."

Far from sharing Galkin's awe at this process, Straustin hears the poet's declaration with great suspicion. If Galkin does not regard what he has written as his property, so Straustin reasons, then he must not respect the proprietary rights of others; in other words, he must be a plagiarist. Straustin finds confirmation for his suspicions in the wildly funny scene that follows. Graphomaniacs of all sorts gather in Galkin's apartment to read their work. Soon they are all reading at once, and in the surreal babble Straustin detects fragments of his own writings. Convinced that he has been the victim of massive plagiarism, he finds further evidence in books pulled at random from the shelf: Everyone, it seems, has been plagiarizing his unpublished works. He does not realize that the "incriminating" passages consist entirely of clichés.

This "discovery" sets him walking the streets of Moscow (an extraordinary number of which, he notes, are named for writers). After a hallucinatory night, he returns home and promises his wife, to her great delight, that he has given up writing. As soon as she leaves for work, however, he addresses his son as an accomplice and, swearing him to secrecy, welcomes him into the fellowship of graphomaniacs: For the first time, Straustin has accepted that designation for himself. Now the parenthetical subtitle takes on a new meaning, for the end of the story loops back to its beginning:

I took a fresh sheet and wrote on the top in capitals the title:

GRAPHOMANIACS

Then I thought for a moment and added in brackets:

(A Story from My Life)

## Themes and Meanings

Abram Tertz has treated many of the themes in "graphomaniacs" in an essay entitled "The Literary Process in Russia." In that essay, Tertz argues that "all true writing—even when no clash with authority is involved—is something forbidden, something reprehensible, and in this illicit element lies the whole excitement, the whole dilemma of being a writer." This view of writing conflicts not only with the dogma of socialist realism, which governed approved literature in the Soviet Union, but also with the prescriptions of the most famous Russian writer in exile, Alexander Solzhenitsyn.

At the beginning of "Graphomaniacs," Straustin is unwilling to admit that by spending his life writing, hunched over a piece of paper, he is doing something intrinsically shameful, illicit, whether or not the product of his labor meets with the world's approval. Despite his diatribes against the worship of the nineteenth century masters ("it's said that in Yalta Chekhov's dried-up spit has been collected in special little packets—yes, the actual spit of Anton Pavlovich Chekhov"), he measures writers and writing strictly in terms of conventional success. In his own writing, he aspires to literature with a vengeance, with grandiloquent phrases and lofty sentiments.

Tertz, however, believes that true writing has nothing to do with "literature." It is only when Straustin abandons his pride and accepts his place among the graphomaniacs that he is able to write anything worthwhile. This is the cunning twist at the heart of "Graphomaniacs," for as one turns the last page one realizes that the author of the (mercifully unpublished) novels *In Search of Joy* and *The Sun Rises Above the Steppe* is also the "author" of the story that the reader has just finished reading.

### Style and Technique

As one might expect from a writer who has said that "whenever I earn any money—and I earn it regularly from my literary works—I am amazed each time it happens and I carry the money away in haste, clutching my pocket, crouching slightly like a burglar," the style of "Graphomaniacs" is tricky, devious, playful. One notable example of this devious style is the manner in which Tertz uses the character of Galkin.

Galkin is something of a buffoon—moreover, a buffoon seen through the eyes of the vain, spiteful Straustin. By using Galkin (instead of a more impressive figure) to express many of his own views on the nature of writing, Tertz avoids a didactic or sententious tone. The same purpose is served by the description of Galkin in the grip of poetic inspiration. Straustin scornfully observes that, at such moments, Galkin would fall silent, sitting motionless for minutes on end. Complaining that these trances distracted him from his own work, Straustin relates that he "would drop some article on the floor—a pencil, a pair of scissors and once, for the sake of experiment, a heavy manuscript, the novel *In Search of Joy*"—but, having been lifted outside himself, "Galkin did not react. From his protuberant lower lip a strand of spittle hung down to his collar." Thus, Tertz suggests that true writing is a selfless discipline in the service of transcendence—but deviously, with a smile.

*John Wilson*

# THE GRASSHOPPER AND THE CRICKET

*Author:* Yasunari Kawabata (1899-1972)
*Type of plot:* Fable
*Time of plot:* The early twentieth century
*Locale:* A university town in Japan
*First published:* "Batta to suzumushi," 1924 (English translation, 1979)

*Principal characters:*
 THE UNNAMED NARRATOR, apparently an academic
 FUJIO, a boy who discovers a singing insect
 KIYOKO, a girl to whom he gives the insect

## The Story

Walking along the wall of a university, the narrator hears an insect's voice from behind the fence of a school playground. The fence gives way to an embankment, at the base of which the narrator sees a cluster of bobbing, multicolored lanterns.

The narrator now imagines that one of the neighborhood children, having heard an insect sing on the slope one night, returns the next night to search for the insect. The next night, another child joins the first one, and so on. When the narrator comes on the insect hunting party, he counts twenty children among its members.

The narrator imagines a scenario in which one child, unable to afford a store-bought red lantern, creates his own from a small carton. Others follow his example. The narrator pictures the children coloring and drawing on paper they then stretch over the various-shaped windows they have cut out of the cartons, each making a singular pattern. Eventually, the child who bought his lantern grows dissatisfied with it and discards it. The narrator supposes that each day the children—whom the narrator likens to artists—create new lanterns. Brought back to the present, the narrator notices on the lanterns the names of the children who made them, cut in letters of the syllabary.

A boy who has been peering into a bush away from the other children suddenly asks if anyone wants a grasshopper. A number of children gather around; he calls again, and more children flock to him. He calls once more; this time one of those who appear is a girl who, coming up behind him, responds that yes, she wants the insect. The boy thrusts out his fist holding the creature to the girl, and she encloses his fist with both hands. He opens his fist and the transfer is made.

The girl, her eyes shining, announces that the insect she now has is not a grasshopper but a cricket. She opens the little insect cage hanging at her side and releases the cricket into it. The boy, meanwhile, behaves sheepishly. The narrator claims to suddenly understand the boy's actions. Surprised, he also notices something that neither the boy nor the girl nor the other children see. On the girl's breast has fallen a faint greenish light with the boy's name discernible in it; the boy's lantern is inscribing his name on the girl's white cotton kimono. At the same time, although the girl's lantern does not project its pattern so clearly, the narrator can still make out, in a patch of red on the boy's waist, the name of the girl.

The narrator contemplates that even if Fujio and Kiyoko remember the incident, they will never know about the chance interplay of colors and names. He addresses the boy he imagines grown to a man to consider the confusion between crickets and grasshoppers he will encounter throughout his life.

### Themes and Meanings

The theme of alienation, which characterizes Yasunari Kawabata's work, resonates throughout this story. The narrator, the boy, and the girl are all intensely united in a brief but highly affecting encounter. Ironically, it is the narrator—that is, the observer and stranger—who, from his perspective of time and distance, feels the full impact of the moment. He is the most sensitive to the sorrow over the transience of things and, consequently, the betrayal of expectations. The story, therefore, becomes a meditation not only on love, loneliness, and loss but also on the nature of time itself, expressing the traditional Japanese sense of *aware* that links beauty with sadness. A feeling of incompleteness pervades life, and the narrator's resigned sadness comes from an acceptance of human helplessness before the flow of time.

The singing insects of the title contribute to the meaning of the story in a multilayered way: The music they produce not only is suggestive of the beauty of nature but also signals the approach of autumn. In the context of Japanese classical literature, which Kawabata acknowledged as an influence, autumn connotes sadness, that is, the sadness of *aware*. The beauty of nature, which is especially evanescent, serves as a metaphor for the transitoriness of life and the elusiveness of human contact. Significantly, singing insects do not live long once they are put in cages.

It is generally agreed in Japan that crickets are better singers than grasshoppers, and the *suzumushi*, the particular type of cricket in the story, is considered among the best music makers. Fujio's chagrin, therefore, at being mistaken is intensified by the implication of his lack of discernment. Eager to impress Kiyoko, he is instead humiliated. He becomes more painfully aware of her unattainability.

Fujio is bound by his own feelings and perceptions. The narrator, however, is able to identify a connection between the boy and girl of which both appear to be unaware. Perhaps it is their innocence that makes them so; perhaps it is the fate of human beings not truly to appreciate the bonds that unite them. Those immersed in an experience may never be able to comprehend it fully. Apparently, the alienation that people sense from one another is compounded by their alienation from their own lives.

### Style and Technique

"The Grasshopper and the Cricket" exemplifies Kawabata's ability, as described by translator Lane Dunlop, to "endow a small space with spaciousness." The sense that Kawabata's stories represent the distillation of a larger world endows them with a powerful suggestive quality.

The Nobel Prize winner's prose, critics generally agree, is highly poetic. It appears to pay homage to the allusiveness and economy of classic Japanese poetry. The storyline of "The Grasshopper and the Cricket," as is characteristic of Kawabata's fiction, proceeds from image to image; leaps of associative logic move the narrative along. The narrative seems constructed, in fact, after the manner of *renga*, or linked verse poetry, in which separate verses are joined to form a longer poem, the linkages dependent on subtle shifts of perspective.

The author's sensitivity to the fleeting gesture reveals itself in an intense awareness of beauty and significance in a briefly perceived instant. Human actions are linked with natural objects and occurrences that, trivial in themselves, evoke strong emotion. As a youngster, Kawabata intended to be a painter, and his exquisitely detailed descriptive passages attest a highly developed visual sense.

The Japanese language itself is enriched by a pictorial component: *kanji*, or the ideogrammic system of characters adapted from Chinese writing. Response to the beauty of a picture conveyed by *kanji* is an essential part of the Japanese reader's experience, as is delight in multiple readings of characters. The opportunity for puns and wordplay, as well as for many-layered meanings, abounds.

The visual qualities of the ideograms, however, are an untranslatable element of the language, so that a dimension of Japanese literature may be lost to the reader of a translated work. Japanese syntax also tends to defy translation, so that the translator must sometimes be forced to add details or be specific where the author has intended to only hint at meaning. Particularly because Kawabata is said to maximize the ambiguity of the Japanese language, a reader who is limited to his works in translation may not fully appreciate his craft. An added impediment to a Western reader's appreciation of Kawabata is the richness of literary allusion in his fiction. As is demonstrated by "The Grasshopper and the Cricket," the author is particularly adept at making use of seasonal associations, a technique traceable in Japanese literature over a thousand years.

"The Grasshopper and the Cricket" is one of more than a hundred or so "palm-sized," or miniature novels, also known as "palm-of-the-hand" stories, that Kawabata wrote. He first experimented with the form in 1923, and although most were published in his early years, one of his final works, written not long before his suicide in 1972, was a "palm-sized" version of his novel *Yukiguni* (1935-1937; *Snow Country*, 1956). The form itself, with its juxtapositions of images and slight but evocative plot, evidently is distinctive to Kawabata. He has written of the "palm-of-the-hand" stories that the "poetic spirit of my young days lives on in them."

*Amy Adelstein*

# THE GRAVE

*Author:* Katherine Anne Porter (1890-1980)
*Type of plot:* Psychological realism
*Time of plot:* 1903 and about 1923
*Locale:* A Texas farm and a foreign city
*First published:* 1935

*Principal characters:*
МIRANDA, a nine-year-old girl; later a grown woman
PAUL, her twelve-year-old brother

*The Story*

The corpse of Miranda and Paul's grandfather has been exhumed three times since his death in about 1870. Twice it was removed by their possessive grandmother and reburied, first in Louisiana and then on her farm in Texas. After the grandmother's death, the land where the burial ground lies is sold, and the grandfather—along with the other occupants of the family cemetery—is removed by his descendants to a public cemetery to lie beside his widow for eternity.

One day following the last exhumation, Miranda, nine years of age, and Paul, who is twelve years old, are hunting for rabbits and birds. Crossing the fence into the old burial ground, they notice the open graves. Miranda leaps into the pit that had held her grandfather's bones and finds a small silver dove. Excited by her discovery, she climbs out to show the dove to Paul, who, in another grave, has found a gold ring. Miranda instinctively wants the ring, Paul the dove, so the two exchange their treasures. Realizing that they are trespassing on land that is no longer theirs, they return to the other side of the fence and pick up their guns. As they walk, Paul declares that the first dove or rabbit they see is his, and Miranda asks if she can have the first snake. The gold ring, now glistening on Miranda's "grubby thumb," shifts her attention from hunting to her boyish clothes; suddenly she resents her overalls and sockless feet and longs to put on a thin, becoming dress.

Just as Miranda decides that she should tell her brother about her change of mind and return home, Paul shoots, without Miranda's competing, and kills a rabbit. After stripping the skin—to be used as a coat for Miranda's dolls—and noticing the animal's bloated belly, he tells Miranda the rabbit was going to have babies. Cutting through the flesh and then into the scarlet bag, Paul exposes a bundle of tiny rabbits, each wrapped in a thin scarlet veil. He removes the veils and reveals their almost featureless blind faces, and Miranda asks to see them. Touching one and noticing the blood running over them, she trembles without knowing why. Seeing the unborn rabbits, which remind her of kittens and human babies, Miranda loses some of her former ignorance and begins to feel a formless intuition in her mind and body. She at once decides not to keep the skin, and Paul buries the babies back in the womb, wraps the loose skin around the body, and hides it in the bushes. With a confidential tone, Paul implores Miranda to keep the event a secret.

One day, nearly twenty years later, as Miranda is picking a path along a market street in a strange city of a strange country, a vendor holds up a tray of dyed candies in the form of little creatures, including birds and rabbits. The candy, in combination with the market's piles of raw flesh and wilting flowers, evokes the memory of that long-ago day, which springs to her mind with such vivid clarity that it stuns her. Until this day, she had remembered the episode only vaguely as the time she and Paul had found treasure in the opened graves. At this moment, the dreadful vision dims, and Miranda imagines young Paul standing in the blazing sunshine, smiling soberly, and turning the silver dove over in his hands.

*Themes and Meanings*

"The Grave" is one in a series of Katherine Anne Porter's stories that relate Miranda's initiation into experience and into a modern world at odds with the traditional world of her grandmother. The initiation in this story is multilayered: seeing and touching the unborn rabbits in their mother's womb, young Miranda discovers the adult secret of pregnancy and birth; applying this new knowledge to her own mind and body while perceiving the incongruity of the gold ring shining on her grubby thumb, she differentiates herself from her brother and comprehends her sex. This knowledge, springing as it does from death, exposes Miranda to the cyclical nature of life, a discovery that informs her vision twenty years later. Her flashback begins with a dreadful vision, suggestive of the rabbit episode, and at once fades to a vision of Paul, a vision charged mostly with life-affirming details: sunshine, youthfulness, the movement of hands, a smile, and the dove—symbolic of innocence, peace, and love. The adult Miranda's layered vision suggests that she has assimilated her childhood initiation, for it reveals a comprehensive, cyclical view of life, one that accepts at once sweetness and corruption, joy and pain, life and death.

The images of incongruity throughout the story help prepare the reader (and young Miranda) for the adult Miranda's vision: for example, children (symbols of innocence) playing inside the graves (symbols of experience, one of the story's many links to the myth of the Fall); the young Miranda scratching aimlessly like an animal (one of several archetypal images); a rabbit (symbol of fertility and rebirth) that is dead; a birth that is arrested by death; a womb that is a grave. Readers are prepared, as well, by the many images of resurrection and rebirth: the brief opening frame presents a grandfather who does not stay buried and a grandmother who keeps digging up the past; the empty graves themselves imply resurrection; the dove's emergence from the grave suggests innocence born from experience; Miranda's sexual awakening is a loss of the tomboy and a birth into womanhood. The closing frame reveals a twenty-year-old memory exhumed and resurrected by a scene in the present, a scene that includes present death (the piles of raw flesh) and icons of past death (the candies).

Graves and treasures represent loss and recovery; together they suggest continuity. The word "grave" has at least three literal and figurative referents in the story: the graves in the old cemetery, the dead rabbit's womb, and Miranda's mind. All these graves conceal secrets and must be opened in the story (note Porter's use of the Hawthornian word "veil"). The word "treasure" refers to all of those things that are revealed: the dove and the ring (representative of cycles and the children's connection with their ancestral past), the unborn rabbits and the mystery of conception, the woman in Miranda, the awareness of continuity, and the image of Paul's childhood face. Miranda's epiphanic vision suggests that, although the mind is a grave, memories are alive and in transit. The mind, like the ancestral graves in the story, is a confluence where all that is remembered converges: the past and the present, the young and the old, the living and the dead.

### Style and Technique

The narrator draws us into "The Grave" through several layers of time and seemingly disjointed events, each layer revealing more than the one before, like the layers that conceal the baby rabbits. At the story's close, the reader, like Miranda, discovers continuity. By returning to a previous time and place, the frame shows that the present leads back into the past as easily and as naturally as the past moves into the present.

"The Grave" is remarkable for its naturalness of tone, part of which comes from its subtle shifts in point of view. Porter's third-person narrator begins the story objectively, but as the story unfolds, one is drawn deeper into Miranda's consciousness, for example, by the narrator's reference to Paul as "Brother" during the rabbit episode. At the end, one discovers through Miranda's mind's eye the connection between the previous experiences.

The story's organic blend of character, event, symbol, and metaphor can be attributed in part to its autobiographical nature: In 1902, young Porter and her brother found a small dove and a ring in their grandfather's grave. Thus, not only did Porter employ real objects and events in the story, but she also carried the event in her mind for some three decades before it emerged and was reborn into fiction.

*M. A. Grubbs*

# GRAVEYARD DAY

*Author:* Bobbie Ann Mason (1940-    )
*Type of plot:* Domestic realism
*Time of plot:* A late spring around 1980
*Locale:* Western Kentucky
*First published:* 1982

> *Principal characters:*
> WALDEEN, the protagonist, a young, recently divorced mother
> HOLLY, her ten-year-old daughter
> JOE MCCLAIN, her thirty-year-old suitor, a Kentucky construction worker
> JOE MURDOCK, her former husband, a construction worker now living in Arizona
> BETTY MATHIS, her best friend
> C. W. REDMON, Betty's live-in companion and Joe McClain's coworker

*The Story*

For less than a year Waldeen has been divorced from Joe Murdock, a wild and irresponsible construction worker whom she married when she was too young to choose wisely. Another construction worker named Joe McClain has now proposed to her, but she does not yet feel ready to marry again. She cannot forget about the first Joe, the failure of her marriage, or her former husband's continuing need for adventure. Although she feels love for Joe McClain, she distrusts her emotions and worries about the future—including the danger of losing her daughter Holly to her former husband.

Waldeen feels that she is only playing family when she, Holly, and Joe McClain eat together, watch television, play cards, and spend weekends at each other's houses. In truth, she believes that family is permanent and its membership cannot change—even though it has. Joe McClain brings Waldeen and Holly food and gifts almost every day, he cuts Waldeen's hair for her, and he tends to his family plot on his "graveyard day" each spring and fall. Although he seems to be a caring person, Waldeen fears that he may become irresponsible like her former husband, Joe Murdock. She tells McClain that she needs time to think about his marriage proposal. She resists marriage as has her best friend, Betty Mathis, who has told her live-in companion, C. W. Redmon, that she does not want to have his child—the condition that he has placed on their getting married.

Waldeen plans a picnic for McClain's "graveyard day" at the cemetery, inviting Betty and C. W. to join her, Holly, and Joe. She does this over McClain's protests that the day will involve much hard work because he takes his responsibility of tending the graves of his relatives quite seriously.

McClain's graveyard day begins poorly when Waldeen oversleeps after having nightmares about her former husband, leaving her with no time in which to prepare food for the picnic. Later at the cemetery, Waldeen drinks beer and eats fried chicken that she has bought on their way there and watches McClain work. He lovingly plants geraniums, washes his grandparents' gravestones, rakes leaves, and toasts his great-great-grandfather, who died in the Civil War. Waldeen hears him tell C. W. that he looks forward to one day being buried in the family plot alongside his ancestors, where he belongs.

McClain's remark makes Waldeen understand how different he is from her former husband. Realizing that his reverence for family is similar to her own, she senses that if she marries him, she too will end her days in the family plot that Joe is tending, with her headstone next to his—a great contrast to the several states and hundreds of miles that separate her from Joe Murdock.

Waldeen springs up and jumps into the pile of leaves that C. W. and Joe have so carefully raked, scattering them. As her daughter, Joe, Betty, and C. W. surround her in a disapproving circle, Waldeen's sudden playfulness signals that her anxiety and fears have ended. She now has a new sense of security that will allow her to make important changes in her life. Her leap into the leaf pile suggests that she is ready to move on with her life by marrying Joe McClain.

*Themes and Meanings*

"Graveyard Day" expresses a central concern of Bobbie Ann Mason's fiction: how impermanence and change in modern American society affects the largely traditional lives of her conventional, working-class Kentucky characters. As with many other characters in Mason's works, Waldeen tries to cling to the past at the same moment that her life is undergoing great changes.

Waldeen's life reflects aspects of the popular culture that enter her home through television. For example, she compares her mutilated and mutable family with Johnny Carson's "Tonight Show," with its many guest hosts. Although her life seems to mirror the flux and change of a larger world beyond, she is bewildered by the complexity of modern society and fears the future. Even her daughter Holly—the one constant in her life—puzzles and frightens her when she converts to a vegetarian diet (which conflicts with Waldeen's belief that meat is necessary for health and growth) and by wearing an Indian bracelet that her father has given her. To Waldeen, the latter is a possible sign that her daughter's loyalty to her father is greater than that to her mother.

Yearning for her family and home to be lasting and unchanging, Waldeen is searching for ways to hold onto family without "shifting" its membership in any way. On McClain's graveyard day, however, she finally learns that she must enter the future in order to find the verities of the past. Only by remarrying and choosing someone who believes in family as she does—someone like Joe McClain—can she have the kind of family life that she craves. Only by forming a new family can she have an old one; only by being progressive can she return to a more old-fashioned way of life. Waldeen confronts the paradoxes and challenges of modern life, even as she seeks the simplicity and permanence of the past.

*Style and Technique*

Mason tells this story through a third-person narrator who conveys Waldeen's thoughts and feelings. She characterizes Waldeen and her friends and family through the plain, unsophisticated, everyday language that they use—filled as it is with colloquialisms such as "youngun" and "okay" as well as with clichés such as "spend a fortune," "gained a ton," or "don't know beans." In this story as in Mason's other works, her characters constantly use popular cultural references from television, business, and the entertainment industry as their frames of reference—the larger world to which they compare their own. They discuss going to the Tastee-Freez, participating in drag races, visiting Florida's Sea World, driving LTD cars, and watching Evel Knievel's daring feats on television. They recognize Colonel Sanders from fried chicken commercials, they name their cat "Mr. Spock" after a "Star Trek" character, they discuss figures such as Johnny Carson, Morley Safer, and Jimmy Durante as though they are close friends, and they compare their own lives to those they see on such television shows as *The Waltons*, *All in the Family*, and *Sixty Minutes*.

Although Mason suggests that her characters share a common culture—drawing on both mainstream American popular culture and western Kentucky traditions—they are less alike than they may appear. Joe Murdock, for example, functions as a foil for Joe McClain; although both are construction workers with roots in Kentucky, one is wild and irresponsible while the other is domestic and dependable. Further, the relationship between C. W. Redmon and Betty Mathis contrasts with that between Joe McClain and Waldeen. C. W. and Betty appear more bold and adventurous; for example, they have just returned from Sea World in Florida. Waldeen not only hesitates to venture far from home, she seems less committed to McClain than Betty is to C. W. However, by the end of the story, the reader recognizes that although Waldeen appears more timid, she is ready to commit herself to marrying McClain, but Betty still refuses to formalize her relationship with C. W.

At the end of the story, several symbols convey the changes that have occurred within Waldeen. For Waldeen, the graveyard site becomes a more appropriate symbol than a diamond ring for "the promise of marriage." Instead of the bright, glittering future promised by a diamond, the graveyard offers the assurance that the wedding vow "til death us do part" will be fulfilled. Waldeen's jump into the pile of leaves is a symbolic leap into the future—believing in the promise of tomorrow, that marriage to Joe McClain will last forever.

*Susan S. Kissel*

# GRAVITY

*Author:* David Leavitt (1961-    )
*Type of plot:* Psychological
*Time of plot:* A May during the 1980's
*Locale:* New Jersey
*First published:* 1990

> *Principal characters:*
> THEO GREENMAN, a terminally ill young man
> SYLVIA GREENMAN, his mother

*The Story*

The first two paragraphs—the opening third of the story's triptych structure—give the background exposition: Theo (probably in his twenties) is dying. Given a choice between a drug that would save his sight and a drug that would keep him alive, he has chosen not to go blind. He has moved back to his mother's house in New Jersey, after living on his own. His mother must give him drug injections four times a day, through a painful catheter in his chest, but she remains cheerful, and each day urges him to go out with her somewhere.

One warm, breezy afternoon in May, Theo and his mother go shopping for revenge. The action of the story proper, in the middle third of the story, begins and concludes with this brief shopping trip. Sylvia drives Theo to a store where she wants his advice about a present she is thinking of giving his cousin Howard, who is about to get married. The revenge involves Theo's Aunt Bibi, who gave him a tacky pen and pencil set for his college graduation. After parking the car in a handicapped parking place, Sylvia guides Theo into the gift shop where she has spotted a large, ridged, 1950's style crystal bowl, stalwart and square-jawed. As Theo observes, the bowl is rather ugly and costs $425. Revenge can be expensive.

Inside the shop, Sylvia picks up the heavy bowl and suddenly tosses it to Theo like a football. The owners of the store can only gasp, but Theo catches the bowl, his cane clattering to the floor. The omniscient narrator observes: "It seemed Sylvia had been looking a long time for something like this, something heavy enough to leave an impression, yet so fragile it could make you sorry." The objects of this thought are not only Bibi and Howard, the intended victims of her revenge, but Theo, the beneficiary of her love.

In the concluding portion of the story, Sylvia and Theo drive home. When Theo reminds his mother that it is almost time for his medicine, she nearly breaks down but recovers. Theo concludes the story wondering about the bowl and his mother, only recognizing "that she was trusting his two feeble hands, out of the whole world, to keep it from shattering. What was she trying to test?"

*Themes and Meanings*

Although Theo's illness is never named, it is clear from his symptoms—the cane, his failing eyesight, the drug injections—that he is dying of acquired immunodeficiency syndrome (AIDS). One level of author David Leavitt's meaning revolves around different attitudes toward the disease. The owners of the gift shop, for example, do not offer to shake hands with Theo: They want no physical contact with the dreaded AIDS. They typify how members of the larger public often treated people with the disease, especially early in its history.

Theo and his mother, however, are dealing with it differently, and in the best way they can. Theo has decided that he would rather have his eyesight than extend his life as a blind person. He has made his choice about the quality of his life, and his death.

The story's actions focus more on Sylvia and her response to her son's sickness than on Theo. She has rented a hospital bed for the duration of his stay, she gives him the necessary injections four times a day with the equanimity of a nurse, and every day she urges Theo out of himself and their house. She knows what is best for him. In the story's only flashback, in the opening expository section, readers are told of a trip to a Broadway show in New York City when Theo was a child, when he did not want to admit he needed glasses. Sylvia forced her own ugly glasses on him then, caring only that he be able to see. Sylvia is pushy, overbearing—and a mother acting in the only way she knows how for the child whom she so dearly loves.

The pressure she is under is noted in her one breakdown in the last part of "Gravity": "For just a moment, but perceptibly, her face broke. She squeezed her eyes shut so tight the blue shadow on the lids cracked." In the very next paragraph, she quickly is back to normal. In the third and final section of the story, Theo worries about "what damage his illness might secretly be doing to her that of course she would never admit." Readers probably will guess that Sylvia will survive; that she is functioning in the only way that she can; and that so long as she can help Theo, she will have her own sense of purpose.

The central image of "Gravity" carries this meaning perfectly. Sylvia throws the heavy bowl at Theo without warning, scaring her son and the store owners simultaneously, but Theo surprises himself and catches it. In the final section of the story, Theo wonders what his mother was testing when she pitched the bowl at him, but he answers his own question with another reference to his childhood: "Was it the assurance that he was there, alive, that he hadn't yet slipped past all her caring, a little boy lost in rhinestone-studded glasses?" Theo has caught the bowl, and thus proved, not only to his mother but also to himself, that he is still alive. Leavitt concludes: "It had pulled his arms down, and from that apish posture he's looked at his mother who smiled broadly, as if, in the war between heaviness and shattering, he's just helped her win some small but sustaining victory."

Although there is no way to defeat the law of gravity—for it is the law that roots humans to their bodies and thus ultimately to death—there are gestures such as the tossing of the bowl that momentarily seem to defy gravity and thus assert the human ability to defy death. Sylvia has done what any mother would do for her son: She has kept him alive, or reminded him that he is alive. However briefly, she has won a victory for them both. At the story's core is the final and undying love of one person for another, and her clever way of proving it. She is plotting an elaborate revenge against Theo's aunt through most of the story; she is even busier plotting her love for her son throughout it all.

## Style and Technique

"Gravity" is relatively straightforward—with the exception of the one long flashback in the first expository section—and gets to its central incident and meaning quickly, with little literary flourish or backtracking. What is most significant about the story's telling are the different levels of figurative language that Leavitt employs in this short, third-person narrative.

On one level, Leavitt uses images and metaphors to make the story's meaning more vivid for the reader; in its first section, for example, Theo thinks "of how wide and unswimmable the gulf was becoming between him and the ever-receding shoreline of the well." Here language is used figuratively to freshen and strengthen meaning. The metaphor of sight—through the many references to eyes, glasses, and vision—has a similar function of helping readers to reach the depth of the story.

The bowl carries that figurative use of language even further into literary symbolism, where the objects represent complex ideas in the story. Twice Leavitt notes the contrast between the bowl's heaviness and its fragility, and this opposition carries one of the central meanings of the story. What is life, and especially Theo's, if not heavy and fragile at the same time, balanced as it is between existence and death? Leavitt's use of language is clever and sure, and it is organically connected to the several meanings of his story.

*David Peck*

# GREASY LAKE

*Author:* T. Coraghessan Boyle (Thomas John Boyle, 1948-     )
*Type of plot:* Adventure
*Time of plot:* The 1960's
*Locale:* A small American town and its environs
*First published:* 1982

> *Principal characters:*
> THE NARRATOR, an unnamed teenage boy
> DIGBY, the narrator's teenage friend
> JEFF, another friend
> BOBBY, a rough character, also a teenager
> AL, a "biker," who is found dead
> A YOUNG WOMAN, unnamed, who is looking for Al

*The Story*

"Greasy Lake" is, on the surface at least, a teenage adventure story replete with high jinks, slapstick, and a good brawl. The good times go decidedly sour before the story is over, however, and the reader realizes that something more serious has been at issue all along.

The story is divided into three major sections. The first introduces the narrator and his two friends, just out of school for the summer, who cruise the streets of their small hometown, drinking, sniffing glue, and in general being what they consider "bad characters."

The longer second section of the story begins when the three drive out to scum- and refuse-clotted Greasy Lake in search of "action." A "chopper" (motorcycle) is parked on one side of the lot next to the lake, no owner in sight. A 1957 Chevy with the inevitable teenage lovers inside is parked on the other. The three friends mistake the car for that of an acquaintance; the narrator pulls his car behind the Chevy and, for a joke, flashes his headlights and honks the horn. Unfortunately, the owner of the car (Bobby) is not their friend after all. A fight ensues. The narrator and his friends are routed, comically so, by Bobby, who is in truth the "bad character" they believe themselves to be.

The relatively harmless fun now begins to sour. The narrator, humiliated by a kick to the mouth, hits Bobby over the head with a tire iron, perhaps hurting him seriously. Bobby's girl emerges screaming from the car, half-clothed, and the three, impassioned and heedless from the recent violence, attempt to rape her. They are stopped not by their consciences but by the headlights of an approaching car. This fresh carload of "bad characters" rescues the girl and chases narrator and friends into the brush surrounding the lake. Dodging rocks hurled into the darkness, the narrator dives into the lake and bumps into a true horror—a floating corpse. The second section ends as the narrator staggers out of the water and hears Bobby (recovered) and his friends battering the narrator's car.

The third section begins as dawn allows the narrator, Digby, and Jeff to survey the damage. It is some consolation, though not much, that the tires were not slashed and the car can still be driven. As they are about to leave, another car pulls into the lot. In it are two young women in their mid-twenties. One approaches and asks if the boys have seen Al, the owner of the chopper across the lake. Al, the narrator realizes, is the corpse he splashed into in the lake, but he denies having seen anyone. The woman takes a good look at the three of them—cut, bruised, and filthy—and says, "Hey, you guys look like some pretty bad characters." The three would have considered this high praise at the beginning of the story, but now they are too stunned by events to react. They decline when she offers them drugs, and the story ends as they drive away from the lake.

## Themes and Meanings

Were it not for the story's obvious dual point of view—an older, mature narrator looking back at his foolish younger self—the reader could be forgiven for dismissing "Greasy Lake" as a sordid and superficial teenage thriller. The very fact that the mature narrator isolates this one night out of all of his youth for dramatization implies its importance. His experience amounts, in fact, to a harrowing "initiation ritual," in anthropological terms, or a "dark night of the soul," in religious terms. By the end he has taken one large step toward maturity.

The principal theme of the story could be summarized quite well in the old Greek saying, "Through suffering comes wisdom." Several details support this reading. Much of the action turns on mistakes that the narrator must recognize as such and atone for— above all, his belief that he and his friends are "bad characters." They attempt to bolster this self-image by "razzing" their friend in the Chevy—another mistake, which is followed by yet another when the narrator drops his car key and cannot flee the enraged Bobby. The narrator, however, becomes "bad" in a moral sense when he hits Bobby with the tire iron, then tries to rape the girl. When he flees into the brush at the approach of the car, he is more shaken by guilt than by fear that Bobby's friends will hurt him. He is, in fact, later overjoyed to hear the sound of Bobby's voice. His punishment comes in several forms: He is kicked in the mouth and then hit on the knee by a rock; he splashes up against the horrible corpse in the lake; he watches his mother's car being demolished (and one can only guess what further punishment awaits him at home).

Two patterns of symbolism support the story's theme. One centers on the lake itself. The narrator's submersion in the lake, in his fear and guilt, amounts to a ritual baptism; the fetid waters are appropriate to his "filthy" moral condition. In the water he encounters what teenagers are generally heedless of but what life and sin inevitably lead one to: the corpse, death. The second pattern of symbolism involves the car key. The lost key is the narrator's "grail and . . . salvation," religious images that prepare the reader for the baptism in the lake. The second time he thinks of the key is after bumping into the corpse—he wants to flee, obviously—but such "nasty little epiphanies" cannot simply be driven away from. He does not find the key until his dark night of the soul is over; dawn reveals the key shining like a "jewel" just where he had dropped it.

Having confronted his own sin (his "bad character") and his mortality (the corpse), the narrator has earned the right to face the dawn (the light of truth) and take up the key (to understanding). In rejecting the offer of drugs at the end he is not merely rejecting a dangerous lifestyle but is accepting, by implication, the responsibilities of adulthood. The end is hardly joyful, but then, as the Greeks well knew, the price of wisdom is suffering.

*Style and Technique*

The dual point of view is crucial to the story's theme, but it is also the most important technical feature, and T. Coraghessan Boyle wields the dual perspective to interesting effects, especially in tone and imagery. In fact, the careful reader will note how often the tone and imagery seem to break into contrasting halves, mirroring the contrasting levels of understanding exhibited by the older narrator and his younger self.

It is the narrator as a nineteen-year-old, for example, who considers his friend Digby a "dangerous character" and who is impressed by the gold star Digby wears in his right ear; the older narrator, however, notes ironically that this dangerous Digby "allowed his father to pay his tuition at Cornell." The boy thinks that it will be a great joke to "razz" their friend in the Chevy; the older narrator casts all this in an ironic light, reflected in his inflated rhetoric, when he speculates that after the joke the friends will "go on to new heights of adventure and daring." The reader would do well, in fact, to remember the difference between "atmosphere" and "tone" throughout the story. "Atmosphere" is the mood evoked by setting and events. "Tone" is the author's (narrator's) perceived attitude toward the story. These may be nearly identical or greatly at variance—the latter in "Greasy Lake."

The dichotomy between tone and atmosphere is supported by contrasting images—between past and present, between nature and civilization, between horror and humor, but most important between the "tough guy" images nurtured by the teenagers and contrasting images of immaturity. The friends assert their toughness by rolling marijuana cigarettes, for example, but the "joints" are "compact as a Tootsie Roll Pop stick." In the fight with Bobby, Digby's karate maneuvers are far less effective than Jeff's more elementary tactics: jumping on Bobby's back and biting his ear. To underscore the childishness of the scene, the narrator immediately recalls that he had not been in a fight since the sixth grade. After bumping into the corpse in the lake, the narrator realizes, "I was nineteen, a mere child, an infant." At the end, when the young woman says that the three look like "pretty bad characters," the narrator's reaction is hardly one of pride: "I thought I was going to cry."

In this last section, the distance between tone and atmosphere is radically reduced and the use of contrasting images largely abandoned, all of which is appropriate; after his painful learning experience, the nineteen-year-old is much closer to the maturity of the older narrator than to his childish self of only a few hours before.

*Dennis Vannatta*

# THE GREAT BEYOND

*Author:* Cyprian Ekwensi (1921-    )
*Type of plot:* Sketch, fantasy
*Time of plot:* The late 1960's or the early 1970's
*Locale:* Lagos, Nigeria
*First published:* 1975

> *Principal characters:*
> IKOLO, the dead man
> JOKEH, his wife
> THE WELL-FED PASTOR
> LITTLE RAIFU, a fourteen-year-old son of an undertaker
> THE PATEY STREET TRADER, who owes Ikolo money

## The Story

The story opens with the funeral of Ikolo, a jovial, convivial man who had predicted that on the day of his funeral he would return "if only to have his last laugh." In Lagos, Nigeria, the length of a funeral procession usually tells "the sort of man who had died." However, although Ikolo was quite popular and was known and appreciated for delighting in making people laugh, his funeral procession is unusually short. Everything about the funeral and the day on which it occurs is strange and ominous: the dreary rain, the "disturbed" singing, the disorganized procession, the general lack of coordination, and the rather awkward, irreverent atmosphere, all of which are noted by the onlookers who line the procession route.

The hearse bearers lead the bare-bones procession, attended only by a small familial group of mourners consisting of Ikolo's mother-in-law, aunts, uncles, sisters, and nephews. Over the combined din of the unsynchronized singing, the mourners' weeping, and the grinding wheels of the hearse, a strange noise arises. At first the sound is barely audible to anyone except Ikolo's mother-in-law but later is loud enough to be heard by others, particularly the hearse bearers, who soon determine that the now thunderous knocking sound is coming from inside the sealed coffin. The mourners are stopped cold in their tracks by a muffled voice, calling out the name of the dead man's wife, Jokeh, asking her to open the casket. Shocked at the now distinctly violent knocking from within the coffin, the panic-stricken hearse bearers drop the casket and flee as if possessed, as do the rest of the mourners and onlookers. Even the pastor momentarily forgets his duty and dashes off, then returns, mortified. He runs frantically from house to house, seeking help in opening the coffin. Little Raifu, the brave fourteen-year-old son and apprentice of his father, an undertaker, offers the pastor tools with which to pry open the coffin. They manage to open the coffin, revealing the cherubic-faced Ikolo, who sits up, decked out in his favorite forty-pound suit, and calls for his grieving, frightened wife who stands rooted before her husband's coffin.

More than one half hour later, Jokeh lurches forward suddenly and carefully lays her husband down in the coffin, and as if to ensure certainty, she nails down the coffin lid for the burial. With bewildering certainty, she acknowledges that she has understood her husband's wordless message and his clear instructions that were otherwise inaudible to the confused pastor who had been standing beside her the entire time. What did Jokeh hear that nobody else could hear? How could they "hear" when they all committed the cowardly, irreverent act of running away? Even the pastor who stuck around did so reluctantly, out of duty, having first indulged his "instinct of self-preservation" like everyone else.

Two weeks later, Jokeh visits a trader, a stranger whom she had never seen before. How she knew exactly where to go and whom to ask for remains a mystery. Emboldened by the transforming power often believed to come from an encounter with spirits from the Great Beyond, Jokeh confidently confronts the Patey Street trader, who tries to dismiss her attempt to execute her dead husband's instructions to collect forty-five pounds, ten shillings, two and a half pence, a debt owed him that he was to have collected on the day he died. Carrying the money carefully wrapped in the folds of her garment, she heads for the pastor's house and tells him that the money is to be distributed as alms on a Friday to the poor and needy, according to her husband's wishes. His faith rattled to the core and befuddled by Jokeh's transformation and ability to hear what he himself could not despite "his daily devotion to the Great Beyond," the pastor recognizes the mystery of the great power of the Great Beyond and the important message of repentance and atonement from one who has experienced it first-hand and returned to tell it to a devoted wife.

*Themes and Meanings*

Like many of Cyprian Ekwensi's works, "The Great Beyond" deals with Nigerian city dwellers, the stock-in-trade characters of most of his novels and short stories. As its title implies, the story is about the city dwellers' preoccupation with and response to death and dying and the questions of existence and mortality that often surface during the funerals of others. In "The Great Beyond," Ekwensi takes up the themes of death, the occult, and clairvoyance, weaving folk belief with humor and irony in a way that neither questions the validity of the folk beliefs about death and the afterlife nor ridicules the characters' belief system. He simply poses the questions of life and death and the idea of the hereafter in an amusingly serious way through characterization. For example, Ekwensi casts Ikolo, the dead protagonist, as a jesting, carefree, life-loving sort whose death affords both his less-than-pious wife and the well-fed pastor an invaluable opportunity not only to broach the serious metaphysical and theological questions about the meaning of existence and the nature of the great beyond but also to attempt to make some sense of good and evil and repentance.

Throughout the story, Ekwensi is able to maintain an undercurrent of seriousness by the very nature of the subject matter and still sustain a humorous tone throughout the story, albeit with his moral finger wagging. However, unlike the sometimes heavy-handed moralizing for which he has come under much criticism in his major works,

Ekwensi frames the story's moral subtly in the final exchange between Jokeh and the pastor who, ironically, is the one of the two that has to ponder the question of morality and the essence of his own calling as a "preparer" of souls.

## Style and Technique

Although Ekwensi has come under much criticism for what some consider his lack of skilled craftsmanship and unrefined prose style, his reputation as one of Nigeria's most prolific popular fiction writers has never been disputed. A self-styled writer for the masses, Ekwensi makes no apologies for the simplicity of plot that characterizes his stories, particularly as his shorter novels and a number of his short stories are directed toward a younger audience. Like his novels, the fifteen short stories in *Restless City and Christmas Gold, with Other Stories* (1975), including "The Great Beyond," have a moral bent.

"The Great Beyond" is written in simple, straightforward English, typical of Ekwensi's journalistic style. Told in the third person, the story laces humor with pathos and irony, especially evident in the characterization of the hearse bearers who, lacking the pastor's somewhat shaky sense of duty, wear their "instinct of self-preservation" on their sleeves. They form a humorous but pathetic bunch as they scramble into nearby buildings for cover when the corpse knocks from inside the coffin.

The pastor's lack of understanding of metaphysics serves as the most glaring example of disconnectedness from an environment in which belief in the coexistence of the supernatural and natural worlds is commonplace and the dead are believed to have the ability to traverse both worlds. It is ironic that Jokeh, the wife of the dead man—not the pastor—gives some meaning and clarity to these folk beliefs. It is also ironic that Jokeh, the once frightened and grieving but now empowered widow, pushes Ikolo back into the coffin and nails it shut, in preparation for his strange burial. Ekwensi's behold-the-way-of-the-world message—illustrated through the irony of the shortness of the funeral procession of the man who made a life of laughing and making others laugh—is suggested through much of the action of the story.

*Pamela J. Olubunmi Smith*

# THE GREAT GOOD PLACE

*Author:* Henry James (1843-1916)
*Type of plot:* Dream vision
*Time of plot:* The late nineteenth century
*Locale:* London
*First published:* 1900

*Principal characters:*
GEORGE DANE, an elderly, successful author
BROWN, his manservant
A WRITER, an unnamed, unsuccessful young man
TWO BROTHERS, shadowy figures within the dream

*The Story*

George Dane, a writer whose success has brought with it a tremendous amount of responsibility in the form of increasingly more reading and writing to be done, wakes up one morning feeling overwhelmed by all the paperwork on his desk. The rain during the night has not washed away the work waiting to be done, the sentence waiting to be completed. Brown, his servant, enters the study to remind him of an engagement and inquire about his luncheon plans. Dane would rather not be bothered. Brown's distractedness leads them to talk at cross-purposes until Dane intones, "There is a happy land—far far away!" Brown is concerned that Dane is not well. On Dane's reassurance, Brown introduces a young man, whose name Dane does not catch, into the room. The story's first scene ends as they shake hands.

The remaining four scenes take place within Dane's dream until he wakes up for the story's last few paragraphs. The second scene begins with Dane feeling as if he is experiencing the rebirth of consciousness in a place of infinite charm, peace, and freshness: the "great good place" of the title. Author Henry James dramatizes the growth of Dane's consciousness through the successive scenes until Dane awakens to the everyday world. Within the dream, Dane is first vaguely aware of a place defined as "such an abyss of negatives, such an absence of everything." Out of a general feeling of peace and contentment, he develops self-consciousness as he becomes aware of a shadowy, human-like figure who seems to be sharing a bath with him. This figure is a "Brother," one who shares Dane's sense of ease, serenity, and security in this place that appears to be a combination of monastery and health spa: a retreat from the world that will invigorate the self. The pleasant sound of bells introduces times and the orders of spatial form and perspective. Dane and the Brother discuss the finding of the place and what it means to them. Dane names it "The Great Good Place." For the Brother, it is "The Great Want Met." They agree that to get to there, the burden of the world had to be dropped. Dane tells how the young man who showed up in his study that morning became his "substitute in the world" by assuming all of his obligations.

As the young man took over the identity of Dane, Dane gained the freedom of becoming nobody.

After what seems like three weeks to Dane, he believes that he has regained his vision, his genius, his way of ordering and understanding the world. Instead of appearing amorphous, everything now seems crystal clear, the creation of a wise consciousness exactly like his own. He is able to analyze the situation. The place has a library containing all the books he has always wanted to read but did not have the time to read. His comparisons become more aesthetic, including references to painting and music. He feels the pleasure of detachment in combination with the impression that everything was a result of his desires and vision. In the company of another, apparently younger, Brother, he comes to believe that he has found what he wanted.

As the final scene commences, it seems to be raining, indicating an element of change that has heretofore been absent in the place. Dane and the Brother compare the place to a convalescent home and a kindergarten, institutions that imply process or development. With this comes a concern that the place will not always be available. They decide that it will. They realize that they must return to life itself. As Dane shakes the hand of the Brother in farewell, he wakes up to find his hand being held by the manservant Brown. He has been sleeping all day while the young visitor has taken care of all of his correspondence.

## Themes and Meanings

The theme of the story, the importance of consciousness, is the primary theme of Henry James's fiction as a whole. The "great good place" is consciousness. The scenes in the study provide the frame for the dramatization of the process of a developing consciousness, which constitutes the dream sequence. George Dane's literary correspondence and obligations have diminished his contact with his own consciousness, the source of his creative abilities and of his sense of identity. Dane's despair and rejection of the work of his everyday life, his distraction, his overall feeling of being overwhelmed by the details of his life brought about by his success, result from this lack of nurturing contact with his consciousness. Dane's withdrawal from the world into his dream is the vehicle for reunification with that inner life of which the principal component is consciousness itself.

The conjunction of "the great good place" with "the great want met" signifies that Dane has come to the right place to fulfill his desire to regain contact with himself even though he does not yet realize exactly what this means. The place is, in effect, consciousness unadulterated by the facts of the world. The "blessed fact of consciousness" antedates all values or perceptions. From being conscious, Dane moves through stages of becoming self-conscious to awareness of the significant patterns of the world of both the inner and outer life. He wakes from his dream with the realization that through consciousness, inner and outer worlds are united.

## Style and Technique

Through the device of the dream story, James is able to render the theme of consciousness more directly than he normally does. He dispenses with the exigencies of plot, characterization, and the defining details necessary for verisimilitude. Within the dream, George Dane is nothing but consciousness. He is what he is aware of being. He encounters nothing but himself in the process of becoming aware of himself. Even those shadowy figures, the Brothers, are merely projections of his desire to communicate with those aspects of himself that validate his work as an author and his vision of life. There is no boundary between inner life and outer world. Within some vaguely defined limits, Dane's consciousness is free to reconstruct itself and the world at the same time, and James is free to dramatize this process. Of "The Great Good Place," James himself wrote that "any gloss or comment would be a tactless challenge." The unity of story and theme validates his assertion.

*William J. McDonald*

# THE GREAT WALL OF CHINA

*Author:* Franz Kafka (1883-1924)
*Type of plot:* Allegory
*Time of plot:* Third century B.C.E.
*Locale:* China
*First published:* "Beim Bau der chinesischen Mauer," 1931 (English translation, 1933)

> *Principal characters:*
> THE NARRATOR, anonymous, apparently an official in the imperial bureaucracy
> THE EMPEROR OF CHINA
> THE STAFF OF THE HIGH COMMAND, in charge of the construction of the Wall

*The Story*

The anonymous speaker of this quasi-historical report on the Great Wall of China speculates not only about the peculiar method of the wall's construction but also about the motives behind the project and the authorities on whose decision it was undertaken. The speaker's focus gradually expands to consider the larger matters of relationship between the emperor and his people, between the empire and the barbarians beyond it, and, ultimately, between the real and the imagined meanings of all these various shapers of the speaker's world.

At the outset, the speaker points out a conspicuous peculiarity in the construction of the wall: Rather than being built continuously from one end to the other, the wall was assembled piecemeal in sections of about a thousand yards each. Isolated from other workers and usually not even in sight of another section of the wall, two crews, beginning at opposite ends of the thousand-yard stretch, would spend as many as five years laboring to make their respective sections meet; after appropriate ceremonies, they would then be dismissed to their homes. After such a lengthy absence, their return would be celebrated in their villages, which were very often many miles from the borders on which their section of the wall had been constructed. After a period of rest and rejuvenation, the workers would be dispatched again to join others with whom they had not worked before and to begin a new section of the wall in some other remote corner of the empire, far from home.

Such a method of construction left many gaps in the wall over the long period of its building, some of which were not closed until after the wall was officially declared complete. This fact, coupled with the apparent motive for the wall itself—namely, to provide security against the barbarian hordes that threatened invasion—gives the speaker the problem that he sets out to resolve by considering the history and development of this imperial project.

Among the considerations that he entertains is the evidence of a central and all-encompassing plan designed by the "high command" in charge of the project, even though—as he remarks—the whereabouts and staff of the high command remain veiled in mystery. Nevertheless, so large a project and so peculiar a method of construction force him to assume that the high command existed and had direct control. Otherwise, he says, how can one account for the long period of preparation before the first stone was laid? for the emphasis on architecture as the greatest of sciences? for the schoolyard games of building pebble-walls? or for the rigorous training and high culture possessed by a mere supervisor of even four workers on the wall? Then, too, the expense of the project, not only material but also psychological, suggests that some greater power and design were at work than even the most advanced and intelligent individual could comprehend.

The high command must have all human designs and all human wishes within its purview, and the wall must therefore represent the cryptic but necessary working out of this truly benevolent design. Or, as the speaker finally admits, it is perhaps not useful or safe to dwell too much on the greater design, or to attempt a complete understanding on one's own; better by far to repose one's trust in the plans of the high command and to submit to its decrees.

Although the speaker confesses this maxim of resignation as useful, it is clear that he is unable to apply it fully. He insists that he is pursuing an inquiry that is historical, not critical or philosophical, but his attempts to reconcile the evidence of the great plan with the experience of his own life nag him into broader considerations. Why should he, for example, whose home is far down in the southeast of China, be involved in the project—or indeed, why should he care about the northern barbarians, who could never penetrate so far into the empire? He questions whether the barbarians exist, because (apart from the frightening pictures that sometimes appeared in children's books) no other representation of the great enemy exists. At its root, therefore, the grand design of the high command must predate even the decree of the emperor that establishes the project, and in that grand design, the actions of the northern barbarians and of the emperor himself have their appropriate place, acquiring meaning only in relation to the design of the high command, eternal, mysterious, and finally unknowable. These things, says the speaker, only those who have meditated on the history of the wall can know.

In the second half of the story, the speaker works out the consequences of this idea about the division between the nominal authority of the emperor and the real authority of the high command. As before, his speculation revolves around the disparity between perception and explanation. The empire is too vast for the emperor's authority to reach all of his subjects: A messenger dispatched from the emperor's bedside could not even struggle through the concentric rings of the palace or reach the surrounding imperial city—to say nothing of the remote provinces—before both the emperor and the one to whom the message was sent had crumbled into dust. There can be no news from the capital because all news becomes obsolete, owing to the long period of its transmission.

Although the living emperor and his provincial subjects depend on each other for their mutual existence, their relationship is unreal because of their remoteness from each other. The emperor must therefore imagine his people, and the people must construct in their imagination the figure and the authority of the emperor whom they will not and cannot ever know. As a result, even the empire must remain largely in the imagination of its subjects, giving them a kind of freedom—because no actual external authority interferes with their lives—but only at the cost of depriving them of the security that these fictions still provide. Having gone so far, the speaker declines to pursue his inquiry further.

## Themes and Meanings

As a fictional and indeed allegorical work, Franz Kafka's story is not really concerned with the Great Wall of China or the process of its building but with the relationship between the abstract structures that give human life its meaning and the quality of life that human beings lead as a result. The only absolutes in the story are the absolutes of experiences: that some sections of the wall have been completed; that many stand in isolation from others, defeating the nominal defensive purpose of the project; that workers come and go; that the daily life of villages, although remote from the wall itself, is nevertheless affected by it in the absence of the workers and, more positively, in the brief but happy celebrations of the workers' return. Against these absolutes of experience, which are the actual shaping forces of the villagers' (and the speaker's) lives, stand the great abstracts, which all the subjects can only imagine to exist: the emperor, the empire, the high command, even the wall itself, now officially declared to be complete. The principal theme of the story is thus the dissociation of modern life: that the realities of experience are in fact too little associated with the abstract ideals and forces (whether economic, social, political, or religious) that modern humanity uses as an explanation of its actions, or as a veil for the essential meaninglessness of many modern concerns.

The inset tale of the emperor's messenger hints that the possibility for meaning still exists, if only connections between abstractions and experiences could be made explicit, but the fate of the message, the emperor, and the receiver shows that such a hope is finally futile. The refusal of the speaker to pursue his inquiry about the wall is thus a representation of a similar modern refusal to question the apparent motives by which actions and circumstances are directed and shaped: For the world, as for the empire, it is better to accept the specious security of illusory ideals than to question their reality and significance.

## Style and Technique

Many of the characteristic marks of Kafka's short-story style appear here. First-person narration from an unnamed narrator, exotic or peculiar locales, and the general tendency to weave together an integrated metaphor—an allegory—for some larger issue are all typical of his general handling of story materials. By far the most conspicuous of Kafka's stylistic markers is the tone of the story as a whole: the flat, quasi-historical, apparently calm and reasonable but clearly single-minded opening masks the much more disturbing, less rational, and finally almost frightening voice of a speaker confronting an unthinkable gap in the order of his experience. The accumulation of subtle but important contradictory details, especially in the mass of obsessively collected and apparently objective data about the wall, leads the reader to question the accuracy of the report that the speaker gives. Although at the outset the speaker seems both lucid and authoritative, this lucidity and authority are quickly obscured by the weight of information not given, so that even the anonymity of the speaker and the proposition of an all-knowing, eternal high command become finally threatening. Kafka's control of tone, so that in the apparently reasonable monologue of the speaker one can discern the shrill overtones of mania, is an indication of his mastery of that anxious and ominous style that is so distinctively his own.

*Dale B. Billingsley*

# THE GREAT WAVE

*Author:* Mary Lavin (1912-1996)
*Type of plot:* Social realism
*Time of plot:* The early twentieth century
*Locale:* West coast of Ireland
*First published:* 1959

*Principal characters:*
THE BISHOP, called "Jimeen" in childhood
FATHER KANE, his secretary
MARY, his mother
SEOINEEN, a friend of his youth, who studied to become a priest

*The Story*

An Irish Roman Catholic bishop sits in the stern of a currach, a small skin-covered boat, wearing his robes and carrying his stiff ecclesiastical vestments inside out in order to protect them. Because he travels to this island only once every four years for a confirmation ceremony, it is fitting that he come in full pomp. His vestments are exceptionally beautiful, including a cope, a capelike garment made with threads of gold, which he commissioned from a convent in Switzerland.

Privately, the bishop, who was born on this poor island, marvels that he has ever learned to appreciate the beauty of these garments. He is mildly irritated that the hem of his robe is wet from water in the bottom of the currach. The rowers warn him that his crosier, the symbol of his office, may also get wet. Although his secretary, hard-eyed Father Kane, offers to hold the staff, the bishop tersely declines.

As he notices the island church perched near the top of a cliff, the bishop becomes nauseated, perhaps by the roughness of the waves, but he says nothing. Instead he recalls how, when he was a boy, he begged to go out fishing with the island men, but his mother would not allow it, having lost her husband to the sea. Worse, she made sure that none of the fishing crews could be coaxed into taking him.

In a flashback, the bishop remembers the day when his friend Seoineen, a young seminarian, returned to the island for a leave before his final year of study for the priesthood. Headstrong Seoineen was the pride of the island, for after many years they would give one of their own to the church. When Seoineen arrived, he jokingly predicted that the herring would spawn the next day. The superstitious islanders marveled at his wisdom.

Next morning, the herring were indeed spawning. The fishermen immediately set out in their boats, but Seoineen's father was too ill to go. His currach, the only one left ashore, had just been tarred. Seoineen declared the currach dry and ready for what appeared to be a huge catch, and he urged young Jimeen (as the bishop was called as a child) to come with him. Because the islanders believed that Seoineen, so near to the priesthood, was under God's special protection, Jimeen's mother was finally persuaded to let him go. Only after the boat was well away from shore did Jimeen realize that the tar on the bottom of the currach had not dried. Seoineen, the future priest, had lied.

To Jimeen, the sea appeared strange, the waves too smooth, like great glass rollers. The fish in the sea were packed so tightly they were near suffocation. Seoineen was elated by such incredible bounty. They cast their nets and began to haul them in.

As Seoineen prepared to lower the nets again, they heard a terrific clap of thunder, and the sky turned black. They could see nothing, but shouts from another boat warned them to let go of the nets or be pulled under. Jimeen's swollen fingers were caught in the heavy mesh, and he could not free himself. Seoineen cut the boy loose but stubbornly clung to the teeming nets. "I'll show them a man is a man, no matter what vows he takes!" he cried. "I'll not let go this net, not if it pull me down to hell." Though he was aware that Jimeen's life could be lost as well as his own, he did not seem to care.

Suddenly, Jimeen saw rising up before them a huge wall of water, a great wave. Sliding down that wall were hundreds of dead fish, and within the wave itself he saw a corpse. He remembered nothing more until he found himself with Seoineen, thrown clear of the sea and lying on the grass atop the island cliff. Jimeen believed they had been saved by a miracle because of Seoineen's presence.

In fact, a massive tidal wave had swept over the island, drowning all the inhabitants as well as those fishing in the boats. Horrified, Seoineen bemoaned his greed; his life had been saved but, with his ruined hands, for what? His dream of the priesthood was swept from his grasp along with the nets that had crippled him. He asked the same question of Jimeen: Jimeen's life had been spared but for what?

Coming back to the present, the bishop prepares to disembark on the island. He thinks of his friend Seoineen, who lives apart from the new village and whom he has not seen since that day. The boy Jimeen, now the bishop, has taken Seoineen's place as the island's offering to the church. Refusing to put on his coat in spite of the cold, he takes care to display his vestments in all their magnificence so that Seoineen, who he knows is watching from the cliff, can see that he has been faithful.

*Themes and Meanings*

Who knows, the bishop asks himself, what will set us on our rightful path? Mary Lavin's story can be seen as a study of the mysterious ways of God, for both the seminarian and the boy undergo a moral and spiritual test. Seoineen challenges God through his overweening pride in his own strength and skill. Heedless of Jimeen's safety as well as his own, he can think only of the marvelous catch that he will bring home to the island. Later, he believes himself somehow responsible for the destruction wrought by the tidal wave and for the deaths of his family and neighbors. God has punished him, and he must live with this knowledge. He goes into self-imposed exile on the island.

Even though Seoineen chooses to set himself, however briefly, against God, his refusal to give up his nets has allowed Jimeen to become the man he is now. Seoineen is undone by pride, but Jimeen takes up his burden without regret.

This is also a story about love. A subtext is about suffering for others, even giving up one's life for them. Jimeen, now the bishop, has dedicated his own life to God, his flock, and his friend. He is fully aware of the responsibility. His frightful boyhood experience has taught him to honor and affirm life and beauty. He has become a great and good man, a true shepherd. The bishop offers up his physical discomfort, and the emotional pain of returning to this terrible scene, as a sacrifice for his friend who lost so much in the tidal wave.

*Style and Technique*

The present action of the story, the bishop's journey across the bay, offers a framework for the flashback that makes up the body of "The Great Wave." Lavin's style and language are colored by the strong Gaelic influence of western Ireland. Dialogue is always a strength in her writing, and here she captures the lilt of the Irish voice and the sensory details of coastal life.

Lavin plants information so subtly that it is easy to misread, and to misjudge, her characters. At first impression, the bishop appears fussy, vain, and excessively proud of his gorgeous vestments. Later, it becomes clear that the bishop keeps his own counsel and that his behavior stems from reasons known only to himself. He understands that the elaborate vestments are part of the ceremony the parishioners expect of him, but he wants to spare his housekeeper the extra ironing of damp garments. He is sad that Father Kane can think only of their cost, not their beauty.

The bishop is nauseated by the boat's movement but does not complain. Actually, his nausea is a psychological reaction to his ghastly memories of the wave. When Father Kane scorns the islanders, the bishop pities him. The bishop has truly joined the ranks of holy men as a living saint, a quiet martyr.

Ironically, what is welcomed as the richest catch of all time destroys all the islanders except the bishop. The fears raised in the story are always of the wrong things—of being left behind with no fish, of wet tar remaining on the currach bottom, of being pulled overboard by the bursting nets, of the currach sinking under its heavy load— but with no awareness of the real terror until it is on them. The utter shock of such a tidal wave in this part of the world leaves one breathless.

*Joanne McCarthy*

# THE GREEK INTERPRETER

*Author:* Arthur Conan Doyle (1859-1930)
*Type of plot:* Mystery and detective
*Time of plot:* The mid-1880's
*Locale:* London, England
*First published:* 1893

>       *Principal characters:*
>           SHERLOCK HOLMES, the world's greatest detective
>           DR. JOHN H. WATSON, his friend and biographer
>           MR. MELAS, the Greek interpreter
>           MYCROFT HOLMES, Sherlock Holmes's elder brother

*The Story*

The story opens in the familiar quarters of Sherlock Holmes and Dr. Watson at 221-B Baker Street in London. It is a warm summer evening, and their conversation wanders from subject to subject until Holmes mentions his family. Despite Watson's sharing the apartment for several years, he has never known Holmes to speak much of his background, and Watson is surprised to hear that Holmes has an elder brother, Mycroft, whom the detective describes as a reasoner even greater than himself. However, Mycroft, Holmes explains, has an absolute aversion to interrupting his daily routine for the sometimes vigorous activity needed to solve crimes.

Holmes has a purpose in mentioning Mycroft precisely at this time, because his corpulent brother has summoned him to what Holmes characterizes as one of the strangest clubs in London. Holmes and Watson, therefore, stroll to the Diogenes Club for Watson's first sight of this strangest member of the city's strangest club. The Diogenes Club was founded for gentlemen who desired the refuge of a club and the privacy of their homes: Conversation is forbidden except in the Strangers' Room, in which Holmes and Watson are joined by Mycroft.

Mycroft sets before Holmes the mystery of the story: A neighbor of his, a Mr. Melas, has come to him with the tale of a very strange experience. Thinking at once of his younger brother, Mycroft has asked Melas to join them at the club so that Holmes may pursue the problem. Melas, a Greek, works as a translator in London, and his adventure began when he was hired for that purpose by a Mr. Latimer. Latimer asked Melas to accompany him to his house; when they entered their carriage, Latimer closed the window shades so that Melas could not see where they were going. Latimer then drew out a blackjack and threatened Melas so effectively that the interpreter made no protest during their ride of almost two hours.

Because night had fallen, Melas was unable to identify his surroundings when the carriage stopped. He was shown into a house and introduced first to a small, mean-looking man, and then to an emaciated figure whose head was crisscrossed and whose mouth was sealed with adhesive tape. The man, obviously a prisoner, was given a slate, and Melas was instructed to ask him questions (in Greek).

During the questioning, the captors insisted that the taped figure sign some papers, an act that he absolutely refused to do. After a session of several hours, Melas was taken back to town in the same furtive manner and warned to tell no one.

Melas immediately went to the police, who refused to credit his story, and he then turned to Mycroft Holmes. The stage is now set, and Sherlock Holmes's work begins. They have a few clues: Melas had been able during his questioning to find out that the captive's name was Paul Kratides, and, during an unexpected intrusion, that the man's young sister was also in the house, although she was unaware that her brother was under the same roof. Unfortunately for Holmes (and for Melas, too, eventually), Mycroft has run an advertisement in the papers for anyone knowing anything about a Paul Kratides or his sister. As Holmes points out, this notice will inform Latimer and his confederate that Melas has talked about their actions.

After leaving the Diogenes Club, Holmes and Watson send some telegrams to some possible sources of information, but when they enter their flat at Baker Street, Mycroft is already there. He says that an answer to his advertisement has identified the house in question. Mycroft wants to interview the writer of the letter, but Holmes rightly observes that the captive man is being starved to death and that they should head immediately for the house.

Watson suggests that they pick up Melas on the way, should they need an interpreter, but when they arrive at Melas's address, he has already gone off with the mean-looking little man he had described to them earlier that day. Knowing that Melas is now in mortal danger as well, Holmes rushes to Scotland Yard to appeal for a warrant to force entry into the sinister house. After a worrisome delay, they receive the warrant and reach the house in question only to find that the captors have escaped. They hear a groan from upstairs and rush up to find two prostrate figures in a room with a burning charcoal fire—the taped man, already suffocated, and Melas, whom they are able to save.

In the quiet aftermath of the action, Holmes pieces together the story of a young Greek woman, obviously with prospects of inheriting some wealth, who fell in love with the Englishman Latimer. When her brother arrived in England, he was taken by Latimer and his confederate, who attempted to force him to sign over the girl's property; keeping his arrival a secret from his sister, they had taped the brother's face so that she would not recognize him should she see him being moved about the house. The story ends with a notice in a European paper that the two Englishmen have been found stabbed, and that the woman with whom they were traveling has vanished.

## Themes and Meanings

One will not find philosophical themes in "The Greek Interpreter." When Arthur Conan Doyle first wrote of Sherlock Holmes, he was interested only in giving the readers of *Strand Magazine* an exciting, well-written story. However, he soon found that he had created in Holmes something of a Frankenstein's monster: The public took the detective to its collective heart. Perhaps it was the detective's lucid intelligence:

Through the power of the mind, the world could be seen to make sense. Holmes lives and moves among the most emotional of people, but his clear sight and keen study of detail allow him (almost always) to help reason to triumph.

Some of Holmes's quirks became set pieces, little bits of introduction that the audience came to expect, such as the detective's revelations about a client from details of the client's appearance. However, even a good thing can be overdone, and Doyle must have felt a need from time to time to get Holmes and Watson out of their flat at Baker Street in order to expand the cast of continuing characters. Something like this may have been the motive behind "The Greek Interpreter." The story's main charm lies in its details about Holmes's life, in particular about his fascinating older brother, Mycroft. Mycroft gives Doyle a chance for one of the set pieces of observation noted above, and the further chance to show in Mycroft someone who is even better at observation than Holmes is. The story furnishes a deeper, more detailed history for the detective. As one of the first continuing characters in short fiction, Holmes needed more depth, more solidity, than would normally be supplied for a character in a short story.

This was an entirely new method—to round out a fictional character through a number of works: One story might demonstrate Holmes's love of music, another his moods of depression, and another his deep friendship with Watson. This story focuses on, one might say, his heredity, through the equally remarkable powers of his brother.

*Style and Technique*

"The Greek Interpreter" is certainly an unusual representative of the sixty-odd stories of Sherlock Holmes written by Doyle. The story contains no mystery whatsoever to display the singular intellect of the great detective: Melas tells Holmes almost everything that he ever learns about the captive man, and almost anyone could guess at the rest, given Melas's account. The mystery of the location of the house is solved in a very prosy way, by Mycroft's placing an advertisement in the newspapers, a notice that at the same time tips off the kidnappers and very conveniently supplies the one piece of information that the rescuers need. Holmes knows this and complains about it to Mycroft.

There are other inconsistencies in the story, too: Holmes knows that both the mysterious, taped man and Melas are in danger of being murdered, yet he waits for a long while until he can obtain a proper search warrant for the house in which they are being held. In other stories Holmes has not strictly observed the laws against breaking and entering when the stake was someone's life.

Many of the Holmes stories that Doyle wrote are better as detective stories; that is, they have a tighter plot, a deeper mystery, or require real imagination and daring on the part of the famous detective. By 1893, however, the character of Sherlock Holmes had come so vividly to life that details of the detective's life were as pleasing to the public as any merely puzzling plot. It is in that characterization of Holmes that the enduring interest of "The Greek Interpreter" lies.

*Walter E. Meyers*

# GREEN TEA

*Author:* Joseph Sheridan Le Fanu (1814-1873)
*Type of plot:* Horror
*Time of plot:* About 1805 and about 1869
*Locale:* London, rural Warwickshire, and Richmond, England
*First published:* 1869

*Principal characters:*

THE ANONYMOUS NARRATOR

DR. MARTIN HESSELIUS, a physician and author of medical works

LADY MARY HEYDUKE, a society woman and friend of Dr. Hesselius and Mr. Jennings

THE REVEREND MR. ROBERT LYNDER JENNINGS, the vicar of a rural parish in Warwickshire

JONES, Mr. Jennings's servant

*The Story*

The anonymous narrator, who was trained as a surgeon, has been arranging the papers of his deceased mentor, Dr. Martin Hesselius. One case in particular, from about sixty-four years before, draws his attention; forthwith the narrator presents a set of letters, with a memorandum, that discuss the doctor's efforts to treat a particularly insidious and vexing complaint.

One evening, Dr. Hesselius meets the Reverend Mr. Robert Lynder Jennings at the house of a mutual friend, Lady Mary Heyduke. In an aside, the hostess informs the doctor of Mr. Jennings's probity and good standing in the community; nevertheless, the clergyman's health is uncertain and he seems subject to sudden and mysterious collapses. With some evident embarrassment, the clergyman engages Dr. Hesselius in a discussion of Metaphysical Medicine, and evinces an active interest in the doctor's publications on the subject. Later, Lady Mary mentions that Mr. Jennings's late father had seen and spoken with a ghost. On the following evening, the clergyman sends his calling card with a note requesting a consultation with Dr. Hesselius.

At Mr. Jennings's house in Richmond, the doctor is received by Jones, the vicar's servant; the clergyman has been detained by work in his parish. While waiting in his host's library, Dr. Hesselius comes on a set of the complete works, in Latin, of Emanuel Swedenborg, the Swedish mystical philosopher; perusal indicates that Mr. Jennings has underscored such passages as "May God compassionate me." As Dr. Hesselius continues, he realizes with a start that "four eyes were reading the passage." Mr. Jennings's unannounced return is revealed by his features reflected in an overhanging mirror. He abruptly embarks on a conversation about the origins of illness, and he confounds the doctor with his spirited denunciation of materialism in medical thought. Dr. Hesselius is taken aback particularly by the abrupt fluctuations of unchecked gloom and brisk gaiety in his host's demeanor.

After five weeks, Mr. Jennings again summons the doctor to his home, and there sets forth his own diagnosis of the maladies that have taken possession of him. Already he has been described as having once been an inveterate tea drinker. Mr. Jennings now maintains that his nervous sensibilities have been upset by the consumption first of black and then, gradually and more insidiously, of green tea. Even a change in his habits has not improved his condition. More than that, he is stalked by a creature that, whether imagined or real, relentlessly insinuates itself into his field of vision at every turn.

Once while riding on an omnibus, Mr. Jennings endeavored to push a small monkey out of his way; his umbrella actually seemed to pierce the animal. Since that time, this small, jet-black primate has followed him, its eyes ever animated with burning malevolence; in the dark, it is enveloped in a glowing reddish aura. Inexplicably it has been absent for fifteen days, but the clergyman suspects it will return. He fears that it will induce a cataleptic state, rendering powerless his own will, and lead him to crime or self-destruction. After this exposition, the first he has made to anyone, Mr. Jennings asks Dr. Hesselius whether the quantities of tea he has taken could have affected his inner eye, the cerebral tissue alongside the optic nerve. He increasingly has become conscious of the monkey's singing speech, which would seem to have entered his mind through some degeneration of his faculties.

Rather soon after his second visit, the doctor receives another, and unmistakably urgent, appeal from the clergyman. It is all in vain. When he arrives, Dr. Hesselius is met by Jones, who leads him to his master's body; Mr. Jennings has opened a deep gash in his neck and left a vast pool of blood on his bedroom floor. During his last night on earth, Mr. Jennings asked his servant whether he could hear the monkey's cursing; evidently the master then did away with himself during the early morning hours.

In his concluding statement, Dr. Hesselius expounds his belief that Mr. Jennings was persistently affected by hereditary suicidal mania. The doctor contends that the optic nerve is the channel by which the inner eye establishes contact with the external world. Prolonged abuse of chemical agents—such as those found in tea—upsets the mental equilibrium and renders those affected vulnerable to innate weaknesses. Dr. Hesselius maintains finally that this combination of predisposed melancholia and morbid overstimulation of the nervous system led Mr. Jennings to take his own life.

*Themes and Meanings*

Victorian writers were markedly prone to ascribe their characters' complaints to brain fever or other, equally vague, maladies. The effects of opium, morphine, and other such agents were also explored in fiction, sometimes with (to the modern mind) extraordinary and indeed implausible results. At first, some readers may regard as preposterous, if not laughable, the notion that drinking strong tea could produce prolonged visions and ultimately death. This story manifestly does not elicit that reaction, although the Reverend Mr. Jennings's green tea figures prominently in it from the title to the conclusion. The active properties in tea are never really demonstrated. At one time, Lady Mary had almost quarreled with the clergyman on this subject; during his longest consultation with the doctor, Mr. Jennings cites green tea specifically as the source of his visions. Evidently the effect is cumulative and possibly irreversible; even abstention cannot dispel the specter that haunts Mr. Jennings. Both he and Dr. Hesselius regard this complaint as much more than mere dyspepsia. Neither believes, however, that his malady may be understood through medical materialism alone.

This curious ambivalence, where neither spiritual nor chemical origins may be established with certainty, is heightened by Joseph Sheridan Le Fanu's presentation of several characters' points of view; the author does not explicitly endorse any of them. The narrator, who introduces the story, regards Dr. Hesselius as highly gifted, but one who alternately takes the standpoints of an intelligent layman or a medical philosopher. In several places the doctor somewhat ponderously expounds his theory that human beings are spiritual beings and that their bodies are merely a material expression of their essential and ideal nature. He can explain Mr. Jennings's affliction only by referring to "a poison which excites the reciprocal action of spirit and nerve." Mr. Jennings himself originally found green tea pleasant and almost soporific in its effects; though later he withdraws from it in horror, he admits candidly that his medical reasoning against it is speculative.

The notion of hereditary trauma, which Lady Mary and the doctor accept in part, is not much discussed by Mr. Jennings; this factor remains lurking in the background, putting in occasional appearances at particularly murky junctures. The peculiarly horrific atmosphere of "Green Tea" is derived in part from the separate explanations that leading characters offer for Mr. Jennings's malevolent visions, none of which needs to be accepted entirely.

### Style and Technique

In its turn, this studied ambiguity is amplified by those stylistic qualities that distinguished Le Fanu from other horror writers of his era. There is no omniscient narrator, only a series of admittedly subjective accounts from the various characters. Trappings that are often featured in ghost stories appear but are not thrust on the reader. The aged volumes of Emanuel Swedenborg and of German medical-philosophical cogitations are shown discreetly; gloomy scenes of the doctor's crepuscular visits to Mr. Jennings's house are presented quite in passing, as part of the larger scheme of Dr. Hesselius's narrative. Some effects are achieved obliquely, as when the doctor realizes that Mr. Jennings is watching him from beyond a mirror. The spectral monkey itself is presented only as the clergyman seems to have perceived it, in colors and outlines; ultimately it becomes a hissing sound that appears to emanate from within Mr. Jennings's very ears.

In other respects the narrative style is understated but forthright, both in the introduction and in the ten letters of Dr. Hesselius. Most sentences are simple and direct, with the exception of a few convoluted passages wherein Dr. Hesselius holds forth on medicine and spiritualism. Very few words are emphasized, and then generally from the characters' direct discourse; there are few exclamations or questions, save for when the characters themselves utter them. The effect, though seemingly subdued and understated, actually intensifies the unfolding sense of approaching doom that imbues this work.

*J. R. Broadus*

# GREENLEAF

*Author:* Flannery O'Connor (1925-1964)
*Type of plot:* Wit and humor
*Time of plot:* The 1950's
*Locale:* The rural South
*First published:* 1956

*Principal characters:*
MRS. MAY, the protagonist and the owner of a dairy farm
MR. GREENLEAF, her hired man
WESLEY, one of her sons, a teacher
SCOFIELD, her other son, an insurance salesperson
O.T. and
E.T., Mr. Greenleaf's sons, successful dairy farmers
MRS. GREENLEAF, the wife of the hired man

*The Story*

Mrs. May, the owner of a dairy farm, awakes in the night from a strange dream in which something was eating everything she owned, herself, her house, her sons, her farm, all except the home of Mr. Greenleaf, her hired man. She looks out the window and discovers a stray scrub bull chewing on the hedge below her window. She considers dressing and driving down the road to Greenleaf's place to get him to catch the bull, lest it get into the pasture with her cows and corrupt the breeding schedule of her purebred cattle. She decides to put it off until morning, not because she is averse to bothering Mr. Greenleaf in the night but because she anticipates his uncomplimentary remarks about her two grown sons, who should be able to help their mother in such emergencies.

One of the long-standing rivalries between Mrs. May and Mr. Greenleaf during the fifteen years of their association has been the relative merits of their sons. Mr. Greenleaf's twins, O. T. and E. T., married two French girls of good family during the war when they were in the army. As Mrs. May rationalizes their good fortune, "disguised in their uniforms, they could not be told from other people's children. You could tell, of course, when they opened their mouths but they did that seldom." They both "managed to get wounded," so they received pensions and went to agricultural school on veterans' benefits. They had become the owners of a prosperous dairy farm nearby and the heads of flourishing bilingual families. As Mrs. May bleakly predicts, in twenty years their children will be "society!"

Mrs. May is secretly envious of such productive sons because her own give her little satisfaction. Wesley has a heart condition, commutes to a teaching job, and has a vile disposition. Mrs. May pretends that he is an "intellectual." Scofield is loud and vulgar, has gained nothing from his two years as a private during the war, and now sells insurance to African Americans. He is what they call the "policy man," a position of considerable mortification to his mother. Neither son has married, and they both refuse to lift a hand to help with the farmwork.

The next day, Mrs. May finds out that the scrub bull belongs to Mr. Greenleaf's sons, that it can apparently escape from almost any confinement, and that it hates trucks and cars. It has already attacked the twins' pickup, causing considerable damage. Mrs. May drives to the twins' house and delivers an ultimatum: Either they pick up the bull or she will have Mr. Greenleaf shoot it the next day. It is no comfort to her to learn that the twins probably do not want it and will be happy that she must destroy it for them.

The bull visits her again that night, munching away under her window. The sound of the bull tearing at the hedge enters her sleeping consciousness as a menacing dream about the sun piercing through the vegetation that surrounds her cultivated fields. The burning sun seems to burst through the trees and is racing toward her. She wakes in panic.

The next morning, she orders the reluctant Mr. Greenleaf to get his gun; they are going to shoot the bull. Mr. Greenleaf is angry, but he finally gets his weapon and joins her in the truck. They drive into the pasture, where Mrs. May has seen the animal in the distance. Mrs. May thinks with some satisfaction, "He'd like to shoot me instead of the bull." They drive into the pasture. Mrs. May waits at the truck while Greenleaf looks for the bull in the grove of trees at the edge of the pasture.

After a considerable wait, during which Mrs. May dozes as she sits on the bumper of the truck, the bull emerges from the wood, but Mr. Greenleaf is nowhere to be seen. She had been vaguely fantasizing about the bull attacking Mr. Greenleaf in the wood. The situation is curiously like her dream. She is standing in the middle of the pasture ringed by trees, a natural amphitheater, and the bull is racing toward her. She seems mesmerized, unable to move, until the bull has "buried his head in her lap like a wild tormented lover." One horn pierces her heart and the other encircles her waist: "and she had the look of a person whose sight has been suddenly restored but who finds the light unbearable." Mr. Greenleaf, running toward her now from the side, pumps four bullets into the eye of the bull.

*Themes and Meanings*

The Greenleafs are members of the social class that was once called "poor white trash." Mrs. May, as a landowner, a user of "correct" English, and the widow of an urban businessperson, considers herself socially superior to the Greenleafs in many ways. She is described as a "country woman only by persuasion." The farm, bought as an investment when land was cheap, is the only legacy that her husband left her. She has exported the urban business orientation to the countryside, determined to wrest a living from nature by sheer strength of will, despising the careless ease with which the Greenleafs exist in that environment. However, the conflict between Mrs. May and her sometimes incompetent hired man is only partially sociological. It suggests a more elemental difficulty with Mrs. May, which may be called philosophical or even religious.

What the Greenleafs unselfconsciously possess that Mrs. May lacks is a sacramental view of nature. Religiously suggestive metaphors, as well as the comic description of Mrs. Greenleaf's grotesque religious rituals, convey this difference. Mrs. May insists on taking credit for whatever success and well-being the Greenleafs enjoy. "They lived like the lilies of the field, off the fat that she struggled to put into the land." She is extremely annoyed when Greenleaf drawls, in one of their several discussions about their sons, "I thank Gawd for ever-thang." Mrs. May obviously believes that she should get the credit, not the Lord. When her city friends visit, Mrs. May complains that everything—the weather, the dirt, the hired help—are in league against her. "There's nothing for it but an iron hand!" The insensitive Scofield holds up her arm mockingly to display "Momma's iron hand," which would "dangle from her wrist like the head of a broken lily."

Mrs. Greenleaf, whom Mrs. May despises even more than she does Mr. Greenleaf, is a "prayer healer." She cuts morbid stories out of the newspaper—accidents, murders, rapes, even divorces of film stars—takes them all out in the woods and buries them. Then she mumbles and groans and calls on Jesus over them, usually ending up sprawled facedown in the dirt in her earnestness to win redemption for the miserable and sinful. Mrs. May is appalled at this vulgar display of piety; she is described as "a good Christian woman with a large respect for religion, though she did not, of course, believe any of it was true."

One remembers Mrs. Greenleaf's shriek as she grovels in the dirt: "Oh, Jesus, stab me in the heart!" The image receives a wildly ironic echo when Mrs. May bends over the horn of the unruly scrub bull that stabs her in the heart. There is also a curious irony in the fact that Greenleaf, who once mistakenly planted a field in clover when she had ordered rye, pierces the bull's eye four times, while running. However, his surprising competence in this crisis comes too late.

## Style and Technique

The names May and Greenleaf, both suggestive of springtime, the symbolic dreams, and especially the suggestive imagery and diction used in the confrontations between Mrs. May and the bull, give this sardonic tale a cast of archetypal myth. In the initial scene, the bull stands in the moonlight under her window "like some patient god come down to woo her." He has ripped loose some of the hedge, which encircles his horns, presumably making him even more like a garlanded Dionysus in his bull form. Later he is likened to "an uncouth country suitor." Moreover, Mrs. May's first words are addressed to the bull in curiously anthropomorphic terms: "Get away from here, Sir!" Before the disappointed lover leaves, he has shaken his head so that the vines have slipped down to the base of the horns, now looking like a "menacing prickly crown," suggesting perhaps the sacrificial role that she imposes on him.

When he comes again to her window, her dream is more menacing; the noise of the bull becomes associated with the sun, which burns through the trees and races toward her. Is the reader to remember the ancient pairing of the sun bull with the moon cow? When Mrs. May wakes and looks out the window, however, she sees the bull only as an "iron shadow," a suggestive echo of the "iron hand" with which she attempted to fight the forces of nature and Greenleaf.

In the last scene, the bull, rejected twice in his nocturnal visits, emerges like a "black heavy shadow" from the trees and starts toward her at a slow gallop, "a gay almost rocking gait as if he were overjoyed to find her again." Soon, however, he becomes the "violent black streak" that pierces and embraces her with his horns. She has the appearance of having a blinding vision. As the bull crumbles to the earth, Mrs. May seems to be bent over, "whispering some last discovery" into the bull's ear.

The tale has many of the distinctive qualities that make Flannery O'Connor one of the most original of American short-story writers: the combination of humor and violence with ironic overtones of revelation. Ordinary, small-minded, and often mean-spirited mortals find out that they have dissipated their lives without recognizing their responsibilities for transcendence. Unusual literary symbols point to some other dimension or interpretation of reality: a scrub bull, or, in other stories, a peacock, a club-foot, an absurd hat, tattoos, even pigs. Whether such emblems actually induce wisdom or bring about redemption for O'Connor's spiritual cripples is often ambiguous.

*Katherine Snipes*

# GREYHOUND PEOPLE

*Author:* Alice Adams (1926-1999)
*Type of plot:* Psychological
*Time of plot:* The 1970's
*Locale:* Northern California
*First published:* 1981

> *Principal characters:*
> THE NARRATOR, the unnamed protagonist, a government
> statistician
> HORTENSE, an older woman with whom the narrator lives

## The Story

Nothing extraordinary happens on the first or any of the subsequent bus rides that the narrator takes between her home in San Francisco and her job in Sacramento, a fact that makes her attitude toward buses and the people on them even more puzzling and interesting. She is never accosted or threatened. Her worst experience is being asked, on her first ride, to move out of a seat claimed by a burly black man: She moves, and the incident is over.

However, the narrator is a study in paranoia. In the first of the eleven unnumbered sections of the story, the narrator is afraid that she has gotten on the wrong bus. Her fellow passengers look strange, intimidating. She puts her briefcase on the adjoining seat so that no one can sit next to her. The bus driver apparently takes the incorrect number of coupons from her ticket book, a circumstance she regards as "mysterious"; a mentally disabled boy makes a "senseless" racket in the back; and so on. However, the narrator's exposure to this apparently hostile environment seems to work a healthy change in her, noticeable even by the end of the first section, where she "yearns to," but does not, join in the general applause for the black woman who has the last word in an argument.

In the second and very brief section of the story, the narrator describes her "situation." She is recently divorced and living with an older woman, Hortense. She lives with Hortense not because of any lesbian tendency, she assures the reader, but out of "sheer dependency." After this brief meditation, the narrator is back on the bus completing the journey to San Francisco. On one leg of the trip she makes friends with a young black woman who works with mentally challenged children. The narrator feels guilty about siding with the black woman against the mother of the troublesome boy until her new acquaintance assures her that challenged children have not only rights but also obligations. The narrator is relieved to find that she was right to be resentful of the noisy child.

In the fourth section, the narrator finally reaches San Francisco, and Hortense's agitation at her late arrival—she had indeed taken the wrong bus, the "local" rather than the express—rekindles her fears concerning the "types" who frequent the bus station.

Whatever slight understanding of and rapport with her fellow passengers the narrator seemed to be moving toward at the end of the first bus trip dissipates after contact with Hortense. Once more, she sits by herself on the trip back to Sacramento. Even the scenery seems duller than before. Later, she sits next to a girl who comes from the same part of upstate New York as she, who even works in the same building. Rather than regarding such a coincidence as grounds for enlivening the conversation, however, the narrator sees it as "ominous." Nearing Sacramento, she sees a profusion of pink and white oleanders along the road; they strike her as "unnaturally hardy" and make her uneasy.

The story's turning point takes place in the seventh section, in which the narrator— deliberately or accidentally (even she is not sure)—once more takes the wrong bus: the "local" on which all the dangerous black people ride. Taking the local will force her to be late once more, she well knows, and force another confrontation with Hortense. Suddenly, however, it occurs to the narrator that such worries are "silly" because both she and Hortense are adults. This realization leads indirectly to a second: that she shares a certain camaraderie with the passengers. All, including her, are in one sense or another "poor people."

The last four sections of the story show the consequences of these realizations. The narrator admires a handsome young man on the bus, her first notice of a man, in "that" way, since her divorce. She tells Hortense that she need not bother picking her up at the bus station anymore, then makes plans to move out of Hortense's apartment altogether. In the last section, the black man who had so intimidated her on the first bus ride greets her, and she returns the greeting with confidence. At the very end, she has decided to purchase a "California pass," which will allow her to travel anywhere in the state. "I could meet anyone at all," she concludes in the story's final line.

*Themes and Meanings*

Although the title seems to indicate that the story will be a sociological dramatization of the lives of a certain segment of society, "Greyhound People" is really a psychological study, a "rite of passage" in which the narrator learns to engage the world as a mature adult.

Although an adult in age at the beginning of the story, in many other ways the narrator is a child. Her fear of riding the bus, of associating with strangers is more childish than cautious. Like a child, she requires approval from a more knowledgeable adult before she feels right about siding with the black woman in her dispute with the mother of the retarded boy. Ironically, it is the retarded boy whom the narrator most resembles early in the story. He, too, is trying to understand the world around him— hence his irritating questions. Like the retarded boy, the narrator lives in "sheer dependency" with a mother figure, Hortense, who worries over and scolds the narrator for her late arrival.

The narrator's childishness and dependency, despite her adult age, are explained by a fact given little emphasis until late in the story: her recent divorce. The reader can conjecture that she moved from being dependent on her parents to being dependent on her husband to being dependent on her parent substitute, Hortense.

Thus, her growing camaraderie with the "Greyhound people"—the independent, functioning adults of the working world—and her estrangement from Hortense occur simultaneously. At the end, she can fearlessly exchange greetings with a black man, can look yearningly at a male other than her husband, and can buy a bus ticket that will allow her to go anywhere that her will and maturity take her.

### Style and Technique

The surface simplicity of "Greyhound People"—its plain prose style and lack of flamboyant characters and action—should not conceal the fact that the author is an artful and sophisticated storyteller. Her skill is noticeable especially in word choice and narrative structure.

Two related examples may serve to illustrate Alice Adams's skillful use of language. The first two pages of the story are filled with nouns and modifiers—"frightened," "anxiety," "fear," "angry," "scared," "apprehensively," "mysterious," "senseless"—that convey not the quality of her surroundings so much as the narrator's fearfulness and lack of confidence. Three sections later, the same sort of diction appears but with a difference. In one paragraph persons in the bus station are described as being "frightened-looking," "belligerent-looking," and "dangerous-looking" (emphasis added), the "looking" implying that the narrator has realized by this point—subconsciously, to be sure—that these are impressions only, as dependent on the attitude of the observer as on the actual qualities of the observed. By the end of the story, the use of such "fearful" word choice is almost totally absent from the prose.

The change in diction over the course of the story emphasizes the story's artful structure. In general, two types of rhythms are evident in the structure: the interplay between the narrator's experiences with the bus people and her experience with Hortense, and the interplay between her meditation on the bus people—not only her experiences with them but also her understanding of them—and her meditation on her own condition. The two rhythms move toward two climaxes: one in which the bus people "win out" over Hortense, so to speak, and one in which the narrator concludes that her own condition is related to her understanding of the bus people. Ultimately, the two rhythms and their two climaxes are interrelated, both showing the narrator's growth toward maturity and independence.

*Dennis Vannatta*

# GRYPHON

*Author:* Charles Baxter (1947-    )
*Type of plot:* Psychological
*Time of plot:* The late twentieth century
*Locale:* Five Oaks, Michigan
*First published:* 1985

*Principal characters:*
TOMMY, the narrator, a fourth-grade student
MISS FERENCZI, his substitute teacher
MR. HIBLER, his regular teacher
CARL WHITESIDE and
WAYNE, his classmates
MRS. MANTEI, the sixth-grade teacher

*The Story*

To the narrator, Tommy, a normal fourth-grade boy, and other pupils at Garfield-Murray School in rural Five Oaks, Michigan, each day is much like another. As their teachers lecture to them about predictable subjects in predictable ways, they memorize facts and repeat them back. Occasionally, the routine is disrupted by a substitute teacher, but with only four substitutes in all of Five Oaks, the students know exactly what to expect from each of them. Oblivious to the dullness of their routine, the students do not know that there are other possibilities, other ways to learn, and other ways to look or think, so they do not feel a lack. Into their mundane world Miss Ferenczi, a new substitute teacher, suddenly arrives.

From the first moment that Miss Ferenczi appears, it is clear that she is different; one student even jokes that she may be from Mars. She carries a purple purse and a checkered lunchbox, her glasses are tinted, and her hair is done up in a strange way. Before class begins, she spends time drawing a tree on the chalkboard because "this room needs a tree." She then introduces herself by telling a long and dramatic story about her grandfather, a Hungarian prince, and her mother, a world-famous pianist. The students are captivated but cautious.

On her first day, Miss Ferenczi covers some of the regularly assigned material; however, during the arithmetic lesson, she accepts a student's answer that six times eleven equals sixty-eight. When several students protest, she encourages them to let go of their orthodoxy. She is a substitute teacher, she says, so it will not hurt them to learn a few substitute facts. The students, however, will not have it. They want to know which answer is correct. Miss Ferenczi closes the discussion: "You are free to think what you like. When your teacher, Mr. Hibler, returns, six times eleven will be sixty-six again, you can rest assured. And it will be that for the rest of your lives in Five Oaks. Too bad, eh?"

The afternoon lesson is on Egypt. Miss Ferenczi ignores the assigned text and instead tells about her own travels in Egypt—where she has seen "much dust and many brutalities," and where she claims to have seen a gryphon in a cage. She talks about the movement of souls, the cosmic powers of pyramids, and the tidal forces of the solar system. Although her sentences are unconnected, they seem profound—sometimes true and sometimes not. Tommy wants to believe everything that Miss Ferenczi says, but his friend Carl Whiteside thinks that she is making it all up. To each boy, it must be one thing or the other: Miss Ferenczi must be right or wrong, a truth-teller or a liar.

Miss Ferenczi teaches for two days, enchanting and confusing the students with her rambling, fabulous ideas. On the playground, the students group together, debating whether she is crazy. On the third day, Mr. Hibler returns, and everything is back to normal.

Several months later, Miss Ferenczi reappears. This time, she ignores the assigned lessons altogether, and takes out a deck of tarot cards with which she tells the students' fortunes. For most of them, she sees nothing exceptional in their futures—merely marriage, the army, and a good life. However, she predicts an early death for one frightened boy, Wayne, who tells the school's principal.

After the children see Miss Ferenczi drive away at lunchtime, never to return, Tommy and Wayne come to blows in the schoolyard. Tommy tries to defend the substitute: "She was right," he yells. "She was always right! She told the truth!" After lunch period, they study insects under the guidance of Mrs. Mantei, the regular sixth-grade teacher, who is "no mystery." She tells them about the parts of an insect's mouth, its four-stage metamorphosis, and its internal anatomy. On the next day, she tells them, Mr. Hibler will test them on their mastery of the facts.

## Themes and Meanings

Many of Charles Baxter's stories feature ordinary people encountering extraordinary strangers who disrupt their normal lives: A woman who visits a psychic and hears of great danger; a man who tries to help a homeless man, only to hurt his own family; a new substitute teacher who turns out to be crazy. In each case, the central character's life is orderly, even dull. However, unchanging day-to-day routines are no protection against peril. Just under the surface of the most orderly existence, disorder always lurks.

Baxter has said that the idea for "Gryphon" came out of his own early experience as an elementary school teacher. One day as he presented a lesson about Egypt, he found his "facts" becoming increasingly fanciful. The experience made him realize that a teacher can enter a classroom and teach anything—facts or substitute facts—without anyone knowing the difference. As is the case with any good writer, this realization led Baxter to more questions than answers. For example, is it necessarily all bad to offer substitute facts occasionally in an educational setting? His fictional Miss Ferenczi is more creative, more engaging, than the "regular" teachers. Is not it important for children to dream and wonder, instead of merely memorizing?

By the end of the story, Miss Ferenczi is a puzzle. She demonstrates less control each time that she teaches Tommy's class, until the final day, on which there is a subtle hint of real danger. Very likely, she should not be in a classroom. However, the reader cannot help regretting this when presented with the dreary alternative implied in the story's last line: "Mrs. Mantei said that our assignment would be to memorize these lists for the next day, when Mr. Hibler would certainly return and test us on our knowledge."

Although Tommy's life has been ordered into careful dullness—predictable routines at school, simple chores at home after school—chaos appears suddenly and unexpectedly. For him, the days with Miss Ferenczi are confusing, even upsetting, but they also are freeing, expanding. His brief encounter with danger is also his first encounter with the wider world.

*Style and Technique*

"Gryphon," the title of this story, is taken from the name of a fabulous mythological creature with the head and wings of an eagle and body of a lion. It also symbolizes Miss Ferenczi, whom Baxter describes as "half-miracle, half-monster." In order to make Miss Ferenczi appear simultaneously miraculous and monstrous, Baxter tells the story through the eyes of Tommy, a young boy who is more sensitive than some of his classmates. Although he has no special powers of perception, he is more aware of his surroundings and more inquisitive. He is also one of the most willing to accept Miss Ferenczi's version of truth. Perhaps because he is more curious about the world, he is more open to new ideas about it.

When Miss Ferenczi appears, the reader sees her through Tommy's eyes, and notices the same things that a child would notice. The reader, however, is likely to be much older than Tommy and far more sophisticated. When Tommy notices Miss Ferenczi's purple purse and checkered lunchbox, the reader agrees with him that this indeed is an unusual woman. However, when Tommy mentions that her hair is done up in "what I would learn years later was called a chignon," and that he has never seen hair done like that before (Tommy's own mother looks like Betty Crocker), the reader is also made aware of just how limited life in Five Oaks must be.

When Tommy and Carl argue on the bus about the gryphon that Miss Ferenczi claims to have seen, Tommy wants to believe her, but Carl does not. The reader knows the truth, but that is not the point. Again, Baxter demonstrates how small the children's frame of reference is. Tommy wins the argument by citing what for both of them is an unimpeachable source—the *National Enquirer.* When Tommy looks up the word "gryphon" in a dictionary and sees it defined as "a fabulous beast," he fails to understand the meaning of the word "fabulous" and takes it only as confirmation of his own feelings.

Throughout the story, the reader is allowed to understand things that Tommy does not. The reader, then, sees the subtle danger presented by Miss Ferenczi—a hidden danger to innocent children. However, at the same time the reader never loses sight of the way Tommy sees her—as "fabulous." In the end, she is both.

*Cynthia A. Bily*

# THE GUEST

*Author:* Albert Camus (1913-1960)
*Type of plot:* Social realism
*Time of plot:* 1952
*Locale:* French Algeria
*First published:* "L'Hôte," 1957 (English translation, 1958)

> *Principal characters:*
> DARU, the protagonist, a young teacher
> BALDUCCI, an old gendarme
> AN UNNAMED ARAB, the prisoner of Balducci and then of Daru

## The Story

A young Frenchman named Daru sees two men climbing toward the schoolhouse where he teaches and resides in the desert mountains of French Algeria. One man, the old Corsican gendarme Balducci, rides on horseback and holds a rope tethered to his prisoner, an unnamed Arab, who proceeds on foot. Balducci informs Daru that he is to receive the prisoner (who has killed a cousin of his in a fight over some grain) and deliver him to police headquarters at Tinguit, some fifteen kilometers away. At first Daru refuses Balducci's order, then relents and takes the prisoner in; having been offended by Daru's reluctance, Balducci leaves in a sullen mood.

As the story progresses, it becomes clear to the reader that Daru would welcome the escape of the prisoner: It would relieve Daru of the demands thrust on him against his will. It is a time of uprising, the Arabs against the French government. The Arab prisoner asks Daru to join him and the other rebels, but it is unlike Daru to make an active commitment to anything. In the inscrutable world in which he lives it would make no difference anyhow, for actions are misconstrued over and over again. Still, one must do what one must do, in spite of the absurd interpretations society might make: This is a central message that runs throughout Albert Camus's work. Daru, after a restless night, walks with his prisoner to a point between two directions, one of which leads to the French administration and the police, the other of which leads to the nomads. Having given the Arab dates, bread, sugar, and a thousand francs, he leaves the choice of directions to him. The Arab remains motionless in indecision as Daru turns his back on him and walks away; when, after a time, Daru turns around, he sees that the Arab is walking on the road to prison.

A little later, as Daru stands before the window of the classroom, he watches, but hardly sees, the panorama of the plateau; behind him, written on the blackboard, are the words: "You handed over our brother. You will pay for this." Daru feels alone.

## Themes and Meanings

The original French title of this story, "L'Hôte," means not only "the guest" but also "the host." There is no English word that conveys the double meaning of the French word. Distinctions are leveled, done away with, in order to show a common humanity between Daru and the Arab; still further opposed meanings suggested by the title (amity and hospitality on one hand, enmity and hostility on the other) add to the ambiguity.

The author is deliberately ambiguous because the circumstances of Daru and his Arab guest are. There is no absolute action that can completely satisfy either character. Daru can neither accept European justice nor ignore the crime for which his guest is guilty. The Arab can neither give himself up to his own people nor go to the nomads. To do the former would be to invite severer penalties on himself; to do the latter would be to surrender his identity in a self-imposed exile.

Because he is opposed to the denial of personal freedom but also respectful of law, Daru does not release his prisoner outright; he does, however, leave to him the choice of directions. It can never be clear to the reader why the Arab prisoner elects to go in the direction of the jail. It may be that he is the victim of conditioning; it may be that, from a sense of guilt, he invites condemnation; it may be that, because his crime has cut him off from his own people, he expects European criminal justice to be less harsh and more sober. One view seems as likely as any other: The Arab merely does what Daru does—that is, surrenders to others the determination of his fate. A noble action, Camus seems to say, cannot always be counted on to bring about a favorable end.

It is ironic that Daru, who has chosen to cut himself off from society, is representative of the best sense of humanity that any society can offer. He is both Everyman and Christ figure, suffering as a citizen of the world and suffering for the world, providing sustenance and comfort and promoting tolerance and understanding. A measure of his tolerance is that he reserves ultimate judgments and generously sees more than one side of any question. His charitable reasonableness does not suffice, though, to counter the cruelties and unreasonableness in the Algerian situation.

For Camus, however, the act of confrontation with absurdity, with the meaninglessness and the contradictoriness of experiences in life, is the duty of the heroic type; it is perpetual, as is the struggle of Sisyphus, the mythological figure who passes eternity pushing a huge rock up a mountain only to have it fall again once he has arrived at the top with it. The confrontation is undertaken by the conscious hero with the understanding that there can be for him no divine hope to sustain him in his struggle. He knows that he is inevitably bound for extinction, but he brings a dignity, a grandness, to his task that sustains him and that lends to his existence the only meaningfulness it can have. Daru is no conscious hero, certainly, but he is representative of the noble person who confronts existence and, usually, ends by having to suffer, and sometimes die, for it.

*Style and Technique*

The style of the story is taut, concise, stripped of inessentials. One sees in this the influence of Ernest Hemingway, whom Camus admired very much. All that is there is there for a reason; accepting that truth, all the reader has to do is relate the making of the story to its meaning. The reader has already seen how the title, with its ambiguity, sets the stage for various reversals, displacements, and contradictions. From the beginning to the end of the story, for example, the two main characters shift roles unexpectedly or do, or have done to them, unexpected things. Daru is a host to the Arab but is a guest in the Arab's homeland, making the Arab Daru's host. Received by Daru as a prisoner, the Arab is set free, made his own host; received in hostility, he is accepted in hospitality and amity. Though he is a gracious host, Daru is treated as, at the very least, an unwelcome guest and, at the end of the story, is condemned to a solitude that is absolute.

The description of solitude and isolation at the beginning of the story prepares the reader for the theme of alienation. Daru is alone at the top of a mountain whose ascent is steep and rocky. The difficulty in scaling the heights (reminiscent, incidentally, of the plight of Sisyphus) defines the difficulty of communication. Daru is far from society. He has no vehicle for transportation and has no significant contact with his family, colleagues, or friends. His only acquaintance (except with his very young students, who have been away for a time because of severe climatic conditions) is with the military. He has tried to put behind him, from not many years before, his war experience; thus, such association as he may have is with those with whom he has no spiritual identity. With one of them, Balducci, he has an immediate falling out. He is an exile in his own homeland.

He and the Arab speak, literally, different languages. This fact further alienates the two men, when the political situation has already made a breach between them. If human beings cannot communicate on one level, they cannot be expected to communicate very easily on another; misunderstanding is bound to be, in such an event, profound and perpetual. Like Meursault, the central character in Camus's *L'Etranger* (1942; *The Stranger*, 1946), Daru is utterly cut off—as much from himself as from the world around him. He is a stranger. Camus is uncharacteristically clear on this point. Almost every line of his story underlines it, artistic structure conveying meanings and themes. The sterile plateau, the steep mountain, the self-imposed apartness, the impossibility of understanding, the cruel ironies—all serve as images or symbols evoking the theme of alienation.

From the evils of human nature one may find consolation in nature; nature—in the usual sense of the word, the natural world of rocks and flowers and trees—is not as unkind as human beings. The author of "The Guest" shows through a technique of contrasts that nature is, at worst, indifferent.

*David Powell*

# GUESTS OF THE NATION

*Author:* Frank O'Connor (Michael Francis O'Donovan, 1903-1966)
*Type of plot:* Social realism
*Time of plot:* The first third of the twentieth century
*Locale:* Ireland
*First published:* 1931

*Principal characters:*

BONAPARTE, the narrator, a common young IRA soldier lacking in formal education

NOBLE, Bonaparte's fellow youthful IRA jailer of the two British captives, who is religious and has a brother serving in the priesthood

JEREMIAH DONOVAN, the immediate superior officer over Bonaparte and Noble, and a dogmatic patriot

HAWKINS, a British common soldier, both communistic and atheistic

BELCHER, a British soldier also held captive with Hawkins, whose large stature and taciturnity belie his sensitive nature

AN IRISH WOMAN, an old rustic at whose cottage the British captives are kept

*The Story*

In the first of the four numbered sections of "Guests of the Nation," the main characters are introduced. Though Ireland and the Irish Republican Army (IRA) are not named explicitly, through mention of names such as Claregalway, reference to the British as foreigners, and dialectal expressions such as "divil" (devil), the implicit premise is established that two ordinary British soldiers have been abducted by the IRA and have been held on a rural farm for a period of several days or weeks. Just as the British soldiers got on well with their prior IRA captors in the Second Battalion, even attending Battalion dances, so they play cards with their present captors and are on friendly terms with them and the somewhat peevish old woman who owns the farm where they are being kept, largely because of Belcher's considerate actions toward her.

The tempo of the plot, which takes place in only two days, quickens in the second through fourth sections. In the second section, after the description of yet another nocturnal argument about religion and capitalism between the devout Irishman Noble and his contentious, atheistic captive Hawkins, Bonaparte discovers (as does the reader) from his superior Donovan that their British prisoners are actually hostages, who soon may be shot in retaliation for the threatened execution of imprisoned IRA members. Indeed, as narrated in the third section, the next evening Donovan calls at the farm to implement the retaliation for the execution that day of four of the Irish "lads" (one of whom was only sixteen years old). With the reluctant help of Noble and Bonaparte, who have grown fond of them, the prisoners are taken out into the marshes near the farm, Hawkins arguing all the way, once he has learned what is in store for him and Belcher.

Finally, in the fourth section, a little later in the evening at the bog, Hawkins—despite his vehement arguments and objections and offering to desert and turn renegade—is suddenly shot by Donovan and then again minutes later (at Belcher's behest) by the disinclined narrator in order to hasten the lingering death caused by Donovan's poor aim. After Bonaparte and Donovan help Belcher with a blindfold, the group listens to a surprising outburst of talk about his life from the usually taciturn soldier. Obviously moved, Noble seems about to intercede when Donovan hastily executes the second prisoner. After Bonaparte and Noble return to the farmhouse that night, they and the old woman have powerful feelings of regret or remorse, which the narrator says forever affected and altered his subsequent experience of life.

## Themes and Meanings

The main theme of the story, the conflict between duty and humanitarianism, is clearly enunciated in two signature passages (technically, places in which the author explicitly articulates his theme). The first is in section 3 in the interchange between Donovan and Bonaparte about duty; the second, in section 4, in the interchange between Donovan and Belcher about the same subject. In these and other passages, the story shows that unlike Donovan, Bonaparte and Belcher, as well as Noble, Hawkins, and the old woman, move beyond a circumscribed conception of nationalistic duty to a sympathy and compassion for their fellow human beings that transcend the borders and politics of separate countries. Thus, unlike Donovan, the other major characters feel that harming another human being who is both friendly and innocent is wrong, even in the name of patriotic duty. The Englishmen's "peculiar" expression "chums," picked up by Bonaparte and Noble and repeated seventeen times in the story, embodies the idea of the paramount importance of friendship or humanitarian sympathy. So, too, does the biblical genealogy that Hawkins scorns as "silly" in one of his arguments with Noble. Hawkins does not realize that Old Testament genealogies suggest by way of descent from a common ancestor the brotherhood of humankind, making humankind a nation that surmounts individual countries—a belief that would have saved his life, which is instead sacrificed because of the conflict between the two countries of England and Ireland.

Hawkins's twice disparaging the "fairytale" about Adam and Eve picking the forbidden fruit highlights an implied moral theme relating to the conflict of duty and humanitarianism. Reinforced by constant explicit references to religion in the story, largely in Bonaparte's description of the arguments between Hawkins and Noble on the subject, the Adam and Eve incident recalls the key concept of God's prohibition against sinful acts, including murder—an issue of central importance in the killings that are contemplated by Donovan and his superiors. Even the old woman's apparent non sequitur in referring to Jupiter Pluvius early in the story has a bearing on the theme by recalling that the planned killings would have been a moral wrong in the ancient classical religions because foreigners and strangers were under the protection of Zeus or Jupiter, who was patron god of hospitality. Because of a larger sense of duty as moral obligation, these two British soldiers, the story implies, deserve to be "guests of the nation" (the story's title) in a true sense rather than as a euphemism for "prisoners."

One of the story's many fine insights into human nature and behavior derives from its portrayal of the conflict between conscience and conformity. Bonaparte and Noble go along with the plan for the execution, despite serious reservations. What overrides their moral objection is the pressure exerted by peers (Donovan and Feeney, the local intelligence officer) and by social situation. Many instances from real life, as in the Holocaust of World War II, demonstrate the applicability of this theme.

*Style and Technique*

One of the most important components of technique in "Guests of the Nation" is Frank O'Connor's masterful use of irony. An early instance of irony, apart from the story's title and the repetition of the word "chum" (underlining the failure of friendship in the plot), is the reference to the Irish dances that Belcher and Hawkins have learned, whose titles ("The Walls of Limerick," "The Siege of Ennis") allude to divisiveness, violence, and war, which undercut the harmony of the social occasion. Further, the narrator's word to describe the timbre of Belcher's speech, "peaceable," ironically contrasts with the reason the British soldiers are kept captive, as well as their fate.

Indeed, ironies run throughout the story: The two soldiers executed are among the most congenial to the country and its culture; the religious doubter Hawkins is the first to discover the truths about the afterlife (by being the first killed); Belcher is so considerate of his executioners that just before he is shot he asks their forgiveness for his sudden outpouring of talk, explains his thoughtful wish to speed things up because he knows the delay is painful to them, and finally absolves them all with consoling words. Finally Belcher's blindfold, made by knotting his handkerchief with Bonaparte's, ironically symbolizes the union that should have prevented Belcher's pitiful death, while it is also connected to the story's motif of blindness—to human community and to the twists of fate, summarized in the repeated key word "unforeseen."

*Norman Prinsky*

# THE GUN SHOP

*Author:* John Updike (1932-    )
*Type of plot:* Realism
*Time of plot:* The early 1970's
*Locale:* Pennsylvania
*First published:* 1972

> *Principal characters:*
> BEN TRUPP, the protagonist, who with his family is visiting his
>    parents for Thanksgiving
> SALLY, his wife
> YOUNG MURRAY, his fourteen-year-old son
> MURRAY, his father

## The Story

Ben and Sally Trupp, their two daughters, and their fourteen-year-old son, Murray, are visiting Ben's parents in Pennsylvania for Thanksgiving. A highlight of the annual trek from the Trupps' home in Boston is the opportunity for Murray to shoot his father's old Remington .22, a gun given to Ben when he was about Murray's age. As the father and son go out to a field to shoot the rifle, Ben remembers his son's last birthday, when he tapped Murray's head to quiet him and the boy, holding the cake knife, threatened to kill him if he were hit again. Sally agreed that Murray was too old to be hit, but Ben, watching his son carrying the rifle, thinks he looks very young.

In the field, the gun does not fire, and Murray curses and throws a tantrum. Ben, unable to help, remembers how his father, also named Murray, taught him to shoot this same gun. The two return to the house, where old Murray, to calm his grandson, promises action and calls Dutch, a local gunsmith. That evening, Ben, his father, and young Murray drive to the gun shop—actually the crowded cellar of Dutch's home.

Ben realizes that neither he nor his son has ever been in such a place, that it is only his father who would have stumbled on it. He reflects on his own cautious and prescribed life as against his father's disorderly but somehow more real one. Old Murray introduces his grandson to Dutch as a perfectionist, a boy with drive, and then extols Dutch's talents to the others. Ben interrupts to explain the gun's malfunction to Dutch, and old Murray praises Ben's conciseness, an ability, he says, which he did not inherit from his father.

As Dutch works on the gun, old Murray begins to tell another customer, Reiner, of young Murray's prowess at sailing, golfing, and skiing. His grandson loves competition, he states, a trait he did not get either from his father or from his grandfather. He voices regret that he could not teach Ben the ability to work with his hands and adds that Ben should have had Dutch as his father. Reiner, a gun lover, tells young Murray bloody stories of Vietnam and of bullets that could tear a man to pieces. Dutch finishes his repair and asks two dollars for the job. Ben protests that it is too little, but his father intervenes, saying that no amount of money can pay for the kind of talent Dutch has.

In the car on the way home, old Murray mentions that Reiner had been in the Navy but, like himself, had not seen combat. As he talks, his voice sounds tired and Ben hopes they have not exhausted his father. Old Murray replies that that is what he is for. Once home, Ben tries to explain the evening to Sally and tells her the shop "smelled of death." He thinks it may have frightened young Murray. In bed, he dreams of himself as a boy killing a bird and awakes to realize it had occurred exactly as he dreamed. He thinks that he has never forgiven himself for the bird's death.

That morning, he and young Murray again take the gun to the field. There, the story states, the dream continues. Although Ben concentrates fully, he cannot hit the cans and bottles used as targets. The bullets seem to go right through them. When young Murray fires, however, the cans leap and the bottles break. Ben yells, "You're killing me!" and then laughs in "pride and relief."

### Themes and Meanings

A familiar theme of John Updike's work is the relationship between generations, particularly the ambivalent feelings of fathers and sons: the combination of guilt, pride, rivalry, and inadequacy. It is clear that Ben feels inadequate both as a father and as a son. In his role as son, he has not been quite what he thinks his father wanted: He does not work with his hands and he does not have the drive that his father sees in young Murray. He has led a cautious, orderly life, never exposing himself in the way his father does. He recognizes that the traits his father praises in young Murray are not inherited from him. As a father, he feels he has not done his job: "to impart the taste of the world" to his son. In paying for Murray's golf lessons or skiing instruction, he has simply purchased amusements for the boy. It is his father, not he, who finds a way to get the rifle fixed on Thanksgiving Day. Similarly, old Murray feels inadequate in his role as a father. He thinks Dutch would have given Ben something more.

On the other hand, although fathers and sons may feel inadequate, they also have a sense of rivalry. Young Murray's threat to kill his father may have been the result of a childish tantrum, but it also expresses the resentment of the younger generation toward the domination of the older one. Sally frequently sides with young Murray, telling Ben that he is too hard on the boy, a suggestion that the hostility young Murray feels may be more than childishness. This rivalry, though, can bring about guilt. When Sally warns Ben to be easier on their son, he replies that his father was nice to him and it only gained old Murray "chest pains. A pain in the old bazoo."

There is a sense, however, in which the rivalry is natural and right. When Ben asks his father if they have worn him out, old Murray says, "That's what I'm here for. . . . We aim to serve." Sons should surpass fathers, and it is the job of fathers to make that possible. Thus, at the end of the story, when Ben shouts that young Murray is killing him, he refers not only to his son's marksmanship but to the larger rivalry as well. The relief he feels may come partly from the fact that the killing is metaphoric, that he is being beaten in a contest. The mingling of pride and relief suggests, however, that he is joyful that young Murray can defeat him. He is proud and relieved that his son is a better man than he.

*Style and Technique*

As in his other stories and novels, Updike here uses images and scenes that are literal and evoke a strong sense of physical reality while at the same time having symbolic resonance. The gun shop itself is particularized with its "cardboard cartons, old chairs and sofas from the Goodwill, a refrigerator, stacked newspapers, shoot posters, and rifle racks." It is also, however, a symbol of adventure and death. Going down into the cellar gun shop, Ben moves into a world that seems not only more disorderly and less safe than his own but also closer to reality. He views Dutch as a man who can "descend into the hard heart of things." Although both Ben and his father are sorry that young Murray has heard Reiner's gory tales, this knowledge of mortality seems necessary for growth and success. In the images used at the end of the story, Ben cannot hit the targets even though he "aimed so carefully his open eye burned." On the other hand, the boy's success comes through his "murderous concentration."

The dialogue is natural and realistic while also conveying more than characters sometimes know. Talking to Dutch, old Murray says of Ben, "My biggest regret is I couldn't teach him the pleasure of working with your hands." The change of person represented by "your" is a typical linguistic error, but it also suggests Murray's wish that his son had Dutch's hands. Throughout the story, Updike draws out the deeper meanings of a realistic surface texture.

*Larry L. Stewart*

# GUSEV

*Author:* Anton Chekhov (1860-1904)
*Type of plot:* Character study
*Time of plot:* 1890
*Locale:* A ship at sea
*First published:* 1890 (English translation, 1917)

> *Principal characters:*
> PAVEL IVANYCH, an intellectual civilian
> GUSEV, a peasant soldier

## The Story

Anton Chekhov's brief tale traces the thoughts and interactions of two sick men being transported in a ship infirmary from the Far East back to their native Russia. The first, an intellectual named Pavel Ivanych, delivers several angry speeches in which he criticizes injustice in Russian society. The second, a peasant soldier on an indefinite leave resulting from a severe case of consumption, listens only intermittently to Pavel Ivanych, preferring to think of life in his native village.

With these two characters, Chekhov presents two differing approaches to life. Pavel Ivanych is acutely sensitive to the way that defenseless or unsuspecting individuals can be mistreated by the authorities in Russia. In particular, he rails against the military, finding it disheartening that a man can be uprooted from his home and family and sent thousands of miles away to serve as a mere orderly for some petty officer. He also criticizes the Russian masses themselves, calling them dark, blind, and crushed, too willing to accept whatever they are told. He considers himself, on the other hand, to be "protest personified." Claiming that he always tells people the truth to their faces, he states that he is not afraid of anything, and that he would continue to protest even if he were to be walled up in a cellar. He asserts that he is proud of his reputation as an insufferable person, and he considers this relentless zeal for protest to be real life.

However, while Pavel Ivanych rants on, Gusev ceases to listen to him. Indeed, as Pavel Ivanych concludes one of his fiercer lectures, Gusev pays no attention but rather looks out a porthole and watches Chinese merchants in small boats selling canaries in cages and shouting "It sings! It sings!" This image serves as an ironic commentary on Pavel Ivanych's ineffectual monologue: He, like the caged canaries, seems merely to be singing an empty song. Shortly thereafter, he succumbs to his illness and dies, and his body is buried at sea.

With the death of Pavel Ivanych, Chekhov's focus swings to Gusev. Unlike Pavel Ivanych, Gusev does not concern himself with social injustice. A simple man, he believes folk myths about the natural world: Storms arise, he thinks, because the world has broken loose from its chains. As for his military service, he believes that he has fulfilled his duty without undue hardship, and he finds such a life to be a decent existence. Returning to his homeland, he thinks only of his family and of village life, and he dreams of driving his sleigh across the snowy landscape. However, he too, like Pavel Ivanych, is destined never to reach his homeland. He also dies and is buried at sea. Chekhov describes the process by which Gusev's body is wrapped in canvas and thrown into the water. He follows the corpse as it sinks into the depths, and he notes how a large shark approaches the body and cautiously rips the canvas wrapping from head to toe. Chekhov then turns away from this scene and concludes his tale with a description of the natural landscape, noting how the sky and the sea merge harmoniously in joyous colors with the setting of the sun. In this final scene, the power and majesty of the natural world dwarf the petty concerns of ordinary humans.

## Themes and Meanings

In "Gusev," Chekhov offers two radically opposed views of life and of possible ways to deal with its hardships. He wrote the story on his return voyage from a visit to the Russian penal colony on the Siberian island of Sakhalin, where he had encountered a series of disturbing scenes of human degradation and cruelty. Pavel Ivanych's indignant criticism of social injustice undoubtedly reflects something of Chekhov's own dismay at the prevalence of brutality and evil in the world. However, Pavel Ivanych's protests are strikingly ineffectual. Gusev pays little attention to his words and does not understand very much of what he hears. For his part, Pavel Ivanych does not try very hard to find the appropriate words with which to make an impression on such listeners as Gusev. One wonders whether he would be capable of transforming his negative words into positive deeds; he appears to be content with his role as an insufferable individual—"protest personified." Such an attitude significantly undermines his validity as a spokesman for Chekhov.

In Gusev's character Chekhov presents a potential alternative to Pavel Ivanych's stance of irritated protest: Gusev humbly accepts all that comes his way and appears content with his lot. His calm complacency recalls the positive heroes depicted by Leo Tolstoy in his fiction, and it is likely that Chekhov intended the character to embody, at least in part, the Tolstoyan ideal of passive acceptance. However, the character of Gusev, like that of Pavel Ivanych, contains evident flaws. In his passivity he appears almost subhuman or animalistic; one detects a penchant for mindless violence beneath his veneer of stolid placidity. When looking out the porthole, Gusev sees a corpulent Chinese man in a boat and thinks of bashing the fat man in the neck. Earlier, he had recounted an episode in which he beat four such men simply because they had come into his courtyard.

Neither Pavel Ivanych's posture of angry protest nor Gusev's manner of blind actions strikes the reader as completely satisfying or worthy of emulation. No character in the story serves as an ideal role model for the reader. Instead Chekhov provides a more elusive or suggestive vision of the proper relationship between the human world and the cosmos at large. Shortly before his death, Gusev had looked out at the sea and sky. In the sky he saw bright stars, peace, and quiet, while below lurked darkness and disorder. After Gusev's death, Chekhov notes the beautiful play of light that occurs at sunset, and he concludes "Looking at the magnificent, enchanting sky, the ocean at first frowns, but soon it also takes on tender, joyful, and passionate colors that are difficult even to name with human words." These scenes carry symbolic implications. Like the realm of the sea, the human realm—the world "below"—is dark and disordered. Neither vehement protest nor dull resignation holds out the promise of lasting fulfillment. Rather, one must observe and absorb the mute lessons of nature. Only through a kind of wordless communion with the natural world can one transcend the limitations of the self and attain a measure of peace and joy.

*Style and Technique*

As the final scene of "Gusev" indicates, Chekhov often utilizes symbolic descriptions to convey implicit messages to his reader. Nature descriptions in particular play an important role in shaping the reader's understanding of the author's designs. The vastness of the natural world and its indifference to the everyday travails of human life are evoked by Chekhov's choice of the seas as the setting for his story and his inclusion of the scene in which the shark casually tears open the canvas sack containing Gusev's body. Similarly, the recurring image of a huge bull's head without eyes that Gusev sees in his daydreams of home serves to underscore his own primitive and animalistic character.

The recurring image of the bull's head itself points to another distinctive feature of Chekhov's narrative technique in "Gusev." His portrait of the peasant provides an interesting blend of internal psychology and external sensory stimuli. To convey the mental state of a man stricken with fever, Chekhov skillfully interweaves Gusev's reveries about his village life with the sounds and sights of his shipboard passage. Things happen on the ship around Gusev without his full knowledge or comprehension. As these sights or sounds penetrate into his consciousness, they at times seem curiously relevant, while at other times they seem chaotic or meaningless. Through this flow of apparently random yet meaningful events, Chekhov highlights the unpredictability and mysteriousness of human existence.

In "Gusev," as in many of his other tales, Chekhov doe not overtly preach to his readers. As he explores possible approaches to life, he creates two characters with contrasting attitudes, and he allows his readers to judge for themselves the merits and drawbacks of each. Avoiding melodrama or bold gestures, he constructs his tale out of small incidents and thereby subtly shapes the readers' perception of events. A master of understatement, Chekhov manages to create a portrait of human experience as nuanced and moving as life itself.

*Julian W. Connolly*

# GUSSUK

*Author:* Mei Mei Evans (1953-    )
*Type of plot:* Social realism
*Time of plot:* The late twentieth century
*Locale:* Kigiak, Alaska
*First published:* 1989

*Principal characters:*
> LUCY, an itinerant Chinese American nurse
> ROBERT, a married Eskimo who is attracted to her
> MERCY, his sister

## The Story

Lucy, an itinerant nurse, arrives in the Eskimo village of Kigiak, Alaska, by bush plane from Anchorage. She is welcomed by Robert and his relatives, who help her settle into a trailer home and into the rhythms of village life. Lucy's period of alienation is mitigated by two factors: her Chinese American features, which resemble those of her Eskimo hosts, and the warm hospitality of her hosts. Although her status as an outsider, a "gussuk," may be mitigated by her own Eskimo-like looks, it is not eliminated. Several times she describes the phenomenon of culture shock and discusses her ambivalent feelings toward her imposing natural surroundings. Lucy's primary concern, however, is being accepted by the locals.

Lucy's trailer is her home, office, and refuge, and a reminder of her transitory status as an outsider. While settling in, she is greeted by Amos and Mary, who become her guides through the Eskimo village. The threesome encounters Robert, Amos and Mary's uncle, who invites the gussuk into his sister Mercy's house. Lucy observes all the ritualistic activities of contemporary Eskimo life, and the sights, sounds, and smells peculiar to the setting: Mercy's toothless grin, the scent of seal oil, a creaky table, a paper plate of dried fish, Mercy's polyester slacks.

After a catalog of impressions of nature peculiar to an Eskimo village in the far north—migrating salmon, mosquitoes, muskeg—Robert reappears. Events reach a climax during the annual Fourth of July bash, which ends with Mercy passing out on the floor and Lucy falling drunkenly into bed with Robert. The tensions and differences between Lucy and Robert become apparent. He feels trapped in Kigiak; she is enthralled by it. He is married, she is single. Although each yearns vainly to leave his or her own world, they are headed in opposite directions: Robert returns to Kigiak after a failed attempt to start life anew in Fairbanks; Lucy resolves to return to Boston after her brief stint as an itinerant nurse in the Alaskan bush. She has come to the profound but disquieting realization that she was and always would be a gussuk; she would never belong in Kigiak.

The story concludes with an epilogue set in Anchorage, two years later. Lucy has a chance encounter with a girl named Anna, who claims to be Robert's cousin and to have met her in Kigiak. Anna informs Lucy that Robert drowned the previous year. The story's final lines sound a note of ambiguity, as Anna remarks on Lucy's physical resemblance to Robert, adding a bittersweet touch of irony to this tale of two lovers whose encounter was characterized more by their differences than their similarities.

*Themes and Meanings*

"Gussuk" captures the realities, tensions, conflicts, contradictions, and ambiguities of living in a bicultural borderland. The three principal characters, Lucy, Robert, and Mercy, are all subject to what has been called the tensions of biculturalism. The effects of that tension are manifested in Robert and Lucy, who are moving in opposite directions on the bicultural continuum, although for the same reasons. Both are seeking escape from the culture into which they were born and bred. After a brief sojourn into an alien culture, each returns to his or her home culture. To the question of whether bicultural differences can be overcome between people in general, and particularly between lovers, "Gussuk" answers "No." The cultural gap is too broad to be bridged. Lucy's experience at least has helped her to crystalize her sense of self, of who she is, and, perhaps as important, who she is not.

The lesson, if not bitter, is at least bittersweet. It has been learned, however, making "Gussuk" an initiation story for its narrator. Her eyes, always keen to her surroundings, have been opened even wider. They see things for what they are, even if that vision is unpleasant, and accept them for what they are. "Gussuk" faithfully renders that bittersweet vision. In the final analysis, Lucy's initial resemblance to her native hosts succumbs to her differences from them. When Mercy says that Lucy's predecessor did not belong there, it applies to Lucy as well. She, too, undergoes an abrupt change in attitude relative to her surroundings, realizing as her predecessor must have realized that she would always be a "gussuk," even if she lived there for another fifty years. This is the tough lesson that Lucy, and outsiders like her, must learn through experience. In the last analysis, her naïve idealism is at odds with the reality she encounters, and her need to help others is not as powerful as her need to be among her own.

*Style and Technique*

The finest feature of Mei Mei Evans's style is the realistic tone she deploys to underscore her theme of cultural dissonance. A wealth of details are provided to demystify and deromanticize the experience of going native. Through the narrator's unblinking eyes, readers watch Mercy picking mosquitoes out of seal oil as she cooks, witness the debilitating effects of alcohol, see the saliva leaking from Mercy's mouth after she has passed out, hear her snoring, rasping breath, see the stretch marks on her belly. These details reinforce the realistic treatment of the story's themes, adding a tonal consistency to it. Even Lucy and Robert's sexual encounter is treated more realistically than romantically, for it occurs in a half-remembered alcoholic haze.

Evans's metaphors also heighten the realistic tone of "Gussuk." For example, Mercy's stretch marks are compared to "caterpillar-like trails," while the alcohol that Lucy drinks is "surging against the front of her skull like surf." From the air, the random cluster of houses "looked as though they'd been shaken out like dice."

Sensory details evoke a strong, realistic sense of place. The immediacy of Kigiak is established through the sights, scents, and sounds that Evans captures—whether it is Lucy's ears "vibrating with the drone of the plane," "the cheap acetate curtains" of her "tacky" trailer, or the lopsided, "three-barred cross" atop the Russian Orthodox church that sits alone atop a hill. The density of detail lends an aura of verisimilitude to the writing.

Impressions are entwined with dialogue to capture the singular, remote nature of the setting. The dialogue not only provides information about Lucy's age, marital status, and upbringing but also serves to initiate her into the ways and idioms of her Eskimo hosts. The treatment is more realistic than romantic, as the tensions of bicultural interactions are given free play. For example, when Mercy asks if Lucy is a virgin, Lucy finds the innocent directness of Eskimo curiosity unsettling, and must control her indignation. The scene serves to accentuate the differences that arise from the collision of two cultures.

From the moment Lucy's float plane feathers onto the surface of Lake Kigiak, the reader feels as if he or she has arrived at this singularly Alaskan setting. As a consequence of Evans's effective use of realism, metaphor, and sensory detail, the reader feels as if she or he is walking in the shoes of a gussuk.

*Stephen G. Brown*

# GUY DE MAUPASSANT

*Author:* Isaac Babel (1894-1940)
*Type of plot:* Impressionistic
*Time of plot:* Winter, 1916-1917
*Locale:* St. Petersburg
*First published:* "Giui de Mopassan," 1932 (English translation, 1955)

> *Principal characters:*
> THE NARRATOR, the protagonist, a freelance journalist and story
> writer, twenty years old
> RAISA BENDERSKY, a woman attempting to translate the works of
> Guy de Maupassant into Russian and requiring the assistance
> of the narrator
> BENDERSKY, her husband, a converted Jew and a lawyer, banker,
> and owner of a publishing house

*The Story*

Although unnamed, the protagonist is approximately identical with the author, as the latter was in the winter of 1916-1917: a young Jewish writer from Odessa who has moved to the capital illegally, on the eve of the February Revolution.

The young writer, though poverty-stricken and selling almost nothing he has written, is so supremely confident that he spurns an offer of a job as a clerk. He sees himself as superior to Leo Tolstoy, whose religion was "all fear. He was frightened by the cold, by old age, by death."

The narrator finds acceptable employment when Bendersky's publishing house decides to bring out a new edition of Guy de Maupassant's works; Bendersky's wife, Raisa, has begun some translations, but they are flat and lifeless. The narrator is summoned to assist Raisa; he meets her at the Bendersky mansion on Nevsky Prospect—a habitation decorated in profoundly poor taste. The Benderskys are converted Jews, in consequence of which they have been allowed to grow rich.

The narrator would despise Raisa as he does her husband—"a yellow-faced Jew with a bald skull"—were it not for the fact that he finds her ravishing on first sight (although, it must be admitted, the young man finds all women ravishing, including his forty-year-old washerwoman, Katya). The fact that Raisa is enfolded in pink layers of fat is all to the good—precisely Isaac Babel's type, as readers may know from his other stories.

The narrator meets Raisa daily to go over her translations and to instruct her in literary style. Although Raisa has almost no feeling for style, her redeeming feature is that she recognizes that fact. Additionally to her credit, she declares that Maupassant is the only passion of her life.

Gradually it becomes apparent that the basic plot fine of Babel's story centers on the attempted seduction of Raisa by her new young assistant, who is probably only half her age. As the two become acquainted, the narrator tells stories of his childhood that, to his "amazement turned out to be "very sordid." He frightens Raisa and moves her to pity.

Babel's continuing discussion of Maupassant throughout the story contributes to an ongoing instruction in art and literary style that is central to the work. Maupassant also becomes an element in the plot, however, in that his story "L'Aveau" ("The Confession"), which Raisa and the narrator work on together for a very long time, is retold in some detail. The reader learns that Monsieur Polyte the coachman, who drives red-haired Celeste to market twice a week, continually attempts to seduce Celeste through innuendo and coarse suggestion. Finally, after two years, he succeeds: "What about having some fun today, Mamselle Celeste?" She replies, "I am at your disposal, Monsieur Polyte." It is interesting that Babel describes Celeste, with her "mighty calves in red stockings," almost as he does Raisa, with her "strong soft calves . . . planted wide apart on the carpet." He mentions also that the cart in which Polyte and Celeste make love is pulled by a white mare that keeps on moving forward at a walking pace.

At this point in the narrative, the young writer is full of wine and is alone with Raisa in her big house. He clumsily kisses her, and she recoils. She pushes him into a far-away chair, but he suddenly lunges for her, knocking all twenty-nine volumes of Maupassant off a shelf.

The reader is not told explicitly what happens next. After the books fall to the floor, however, the narrator remarks "and the white mare of my fate went on at a walking pace"—an obvious reference to "The Confession." The reader also learns that the young man has spent enough additional time at the Bendersky house to become sober. He leaves for home near midnight, wonderfully happy, swaying from side to side (though sober) and singing in a language that he has "just invented." It is impossible not to conclude from this joyful epiphany (added to the earlier evidence) that the seduction has occurred.

The story requires this seduction so that the conclusion, presented as contrast, may be better appreciated. The young man spends the rest of the night reading a biography of Maupassant; he learns that the great writer died insane, from syphilis, at age forty-two, crawling on his hands and knees and "devouring his own excrement." The young writer looks out the window at the morning fog, perceiving that the world is hidden from him and realizing that there is much more for him to learn in life.

### Themes and Meanings

The ending of "Guy de Maupassant" is significant for several reasons. First, it marks the transition of the young writer from a state of cockiness and overconfidence (recall his disdain as a "young genius" for Tolstoy) to one of doubt and anxiety. The author writes, "My heart contracted as the foreboding of some essential truth touched me with fight fingers." This truth includes the understanding that great art is seldom achieved without great suffering: The young man now realizes the full implication of his choice of writing as a career.

In general, the story treats the theme of illusion seen against the truth of life. The narrator's roommate, Kazantsev, lives in an imaginary Spain—his permanent escape from the St. Petersburg snows. Raisa's one passion is Maupassant. Though Babel "forgives" Raisa this, he has little use for the whole Bendersky clan, who have deceived themselves into believing that by worshiping Jesus they will escape Russian anti-Semitism and get to keep their money, too. Babel's disdain for such converted Jews is nicely contained in the narrator's remark about Raisa after she has pressed herself against the wall and "stretched out her arms": "Of all the gods ever put on the crucifix, this was the most ravishing."

The theme of illusion contrasted with truth also occurs in the dream of the young writer about Katya, the washerwoman: In the dream they do "godawful things together" and almost "destroyed each other with kisses." In the morning, however, he sees a "wan woman" with "ash-gray hair" and "laborworn" hands. The young man also has sexual fantasies about Raisa's maid. Probably the treatment of sex in this story is meant to be positive: Sex, passion, and love are essential to life and must be seized with zest and joy. This is not all of life, however: hence, the somber ending. However, the ending should not be read as a puritanical, Tolstoyan castigation of Maupassant (or the narrator) for sexual promiscuity.

"Guy de Maupassant" is famous for its observations on literary style. The narrator (clearly speaking for the mature Babel) declares: "A phrase is born into the world both good and bad at the same time. The secret lies in a slight, an almost invisible twist. The lever should rest in your hand, getting warm, and you can only turn it once, not twice." Then, in speaking of style to Raisa, the young writer asserts, "No iron can stab the heart with such force as a period put just at the right place."

*Style and Technique*

The remarks on style quoted earlier reflect the author's attitude toward his own writing. His story is like an icon painted with perfect phrases.

In describing the stairway of the Bendersky mansion, Babel writes: "On the landings, upon their hind legs, stood plush bears. Crystal lamps burned in their open mouths." Avoiding all authorial commentary, Babel gives the reader in seventeen words a perfect description of nouveau-riche bad taste. (The word for this in Russian is *poshlost'*; in German, *kitsch*.) Babel's effectiveness as a writer owes much to his laconism and detachment.

The author's treatment of the sexual theme is enhanced by repetition, until the whole story seems suffused with sexual imagery—as is the inside of the young writer's head. Three times a Bendersky servant is described as "the high-breasted maid." "In her open gray eyes," writes Babel, "one saw a petrified lewdness." The narrator imagines that she makes love with an "unheard-of agility." There is often exaggeration, humor, and vivid color in Babel's images: The narrator and his friends get "as drunk as a flock of drugged geese." The dinners at the Bendersky house are always noisy: "It was a Jewish noise, rolling and tripping and ending up on a melodious singsong note."

Maupassant and the narrator's tale are linked by a motif using images of the sun. In referring to the twenty-nine volumes of Maupassant's collected works, Babel writes: "The sun with its fingers of melting dissolution touched the morocco backs of the books—the magnificent grave of a human heart." When the story "The Confession" is retold, Babel informs the reader that "the sun is the hero of this story": Molten drops of it patter on the red-haired Celeste. When she and Polyte make love, "the gay sun of France pours down on the ancient coach."

Although the closing summary of Maupassant's life is both frightening and repellent, one must balance it against a compelling image of the writer's greatness: Earlier, the narrator refers to the set of Maupassant's works as "twenty-nine bombs stuffed with pity, genius and passion."

*Donald M. Fiene*

# HAIRCUT

*Author:* Ring Lardner (1885-1933)
*Type of plot:* Social realism
*Time of plot:* The 1920's
*Locale:* A small, unnamed town in Michigan
*First published:* 1925

> *Principal characters:*
> DICK, the barber and narrator
> DOC RALPH STAIR, a doctor and coroner
> JIM KENDALL, the town practical joker
> PAUL DICKSON, a mentally retarded boy
> JULIE GREGG, a young, sophisticated woman in love with Doc
> Stair

*The Story*

"Haircut" takes its title from the frame story, in which a barber is talking to a stranger in town as he cuts his hair. The barber is a naïve narrator who does not grasp the full impact of the story that he is telling. His narration concerns the town practical joker, Jim Kendall, who was recently killed in what everyone supposes was an accident.

The barber is a typical resident of a small, unnamed Michigan town near Carterville, who is telling the newcomer how, in his opinion, the liveliness of the town has diminished since the demise of Jim Kendall, whose shaving mug the barber still keeps on the shelf. He begins to illustrate Jim's sense of humor by relating some of the practical jokes that Jim played, such as sending letters to men whose names he would see on signs of establishments in the towns that he passed through on the train. In the letters, he hinted that their wives were being unfaithful. The barber then fills in Jim's background, describing how Jim lost his sales job and was reduced to taking odd jobs around town, spending most of what he earned on drink. Then, when his wife began trying to collect his salary before he got to it, he began borrowing against his wages in order to foil her plan, and, the barber adds, Jim punished her by inviting her and their two children to the circus, where he left them waiting at the tent entrance and never appeared with the tickets.

At this point in the narrative, the barber tells of how Doc Stair, a new doctor in the town, saw them and paid their way into the circus, thus incurring the enmity of Jim. The barber then describes how Doc Stair came to town and gradually built up a good practice, and how he was very lenient with those who could not pay their bills. He relates how the doctor became coroner when the old coroner died because he was the type of person who could not refuse when asked to do a favor.

He then relates the background of another town resident, Paul Dickson, who received a head injury when he was ten years old and is slightly retarded, and who was a frequent butt of Jim Kendall's practical jokes. Because of these jokes, the barber says, Paul has nothing to do with most people except Doc Stair and Julie Gregg, the only two residents of the town who show him kindness. This thought leads him to relate how Julie Gregg fell in love with Doc Stair when she took her invalid mother in to see him.

The plot of the central incident begins as the barber tells of Jim Kendall's attempt to rape Julie. After she called the marshal, Jim decided to revenge himself on her by playing one of his tricks. At a time when he knew that Doc Stair was out of town, he phoned her, disguising his voice as the doctor's, and asked her to come and see him. When she arrived at the doctor's office and called for him, Jim and all of his friends, who were hiding under the stairs, came out, shouting and ridiculing her.

The barber says that later, when Jim came looking for someone with whom to go duck shooting, Paul Dickson volunteered to join him. According to the barber, Paul accidentally shot Jim in the boat while handling a gun for the first time in his life. He ends his tale by saying that it was probably Jim's fault for letting a "half-wit" use a gun with which he was not familiar, but he adds that the town certainly misses Jim Kendall. The barber has ignored the fact that Paul acted deliberately after Doc Stair had told Paul that a person who would play such a trick on a person such as Julie "ought not to be let live."

## Themes and Meanings

The real meaning of "Haircut" is conveyed as the reader begins to understand the situation in the small town as told, but not understood, by the barber. The barber is insensitive and imperceptive. His recounting of the crude jokes told in his barbershop, which are the counterparts of the cruel tricks played by Jim Kendall, and his appreciation of those jokes, shows his insensitivity. He speaks of Jim as being the life of the town who is sorely missed rather than as the sadistic, violent, and insensitive bully he really was.

Ring Lardner is satirizing the smug values of people who live in isolated, small communities (and, by extension, any closed community in which evil is condoned). Although the barber seems to believe that his town is unique in having an entertaining practical joker, he is unaware of how typical a character such as Jim Kendall is and how many other towns are populated by Jim Kendalls. By not recognizing the cruelty that lurked beneath the surface of the tricks played by Jim Kendall, the barber, in a sense, is vicariously participating in it. His appreciation of Jim Kendall's not-so-amusing stories and practical jokes stems from his own insensitivity, ignorance, and latent cruelty.

The theme is conveyed by the dramatic irony of the narrator's thickheaded obliviousness to the cruelty perpetrated by Kendall, and the shock at the end when it becomes apparent that Paul Dickson deliberately killed Kendall. The barber, although he has access to all the facts, fails to put these details together or to realize that the shooting was anything but accidental.

The primary effect of the story is to shock the reader with the realization of what has been called "the banality of evil." Jim Kendall, who is in reality a sadistic person- ality, is described by the barber as being "all right at heart, but just bubblin' over with mischief." Evil can often be ignored or rationalized, especially when it is condoned or explained away by "good" people.

*Style and Technique*

The primary technique employed in this story is the use of irony in having an im- perceptive, naïve narrator relate a story, the impact of which he fails to understand himself. This frame story maintains some subtlety in what would otherwise be a fairly obvious tale about a cruel, mean-spirited character who gets the punishment that he deserves.

Lardner's story is related through the use of a dramatic monologue; the barber is the only character who speaks. The full setting and the understanding that the customer in his chair is a stranger in town become clear entirely through the barber's conversation. Through his speech, the barber shows himself to be a rather crude, unintelligent, and insensitive observer. He narrates the events in a fashion sympathetic to the jokester, without analyzing or commenting on them except to indicate how amusing he thought all of Jim Kendall's jokes were.

The entire narration is in a consistent conversational tone typifying a small-town man. The diction, syntax, and pronunciation show the narrator to be provincial and uneducated. For example, he says, "I bet they was more laughin' done here than any town its size in America," and "he'd be settin' in this chair part of the time," and "she'd of divorced him only they wasn't no chance to get alimony and she didn't have no way to take care of herself and the kids. She couldn't never understand Jim." Such lan- guage (at which Lardner was especially skilled), along with the observations and in- terpretations of the barber, juxtaposed to the obvious cruelty of the tricks played, make the reader aware of the unreliability of the speaker and heighten the impact of the events narrated.

*Roger Geimer*

# THE HALF-SKINNED STEER

*Author:* E. Annie Proulx (1935-    )
*Type of plot:* Domestic realism, regional, frame story
*Time of plot:* The 1990's
*Locale:* Rural Wyoming
*First published:* 1997

*Principal characters:*
MERO, an elderly man, who sets out for Wyoming
ROLLO, his brother, whose death prompts his journey
TIN HEAD, character in a story that Mero remembers

*The Story*

"The Half-Skinned Steer" is told in the third person with frequent flashbacks that reveal various memories of Mero. The flashbacks function as a story-within-a-story, with the girlfriend of Mero's father serving as the narrative voice of those portions of the larger story. The action is both internal and external, either occurring on or resulting from Mero's journey to Wyoming to witness the burial of his brother.

Mero and Rollo were raised on an impoverished ranch in rural Wyoming. Mero left the ranch to go to war, then eventually permanently left his place of origin, settling in Massachusetts and living a lifestyle quite different from that of his brother, who continued to ranch with his son and family.

The story is set in motion when the eighty-three-year-old Mero receives a phone call and learns of his brother's death. He begins an adventurous drive across country during which he rarely eats, wrecks his Cadillac, and buys another one. The journey provides an opportunity for internal action that reveals the subtle conflicts within Mero. He reminisces about his youthful interactions with his father and brother on the ranch. He also recalls a particular story he was told about Tin Head, who had the misfortune of having a galvanized plate sewn into his head. While butchering a steer, Tin Head pauses halfway into the job to eat half of his dinner before taking a nap. When he awakes, the steer is gone. Eventually Tin Head finds the half-skinned steer alive and vindictively staring at his would-be butcher.

In the process of remembering his younger days, as well as the saga of Tin Head and the steer, Mero arrives in the Wyoming countryside near his boyhood home. He drives the last miles through snow. Not having been to the old place in sixty years and arriving at night, he cannot remember the right road. His unfamiliar car becomes stuck in the snow, and Mero becomes disoriented. Confused, hungry, and disappointed in his failure, he finds himself in a serious predicament in the middle of nowhere. He finally decides to try to walk some ten miles to a ranch he believes he can find and then wait until morning to complete his odyssey. As he walks in the snow, a steer follows him. Mero dies in the snow under the angry glare of the half-skinned steer's red eye.

*Themes and Meanings*

As is common in E. Annie Proulx's stories, landscape plays a critical role. In this story, the rural setting in the foothills of the Big Horns is a powerful force that contributes to the main character's demise. Mero had long ago abandoned this harsh environment, but he naturally feels compelled to return on receiving the news of his brother's death. The landscape theme becomes pronounced as the story reaches its climactic moment. The environment kills Mero as he struggles to find shelter from the snow. The plight of a struggling human in the midst of an indifferent and dangerous landscape hearkens back to the works of naturalist writers of the late nineteenth century such as Stephen Crane and Jack London. Mero's conflict, like the conflicts in many of the naturalists' stories, suggests a human struggle against ominous environmental forces in which survival is largely a matter of chance.

Another important theme in the story is the notion of returning home. Mero has been away sixty years, but the story is framed with his origins and death in the harsh West. Apparently, Mero abandoned the poverty of his ranching family to reinvent himself in an eastern urban setting, but the compulsion to see his brother causes him to return to his place of origin and former life.

The story also suggests that life is a journey, and the episodes encountered along the road define human character and destiny. The related theme of unfinished business is expressed through the tale of the steer. The story hints that there are unpleasant consequences for not finishing jobs, for quitting before the appropriate time.

In a more pessimistic existential sense, the story puts forth the idea that human activity is essentially futile when the greater context of imminent death is considered. Mero cannot evade the symbolic steer, just as one cannot evade death. Attempts at redefining oneself are, in the end, relatively pointless or at least temporary and therefore limited.

These themes correlate with the implied theme of brothers living united in purpose and spirit. Though the story does not reveal any overt antipathy between Rollo and Mero, they have lived in separation from each other. Rollo had intended to one day check up on Mero, but he did not fulfill that intention. In the end, this separation is problematic.

*Style and Technique*

The story opens with a general overview of the history and lineage of the Wyoming family, then describes the particular events and ideas linked to the general opening. Proulx packs a lot of information into a short amount of space, but the background information allows for the themes to be carried out in a deeply meaningful way because readers can see and appreciate the biological and sociological connections inherent to the characterization and plot.

Proulx's story makes infrequent but effective use of dialogue. There is some exchange between Mero and his niece, who informs him of Rollo's death. There is also effective use of dialogue in the flashback memories when the narrator of those flashbacks converses with Mero.

Proulx's use of flashback reveals a stream of consciousness within Mero, and it is strikingly effective for a story about an old man driving across country on such an occasion. People tend to recall things not frequently thought of when driving along and feeling the hypnotic rhythm of the tires meeting the pavement. This phenomenon is certainly accentuated when people are traveling to a funeral, where introspection and contemplation of one's time and place in the world are significantly pronounced.

The author also uses the story-within-a-story technique (one story in the present and the other in memory), with the effect that one story foils the other. In the end, Mero's unfinished business is not unrelated to Tin Head's unfinished business. Proulx then unifies the two stories by the mythic symbol suggested by the half-skinned steer. The animal in the flashback exists in myth and legend, and when Mero dies at the end of his journey, the same steer is following him. The wounded animal is a bloody reminder of the consequences of unfinished business and of the violent and vindictive qualities of living and dying. The glaring red eye suggests the human inability to escape fate. The transitory nature of life and the certainty of death are confirmed by the animal's all-seeing presence.

The journey theme seems to be a postmodern odyssey in which an apparently self-satisfied, estranged brother attempts to redeem his absence from his brother's life by making a problematic cross-country journey. The end of Mero's travels indicates the ultimate passing of life into death.

The journey also reverses the direction of the archetypal westward movement. Especially in the American frontier, the movement has been from the civilized east to the untamed west. In this story, the journey opposes that formula, with Mero leaving home and traveling east to establish his identity.

Proulx employs what might be described as a brutal lyricism by her word usage and imagery. The implied beauty of the landscape is terrifying and unforgiving. She is sometimes innovative, using language harshly to parallel her harsh themes, as in the following constructions: "dotting around on a cane," "goggling at her bloody bitten fingers," "the damnedest curl to his hat brim," "twitched the wheel," and "sheeted off him like water."

*Kenneth Hada*

# THE HALFWAY DINER

*Author:* John Sayles (1950-     )
*Type of plot:* Social realism
*Time of plot:* The late twentieth century
*Locale:* An arid region of the southern United States
*First published:* 1987

>            *Principal characters:*
>            LOURDES, the narrator, the wife of a prison inmate
>            LEE, a passenger on the bus
>            DELPHINE, a passenger and friend of Lee's
>            MRS. TUCKER, the eldest passenger
>            PAM, a newcomer to the bus

*The Story*

A group of women, diverse in age and ethnicity, travel by bus each weekend to visit their husbands and lovers in prison. Their round-trip journey takes twelve hours, and they are allowed only one hour of visiting time. Spending more time traveling than visiting, they get to know one another better than they know their men.

As the women board for departure, Lourdes notices Pam, a young blond, visibly anxious in her search for a seat. Lourdes, a Mexican American, sarcastically refers to Pam as Goldilocks but is kind enough to warn Pam against her first choice: Renee's usual seat. Renee travels with a display case of cosmetics to sell to her companions; her seat also serves as her place of business.

Lourdes offers Pam the seat by her own. Their ensuing dialogue sketches a portrait of prison wife etiquette—for example, it is allowable to ask the length of a man's sentence, but to ask what his crime was is considered too personal. Lourdes introduces others as they arrive, such as Mrs. Tucker, who has traveled this route every weekend for thirty years, and Lee and Delphine, two nurses who enjoy an atypical crossracial friendship. In a big-sisterly way, Lourdes is amused by Pam's naïveté and enjoys the diversion that she offers from the tedium of the long bus ride. There are awkward stretches of silence, however, and when the bus stops for lunch, there is a noticeable air of relief.

The Halfway Diner takes its name from the motto of its owner, Elvira: "Everyplace on earth is halfway between somewhere and somewhere else." The diner is halfway between the prison and the women's point of departure, and the bus routinely stops there en route and on return. It is a typical, 1950's-style eatery located on a lonely stretch of desert highway. Elvira welcomes the sudden onslaught of customers to her otherwise sparsely occupied diner. She knows everyone except Pam by name, shuffling them through the process of ordering lunch like a gum-snapping schoolmarm. Pam has brought sandwiches for her husband, which Lourdes tells her she will not be allowed to give him. Instead of eating them herself, she follows the crowd in ordering from the menu by number.

During the prison visit, everyone but Pam learns that Lee's husband has stabbed Delphine's husband in a racially motivated fight the previous day. The return trip is rife with tension, as Lee and Delphine avoid each other so conspicuously as to effect an overall chill. Disappointed to find Lee sitting next to Lourdes, Pam takes the seat beside Delphine. She wants to talk about her impressions of the prison, but Delphine snaps that she is not interested in her problems. The bus ride continues in silence until reaching the Halfway Diner. Pam is relieved to be able to sit with Lourdes again at the restaurant, and finally to be told the reason for everyone's tense behavior.

Mrs. Tucker suddenly collapses, and it is up to Lee and Delphine to deal with the emergency until an ambulance arrives. Once the situation is under control, everyone reboards for the final leg of the trip. Lee and Delphine take their normal places beside each other, while Pam and Lourdes are also reunited, directly behind them. An air of apparent normalcy resumes between them, along with a deflated sense of resignation that they are not ultimately friends in any normal way, that perhaps they are no more than two nurses estranged from their petty criminal husbands.

## Themes and Meanings

Friendship, trust, intimacy, and the need for protection from emotional injuries are pervasive elements in John Sayles's story. Each of its women has fallen in love with a man whose crimes have made her life harsh and problematic. Like their male counterparts, the women are mistrustful of, yet finally dependent on, one another. Lourdes excuses the act of taking a newcomer under her wing by claiming boredom, but through Pam, sees her own first visit four years earlier. She too had feared that the other women would be radically different, former convicts themselves and capable of the prison violence they constantly discuss. Pam, like Lourdes, however, will eventually adapt.

The relationship between Lee and Delphine is the closest to an actual friendship, although Delphine is African American and Lee is another goldilocks. Ethnic barriers here are not strict but still exist. Whites, Hispanics, and blacks occupy the front, middle, and rear sections of the bus, respectively. Sharing their careers, Lee and Delphine discover more common ground as they pass the time comparing notes on marriage and disastrous honeymoons, and knowing the emptiness of it, they continually promise to socialize as couples when their husbands return to them. It appears that Lee and Delphine could enjoy a more conventional friendship were it not for the strict racial barriers dividing their husbands. It is as if they are dutybound by marriage to mirror the antagonism that exists between their husbands.

That Lee and Delphine can heal their rift is a small triumph for all the passengers. As Mrs. Tucker has shown them a glimpse of the austere road ahead, Lee and Delphine prove that they are not so accountable for their husbands' mistakes as it seems. Although their men must adhere to an aberrant code of prison ethics, it is no fault of the wives, and the price the women must pay need not be as steep.

Pam and Lourdes appear to be on the road to forming a bond similar to Lee and Delphine's, even with the notion that white-versus-Hispanic violence is as possible between their husbands as the white-versus-black violence between Lee's and Delphine's. These sisterly bonds are finally stronger than those of their long-distance marriages. As Lourdes suggests, "If there's life in hell this is what the field trips are like."

*Style and Technique*

It has been noted that Sayles's work, both as filmmaker and writer, is remarkable for creating community as character. This work is a clear example. It is a story that places its characters on particularly common ground. The totemic sense of territory is remarkably like that of a school bus. One may come to know Lourdes most closely in her role as narrator, but she is no more or less changed by the story's turns of event than anyone else. Even Lee and Delphine are little changed by the resonance of their husbands' fight. They are simply shaken momentarily by the realization of a possibility they knew existed all along.

Mrs. Tucker's apparent stroke is the catalyst for thawing the chill that arises between Lee and Delphine. They must work together as nurses to keep the older woman alive until the ambulance arrives, a reminder of their striking similarities. It is also a reminder to all that any one of them could easily find herself alone in thirty years, having a stroke in a remote eatery, hanging on to a marriage that has long since ceased to be a marriage.

Because it is Delphine who breaks the silence, tentatively urging Lee to continue the story she had been telling earlier about her honeymoon, their prior tension is eased more effectively for her husband's having been the injured party. It is as if losing her closest traveling companion could only make the news of her husband's injury that much more difficult.

Voice is a main factor in creating this story's character distinctions as well as its atmospheric sense of narrative. Lourdes's voice, the narrative voice, is one of colloquial eloquence. A highly educated woman would be noticeably out of place in this group, as the dialogue throughout proves. Sayles's keen ear for voices makes for a trustworthy, working-class sense of narrative. Lourdes breaks into Spanish at appropriate turns, without making undue demands on readers who are not bilingual. Although she may talk tough, the unselfishness of her actions and the clarity of her observations create the appeal of a benevolent journalist.

As in other works by Sayles, the peaks and valleys of dramatic tension in "The Halfway Diner" are intensified by an underlying sense of understatement. The narrator's editorial eye has much to focus on, and the matters of Mrs. Tucker's stroke as well as Lee and Delphine's rift are taken and spoken of in stride. The power of the story lies in the juxtaposition of a deceptively ordinary voice and the simple yet extraordinary tale it has to tell.

*Jon Lavieri*

# HAMLET OF THE SHCHIGROVSKY DISTRICT

*Author:* Ivan Turgenev (1818-1883)
*Type of plot:* Sketch
*Time of plot:* The 1840's
*Locale:* A backwater village in the Shchigrovsky District of Russia
*First published:* "Gamlet Shchigrovskogo uezda," 1849 (English translation, 1855)

*Principal characters:*
> THE SPORTSMAN, the narrator and assumed voice of the writer, a traveling hunter
> VASILY VASILYCH, the main character, an embittered, poor landowner
> PYOTR PETROVICH LUPIKHIN, the sharp-tongued village wit

## The Story

The first-person narrator begins this story by establishing a frank and straightforward camaraderie with his audience. A well-mannered, cultured, and polite man, the narrator informs his readers that he had, on one of his hunting trips, been invited to a dinner party that was given by one Alexander Mikhailych. The host's surname is unimportant. A minor character, he is a representative of his class: a small-minded, provincial landowner who nearly starves his guests because he must wait for the arrival of an important dignitary.

Using the party as a vehicle to satirize provincial aristocracy, the narrator gives a blow-by-blow account of the evening's festivities: when he arrived, how he was greeted, who was there and what was said. He minutely details how he watched the provincials playing cards, their stomachs drooping over the tables; how he nearly fell asleep; and how he was first whisked away by Voinitsyn, a college failure, and then by Pyotr Lupikhin, the local satirist. This traveling hunter is far too reserved and polished to direct more than a subtle, pointed attack on what he witnessed. In this story he uses first Lupikhin and then Vasily Vasilych as mouthpieces for broad, virulent satire.

Lupikhin mocks the pageant of landowners who parade in front of him: They are a fat, ignorant lot, and Lupikhin sees them as so many animals. One is said to be "as stupid as a couple of merchants' horses"; another is described as a sly predator, "stealing along by the wall, glancing all around him like a veritable wolf."

While pleading disgust and claiming that it is hardly necessary for him to describe such a dinner, the narrator, humorously enough, describes it anyway. He captures snapshots of hypocritical stances: The boorish landowners, attempting to appear sophisticated, wear French manners as one wears a tight girdle. The tardy dignitary graces his fellow guests with a high-sounding after-dinner speech; this high official's remarks are as fatuous as the philosophizing of William Shakespeare's Polonius.

The party described, the narrator slowly moves toward the core of his story. Something happened that evening, he tells his readers, that made the party worth mentioning: He met "a certain remarkable person." This is where the story-within-a-story begins. In a thoroughly unappealing room, the narrator meets one Vasily Vasilych. The latter, seeing that the narrator cannot sleep just as he cannot, begins a long dramatic monologue on the story of his life: the circumstances of his birth, his mama's efforts to educate her boy of the steppes, and his foolish boyhood. What Vasily Vasilych reiterates, in this confessional tirade, is his awareness of his mediocrity. He knows that, like everyone else, he lacks originality. He differs from those pretentious party guests only in that he knows that he is common; he suffers, Vasily Vasilych tells the narrator (and the narrator retells his readers) because he is sensitive to his condition.

Who knows what one will say in the middle of the night, in a strange house, to a bedfellow who is a complete stranger whom one will never see again? The narrator, merely acting as a drum on which Vasily Vasilych beats, documents a moment in time. It is a moment in which he is placed in a situation wherein he hears the most pitiful of stories from a man who really is not remarkable. Really, the narrator implies, Vasily Vasilych is a man of his time, a man of his place, a representative of his generation.

Vasily Vasilych recounts how he came to be fully repulsed by his very being. One day he was accosted by a local inspector for not repairing his bridge. A conversation ensued, in which the poor landowner derided a certain party who was running for office. The inspector chided Vasily Vasilych, saying that persons of no consequence such as the two of them have no business passing judgment on the higher-ups. Vasily Vasilych, a man who is consumed by self-hatred and an abject sense of smallness, relates how he retreated into his room, scrutinized his face in the mirror, then, slowly, stuck out his tongue at his own reflection.

Interrupted by a sleepy, irritated neighbor, the main character sheepishly hides beneath the bedding. When the narrator presses him at least to state his full name, he alludes to another self-absorbed man, a man who is fated to live and die in a rotten world: the prince in Shakespeare's *Hamlet, Prince of Denmark* (c. 1600-1601): "But if you earnestly want to give me some kind of title, then call me . . . call me Hamlet of the Shchigrovsky District. There are many such Hamlets in every district."

### Themes and Meanings

Hamletism, both in the Russian people and in an individual's personality, was an issue that Ivan Turgenev explored, initially in his early sketches and later in his novels. In 1860, Turgenev actually gave a lecture entitled "Hamlet and Don Quixote," in which he delineated two basic personality types. In "Hamlet of the Shchigrovsky District," Vasily Vasilych utters what became the subtext for some of the author's later characters: those highly sensitive, cultured intellectuals who cry out against the petty conventions of their fathers yet ultimately succumb to these very same conventions because of a kind of spinelessness—a lack of will. Turgenev's Hamlets, feeling themselves alone in a hostile, corrupt world, rail not only against society but also against themselves. They berate themselves for doing nothing, and they persist in doing nothing. They wear themselves out with philosophical talk, yet they are afraid to act on their words.

Perhaps the people despair that action will ever do any good, or perhaps they lack a kind of faith in human nature. They are cynical, self-deprecating men who thrive on self-pity and who, like Vasily Vasilych, "become reconciled" to their meaninglessness. They will make no mark on their world; they will change nothing; they will blame fate for their failure. They are, according to Turgenev, "superfluous" men.

Turgenev first introduced this type of character into his works because he believed that the youth of Russia was falling into Hamletism. In 1849, the date when "Hamlet of the Shchigrovsky District" was published in a Russian journal called *The Contemporary*, Russia was a country caught between two modes of being. It could no longer remain isolated from Western influence. Napoleon had done the unthinkable: He and his horses and his men had marched on Moscow; whether Russians liked it or not, they felt the imprint of Western ideas. However, Russia, in 1849, was still operating under feudal codes.

Twelve more years would pass before the emancipation of the serfs. The younger generation revolted against the feudal hierarchy. Turgenev, a man influenced by Western ideas, sometimes more at home in Paris than in Russia, advocated change: a slow process of change. He decried the horror of a caste system in which capricious, petty landowners had full power over their serfs. However, he believed that his country's youth were not strong enough to move Russia into a modern age. A man who saw people as either Hamlets (passive intellectuals) or Don Quixotes (blind idealists), Turgenev attacked the younger generation through his creation of these types. The self-pitying Vasily Vasilych is Turgenev's indictment of Russian youth; the petty landowners at the party are caricatures of these youths' fathers.

*Style and Technique*

Written more as a character study than a short story, "Hamlet of the Shchigrovsky District" is one of twenty-five sketches that Turgenev wrote between 1847 and 1851. It was included in Turgenev's first published work, a collection of the most important of these sketches, entitled *Zapiski okhotnika* (1852; *Russian Life in the Interior*, 1855; better known as *A Sportsman's Sketches*, 1932). Each sketch is a minutely detailed portrait of a Russian type: a representative of the kinds of people whom Turgenev met while he hunted through the Russian countryside. The sketches are linked by an objective narrator, a discerning hunter who is able to hear the voices of provincial landowners and peasants, who is able to hear the land and its peasant boys speak; yet this huntsman cannot answer. He is a nearly mute narrator, an instrument on which the people he encounters play a uniquely poignant Russian tune.

Although the role of the narrator in this story is typical of the collection, in other ways this is an atypical piece. It is one of Turgenev's broadest satires; whereas some of Turgenev's sketches, such as "Bezhin Meadow," are poetically descriptive and capture the beauty of the Russian countryside, and others, such as "Khos and Kalinych," document peasant life, this piece concentrates on the landowning class. Dialogue is minimal. Vasily Vasilych's speech, imitative of Hamlet's soliloquies, indicates how form fits meaning: The dramatic monologue is an ideal form for this self-absorbed, overly sensitive man. Although Hamlet directs his words to his audience, Vasily Vasilych uses the narrator (and consequently the reader) as an audience. Not only is Vasilych a Hamlet-type, but also he acts as Hamlet, and the tiny, damp bedroom becomes his stage.

This particular sketch is like the others in Turgenev's first published work, however, in that it captures and holds a moment in time. All the sketches, enduring works of art in their own right, allowed Turgenev a means to perfect his craft.

*Miriam Bat-Ami*

# THE HAMMER OF GOD

*Author:* G. K. Chesterton (1874-1936)
*Type of plot:* Mystery and detective
*Time of plot:* The early twentieth century
*Locale:* The fictitious village of Bohun Beacon, in England
*First published:* 1911

> *Principal characters:*
> FATHER BROWN, a Roman Catholic priest and detective
> THE REVEREND WILFRED BOHUN, the Anglican curate of Bohun Beacon
> COLONEL NORMAN BOHUN, his brother
> SIMEON BARNES, the village blacksmith

## The Story

The Reverend Wilfred Bohun is pleading with his wanton brother, the colonel, to leave the blacksmith's wife alone while the blacksmith is away. Angry at his brother's unrepentant lust, the curate warns him that God may strike him dead and runs into the old Gothic church to pray. Half an hour later, the village cobbler enters the church to tell the curate that his brother is dead. They run out to find Colonel Bohun's corpse stretched out in the courtyard of the smithy, his head smashed in by a small hammer. The local police inspector and doctor are already trying to reconstruct the crime. At first it seems obvious: The blow was so powerful, smashing even the colonel's metal helmet, that only the smith could have delivered it—and the smith, indignantly aware of the colonel's trifling with his wife, had ample motive. The smith, however, is soon cleared by unimpeachable witnesses who place him in the next town at the time of the crime.

The hammer's smallness moves the doctor to guess that the smith's wife killed the colonel. This theory is discarded, however, because the fatal blow was too powerful for her to have dealt. The curate suggests that the village idiot, Mad Joe, might be capable of such a blow. He recalls seeing Mad Joe, the smith's nephew, praying in the chapel just before the murder, and seeing his brother, the colonel, mercilessly teasing the poor soul as he left the chapel.

The only one who does not seem content with the curate's solution to the mystery is Father Brown, who suddenly becomes noticeable in the crowd. When he is alone with Reverend Bohun in the spire of the church, he offers his own solution to the mystery: The murderer is Bohun himself, and the mysterious force that crushed his brother's metal helmet with such a small hammer is a natural one: gravity. Having picked up a hammer while pleading with the colonel at the smithy, Bohun threw it from the top of the belfry onto his brother's head, the acceleration giving the tiny tool tremendous force. Father Brown swears that he will not reveal Bohun's secret but urges him to give himself up, which the curate does immediately.

*Themes and Meanings*

The towering presence of the Gothic church in the hillside village dominates G. K. Chesterton's story, both as an image and as the final key to the mystery. Father Brown explicitly connects the height of the church with the self-perceived spiritual elevations of the various characters. The smith, Simeon Barnes, is presented as a Puritan, a Scots Presbyterian, who condemns the sins of others from the lofty height of his smug sanctity. Barnes's spiritual condescension may be the reason Chesterton names the character "Simeon." The Syrian Christian ascetic St. Simeon Stylites lived atop a sixty-foot pillar of his own construction, from which he preached repentance for sins. Father Brown connects the modern Simeon's self-styled spiritual elevation with the Scottish highlands that produced his brand of Puritanism. "His Scotch religion," says Father Brown, "was made up by men who prayed on hills and high crags, and learnt to look down on the world more than to look up at heaven." He tells this to the Reverend Bohun, hoping that the Protestant curate will make the connection with his own spiritual pride in looking down spiritually on his profligate brother.

At the time Father Brown says this, he is looking down, and notes that from the belfry's height, people below look like insects. The visual perspective symbolizes the spiritual one that makes the murder possible: When one ceases to think of sinners as human, murder becomes more simple for even the most pious. However, the symbolic height of Bohun's spiritual condescension matches the physical height of the church spire, for it is the physical height that gives the falling hammer the power to crush the colonel's skull. The symbolic and literal levels are deftly interconnected in this story.

The connection of spiritual elevation and Gothic architecture is a significant part of Chesterton's thought. In the fifth chapter of his biography of Saint Francis of Assisi, Chesterton describes the saint's spiritual vision as that of a man looking at a medieval cathedral upside down. The very massiveness of the masonry, which right side up gives the viewer a sense of stability, conveys a frightening sense of precariousness upside down. With Francis, Chesterton is making quite a different point: The sense of precariousness leads to an acknowledgement of humanity's radical dependence on God. Nevertheless, the terror of the reversed point of view comes from the same source as the murderous power of the deathblow in "The Hammer of God": the potential energy locked in a massive medieval church.

The Reverend Bohun experiences his own topsy-turvy vision, and Father Brown endeavors to set it right. Chesterton plants the image of inversion when Bohun tells of seeing Mad Joe praying just before the colonel's death. "God knows what he prayed; but with strange folk it is not incredible to suppose that their prayers are all upside down." On first reading, the curate's words sound innocent enough, but they gain a fine irony after Bohun is revealed as the killer. Father Brown makes the curate realize that it is not Mad Joe's theology that is upside down; it is the curate's, if only temporarily. Gothic architecture is intended to make the faithful look up; praying in the spire, the curate momentarily looked down, and as Father Brown put it, "fancied he was God."

*Style and Technique*

Chesterton is a master of the aphoristic style, weaving his philosophical and theological ideas into brief, readily quotable aphorisms that pepper all of his writings, fiction and nonfiction alike. "The Hammer of God" abounds in terse, well-crafted sentences that can stand on their own as proverbs: "Few except the poor preserve traditions"; "No man is such a legalist as the good Secularist"; "Heights were made to be looked at, not to be looked from"; "Humility is the mother of giants"; "I am a man . . . and therefore have all devils in my heart." However, despite the proverbial quality of each of these sentences, they are not merely decoration; each is essentially integrated into the story at the point at which it appears. Each strikes the reader not only as a well-turned phrase but also as just the right thing to say at that moment to capture what is happening in the story.

Chesterton's Father Brown stories always express theological ideas, yet, like his aphorisms, they are so well integrated into the story that they seldom intrude as mere didacticism or preaching. The religious theme within "The Hammer of God" is expressed through his characterizations by theological types. Readers first encounter two extremes in the brothers Bohun: the pious Wilfred and the prodigal Norman. When Gibbs the cobbler enters with the news of the murder, he is described as an atheist. His atheism is no extraneous matter: It is necessary to present a counterbalancing skepticism to Barnes's supernatural explanation of Colonel Bohun's death. When the prime suspect Barnes appears, one notes his piety, but it is of a stern, uncharitable, judgmental type contrasting the Reverend Bohun's.

The ideal balance among these various theological positions is provided by Father Brown. Unlike the colonel before his death and Gibbs afterward, he does not scoff at the idea of the hand of God in the colonel's death; he does, however, doubt that it was achieved by miraculous means. The Reverend Bohun had warned his brother that God might strike him down for his sins, although it is clear he did not really believe it likely. The smith, Barnes, implies that God did strike down his rival, but Father Brown points out that, despite the smith's piety, he doesn't really believe in true miracles any more than an atheist: When his accusers pointed to the hammer in his hand, he scornfully replied, "My hammer hasn't got wings that it should come flying half a mile over hedges and fields." In a pinch, the first appeal of even the religious mind is to natural law, and it is to natural law that Father Brown turns to solve the mystery. Here again, the literary device does not act independently of the story: Characterization by theological type is directly connected to the plot. Just as each character's religious position presents a partial truth from the point of view of Father Brown (and Chesterton), so each grasps a portion of the mystery, leaving it to Father Brown to piece together the whole.

*John R. Holmes*

# THE HAMMON AND THE BEANS

*Author:* Américo Parédes (1915-1999)
*Type of plot:* Social realism
*Time of plot:* The 1920's
*Locale:* Jonesville-on-the-Grande, a fictitious Texas town
*First published:* 1963

*Principal characters:*

THE NARRATOR, a young child at the time of the story
HIS FATHER
HIS MOTHER
CHONITA, a young girl
DR. ZAPATA, a friend of the narrator's father

*The Story*

The narrator recalls his boyhood during the 1920's, when he was growing up in Jonesville-on-the-Grande, a small town on the Texas side of the Rio Grande.

The boy lives a block away from Fort Jones in his grandfather's large frame house, where his mother complains about pigeons in the eaves bringing fleas. The town regulates its activities by the trumpet and cannon signals emanating from the fort, where soldiers have been stationed since border troubles ten or so years earlier.

In the evenings, children gather by the fence outside the fort to watch the flag lowered. On the days when they study in school about heroes of the American Revolution, such as George Washington and Marion the Fox, they cheer and salute as the fort's soldiers lower the flag. On days when they hear local men discussing the border incidents of the previous decade, they jeer. Whether the children cheer or jeer, however, the soldiers in the fort are indifferent to them.

None of the children ever goes inside Fort Jones except Chonita. Entering through the entrance leading to the poorest part of town, she watches the soldiers eat; afterward, the cooks come out, scold her for coming inside, and give her food. Chonita's family lives in a shack that was originally a shed on a vacant lot that the narrator's grandfather owns. He charges them no rent, but as a kind of payment, Chonita's mother does washing for the narrator's family. Thanks to a building boom in the Rio Grande Valley, Chonita's father is now working. Although he spends most of the money that he earns on drink, enough remains to buy corn for the family. "He was the breadwinner, you might say, while Chonita furnished the luxuries."

In the evenings, the neighborhood children gather to urge Chonita to speak English to them. She tries to repeat what she has heard the soldiers saying as they eat in the fort. Perched on a fence in an alley with the children in front of her, she says, "Give me the hammon and the beans." Her younger siblings are proud of her, but the other children merely laugh, telling her that she speaks English better than the teachers in school. The narrator thinks that all of this is a bad joke, which he wants to end so that they can play.

After the narrator contracts malaria, he is unaware that Chonita has also become sick. One night, Dr. Zapata comes to his house and announces that Chonita is dead. The narrator's father regrets not having known how sick Chonita was, although he says that her passing is not really his affair. The mother comments that Chonita is now in heaven and happy, but the doctor is upset because Chonita's father was drinking and laughing with friends when he left Chonita's house. The narrator's father points out that the man is actually Chonita's stepfather; however, the narrator's mother says that no one can tell what the poor man was feeling.

Dr. Zapata then says that in classical times, the people were more "humane": When the Greeks conquered Troy, they "grabbed the babies by the heels and dashed them against the wall." The narrator's father accuses the doctor of sounding like his relative, the Mexican revolutionary leader Emiliano Zapata. The doctor denies that he is related to the famous revolutionary and insists that he is conservative.

The narrator himself is not fully recovered from his illness, so his mother sends him back to bed. He imagines Chonita in heaven, wearing "her torn and dirty dress, with a pair of bright wings attached, flying round and round like a butterfly shouting, 'Give me the hammon and the beans.'" Then, he cries and feels better.

*Themes and Meanings*

Américo Parédes has written a complex story about problems relating to poverty, dual cultural heritage, and government indifference. The soldiers in Fort Jones are depicted—particularly by Dr. Zapata—as a kind of occupying power totally indifferent to the townspeople. The soldiers pay no attention to the children who gather outside their fence to watch the activities in the fort. Even Chonita, who is brave enough to enter the fort, must put up with scolding before the cooks will give her ham and beans left over from the soldiers' meal. Although the soldiers have plenty to eat, many of the town's children suffer from malnutrition, and Chonita's family lives in abject poverty. For them, the ham and beans that she brings home are luxuries.

In addition to government indifference, Chonita must face the teasing of the other children who deride her limited English. Only the narrator seems to recognize the cruelty behind their fun. Chonita also must endure the extra problems caused by an alcoholic father, who earns more than enough money to support his drinking but not enough for his family to live well. Seemingly fated not to have a chance in life, Chonita dies at a young age. When asked of what she died, the doctor says, "What the hell difference does it make?" voicing his own feeling of helplessness.

The narrator's father explains that Chonita's biological father was killed while working close to railroad tracks when a train derailed. He, too, was a victim, the father implies, of an indifferent or even hostile government.

The town's children learn about the American Revolution in school, but they learn nothing about the Mexican Revolution that led to the recent border troubles, except what they hear from men on the streets. To the children, the fort's soldiers are alter-

1706 Masterplots II

nately the bearers of the proud tradition of George Washington and the ruthless conquerors who fought against men such as Pancho Villa, an important Mexican revolutionary leader who was a central figure in the border trouble.

The narrator and his family are much better off than Chonita and her family, but even they are far from wealthy, as their problems with fleas and pigeons suggest. Nevertheless, of all the local children, only the narrator seems to feel true sympathy for Chonita. His final vision of Chonita follows an earlier one of what she would have been like had she lived into the 1930's: He often imagines her, he says, in picket lines demanding not bread but "hammon and beans." In his final vision, Chonita even in heaven remains in poverty, wearing her ragged dress and asking for "hammon and beans." Thus, the author indicates that in spite of the horrible conditions in which Chonita lives and in spite of Dr. Zapata's cynicism in saying that the Greeks who conquered Troy were more humane than the soldiers in Fort Jones, there is hope for humanity because people like the narrator are compassionate.

*Style and Technique*

Although the first-person narrator tells his story years after it takes place—as his reference to the 1930's indicates—he speaks from the point of view of a young child not fully aware of the implications of his own words. This fact makes it possible for the author to achieve a kind of objectivity. More important, he avoids the kind of sentimentality that one is tempted to use when writing about an impoverished child who dies before she has a real chance to live.

Central to the story is Parédes's ironic vision. Political, economic, ethnic, and personal circumstances deprive Chonita of an opportunity for happiness and success. All of these things, connected with human biology and lack of medical knowledge, lead to her early death. The narrator sees these problems pursuing her even into heaven. The irony is compounded by the glorification in school of revolutionaries such as George Washington and Francis Marion the Swamp Fox along with the official condemnation of revolutionaries such as Emiliano Zapata. As a result, irony of circumstance pervades the story. Nonetheless, the narrator's feelings of sympathy for Chonita provide some relief from the bleak irony that pervades the story.

Richard Tuerk

# HANDS

*Author:* Sherwood Anderson (1876-1941)
*Type of plot:* Psychological
*Time of plot:* The early 1900's
*Locale:* Rural Ohio
*First published:* 1919

> *Principal characters:*
> WING BIDDLEBAUM, a forty-year-old recluse
> GEORGE WILLARD, his only confidant

### The Story

Wing Biddlebaum, a fat little old man, lives an isolated life in a small frame house outside Winesburg, a small, provincial Ohio town. Beset by troubling doubts, he does not think of himself as a part of the life of the town where he has lived for twenty years. In fact, only with George Willard, the young son of the proprietor of the New Willard House, does Wing have anything close to a friendship, and only in George's presence does Wing lose some of his timidity. On this single day of the story's action, Wing hopes that George will spend the evening with him. George never appears, and most of the story's action occurs not in the present but in flashbacks.

During an earlier meeting between the two men, Wing became "wholly inspired" and told the younger man that he cared too much about the opinions of others, and should shut his ears to the roaring of other people's voices and begin to dream. Wing "raised the hands to caress the boy and then a look of horror swept over his face."

After Wing flees this scene, George thinks Wing's hands have something to do with his fear of him and everyone. Here begins a major flashback, "the story of the hands. Perhaps our talking of them will arouse the poet who will tell the hidden wonder story of the influence for which the hands were but fluttering pennants of promise."

Wing had an earlier existence as Adolph Myers, a twenty-year-old school teacher in rural Pennsylvania. Adolph Myers was much loved by the boys of his school, for he was meant by nature to teach young people. His voice and his hands were both expressive. "He was one of those men in whom the force that creates life is diffused, not centralized. Under the caress of his hands, doubt and disbelief went out of the minds of the boys and they began also to dream." Then tragedy struck. One of the boys became enamored of Wing, dreamed unspeakable things, and spoke them to others. The hysteria against Adolph grew quickly. Henry Bradford, a saloon keeper, called Adolph out from the schoolhouse and beat and kicked him, and a mob drove Adolph out of town that night. Wing moved to Winesburg to stay with an old aunt, and lived with her until she died. He was ill for a year after the incident in Pennsylvania and has worked since as a day laborer in the fields around Winesburg.

Back in the present time of the story, in its final paragraph, Wing walks up and down the veranda of his house, prepares and eats a simple meal, washes his dishes, and then gets ready for bed. "A few stray white bread crumbs lay on the cleanly washed floor by the table; putting the lamp upon a low stool he began to pick up the crumbs, carrying them to his mouth one by one with unbelievable rapidity." He looks like a priest engaged in a church service. The sad, lonely figure of Wing Biddlebaum is transformed in this last image into a transcendent spiritual being.

*Themes and Meanings*

"Hands" is the first of some two dozen stories that Sherwood Anderson brought together in *Winesburg, Ohio* (1919) and one of the most realistic and powerful in that collection. Like many of the stories in *Winesburg, Ohio*, "Hands" is about a character estranged from society, "grotesques," as Anderson called them in the preface to the story cycle, misfits forced to live lives of quiet desperation outside the circle of the human community.

The stories in *Winesburg, Ohio* are in fact linked by theme, geography, and a central character (George Willard) who wanders through them connecting different characters. Part of the New Realism that sprang up in the United States after World War I and that included other essentially Midwestern writers such as Sinclair Lewis and Ernest Hemingway, Anderson's short stories often focus on the estrangement and disillusionment of their protagonists.

Although a story of little action, "Hands" has multiple meanings. On one level, the story is a psychosexual portrait of a man driven out of society by his odd behavior, or by behavior that society can neither understand nor tolerate. Clearly there is a sexual element to the accusations against Adolph/Wing, for he was earlier driven out of town by people who misinterpreted his behavior. As a number of critics have pointed out, however, the real conflict is not sexual but the clash of the spiritual with the physical. The tragedy occurs when the Pennsylvania townspeople fail to recognize how Wing's hands (his physical dimension) really express his spiritual side (the dreams he talks to George about, as he did earlier to his students). For one brief moment, the young teacher had brought the two together: "In a way the voice and the hands, the stroking of the shoulders and the touching of the hair were a part of the schoolmaster's effort to carry a dream into the young minds." Society, unfortunately, cannot tolerate that union, and now, when George Willard knows Wing, a forty-year-old man who looks much older, his hands have become his marks of shame, his human condition one of loneliness. "Although [Wing] did not understand what had happened he felt that the hands must be to blame."

In the final image of the story—Wing kneeling "like a priest engaged in some service of his church"—Anderson brings the physical and the spiritual together again in his concluding sentence: "The nervous expressive fingers, flashing in and out of the light, might well have been mistaken for the fingers of the devotee going swiftly through decade after decade of his rosary." The story is thus not only about the tragedy of someone estranged from the human community but also about the rarity of joining the physical and the spiritual in this life. Like James Joyce's story "Araby," the religious symbolism of the story's conclusion leads to an epiphany or recognition, and the reader's sympathy and identification with Wing Biddlebaum—as with the essential loneliness of the human condition—are completed.

*Style and Technique*

A masterful story on several levels, "Hands" is particularly remarkable for its structure. Little actually happens in the present: Wing waits for George, who does not appear; he eats his supper and cleans up. Through a series of flashbacks, or stories within stories, like a series of Chinese boxes, Anderson reveals Wing/Adolph in all his human frailty. The very structure of the story is a worthwhile object of study in and of itself.

The figurative language of the story is also exceptional. Wing's story demands a poet, so Anderson employs images here that transcend language. The central image of the story, Wing's hands, conveys much of the meaning of the story: "Their restless activity, like unto the beating of the wings of an imprisoned bird, had given him his name." Wing's hands thus represent his estrangement, appendages almost unconnected to his body, as Wing himself is physically cut off from Winesburg. Wing's hands also represent the split in human life. They can express or represent his spirit, but they can also become something uglier: Walking earlier with George Willard, Wing stopped near a fence and, "beating like a woodpecker upon the top board had shouted at George Willard." Of course, Wing is beaten by hands as well, by Henry Bradford, who beat him with his fists. Hands can thus be used in diametrically opposite ways, to express the inexpressible (dreams) or to convey the purely physical (violence). In the concluding image of the story, hands are still central, and resemble objects in religious acts. In this final scene, the spiritual and the physical are once again combined in a mystical and positive way.

*David Peck*

# THE HANDSOMEST DROWNED MAN IN THE WORLD

*Author:* Gabriel García Márquez (1928-    )
*Type of plot:* Magical Realism
*Time of plot:* The twentieth century
*Locale:* A small, barren fishing village, perhaps in colonial South America
*First published:* "El abogado más hermoso del mundo," 1968 (English translation, 1971)

*Principal characters:*
THE HANDSOME DROWNED MAN, named Esteban by the villagers
THE VILLAGERS, grouped by children, women, and men
THE OLDEST WOMAN, who leads the villagers' reactions

*The Story*

Significantly, "The Handsomest Drowned Man in the World" begins with the children of the seaside fishing village. They see the drowned man floating ashore; at first they think he is an enemy ship, then a whale. The discovery that he is a drowned man does not dampen their sense of play at all: They proceed, in the beach sand, to bury and dig him up repeatedly. Responsible adults see the drowned man and take over. The village men carry the body to the village, noting that the drowned man is enormously heavy, tall, and encrusted with ocean debris. Even though his face is covered, they know he is a stranger because no man in the village is missing. Instead of going fishing that night, the men leave the body with the women and visit neighboring villages to check if the drowned man belongs to one of them.

The women prepare the body for burial. As they clean off the encrusted vegetation, they observe that the material comes from faraway places. The man's shredded clothes also indicate a long ocean voyage. The most astounding thing about him, however, once the crust is removed, is his handsome appearance: "Not only was he the tallest, strongest, most virile, and best built man they had ever seen, but even though they were looking at him there was no room for him in their imagination."

As they sit through the evening sewing new clothes for him and admiring his body, the village women fantasize about the drowned man. They imagine the disturbed sea outside roaring in his honor. They imagine him as the village's leading man, who has the best house, who makes fish leap out of the sea, and who digs springs and makes the barren cliffs bloom. Most of all, they fantasize about the happiness of his wife, and in their secret thoughts they compare the drowned man with their own men, who seem like "the weakest, meanest, and most useless creatures on earth."

Their thoughts are redirected by the oldest woman, who feels "more compassion than passion" for the drowned man and who announces around midnight that his name must be Esteban. Another school of thought among the youngest women is that his name is Lautaro. This romantic notion is dispelled by the ill-fitting new clothes, however, which make it clear that he is Esteban. Once his name is settled, the women launch into compassionate fantasies, imagining Esteban suffering through life with his huge body, so ill-suited for parlor visits. When dawn breaks and they cover his face with a handkerchief, the women begin identifying Esteban with their own men, and finally they break into an orgy of weeping.

The village men find the women thus when they return from the neighboring villages. The women's weeping turns to delight, though, when they learn that the drowned man does not belong to the other villages: He is theirs. They start making a fuss about him, adorning him for burial. The men cannot understand the women's behavior until the handkerchief is taken off the drowned man's face. Then the men, stunned, also see that he is Esteban, the handsomest drowned man in the world. They give the drowned man a fabulous funeral. The women go to the neighboring villages for flowers, and other women return with them. Soon the village is overrun with flowers and people. Rather than let Esteban remain "an orphan," the villagers choose relatives for him from among themselves, "so that through him all the inhabitants of the village became kinsmen." Bearing his handsome corpse to the cliffs to toss it back to the sea, the grief-stricken villagers become "aware for the first time of the desolation of their streets, the dryness of their courtyards, the narrowness of their dreams." However, from now on, things are going to be "different": Through their hard work, they are going to make the barren village prosper and bloom. It will become so famous that passing ocean travelers, overcome by the waiting fragrance, will point to "the promontory of roses on the horizon" and say "yes . . . that's Esteban's village.'

### Themes and Meanings

It is easy, in a cynical fashion, to make fun of the villagers in this little story, which Gabriel García Márquez wrote shortly after finishing his great masterpiece, *Cien anios de soledad* (1967; *One Hundred Years of Solitude*, 1970). *One Hundred Years of Solitude* chronicles the rise and decline of Macondo, a mythical city representing Latin American society in the period of independence. In some ways, the fishing village in this story is a stripped-down Macondo: The villagers are even more backward, provincial, ignorant, and gullible than the inhabitants of Macondo. Their village is the center of the universe, so instead of moving to a more promising location, they resolve to "break their backs" to turn a rocky promontory into a rose garden. They are inspired by a waterlogged corpse and led by emotional women. For all they know, the drowned man was a scoundrel, and there is no guarantee that their resolutions will ever lead to anything, that the rose garden will become a reality. If *One Hundred Years of Solitude* mirrors the history of Latin America's big hopes and bigger failures, is this story a boiled-down version of how the historical cycle begins?

The answer is no. "The Handsomest Drowned Man in the World" is not so much a repetition of *One Hundred Years of Solitude* as a coda with a counterpoint theme. The story takes an even more unpromising situation than the one in Macondo and proposes a solution. The solution is the imagination, which might be circumscribed by circumstances but can be stimulated by outside influences, represented by the drowned man. In *One Hundred Years of Solitude*, an obsession with incest suggests cultural inbreeding and degeneracy; here, the villagers become kinsmen only through their imagined relationships with the corpse. What does it matter that the corpse is waterlogged, possibly a former scoundrel? He still inspires the villagers to see their desolate lives and try to fill them with beauty. He is the poor villagers' Grecian urn.

As a story about the imagination, "The Handsomest Drowned Man in the World" has some powerful undercurrents appealing to the unconscious. The drowned man's long journey through the ocean deeps suggests the mysterious workings of the imagination. The drowned man is also an old motif in literature, where he frequently has positive associations, representing the preferred form of death (with overtones of baptism and spiritual rebirth, as in T. S. Eliot's poem *The Waste Land*, 1922) or even the triumph of the imagination over death (as in William Shakespeare's play *The Tempest*, 1611: "Those are pearls that were his eyes"). Here the drowned man's handsome looks symbolize such a triumph, as does his effect on the villagers. The story is a reminder that most of the people who inspire the world are dead.

Finally, one does not have to know anything about Latin American history, *One Hundred Years of Solitude*, the unconscious, or García Márquez in order to appreciate "The Handsomest Drowned Man in the World." The reader can readily enjoy this story without these outside references, which merely provide its rich context. It is, at heart, a fable of the imagination. The English version of the story is appropriately subtitled "A Tale for Children," just as it is appropriate that the village children should discover the drowned man. They show the most imagination among the villagers, followed by the women, though ultimately everyone's imagination is sparked.

*Style and Technique*

Whether children could grasp the occasionally long Faulknerian sentences in this story is debatable, but they could probably follow the switches of voice within the sentences better than adults. The switches of voice reflect the villagers' thoughts, including what they think the corpse is thinking; this complexity is all subsumed and remarkably controlled by the humorous voice of the omniscient narrator, who makes it seem like child's play. The style is known as García Márquez's Magical Realism, made famous in *One Hundred Years of Solitude*. The style also features exaggeration (as in the size of the corpse here) and imaginative thrusts ("the men began to feel mistrust in their livers") that now and then verge into fantasy.

It is certainly fantasy that the drowned man's corpse does not stink, a fantasy that enables García Márquez to construct a symbolism of smells reminiscent of the one in William Faulkner's "A Rose for Emily" (1930). Although Faulkner is perhaps the greatest influence on García Márquez, here the pupil reverses the master. Whereas Faulkner's story begins with a strong smell and ends with a decayed corpse, García Márquez's story begins with a remarkably preserved corpse and ends up smelling like roses. The symbolism typifies García Márquez's style, his gift to the world.

*Harold Branam*

# HAPPINESS

*Author:* Mary Lavin (1912-1996)
*Type of plot:* Domestic realism
*Time of plot:* The twentieth century
*Locale:* Ireland
*First published:* 1968

*Principal characters:*
VERA TRASKE, a mother
BEA TRASKE, her daughter
FATHER HUGH, a friend and adviser to Vera

*The Story*

"Happiness" begins rather abruptly as the narrator speaks of her mother, Vera, as having "a lot to say." What the mother discussed, almost incessantly, was her own happiness and happiness as a way to live. However, nearly every other character in the story challenges her assertion of the importance of happiness. For example, Father Hugh, a friend and supporter from a local monastery, challenges it directly by claiming that sorrow is a "necessary ingredient" in happiness, a view that Vera rejects. He also feels that Vera places far too much emphasis on happiness, especially happiness in this world. Vera's own children question her sharply about her supposed happiness, and they suggest that happiness is not really defined by Vera, that it is not that important, and that one can live without it. Her daughter Bea calls Vera's insistence on her happiness a "sham." At times, Vera's children redefine their mother's concept of happiness as courage, or persistence; it certainly is something that they notice in their mother's efforts to maintain happiness in the midst of chaos and loss.

Vera's mother acts as a foil to her daughter's insistent happiness. She resolutely refuses to be pleased by anything, and if something seems momentarily pleasant, she comments on its eventual loss. Father Hugh says, "God Almighty couldn't make that woman happy." In contrast, Vera's father was a happy man, even on his deathbed. He nurtured Vera's happiness and passed along his positive outlook, even though he could not pass it on to his wife.

Vera's happiness persists in the midst of disappointment and even tragedy. She loses her husband at an early age, but this loss makes her even more determined to maintain her happiness. Indeed, she finds it a continual struggle not to give in to the opposite side and become despondent and reject the joy she finds in the world.

She continually celebrates and embraces life rather than death. When her husband is dying, she brings him pots of daffodils to brighten up his room. She insists on nurturing and protecting the living, even a wasp that has wandered into the house. This may explain why the garden is the one place where she is happy and at rest. It is in the garden that she overdoes her search for happiness. She stays late working in the damp garden and catches a disease that soon after leads to her death.

The climax of the story comes when Vera has to face death and leave the world that she associates with happiness. She says that she cannot face it; she cannot deal with the loss of what has sustained her. Finally, her daughter, Bea, who is described as the family "oracle," takes charge and takes the role of a mother who is comforting her child. She tells her mother, "It's all right, Mother. You don't have to face it. It's over." She tells her mother, "You're finished with this world, Mother." She is then described as sinking into her pillow so deeply that she would have dented it "had it been a pillow of stone." It is a final surrender of the struggle to maintain happiness in this world.

*Themes and Meanings*

The theme of the story is happiness. However, the concept of "happiness" as seen by Vera is subject to debate, challenge, and final qualification in the story. Vera announces her happiness very early in the story and defends it against all onslaughts until the ending. The challenge to define happiness by her daughters, especially Bea, does seem to provide a different perspective; they see happiness more realistically than Vera's desperate struggle. In one scene, they see her swimming and are afraid she has gone too far to return to shore and may die. They notice that their mother's happiness is something that is "dearly bought." Happiness is, for Vera, a continual struggle rather than a state of being.

Above all, Vera's happiness is rooted in this world. The daughters describe Father Hugh as being close to Vera to make sure of her salvation in the next world. He is less concerned with happiness in this world. She demands that the flowers not be given to the church because they would only end up on the altar; she claims that God made the flowers for people in this world rather than for himself or religious purposes. She seems to feel that she is a good Catholic, but her emphasis on this world is not traditionally Christian. In another episode, she brings daffodils to her dying husband but is rebuked by a nun at the hospital who tells her she should be praying for her husband rather than bringing him flowers. Vera rejects this point of view throughout the story. She does not think of the other world as a possibility for her or a compensation for suffering, as Father Hugh does. She is so oriented in this world that the Christian heaven is not a possibility she can make part of her thinking and that conventional hope is never mentioned by her. However, at the end of the story, Bea tells her that she is done with this world and seems to feel that it is "joyous" news. The description of Vera sinking into her pillow so deeply that it "would have dented stone" does not seem to be a "joyous" acceptance of another world but a regret at losing this one and the end of the struggle to maintain happiness in it.

The meaning of the story is revealed in the debate concerning the nature of happiness and Vera's special claim to being happy. There is little change in the main character until the conclusion of the story, but her claim to happiness is never a settled state but one that is in question until the end.

*Style and Technique*

The first fictional technique to observe in the story is the use of a secondary character, one of the daughters who is not named, as the narrator. She tells the story in the first person and is obviously a close part of the main character's struggle, but she can be far enough removed so as to judge her character and her claim to "happiness." She is an observer of her mother's life and her forcefully declared way of living, so the reader sees her mother primarily through the daughter's eyes and her judgments.

Another technique that Mary Lavin uses is to place the story in a middle-class, Roman Catholic setting in Ireland, a society that typically pays less attention to this world and more to one's eventual salvation. Father Hugh, for example, clearly rejects Vera's demand that it is in this world that she has her hard-won happiness. However, she is opposed to placing flowers on the altar, since "God made them for us." She has no thoughts about the afterlife with which a Roman Catholic should be concerned. Furthermore, when she is faced with death and the possibility of that afterlife, she is terrified. She lacks the faith that seems to govern Father Hugh's life.

Characterization is one of the most important fictional elements in the story. The characterization of Vera is exuberantly imperative in her constantly urging others to pay attention to her views: "Take me," or "Take Father Hugh." She challenges people that she knows by asking, "But are you happy?" However, as the story goes on, it reveals the disorder that makes up her life. In one scene, Father Hugh has to send her off to London with her papers and makes her give up the attempt to impose order on chaos. This disorder seems to be at odds with her claim to happiness.

The relationship between Vera and Father Hugh is especially interesting. Early in the story, Vera rejects any implication that there is anything wrong with her spending so much time alone with a priest. Father Hugh even spends the night on occasion. The story is autobiographical, and Lavin did marry a Jesuit priest who left the church. This followed the death of her own husband in 1954. At the end of the story, Father Hugh carries Vera from the garden and he is described as being like a "lover," so there are implications of a deeper relationship.

Toward her daughter, Vera is an unconventional but loving mother. She allows the daughters to bring scores of friends to the house and increase the chaos that is already there. She also took them on a tour of Europe soon after the death of her husband. The daughters do challenge her and her cherished happiness, but the closeness between them is always evident.

There is not much dialogue in the story. The first-person narrrator provides a view of the characters and their situation. The structure of the story is a debate over Vera's happiness and a final epiphany that reveals its limitations.

*James Sullivan*

# HAPPY AUGUST THE TENTH

*Author:* Tennessee Williams (Thomas Lanier Williams, 1911-1983)
*Type of plot:* Psychological
*Time of plot:* The 1960's
*Locale:* New York City and rural Connecticut
*First published:* 1971

*Principal characters:*
ELPHINSTONE, a self-employed genealogist
HORNE, her apartment mate, a social researcher
HER MOTHER, unnamed

*The Story*

For ten years, Elphinstone and Horne, two unmarried women in their forties, have shared a small apartment on the fifth floor of a brownstone on East Sixty-first Street. They have abided by their original agreement to swap bedrooms during the dog days of August and September every year so that Elphinstone will have the one air-conditioned bedroom during the hottest time of the year. The story opens on the morning of August tenth with Horne popping her head into Elphinstone's cool bedroom and shrieking, "Happy August the Tenth!" at her apartment mate, waking her.

Horne leaves the house every day to go to her job in the research department of the *National Journal of Social Commentary.* Elphinstone works at home as a freelance genealogist. She awaits the death of her decrepit mother, who lives in Connecticut attended by servants. She worries about whether her mother will leave her estate equally to her and her sister, or whether she will leave the bulk of it to the sister, who is married and has three children. Horne's genuine concern for Elphinstone is apparent. She urges Elphinstone to have a polio shot, and, although they have some unpleasant words about that matter, it is clear that Horne cares about Elphinstone's welfare and that Elphinstone, who regularly visits a psychiatrist, Dr. Schreiber, realizes that Horne is truly concerned about her and, in her own way, appreciates that concern.

Horne has the temerity to waken Elphinstone early on this particular morning because she knows that Dr. Schreiber has scheduled her for a nine o'clock appointment "in order," she relates, "to observe your state of mind in the morning." Elphinstone, nevertheless, is annoyed at having her sleep disturbed. She and Horne bicker, and it soon becomes evident that bickering is an established pattern in their relationship. Elphinstone, whose social circle is confined to a small group of other alumnae of Sarah Lawrence College, does not approve of Horne's friends. Although Horne wants to include her in social gatherings, Elphinstone, who has behaved badly at one such affair, resists her efforts, and the two have quite separate social lives.

Elphinstone casually reveals that she has talked with Dr. Schreiber about Horne's friends, whom she considers Village hippies, and that he has called them "instinctively destructive." Horne is outraged not only that Elphinstone has discussed her friends with the psychiatrist but also that he has made judgments about her friends, whom he does not know. She considers Dr. Schreiber's conduct unprofessional. Elphinstone upbraids Horne for her compulsion to use shocking language, and also reveals to her that Dr. Schreiber has described her as sick because she considers the buildings of New York to be giant tombstones that mark a city of the dead.

Much of the furniture in the apartment is Elphinstone's and has been handed down to her through her family. Horne lets it be known that she feels crowded by all the family relics that Elphinstone has crammed into their small apartment. She tells Elphinstone that she is going to check into the Chelsea Hotel for the weekend and then move out. She needs to assert herself as an individual.

By noon, Elphinstone has come to regret the unpleasantness of the morning. She calls Horne at work to apologize. They have a civilized conversation in which Elphinstone, without any additional prodding from Horne, agrees to go for her polio shot, even though she dreads "the prick of the needle." They both weep before they say good-bye. Elphinstone sees Dr. Schreiber that afternoon. He dismisses her after only twenty minutes of the hour she is paying for. On an impulse she decides to go to Connecticut to see her mother, and on another quite cruel impulse, she packs Horne's bags and puts them at the door where Horne will see them when she comes home.

In Connecticut, Elphinstone begins to regret her treatment of Horne. She spends eighty dollars—less than half of the cost of two sessions with Dr. Schreiber, she tells herself—to rush back to Horne by taxicab. When she gets home, she finds Horne asleep before the television set. She sinks to the floor, hugs Horne's knees, wishes her a happy August the eleventh, and promises to go for her polio shot soon.

In the end, the two women are probably back where they started. The bickering will continue, but the interdependence of the relationship will keep them together, as will the fear of being alone.

## Themes and Meanings

"Happy August the Tenth" was written during a crucial period in Tennessee Williams's own life, and Elphinstone clearly represents Williams, who had himself been in psychoanalysis. Williams had broken up with Frank Merlo, his lover of several years. After the breakup, which was caused in part by Williams's flagrant infidelities, Merlo became seriously ill and finally died. Williams, who spent much of his time at Merlo's bedside during the final months of Merlo's life, felt great guilt about his treatment of Merlo, whom he loved deeply. In many respects, "Happy August the Tenth" provides insights into Williams's relationship with Merlo. More important, the story points to what might have been. It suggests that they could have gone on together, although in the continuation of their relationship they would have been quite unlikely to find peace or even what most people would regard as happiness.

The story suggests that people are essentially in a trap. They engage regularly in love-hate relationships, but interdependence keeps these relationships together in spite of the incredible cruelty that frequently characterizes them. If this story is a comment on the nature of people, it suggests that people feel very much alone, very much excluded, and that they reach out for any kind of relationship that will make them feel a part of something.

A naturalistic determinism pervades most of Williams's major dramas, and that determinism is also a part of this story. When Horne views New York City as a great necropolis, when she views its tall buildings as tombstones, she is essentially suggesting that people have little control over their own destinies. She is better resigned to this reality than Elphinstone is. Elphinstone wants more from life—she searches genealogies, ferrets out past greatness. Horne more realistically works for a journal that deals with social commentary, that deals with the here and the now. Elements of the kind of nihilism that pervades the work of Jean-Paul Sartre, Albert Camus, Edward Albee, and Samuel Beckett are present in this story and in much of Williams's other work.

*Style and Technique*

In "Happy August the Tenth," Williams shows through the use of carefully selected details that it is the small things in one's day-to-day existence that lead to immediate tensions among people. The story also suggests that it is elemental anger rather than the small occurrences that precipitate the bickering that most people have to deal with essentially. The bickering is a symptom of deep anger. Perhaps this realization has led Elphinstone to go to the psychiatrist, but even the psychiatrist has his limits. In Elphinstone's August the tenth session with him, he dismisses her when they are not even halfway through the session. On the mundane level, this act has economic implications because Elphinstone is paying for the hour; on a different level, it suggests that there are times when people cannot even pay a professional to put up with them.

Williams understood tension and depicted it with an accuracy that helps to define him as a literary master. For example, during the bickering between Elphinstone and Horne, "another pause occurred in the conversation. Both of them made little noises in their throats and took little sips of coffee and didn't glance at each other; the warm air trembled between them." Williams makes optimal use of every prop available to him. The heat of August, the futility of August, a time when many people have abandoned the city to go on holiday, work for him as the heat of New Orleans in the summer worked for him in *A Streetcar Named Desire* (1947).

Elphinstone and Horne have a parrot, Lorita, which is permitted to move about the apartment at will, but which apparently does not know that it can fly. During the story, it confines itself voluntarily to its "summer palace," its cage out on the balcony. Elphinstone and Horne are just as able to get out of their confining situation as Lorita is, but they apparently do not know that they, too, are free. Indeed, their freedom is merely physical. They are not free in spirit, and as the story ends, it is clear that they never will be. The best they can hope for is that they will have each other, that their interdependence will keep them in their little brownstone cage, bickering with each other just as Lorita, in her summer palace, makes clucking sounds and whistles.

*R. Baird Shuman*

# THE HAPPY AUTUMN FIELDS

*Author:* Elizabeth Bowen (1899-1973)
*Type of plot:* Psychological
*Time of plot:* The late 1800's and the early 1940's
*Locale:* The English countryside and London
*First published:* 1944

*Principal characters:*

SARAH and
HENRIETTA, young sisters in Victorian England
THEIR FAMILY, their parents and their seven brothers and sisters
EUGENE, a suitor to Sarah
MARY, a young woman in London during World War II
TRAVIS, her fiancé

*The Story*

The story is told in four parts, sharply divided, differing in time, place, and characters and alternating between a Victorian country estate and a bombed-out London house during World War II. The focus of the whole is on the perception of a London woman, Mary, who learns about (or dreams) the experiences of the Victorian family and strongly identifies with Sarah, one of the daughters.

In the first episode, Papa and his family form a walking party to stroll through the stubbled autumn fields of his extensive land. The gathering honors three of his sons, who will leave the next day for boarding school. There is a sense of order and stability in their procession, a feeling of permanence. Details of action and conversation emphasize the extraordinary closeness between the two younger sisters, Henrietta and Sarah; they have shared all of their thoughts and all of their lives, and nothing, says Sarah, "can touch one without touching the other."

The walkers are joined by two horseback riders, Papa's eldest son and his friend Eugene. It is clear that the initiative to dismount and stroll with the others is Eugene's, and it is clear that he is in love with Sarah. Leading his horse, he walks beside Sarah, separating her from Henrietta. Henrietta, thus isolated, begins a plaintive song that pierces her sister's heart and makes Sarah long to call out her sister's name and to restore the old sense of communion.

There is a sudden break. The name Henrietta is spoken not by her sister but by Mary, waking from sleep in a half-destroyed London house, in about 1942. The reader becomes aware that reality lies not in the happy autumn fields but in Mary's mind. Somehow, perhaps through a box of old letters that she has found, Mary knows about and empathizes with Sarah's conflicting emotions, her established love for Henrietta fighting against her awakening love for Eugene; Mary identifies with Sarah. More important, she finds the world of fifty years ago a better place to be than the present world, and she resists the effort of her fiancé, Travis, to get her out of the dangerously damaged house. They compromise: She will have two hours alone with her house and her dreams. Travis, however, takes the box with him as he leaves.

The dreamworld returns. Papa's family is now gathered in the drawing room at the end of the day. Eugene is there, his love evident and still unspoken. When he says, "I shall be back tomorrow," both sisters understand that he will speak then, and both are frightened of impending change. Sarah has an ominous sense that "something terrible" might happen. Henrietta promises to stay with her and protect her, and she tells Eugene imperiously, "Whatever tries to come between me and Sarah becomes nothing." She begs Sarah to confirm that, but Sarah cannot speak.

As before, Sarah's unspoken word awakens Mary's consciousness; in her London world, she is aroused by a bomb falling nearby. Travis returns, anxious about her, and as she slowly returns to the war world, she speaks of the other: "I am left with a fragment torn out of a day, a day I don't even know where or when; and now how am I to help laying that like a pattern against the poor stuff of everything else?" She wonders if she is descended from Sarah, which might explain her close identification. However, Travis has spent the two hours reading letters from the box, and he finds such a kinship impossible; the letters soon cease to mention Henrietta and Sarah, suggesting that they died young and unmarried. Another letter, written by a brother in his old age, mentions a friend who, in his youth, was killed when his horse threw him on an autumn evening after a visit to their home. In the last fine of the story, as Mary and Travis leave the London house, Travis says that the brother had always wondered "what made the horse shy in those empty fields."

*Themes and Meanings*

The title is taken from Alfred, Lord Tennyson's poem "Tears, Idle Tears":

> Tears from the depth of some divine despair
> Rise in the heart, and gather to the eyes,
> In looking on the happy autumn fields,
> And thinking of the days that are no more.

Many stories have been told about people who yearn for bygone days. What is unusual about Elizabeth Bowen's story is that her central character yearns not for her own more peaceful past but for that of people she has never known, in a place and time she has never known. This kind of hallucinatory experience appears in other stories in *Ivy Gripped the Steps* (1946), and Bowen uses it as a unifying factor in her preface to the collection. The hallucinations, she says, "are an unconscious, instinctive, saving resort. . . . [L]ife, mechanised by the controls of wartime, and emotionally torn and impoverished by changes, had to complete itself in some other way."

Thus Mary completes herself through Sarah. When the reader first sees her and hears her cry out for Henrietta, Mary is lying on a bare mattress in a room covered with gritty white dust, in a house that she has loved and in which she can no longer stay. The destruction and loss incurred by the blitz make Sarah's long-ago, long-resolved emotional crisis—even with its tragic end—seem a thing of peace and permanence compared with the unending crisis and change of the war. Travis tells her, "You don't like it here. . . . Your will keeps driving your self, but it can't be driven the whole way—it makes its own get-out: sleep." Sleep—perchance to dream. It is Travis and London that seem unreal to her.

The meaning of the story for Mary is a desperate search for stability amid constant, uncontrollable change; the theme involved in the relationship of Henrietta and Sarah is a response to impending change. Eugene's courtship will force Sarah to grow up; she is not sure that she wants to, and Henrietta is certainly opposed. The passing of childhood, the beginning of life's inevitable mutations, is unwelcome and frightening. Is it possible that the story's final question—What made the horse shy?—has an answer involving Henrietta's white handkerchief?

*Style and Technique*

There is considerable ambiguity in the telling of "The Happy Autumn Fields," made possible by the use of an omniscient narrator. Had the story been told in Mary's voice, the details about Sarah's family would have been solidified by Mary's interpretation and the ambiguity lost. The omniscient narrator, however, instead of explaining overtly, drops hints from which the reader may draw interpretations—sometimes slightly differing ones.

The most cogent example is the final question and its possible connection with the flying flag of Henrietta's white handkerchief. The latter is mentioned once a fourth of the way into the story and alluded to once again; yet in the last lines, in another place and time and a different context, the reader may remember it and may remember Henrietta's determination never to lose her sister.

The most all-encompassing example involves Mary's consciousness. The narrator never says explicitly how Mary came to know Sarah's family—whether the detailed impressions of the Victorian afternoon are dreams or imaginative waking reconstructions. Both times when the story shifts to Mary, there are hints that she has wakened from sleep, but she might well have been seeking refuge in daydreams of happy autumn fields. Similarly, the box of letters and pictures is never explained; the reader may assume that it was shaken out of the house's walls or closets by an explosion, but how it came to London and to Mary's attention is never said.

Bowen uses much impressionistic detail as well as dialogue; these techniques, like the voice of the narrator, set up echoes that the reader may interpret. Impressionistic details inform and fill out setting and character. Henrietta, too young for floor-length skirts, is "still ankle-free" and free also from other burdens of maturity. The youngest boy's hand is a "twisting prisoner" in the restraint of his father's hand. Smoke from a cottage chimney is the "colour of valediction." In London, Mary sees that her watch has stopped and "through the torn window appeared the timelessness of an impermeably clouded late summer afternoon."

Dialogue, even more than detail, encourages the reader's interpretation. When Henrietta pauses during the afternoon stroll, Sarah says to her, "We cannot stay here forever." Sarah means that they must join the others, but the reader knows that it is their childhood that cannot stay. Eugene, on the point of leaving for his last ride, says gravely, "There cannot fail to be tomorrow," and Henrietta answers, "I will see that there is tomorrow." When Travis comments on the junk in the old leather box, Mary says, "Everything one unburies seems the same age." Thus the two women, Mary and Sarah, and the two time periods, fifty years apart, are one.

*Rosamond Putzel*

# HARMONY

*Author:* Ring Lardner (1885-1933)
*Type of plot:* Realism
*Time of plot:* The 1920's
*Locale:* A train en route to Boston
*First published:* 1915

> *Principal characters:*
> THE NARRATOR, a baseball writer
> WALDRON, a new outfielder and a tenor
> ART GRAHAM, an outfielder who has a passion for quartet singing
> BILL COLE, a pitcher and a member of Waldron's quartet
> LEFTY PARKS, the fourth member of the quartet
> RYAN, the baseball club manager

*The Story*

"Harmony" is both a baseball story and a mystery story. The setting is a train full of baseball players on their way east to a game in Boston; the narrator is a baseball writer; the mystery that the writer is trying to solve through talking to the manager and to various players is how the club recruited Waldron, the unknown player whose batting has put the team in first place.

Ring Lardner's structure is fairly complex, involving stories within stories. There are five people who contribute information about the mystery: the narrator, who begins and ends "Harmony"; Ryan, who gives the first account but who disagrees with the narrator's final version; Dick Hodges, the Jackson coach, who originally acquired Waldron and who is quoted by Ryan; Art Graham, who recruited Waldron but who is secretive about the details; and Bill Cole, whose story the narrator accepts as the truth.

The story begins on a train moving east toward Springfield, Massachusetts, where the narrator must file a story about the team with which he is traveling. The hottest news is the new outfielder, Waldron, who is setting records at bat. The only story about him that has not been told, however, is how Ryan, the club manager, found him. According to Ryan, there is no mystery. Art Graham spotted Waldron and recommended him even though both men were outfielders, and Waldron might well take Graham's place. Ryan accepted Graham's explanation that his motive was the good of the club and drafted Waldron.

However, the Jackson coach, Hodges, is still puzzled. Ryan quotes a conversation with him in which Hodges described his plan to conceal Waldron for a season and insisted that Graham could not possibly have been impressed with his single performance when Waldron batted under a false name and popped out, at that. Did a Jackson player tell Graham about Waldron? Or could Graham spot a great batter, as he insists, simply by the way he swung?

Although there are still some loose ends, the narrator files his story at Springfield and does not inquire further until he encounters Graham at dinnertime. Graham is noncommittal, and it is not until the narrator finds himself in the diner with Cole that he hears what Cole insists is the true story. Graham had never gone to the ballpark in Jackson, it seems. He had recruited Waldron not for his ball-playing abilities but for his fine tenor voice. Graham's great passion is barbershop quartet harmony, Cole says, and the happiest times in Graham's life have been those periods when the team included three other good singers, one of them the essential tenor, who were willing to sing with Graham for the long hours that he demanded. To keep his quartet going, Graham was willing to do almost anything. He had talked Lefty Parks out of a romantic involvement, which Graham thought was taking too much time away from his singing; he had rallied the team around Mike McCann, his tenor, in an attempt to keep McCann from being shipped out after his pitching deteriorated; in fact, he had been so concerned about McCann that he missed a fly he should have caught, thus ensuring the pitcher's departure.

With such an obsession, it is no wonder, says Cole, that Graham decided to get Waldron on his team after he heard him sing during a casual meeting on the fateful day in Jackson. Graham had no idea that Waldron would turn out to be a star player. He only hoped to keep a good tenor for a season. That, says Cole, is the real story, but it must not be published until Graham is off the team.

Two years later, after Graham has been let out, the narrator does tell Ryan the story that Cole had told him, but Ryan refuses to believe it. He cannot think that anyone would be so obsessed by quartet harmony. The narrator, however, does believe Cole, and concludes that despite Waldron's fine playing, the team is not doing as well in baseball as it had done during the great days of musical harmony before Graham, Cole, and Parks were retired.

*Themes and Meanings*

The theme of "Harmony" is indicated both by the title and by the narrator's final comment. The story involves two kinds of group effort: baseball and close-harmony singing. To most of the characters in the story, singing is a spare-time activity. Baseball is their primary interest, even though they know that their big-league careers will be over when their skills decline. To Graham, however, the quartet makes life worthwhile, and baseball is simply a necessary adjunct to the quartet. The comedy in "Harmony" comes from Graham's attempts to use the baseball system for the purposes of his quartet, attempts that are doomed by the perishable nature of baseball talent.

In keeping his quartet together, Graham must always battle the clock and the calendar. He fights for the players' time, hurrying them out of bed on the train, gathering them from the dining car, resenting their leisure activities, even breaking up Parks's romance. He would, if he could, put quartet practice ahead of baseball practice. Though he must let the players stop singing long enough to play ball, however, Graham has considerable success in dominating the rest of their time. It is the calendar that defeats him, first taking McCann from him and finally removing Graham himself, who probably leaves the team sooner because the tenor he scouted happens to play Graham's own position.

Although the story is built on Graham's attempt to serve the needs of his quartet while seeming to live for his sport, an attempt in which the victories are necessarily temporary, in his conclusion the narrator suggests that the harmonizing of the quartet may have resulted in better play on the ball field. One recalls Graham's insistence that he could not be a scout because he would be too lonely. Perhaps the same spirit that brings the quartet together, sometimes half unwilling, but submitting to Graham's demands in part simply to make him happy, is the spirit that took the team to first place. Somehow, once the habit of musical harmony has gone with three of the harmonizers, says the narrator, the baseball team itself is not the same.

## Style and Technique

The realism for which Lardner was praised is evident in "Harmony." The setting is everyday and undramatic—a train running behind schedule, a diner with good minced ham and inferior asparagus. The ball players talk, sing, and eat. The talk itself is both matter-of-fact in tone and authentic in detail, revealing Lardner's ear for slang, baseball jargon, and the peculiarities of spoken English. Talking about Mike McCann, for example, Cole says, "You know what a pitcher Mike was. He could go in there stone cold and stick ten out o' twelve over that old plate with somethin' on 'em." The passage rings true, and it is typical. The asparagus, says Cole, for example, is "tougher'n a doubleheader in St. Louis." When McCann's pitching fails, Cole says, "I'll swear that what he throwed up there didn't have no more on it than September Morning." The beauty of Lardner's language is that it seems transcribed rather than invented.

Lardner has been criticized for his objectivity, which it has been argued indicates a dislike of his own characters. In his satiric stories, the dislike is justifiable, and Lardner should not be faulted for letting the characters condemn themselves as they talk. Lardner, however, is also capable of tenderness, of an appreciation of the human condition in a story more poignant because it is told objectively, perhaps, as in "Harmony," by a number of tellers. In Art Graham, a middling ball player and a fair singer, Lardner has drawn his portrait of the artist.

*Rosemary M. Canfield Reisman*

# HARRISON BERGERON

*Author:* Kurt Vonnegut (1922-      )
*Type of plot:* Dystopian
*Time of plot:* 2081
*Locale:* The United States
*First published:* 1968

> *Principal characters:*
> HARRISON BERGERON, a fourteen-year-old genius who escapes
>     from an insane asylum
> GEORGE and HAZEL BERGERON, his parents
> DIANA MOON GLAMPERS, the Handicapper General

*The Story*

By the year 2081, the search for true equality of all U.S. citizens has led to the creation of scores of amendments to the Constitution. In every case, the effort has not been to raise the standards of those handicapped by their differences or inadequacies. Instead, those who are gifted with superior intellect, physical beauty, or strength are penalized.

Those who are beautiful must wear hideous masks, intelligent people must wear headsets that jangle their brains and nerves with a series of loud, annoying sounds, and those with physical agility or strength must carry sacks of birdshot to weigh them down. Thus, in the race of life, all Americans are handicapped so that no one must ever feel ugly, stupid, or "like something the cat dragged in."

Diana Moon Glampers is the Handicapper General, whose job is to track down violators of the law and rid society of those who menace the average, the inadequate, the mediocre. If a man wants to rest from the drudgery of carting around fifty pounds of birdshot by removing some pellets, he can be killed. Those, such as Harrison Bergeron, who learn to overcome their handicaps are forced to shoulder ever larger burdens, or noisier apparatus, or face incarceration or execution.

Society has become so repressive that no one dares question the increasing numbers of new laws that call for more handicaps and punishments. All those who oppose the Handicapper General are arrested, thrown into mental institutions, or shot because they threaten the fabric of society. The effects of these governmental policies are appalling. Society is stagnant because those smart enough to develop new technology, medicine, and literature have been permanently handicapped, exiled, or killed.

Television announcers have speech impediments, dancers cannot dance, musicians are tone deaf, and families lose all purpose, continuity, compassion, and love. A good example of this is Harrison Bergeron's story. Harrison escapes from an asylum that was meant to protect society from him. Fourteen years old and already seven feet tall, he is the handsomest young man possible, and possesses an intellect that would stagger even Albert Einstein. George and Hazel, his parents, are aware of his exploits from reports on television. Harrison threatens the regime, for he would remove all artificial handicaps and enable people to achieve beyond the limits set by their inadequacies.

Instead of attempting to rally support to overthrow the government and create a better society, Harrison merely breaks into a television studio, disrupting the musical show by removing everyone's masks and handicaps. Choosing the most beautiful of the dancers, he dances higher and higher as the musicians play brilliantly. As the couple leap, they appear to fly in the air as they kiss the ceiling—this is freedom! The sound of two shotgun blasts signals that Harrison and the ballerina have been shot down by the Handicapper General.

Harrison's parents witness the entire affair on their television, but when George goes to the kitchen for something and Hazel gets sidetracked, neither can remember why they are crying—something sad on television, no doubt.

## Themes and Meanings

Kurt Vonnegut's purpose in "Harrison Bergeron" is clear and unequivocal. He wants to show that a society that exalts the lowest common denominator (the homely, the stupid, the mediocre) by handicapping all those with talent, intellect, and beauty, can never help those with natural disabilities. For Vonnegut, fundamental human decency demands that society give such people more assistance in reaching up, aspiring to be more than the mere appendages of society. It is the exceptional people who improve society—the nonconformists, the dreamers, the different. Failure to inspire all people will lead inevitably to the destruction of such a society. It is appropriate to legislate equality before the law in the areas of education, employment, and justice, the author suggests. Too often, he warns, people assume that equality means being the same. This is simply not realistic. Conformity for its own sake can be frightening, as seen in Nazi Germany, which attempted to rid Europe of people who were different—Jews, Poles, Czechs, gays, and the mentally and physically disabled.

Although one may laugh at the seeming absurdity of Vonnegut's story, he asserts that society has gone far down that road already. Because some people are stupid, labels on poison must instruct all users not to eat it, shampoo bottles come with instructions for use, and cigarette labels proclaim that they cause cancer while people continue to smoke them. Society has been forced to protect the innocent, which is noble, but it also must protect the lazy, the incompetent, the mediocre, so that no one accepts responsibility for their actions.

In "Harrison Bergeron," as elsewhere in his writings, Vonnegut carefully suggests that humanity is at once noble and the cause of much unnecessary suffering. Democratic institutions may help to control people's baser natures, but even the most well-meaning behavior can create new problems. Civil rights laws, affirmative action laws, and equal employment opportunities committees have all been seen as either the best efforts of humanity or the worst of fuzzy thinking.

It might appear optimistic that, despite the almost pathological efforts to destroy all that is beautiful, brilliant, or talented here, Vonnegut implies that a champion will defend these values. His pessimistic view, however, is revealed when Harrison Bergeron throws off his shackles and weights and mask and those of the dancers and musicians, but his only revolutionary act is to dance. That is Vonnegut's point—that society needs rebels to risk everything in order to make life better. The ironic reality that in order to be fair to one group, society must be unfair or unjust to others is the basis of "Harrison Bergeron" and much of Vonnegut's fiction. The ignorance and hatefulness of humankind are attacked again and again. Here, as elsewhere, Vonnegut asks what are people for? If there is a grand design to life, a true purpose for suffering, why can it not be discovered?

*Style and Technique*

Since writing his earliest stories, Vonnegut has been called a science fiction writer, a term, he says, that for many people is another word for a bathroom receptacle. Although there are elements of science fiction in his stories, he is more clearly a fantasist—one who creates a believable but purely imaginary world such as one finds in Lewis Carroll's *Alice's Adventures in Wonderland* (1865). He frequently resorts to dystopias (negative views of the future) to comment on modern society.

His style here is straightforward and matter-of-fact, as if he were sharing a story with his fishing buddies. Vonnegut does not interfere with the narration of this story to wink at the reader, implying that it is all a joke. Here, as in other stories and novels, Vonnegut appears to be a serious writer who uses the trappings of a futuristic science fiction world to entertain readers while he "poisons our minds with humanity."

The story's narrator never passes judgment on the words or deeds of the characters. Instead, his description of those actions becomes increasingly unbelievable. For example, as Harrison Bergeron and his dance partner dance and leap into the air, they finally manage to kiss the ceiling. Thus Vonnegut shows that Harrison represents someone so alien to his society that he can even defy the laws of gravity by seeming to float as easily as he was able to toss aside his shackles and handicaps.

Vonnegut's outstanding stylistic trait is his use of black humor—humor that relies on the use of darker, more pessimistic, even depressing views of the absurdities of life. In a century when science and technology have been used to harm rather than help humankind, Vonnegut's bitter antimachine, antitechnology images clearly reinforce the themes of the story. Instead of improving machines to make life easier, Harrison's society—and thus ours—relies on outdated, nineteenth century tools to encumber the superior members of his culture to prevent either growth or experimentation. This is Vonnegut's effort to make readers rethink their comfortable complacency and imagine instead what life would be like in such a world. The irony is that humans already inhabit such a world.

*Linda L. Labin*

# A HAUNTED HOUSE

*Author:* Virginia Woolf (1882-1941)
*Type of plot:* Fantasy
*Time of plot:* The early 1900's
*Locale:* An English house and garden
*First published:* 1921

*Principal characters:*
A LIVING COUPLE, the present inhabitants of the house
A GHOST COUPLE, the house's former inhabitants

*The Story*

The narrator, apparently a woman, begins: "Whatever hour you woke there was a door shutting." Along with her husband, the narrator experiences the sensations of a home literally alive with memories. She does not, however, try to keep the reader in suspense regarding the mysterious openings and closings of doors and windows that she and her husband witness. Despite the fact that she knows two ghosts wander through her home, she is not afraid. The ghosts, after all, mean the narrator and her husband no harm.

The ghosts clearly are conducting a search. They look for something that may have been left out in the garden, or perhaps up in the loft. The narrator is anxious to discover what the object of the ghosts' search can be. The mystery is deepened by the response of the house itself to the searchers; it has a pulse that quickens as the ghosts seem on the verge of recovering whatever it is they have lost. The narrator hears the house's heartbeat as the word "safe" repeated rhythmically. The house also speaks of a treasure hidden somewhere within its rooms. This must be what the ghosts are looking for.

Although she does not tell how, the narrator has learned a few details from the ghosts' past. They lived in the house as man and wife hundreds of years before. After the woman died suddenly, the man abandoned the house and wandered throughout the globe. After his death, he returned to be reunited with his wife. The narrator realizes that what the man could not find on his journey, and what the ghost couple still seek, is the joy of a loving relationship. She overhears the ghost husband tell his wife that their lives were full of kisses without number.

Eventually the ghosts come on the narrator and her husband asleep in their bed. The ghosts seem to realize that the living couple may feel the kind of love that themselves once shared. The narrator is awakened by the light of the dead couple's silver lantern and by the realization that she knows, in fact she possesses, what the ghosts have been searching for. The ghosts have buried their emotional treasure in the narrator and her husband—in their living love. She calls this feeling of joy and love the light in the heart.

*Themes and Meanings*

"A Haunted House" employs several themes that became the focus of Virginia Woolf's later fiction. The permanence of love, the difficulties of marriage, the inevitability of death, and the connections between all souls, living and dead, are concepts that Woolf treats with great complexity in the ten paragraphs of this short story, as well as in the many pages of her best-known novels. She attempts to uncover the profound, unspoken aspects of human relationships.

Love endures in "A Haunted House." Not even cruel fate can keep the ghostly lovers apart. By locating their old sense of joy in the living couple that shares their house, Woolf raises the hope that both this life and the afterlife will be kingdoms of the heart. This is as optimistic a vision of human relationships as Woolf will ever offer. Although many of the characters in *Mrs. Dalloway* (1925) can never forget the first, most enduring loves of their lives, there is no suggestion in that novel that lost love can be recovered, even in the afterlife, as it is in "A Haunted House." In Woolf's novels, love, particularly love expressed through the institution of marriage, rarely runs a smooth course.

The interruption of the ghostly lovers' marriage by death forecasts many such occurrences in Woolf's major fiction. Her first heroine, Rachel Ambrose of *The Voyage Out* (1915), dies before her wedding. Septimus Smith commits suicide in *Mrs. Dalloway*, leaving his bride alone in the world. Mrs. Ramsay's death leaves the characters of *To the Lighthouse* (1927) without their main source of love and security. Although Woolf continually reinforces the observation that physical existence is fleeting, she also explores a variety of ways in which the communion of all souls extends individuals' life beyond their own time on earth. The lovers who return to their home hundreds of years after their death are clearly an early example of the thinking that develops into Mrs. Dalloway's "transcendental theory" of life, which holds that people attach themselves to the people they have known and the places they have been. Mrs. Dalloway even uses the word "haunting" to characterize this sense of spiritual immortality. It is perhaps because of lingering spirits that places, houses in particular, play such an important role in Woolf's fiction. Just as she makes the house itself a breathing, speaking character in "A Haunted House," Woolf devotes several pages of *To the Lighthouse* to a description of the Ramsays' house as it temporarily stands empty, its solitary state seeming to mourn the loss of Mrs. Ramsay.

*Style and Technique*

Woolf's unique style is often characterized as stream-of-consciousness narrative. She creates a fluid movement that captures a subject's thought processes as they drift back and forth from a recognition of sensations encountered in the present moment to ones remembered from the past. With this same ease of movement, Woolf is able to jump in and out of the minds of all her characters. This method of narration is certainly in evidence in "A Haunted House," and serves to explain how the narrator is able to relate details of the lives of people she does not know.

Because detail is presented through the eyes of the characters who notice it, descriptions of ordinary objects often carry a great emotional weight. This gives "A Haunted House," like much of Woolf's fiction, a melodramatic tone. When the shadow of a bird crosses the carpet of the house, the reader understands that this is both an intricate physical detail and a symbol of the mysterious presence that visits the narrator in fleeting moments. The bird's shadow is cast through the window, an object that also takes on great symbolic importance. The pane of glass through which the narrator often gazes comes to represent an invisible barrier to understanding and satisfaction, states of being that are represented by various kinds of light. The glass keeps the light of revelation, a sunbeam, from reaching the narrator, and then becomes a symbol of the death that separated the lovers centuries ago.

It is only when there is no glass between the narrator and the ghosts that light, this time not from the sun or the moon but from the lovers' lantern, enlightens the narrator. It is remarkable that in such a brief work, Woolf uses the device of repetition so effectively. Not only are these symbols repeated, but the house's murmur of "safe, safe" is a persistent drumbeat. Through repetition, Woolf puts before the reader the proposition that life forms itself into patterns or cycles that must be investigated for the deep meanings they convey.

In putting words in the mouth of her haunted house, Woolf employs the device of personification. Woolf often uses this kind of metaphor to draw existence in larger terms than the boundary of an individual human life would permit. The haunted house here is both a container of souls and a soul of its own, just as the narrator is her own person as well as a place in which the ghosts who visit her have stored their emotions. The presence of a living house and ghosts raises the question of the supernatural. Throughout her career, Woolf experiments freely with devices that add a touch of fantasy to her otherwise realistic fiction. In "A Haunted House," the lovers appear centuries after their time because they are ghosts. When they find their reflections in the presence of the living lovers, the continuity of human existence and the timelessness of love are established. Woolf would span the centuries in search of emotional connection again in the person of Orlando, a character who, in the novel by the same name, is inexplicably able to live for centuries. The artistic freedom exercised by Woolf in *Orlando* (1928) was certainly established as early as "A Haunted House."

*Nick David Smart*

# THE HEADLESS HAWK

*Author:* Truman Capote (Truman Streckfus Persons, 1924-1984)
*Type of plot:* Fantasy
*Time of plot:* The 1940's
*Locale:* New York City
*First published:* 1946

> *Principal characters:*
> VINCENT WATERS, the manager of an art gallery
> D. J., an odd young woman

*The Story*

Considered one of the most complex of the author's stories, "The Headless Hawk" resembles several of Truman Capote's other pieces in its use of flashback. In the first part, the protagonist, Vincent Waters, is followed home by an unusual-looking girl; the middle section flashes back to their earlier meeting, romance, and separation; and the ending of the story returns to the beginning—the present—and accentuates the stasis of the situation, the impossibility of any resolution short of violence.

Vincent is shown in the first and last segments in a state of disintegration, uncertain about everything, as if he has lost contact with reality. When he leaves his art gallery one hot July evening, he begins to look for and soon notices the young woman whom he expects to see. Neither speaks to the other, yet there appears to be a pattern to the encounter: First she walks and he follows; she waits, he catches up, they pause, and then he sets off with her trailing behind him as he makes his way to his apartment. There she stands outside, always waiting.

At that point the story flashes back to their first meeting, the previous winter. A peculiarly dressed young woman, with unusual eyes and haircut, appears in the gallery to sell Vincent a strange self-portrait. In it, her severed head lies alongside her body, and in the background is a headless hawk. Although the girl tells Vincent a few things about herself, mentioning a Mr. Destronelli, a name that will become very familiar to him in the future, she is also curiously remote.

Impressed by the power of the painting and by the affinity that he feels for it, Vincent decides to buy it. He is also attracted by the girl herself, though he recognizes that he has a history of falling in love with eccentrics for brief periods. He knows that ultimately he will dislike the very quality that draws him to her.

When he is distracted by a phone call, the girl disappears, leaving behind on a piece of paper only her initials, D. J., and an open-ended address, the YWCA. Because of that, Vincent cannot trace her. He spends lonely nights speaking to the painting, confessing his feelings about himself, his sense of failure and incompleteness.

Several months pass, during which Vincent is disturbed and upset. Then, one April evening as he wanders through the streets of New York City, he encounters D. J.

Frightened of him at first, it is not long before she agrees to go home with him. They become lovers, and occasionally D. J. tells Vincent a little about her past, always invoking the name of the mysterious Mr. Destronelli. When Vincent wants to know more about Destronelli, he learns only that the man resembles everybody.

The affair ends in a month, after the two have celebrated D. J.'s birthday. That night Vincent has a terrifying dream, in which he sees himself at a party, carrying the burden of another self, a horrible old man. Lovers whom he has betrayed also appear in the dream. When he dances with D. J., he floats away from her. At that moment, he is attacked by a headless hawk, which the freakish host has been holding. With that he knows there can be neither love nor freedom from his fate.

Awakening from his dream, Vincent finds D. J. outside in the neglected garden, behaving in a way that leads him to question her sanity. As soon as he does that, he realizes that he has destroyed his love for her. The next day, sick in body and spirit, he cuts up her painting and puts her suitcase out in the hall.

The story returns to the present and ends quickly with a scene in front of the apartment house. Vincent, ill and indecisive, stands for a moment next to a lamppost. The rain that has been threatening all day comes, and, as everyone else goes indoors, D. J. walks up to Vincent and waits in the silence and the rain.

*Themes and Meanings*

Vincent is a solitary figure who cannot escape from himself any more than he can flee from D. J. All of his previous love affairs have been failures, and he has abandoned everyone with whom he has been intimate. Like all mortals, each of his lovers had some imperfection; Vincent, in spite of his brief infatuation with each, grew to despise them, both male and female. Although he has escaped from all of them, he knows, or suspects, that he has injured them beyond healing. Until his affair with D. J., however, he evaded the responsibility for their destruction. However, D. J. is not to be eluded. She remains his waking reminder that he is a destroyer, a victimizer, a Mr. Destronelli, the one who has pursued D. J. throughout her life, the stranger who looks like everyone.

Vincent has also destroyed himself, though, becoming his own victim. Before meeting D. J., he was able to exist in his usual way, to work, to spend some time with friends, and to avoid examining his behavior too closely. However, when he sees her painting of the headless hawk, two things happen to him: He has the sensation that the artist must know and understand his inner being, and he finds that he identifies with the hawk itself. Lacking its head, the hawk is without direction. Vincent recognizes his own directionless self, a man who has talents and abilities that have never been utilized, a man who has never really loved anyone. If, then, the hawk is a representation of Vincent, his dream in which the hawk assaults him reveals Vincent to be his own victim. Furthermore, his attack on the painting suggests self-destruction.

As to D. J.'s knowing his secret self even before she meets him, Vincent is only partly right. The deception and betrayal that she has experienced and that she attributes to Mr. Destronelli are characteristic of Vincent. That D. J. is an innocent, an eternal child, is shown through Vincent's dream. She is also his last opportunity for love, for she is symbolically his last dancing partner in his dream. On awakening from his dream, however, Vincent speaks the terrible words that bring about the death of love. Instead of accepting D. J. as she is, he rejects her.

*Style and Technique*

In writing "The Headless Hawk," Capote worked with many of the same components that he used in other short stories of the same period, as well as in his first novel: dreams, nightmares, and distortions, all characteristic of the gothic mode that is typical of much of his work. The intent of this style is to reveal psychological states that cannot be portrayed in other ways, to show fear and horror within the inner core of many lives.

The dreams, the painting, and the fantasy of Mr. Destronelli compose the major symbols of the story, but there are many more, in addition to multiple images. Directionlessness, for example, is seen not only in the symbol of the headless hawk but also in other phases of the story: in Vincent's dream of waltzing, in his uncertainty as he walks the street, and in his use of an umbrella, which makes the tapping sound of a blind man with a cane.

Images of imprisonment, entrapment, and death recur throughout the story. The word "locked" appears in several places, and at the end it is clear that the two characters are locked together figuratively, imprisoned in their lives, bound to their individual selves and to each other. A fan that turns around and around in a store window is still another emblem of the inescapable circularity of their lives.

The separation of Vincent and D. J. from the ordinary world is shown through nightmarish images. The people on a New York avenue appear to Vincent as underwater creatures in a green sea. D. J. appears in a green raincoat; her reflection in a store window is green; her eyes are green; the popcorn she buys is put into a green bag. The emphasis on the color green simultaneously suggests distortion and unreality; it symbolizes a lack of connection with human existence; and, most important, it serves as an image of drowning and death. The use of the color green is representative of Capote's style.

Light, dark, and shadow are utilized not only for setting but also to symbolize states of mind. Reflections are distorted; mirrors are either blank or hazy, or they give false images. Nothing is dependable; everything shifts and changes. Only the relationship of Vincent and D. J. seems fixed, like the fan in its endless turnings. In the final scene, they stand together yet separated by the rain that falls between them as if it were an uncrossable barrier.

*Helen S. Garson*

# HEALTH

*Author:* Joy Williams (1944-    )
*Type of plot:* Coming of age
*Time of plot:* The 1980's
*Locale:* Texas
*First published:* 1985

*Principal characters:*
> PAMMY, the protagonist, a twelve-year-old girl
> MORRIS, her father, a college teacher
> MARGE, her mother, an art student
> WANDA, her girlfriend
> AURORA, a health spa receptionist

*The Story*

Shortly after her twelfth birthday, Pammy is riding with her father, Morris, to a health spa, where she will receive one of the ten tanning sessions that she requested as a birthday gift. Tanning and roller-skating—two of her passions in her final preteen year—help mitigate the worries that beset her youth. As she and her father drive to the spa, some of these concerns begin to surface.

The condition of Pammy's family, in relation to families around her, both comforts and disturbs her. Her father, who teaches petroleum science at a local university, is an imaginative man who delights in such little things as the pure act of driving; he is good at it, as Pammy notes, and uses their time together in the car to instruct her in the intricacies of geared and fluid movement. His joy in movement is mirrored in the pleasure that Pammy takes in roller-skating. Pammy's mother, Marge, is a student of art history and film at the university where her husband teaches; she keeps a chip of paint that fell from a Goya painting in a small glass box.

Morris's fondness for travel has taken the family to many places—including Mexico, where six months earlier Pammy achieved her best-ever tan and also contracted tuberculosis. Pammy's mother blames her father for her illness; scorning the safe hotel pools, Morris took Pammy to a mountain spa to swim. At this same place he later bought blue tiles for the family kitchen—the same kitchen in which Pammy now takes her orange juice and isoniazid.

Pammy also compares her own family to that of her good friend Wanda, who was adopted in infancy. Unlike her own parents, Wanda's parents like to drink. In contrast to Pammy's father, who drinks coffee in his car, Wanda's father drinks bourbon and water. Wanda's parents make Pammy nervous; she thinks of them as not very "steadfast." She is also bothered by a freak accident that once occurred in Wanda's home. During a vacation, the family had their house tented and fumigated for termites; on their return, they found a dead housebreaker in their living room—killed by the deadly insecticide fumes.

All of these thoughts intrude on Pammy's imagination as she finally lies down naked on the spa's tanning bed and draws its cover over her. She thinks of Snow White lying similarly in her glass coffin—an image that recalls her lingering worry over her tuberculosis. She overhears people in the next room discussing familial diseases and deaths. Near the end of her session she hears the door to her tanning room open and sees the vague image of a man standing, staring at her. The figure leaves the room, and Pammy ends her session.

The incident disturbs Pammy but not enough to keep her from signing up for another session. As she leaves the spa with her mother, she considers the blank coldness of the man's image and realizes that it is something that she never wants to envision again in her world. It is an image that she wishes not even to imagine.

### Themes and Meanings

In "Health," as in many other stories, Joy Williams assumes the perspective and describes the world of an adolescent female. She is fond of placing characters at this crucial age in order to explore the developmental crises that can emerge. As a result, her stories are often coming-of-age tales that detail the experiences of initiation, instruction, and awareness. As a twelve-year-old American girl, Pammy has witnessed the failures of familial and personal love all around her, so she looks for assurances of such love within her own family. Evidence for such love does exist: Morris and Marge demonstrate a kind of marital health that satisfies Pammy's concerns.

Moreover, that love is made especially important in light of Pammy's illness. The tuberculosis that rests in her young body heightens her desire for love. Although the disease does not make Pammy physically ill, it represents a potential for serious illness and possibly even death. Indeed, death shadows Pammy's imagination and her everyday existence. Though the shadowing is made subtle through Williams's art, it still darkens the corners of Pammy's world—a world that she works to make safe for herself amid the perils of words and knowledge.

Pammy comes to understand that language and words are powerful, often threatening elements of one's conscious life. Words such as "germs," "infection," and "cancer" can shape one's perception of how the world operates and how one fits within that world. Pammy herself is touched by illness, but more by the words of that illness than by its actual physical essence. Through these words she examines herself from new perspectives; she considers her changing body and its relative health. Although it is infected by a dangerous bacterium, her body has worked the magic of its youth and vigor in quieting her disease. This fact offers Pammy reassuring knowledge of her own vitality, of her own physical possibility, and to some degree offsets the disquieting knowledge of her own mortality. However, this darker knowledge that haunts the edges of Pammy's life is inescapable and undeniable in its presence.

More important, Pammy realizes the tremendous power wielded by the imagination as it creates, through word and language, whole new worlds and whole new truths. Words become part of a tactical exercise in defense. Words mask the reality of things; they signify both truths and nontruths that frequently are too horrid to share.

So Pammy works to construct—to imagine—a world that enjoys order and meaning. Hers is the adolescent imagination trying to make sense of an adult world; perched precariously on the fine edge of experience, Pammy strives to reconcile the remnants of her innocence with the hard knowledge of her adult world-to-come.

When the bleak, cold intruder steps into Pammy's tanning room—where the young girl lies literally stripped and figuratively in a coffin—Williams wants the reader to consider the imaginative potentiality of that experience to a twelve-year-old consciousness. Death is the odd, inevitable event that blurs all easy definition and shades the brightest light, and knowledge is the rude collection of fact that forever estranges the innocent heart from the experienced soul.

When Pammy leaves the health spa, she stops at a store called "Imagine," in whose window display rests a heart-shaped satin pillow split by a heavy metal zipper. This image of the zippered heart speaks both to the desire to close the heart off to hurt and pain, and to the strategy of repair that labors to mend the damage inflicted by the world-at-large.

## Style and Technique

Williams is often associated with a style of fiction writing that is loosely called minimalism. Minimalist writers are frequently characterized as those who strip their stories of all extraneous description and narration, supporting their stories more on dialogue than on exposition. Their stories often have an edge of despair, of bleakness to them, as they chronicle lives caught in the contemporary anguishes of failed love and failed family.

Williams is fond of describing the modern American scene, with all of its cultural—and pop cultural—detritus. In "Health," she employs the American cult-fondness for physical health and beauty—the artificially tanned body as a symbol (often a false one) of bodily well-being and success. The health spa thus becomes a potentially comic paradox of America's search for the artificially produced (or induced) healthy American.

Williams also enjoys catching the off-beat and off-center elements of our daily lives. The impulse toward movement and mobility, here expressed in automobiles and roller skates, is a motif that Williams frequently uses and one that she sees as part of the American character. What we see and hear on the road in "Health"—a television with a single bullet hole in the center of its screen, a car radio playing "Tainted Love"—provides a discordant counterpoint to Pammy's experience.

Finally, Williams tells her story in the present tense, as do so many contemporary fiction writers. This technique allows her to emphasize the immediacy of Pammy's experience, and to heighten our awareness of what might be called "the American present." We are taken directly into Pammy's maturing consciousness as it attempts to assimilate the varieties of experience—the varieties of health and un-health—that make up her American scene.

*Gregory L. Morris*

# THE HEART OF THE ARTICHOKE

*Author:* Herbert Gold (1924-    )
*Type of plot:* Domestic realism
*Time of plot:* Probably the mid-1930's
*Locale:* Unspecified, but apparently the Northeastern United States
*First published:* 1951

### Principal characters:

DANIEL BERMAN, a twelve-year-old boy, the eldest son of a
    working-class family
JAKE (JACK), his immigrant father
ROSE, his mother
PATTIE DONAHUE, his well-to-do classmate

### The Story

Now an adult, the narrator remembers conflicts he had with his parents, mainly his father, when he was twelve years old. The story begins with three quick vignettes of his father: striking a kitchen match with one hand to light his cigar; talking about his first job in America, selling water to men building skyscrapers; and peeling an artichoke "with both hands simultaneously . . . until with a groan that was the trumpet of all satisfaction he attained the heart." Interspersed with general anecdotes about his family, most of which involve food, the narrator reveals his adolescent crush on Pattie Donahue, a patrician classmate. As he attempts telepathically to turn Pattie's disinterest into a devotion to match his own, his parents decide that he should begin working in his father's grocery store.

Daniel envies his carefree classmates but is forced to follow his cousins' examples and spend his Saturdays working. He is embarrassed to be working while his friends play, and even more so when Pattie comes in to shop with her mother. He is also embarrassed by his father's job; he wants him to "commute instead of work, like the others." He resents his father's wanting to mold him in his own fashion: "The constant pouring of commands from a triumphant father shivered and shattered my sense for work; he wanted me by his side, proud of an eldest son, any eldest son. . . . he had been poor, he wanted me to see what he had done for himself and for us all." At the same time, he loves and admires his father tremendously; when he is invited to join his father for lunch, he is proud. Having the "Business Men's special" with Dad in a restaurant is one of the compensations; he sees choosing food as the act of a god—"only gods and businessmen don't have mothers to tell them what to eat."

A crisis does not come immediately. Some months later, Daniel enters junior high and is taking social dancing, while artichokes are coming back into season. Jake tries to interest Daniel in the store, even asking his son to write copy for a newspaper advertisement. A devotee of Edgar Allan Poe, Daniel patterns his copy after "The Raven." His efforts, however, are rejected by the shortening manufacturer who is paying half the cost of the ad. Still resentful of his duties at the store, Daniel consistently pretends to be asleep when it is time to go to work. His mother pleads for him against his father's irritation, reminding Jake that growing boys need their sleep, then chastises Daniel angrily when he finally rises.

One day, Daniel sneaks out early to see a gangster movie with his best friend. Arriving home after his parents have gone to bed, he must crawl into the house from its basement, from which he has no access to the upstairs. Filled with angst, he alternately believes that the gas stove has leaked and that his parents have died in their beds. He also envisions the basement crawling with huge Paris sewer rats and fantasizes that the water pipes will break and that he will drown. Finally, he decides that he surely will get consumption from sleeping in the damp basement before he finally curls up on a pile of dirty laundry and goes to sleep.

The next Saturday, after Daniel works diligently at the store all day, he discusses the business with his parents and enjoys having his opinion solicited on the various types of canned goods displays. He views this as a real truce but wonders if anything has been altered. Within days, the equilibrium is threatened by an opportunity to go on a field trip that is scheduled for one of the store's busiest days of the year. After hearing that Pattie Donahue is going, Daniel decides to sneak away before noon in order to join the field trip.

At first, it seems that his dreams of Pattie will be fulfilled. Seeing that he has no lunch, she shares hers with him, and afterward lets him walk her home and buy her ice cream. However, when he opens up to tell her he likes her and ask if she likes him, she replies, "Sure I like you but . . . you're just a *grocery* boy, you."

Daniel morosely returns home. The story concludes with the emotional conflict between Daniel and his father escalating into physical confrontation, shattering both Daniel's and his father's sense of security.

*Themes and Meanings*

"The Heart of the Artichoke" illustrates the conflicts inherent in an adolescent's struggle to make his own way independent of the family, intensified by the additional problems between immigrant parents and their America-born children. As the narrator recalls, "His sons were strange animals, born in America." Despite the love between Daniel and his parents, and the strong bond Daniel has with his father, Daniel feels that he must fight against his parents' life in order to build his own. The conflict is set up to explode with his parents' insistence that he work in the family store, which his father sees as their joint future. Not only does this deprive Daniel of chances to goof off with his friends on Saturdays, it marks him as a lower-class immigrant in his own eyes and, worse, in the eyes of his adored Pattie. He believes he has only two choices: to surrender to his father's world, or defy it. His father, who defied his own father in order to come to the United States and start a new life, does not acknowledge that Daniel faces the same conflict that he did as a teenager.

Pattie's rejection of the worshipful "grocery boy" focuses Daniel's anger on his parents' loving but old-fashioned way of life. The story ends with him returning home to face his parents. Initially he is ashamed of having disappointed them and is on the verge of tears—until he thinks of how Pattie would laugh at his father's pronouncing "kids" as "kits." He rages at his father, until his father responds physically. In the ensuing battle, his father's greater strength and experience easily prevail, but when he releases Daniel, Daniel throws himself at his father's legs and is as shocked as his parents when his father is knocked down. Not yet ready to take his place as a man, he tries to convince himself that his father let him win. For an instant, however, he is the adult, and his father retreats to the bathroom, crying "those first tears of old age."

*Style and Technique*

"The Heart of the Artichoke" is an excellent example of a unified plot that is advanced by vividly drawn and believable characters, not chance or coincidence. Herbert Gold uses language as rich and textured as the ethnic foods that dominate his symbolism. Food is a family symbol of love, security, and abundance. Jake's store is called Jack's Fruit and Vegetable, although it sells more than just produce, and Jake seemingly gets as much pleasure from procuring and selling excellent food as he does from eating it.

Using the artichoke—a comparatively scarce vegetable at the time the story was written—for the central metaphor, rather than a more ordinary symbol such as a rose, may seem an odd choice at first, but it works beautifully in the author's talented hands. From the opening scene in which the father skillfully tears through the artichoke to achieve the hidden treasure of the tender heart, through descriptions of his father "giving himself to a snack of artichoke with Kraft's dressing, the heart his end but the money-colored leaves loved for what they were," "listening to the artichokes at the top of a load," and accepting "being stuck with thorns," the analogy of the artichoke is echoed in the adult narrator's realization that life's treasures are only reached by persistently negotiating through the thorns.

*Irene Struthers Rush*

# HEAT

*Author:* Joyce Carol Oates (1938-      )
*Type of plot:* Psychological
*Time of plot:* The 1930's
*Locale:* A small town in the United States
*First published:* 1989

*Principal characters:*
RHEA KUNKEL and
RHODA KUNKEL, identical twins
THE NARRATOR, their friend
ROGER WHIPPLE, the murderer

## The Story

"Heat" tells the story of the murder of eleven-year-old identical twins, Rhea and Rhoda Kunkel, through the eyes of a childhood friend who is now an adult. Joyce Carol Oates weaves the story together like bursts of heat on a sultry day. The story begins with a reference to the "rippling" heat of the summer day as the girls ride their bicycles toward Whipple's Ice.

In the next scene, the twins are in matching white caskets in a funeral parlor. Again, reference is made to the heat. In a narrative that boarders on stream of consciousness, Oates introduces the girls, the narrator, and Roger Whipple. The child narrator describes the girls as inseparable, full of life, and drawing energy and power from each other. She describes their lives and their death with the innocence of a child's perceptions as she relates her experiences with the twins, who were lively and nice but would steal from their own grandmother.

The twins were active and freckle-faced with bright red hair; then they were dead. The narrator questions whether their death is related to their stealing. She philosophizes about fate and God and relates her image of what the murder must have been like, with an eleven-year-old's perspective. She was not there, but she *knows* what happened in Roger Whipple's upstairs room. Even as an adult, she continues to be haunted by the murder; the violence has become a part of her being. The narrator is a victim as well.

The twins are seen as one girl. They go everywhere together; they seem to function as a unit. They seem to know instinctively that one must have the other as a source of strength or both will die. Always known as "Rhea-and-Rhoda," they seem to have one voice. Alone each appears voiceless and powerless. In the scene under the Kunkels' veranda, when the twins force the narrator to strip, they do so too. They are energized by the power they have together. There was no touching, no harm done, just the realization that the three young girls have much in common.

The Kunkel twins stand out from other children. They share a special bond that only twins can fully understand. They do everything together. They plan to steal from their grandmother together, and they ride their bikes together. They visit the ice house together; they suck ice chunks and tease Roger together in the heat of the day. Rhea, the first born, always must be first, so when Roger invites the twins to visit his room to see the "secret things" that belong to his brother Eamon, it is she who goes up the stairs to his room first. Rhoda stays behind, but suddenly, having lost the power and the confidence she shares with Rhea, she experiences first fear, then anger at having been left out of whatever is happening in the bedroom.

Rhoda tries to leave, to go out on her own, but she cannot leave Rhea. *Something*, be it fate, God, or simple intuition, tells her she must go back for her sister. She turns her bicycle around in the driveway and seals her fate. She knows they must stay together, and so she returns to get her sister. The terrible events that happened in Roger's room are not described in detail, but the reader knows that these girls die together. There can be no other outcome.

The bodies, hidden in the icehouse, are discovered by Roger's father. The girls are buried together in perfect little white coffins, side by side. Roger is institutionalized, and blame is tossed around in the town. Some blame the girls; some blame the Whipples for not supervising Roger. All involved, directly or indirectly, are forever changed by the tragedy. The narrator carries the unseen scars of the incident with her into adulthood. She still sees the murder scene in her mind's eye. It is a permanent part of her psyche, affecting all of her interactions. The Kunkel twins seem to retain some power over her, in that the fear that was generated by their murder has been ameliorated over time, but the scars of lost innocence will never leave her damaged soul.

*Themes and Meanings*

The main focus of "Heat" is the reality of violence in the world. As she does in many of her stories, Joyce Carol Oates examines the mysterious and more horrifying aspects of life. What happened to the little girls is revealed by inference and minimal description of the scene. Clearly, they were sexually assaulted and bloodied by Roger Whipple, a character who represents the negative components of humanity in general and American society in particular. He represents the strong, simplistic male force that is seen as stronger than innocence, laughter, or good. The violence in this story is overwhelming to the reader because it is not graphically described. Readers are allowed to imagine the terrible reality based on their experiences.

Another theme that runs through this story is the eternal question of fate or God in the lives of human beings. Oates says that death waits for everyone. Sometimes people see it coming, sometimes they do not. The child narrator questions whether the children were punished for stealing from their own grandmother, even as she ponders the reality of death. The murders are exciting—even fun—for innocent eyes to read about in some ways. However, the finality of death is a hard lesson learned: The narrator sadly notes that the twin's friends missed them.

The adult narrator still carries that sorrow in her heart, along with a sense of guilt at having survived the twins. She is drawn back to the scene of the murders as she experiences her own sexual adventure in the form of an affair. While she has sex with her nameless partner, the murdered girls are constantly in her thoughts. She cannot escape her past. The power of the interconnections between fate and personal choice permeates every word of this story. The reader is constantly drawn into not only the events of this story but also into the thoughts of the characters. As the reader learns more and more about the twins, the Kunkels, the narrator, and the Whipples, questions about individual mortality and morality come into play. Oates forces her reader to examine personal beliefs, based on individual experiences, circumstances, and how one perceives the order of the universe, within the context of daily living in a small town.

### Style and Technique

This story raises the everyday questions of life to new heights. Oates uses minimalistic descriptions of the girls and the events in the story and leaves it to the reader to fill in the gaps. She parallels the themes of the twins, life, death, and fate in a way that resembles snapshots of life. First, the girls are portrayed as happy and alive on their rusted bicycles, which are often placed side by side in the same direction on the ground. Death is foreshadowed, and soon the freckle-faced imperfect twins are together again, porcelain perfect faces, still and lifeless in their perfectly pure white coffins, side by side in the funeral parlor.

Oates writes with a biting clarity that rips at the soul, and yet she does so with images that are purely poetic. The oppressive heat of the day serves as a metaphor for the sexual tension in the story. The scene with the ice chunks, in which the girls tease Roger, foreshadows a kind of formidable foreplay, leading to their demise. They played, unaware of death lurking in the upstairs room. Her language is at once gritty and as searing as the heat referenced in the title and at the same time alliterative and engaging. Her choice of narrative voice moves the story along. The first-person child narrator describes her experiences with Rhea and Rhoda. The omniscient narrator tells the horrors of the murder and delves into the thoughts of the girls and Roger. The adult narrator reflects on her memories with the innocence of childhood recalled but with the clear vision of a grown woman who has been victimized by her past and is still held captive in some ways by the violence that claimed her friends, even as she seeks to reclaim her place in the world.

*Kathleen Schongar*

# THE HECTOR QUESADILLA STORY

*Author:* T. Coraghessan Boyle (Thomas John Boyle, 1948-    )
*Type of plot:* Fantasy
*Time of plot:* The 1980's
*Locale:* Los Angeles
*First published:* 1984

> *Principal characters:*
> HECTOR QUESADILLA, an aging major league baseball player
> ASUNCIÓN QUESADILLA, his wife
> HECTOR QUESADILLA, JR., their son, a graduate student
> REINA, their daughter, who is expecting her fifth child
> BERNARD DUPUY, the Dodgers manager

*The Story*

Hector Hernán Jesús y María Quesadilla, an aging baseball player, bemoans the pains of growing old. Of indefinite age, he has played for five teams in the major leagues, compiling a lifetime batting average of .296. He fondly recalls how good he was when he was a nineteen-year-old star in the Mexican League. Now, he is a short, fat pinch-hitter for the Los Angeles Dodgers. Although he has not played regularly for ten years and can barely run, he hopes to play one more full season. He refuses to acknowledge his own age, but his son, Hector, Jr., is about to turn twenty-nine, and his daughter, Reina, is expecting her fifth child. Hector considers himself indestructible, an essential part of the game, "eternal as a monument."

On a game day late in the season, with the Dodgers battling the Atlanta Braves for first place in their division, Hector awakens sensing something unusual. "Today is different, a sainted day," he thinks. It is his birthday, so his wife, Asunción, cooks him special breakfast treats. After Hector receives gifts from his children and grandchildren, he senses that today he will play and he has no doubt that he will hit. In the baseball game later that day, in the bottom of the ninth inning, the score is tied. Bernard Dupuy, the Gelusil-guzzling manager, calls for Hector to bat. With two outs and a runner on second, it is a moment of catharsis, a moment to hit a home run. Suddenly Corcoran, the Atlanta pitcher, collapses in pain. He is replaced by star reliever Kerensky, Hector's personal nemesis. However, because it is his birthday, the aged pinch-hitter sees these developments as providential. Unexpectedly, Dupuy replaces Hector with Dave Tool, a lumbering, inconsistent power hitter, before Hector even gets his chance to bat. Hector screams at this injustice as Tool makes an easy out and the game goes into extra innings.

By the time that Atlanta takes the lead in the fourteenth inning, more than half the spectators have left. In the bottom of the inning the Dodgers tie the score. In the twentieth inning, Hector begs Dupuy for a chance to bat, but the manager cannot risk it. If the overweight Hector were to bat and not help the Dodgers win the game, he would have to take a position in the outfield, as the Dodgers are now out of substitute players. As the tie game approaches the league record for most innings played, Hector becomes glad that Dupuy has held him back and thinks that "the Niño and Santa Griselda have been saving him for something greater." He now knows in his bones that he will become the hero of the longest game in history.

As Hector's teammates grow exhausted, Hector himself feels stronger and more alert. When the Braves go ahead again in the top of the thirty-first inning, the Dodgers' situation looks bleak. With the pitcher's batting spot coming up second in the bottom of the inning, Hector finally gets his chance at the plate.

After Hector's count reaches two strikes, he hits the ball over the centerfielder's head for an easy double; however, he is tagged out when he tries to take third base and the remaining fans erupt in verbal abuse and throw debris at him for his failure. After the next batter hits a home run, Dupuy explodes at Hector, telling him that the game would be over, "but for you, you crazy gimpy old beaner washout!" Soon, however, the manager is on his knees, begging Hector—who has not pitched since he was a boy—to take the mound in the thirty-second inning. Miraculously, Hector strikes out the first two hitters, only to walk the next three and then give up a home run. With the Dodgers down by four runs in the bottom of the inning, Hector gets yet another chance to redeem himself when he goes to bat with the bases loaded. "The wind-up, the delivery, the ball hanging there like a piñata, like a birthday gift, and then the stick flashes in your hands like an archangel's sword, and the game goes on forever."

### Themes and Meanings

The fictional Hector Quesadilla is loosely based on Manny Mota, a Dominican baseball player who spent twenty seasons in the major leagues. During Mota's last seven seasons, he was almost exclusively a pinch-hitter for the Dodgers. Officially forty-four years old when he played his last game in 1982, Mota set the record for most pinch-hits in a career. T. Coraghessan Boyle uses Hector to make observations about baseball, age, time, and myth.

As Hector points out, baseball is "a game of infinite surprises." Although it may be impossible to prove that the unexpected happens more often in baseball than it does in other team sports, it is clear that the game offers possibilities that are absent in basketball, football, hockey, and soccer because the length of a baseball game is determined solely by how long it takes to make three outs in each inning. In theory, any game—such as the one that Boyle imagines in this story—could last forever.

The absence of time restraints in baseball contributes to Hector's considering himself similarly free of such boundaries: "How can he get old? The grass is always green, the lights always shining, no clocks or periods or halves or quarters, no punch-in and punch-out: this is the game that never ends." Baseball's freedom from time restrictions assumes an almost religious aura: "The new inning dawns as inevitably as the new minute, the new hour, the new day, endless, implacable, world without end." Despite his infirmities, Hector is reborn as he prepares for a game, feeling "the pain stripped from his body as if at the touch of a healer's fingertips." Because the game with its sacred statistics goes on endlessly and keeps renewing itself, why cannot one of its players do the same?

For Hector, baseball and life are inseparable. He sees the confrontation between the batter and pitcher at crucial moments as the essence of life: "My record, my career, my house, my family, my life, my mutual funds and beer distributorship against yours." Baseball, however, may be simpler than life: Hector is a hero if he produces and a bum if he does not. Baseball, as with other sports, draws a thin line between success and failure. However, failures can be redeemed. If Hector fails once, he will get another chance—so long as he and the game go on.

"The Hector Quesadilla Story" takes on mythic proportions as it depicts humanity's constant quest for redemption. This quest may be spiritual—witness Hector's frequent invocation of saints—or physical, as Hector's feats belie the reality of his deteriorating body. Like his namesake in Homer's *Iliad* (c. 750 B.C.E.; English translation, 1611), Hector is a heroic warrior. He also resembles William Shakespeare's aging King Lear: On the pitching mound, he is "elevated like some half-mad old king in a play." Hector's son is a graduate student in English at the University of Southern California, where he is working on a thesis about a poet unknown to his father, "writing about the mystical so-and-so and the way he illustrates his poems with gods and men and serpents." Hector, Sr., can thus be seen as a mystic on a quest to unite spiritual and natural forces by smashing a baseball.

*Style and Technique*

"The Hector Quesadilla Story" resembles Boyle's other short fiction in its explorations of the clichés and mythologies of popular culture and in its loving attention to the details of the senses. In addition to being in tune with his pain, Hector is acutely alert to all his senses, loving the fact that his sheets "smell of starch and soap and flowers." His greatest sensual delight, however, comes from eating.

Food is a unifying device in Hector's story. Although it may revive him, it also weighs him down: "He ate too much, that was the problem. Ate prodigiously, ate mightily, ate as if there were a hidden thing inside him, a creature all of jaws with an infinite trailing ribbon of gut." (His appetite is one of the serpents the mystic warrior must battle.) Boyle's accounts of Hector's quest for good meals allow him to display the writer's gift for colorful metaphors and comic exaggeration and his love of lists, as when he describes each dish in the athlete's multi-course breakfasts.

Baseball and food even overlap. When Hector is hitting well, it is because he sees the ball as being larger: "like an orange, a mango, a muskmelon." In unusual circumstances, however, as with the endless game, even food can be forsaken: "Though he hasn't had a bite since breakfast he feels impervious to the pangs of hunger, as if he were preparing himself, mortifying his flesh like a saint in the desert." Only the quest for baseball sainthood or immortality can overshadow Hector's more basic need.

*Michael Adams*

# HELIX

*Author:* Mahoko Yoshimoto
*Type of plot:* Psychological
*Time of plot:* The 1990's
*Locale:* Japan
*First published:* "Rasen," 1993 (English translation, 1995)

> *Principal characters:*
> A YOUNG MAN, a writer
> HIS GIRLFRIEND

## The Story

A writer wakes from a night of heavy drinking to find his head is throbbing. The discordant sounds of his neighbor practicing the violin add to his discomfort as he lies contemplating the intensely blue sky and thinking of his girlfriend. The blue expanse somehow reminds him of her peculiar habit of blinking when she is searching for a word. This small detail somehow sums up his girlfriend's personality for him, and he fears that this understanding of her dooms their relationship. With other women, knowing them too well has destroyed his feelings for them.

His girlfriend has arranged for them to meet that evening at their favorite café after it closes. Sensing that she wants to tell him something important, perhaps that she wants to end their relationship, the young man telephones her, trying to cancel, but she does not answer, so he decides to keep their date. At the café, they enter with a key borrowed from the manager. The young man wants the lights turned on, but she prefers the darkness; she brings them apple juice, but he wants beer. She tells him of a seminar a friend of hers plans to attend. The seminar teaches people how to rid their minds of bad memories. She likes the idea, for it gives people the freedom to choose what to think about, but he thinks the idea too radical and asks her not to go. She replies that she will go but will not forget the memories they have accumulated together. To forget them, she says, would be like dying. This reassurance raises his spirits.

They leave the café, and as his girlfriend describes some of the memories that remind her of him, they hear an explosion, and a flash of light erupts from a nearby building. Glass shards rain down on them as people hurry into the street. The turmoil does not frighten her; she is strangely cheered, for the flash of light reminds her of fireworks. She hopes that the blast has not injured anyone and enjoys its beauty. Her response makes the young man realize that although they are very different from each other and think very differently, they can still share their love. The night sky and this revelation also make him see that they represent all couples and are part of a universal continuum. Their souls entwine, he finally realizes, like the helix spiraling in universal time and space.

*Themes and Meanings*

Mahoko Yoshimoto begins and ends her story with an elaborate reference to the sky. The expansive blue sky outside the young man's bedroom window reminds him of his girlfriend's eyes, which look like half moons fringed by dark circles. In the final moments of the story, her eyes represent the universe that engulfs every part of him. If she did not love him or if she cleared her mind of memories of him, he thinks that he would cease to exist in some way, and the helix of their entwined souls would disappear. The young woman's discussion of memory suggests that time is also a helix that entwines experience and spirit: The young woman's spiritual world is woven in time from experience, and she intuitively realizes that beauty, freedom, and selfhood are entwined. The explosion outside the café marks a turning point in the story, concluding it and bringing focus on people's ability to discover beauty in the world, even when destructive forces are encountered. The young woman's thoughts on the seminar highlight her belief that people can choose their own thoughts; the explosion demonstrates her ability to see in the flash a beautiful display of light and color. Her response to the explosion makes the young man finally see the significance of their togetherness, which is both a beginning and a continuation.

Like Adam and Eve, the young man and his girlfriend stand at the head of generations, and their entwined souls form a helix that symbolizes the interweaving of past and present, the continuum of time and spirit. They are representative of man and woman, and the image of a helix expresses the union of time and feeling, of spirit and flesh, and of the growth and connectivity that binds all men and women who share a love like theirs. Their spiritual selves entwine as their romantic feelings are brought to light. The fact that the two characters are given no names highlights their universal nature. They are generic, representative of all who are willing and able to discover beauty and take control of their own minds. Their names are left blank, inviting readers to insert their own names.

Yoshimoto has said that her writing reflects the outlook of Japanese young people, who seek freedom and independence in a material world. Her worldwide popularity suggests that she speaks for the youthful spirit everywhere. This short story is set in the heart of a city, which could stand for any modern city, and the explosion is a reminder that danger can erupt randomly without warning. The young woman demonstrates that the individual is free to choose how to live in this environment, in fear or with the knowledge that people can choose to see beauty everywhere. The story shows that her control is pervasive: She chooses to continue their relationship by choosing to retain memories of their relationship.

The explosion ironically fuses the story's themes and principal images. The flash that splits the dark night reflects the relation of spiritual and physical light and darkness; the young woman's seeing beauty in the flash reflects the relation of the spirit, emotion, and experience. The explosion symbolizes the light of spiritual discovery, which illuminates the darkness and, for those who choose to see, offers the revelation of beauty. The young woman's independent spirit enables her to choose how she responds to her environment. The implication is that if she can control her own thoughts, she can control her own happiness.

## Style and Technique

The interplay of dark and light works on several levels and is conveyed in several images that form a continuum that comes full circle by the end of the story. The narrator wakes from a night of drinking; figuratively speaking, he is still in the dark about his relationship with his girlfriend. He is brought into the light by her revelation that she loves him, a revelation that takes place in the darkness. The helix, too, represents a continuum between the dark past and the bright present. To break this continuum by forgetting the past would alienate the pair not only from their past but also from each other and from the universal spirit that is in them by virtue of their mutual love.

The mood of the story is reflective, befitting the central subject, memory, and a spiritual quality infuses the young woman's conversation about the role memory plays in her relationship with the young man. A series of sharply focused images emphasizes the importance of seeing significance in the representative detail. The young woman's love for the young man becomes increasingly evident in the images that remind her of him: an elderly man, dogs and cats in alleyways, the warm rush of air from a subway station, and a ringing telephone in the night. When the young man recalls his girlfriend's way of blinking when she is at a loss for words, he fears his interest in her will fade. The story traces the unraveling of this fear in images of light, starting from his initial mental darkness and leading to his intellectual awakening. Her response to the explosion and her revelation that her memories of him express her love make him see the error in his thinking.

Toward the end of the story, the focus shifts to the young woman, whose own way of seeing supervenes and enlarges the significance of light and darkness in discovering beauty, as demonstrated by her reaction to the explosion. In the darkened café, he wants to turn the lights on, but she prefers the darkness, which provides a backdrop to the explosion and his own enlightenment. These images enable the reader both to see Yoshimoto's meaning in spiritual and symbolic terms and to feel their significance emotionally.

*Bernard E. Morris*

# HELPING

*Author:* Robert Stone (1937-    )
*Type of plot:* Psychological
*Time of plot:* The 1980's
*Locale:* The suburbs around Boston
*First published:* 1987

> *Principal characters:*
> CHARLES ("CHAS") ELLIOT, a Vietnam veteran and veteran's counselor
> GRACE, his wife, a conscientious social worker
> BLANKENSHIP, one of his clients
> LOYALL ANDERSON, his nearest neighbor
> CANDACE, a librarian

*The Story*

"Helping" follows Charles "Chas" Elliot, a sensitive, sardonic Vietnam veteran prone to alcoholic binges when he is frustrated or angry, through a time in his life when his marriage, job, and social interactions have fused into a flux of turmoil and disappointment. The omniscient narrative operates primarily as an unfolding present, with long passages of dialogue illuminating Elliot's evolving psychological response to the circumstances of his life. The stresses he feels have led to a return to the alcoholic escapism that he has previously managed partially to control.

As the narrative begins, Elliot has been attending meetings of Alcoholics Anonymous for fifteen months, maintaining a fragile sobriety. His resolve is tested by sudden perceptions of ways in which his plans have been thwarted and by moments of keen awareness of aspects of the natural world that tend to unsettle his mental equilibrium. Nonetheless, he is able to control himself until a client named Blankenship, a thief, liar, and leech, arrives at the state hospital for counseling.

Following a particularly enraging session with Blankenship, Elliot leaves the hospital feeling anxious and impatient. He stops at the local library, but his conversation with Candace, a good friend and amateur Greek scholar, fails to cheer him. Returning to an old pattern of behavior, he buys a bottle of Scotch, and in a mood mingling expectation and apprehension, he stops at a familiar tavern. His drive home is conducted in a mood of "baroque ecstasy, swinging and swaying and singing along," and when his wife realizes that he has been drinking, Elliot's forced humor juxtaposed with her distress reduces his euphoric state to one of defensive contrition. The tension between them escalates into a lacerating verbal exchange, suspended when one of Grace's recalcitrant clients phones the house. Elliot picks up the phone and unleashes a justifiable barrage of invective at the abusive caller, resulting in a cursing spree that leads to Elliot settling in the darkened living room with a bottle and a shotgun.

The next morning, Elliot sets out across a snow-covered field, carrying the shotgun, a massive hangover, and a heavy burden of guilt. When he meets Loyall Anderson, a neighbor he resents for his smug moral complacency and instinctively wants to provoke with antic gestures, Elliot is querulous and deferential, his manner indicating his confusion and his smoldering, unfocused anger. After a strained conversation rife with implied threats, Elliot heads back toward his home, stopping to fire ineffectually at a passing pheasant before trudging through the snow onward to his house. As he approaches the building, he sees his wife at the bedroom window, standing "perfectly still, and the morning sun lit her nakedness." This is a transcendent vision for Elliot, and he finds himself imagining her thoughts and feelings in a piercing instant of shared consciousness.

Still caught in a welter of emotions, Elliot has a moment of self-insight that gives him the recognition that he needs help and that Grace is probably the only person who might provide it. In a gesture of supplication, he raises his hand, acknowledging his failings, his hopes for forgiveness, and the degree to which his love for his wife endures in spite of his blatant exhibition of rotten behavior.

### Themes and Meanings

In an observation similar to others that Robert Stone has made in various interviews, he mentioned seeing a famous writer "drunk and pissed off, a situation I understand very well." Stone's interest in the nature of addiction, a subject he examined in considerable detail in his novel *Dog Soldiers* (1974) and in the short story "Porque No Tiene, Porque Le Falta," is the central concern of "Helping," a vivid and very convincing rendering of a man who is fully aware of the damage that his drinking has done to his life and to his relationship with his wife but who cannot completely resist the temporary elation he experiences in anticipating and then submitting to the allure of alcohol.

Compounding Elliot's confusion is a chaotic social situation that Stone uses as a register of his dissatisfaction with society in the decades following the Vietnam War and its effects on American life. Although it is not offered as an excuse for Elliot's alcoholism—neither by the narrative perspective nor by Elliot himself—the lingering effects of American involvement in Vietnam are evident in Elliot's barely suppressed rage toward Blankenship, who lies about serving there, and by Elliot's tendencies toward violence in speech and gesture that he regrets to an extent but does not really try to suppress.

Stone is clearly sympathetic toward Elliot, and the reader can understand why Elliot explodes when the parasitic Votopiks places impossible demands on Grace, why Elliot feels patronized by Anderson's casual assumption of moral superiority, why he purposely departs from standard counseling styles when the irritating Blankenship persists with constant demands, and even why he resorts to alcohol as a palliative for his psychic pain. What is harder to accept is Elliot's badgering, bullying attitude toward his wife, who not only deserves much better treatment but also whose willingness to stay with Elliot is either a measure of immense love and devotion or a perverse need to absorb verbal abuse as a demonstration of sanctity. Stone uses Grace's name as an obvious symbol but avoids a too-simplistic conception of her character by skillfully showing both her desire to assist people who have no other place to turn, as well as her irritation with Elliot expressed in biting ripostes to Elliot's cheap sarcasm. Ultimately, her sense of herself is based so strongly on an ethic of caring and assistance that she persists in her efforts to stand by and with Elliot. When she speaks of leaving him, it is clear that she has been tested to the limits of her endurance so that Elliot's final plea for help may not be sufficient to re-engage her affection.

At the crux of Elliot's behavior is a kind of negotiation with his perceived need for alcohol and his knowledge that there is at least an equal chance that drinking will make everything worse. There is no fully adequate explanation for alcoholism— genetic inheritance, individual difficulties, social pressures, and other apparent contributing factors not withstanding. Stone confronts the question by attempting to show why a man like Elliot not only returns periodically to alcohol but also can say to his wife, "What you have to understand, Grace, is that this drink I'm having . . . is the only worthwhile thing I've done in the last year and a half," and by having the reader, perhaps, agree that this statement is not without some validity. The manner in which Stone does this is through the employment of a very powerful version of realistic description and by the establishment of a vocal style for each significant character that corresponds to the psychological foundations of his or her personality.

*Style and Technique*

Although Stone has observed that the traditional concept of realism was a "fallacy," he has qualified this position by saying that since he does not "believe in it to start with," he does not "feel the necessity of reacting against it." His somewhat paradoxical and protective position has enabled him to use a kind of intensely realistic description as a means for drawing the reader into scenes of action that reveal and illuminate character.

This technique makes Elliot's moments of anguish especially poignant, as when he rages against the loathsome Vopotiks or when he goads his wife into lashing back at him as a compensation for his loss of control. Consequently, even with an omniscient narrator, the narration is close enough to Elliot's psyche to encourage the reader's identification with him throughout moments of clearly self-destructive behavior.

In addition, both Elliot and his wife are hyperarticulate, well-educated, and self-aware people involved in professions that require a constant dialogue with the people they are trying to help. Grace's sincerity is evident in her patterns of speech, as is Elliot's defensive irony, which he resorts to when coworkers and clients press him too closely. When they are involved in an extended conversation at the center of the story, the dialogue is both riveting and forbidding, fascinating in its naked revelation of their needs and horrifying in the way something usually unseen has been exposed. The individuality of their speech patterns permits Stone to hold the reader's attention through the long section in which, aside from consumption of alcohol, hardly anything other than talk takes place.

Because the dominant mode of the narration is a kind of realism, the use of symbolism in terms of Grace's name and her appearance at the conclusion of the story is an effective exception suggesting that Elliot might still be rescued. As Stone depicts her, unclothed in the window in the pale morning light, Grace is an emblem of hope, open and vulnerable. Elliot responds to this vision of grace—the word play obviously intentional—with the realization "that he could build another day on it." This phrase is a variant of the well-known Alcoholic's Anonymous credo of taking one day at a time and indicates that the "help" Elliot has received from alcohol may not be the only help available to him in his hours of deepest need.

*Leon Lewis*

# HER FIRST BALL

*Author:* Katherine Mansfield (Katherine Mansfield Beauchamp, 1888-1923)
*Type of plot:* Domestic realism
*Time of plot:* The early nineteenth century
*Locale:* England
*First published:* 1921

> *Principal characters:*
> LEILA, the protagonist, a girl attending her first ball
> THE FAT MAN, one of Leila's dancing partners, a jaded cynic

## The Story

Leila, the young protagonist of "Her First Ball," is thrilled though extremely self-conscious at the prospect of attending her first formal ball. Every detail, from the shared cab that takes her there to the coach bolster, which feels like the sleeve of an escort's dress suit, contributes to her pleasure. Not even the Sheridan girls, amazed that she has never been to a ball before, can dampen her enthusiasm. She does feel less sophisticated than her companions; after all, she has been reared in the country, fifteen miles from the nearest neighbor, and her friends have had such evenings before.

She admires the easy gallantry of her cousin Laurie when he arranges, as usual, to have the third and ninth dances with his sister Laura. Though sad almost to the point of tears that she herself does not have a brother to make such casual agreements with her ("no brother had ever said 'Twig?' to her"), the whole experience is so overwhelming that Leila seems almost lifted past the big golden lantern, and the couples seem to float through the air: Their "little satin shoes chased each other like birds."

Leila acts with instinctive grace and is courteous even to the boorish fat man who presumptuously compares his program with hers to schedule a dance. The fat man asks himself aloud whether he remembers Leila's "bright little face," whether he had known it "of yore," but his condescension does not faze her. She dances beautifully, even though she learned to dance in "a little corrugated iron mission hall" near her boarding school. Indeed, Leila has a series of partners, and Jose's wink tells the reader, though apparently not Leila, that her exuberance, grace, and beauty have quickly made Leila the "belle of the ball." Her partners, aware of her instinctive elegance and grace, try with varying degrees of success to appear nonchalant and to make the usual small talk. Leila herself seems unaware of the splendid impression that she is making; she knows only that she is enjoying herself immensely and that the evening is passing very quickly.

Then the fat man reappears for the dance he himself had scheduled, and the tone of the story changes completely. To this point, the words have flown by in a series of vignettes, almost a catalog of Leila's quick, vivid impressions of the scene. Instead of the expected awkward pleasantries about the quick and slippery dance floor, the fat man tells Leila that she "can't hope to last," that "long before that you'll be sitting up there on the stage, looking on, in your nice black velvet," that her "pretty arms will have turned to short fat ones," and that her fan will be "a black bony one."

Leila laughs at the fat man's words, though they bother her inwardly because she realizes that they are essentially true. One day she will grow old; then no one will dance with her, and she will become one of the chaperons. The music, which had seemed gay, suddenly seems sad to her. For a moment, Leila feels like a little girl wanting to throw her pinafore over her head and sob. Even so, she never loses her composure; she tells the fat man that she does not take his words seriously.

Leila's gloomy mood does not last. When the couples parade for the next dance and a new partner, "a young man with curly hair," escorts her to the center of the dance floor, Leila's feet "glided, glided," and she even smiles radiantly and without recognition when her next partner accidently bumps her into the fat man.

## Themes and Meanings

Leila's first ball is her first social triumph, even as it is her first disillusionment. She knows, even before she dances with the fat man, that time will take her beauty, that she will not always be *la belle du bal*; even so, these are things that she need not consider on the evening of her first formal. What bothers her is not so much the fat man's words as his callousness in saying them. Indeed, what Leila discovers at the ball is human cruelty, that it is usually aimed at the naïvely innocent for the perverse pleasure it gives to its wicked agent. She also discovers how brief and fragile periods of absolute happiness are. Fortunately, however, youth is buoyant, and the fat man's remarks, though noted and stored away, do not mar Leila's perfect evening.

Because she has been reared in an isolated place and as an only child, Leila's sensitivity is more acute than that of others her age. This gives her greater capacity for joy, even as it makes her vulnerable to greater pain. One moment, the lanterns, the azaleas, the gowns, the music make her float on air; the next, an aging cynic's cruelty punctures all of her joy, and Leila wishes that she were at home listening to the baby owls in their nest near the veranda. In short, Katherine Mansfield's story, for all its brevity, encapsulates the bittersweetness of growing up.

## Style and Technique

When scholars pored over Mansfield's autograph manuscripts and journals, they were struck by her poor spelling and her eccentric grammar. Even so, Mansfield's style is geared to pictorial rather than verbal vividness. For example, "Her First Ball," though narrated in the third person, re-creates the ball as Leila sees it: vivid colors, swift movements, ravishing music. It presents an important moment, perceived with the intensity possible only for a sensitive and impressionable young person. Indeed, the story is told with the manic mood swings of an adolescent. Like a musical composition, its tempos vary from *allegro* (the quickly narrated sections of Leila's arrival and first dances) to *maestoso* (the melancholy sadness following the fat man's words) to *allegro vivace* (when Leila dances with the curly haired young man). Often the words reproduce a waltz rhythm: "in one minute, in one turn, her feet glided, glided. The lights, the azaleas, the dresses, the pink faces, the velvet chairs, all became one beautiful flying wheel."

Mansfield was born Kathleen Beauchamp in Wellington, New Zealand. When she became nineteen she changed her name to Katherine Mansfield, joining an altered first name to her mother's maiden name. She was not an only child, but she was lonely, and her early trip to Europe made her bloom as surely as Leila at her first ball. Mansfield's pictorial intensity is the single most distinguishing element of her writing technique; it brought her to the notice of the Bloomsbury writers and caused Virginia Woolf to say, "I was jealous of her writing. The only writing I have ever been jealous of."

*Robert J. Forman*

# HER QUAINT HONOR

*Author:* Caroline Gordon (1895-1981)
*Type of plot:* Psychological
*Time of plot:* The 1930's
*Locale:* Kentucky's tobacco-growing region
*First published:* 1945

> *Principal characters:*
>> JIM TAYLOR, the narrator, a white man who returns to his family home to grow tobacco
>> TOM DOTY, an African American sharecropper
>> FRANKIE DOTY, Tom's wife, the great-granddaughter of a white plantation owner
>> MISS JINNY TAYLOR, Jim's seventy-five-year-old grandmother
>> BUD ASBURY, an alcoholic tobacco expert
>> UNCLE PHIL, Miss Jinny's seventy-year-old brother and manager

*The Story*

After Jim Taylor's business in the city failed, he returned to Taylor's Grove, his family's home for generations. Soon discontented there, he moved to Louisville, where he ran a gas station until the Great Depression brought financial ruin. Now he is home again, trying his hand at tobacco farming. As his narrative begins, he expresses his disappointment at earning only fifteen cents per leaf on his first crop instead of the thirty cents that he expected. Jim's latest venture depends on the cooperation of other people. Although he has no hesitation about living with his grandmother "Miss Jinny" again, it is risky to approach her with his idea of using her land. He must also get permission from his uncle Phil, who he expects to teach him how to cure tobacco. Before approaching his relatives, he asks Tom Doty, a former family servant, to work with him in return for a share in the profits.

Jim calls Tom "the smartest nigger and the fastest worker I ever knew." Their affection for each other is genuine, although the racial caste system left over from the days of slavery inhibits their relationship. Tom agrees to sharecrop with "Mister Jim" if they can keep the volatile "Miss Jinny" at bay. Notoriously difficult to deal with, Jim's grandmother is the last person in the county who can remember growing up with slaves. The black residents in the county know her best, as virtually all of them have worked for her family. Tom started working in her house when he was a young boy.

In addition to their having shared their early years on the farm, Jim and Tom now share the desire to work for profit together, and they recognize the need to handle Miss Jinny carefully. With this end in mind, Tom introduces his wife, Frankie, to the old woman, suggesting that Frankie can help her with housework and keep the atmosphere pleasant.

Jim has ambivalent feelings about Tom's attractive wife. A member of a respected African American family that has inherited land, Frankie has some financial security. Jim thinks that he dislikes her because, with her light skin and makeup, she appears "sassy." However, Frankie seems to be sufficiently good-natured to serve his and Tom's purpose, and Jim feels reassured by the love that Tom and Frankie demonstrate for each other. Jim also has ambivalent feelings about his grandmother, who is weakening physically but not mentally. She puzzles him with her interest in radio broadcasts, especially the news of Soviet Russia and China. She took care of him after his mother died when he was young, so he feels responsible for her now. Although everybody agrees that Miss Jinny is cantankerous, the reader sees her only as a generous and accommodating woman.

As Jim and Tom work the land, Frankie ingratiates herself with Miss Jinny, as planned. Tom and Frankie grow more loving, and Frankie keeps everybody happy. However, curing tobacco is an art that neither Jim nor Tom has mastered, so Uncle Phil sends Jim to Bud Asbury to gain the necessary expertise. At this moment, Bud happens to be in jail for taking a friend's automobile during a drunken spree. Jim gets Bud out of jail and brings him home for one of Frankie's delicious suppers. Everyone enjoys the food, but Bud especially enjoys Frankie. His obvious flirtation angers Tom, who must remain quietly in his place in the white household. Uncomfortable with the tension, Jim leads the men down to the barn to start the fires for curing tobacco. Bud shares his knowledge but leaves at intervals for solitary drinks.

Later the three men return to the house for a midnight snack. Emboldened by liquor, Bud dominates the gathering. He lustfully grabs Frankie's ankle, but she tactfully pretends to have stumbled. Though horrified by what is going on, Jim remains quiet until Bud asks Frankie to go outside with him. At that point Tom, who has never been impolite to anyone, reclaims Frankie from Bud and flashes an old-fashioned straight-edged razor. Jim now takes charge, ordering Tom and Frankie to stay inside as he reprimands Bud. The two white men get into a fight, which ends only when Jim hits Bud with an oak stick several times. After Bud leaves, Tom and Jim return to the untended fires in the cold barn. Although they resume the curing process, the tobacco leaves have passed their peak, resulting in a major loss of profits. As he had hinted at the beginning, Jim blames Frankie for their problem.

## Themes and Meanings

Caroline Gordon's story deals primarily with relationships and how human beings treat one another respectfully or disrespectfully. The value of personal relationships is most important to the author, but it is made more complex by her addition of multiple layers of racial customs, sexual mores, and economic pressures derived from the story's locale and its era. Most striking is Jim's ambivalent attitude toward the black characters. Jim wants to share work and profits with Tom, a friend from childhood. He recognizes Tom's intelligence and ability, and he has greater respect for him than for the white man Bud.

Frankie, however, bewilders Jim. He cannot acknowledge her physical attractive-

ness, so he labels his attitude toward her as dislike. In response to Bud's drunken escapade, which repulses him, he wants to rationalize his behavior by using the old racial
code instead of common sense and morality. Has he done the right thing—preventing
a rape and a possible killing—for the wrong reason? He does not know, or will not tell,
whether he has fought with Bud because he feels responsible for protecting Tom and
Frankie because he feels attracted to Frankie, or because he has higher standards of
sexual morality than Bud has. Jim's claim that he has acted in order to stop a black
man from attacking a white man is shocking, as the reader knows that he is morally
right in refusing to permit the white man to indulge in a reprehensible custom.

In the end, this ambiguity concerning southern racial relationships is viewed
harshly; however, it is anticipated in the sexual connotations of the story's title. As a
potential victim and scapegoat, Frankie has honor and she deserves respect. If her
honor is merely "quaint," or if a sexual pun is suggested here, Gordon is asserting that
men of this time and place consider woman's honor out-of-date.

## Style and Technique

Irony is Gordon's primary technique for presenting the complex relationships
among southerners in the early twentieth century. Her first-person narrator, who un-
wittingly reveals more than he intends, is the basis for this irony. The rough living
conditions and the brutality that interrupt relationships are offset in the early parts of
the story by Jim's basically good-natured acceptance of the bad luck that sends him
back home. His language is a major component of the light humor as well as the shock
of the story.

Gordon's command of early twentieth century southern dialect is a natural device
for grounding her story in reality. Although both her white and black characters speak
generally the same way, she follows the custom of her era by using certain spellings
associated exclusively with early black English usage. Modern readers may be
shocked by the number of times that the white narrator utters such words as "nigger,"
"colored," "boy," and "girl"; however, they are a part of the harsh reality of the story's
setting. They convey cultural attitudes that surface in the violence of the ending. To a
certain extent, they also prepare the reader for Jim's confused reasoning at the end and
his attempt to blame his failed tobacco-curing effort on Frankie, who is the true victim. By showing Jim's reliance on stereotypical attitudes, Gordon shocks her reader
into recognition.

These characters, their setting, and their language are familiar through the works of
better known writers such as William Faulkner and Flannery O'Connor. However,
with stories such as "Her Quaint Honor," Gordon joined her husband, Allen Tate, in
preparing critics and later the general public for twentieth century formalist criticism.
Their works and those of other New Critics attempted to demonstrate how technical
issues of unity, irony, and ambiguity were to coexist with values generated in a context
of family, religion, and the agrarian South.

*Emma Coburn Norris*

# HER SWEET JEROME

*Author:* Alice Walker (1944-    )
*Type of plot:* Social realism
*Time of plot:* The late 1960's and early 1970's
*Locale:* The American South
*First published:* 1973

> *Principal characters:*
> MRS. JEROME FRANKLIN WASHINGTON, III, owner of a small
>    beauty shop
> MR. JEROME FRANKLIN WASHINGTON, III, her husband, a
>    schoolteacher and "black revolutionist"

## The Story

The protagonist owns a small beauty shop in the South. She is a big, awkward woman with short arms that end in ham hands, plump molelike freckles down her cheeks, and a neck that is a squat roll of fat protruding behind her head as a big bump. To many people, she is anything but lovely.

The woman's trouble starts one day when Jerome, a neat and cute local schoolteacher, walks past the window of her shop. Although she is ten years his senior and knows very well that she should not desire him, she cannot resist the temptation of being called "Mrs. Jerome Franklin Washington, the third." Being married to a schoolteacher would greatly enhance her social status. Her family is known as "colored folks with money," but there is not yet a schoolteacher to grace the family name. Marriage does take place between the two, but it is a marriage marked by her total devotion and his complete oblivion. Her efforts to make herself sexy and pretty have no effect on him; instead, they drive him away from her. Married more to his revolutionary beliefs than to her, he is buried in his books and meetings, hardly showing any interest in her.

A rumor spreads that Jerome is interested in other women. Feeling rejected and cheated, his wife sets out searching for his lovers in order to destroy them. Rage and suspicion lead her to taverns and churches, from whorehouses to prayer meetings, through parks and outside the city limits, all the while armed with axes, pistols, and knives of all descriptions. She looks at white girls, black women, brown beauties, ugly hags of all shades, asking them if they have been messing with her Jerome. Soon, she is consumed by all this and stops operating her beauty shop. Her madness is obvious to all but her husband.

One hot night, made bold by a drink, she bursts into her husband's school principal's house, where she has seen her husband go in and out, and where she has been watching night after night to figure out what is going on inside the house. She is bewildered and astonished to find the women she has suspected sitting in one corner, and men in another, debating about things that she cannot comprehend. Her husband, without paying any attention to her, starts reciting some of the nastiest-sounding poetry she has ever heard. When the only woman in the room who acknowledges her asks laughingly if she has come to join the revolution, she leaves the room in shame and confusion.

At home, she hunts through her husband's clothes for a clue. It does not take her long to figure out that her rival is not a woman, but the revolution in which her husband believes. In a second, she gets down on the floor and takes out the books that have fallen from her husband's hands behind the bed over the months of their marriage. The word "Black" appears on every cover: *Black Rage, Black Revolution*, and so on. She looks with wonder at the books that are her husband's preoccupation, enraged that the obvious is what she has never guessed before.

Stacking the books neatly on his pillow, she uses the largest of her knives to rip and stab them through. Failing to make the words disappear, she hastens with kerosene to set the marriage bed afire. Calling the books trash and crying, "I kill you! I kill you!" as if they were his mistresses, she herself is on fire.

## Themes and Meanings

In an interview Alice Walker said, "In my new book *In Love and Trouble: Stories of Black Women* (1984), thirteen women—mad, raging, loving, resentful, hateful, strong, ugly, weak, pitiful, and magnificent, try to live with the loyalty to black men that characterizes all of their lives." Indeed, like all the stories in this collection, "Her Sweet Jerome" has taken on itself to examine the most intimate aspect of the female and male relationship, that is, love.

Walker portrays a troubled relationship in the story and demonstrates how larger social issues intrude into the individual lives of black men and women. In this story, the particular social issue is the African American revolution that aimed at liberating all black people. Fighting for the rights of black people should be a common goal to connect the couple in the story, but it is not. The couple's different understandings of what this revolution means and their inability to communicate with each other literally drive them apart.

Walker further points out that the couple's marriage failure is caused by their identity confusion, and she is critical of both sides. The female character's loyalty is apparently misplaced. Although other blacks in the story strive for everything African—African hairstyles, African dress, African names—she tries her best to look white. She has internalized the roles and images imposed on her by a society that advocates that white alone is beautiful. As a result, she is at a loss to situate herself either in the relationship or in the larger society.

The male character is not clear of his position, either. Jerome is definitely not a positive male figure in the story. He is not a real revolutionist who fights for the rights of his people, but a man interested only in theory, in the big-sounding words, not in action; especially not in those actions that will radically change his status of being superior to women. It is as if he enjoys treating his wife with cruelty and contempt, playing the master in the house. He identifies with his white oppressors and shows no remorse for oppressing his wife, abusing her physically and emotionally.

*Style and Technique*

"Her Sweet Jerome" is narrated in a very quiet and controlled manner, and written with an ironic touch. Readers are led to see what goes wrong with the relationship of the two characters and discover for themselves the "sweetness" of Jerome. Her sweet Jerome beats her black and blue even before they marry; he quietly carries out his sweet readings, knowing that his wife is raging all over the town looking for his lovers. Ostensibly, he is very involved in the black revolutionary struggle for the rights and justice of his people, but his struggle is so narrow that it excludes his own wife's sufferings. The reader soon sees the discrepancy between Jerome's alleged fight and his cruel treatment of his wife.

In this story, Walker deliberately uses narrative description, rather than dialogue, to present her characters. A heated argument between the couple in the form of dialogue would too clearly betray their inner feelings of love and hatred. Instead, as an impassive spectator, one reads the descriptions of Jerome's beating his wife black and blue; his muttered curses when she tries to kiss him good-bye, making her not know whether to laugh or cry; her mad searching for his lovers; and her almost ritualistic setting of his books on fire. It is this matter-of-fact description, rather than angry dialogue, that upsets the reader, haunting her or him with a picture that is clearer than the sound of words would be.

The ironic touch is best exemplified by the last scene in the story: the igniting of Jerome's books. Here, Walker makes an ironic twist to demonstrate her female character's madness. Mrs. Jerome Franklin Washington, III, is certainly not mad when she decides to destroy her husband's books by fire because they are the very cause of her sufferings: like a human mistress, those books have usurped her rightful place as the wife of her husband; like an accomplice, they have joined with her husband in making a fool of her. She is sane enough to take her revenge by burning her husband's books, the very things that he loves best; but she is crazy enough to think she can hide her face in her sizzling arms.

*Weihua Zhang*

# HER TABLE SPREAD

*Author:* Elizabeth Bowen (1899-1973)
*Type of plot:* Psychological
*Time of plot:* The early twentieth century
*Locale:* The coast of Ireland
*First published:* 1930

> *Principal characters:*
> VALERIA CUFFE, an heiress and owner of the Castle
> MRS. TREYE, her aunt
> ROBERT ROSSITER, Mrs. Treye's uncle
> MISS CARBIN, a friend of Mrs. Treye
> MR. ALBAN, a guest from London

*The Story*

"Her Table Spread" is the account of the events of one evening in an Irish castle. The title suggests the purpose of the lavish dinner party that has been staged by Valeria Cuffe, the young heiress who is also the owner of the Castle. She is twenty-five; it is time that she married. Mr. Alban is aware that he may be a likely candidate. What he discovers only gradually is that he is not the primary prospect for whom the Castle and Valeria are waiting.

As the story begins, the hostess and the guests come down to dinner. With the assurance of a guest of honor and a courted prospective husband, Alban observes the simple Valeria, to whom he is not particularly drawn. Alban's self-satisfaction diminishes, however, when he discovers that the ladies are hoping for a visit from the officers of a destroyer that is anchored in the estuary, perhaps the same destroyer whose officers, a Mr. Garrett and a Mr. Graves, visited at the Castle previously and were entertained at the Castle by friends living there during the absence of Valeria and her dependents.

After dinner, Alban's discontent increases. Although he plays the piano, he is ignored. Indeed, Valeria is not even present, but is racing about in the rain, careless of her satin evening dress, hoping to attract the officers, even if she must row out to their ship. Although she considered marrying Alban, she has now decided that her husband must be one of the officers; she assumes that the destroyer is the ship on which Garrett and Graves serve, and she tries to choose between them, remembering her friends' descriptions.

Fearing that Valeria will come for a boat, Robert Rossiter, an uncle of hers, and Alban guard the boathouse until Alban is frightened out by a bat. On his way back to the Castle, he hears sobbing in the darkness and realizes that it is Valeria. She is certain that it is Garrett, the tall young officer, and she calls joyfully, "Mr. Garrett has landed." Suddenly Alban is touched by emotion; he feels himself a man desired by women. The next morning the destroyer leaves.

*Themes and Meanings*

Although Elizabeth Bowen penetrates the minds of both Alban and Valeria, it is the change in Alban that involves the theme of the story. Valeria is immature, childish, ruled by whims, perhaps a bit simple, but she is at least fully alive. Although her dreams of a visit from the naval officers are based on the flimsiest of chances, both her initial joy and her later grief indicate that she is certainly a woman.

On the other hand, Alban is aware that he is not fully a man, but he blames his lack of feeling on the other sex. In the first sentence of "Her Table Spread," Bowen points out that Alban dislikes women. The reason for his dislike becomes clear after he discovers that the candles, the delayed dinner, the air of expectation are all evidence that the guests to be truly honored are the officers who Valeria hopes will come to the Castle. Evidently, Alban is generally ignored by women. As a result, he dislikes them. Surely, he feels, some woman could have caused him to love her and, thus, could have cured his emptiness.

Bowen makes it clear, however, that Alban's unattractiveness to women is not their fault. When he plays the piano, he swings around on the stool "rather fussily"; later, in the boathouse, he runs away from the bat; he worries about his evening pumps, which are soaked by the rain. Clearly he projects the image of a male spinster, waiting for life to come to him but only on his terms. His loneliness is his own doing.

When Valeria mistakes him for Garrett, when at her cry the other women come out onto the lamplit terrace, suddenly the magic touches Alban. He responds to the bare shoulders of the two women on the terrace above him; hearing Valeria's laughter, he thinks of her as the princess she imagines herself. For a moment he feels like a man, to whom all the women are reaching out. In a sense, he becomes the desired Garrett.

There the story ends. The destroyer leaves the next morning; the Castle is "extinguished," and Valeria's arms are empty. Bowen does not trace the results of the strange evening episode. With the destroyer fortuitously gone, will Valeria turn to Alban? Will he be able to become the prince of her dreams? In the daylight, will her eccentricities drive him away? The questions are left unanswered, and in a sense they are irrelevant. For Alban, there has been a difference. At the beginning of "Her Table Spread," he is alone, dead to feeling, unmanly and therefore inhuman. At the end of the story, he has, if only briefly, responded to women's beauty with manly strength; he has felt desired.

*Style and Technique*

In her spare, carefully crafted narratives, Bowen utilizes every character and every image to develop her theme. In "Her Table Spread," only five characters appear. Every one of them is important to the author's theme. For example, Mrs. Treye and Miss Carbin represent the dependents, to whom the marriage of the heiress is of practical importance. Should she not establish a permanent home and continue the line, their own security will be imperiled. In contrast, Valeria Cuffe herself wishes to marry for more romantic reasons. Even though she has not selected the man, she imagines an exciting life; childish though she is, she wisely understands her need for someone with whom to spend her life. Similarly, the elderly Robert Rossiter contrasts with young Alban. Old though he is, Rossiter is still part of life, chasing the parlor maid, drinking in the boathouse, despite the bats. His participation in life underlines Alban's flight from it.

In this story, the dominant symbols are light and darkness. The women may almost be said to be the carriers of light; from the gleam of Valeria's red satin dress to the sparkle of the other ladies' beaded dresses, feminine garb is intended to entice men into liveliness. Valeria deliberately uses light to attract her naval officers. The candles are lit so that they will be seen from the ship; later, the lantern Valeria carries is as much a signal as a light for her wanderings outdoors. On the other hand, though he is in the lamplit drawing room, Alban, at the piano, muses that he is "fixed in the dark rain."

At the end of the story, the light-dark symbolism becomes more complex. Valerie's lantern goes out, and she encounters Alban in the darkness. Although light streams from the terrace, Alban sees the beauty of the three women without seeing their faces; transformed in the darkness, he stands in the "flame" of their warmth toward him, or, indeed, toward the supposed Garrett. The fact that the Castle is "extinguished" in the morning leaves the issue in doubt; perhaps, having felt warmth, Alban will not be extinguished so easily.

*Rosemary M. Canfield Reisman*

# HERAKLEITOS

*Author:* Guy Davenport (1927-    )
*Type of plot:* Mythological
*Time of plot:* 500-400 B.C.E.
*Locale:* Ephesos
*First published:* 1974

> *Principal characters:*
> HERAKLEITOS, the Greek philosopher
> KNAPS, his visitor and student
> SELENA, his female housekeeper
> TMOLOS, his mute slave

## The Story

Knaps, stranger to Ephesos, materializes one late summer morning at the home of Herakleitos, the thinker, whom Knaps presumes to visit without asking first. Knaps receives a gracious welcome from Herakleitos and his two companions, housekeeper Selena and slave Tmolos. Propriety and proper measure are important to Herakleitos; accordingly, Knaps, after sharing their breakfast, will be expected to observe the usual morning routine, including music and dancing performed by the three, the strangeness and intricacy of which Knaps can only gape at. Herakleitos explains: "Were I to visit you in your rocky Arkadia, I should not expect you to discompose your day." The philosopher of flux and perpetual change silently observes and relishes the barbaric fashion of Knaps's hairstyle. Each is strange to the other, the difference being Herakleitos's at-homeness with contrariness and variety, out of which he has fashioned his famous thoughts.

Knaps's first impression of Herakleitos is of a man blending the exotic and the conventional. The strange musical performance is then followed by a session of philosophy, which Herakleitos initiates by crushing a leaf of sage and smelling his fingers, a religious observance. Herakleitos's "prayers"—whether before a session of thinking or at dinner—Knaps finds beside the point. When asked by the philosopher about the honor given Artemis in Arkadia, Knaps's home, the grave young man politely debunks the goddess: "There are country people who shout at the full of the moon." He admits to finding Artemis no more than a comfort for dull minds and women.

Knaps's secularity serves as a springboard for Herakleitos. Knaps is so philosophical that he has dismissed all customary acknowledgment of the mysterious or magical—Herakleitos pointing out the cosmic significance of Knaps's name he dismisses as a whim of his parents. Because Knaps is skeptical, and gently so, rather than cynical, he is no match for Herakleitos, whose penetrating vision repeatedly exposes the strangeness and harmony hiding beneath the obvious surface of nearly everything about which a mind can think. The old thinker's sense of paradox in nature, and in the way a mind works, soon reduces Knaps to a silent secretary, papyrus and quill at the ready. Herakleitos's utterances he records with proverb-like succinctness. Asked if he does not find it remarkable that a thread drawn absolutely tight should still be composed of curly fibers, Knaps writes: "Spun wool, . . . straight thread." For the duration of the story Knaps is an auditor, and gradually a disciple. He dances with Herakleitos, Selena, and Tmolos in the morning music rituals, even teaching the three new friends a wild partridge dance from his home region.

As summer changes to fall, Knaps accumulates a load of the sage's statements, which Herakleitos seems never at a loss to deliver while keeping each one in tune with his central theme: That which seems to be is often the opposite of what is. Thus, he intuits the motion in stone without the benefit of modern physics. Herakleitos's science is oracular, poetic, and very moving to Knaps's sense of wonder. Mesmerized, Knaps records:

> *Justice is contention.*
> *War is the father of all that is.*
> *Ephesians, be rich! I cannot wish you worse.*
> *Pigs wash in mud, chickens in dust.*
> *Even sleeping men are doing the world's business.*
> *The river we stepped into is not the river in which we stand.*

At the end of the story, Knaps accompanies Herakleitos, Selena, and Tmolos to the temple of Artemis. As Herakleitos offers his book of philosophy to the multibreasted image whose garments are adorned with bears, cows, lions, bees, flowers, and frogs, Knaps offers a carved wooden horse. The secular Knaps is born again to the awe of nature through the witness to her by the philosopher, whose concentrated attention is the most convincing kind of worship.

## Themes and Meanings

"When Herakleitos finished his book on nature and the mind, he put it on the altar of the Artemis of Ephesos, for whatever nature is, we know it first through her knowing eyes, her knowing hands." These words are spoken by a character in another story in the same book (*Tatlin!*, 1974), which contains "Herakleitos." The speaker is also a philosopher, though living in the twentieth century. Guy Davenport, the author, has provided this "footnote" in the later story to emphasize the theme of knowledge. The archaic Herakleitos saw human knowing as a response to the signs, the *logos*, which nature offers to a man's senses. For Davenport, what is most crucial is Herakleitos's ability to have seen and interpreted the world with a clarity and rightness that the most current modern science only restates, albeit with more complexity and an array of technological "proof." This *logos*, the speech of the universe, is a constant down through the centuries.

Hence, Knaps's initiation by Herakleitos proceeds from the master's first official philosophical pronouncement: "Let us begin by noting that understanding is common to all men." Why, Herakleitos asks Knaps, should a man act as if his intelligence were private, an extension of his inner self, belonging to him alone? The eyes, nose, ears, hands, nervous system, and brain he uses to know things together constitute an organic structure, marvelous when attuned to the universe of which it is part, but tending frequently to forget its basis in process, the flow of miraculous creation for which the Greeks worshiped Artemis, the giver and sustainer of life's rich bounty. Whenever a thinker breaks his connection with the *logos*, Artemis's voice, he becomes less intelligent, for, as Herakleitos instructs Knaps, "Men are not intelligent . . . the gods are intelligent."

## Style and Technique

Readers of this story will likely feel that they are experiencing something of the "real Herakleitos." That Herakleitos's life is a subject for conjecture, eluding documentation, matters not; Davenport's specificity in descriptions conjures the veritable. When Knaps first sees Herakleitos, the philosopher is "sprinkling crushed herbs into his wine, basil, tarragon and sage." The story's first three pages are crowded with sensuousness, from the fragrances mentioned to mouths "full of figs and spiced wine," to the sounds of barbitos, lyre, and a "chittering of sticks" accompanying the dance, a wild kinetic performance by Tmolos, the slave. Davenport's theme of knowing is played forte from the story's opening sentences, where the sensations of a rooster responding to sunrise and remembering other sunrises are conveyed through bright omniscience: "When he closed his eyes he sometimes saw a mare nursing her foal under the yellow leaves of a gingko, and heard the *tap tap* of the horseskin drum."

The author's language is applied to the page as if it were paint. The words call attention to themselves as words, as sounds. Selena walks around with her sandals "slapping the stone floor." Weather is frequently mentioned, the brightness of the sun on the sea. Sentences become paintings, imagistic and bright: "Herakleitos and Knaps stood in wild wheat above the olive groves, the royal blue of thistles beside the fluting of their cloaks." Davenport registers his vision by driving the language into the realm of iconography, the characters appearing in a visual stateliness, like figures drawn in frozen movement on an urn or carved in stone. The sentence rhythms create this "felt sense" as well, adding a weightiness and gong-like resonance to the description of Artemis in the temple: "Her golden hands were open in solicitude and blessing. A citadel crowned her neatly bound hair." The style makes the reader think about the artifice, which is the ordered language, at the same time as he is dazzled by the images—appropriate dilemma for someone reading a story about the man whose name is now trite with its association with the perception that everything perceived is something other than what it appears and is constantly moving even though standing still.

*Bruce Wiebe*

# THE HERMIT'S STORY

*Author:* Rick Bass (1958-      )
*Type of plot:* Magical Realism, frame story
*Time of plot:* The 1970's and the 1990's
*Locale:* Montana and Saskatchewan, Canada
*First published:* 1998

> *Principal characters:*
> ANN, a dog trainer
> ROGER, her husband
> THE NARRATOR AND HIS WIFE, visitors at Ann's home
> GRAY OWL, a man who hires Ann to train his dogs

### The Story

"The Hermit's Story," a magical tale about entry into an alternative reality, begins with a sort of poetic overture about the blue color of an ice storm. The narrator and his wife have gone to the home of Ann and Roger for Thanksgiving dinner. The power is out, and after the two couples eat pie and drink wine before a roaring fire, Ann tells a story about an experience she had twenty years earlier in Saskatchewan with a man named Gray Owl, who hired Ann to train six German shorthair pointers.

After Ann has trained the dogs all summer and into the fall, she takes them back to Gray Owl to show him how to continue to work them. She and Gray Owl take the dogs out into the snow, and Ann uses live quail to show Gray Owl how the dogs will follow the birds and point them. They work the dogs for a week until they get lost in a heavy snowstorm, drifting away from their base by as much as ten miles. When they come to a frozen lake and Gray Owl walks out on its surface and kicks at it to find some water for the dogs, he abruptly disappears below the ice.

Ann decides to go into the water after Gray Owl, for even if he is already drowned, he has their tent and emergency rations. However, when she crawls out onto the ice and peers down into the hole through which Gray Owl has disappeared, she sees him standing below waving at her. When he helps her climb down, he says that what has happened is that a cold snap in October has frozen a skin of ice over the shallow lake and then a snowfall insulated it. When the lake drained in the winter, the ice on top remained. Ann goes back to the shore and hands the dogs down into the warmth created by the enclosed space beneath the ice.

The world under the ice is a magical one, the air unlike anything they have ever breathed before. The cold air from the hole they made meets with the warm air from the earth beneath the lake to create breezes. Although the ice above them contracts and groans, they feel they are safe beneath a sea, watching waves of starlight sweep across their hiding place. When they build a fire from cattails, small pockets of swamp gas ignite with explosions of brilliance.

The two head for what they hope is the southern shore, the dogs chasing and point-ing snipe and other birds. They finally reach the other shore and walk south for a half a day until they reach their truck. That night they are back at Gray Owl's cabin, and by the next night, Ann is home again. The story ends with the narrator considering that Ann is the only one who carries the memory of that underworld passage. He thinks that it perhaps gave her a model for what things are like for her dogs when they are hunting and enter a zone in which the essences of things are revealed.

*Themes and Meanings*

When "The Hermit's Story," appeared in *The Best American Short Stories, 1999*, Rick Bass said in his contributor's note that as soon as he heard about a frozen lake with no water in it, he knew he wanted to write a story about that. Because he was try-ing to train two bird dogs at the time, he created a bird-dog trainer character and had her go up to Canada and fall into such a lake.

Such an event alone, despite its dramatic potential, does not make a story. What makes the event a story is Bass's exploration of the symbolic significance of the magi-cal world into which the characters enter. That magical world is presaged even before they break through the ice by the narrator's description in the opening paragraphs of the blue world of the ice storm, in which the blue is like a scent trapped in the ice. The magicality is further emphasized by the fact that the storm has knocked out the elec-tricity, creating a world of darkness. In the midst of this cold, blue, dark world, the two couples sit before a fire, creating the classic setting for a story to be told.

When Ann and Gray Wolf work the dogs in the snow of Saskatchewan, they travel across snowy hills, the sky the color of snow so that it seems they are moving in a dream. Except for the rasp of the snowshoes and the pull of gravity, they might believe they had ascended into a sky-place where the entire world was snow. All this is prepa-ration for their descent into the improbable, magical world underneath the frozen lake. When they look up, the ice is clear, and they can see stars as if they were up there among them or else as if the stars were embedded in the ice.

The closest the narrator can come to articulating the meaning of the experience is to suggest that it perhaps was a zone in which the appearances of things disappeared, where surfaces faded away and instead their very essence was "revealed, illuminated, circumscribed, possessed." Much like a magical journey in a fairy tale, the experience under the ice is a journey into a realm of dream and desire, which suggests that the world is a much more magical and mysterious place than it is usually believed to be.

*Style and Technique*

Style is especially important to this story, for without Bass's poetic descriptions, his rhythmic prose, and his suggestions about the mythic significance of the experience, it would be merely an interesting anecdote, depending solely on the unusual nature of the frozen, waterless lake. The opening paragraph, by repeating the reference to the color blue and the fictional metaphoric phrase "as if," sets up the entry into the fairy-tale world. This "as if" metaphoric quality also is used to refer to Ann's transformation of the dogs from wild and unruly pups into well-trained hunting dogs, "as if" they are rough blocks of stone with their internal form existing already, waiting to be chiseled free. If the training is neglected, they have a tendency to revert to their old selves, "as if" the dogs' greatness can disappear back into the stone.

Although often metaphoric, Bass's style is not flowery, but rather simple and straightforward. He does not tell the story in Ann's words, but rather has the narrator retell it, thus filtering the story through two points of view. Neither Ann nor Gray Owl talk much during their experience, and when they do, it is in the simple straightforward language of people reduced to basic states. In telling Ann about the lake, he says, "It's not really a phenomenon; it's just what happens." When she asks if he knew it would be like this, he says, "No. I was looking for water. I just got lucky." Although there is no indication, other than his name, that Gray Owl is Native American, his dialogue reflects the common literary convention of having Native Americans speak in short declarative sentences.

Bass, a naturalist who has written nonfiction books about the Yaak Valley in Montana, also devotes much of the story to his fascination with the natural world in addition to the dogs and the birds they hunt. For example, when the dogs flush out snipe from the cattails underneath the ice, Bass spends at least two pages pondering the presence of the birds, wondering if they had been unable to migrate because of injuries or a genetic absence. With the curiosity of the naturalist, he wonders if the snipe had tried to carve out new ways of being in the stark and severe landscape, holding on until the spring would come like green fire. If the snipe survived, the narrator reckons, they would be among the first to see the spring; they would think that the torches of Ann and Gray Owl were merely one of winter's dreams.

The fairy-tale, folklore nature of the story persists throughout, with the narrator considering at the end that Ann holds on to her experience as one might hold on to a valuable gem found while out for a walk and thus containing some great magic or strength.

*Charles E. May*

# HÉRODIAS

*Author:* Gustave Flaubert (1821-1880)
*Type of plot:* Psychological
*Time of plot:* About 30 C.E.
*Locale:* Machaerous citadel, on the outskirts of ancient Jerusalem
*First published:* 1877 (English translation, 1903)

*Principal characters:*
HEROD ANTIPAS, the tetrarch of Jerusalem
MANNAEI, a Samaritan, jailer, and executioner
HÉRODIAS, Herod's wife and former sister-in-law
IAOKANANN (JOHN THE BAPTIST), a prisoner and prophet
LUCIUS VITELLIUS, a Roman proconsul
AULUS VITELLIUS, his son, a favorite of Tiberius
SALOME, the daughter of Hérodias by her first marriage

*The Story*

"Hérodias" opens with a harsh and unsparing landscape, the powerful citadel of Machaerous as it looms over the desert, no city of human beings but an incarnation of power, a huge, pointed crown suspended over an abyss. Great forces are at work in this unforgiving land, against whose barren geometry of forms human figures are dwarfed. Herod Antipas and his wife, Hérodias, dominate the foreground of the opening scene. He is surrounded by political factions and wracked by doubts, shaken by the voice of his prisoner Iaokanann. She is engaged in a remorseless pursuit of power, a pursuit furthered for her by Herod's love, at the expense of divorce and the loss of her daughter. Herod's love has died, but she still works to further his power because she may yet rule through him. Thus she arranges the death of her own brother in prison; such intrafamilial killings are as commonplace to her as they are to Herod. Their very marriage is founded on her divorce from Herod's own brother. In Rome, such machinations are taken for granted, but to the peoples they rule, the marriage of Hérodias and Herod is incestuous, an abomination.

Iaokanann, whose last day this story chronicles from rising sun to rising sun, is the opposite of Hérodias; he denounces her as a Jezebel and threatens her power, his voice cuts off her breath, and she desires nothing so much as his death. All of her wiles are bent to this end from the moment that she appears on the scene. Because Herod is now dead to her charms, she does not hesitate to use other means: The first hint of the arrival of Salome comes through Hérodias's reproaches to Herod. In Herod's mind, Iaokanann is still valuable in bargaining with the many sects that he must manipulate to control Jerusalem. Locked deep in the bowels of the citadel, the prisoner seems harmless, though the rumble of his voice arises at times to trouble the already troubled ruler.

Herod is preparing to celebrate his birthday. The most important leaders of Jerusalem, religious and secular, the Roman proconsul Lucius Vitellius and his son, and the most important of his allies and political opponents are invited. Outside the citadel the king of the Arabs, Herod's insulted first father-in-law, gathers forces for an attack. The progression of the day sees the interplay of these political forces as Herod attempts to maneuver himself into a position of safety and strength. There has even been a prophecy: Someone important will die in the citadel this day.

The arrival of various guests, especially of Lucius Vitellius and his son Aulus Vitellius, swamps the reader with names and a catalog of warring political and religious interests. Herod must meet and propitiate Samaritans, Essenes, Galileans, Pharisees, Nazarenes, Sadducees, Romans, and publicans, each of whom clamors for attention. Lucius Vitellius, representing the power of Tiberius Caesar, insists on inspecting the citadel and is led into all the storage rooms, the great beehive of the hollowed cliff under the fortress. Here armaments of all kinds are stockpiled, enough for forty thousand men.

There is even a subterranean stable with a hundred white war-horses, trained and groomed by a Babylonian. During this inspection, the underground cell of Iaokanann is discovered and opened. The powerful voice, rising from darkness into a scene where sunlight glints from armor and jewels, blasts Herod and his wife. The leaders of the Jewish sects are set abuzz; the Romans find Iaokanann's accusations of adultery and incest against their host amusing but are more troubled to hear that he opposes paying taxes to Rome. So passes the afternoon of confusion and bargaining, in preparation for the evening's feast. In the course of the afternoon, Herod twice catches a glimpse of a young girl—a stranger, but very beautiful—first from a distance, then in the rooms of Hérodias herself.

The feast is described in the most lavish of terms, a heaping up of all the excesses of Roman orgiastic cuisine for the benefit of the young Aulus Vitellius, who is already renowned as a glutton. The two cultures, Roman and Jewish, clash, and there are many conflicts of interest, both political and religious. Lucius Vitellius affects an interpreter but can understand the language of the people surrounding him; he hears them speak of a Messiah in connection with Iaokanann, one Jesus Christ, and must ask the definition of the term from the priests.

The climax of the evening is reached with the entrance of the lovely Salome, glimpsed earlier in the day. At her mother's orders, Salome dances in such a seductive manner that she arouses all the men at the feast, and Herod, seeing in her the beauty that Hérodias has lost, offers her any reward she wishes. Her answer? The head of Iaokanann.

The actual execution is not described. Mannaei brings the severed head on a platter to Salome, then displays it to the guests. The banquet ends, and Herod remains, staring at the head and weeping. Phanuel, an Essene who had delivered the prophecy of death to Herod and had pleaded for the life of Iaokanann, prays.

At dawn the next day, Phanuel leaves the citadel with the head still on its platter. He meets two men, messengers returning to Iaokanann. The three continue together on the road to Galilee, carrying the heavy load by turns.

## Themes and Meanings

The late nineteenth and early twentieth centuries saw many adaptations of the biblical story of John the Baptist and Salome. Notable examples are the verse drama *Hérodias* (1940) by Stephane Mallarme and Richard Strauss's opera *Salome* (1905), which was based on a play of the same name by Oscar Wilde. In "Hérodias," Gustave Flaubert focuses on the struggle between the worldly Hérodias and the righteous Iaokanann. The swirl of political and religious interests that surrounds Herod Antipas and his wife is the antithesis of the simple yet terrible preaching of the Baptist. Hérodias's power is doubled in the person of the young Salome, the incarnation of the sensuous life, while Iaokanann effaces himself as a double for Jesus, the Messiah. Iaokanann speaks from the shadows, a powerful voice whose echoes rock the citadel, while Hérodias strikes the reader visually; she stands in the light, bright in color, sharp-edged. The pivotal point in this struggle is reached in the familiar scene of Salome's dance, the trap for the wavering Herod, who finds a kind of relief in seeing his decision made for him by Hérodias's ruse. The execution of her enemy seems a victory for Hérodias, yet it is only through the death of Iaokanann that Jesus can rise; the personal diminishment of the Baptist contributes to the eventual triumph of the Messiah.

## Style and Technique

Flaubert is said to have done extensive historical research before writing the opening words of "Hérodias." His arid painting of a geometric and empty world, where a great fortress stares across the desert to Jerusalem, expresses the spiritual vacuum behind the power of Herod's house. As the story progresses, the author continues to make every word count. His descriptions pile up, proliferating details on the fortress itself and the people who pass through its gates on this fateful day. Tribes are named and individuals listed and described in all their exotic and sometimes grotesque detail. In Herod's subterranean storerooms are a confusion of numbers and an exhaustive listing of armaments, such as the hundred blue-maned war-horses, gentle as sheep yet trained to eviscerate the enemy and fight all day.

Against this world of proliferating detail is set Iaokanann, little more than a shadow with a voice, but this voice speaks in biblical phrases and rocks the foundations of the worldly power of the captors. During the banquet, Flaubert again heaps up details of food, arguments, personalities, adding to the masculine political world the raw sensuality of Salome and her dancing. This dance is the climax of all that has gone before. The execution of Iaokanann is anticlimactic; his head is presented to the reader in the flattest and simplest of terms. Absent are the lavish descriptions and listings, absent the lyric sensuality of Salome's dance. Iaokanann, deprived of his voice, has given way to a story yet to be told, that of the Messiah. The last glimpse of him is of his head, reduced to an object remarkable mainly for its weight, being carried toward Galilee.

Flaubert does not mention Hérodias again after the Baptist's death is assured; her place in the stylistic considerations of the story, as in thematic development, lies in descriptions of excess. There is no room for her in the cool and understated phrases that end the narration.

It is interesting to note that Flaubert has divided his action into three main parts and that he stays within the limits of the three classical unities of French tragedy: time (within the space of twenty-four hours), place (all action is in or about the fortress), and action (the story is devoted to the development of one narrative line, and it does not deviate from it.) Within these strict formal limitations, the author produces a story of remarkable power.

*Anne W. Sienkewicz*

# THE HEROES IN THE DARK HOUSE

*Author:* Benedict Kiely (1919-     )
*Type of plot:* Frame story
*Time of plot:* 1944
*Locale:* Northern Ireland
*First published:* 1963

*Principal characters:*
ARTHUR BRODERICK, an elderly folktale collector and storyteller
A YOUNG SCHOLAR, unnamed, interested in Broderick's tales
PATRICK, a village public-house keeper
AMERICAN SOLDIERS, stationed briefly in Northern Ireland

*The Story*

Benedict Kiely's "The Heroes in the Dark House" is both a story of the sudden arrival and disappearance of modern-day heroes and the story of the narrator's visit with a young admirer who would hear one of his best Irish tales. Its dramatic impact comes from the juxtaposition of the exploits of ancient heroes such as Shawn of Kinsale with those of ordinary American G.I.'s stationed for a time in a Northern Irish village.

The story begins with Arthur Broderick, a collector of stories dealing with heroes, ending his tale about the American soldiers. The third-person narrator of the story indicates that Broderick has enthralled his young listener with an account of how dashing, even gallant Americans forever transformed the life of his village, then were gone to fight in France without any good-byes. Like true heroes, they went into the realm of myth and left behind no physical trace of their visitation. A bulldozer smashed everything they cast off, from bicycles to bayonets.

Most of the tales that Broderick collects from old people with long memories deal with events set in pre-Christian Ireland, but he insists to his scholar-visitor that the story of the American soldiers is a genuine folktale in its own right.

The "dark house" of the title is Broderick's old dwelling, which is both reminiscent of the smoke-filled castles of ancient Irish warriors and a reminder of the rebellion of 1798, when the house was used as a gathering place for conspirators against the Crown. Broderick makes much of the fact that the handsome oak table in front of the scholar was fashioned from a bellows in a smithy that was destroyed by British redcoats, who feared that it would be used to fashion the deadly Irish rebels' pikes. His mentioning the "men of '98" reemphasizes the heroic motif introduced when he spoke of the deeds of Shawn of Kinsale, who battled seven mile-high crags and seven miles of angry sea to gain the hand of his love.

The presence of departed heroes, the narrator notes, hangs about Broderick's house like smoke. Smoke and darkness are used throughout the story to establish the continuity of past and present.

After letting the reader know something about Broderick's house, the narrator then discusses some of the sources of his tales, people such as Peader Haughey of Creggan Cross, a wizened man recalling the struggles of the king of Antua and the tyranny of the giant of Reibhlean, and an eighty-year-old woman named Maire John who remembers the tale of the three princesses and a wishing chair. The narrator emphasizes that such tales grow spontaneously in Ireland. Whenever a magical event occurs, it is transformed into a folk story by someone and thereafter is polished and reworked by tellers down the ages.

Next, the narrator is taken on a walk with Broderick during which he enters into the recent past and sees soldiers waving as they casually pass by and the dust clouds announce their passing. They stand out against the life of the village as the heroes of the past would have done; they are larger-than-life figures invigorating the world with their youth and vitality.

Patrick the pub keeper, a local trickster and character, cannot understand the Americans' lack of decorum and discipline, nor can he figure out why one large Texan would stoop so low as to assist a local prostitute struggling with a milk pail. Broderick counters that perhaps what every Irishwoman needs is a bit of chivalry.

A few days later, the shouting, friendly, gallant men are gone off to battle in Normandy to encounter the mighty and terrible weapons of Adolf Hitler's German army and air force. Broderick lets his listener know that the tests the American soldiers would face in Normandy would be as terrible as those faced by heroes of ancient times. Instead of mountains of fire, they would have to contend with mortars, rockets, and grenades. The story ends as it began: with an empty barracks and a quiet village.

## Themes and Meanings

One of the central themes of "The Heroes in the Dark House" is that heroes are found whenever there is a monstrous evil in the world that must be overcome. The hero's characteristics remain unchanged throughout the ages. Cheerfulness despite the threat of injury and death, a compelling love for others that allows one to fight for their well-being, a bold resolution to act: These traits always have been those of the hero. The heroes of the story, for all their collective importance, are not given individual identities, a fact that points to another trait of the hero: Often he is not a three-dimensional personality, but rather, a kind of ennobled Everyman, one to whom everyone can relate.

A second theme is that history is cyclic, and because it is, tyranny, though it takes many forms, is a recurring phenomenon in human affairs that demands either total submission to it or total defiance of it.

The heroes conjured forth in Broderick's dark house are giant-slayers, witch-destroyers, fighters against tyrannical kings, and the antagonists of evil, monstrous regimes. Because of them, civilization survives. Certainly, all about them is a magical, supernatural quality that comes from their ability to suspend their fear of death and fight for liberty.

If tyranny is cyclic and the nations of the world never see the end of it, so, too, hope is never-ending. At every challenge to civilization, heroes will come forth, often from the most unexpected quarters.

*Style and Technique*

By using the story-within-a-story technique to create a certain distance between the author/narrator and Arthur Broderick, teller of tales, Kiely expands on the historic and mythic meaning of Broderick's dark house and Broderick's resemblance to a bard and a wizard, while allowing the old man to tell a spellbinding story. Thus, Broderick becomes as important a figure as the subjects of his account, and the reader discovers how significant is the local storyteller's contribution to his culture. By recording the great tales in written form, he assures their continued life.

In a large sense, then, this is a story not only about American soldiers in Ulster province but also about the storyteller's art. By extension, it is about the soul of Ireland, for storytellers have been fashioning a bold enchanted Ireland from stories for centuries. To Kiely, the Brodericks of Ireland weave together the past and the present into one remarkable tapestry, the very chronicle of everything heroic and sublime.

*John D. Raymer*

# HE'S AT THE OFFICE

*Author:* Allan Gurganus (1947-     )
*Type of plot:* Realism, war
*Time of plot:* The late 1990's
*Locale:* An eastern U.S. city
*First published:* 1999

> *Principal characters:*
> DICK MARKHAM, a businessperson
> MISS GREEN, his secretary
> BETTY MARKHAM, his wife
> DICK MARKHAM, JR., his son

*The Story*

"He's at the Office" is the story of an aging man forced from his job because of his increasingly common memory lapses and of his wife and son, who try to care for him. The father has severe trouble dealing with retirement, for reasons that stretch back more than fifty years, to the 1940's.

Before his forced retirement, Dick Markham was a devoted employee of Integrity Office Supplier, a manufacturer of high-quality office goods. The company did a thriving business from the 1940's into the 1970's, when it was bought by a German firm. With the onset of computers, the steadfastly conservative nature of the business spelled its slow decline. Markham seemed intent on making up for the slowing business by increasing his efforts. Always a hard worker, he spent more time in the office than before.

Markham had not always been so heavily devoted to the working world. As fun-loving as any other young man before World War II, his experience in that conflict had turned him into a sober-minded man of business. Something about his entry to the working world, moreover, deeply affected him. This was apparent in his daily apparel. He never abandoned the styles of the 1940's, affecting them to his last day.

Dick Markham, Jr., narrates his father's story. He relates that four years earlier, he received a phone call from someone in his father's office building. His father, he learned, had become disoriented and was banging on the door of the office a floor above his own, demanding that they let him in and also that they release his secretary, Miss Green, who he supposed was being held hostage. Dick, Jr., went to help his father and escorted him to the correct floor. He then quizzed Miss Green about his father and learned that she had been covering for his father's small lapses of memory for some time. Now, however, they were increasing in frequency, and were becoming more serious. Throughout the older Markham's career, Miss Green had been his perfect match in the business. Like him, she had continued wearing styles made popular in the 1940's.

Once he is forced into retirement, Markham becomes a burden to his wife, Betty, who had enjoyed a considerable social life and now finds herself in the role of caretaker. Markham's inability to adjust to a life of being constantly at home occasionally takes a violent turn, which leads Betty to consider surrendering their savings in order to put him in a care facility.

Dick, Jr., wanting to keep Miss Green abreast of developments, visits her in a retirement home and is surprised to find her now looking up-to-date in appearance. He learns she had maintained her look all those years for the sake of his father's peace of mind. He had been unable to cope, otherwise. When Dick, Jr., then visits a local Salvation Army and sees a homeless man asleep at some old office furniture, an idea is born in his mind that seems to offer a solution to his father's problems.

With the help of his mother, he recreates his father's old Integrity office in a spare room and scatters some old paperwork. Making the elder Markham dress for work and put on his hat, Dick, Jr., walks him around the block, then escorts the old man back inside to his new office at home. Even though the elder Markham is aware of the ruse, he accepts it. The balance of household life is restored. Thereafter, Markham daily goes to his office, where old habit and routine can still comfortably guide his actions. Meanwhile, his wife regains the freedom she needs to pursue a satisfying social life.

When Dick, Jr., finally relaxes enough to take a vacation with his own family, he receives a call from his mother, saying his father has died, peacefully, in his office.

## Themes and Meanings

In "He's at the Office," Allan Gurganus uses the figure of Dick Markham to embody a generation deeply affected by World War II. The war resonates in Markham's life decades later, although the resonance rarely emerges into direct reference. The indirect references, however, are abundant, even in Markham's own spoken and written words. He refers to Miss Green as being "something of a bombshell," and, when confused about which office is his, refers to his son's appearance as the arrival of "reinforcements" and to the incident as "a hostage situation."

The speed of social change is introduced as an important element in the story's opening paragraphs, which describe a walk the father and son take along the road. Markham is dressed in his 1940's business suit, complete with the appropriate hat for the season. They encounter a youth who is impressed by the apparel: "Way bad look on you, guy," he says to Markham. The son has to translate the phrase for his father, saying only that it was positive praise. He is unable, however, to explain the changing waves of fashion trends, toward which the man had turned a blind eye through all the postwar years.

The sadness of Markham's life extends to the situation being depicted. Markham is a damaged man, having entered the war as a enthusiastic and energetic young man and having emerged from it as the single-minded businessperson he remained for the rest of his life. That he witnessed horrors goes unspoken, beyond the notation that he had enlisted with friends and he alone had emerged whole. What was lost from his life, however, was something not to be recovered any more easily than a lost limb.

The theme of the damaged soul trying to cope within society is tied to the theme of the charade. Markham lives within a long series of illusions. His business persona may have been the first, an illusion designed to conceal the damaged man inside. His maintenance of his 1940's clothing styles, an effort in which he was willingly aided by Miss Green, was another such protective illusion. His having an office at home is the final illusion of his life. Like the others, it is a protective illusion.

Markham's life seems limited and constrained to his family and is clearly anchored too strongly in the past. Even so, his family helps him continue that limited and constrained life by creating an office for him at home. This turns out to be as rewarding for his wife and son as it is for him. Undoubtedly because of the unmentioned damage he suffered in the war, Markham throughout his life continued to be a soldier. His personal war could not end until he himself could reach an end. By creating Markham's office at home, the wife and son finally reconcile themselves to this fact of his nature.

*Style and Technique*

Gurganus uses a set of terms and phrases that emerged during World War II to convey the lingering effects of that pivotal event. Not only does the elder Dick Markham use these terms and phrases himself, but also his son employs them throughout his narration. In the introductory scene, in which the pair meet the "young hipster" who approves of the older man's 1940's vintage clothing, the son regards his father as "the fifty-two-year veteran of Integrity Office Supplier." When he later considers his father's office, he likens the ashtray to a torpedo, and the color of the metal desks to the color of battleships. The son also projects himself into his father's shoes, and imagines the older man viewing their visit to the hospital as being subjected to a "Nazi medical experiment."

Miss Green serves as another embodiment of Dick Markham's attachment to the past. She retains the hairstyles, clothing, and high-heel shoes of the decade within which the man is trapped. That she herself is free of that decade in her personal life is something the younger Markham discovers only after his father moves back home.

One of the strongest symbols of the elder Markham's clinging to the past is his hat. Introduced in the first paragraph, the hat is presented as a relic of the past. "Till the Japanese bombed Pearl Harbor," the story begins, "most American men wore hats to work." Markham's three hats serve him throughout the year. Because he changes his hat with the season, the old hats serve as a way of keeping each season the same as the one before. At the end, it seems to be the act of putting on his hat beforehand that allows him to accept his office at home as a real office.

In the end of the story, Betty Markham reveals her husband's closing act: "He died at the office." This is in itself symbolic. Dick Markham's life of obsessive work had served somehow to hold negative forces, which he repeatedly identified as the Nazis, at bay. By dying in his office, he had died in the line of duty.

*Mark Rich*

# THE HIGGLER

*Author:* A. E. Coppard (1878-1957)
*Type of plot:* Realism
*Time of plot:* Shortly after World War I
*Locale:* Rural England
*First published:* 1924

#### Principal characters:

HARVEY WITLOW, the main character, an attractive young higgler
ELIZABETH SADGROVE, a prosperous widow
MARY SADGROVE, her daughter

*The Story*

Harvey Witlow, the higgler, is driving his cart along a road on a remote moor. (A higgler is an itinerant dealer who buys poultry and dairy products from farms and supplies them with small items from the shops in town.) He has recently been discharged from the army and is meeting with little success in his business. His financial situation is getting worse, but it is generally expected in his village that he will marry Sophy Dawson, the daughter of a gamekeeper. Although they are not formally engaged, Sophy clearly expects the marriage to take place soon.

Just when Harvey is wishing that his affairs will "take a turn," he comes to the neatly maintained and obviously prosperous farm owned by Elizabeth Sadgrove. After some brief negotiations with Mrs. Sadgrove, he buys fifteen score eggs and some pullets from her. It is evident that the hoped-for turn for the better has occurred. Mrs. Sadgrove, a widow, also has a beautiful red-haired daughter named Mary, who has "the hands of a lady." Although Mary says almost nothing to the higgler, she appears to be impressed by him. For his part, Harvey momentarily forgets everything.

Harvey begins to call regularly at Mrs. Sadgrove's farm, and his business flourishes. He discovers that Mrs. Sadgrove, who has the reputation of driving a hard bargain, is quite well-to-do. Mary has attended a "seminary for gentlefolks' females," and her superior education seems to have spoiled her for the work for a farm. When, for example, she goes out, heavily veiled, to collect a swarm of bees into a hive, her movements are tentative and ineffectual; Harvey, without protective clothing, comes to her rescue and confidently collects the swarm. Harvey is attracted to Mary but is puzzled by her quietness in his presence. They spend an entire day in the orchard, where Harvey is picking cherries and Mary is walking back and forth with a clapper to frighten away the birds, but she never speaks to him. On the occasions when Harvey takes tea with the Sadgroves, her responses to his conversational overtures are brief and confused. Harvey wonders if there is anything wrong with her.

Harvey's doubts are increased when Mrs. Sadgrove invites him to have Sunday dinner with them. He dresses gallantly, putting a pink rose, which he plans to give to

Mary, in his buttonhole. During dinner, he talks volubly about his war experiences, but Mary says almost nothing. After the meal, Mary withdraws and Mrs. Sadgrove invites Harvey to take a walk in the meadow. To his consternation, she asks if he has a sweetheart and then pointedly says that she wants to see Mary married before she dies. She estimates the worth of her farm at three thousand pounds and reveals that Mary will inherit five hundred pounds of her own when she is twenty-five. She describes Mary as healthy, quiet, and sensible but declares that she has "a strong will of her own, though you might not think it or believe it." Although she does not press him for an immediate answer, she says that she is not a "long-living woman." Astonished by Mrs. Sadgrove's businesslike proposal, Harvey remembers as he drives away with the rose still in his buttonhole that he did not ask if Mary were willing to marry him.

When Harvey tells his mother, who also has the reputation of shrewdness, about Mrs. Sadgrove's proposition, Mrs. Witlow is surprised at her son's hesitation but asks if there is anything wrong with Mary. Harvey maintains that there is no problem with Mary, but he assumes that there must be a catch somewhere. On his subsequent visits to the farm, Mary does not even look at him; for his part, Harvey is now so inhibited in her presence that he can say nothing to her. He is powerfully attracted to Mary, but his "native cunning" persuades him that she is unaware of her mother's "queer project." Convinced that there is a trick somewhere, he makes up his mind to marry Sophy and stops calling at the Sadgrove farm altogether.

Harvey and Sophy's wedding is a rather strange affair, partly because Sophy's grandmother, who has come to the wedding with her aged third husband, takes this occasion to reveal that she was begotten by a wealthy gentleman who was having an affair with her mother. The couple cannot afford a honeymoon but move in with Mrs. Witlow. Within four or five months after his marriage, Harvey's affairs have again declined. Sophy and his mother quarrel continually; Sophy wants a home of her own, but Harvey cannot afford to buy a separate cottage for his mother. Without the rich produce of the Sadgrove farm, his higgling business declines drastically. His horse has died, and he is compelled to hire a replacement. He needs desperately to borrow money but knows no one who can lend him any.

Finally, his desperation impels him to call again at the Sadgrove farm, hoping that Mrs. Sadgrove will make him a loan. When he arrives at the farm just at evening on a wildly windy day, Mary meets him at the door. She tells him that her mother died the previous night. The doctor that she sent for has not arrived, and Mary has been attempting all day to wash her mother's body and dress it for burial, a task that is now almost impossible because of rigor mortis. Harvey takes over and, although he has to tie one stiffened arm in place, succeeds in preparing Mrs. Sadgrove's body for burial. Harvey then inquires in a kindly way about Mary's circumstances. She has no other relatives, but she has been left well-off financially. She plans to get a working bailiff to look after her farm. Rather impetuously, Harvey asks if Mary knew that her mother had once asked him to marry her and wonders why she did. Mary reveals that her mother had actually opposed the marriage but had made the request only because Mary had insisted that she do so since, as Mary says, "I was fond of you—then."

As Harvey drives away in the wind and darkness, his thoughts are "strange and bitter" as he realizes that he has thrown away both love and a fortune. He recollects that he has even forgotten to ask about the loan. He decides that he must give up higgling and take on some other job; a job as a working bailiff, he concludes, would suit him. However, he recalls, there is still Sophy.

*Themes and Meanings*

This story is a variation on the familiar motif of the trickster tricked, a plot pattern that can be traced back to dozens of folktales, in which a person with a reputation for shrewd bargaining outsmarts himself and loses everything. A successful higgler must be able to recognize a bargain and must be willing to extract advantageous terms from the person with whom he higgles. (Mrs. Witlow, also a higgler, is "perhaps more enlightened" than Harvey; it is "almost a misfortune to get into her clutches.") However, Harvey, who is presented with the opportunity of marrying a beautiful, well-educated girl who not only cares about him but also is heir to a prosperous farm and a cash legacy, misses the opportunity because he suspects that there is a trick where there really is none. It is small wonder that he is not successful as a higgler except when he can draw on the resources of the Sadgrove farm.

As the trickster-tricked motif is usually developed, the reader delights to see the trickster outsmarted, or, better yet, outsmart himself by being too shrewd. In this story, however, the reader's sympathies lie with Harvey, who is clearly a decent young man, but one who misses a great bargain by suspecting a catch where there is none.

*Style and Technique*

In the foreword to the American edition of *The Collected Tales of A. E. Coppard* (1948), A. E. Coppard states that one of the two principles of storytelling is "that unity, verisimilitude, and completeness of contour are best obtained by plotting your story through the mind or consciousness of only one of your characters." Clearly, for the particular effect of this story, it is essential that the point of view be handled in such a way that the events are seen through the mind of Harvey. For one thing, plotting the story through Harvey's mind tends to persuade the reader to sympathize with him because his are the only thoughts revealed to the reader. It is equally important that neither Harvey nor the reader know what Mrs. Sadgrove and Mary are thinking. Because Coppard carefully establishes the fact that Mrs. Sadgrove has a reputation for driving a hard bargain and because Mary's reserve seems almost pathological, the reader is likely to agree with Harvey that there is a catch somewhere in Mrs. Sadgrove's offer. The fact that Mrs. Witlow favors the marriage to Mary only contributes to the reader's suspicions because Mrs. Witlow herself seems excessively hard and materialistic. Mary's revelation that she was fond of Harvey—then—is almost as much of a surprise to the reader as to Harvey, but like all good "surprise" endings, it has been carefully prepared for.

*Erwin Hester*

# HILLS LIKE WHITE ELEPHANTS

*Author:* Ernest Hemingway (1899-1961)
*Type of plot:* Vignette
*Time of plot:* About 1920
*Locale:* A train station in rural Spain
*First published:* 1927

> *Principal characters:*
> AN UNNAMED MAN, an American
> JIG, his young female companion and lover, perhaps his wife

*The Story*

An unnamed American man and a young woman, Jig, are waiting for the express train from Barcelona; they are on the terrace of a small station-bar and seem to be on their way to Madrid. The story consists entirely of a seemingly objective documentation of their words and actions during their forty-minute wait for the train. The surface events are very simple. The woman looks at the hills across the valley of the Ebro, suggests that they order a drink, tries to engage the man in light conversation, responds briefly and unhappily to his assertion that an operation that she is to have is "really not anything . . . it's all perfectly natural"; she then stands up, walks to the end of the station, looks at the hills again, speaks angrily, sits back down, demands that he "stop talking," drinks in silence, and finally assures him that she feels "fine." The only actions of the man not accounted for in this detailing of the woman's movements occur after she asks him to "stop talking" and before she asserts that she is "fine." During that brief period, he carries their bags "around the station to the other tracks" and stops to drink an anisette at the bar alone.

Clearly, little happens and not much is said, but just beneath the surface of these spare and dull events, a quiet but crucial struggle between these two characters has been resolved. The future course of their relationship appears to have been charted in these moments, and the fate of their unborn child determined. Their very first words not only reveal tension between these two but also suggest that there are perhaps fundamental differences between them. The woman is interested in the world around her, concerned with being friendly, vital, and imaginative; the man, on the other hand, is self-involved, phlegmatic, and literal.

> "They look like white elephants," she said.
> "I've never seen one," the man drank his beer.
> "No, you wouldn't have."
> "I might have," the man said.

What is critical in this story, as in Hemingway's fiction generally, is the ironic gap between appearance and reality. The seemingly petty conversation here about hills and drinks and an unspecified operation is in actuality an unarticulated but decisive struggle over whether they continue to live the sterile, self-indulgent, decadent life preferred by the man or elect to have the child that Jig is carrying and settle down to a conventional but, in Jig's view, rewarding, fruitful, and peaceful life.

In spite of his transparent assertions to the contrary ("I don't want you to do it if you don't really want to"), it is clear that the man wants Jig to have an abortion so that they can be "just like we were before." Their life together up to this point seems to have been composed primarily of travel and aimless self-gratification: "That's all we do, isn't it—look at things and try new drinks?" "I guess so." The woman apparently yields to his unacknowledged insistence that she get an abortion; in order to do so, however, she must give up her self-respect and her dreams of a fruitful life: "I'll do it. Because I don't care about me." She does not seem to have the strength to resist his demands, but she is aware of the significance of her capitulation. She looks at the beauty, the life, the bounty across the tracks—fields of grain, trees, the river, mountains. "'We could have all this,' she said. 'And we could have everything and everyday we make it more impossible.'" The abortion is not merely a "perfectly natural" or "simple operation" to her; it is a symbolic act as well, which will cut her off irrevocably from what is good and alive in the world: "It isn't ours any more." The man takes exception to her powerfully negative vision of their situation, but she has heard enough: "Would you please please please please please please please stop talking?" He desists, moves their bags, wonders, while he drinks his anisette, why she cannot act "reasonably" like other people, and then returns to her as if nothing had happened. Perhaps Jig's perception that their lives are sterile and that the man does not truly love, or know, or care for her will enable her to leave him and struggle alone to live a meaningful life; yet Hemingway gives the reader no solid reason to believe that she will do so. The story ends with an apparent lie: "There's nothing wrong with me. I feel fine." Presumably they board the train; she has the abortion; and their relationship continues its downward drift into emptiness and hypocrisy.

*Themes and Meanings*

"Hills Like White Elephants" calls to mind the "A Game of Chess" section of T. S. Eliot's *The Waste Land* (1922); like Eliot's masterpiece, Hemingway's story deals with the sterility and vacuity of the modern world. The boredom of the man and the desperation of the girl reveal the emptiness of the postwar generation and the crucial necessity of taking responsibility for the quality of one's own life. Both Eliot's poetry and Hemingway's fiction are filled with a sense of missed opportunities and failed love, of a fullness of life lost and never to be regained: "Once they take it away, you never get it back." As in Eliot's poem, the landscape takes on powerful symbolic dimensions here. On the side of the tracks where the couple is waiting, the country is "brown and dry"; "on the other side, were fields of grain and frees . . . the river . . . mountains." The girl calls attention to the symbolic value of the setting and indicates that in choosing to have an abortion and to continue to drift through life they are choosing emotional and spiritual desiccation.

Hemingway's characters seem to live in a world without a God, without traditions or clear and established values; they are, in Jean-Paul Sartre's words, "condemned to be free" and consequently are responsible for their own meaning. The man here is unequal to the challenge; he is a bored and listless fragment of a human being. He resolutely refuses to speak truthfully, to acknowledge his own hypocrisy. His unwillingness to be honest—and, by extension, modern humanity's refusal to live honestly—is a consistent motif of this sketch. The girl is, at least, profoundly distressed by the aimless and sterile nature of their existence and does not give in to vacuity without a struggle.

One particularly interesting aspect of Hemingway's uncompromising dissection of the poverty of the modern world in this story is the juxtaposition of reason and emotion or imagination. The man is perfectly reasonable. He lives in a senseless and violent world; he has the financial resources to do as he pleases; he reasonably concludes that he should enjoy his life, not encumber himself with unnecessary conflicts or responsibilities, certainly not trouble himself with relationships that are demanding or in the least unpleasant. He is quite literal-minded, quite pragmatic, quite unemotional: an admirable fellow by modern patriarchal standards. The woman, on the other hand, is unreasonable enough to imagine that hills look like white elephants and that there might be some virtue to having a child who would surely be like a "white elephant," a sacred beast in some cultures, but in Europe and America something that is only apparently valuable and is in actuality more trouble than it is worth. Reason here is associated with dissimulation, death, nonmeaning; emotion with life, imagination, growth. Hemingway suggests that reason (the God of modern humanity) is an insufficient standard by which to live. The reasonable male here is a cipher, a man of straw who declines to acknowledge the necessity of making his every moment intense, honest, full.

Another interesting facet of this story in the context of Hemingway's fiction is the clear superiority of the woman to the man. Hemingway is not particularly kind to women generally, certainly not to women who want to have children. Usually such women are interested in asserting their sexual power over men and in depriving men of their freedom and their maleness. This girl may prove to be angry and frustrated enough to evolve into a castrating harridan; in this story, however, she is a tragic figure seemingly driven into a barren and empty existence by her love for this man.

Hemingway's brief and seemingly objective story is a powerful condemnation of the aimlessness, hypocrisy, and moral and spiritual poverty of the modern world.

## Style and Technique

The impassive, documentary style of "Hills Like White Elephants" is typical of much of Hemingway's fiction. It manifests the care, restraint, intensity, and control, the economy and precision that characterize his best prose. The author seems to be indifferent both to the characters and to the reader; he pretends to be merely an objective observer content to report without comment the words and actions of these two people. He has virtually no access to their thoughts and does not even interpret the emotional quality of their words or movements by using adverbs; he simply records. Hemingway believed in a precise, naturalistic rendering of the surface; he insisted on presenting things truly.

As was indicated earlier, Hemingway's ironic technique plays an important role in this story. The very use of a clear and economical style to reveal a relationship that is troubled and complex is ironic. The story seems to be void of artifice and emotion yet is carefully fashioned and powerfully felt. The dispassionate style appears to be absolutely appropriate to the cold, sophisticated, literal-minded, modern sensibility of the protagonist, yet in fact the man is revealed to be disingenuous and destructive. The deeper levels of this story are disclosed by examining not only what is implied through the irony but also what is indicated by symbolism and repetition.

The symbolism has already been remarked, and only one other observation seems necessary here. It is important to note that anything that can be said to operate symbolically does so without violating the realism of the story in any way. Hemingway uses banal repetition quite effectively here. The insincerity of the man is apparent in his dependence on empty phrases: "it's perfectly simple"; "if you don't want to you don't have to." Both the man's duplicity and the girl's perceptiveness, anger, and despair are evident in the way in which she echoes his transparent lies: "And afterward they were all so happy . . . I don't care about me. . . . Yes, you know it's perfectly simple."

In terms of style and technique, "Hills Like White Elephants" is a quintessential early Hemingway story. The use of the language of speech as the basis for the story, the insistence on presentation rather than commentary, the condensation, and the intensity are all basic elements of his theory of fiction.

*Hal Holladay*

# THE HINT OF AN EXPLANATION

*Author:* Graham Greene (1904-1991)
*Type of plot:* Psychological
*Time of plot:* December, 1948
*Locale:* A train traveling from Scotland to England
*First published:* 1949

*Principal characters:*
THE UNNAMED NARRATOR, an agnostic taking a train ride
DAVID, another traveler on the train
BLACKER, the atheistic baker recalled from David's childhood

*The Story*

On a long train journey from Scotland to England, the unnamed narrator listens to another traveler, a man named David, tell about an incident in his childhood that gave him a hint of an explanation about God's mysterious ways. The narrator (who resembles Graham Greene during his agnostic days at Oxford University) says that he has a certain intuition, which he does not trust, founded as it is on childish experiences and needs, that God exists, and that he is surprised occasionally into belief by the extraordinary coincidences that people encounter in life, like leopard traps in the jungle. He is, however, intellectually revolted by the notion of a God "who can abandon his creatures to the enormities of Free Will." The skeptical narrator is a perfect audience for David's ironic story of religious faith, for the story itself is structured like a providential trap.

David's tale has some of the features of a fairy tale: An innocent boy heroically overpowers a threatening monster and is rewarded for his bravery with a happy life. A terrifying character named Blacker, a baker by trade, bribed the ten-year-old David with an electric train set if he would bring him the communion host. To enhance his control over the boy, Blacker showed him a razor that he kept to bleed people. Obsessed with his atheism, Blacker wanted to examine the host to prove once and for all that Christ's body and blood are not present in the communion wafer. He told the boy, "I want to see what your God tastes like." David recalls that when Blacker asserted that he wanted to get one of those consecrated hosts in his mouth, for the first time the idea of transubstantiation lodged in his mind, for he was in the presence of a man who looked on the idea with a deadly seriousness.

According to David, Blacker was seeking revenge on the Catholics of the town, all of whom refused to patronize his store; on David's father, a banker who may have had dealings with Blacker; and on God himself. Driven by his fear of Blacker, David went to communion and lodged the host under his tongue. When he was alone, he wrapped the host in a piece of newspaper and carried it home so that he could give it to Blacker the next day.

Through Blacker's obsession, the boy realized for the first time that the host involves something special: "I knew that this which I had beside my bed was something of infinite value—something a man would pay for with his whole peace of mind, something that was so hated one could love it as one loves an outcast or bullied child." No longer viewing the host as part of a mechanical religious routine, David began to sense the power of God and grow firm in his resistance to temptation and fear. The overwhelming presence of Blacker and the evil he represented was diminished in that illuminating moment. At the last minute, David swallowed the host instead of turning it over to Blacker.

Then something happened, David recalls, which seemed more terrible to him than Blacker's desire to corrupt or his own thoughtless act: Blacker began to weep. The powerful image of evil and corruption was suddenly rendered human and pathetic in the boy's eyes. As Blacker transformed from a monster to a pathetic human being, David's unexamined life as a Catholic began to change into a life of service to God.

After David finishes his story, the narrator glimpses a priest's collar beneath his overcoat. David's earlier remark about the hint of an explanation suddenly makes sense to the narrator. Filled with hatred and finally with the anguish of frustration, the demonic Blacker led the indifferent boy into the powerful mysteries of his own religion. When the narrator suggests that David must owe a lot to Blacker, David replies, "Yes. You see, I am a very happy man."

*Themes and Meanings*

By the end of the 1940's, Graham Greene had written several major novels dealing with Roman Catholicism, but "The Hint of an Explanation" is the first of his many short stories to focus on Roman Catholic subject matter.

The central theme of David's story is that God works in mysterious and ironic ways to win the faith of his subjects. In the light of such irony and of the religious role played by the adversary of Christian providence, Greene's atheistic character, Blacker, functions with a significant ambiguity. From the child's point of view, Blacker is a simple villain, an oppressive force that threatens both the boy and the sanctity of the host. As an unwitting instrument of God's providence, however, he becomes the catalyst of the boy's faith. He is thus portrayed with a muffled sympathy. Catholics in Blacker's village did not patronize his bakery because he was a freethinker. Furthermore, he was ugly, having only one walleye and a turnip-shaped head, and he had no family. When the young David swallowed the host, the reader sees Blacker break down and hopelessly weep like a child.

It may be that Blacker was possessed by Satan (or the "Thing," as David prefers to call him), which would allow the reader to see him as pure evil, but his grotesquely flawed body and mind and his outcast position in the largely Catholic community permit the reader also to pity him, especially in light of his unwitting service to the God whom he denied.

*Style and Technique*

Greene employs a first-person narrator in order to arrange a surprise ending for the story. Like the skeptical narrator, the reader must wait until he obtains a glimpse of David's collar at the conclusion to the story before he realizes that Blacker was the catalyst that led the young David to become a priest and a happy man.

Greene is careful to keep his agnostic narrator from drawing any conclusions about David's providential tale and from articulating any moral judgments about either David or Blacker. This allows the reader to frame his or her own interpretation of the story. Is Blacker, as his name implies, a creature of pure evil? Is Blacker actually an unwitting servant of God's divine providence? Is David, perhaps, the self-proclaimed hero of his own adventures? David's assertion at the end of the story that he is a very happy man may, indeed, indicate a troubling complacency in one who is a priest. Where is his sympathy or compassion for Blacker, who is, after all, one of God's creatures? The pity that David recalls feeling for Blacker is not a redemptive emotion; rather, it indicates his sense of superiority over the deformed and obsessed baker.

Adding to the story's ambiguity, David was raised in a predominantly Protestant market town in East Anglia, and the Protestants were quite hostile toward the few Roman Catholics. David's school nickname, for example, was "Popey Martin," and his father was nearly excluded from a local club because of his religion. Given this sense of isolation from the community at large, David might understandably develop a distorted view of people outside of his own religious circle, a distortion that could inevitably lead to an exaggerated sense of his own victory over Blacker's villainy.

The narrator's final remark to David, "I suppose you think you owe a lot to Blacker," furthers the ambiguity of the tale. Recalling that the narrator is an agnostic, the reader is inclined to emphasize the phrase "you think" in that last statement. The implication is that although Blacker may indeed be the unwitting servant of God's providence, he may be so only in the narrow focus of David's dramatic and self-serving account of his childhood. After all, David clearly makes himself the hero of his own story.

*Richard Kelly*

# HIS FINAL MOTHER

*Author:* Reynolds Price (1933-    )
*Type of plot:* Psychological
*Time of plot:* The twentieth century
*Locale:* Southern United States
*First published:* 1990

> *Principal characters:*
> CRAWFORD LANGLEY, a twelve-year-old boy
> HIS FATHER
> ADELE, his mother

*The Story*

Adele Langley, the mother of twelve-year-old Crawford, drops dead while hanging a quilt on the backyard clothesline. All the family had been sure her racing heart would shorten her life. Now Crawford must face the crisis that everyone expected. The boy directs the ambulance, sends the body to the funeral home, and waits for his father, who is away on an errand, to arrive. In his attempt to become grown up, Crawford tries to assume an adult role, taking charge in his father's absence.

Crawford analyzes each stage of his own maturation. Bravery, he thinks, is his main ambition. Rather than cry, he goes to his room to pray for strength and passes the time by reading *Robinson Crusoe*. When his father returns, Crawford braces himself as he prepares to break the tragic news. He worries about how his father will react to the sudden loss of his wife.

Later that night, Crawford accompanies his father on a walk in the woods. Once they forge through the trees and come to a river bank, the father suggests that drowning would be better than living. The boy reassures him that his mother is in heaven waiting for them, but the father rebuffs his attempts at comfort, answering that much of what the boy knows is a lie. The father's sudden lack of belief frightens Crawford.

When the child asks his father to be calm, the father impulsively seizes his son by the neck. Just as suddenly, he releases his grip and walks away. When the boy asks if he is alone, his father answers that he always was. As Crawford makes his way back home, his mind begins to play tricks on him. He suspects that his father has gone mad.

The house is dark. Crawford imagines that his father is holding a butcher knife and waiting for him in the shadows. The boy summons his courage and makes his way upstairs to his bedroom. Unable to sleep or pray, Crawford examines himself and his past actions to see if he is at fault for the tragic events that have occurred. After he slips into a fitful sleep, a light awakens him. The light he sees is not the morning sun, however, but a strange glow emanating from the hallway.

As the boy approaches his parents' room, he sees an apparition of his mother as a young woman, looking as she did long before Crawford was born. Adele appears in the image of the girl his father loved and married; it seems her visionary presence has lulled his father to sleep. Crawford returns to his bedroom less afraid, comforted by his vision and his own memory of his mother. Although her face is gone from his daily world, Crawford decides that her memory is changeless and better in dreams.

## Themes and Meanings

"His Final Mother," a psychological exploration of Crawford's development, uses stream of consciousness in its telling. Consequently, the story is not so much about the events that occur in one day of Crawford's life as about the perceptions and impact of his mother's death, which occurs at the same time that Crawford is grappling with puberty and adolescence.

In childhood, Crawford's world was kind. He basked in the unconditional love of his father and the good-natured teasing of his mother. When his mother succumbs to a weak heart and his grieving father becomes irrational, the child realizes that his parents are vulnerable. His father's shaken faith produces doubt and fear in the child, leaving the boy to wonder if God and heaven exist as he has been taught. The turbulent situation creates insecurity for the boy. He now needs to be mature and independent, but without the presence of his mother and father, his rite of passage is more frightening. Crawford grows unsure about the nature of the world; the universe that once seemed benevolent now appears cruel or, at best, unpredictable.

Reynolds Price is demonstrating the complexities of human consciousness and experience. The tale is a retrospective on life, death, and growing up. Crawford's mourning for his mother is complicated by his father's grieving. Juxtaposed with the child's sense of loss is his desire to be mature; however, his path from childhood to adulthood is perilous. Crawford must learn to see the world not as an innocent child but as an experienced adult, aware of pain and loss. He learns that he can survive. No one is waiting to murder him in the dark of the kitchen, and, just as his father can conjure a vision of his wife, Crawford succeeds in conjuring his own image of his mother.

Crawford finds strength in what he knows; the presence of Adele that he summons at the close of the story is his attempt to find security in a hostile world. The mother's image can be recalled; his visionary memories of her sustain him; they become his final remembrance of her—his final mother. The young boy endures his test. Following his father's footsteps out of the forest, Crawford returns to bed, naked as he was in birth, to reemerge as the newborn man he desires to be.

## Style and Technique

Price's style is both poetic and enigmatic; he uses powerful images to communicate both conscious and unconscious elements of human experience and emotion. "His Final Mother" is told in the past tense, a memory. The narrative reveals the thoughts and struggles of Crawford only as he perceives them; the action is not clarified for the reader. The incidents in the story are ordered in disconnected sections of three to five paragraphs. Recollection and memory seem to overlap in the narrative. Price presents the protagonist's conflict using the stream-of-consciousness technique, so that much of the action takes place in Crawford's mind. His reality is clouded by his immaturity, fear, confusion, and imagination. Because Crawford has trouble deciding what is real and what is imagined, Price's audience must view the plot from the character's limited, subjective experience.

Price conveys his message through symbols; the protagonist's archetypal journey lies at the center of the plot. Price uses Daniel Defoe's *Robinson Crusoe* (1719), the novel that Crawford reads in the first part of the story, to foreshadow the child's journey. Like Defoe's Crusoe, Crawford feels shipwrecked and alone. The forest symbolizes the chaos and mental darkness that both father and son are experiencing. When the boy enters the forest with his father, the incident becomes a turning point. Left alone in the woods, he must struggle against fear to return home safely. Crawford's return to the house in the night marks his move toward maturity. This part of the story contains less external action and increased internal action, which depicts Crawford's psychological struggle to find safety or equilibrium from the disturbing events surrounding his family's tragedy. Hence, much of what Crawford experiences in the last part of the story takes place in his mind. He sees his father crouched in the blackness of the kitchen brandishing a butcher knife. Later he sees a mysterious bright light, and Price again reminds his audience that Crawford sees with his mind.

The vision of Adele Langley, both wife and mother, returns as a unifying force for father and son. She is captured in an aging photograph as the young woman the father married. To Crawford, she takes the shape of the young mother who gave him life. The boy cannot share the same vision of the dead woman that his father shares because the girl's face belonged only to his father. Crawford conjures up his own visionary memory of his mother, clinging to the bond that was formed with his birth. This time, however, labor pains do not produce a newborn baby but a newly formed young man. Crawford's passage from childhood to the threshold of adulthood has been a painful journey, much like the birth process itself. Price declares that Crawford is testing his newborn strength.

*Paula M. Miller*

# HIS SON, IN HIS ARMS, IN LIGHT, ALOFT

*Author:* Harold Brodkey (1930-1996)
*Type of plot:* Psychological
*Time of plot:* About 1975
*Locale:* An unspecified Midwestern American city
*First published:* 1975

*Principal characters:*
THE NARRATOR
THE NARRATOR'S FATHER
THE NARRATOR'S MOTHER
THE NARRATOR'S SISTER

## *The Story*

This story has no plot in the conventional sense; its narrator does not tell a tale with sequential events. Rather, he recalls from his childhood various sensations, emotions, and incidents arising from his relationship at that time with his father. The story is not solely about what he felt as a child; it is, more important, also a presentation of the sensations and emotions that his recollections arouse in him as he dredges them up from the past. The story is, then, in part a study of an emotional state in a man who is recalling and interpreting emotional states experienced in his childhood.

The narrator is an adult of unspecified age; the events that he describes happened when he was quite young, probably about six or seven. Among a far more extensive exploration of psychological states, his narrative includes several incidents from his childhood. Often, he recalls, he would be dispatched by his mother to cheer up his father, an exceedingly moody man. Once, when the narrator, as a young boy, was upset, his father came out onto the porch of the family home to reassure him. On another occasion, the father came home with several thousand dollars in bank notes and was chastised by his wife, whom he accused of being a spoilsport. He took his son and daughter outside, but when he was confronted with what he perceived as materialism in his daughter, he returned to the house to blame his wife for teaching that vice to her daughter.

These keys to the kind of family life that the narrator had are not told sequentially and are not even a framework on which the psychological exploration is based, but they do provide the backdrop for an investigation of more shifting, elusive emotions. That exploration is halting, detailed, and very introspective. Although the few details of the domestic incidents are remembered relatively clearly and described briefly, the narrator's recollection of the emotions surrounding them is expressed less decisively; each element of the emotions is inspected, each conclusion reinspected and refined.

The narrator's descriptions and development of his recollections depend only in part on what actually occurred in his childhood. More important is what he can now make of what happened: "Some memories huddle in a grainy light. What it is is a number of similar events bunching themselves, superimposing themselves, to make a false memory, a collage, a mental artifact." The narrator is aware that he may well be reinventing, as in fiction—he likens what he is doing to the creation of fiction.

The most important category of "mental artifact" constructed by the narrator consists of several instances of being lifted into the air by his father. This is the central motif of the story, and the most emotionally charged recollection. In recalling such instances of fatherly affection or protection, the narrator experiences, as the title suggests, an exultant emotional state, a mixture of the sublime and the awestruck.

The first such instance is at the beginning of the story. The narrator remembers his father chasing him; he describes it as if it were happening at the moment he recalls it. In a sense, it is: He is compelled to remember and interpret the influence that his father has had on him, and this makes him feel it again now. At the story's opening, he is being chased by his father; he recalls all the childlike emotions that the event aroused in him. His father is enormous; his hands are giant; even his breath, the narrator recalls, seemed overwhelming: He feels "the huge ramming increment of his breath as he draws near."

Being lifted by his father has, each time it happens, the effect of profoundly moving the boy emotionally. Sometimes he is liberated or deeply reassured; each time he is awestruck and feels physically or emotionally helpless in the face of his father's physical force and force of personality. On the first occasion, the boy has been running from his father, who snatches him up and carries him home. Lifted aloft in his father's arms, the boy senses a oneness with his father: "I feel myself attached by my heated-by-running dampness to him: we are attached, there are binding oval stains of warmth." As the narrator recalls the event, details of the setting come to him, enriching his recollections; he sees—remembers—a path, a bed of flowers, and other very distinct features of his childhood world.

As memories come to him, he attributes various characteristics to his father: He has a distinct smell, which the narrator imagines changed to indicate his mood. His mood changes often and erratically. Even when in a dark mood, he adopts easily a protective, paternal demeanor if he sees that his son is suffering too. He is strong where the boy is defenseless. He is a sentimentalist, and when his sentimentality is engaged, he is profligate; the narrator explains that on one occasion, his father gave a car to a financially troubled man. The narrator also suggests the nature of the father-son relationship. It was a mutually dependent one, the son considering the father massively powerful, the father turning to the son for refuge from the animosity he feels toward his wife and daughter, and toward life itself.

Another instance of being lifted high in his father's arms, the narrator recalls, came after the father had tried to console the son, who had been overwhelmed by a characteristic, fretful insecurity. Again the son experiences a liberating sensation, heightened on this occasion by his being placed on top of a stone wall that overlooks a bluff and that he is usually forbidden to climb. The experience engages all the boy's senses: Wind flicks in his face; the view is so panoramic that he imagines it is audible, that he can hear it buzzing. All of his doubts and fears evaporate, and he senses a mixture of pleasure and "oblivion."

## Themes and Meanings

The unifying characteristic of this highly idiosyncratic story is the way that it relates the nature of memory to particular memories involving a particular person. At the beginning of the story, the narrator says that he is being chased: The counterpart to his urgency as a child as he fled his father is the urgency that he feels as an adult to recall what his relationship with his father was, and in this way to make that relationship real again.

The narrator's attention returns repeatedly to the power of his father: "He kneeled— a mountain of shirt-front and trousers." That he feels unworthy of his father's doting attention, and at times even feels that he is blackmailing his father, is explained by his father's erratic personality, by his "disorderly massiveness." Just as the narrator describes his urgency to recall the past, he recalls the feelings of urgency that his father provoked in him. What he felt was not a sense of physical danger, although his father clearly was a physically overwhelming presence for the young boy; rather, he felt the danger of being bereft of the protection and identity that a father provides: "I could not live without the pride and belonging-to-himness of being that man's consolation." The father is recalled as far more than a mere life-sustaining force. He was able to transport his son into a heightened state: "I understood that he was proffering me oblivion plus pleasure."

Harold Brodkey accords these recollections a lofty status. At the end of the story, that narrator says that as his father lifts him up in the early morning light, the sights and sensations that make their mark on his senses and mind have "the aliveness of myth." Under the influence of his father's hoisting him up in his arms, he experiences a transcendence expressed through images of bright, hot, alien light, one that is "not really friendly, yet reassuring." There was a "luminousness all around us." Such imagery of light is central to the story. Light is the essence of seeing and recollecting, of making the past actual: "I can, if I concentrate, whiten the light—or yellow-whiten it, actually—and when the graininess goes, it is suddenly one afternoon."

Although it is the father who triggers and sustains the narrator's sensation, the narrator certainly depicts his father as far from divine or even humanly ideal. He attributes to him an almost supernatural stature, but he also recalls that his father was very erratic in his behavior. At the end of the story, his face bathed in early morning sunlight, the father gains, not an unadulterated, divine glory but "an accidental glory."

## Style and Technique

Virtually all of Brodkey's writing involves the extremely involved investigation of memories of his own life. Memories are excavated from the past with a precision and sensitivity that is indulged and then indulged further. In this story, as elsewhere, his style suggests a process of profound, persistent reflection and constant refinement of memory.

In order to suggest, for example, that the past occurrences, when recalled by the narrator, produce in him elaborate emotional responses, Brodkey moves repeatedly from past to present tense, blurring the distinction between what happened in the past and what happens as the narrator explores his love for his father.

Brodkey's highly idiosyncratic, fragmented style expresses the way in which the act of remembering intensifies the past for the narrator and transports him to euphoria. Brodkey prevents this euphoria from appearing merely indulgent, nostalgic, facile, or incredible by underpinning it with more mundane elements. For example, at the end of the story, in a skillful touch of bathos, he writes that the luminousness that surrounds the narrator and his father has an effect like that of wearing a simple woolen cap—it is "very dimly sweaty; and it grew, it spread: this light turned into a knitted cap of light, fuzzy, warm, woven, itchy."

*Peter Monaghan*

# THE HITCHHIKING GAME

*Author:* Milan Kundera (1929-      )
*Type of plot:* Psychological
*Time of plot:* The 1960's
*Locale:* Czechoslovakia
*First published:* "Falešný autostop," 1969 (English translation, 1974)

> *Principal characters:*
> A YOUNG MAN, who is on a vacation
> A YOUNG WOMAN, also on a vacation

*The Story*

After having been lovers for a year, a girl and a man embark on a two-week vacation, but by the end of the first day they discover more about themselves than most couples discover in a lifetime. The mechanism of discovery is the hitchhiking game, a game in which role-playing takes on a dangerous and irreversible intensity.

The "girl" is twenty-two, shy, jealous, uncomfortable with her body, and embarrassed by her need to use the bathroom. However, she trusts her lover "wholly," because "he never separated her body from her soul." When she pretends to be a hitchhiker whom her lover picks up, she leaves behind her shy, embarrassed self, and takes on a role "out of trashy literature." She becomes a seductress and slips into "this silly, romantic part with an ease that astonished her and held her spellbound."

The twenty-eight-year-old man is not only older but also considerably more worldly than the girl. A former playboy who believes that he knows "everything that a man could know about women," this man admires his current lover for what his previous lovers have lacked: purity. He is, therefore, surprised and angry when the girl assumes her new role; he is furious with her for "refusing to be herself when that was what he wanted." His anger, in turn, makes him adopt the role of "a heartless tough guy," and he becomes willful, sarcastic, and mean. In an act of defiance directed at both his communistic country and his girl, he deviates from their original travel route and heads for an unfamiliar city, an action that makes him feel like "a free man."

Once in Nove Zamky, the girl continues her role-playing, and her lover becomes increasingly irritated at "how well able the girl was to become the lascivious miss." Their conversation becomes more brazen; she even exclaims that she has to "piss," a word the girl would have been too embarrassed to use at the beginning of the story. She is pleased with how astounded her lover is at her new vocabulary, and on the way to the bathroom, she notices how the other men in the hotel look at her. No longer self-conscious about her body, she thrusts out her breasts and sways her hips. She is even accosted as a prostitute, but she does not mind.

This freedom, however, has its price. The game, after all, is a "trap"; the more involved the girl becomes in the game, "the more obediently she would have to play it." When her lover decides that they will act out the roles of customer and prostitute, she plays along. In the hotel room, when her lover actually humiliates her by forcing her to strip and take obscene poses, she obliges, though she is frightened and confused. She does not realize that, for the man, the game has "merged with life," and that he "simply hated the woman standing in front of him." It is not until after their passionate but emotionless lovemaking that the game ends. In the aftermath of the game, the girl begins to sob, "I am me, I am me," and though he does not understand her plea and is reluctant to respond to it, the man eventually does console her.

### Themes and Meanings

Who is the true person, the real "me"? When, at the end of the story, the girl hysterically asserts, "I am me, I am me, I am me," she asserts that she is both naughty and nice, both whore and madonna, capable of, as her lover discovers, "everything." Her lover, however, cannot accept this to be his girl. He wants her to remain a "nice" girl, a pure girl, a girl who fulfills an unambiguous role. For the most part, she plays her role beautifully; she is shy, pure, and frequently embarrassed by her body. She does not question this role, for it is the one that Western society expects most of its women to play; as soon as she has an opportunity to act other than shy and pure, however, she does so with great zeal. In her new role, the girl becomes sexually assertive and positively aware of her body; she becomes a powerful female. Her lover, however, is threatened by her, and in order to maintain his male dominance, he must frighten and humiliate her.

The most telling moment in the story regarding the male need to dominate a threatening female is the scene in the hotel room when the man makes the girl get up on a table. This is an ironic comment on the image of woman on a pedestal. Before she climbs on the table—which is not only the proverbial pedestal but also the go-go dancer's platform, the beauty contestant's runway, the bride-to-be's church aisle—the girl stops "playing the game." Stripped naked before her lover, she believes nothing else remains of herself to be exposed. She is "now herself." However, a provocative and powerfully naked woman is not what the man wants; therefore, he longs to "treat her like a whore." He needs to treat her this way and manipulates her through various postures because this is the only way he can control and objectify her. Up on the wobbly table, squatting and wiggling, she is an object, something that has been purchased and is soon to be used.

This story presents other ironies: the subtle but important difference between worship and love; the need, especially for women, to romanticize their physical passions; the uncomfortable fact that personal growth is always attended by pain; and the recognition of how limiting and debilitating fixed gender roles are for both sexes.

Milan Kundera, however, does not want the reader to dismiss roles altogether as negative and unnecessary. He strongly suggests that only through such role-playing does the young woman discover how to assert her true self. Similarly, the man's closing gesture of compassion, albeit weak, suggests that he has learned to look behind a given role and to accept the ambiguity of character that is inherent in all human beings, male and female.

### Style and Technique

Kundera's story is gamelike in a fundamental way: Two players take turns until the game is over. Because the story is divided into twelve sections, each player has six turns. Each section identifies and focuses on its particular player. Like any good omniscient narrator, Kundera's does not play favorites: The sections are equally divided between the male and female points of view. The reader gets to know the characters, both their past and present selves, in equal doses.

Because the story zigzags back and forth between the man and the woman, the reader experiences a strange kind of suspense as one role dissolves and another is shaped. The reader is also asked to identify alternately with first the male and then the female, a request that, perforce, requires of the reader a rapid and frequent modulation of roles. The more involved the reader becomes in the story, the closer he or she comes to being one of the players. Kundera seems to suggest that reading itself, then, is a game, a game in which all readers knowingly or unknowingly participate.

*Sylvia G. O'Sullivan*

# HODEL

*Author:* Sholom Aleichem (Sholom Rabinowitz, 1859-1916)
*Type of plot:* Wit and humor
*Time of plot:* The late 1800's
*Locale:* Anatevka, a fictitious village in Russia, and environs
*First published:* 1894 (English translation, 1949)

> *Principal characters:*
> SHOLOM ALEICHEM, the listener-recorder and primary narrator, an author
> TEVYE THE MILKMAN, the story's secondary narrator
> HODEL, Tevye's second eldest daughter
> PERTSCHIK (KNOWN AS FEFEREL), Hodel's teacher and husband, a revolutionary-minded socialist student
> GOLDE, Tevye's wife

*The Story*

After some time of not meeting him, Tevye the Milkman meets Sholom Aleichem, the story's primary narrator as well as its author, and begins to tell of the troubles that have come on him (turning his hair gray) because of his gullibility, fatalism, and obedience to God, which make him an easy target for misfortune.

His latest trouble, as most always, involves marrying off his daughters by means of the traditional arrangements. Hodel, like many young people of her age, is thirsty for an education and has learned to read both Yiddish and Russian from a young university student, Pertschik (known as Feferel). Hodel met Feferel because of a chance happening in which her father played a part. One day, on his way home from delivering his dairy goods to the nearby summer vacation spot for the well-to-do of Boiberik (Aleichem's fictional name for the town of Boira), Tevye sees Feferel and offers the young man a ride.

Tevye's conversation with the sharp-tongued youth (as they ride together) reveals the latter's socialistic sentiments; the son of a local cigarette maker, Feferel expresses contempt for his own class for not sharing their possessions with the poor. Impressed by the lad's talkativeness, Tevye invites him for dinner, which henceforth precipitates Feferel's daily return visits. In return for his meals, the young man agrees to provide Tevye's daughters (six are left now) with lessons.

The only fault that Tevye finds in Feferel is his tendency to vanish suddenly, only to return several days later venting his anger toward the wealthy classes—possessors of money, the root of all evil on earth—while extolling the simple virtues of the poor.

Along with their "philosophical" conversations, Tevye soon learns of Feferel's admiration for his daughter Hodel. On the following day, while in Boiberik, Tevye happens on Ephraim the matchmaker, who offers him an ideal match with a man from a fine family, educated in the holy books of Judaism—and rich. Although not a spring chicken, the prospective groom's credentials intrigue Tevye sufficiently so that he agrees to bring his daughter Hodel with him on his next week's journey.

Driving home, daydreaming about becoming a wealthy and influential man through the marriage of Hodel, Tevye recognizes Feferel walking out of the woods with her. Confronting them, Tevye soon realizes that his new hopes are about to be shattered, for Feferel and Hodel have become engaged without going through the traditional procedures of matchmaking, contract, or parental blessing. Tevye, accustomed by now to the modern notion of love, still cannot accept the young couple's decision to marry outside the traditional customs. Furthermore, Feferel's intention to leave immediately after the wedding, and leave Hodel behind, confounds Tevye. Adding to his consternation, Hodel and Feferel declare their plans to dispense with the pre-matrimonial customs; they want only a modest ceremony. That is how things happen, while Tevye placates his wife Golde with lies about Feferel's rich inheritance. After the wedding, while driving the young couple to the railroad station to see Feferel off, Tevye is still uncertain about Feferel's reasons for leaving; Hodel tells her father that he would not understand even if she were to tell him.

Some months later—after Tevye's worries bring him closer to Hodel's plight—news arrives for Hodel of Feferel's arrest. Thereupon she confides to Tevye her decision to follow Feferel to his distant place of exile, perhaps never again to see her mother, father, and sisters. Tevye, whose heart grieves over the news, feigns a cheerful expression and controls his emotions, knowing that no amount of pleading or anger can sway one of his daughters once her mind is made up. He thus becomes resigned to the differences in their views and values (as different as a hen is from a duck, they agree) and reluctantly agrees to help her.

To conceal the truth from Golde, Tevye fabricates a tale about an inheritance to justify Hodel's need to pack some bedding and belongings and depart on the following morning on a long journey. While the women cry, Tevye maintains a cool, sober exterior until he and Hodel arrive at the railroad station, where Hodel breaks down, crying on her father's shoulder, and he too appears to lose his composure.

Cutting his narrative at this point, Tevye asks Aleichem's forgiveness for becoming so emotional about his daughter (whose letters continue to arrive) and asks to talk about more cheerful things, such as the recent outbreak of cholera in Odessa.

## Themes and Meanings

"Hodel" is the third in a cycle of stories concerning, and narrated by, Tevye the Milkman, one of Aleichem's most famous characters. In these tales, Tevye undergoes a series of educational and tragic encounters with life. The account of Hodel, the second eldest of his seven daughters, represents only a partial loss in Tevye's values, whereas most of the subsequent episodes are marked by more tragic events, as one daughter converts, another dies, and others lead lives of misery.

The incremental fragmentation and destruction of Tevye's family evokes the biblical archetype of Job, the man of patience, suffering in faith. Although juxtaposed against the story of Job, Aleichem's Tevye also departs from the biblical analogue. Whereas both Job and Tevye appear to maintain their faith in the Creator, it is Tevye who copes better with his world by laughing his fate away and adopting a humorous stance against all that befalls him. By doing so, Tevye seems to reject the past's hold on him. The stories consist of largely tragic events related in a humorous tone, and the reader becomes witness to the hero's cyclic downfall and recovery.

This central theme of Tevye's fall and recovery is what characterizes the core of this story (and the others in the cycle). It is Tevye who is the story's main protagonist, the man who weathers the onslaught of events, revolutions, social upheavals, and personal calamities. His ability to remain standing in the face of these adversities is a demonstration of the human capacity to affirm life despite all of its miseries.

Tevye's perseverance is in part attributable to his flexibility, his capacity to adapt to the changes of the times. Among these are the recognition of the notion of romantic love as a precursor to marriage and the shifting regard each generation has for material possessions, dress, and government. Thus, Tevye's ability to accept Hodel's departure is a mark of his strength.

"Hodel" is also an account of the changes in the status of the father in the Jewish family. Whereas in the past the father was invested with nearly absolute authority, Aleichem depicts in Tevye one who most readily abdicates this role not only out of a love for his family but also out of a realization that a new world is about to dawn on him and that he must accept it and its ways in order to survive.

The very fact that Tevye has seven daughters and not a single son (in a society favoring sons over daughters) is significant: His contentment with this circumstance provides further evidence of his broadmindedness, his flexibility, his ability to live in the modern world.

Thus, the story is a call by Aleichem for understanding, compassion, and compromise. As a document—as well as a work of fiction—it stands at the threshold of the process of modernization (and Westernization) of a large segment of East European Jewry.

*Style and Technique*

The narrative technique of this story, as in all the Tevye stories, is that of the first-person, dramatic monologue. In using this technique, Aleichem implies the existence of a certain distance, emotional and temporal, between the events recounted and the present mind-set of Tevye, narrator of these events. The effect is that of a measure of objectivity and aesthetic organization. In "Hodel," Tevye's relatively cool, unemotional, and cheerful posture is maintained until the tearful moment at the railroad station; the heightened emotionalism at this point furnishes the motive for the story's closing while underscoring the lasting emotional impact that these events have had on Tevye.

"Hodel" also demonstrates some of the devices of humor and comedy that have made the Tevye stories—regardless of their ominous message concerning the disintegration and downfall of a Jewish way of life—among the most popular works by this author.

Particularly notable are the comic effects of Tevye's narrative style. Tevye tells his story in a torrent of words interspersed with references and allusions to traditional Jewish sources, particularly the Bible, to lend credence to his views. Tevye thus imitates the manner of a Talmudic scholar's discourse, where every assertion is supported with scriptural citations. Tevye's accounts, however, do not involve study but rather his day-to-day affairs. Comical juxtapositions are thereby established between the traditional and the modern, the lofty and the everyday, the sacred and the profane.

Furthermore, Tevye makes himself the target of the reader's laughter by his use of biblical verses out of their appropriate context. One such instance in "Hodel" occurs when Tevye compares his daughter's beauty to that of Queen Esther; clearly, Hodel's fate is not as glorious as that of the biblical heroine, but Tevye is unaware of the irony. Furthermore, the citation is slightly off in that the biblical words (in the original Hebrew, while the story was written in Yiddish), from Esther 1:11, refer to Queen Vashti and not to Esther.

The biblical narrative, wherein the beauty of Vashti is noted, also tells of her refusal to appear before her king. According to one Jewish legend, her refusal to show her face in public was because of a horn that sprouted on her forehead, making her features hideous and grotesque. Describing Hodel in the words meant for Vashti, a Gentile woman, Tevye is again the unwitting victim of Aleichem's irony.

*Stephen Katz*

# HOMAGE FOR ISAAC BABEL

*Author:* Doris Lessing (1919-    )
*Type of plot:* Sketch
*Time of plot:* 1961
*Locale:* A small town near London
*First published:* 1961

*Principal characters:*
THE NARRATOR, a woman living in a London flat
PHILIP, a fifteen-year-old student at a boarding school near
London
CATHERINE, the narrator's thirteen-year-old neighbor, who has a
crush on Philip

*The Story*

The unnamed narrator takes Catherine, a neighbor child, on an afternoon outing to visit their friend Philip at his boarding school outside London. Catherine, who is thirteen years old, idolizes both the fifteen-year-old Philip and the narrator, an older woman who lives in a nearby apartment. Catherine borrows a collection of short stories by the Russian Jewish author Isaac Babel to read on the train because she knows that Philip is reading them.

The visit to Philip is a success. The three walk through the school's beautiful playing fields, as Catherine carries the Babel book in her left hand. After lunch, they go to a movie matinee, to see *The Hoodlum Priest* (1961), a new Hollywood film about a Jesuit priest who rescues juvenile delinquents, but who cannot save one of them from being executed. The film has a strong, moving, sentimental ending sequence in a prison gas chamber that causes many theatergoers, including Catherine, to cry. As they leave the theater, they pass the doorman, who loudly criticizes the red-eyed patrons for being soft on crime.

On the return train trip to London, Catherine asks the narrator why Isaac Babel is a famous writer. The narrator explains that Babel's writing style is simple, spare, and clear. Catherine is shocked to learn that Babel was killed twenty years earlier. She tries to read the narrator's favorite Babel story, "My First Goose," but does not understand much of it and what she does understand she finds too morbid. The narrator suggests that Catherine might like Babel better when she is a little older. She agrees, remarking that Philip is older.

A week later, the narrator receives a thank-you letter from Catherine, who writes that the visit was the most lovely day in her life. She tells the narrator that *The Hoodlum Priest* has convinced her that capital punishment is wrong. She also writes that she has been meditating on Isaac Babel, and has concluded that the conscious simplicity of his style is what makes him a great writer. Catherine closes the note by asking the narrator whether Philip has said anything about coming to her party but begs in a postscript that she not tell him that she has asked, for she would die if he knew.

## Themes and Meanings

In "Homage for Isaac Babel," Doris Lessing treats two major themes: the nature of early adolescent girlhood and the response to the cruelty of the world. Lessing uses Catherine's two experiences—seeing a film and trying to read a short story—to explore what it is like to be an intelligent young girl.

Catherine clearly is intelligent. She can hold up her end in serious conversations with the adult narrator, who does not condescend to her. When she goes to films, she thinks about what she sees rather than simply watching passively for momentary entertainment. Similarly, she thinks about what she reads, rather than reading for mere escapism, and is willing to try demanding books.

Catherine also reflects the interests and patterns of behavior of early adolescents. Her admiration for others takes the form of exaggerated and romanticized devotion. Because she admires the narrator, she helps straighten up the narrator's flat, showing that for her small flats are more romantic and desirable than large houses, such as the house in which she lives. Because she idolizes Philip, she wants to like the same things that he likes, adjusts her reading tastes to his, and picks the film that he would want to watch. Philip, his tastes in books, food, and music, and his opinions on issues of the day are the focus of her conversation.

Catherine's schoolgirl idolatry extends to ideas. She appropriates the ideas of those she admires, experiments with making them her own, and adopts them with enthusiasm. After watching *The Hoodlum Priest* she is upset at the world's cruelty and wants to stop thinking about it, but Philip declares, "We've got to think about it, don't you see, because if we don't it'll just go on and on, don't you see?" On the train home to London, the narrator shares her opinion that Babel's strong point as an author is his spare style. Catherine appropriates these views and expresses them as her own a week later in her thank-you letter to the narrator. "I have been thinking about *The Hoodlum Priest*. That was a film which demonstrated to me beyond any shadow of a doubt that Capital Punishment is a Wicked Thing. . . . I have been meditating about what you said about Isaac Babel, the famed Russian short story writer, and I now see that the conscious simplicity of his style is what makes him, beyond the shadow of a doubt, the great writer that he is." Catherine also shows the absolutism that often characterizes young adolescent enthusiasms; for her there are no shades of gray. She comes to the flat two hours early, so keen is she to be with her friends. She declares that a Babel-like simplicity is the only basis for a brilliant writing style.

The response to the world's cruelty is the second major theme of this short story. Lessing's choice of Babel is important, for his work deals with this theme. As a Russian Jew, he experienced horrible pogroms during the Czarist days before Russia's Bolshevist Revolution. Most of his stories emerge from his service in the Red Army during the ferocious Russian civil war of 1918-1922. (His story "My First Goose" tells of the conflict between the life of the mind and the life of action; the young, bespectacled university graduate is accepted by his fellow soldiers only after he kills a goose for his dinner.) He was executed in one of Joseph Stalin's prison camps. Babel's life reflects in microcosm the history of the twentieth century.

The narrator wants to protect Catherine from the reality that Babel describes, but Catherine is unable to believe that humans can behave as badly as the narrator suggests they do. She naïvely thinks that Babel's killers felt sorry once they realized they had killed a famous writer. Nevertheless, Catherine's admiration for Philip leads her to accept the importance of opposing evil in the world.

*Style and Technique*

"Homage for Isaac Babel" is one of several deceptively simple Lessing stories. Lessing describes a little slice of life, a few hours of some people's interaction. On the surface, the story appears simple, even slight—what could be simpler, or less significant, than being with a thirteen-year-old for half a day? However, in Lessing's hands, the little slice of life becomes the vehicle for the exploration of important issues.

Lessing conveys her messages and explores her themes by way of uninflected and nonjudgmental description. She writes almost as a reporter might, describing what she sees and what she hears Catherine saying. She does not vary the tone of her prose in order to convey her ideas, nor does she judge her characters or attach labels to them. Rather, she uses description and dialogue to depict characters and to give the reader information to use in forming a conclusion.

From time to time, Lessing uses little flashes of humor to provide telling illuminations of her characters. For example, she remarks that Philip "has pure stern tastes in everything from food to music" precisely because he is fifteen. These little touches of humor, however, do not come at the expense of her characters; she treats them with respect.

Finally, Lessing draws her pictures of the characters by juxtaposing incongruous sentiments or comments to produce the effect she wants. For example, on the train returning to London, Catherine begins the conversation by remarking on a girl—a potential rival for Philip's attention—who had said hello to him in the garden: "They must be great friends. I wish my mother would let me have a dress like that, it's not fair." Catherine then shifts away from jealousy, covetousness, and petulance to Babel, asking adult questions about his literary reputation. Another example is that of Catherine's thank-you letter, which begins with high sentiments about capital punishment and literary style but ends with girlish concern over whether Philip will come to her party.

*D. G. Paz*

# HOME

*Author:* Jayne Anne Phillips (1952-    )
*Type of plot:* Domestic realism
*Time of plot:* The mid-1970's
*Locale:* A small town in the United States
*First published:* 1978

*Principal characters:*
THE NARRATOR, a young woman returned home
HER MOTHER, a local school administrator, divorced
HER FATHER, whom the narrator no longer sees
JASON, her high school boyfriend
DANIEL, one of her more recent boyfriends

## The Story

The unnamed twenty-three-year-old narrator/protagonist, finding herself "out of money" and not "in love," returns home to live temporarily with her mother, who secures her a tutoring job. Her mother, a divorced school administrator, leads a quiet life in a small town resembling the author's West Virginia hometown. The mother spends evenings knitting and watching television; the closest she comes to a man is watching Walter Cronkite, television's grandfatherly news anchorman, who she fears has cancer. After a liberated life in college and later in California, the narrator finds the home routine dull. Rather than watch television, she starts going to her room at night to read and think. She offers her mother "a subscription to something mildly informative: *Ms., Rolling Stone, Scientific American.*" Her mother declines.

One subject that the narrator thinks about is her mother's early life, recalled in old photographs. The mother attended college, then became a cadet nurse, but World War II ended before she finished her nurse's training. She came home to care for her sick mother and eventually to marry the narrator's father: "She married him in two weeks. It took twenty years to divorce him." The mother, it appears, married him for strictly practical purposes: "He was older, she said. He had a job and a car. And Mother was so sick." Perhaps a related reason for the marriage's failure was sex—or the lack thereof. After reading in her mother's *Reader's Digest* about a girl carried off by a grizzly bear, the narrator dreams that her father approaches her sexually: "I think to myself, it's been years since he's had an erection." In the final years of their marriage, the mother refused to have sex with the father.

On weekends, the narrator gets away from home by attending rummage sales, but these, too, recall the past and raise the specter of sexuality. An old football sweater for sale reminds the narrator of Jason, her high school boyfriend who "made All-State but . . . hated football." They would park and try to make love on his sweater, but she was evidently so inhibited that their futile efforts only caused her pain. The narrator does not buy the sweater, but she does purchase "an old robe to wear in the mornings"

because "it upsets my mother to see me naked." She also buys her mother an old record, *The Sound of Music*, but the record reminds them both of Jason.

The subject of Jason and sex finally causes the differences between mother and
daughter to erupt in an argument. It begins when they see Hubert Humphrey, the former vice president, now shockingly old and frail, on television. The mother immediately cries "cancer," but the daughter disagrees:

> All Hubert needs, I tell her, is a good roll in the hay.
> You think that's what everyone needs.
> Everyone does need it.
> They do not. . . . I seem to manage perfectly well without it, don't I?
> No, I wouldn't say that you do.

The mother lectures the daughter—"your attitude will make you miserable. . . . One
man after another"—concluding with the declaration that Jason "lost respect" for the
daughter when the two cohabited at college. The daughter screams back with an ob-
scenity, for Jason eventually suffered some kind of mental breakdown—what he "lost"
was his mind. Refusing to talk about it anymore, the mother retires to the bathroom for
"hydrotherapy," a relaxing bath. When she has to ask the daughter for a towel, the two
make up. The mother is apologetic, and the daughter is shocked to see her mother naked
and scarred: "She has two long scars on her belly, operations of the womb, and one
breast is misshapen, sunken, indented near the nipple" where a lump was removed.

Insult is soon added to the mother's injuries, however, when, in the story's climax, the daughter puts her sexual theories into practice. The daughter gets a phone
call from Daniel, an old California boyfriend who has come east. When they lived
together, both had their problems. He smashed dishes, "ran out of the house with
his hands across his eyes," and was touchy about his Vietnam war wounds, while
she finally developed total frigidity. Still, the daughter, who has been considering a trip to the university to find "an old lover," invites him for a visit. On his best
behavior, Daniel at first delights the mother, but her impression of him changes
when, on Sunday morning, she hears him and her daughter making love in the bedroom above her head. The mother slams the door angrily as she leaves for church.

When she returns, Daniel has left, but her anger remains. Seeing the daughter, the
mother goes to the sink and starts washing the clean dishes again. Fearfully, the
daughter embraces her, and the mother complains bitterly that "I heard you. . . . Here,
in my own house." Then she hushes and stares into the water while the daughter continues holding her.

*Themes and Meanings*

At its most obvious level, "Home" is a simple story about a classic subject, the generation gap. The gap is well documented by the differences between mother and
daughter in lifestyles, tastes (for television, books, magazines, politics), and attitudes
toward sex. On this level, the story is almost comic. As youth must, the daughter re-

turns, confronts the beast in its den (that is, her mother and her mother's attitude toward sex), and triumphs.

There are complicating factors in the story, however, some with tragic overtones. One such factor is American history, ever-present in the "sorrowful" countenance of Walter Cronkite, who helped television introduce history into the American home and who "understood that here at home, as well as in starving India, we would pass our next lives as meager cows." In the context of U.S. history, which the author skillfully evokes, the mother represents the World War II generation and the daughter represents the Vietnam generation—and it is no accident that these two generations are named here after wars. Both generations were scarred, in different ways.

Another complicating factor is that mother and daughter are as much alike as different—two sides of the same coin. The mother handed on her antisexual attitudes to the daughter, in whom they appear either as inhibition or a theory of liberation. In actual practice, both women have difficulty in bed, though the mother appears to have enjoyed sex more than the daughter, despite limited opportunity. The mother is not so much against sex for puritanical reasons as she is against further involvement with men. Although much involved with men, the daughter has not escaped the mother's pattern. Both women callously use men, either as financial support or as sexual partners, and each has apparently helped send a good man, the father and Jason, respectively, to his doom (Daniel moves on quickly). Finally, the two women treat each other with a similar mixture of love and hidden resentment.

*Style and Technique*

The symbolism in "Home" is worthy of a latter-day Nathaniel Hawthorne. Images of masculine sexuality suggest the two women's warped views: The grizzly bear in the *Reader's Digest* story resurfaces as the father in the daughter's dream, and Jason the football star plays "a threatening Nazi colonel"; wounded Daniel, with "his white and feminine hands" seems more to the daughter's taste. Physical scarring represents deeper psychic states: There are Daniel's war wounds and the mother's "operations of the womb," while the girl carried off by a grizzly reappears with "a long thin scar near her mouth." Home is where people go to die, like the submarine crew in an old movie on television (recognizable as Stanley Kramer's *On the Beach*, 1959). Home is where the mother's young aspirations died when she returned to care for her sick mother and to marry an older man, where the family died, and where the mother now lives her hermetic existence and sings out "cancer" at the images on television.

Enter the daughter, who is as obsessed with sex as the mother is with cancer—it is a case of life against death, in the best manner of D. H. Lawrence. Because the story is told from the daughter's point of view, life wins: The daughter overcomes her instilled sexual fears by violating the taboos of her mother's house. The main trouble with the story, however, is the point of view, which appears too short on irony: The daughter is so smug and superior that some readers might find themselves rooting for the mother.

*Harold Branam*

# HOME SICKNESS

*Author:* George Moore (1852-1933)
*Type of plot:* Social realism
*Time of plot:* Around 1900
*Locale:* New York City and Duncannon, Ireland
*First published:* 1903

*Principal characters:*
JAMES BRYDEN, an Irish immigrant to the United States
MIKE SCULLY, a Duncannon villager
MARGARET DIRKIN, Bryden's fiancé

## The Story

James Bryden, an Irish immigrant suffering from blood poisoning, is advised by his doctor to take a long sea voyage to recover his health. He decides that he would like to see Ireland again, and the doctor agrees that a long visit to Bryden's native Irish village of Duncannon will speed his convalescence.

Bryden enjoys his return home. The cozy village is so different from his life in the Bowery of New York City, where he has a job in a barroom. As he grows stronger, he begins to appreciate the slow, deliberate rhythms of village life. Absent are the hectic, demanding city routines; people are comfortable and relaxed, although most are poor and have few prospects for improving their lives. They say little about themselves and want to know all about the United States, having heard of the high wages a man can make, even if the hours of labor are long.

A soothing sense of home spurs Bryden's recovery. He is welcomed by Mike Scully, one of the few villagers who has prospered, who provides Bryden with a place to live. In truth, all Bryden wants is to be left alone. Gaining strength, he finds that he is not interested in the villagers. Both their troubles and their curiosity about him leave him unmoved. At such times, he feels that he belongs back in the Bowery, even if it is a slum, but his returning health is enough to keep him rooted in Duncannon. He is in no hurry to return to the rigors of his Bowery existence.

Satisfying his urge to exercise, and feeling the need for company, Bryden meets Margaret Dirkin driving cows home for milking. Her company delights him and relieves his isolation and loneliness. However, Margaret warns him that they cannot walk together without being observed; it is not the custom for men to court women so openly and she fears the community's censure. They continue their romance, and it is soon understood in the village that they are to be married. With his savings in New York, Bryden knows he can set himself up in the village as a prosperous man. However, he chafes at the narrowness of village ways, at the priest who forbids his parishioners to dance and drink. Then Bryden receives a letter from a friend in the United States, and he is reminded of how free things are there. Even the smell of the Bowery, as Bryden remembers it, seems enticing—the noises, the hoards of people, the heady exchange of money, the politicians talking—all the busy life he thought he had left behind. Ireland seems bleak, ignorant, and servile compared with the United States. Bryden realizes that he cannot marry Margaret and that he must return to the Bowery. He hurriedly leaves Duncannon, and Margaret realizes that he will never return, although he promises to do so.

Bryden later marries and has children, but in his old age he thinks back to Margaret, to that simpler village life, to the home he cannot forget, and it seems that it is the only real thing he has ever possessed.

## Themes and Meanings

Homesickness in George Moore's story is clearly a complicated emotion. When Bryden returns to Duncannon, he regards it with curiosity, but he seems to have lost his feeling for it as a home. He is estranged from nearly everyone except the successful Mike Scully. The villagers treat Bryden as a successful man more than as one of their own. They are more interested in welcoming him as a new American than they are in renewing ties with a native-born neighbor. Bryden confirms their attitude by taking little interest in them. He is curious about them but not very attached to their lives. His home, it seems, is now in the United States.

The atmosphere of village life is so powerful that Bryden begins to relax and feel at home. He gradually accustoms himself to the simplicity of the people and enjoys drinking and dancing with them. He has made a place for himself and recovered his sense of home. When he falls in love with Margaret Dirkin, he fulfills the cliché that home is where the heart is. He knows that her family will welcome him as a good match who will make her life far better than she ever could have dreamed.

Bryden's homesickness, however, is an afflicted state of mind that neither Duncannon nor the Bowery can entirely cure. Neither place can be a complete home to him because he is caught between living his life on two contradictory scales. Duncannon offers peace and quiet, an abiding sense of identity with the land and its people; the Bowery, even though it is a slum, offers personal advancement, diversion, and freedom. Each place exacts its toll. In Duncannon, it is hard to be his own man without incurring the disapproval of the parish priest; in the Bowery, his health has been broken once already and he dreads the pressures of its competitive life.

If Bryden returns home and seems to make his peace with the United States, the story suggests it is an uneasy compromise. Homesickness returns as Bryden envisions his life against the horizon of his native village; the confines of the barroom in the Bowery give way to his dreams of the village and the green hillside, the bog lake, and the "greater lake in the distance, and behind it the blue line of wandering hills." The landscape is itself a metaphor for Bryden's wandering soul, his desire to experience the limitless, and his yearning for a home that would anchor that desire and give him a place to return to. The place is a state of mind, a work of the imagination as much as it is a literal location.

*Style and Technique*

Moore writes in a direct, unadorned style. He seems to be telling no more than the story of one man's life, of one episode that defines that life. In a sense, it has been a life of homesickness in a number of different senses. Bryden initially leaves Ireland, it is implied, because he is sick of it; he returns because he is sick without it. The land remains a touchstone for him, measuring everything he thinks about himself and his new life across the Atlantic.

Much of the story is told in an objective fashion: The narrator explains Bryden's experiences and his feelings about them but does not comment on the validity of his thoughts. How other people treat him is merely reported. That Bryden thinks the village priest is a tyrant is Bryden's opinion; the narrator does not judge him or the priest. Bryden's opinions about the Bowery are his alone, tersely reported by the narrator, but not otherwise discussed.

The tone of the story is that of a report, fleshed out with revealing dialogue and brief but superbly etched descriptions of scenery and characters. The narrator serves as a historian and guide, who also conveys the grace and hardship of people's lives and the inner struggle of Bryden's homesickness. The story's authority derives from the narrator's meticulous accumulation of revealing details. The story's power is a result of picking just the right dramatic moments to convey Bryden's subtle shifts of attitude—meeting Margaret for the first time by chance and at a vulnerable moment, his receiving a letter from the United States, the confrontation with the parish priest.

Only in the story's last paragraph is it revealed how the pacing of the narrative, the strategic placement of details and scenes, leads to an outcome that is philosophical as much as it is psychological. In the conclusion, the narrator's tone shifts and expands to incorporate Bryden's life into a vision of homesickness, a vision that transcends Bryden even as it is called into life by Bryden's example. Bryden's biography illustrates a truth, a generalization that arises naturally out of his predicament: "There is an unchanging, silent life within every man that none knows but himself, and his unchanging, silent life was his memory of Margaret Dirkin." This life that no one else knows is exactly what has been rendered in "Home Sickness." The particularity of one life has become a way of understanding a principle of life itself, of homesickness.

*Carl Rollyson*

# HOMELAND

*Author:* Barbara Kingsolver (1955-      )
*Type of plot:* Coming of age, social realism
*Time of plot:* The 1950's
*Locale:* Kentucky and Tennessee
*First published:* 1989

*Principal characters:*

GLORIA ST. CLAIR, an eleven year-old girl and the narrator
GREAT MAM, her great-grandmother
FLORENCE ANN, her mother
PAPA, her father

*The Story*

In the three-part story "Homeland," eleven-year-old Gloria St. Clair travels the path cleared by her great-grandmother, Great Mam, an elder of the Cherokee Bird Clan. Young Gloria is destined to grow up and become a Beloved Woman, the one who stores her family history and her tribe's myths and legends in memory. The youngster worries about the weight of this responsibility: How will she ever be able to remember Great Mam's immense knowledge of family, nature, and Cherokee myth? In the end, she succeeds brilliantly.

The first part begins with a brief overview of the tribal history of Great Mam, a member of the Bird Clan, which resisted General Winfield Scott's attempts to move the Cherokee westward. In the second part of the story, the first-person narrator interjects herself into the narrative by providing her American name, Gloria St. Clair, followed by her other name, Waterbug, which Great Mam gave to the eleven-year-old Gloria, promising someday to explain its significance to the girl. Gloria and her great-grandmother spend their evenings on the porch, apart from the rest of the family: Gloria's mother, Florence Ann; her coal-miner father, known throughout as Papa; and her brothers, Nathan and Jack.

Although Great Mam rarely speaks of her own life, preferring instead to talk of family history and tribal legend, Gloria has heard her great-grandmother's story from her mother. Florence Ann is not a Beloved Woman as Gloria will be but rather a Baptist and therefore is mired in guilt over her family history. It seems Great Mam was brought, on a stolen horse, from her tribal home in the Hiwassee Valley of Tennessee to Kentucky, to live without the benefit of a Christian marriage with a coal miner, Gloria's great-grandfather Murray. Although Great Mam was originally named Green-Leaf, everyone in Kentucky called her the more "respectable" name of Ruth.

The family lives in Morning Glory, a small town nestled in the coal-mining region of eastern Kentucky. Like many other town families, dependent on the whims of the mine owners, they live in poverty, constantly in need of staples such as meat, and often go without new shoes. When Gloria's father is laid off, the family takes its first trip ever, to visit Great Mam's homeland, the Hiwassee Valley of Tennessee. The trip proves to be a disaster. After two days of traveling in a truck without stopping overnight, they reach their destination. The parents bicker, and the children fall asleep, exhausted, in the back of the truck under a tarp. All they find left of Great Mam's homeland is a town named Cherokee, filled with one souvenir shop after another, selling tomahawks and garish plastic dolls. The only people Great Mam ever sees are Native Americans performing rain dances wearing war-bonnets on the main street and tourists taking pictures. The young narrator feels ashamed and saddened that her great-grandmother witnesses this travesty.

The dejected family returns home to Kentucky, and Great Mam dies soon after, but not before imparting the story of the waterbug to Gloria, her descendant whom she charges with keeping her memories alive.

The third part presents the waterbug creation myth that details the beginning of the Cherokee people. According to the legend, when those who inhabit the stars become curious about the ocean, they send a waterbug to explore it. The waterbug brings back a piece of mud from the ocean's bottom, and this mud becomes Earth.

"Homeland" ends with Great Mam's death. Although Florence Ann has placed cut flowers on her grave—a practice that goes against Great Mam's tribal beliefs—Gloria is not disturbed because she knows the little people will pick up the flowers. The young girl has successfully incorporated the dead woman's mythic knowledge and made it her own.

*Themes and Meanings*

Like many of Barbara Kingsolver's stories, "Homeland" deals with the power of family resistence and endurance, with cultural survival, and with the sacredness of nature. From the beginning, Great Mam's tribe resists the efforts of the United States government to move them west, away from their homeland. Although Great Mam has no choice but to move because she must marry outside her tribe, she retains her cultural heritage inside her head. Through the Native American oral tradition, she passes down her knowledge to her great-granddaughter, Gloria. Great Mam honors her Native American background and feels no shame about her marriage, which was never sanctioned by a Christian church. However, Gloria's mother, the Baptist, who wears white gloves and polishes her scuffed purse with white shoe polish, worries all the while what the neighbors might think. Despite her shame regarding her family roots, Florence Ann is a good mother, caring all the while for her family. Similarly, Gloria's father's love and deep concern for Great Mam prompts the family trip to her homeland in Tennessee.

Kingsolver demonstrates that narrative, particularly the oral form, plays a major role in the preservation of cultural identity. The only remnant that the family finds of Great Mam's homeland in the midst of the tacky souvenir shops is a mangy, one-eyed buffalo. Great-grandmother seems to float above this gruesome evidence of her people's demise and speeds up Gloria's cultural education. Thus, Great Mam's heritage survives in the knowledge she imparts to her great-granddaughter.

In many of her works, Kingsolver, a highly acclaimed novelist, views nature as sacred, and her characters demonstrate great concern with its preservation. Her work has been described as eco-feminism because female characters are usually her choice to praise and preserve nature. Great Mam is described as an old pine. When the family finds it difficult to buy meat, she tells Florence Ann, who feels ashamed of her Native American background, that people can live on vegetables. She herself eats her beans with reverence, realizing how each one nourishes her body.

When Gloria picks morning glories for Great Mam, the old lady counters the child's act of kindness and passes along her tribal knowledge by heightening Gloria's awareness with another point of view. Great Mam cannot reconcile killing plants just to make room for a garden. Flowers, she believes, are to be enjoyed by everyone and should not be picked. Indeed, she explains to young Gloria that flowers are the young girl's cousins and that she has committed a sin by killing them. Flowers should grow where they wish and be allowed to die naturally, so that they can set seeds for future generations.

At the end of the story, when Florence Ann cuts cultivated gladiolas with a serrated bread knife, puts them in a jar, and places them on Great Mam's grave, Gloria remembers Great Mam's lesson and notices how the cut flowers immediately begin to shrivel up with thirst.

## Style and Technique

Kingsolver demonstrates her twin themes of family and cultural endurance as well as pride and preservation of nature by structuring the plot around these thematic concerns. She characterizes people going about their everyday lives with great dignity—working, eating, playing, or even smoking a pipe. When the father is laid off from his mining job, instead of bemoaning his situation, he uses the downtime as an opportunity to take the family on a trip to view their great-grandmother's homeland. However, the trip is not simply for pleasure but to convey the lesson that families should know their roots. A meal together should not produce complaints about missing meat but should provide an opportunity to educate children in family and tribal history and knowledge. The games of cowboys and Indians played by Gloria's brothers are a sign that some family members are out of tune with their heritage. A young girl playing with morning glories presents an opportunity to learn a lifetime lesson on the interconnectedness of all living things. An old lady smoking a pipe on the porch demonstrates the sacred bond between god and humans.

*M. Casey Diana*

# AN HONEST THIEF

*Author:* Fyodor Dostoevski (1821-1881)
*Type of plot:* Psychological
*Time of plot:* The nineteenth century
*Locale:* A Russian town
*First published:* "Chestnyi vor," 1848 (English translation, 1919)

*Principal characters:*
AGRAFENA, a housekeeper
ASTAFY IVANOVITCH, the narrator, an old soldier
EMELYAN ILYITCH, an indigent and drunkard

## The Story

An anonymous frame narrator tells how his housekeeper, Agrafena, introduces an old soldier named Astafy Ivanovitch into the household as a lodger. Astafy proves to be an affable companion, breaking the monotony and loneliness of the reclusive narrator's existence by relating incidents from his past life.

One day, a stranger enters the apartment and asks for someone who does not live there. He leaves when told to do so but returns the following day and boldly steals a coat from the front hallway. This event incenses Astafy, who professes disgust with thievery. He mutters and exclaims over it repeatedly, commenting that a thief is the worst sort of vermin. The incident, however, reminds Astafy of a former acquaintance who was, in his opinion, an honest thief.

Astafy tells how he met this man, Emelyan Ilyitch, in a public house. Emelyan is a drunkard, habitually out of work and homeless. Nevertheless, his gentle nature arouses Astafy's kindness, and soon Emelyan is following Astafy everywhere and even staying all night at Astafy's lodgings. Astafy tries to get Emelyan to leave and seek employment but to no avail. Emelyan merely responds with tearful passivity, and Astafy is unable to turn him out. Astafy attempts to escape by moving to different quarters, but Emelyan finds him and moves in with him again. By this time, Astafy is himself quite impoverished but determines that perhaps Emelyan won't be so much trouble after all and goes on sharing his food and drink with him. Emelyan, however, continues to drink excessively. At first, Astafy is dismayed and disgusted but then is inspired to reform his friend. Suddenly, Astafy feels he has a whole new purpose in life.

Although Emelyan listens meekly to Astafy's exhortations to mend his ways, he responds only by talking of inconsequentialities. One day when Astafy gets particularly angry, Emelyan goes out all night and comes back to sleep on the freezing steps. Astafy becomes so enraged that Emelyan is frightened into stopping drinking for a time. Thinking his friend has finally turned over a new leaf, Astafy goes to a church service. On returning, he finds that a good pair of breeches is missing, and Emelyan is drunk. Obviously, Emelyan has sold them in order to buy liquor. Emelyan professes not to have touched the breeches, even pretending to look under the bed for them, but Astafy is deeply suspicious and angry.

Emelyan is overcome by guilt and runs off. Astafy, to his surprise, is worried and upset when his friend fails to return. Cursing himself for letting Emelyan leave, Astafy finally goes out to search for him. Finding him cold and ill from sleeping several nights on the street, Astafy realizes that he is no longer angry at his friend and takes him home. Astafy offers his friend food, but when he offers him a drink, Emelyan refuses. Emelyan's nights of wandering in the cold combine with his acute shame for having stolen the breeches to cause him severe illness. As he slowly succumbs, Emelyan asks his benefactor to sell his coat when he dies. Just before dying, Emelyan remorsefully confesses to having stolen the breeches, and Astafy forgives him.

### Themes and Meanings

The title of Fyodor Dostoevski's story appears to represent a moral impossibility. The purpose of the narrative is to examine this apparently self-contradictory idea by dramatizing some of the opposing motivations that can exist within a single human spirit. Emelyan is that honest thief, a man who steals, yet whose repentance is deeply sincere. Throughout the story, Emelyan is a thoroughly pathetic figure. He extracts the bare means of livelihood as well as free drinks by means of his meek yet stubbornly parasitic behavior. His theft of the breeches takes place at a time when he has become greatly weakened by drink, both mentally and physically. Moreover, it appears to be an impulsive, rather than a planned or malicious act. The description of Emelyan's remorse is dramatic and heart-rending. Astafy tells how Emelyan stays drunk for a fortnight, then sits wordlessly "as though grief was gnawing at his heart, or as though he wanted to do for himself completely." Emelyan's departure to the freezing streets is an act of self-punishment that further expresses his guilt. When he finally confesses to the theft just before dying, the reader feels that this character has a genuine desire to live virtuously, despite his failure to have done so.

Astafy also exhibits contradictory impulses throughout the story. Like Emelyan, Astafy is constantly torn between base and noble desires. He despises Emelyan's weakness and sloth, yet compassion and a desire to help always succeed these moments of disgust. Often, Astafy's feelings towards Emelyan change abruptly. "He'll ruin me with his drinking, I thought, but then another idea came into my head, sir, and took great hold on me. . . . I determined on the spot to be a father and guardian to him." Astafy's ability to ultimately choose compassion over condemnation mirrors Emelyan's final choice to confess to the theft.

The conflict between the two characters is less important than the private moral struggles each one faces within himself. Astafy, an ordinary and sensible man of humble origins, discovers that he has an almost miraculous capacity for compassion, despite his natural and justified feelings of resentment toward the pathetic Emelyan. Emelyan, a drunkard who appears to have lost his last shred of willpower, is nevertheless deeply conscious of having done wrong and finds the courage to admit to the theft before he dies. In these struggles, the reader sees the pain and difficulty of reconciling high moral aspirations with ordinary human fallibility. Although the story's prevailing mood is one of deep sadness, the conclusion suggests that even the most degraded human beings have the ability to choose goodness over evil.

## Style and Technique

"An Honest Thief" is a story-within-a-story. The frame story presents the bold, calculating thief who steals the anonymous narrator's coat and excites Astafy's contempt. This unrepentant thief is a vivid contrast to Emelyan, who steals on impulse and bitterly regrets his dishonesty. The contrast between these two thieves suggests the story of the good thief from the New Testament (Luke 23: 39-43), in which Christ converses with two robbers who are hanging on crosses next to him. One criminal mocks Christ, but the other speaks meekly to him. Christ promises salvation to the good thief. Dostoevski's allusion to the New Testament story emphasizes the moral purpose of "An Honest Thief." The reader sees that Christian virtues can be attained even in the humble or sordid circumstances of everyday life.

Much of the story is told through naturalistic dialogue, so that the reader has an impression of immediacy and spontaneity. Astafy pours out his story passionately and sincerely, without artifice or elegance. He describes his reactions to each event as it occurs, so that the reader feels he or she is living through the story with the narrator. Astafy does not attempt to present himself in a flattering light; he discloses his angry and impatient thoughts about Emelyan as unreservedly as his charitable ones, so that the reader senses a remarkable degree of human authenticity in his account. Although the reader does not have direct access to Emelyan's thoughts, Astafy comments on his friend's moods frequently and sympathetically.

This unguarded, self-revelatory tone creates an intense, almost claustrophobic concentration on psychological states. Although the narrator tells much about his and Astafy's feelings, he divulges only a little about physical appearances or setting. This emphasis on emotions focuses the reader's attention closely on the characters' moral conflicts so that there is an almost unbearable level of intensity by the time the story concludes. The end is appropriately abrupt, releasing the dramatic tension in a short scene of reconciliation between Astafy and Emelyan.

Although the story's moral values are lofty, the characters and setting are ordinary, even sordid. The frame story takes place in modest bachelor quarters, and Astafy's narrative refers to a corner of an old woman's room, where he stays alive on bread, onions, and kvass. Emelyan wears a shabby old coat, arranged so as to hide its many holes. These coarse circumstances, although briefly sketched, create a poignant contrast with the characters' sensitive and deeply felt spiritual reflections about themselves and each other. This contrast reinforces Dostoevski's contention that virtue can be attained by weak and fallible human beings in humble walks of life.

*Constance Vidor*

# HOOK

*Author:* Walter Van Tilburg Clark (1909-1971)
*Type of plot:* Fable
*Time of plot:* The 1930's
*Locale:* The central California coast
*First published:* 1940

*Principal characters:*
HOOK, a hawk
A JAPANESE FARMER

*The Story*

As a fledgling hawk, Hook is matter-of-factly pushed from the nest by his parents during one of the recurring droughts common to the semi-arid terrain of the central California coast. Preoccupied with their own survival, his parents abandon him to the sand and brush along the dry river bed. As hunger takes precedence over parental and reproductive urges, the father and mother go their separate ways to course about the dry hillsides looking for prey, leaving their undeveloped fledgling to his fate. Still partially covered with down, lacking flight feathers, thin and inept at hunting for food, Hook is a creature of hunger and fear. Unable to fly, he struggles for existence in a dangerous and disinterested world. Hiding in the brush, feeding on insects and the small fish left by the receding water of the river, Hook manages to survive. Only the infuriating sound of the seagulls crying in the sky above him intrudes into Hook's truncated existence. The seagulls at easy play in the sky contrast starkly with the undeveloped hawk frantically scuttling about in a desiccated world of dead or dying things.

During one of his forays for food, Hook kills a small mouse. The taste of blood awakens the first of his primordial drives, the instinct to hunt. When he makes his first successful flight, striking a ground squirrel large enough to wound Hook in its struggle for life, Hook becomes a hawk. His entry into the mature world of the predator gives him a wild delight. Hook senses that his world is a great arena for killing.

Having learned to fly, Hook becomes master of the valley and the hills of grass that nourish his prey. He drives the weaponless gulls back to the seashore and turns away challenges from his own kind. His maturity is complete when he consummates a violent courtship, establishing a brood of his own. Nothing disturbs that completeness save a Japanese farmer in the valley below. Only the farmer causes Hook to veer away in the flights across his domain.

Because the farmer suspects that the hawk takes his chickens, he carefully watches the patterns of its flight, waiting for the opportunity to kill Hook with his shotgun. One of Hook's flights carries him within range of the farmer's shotgun, and he is brought to the ground, badly crippled, fierce with fear. The broken-winged hawk, no longer able to hunt, must return to scrabbling for bugs and lizards in the dust and dirt. Hook's existence becomes abject. When the seagulls discover that Hook is a helpless creature of the ground, they catch him in the open and peck out an eye, but his remaining eye burns with rage. Now suffering from starvation, unable to catch and kill wild creatures, Hook raids the farmer's chicken coop, killing the helpless birds in a mad frenzy. Awakened by the noise of the terrified and dying chickens, the farmer and his dog find the crippled hawk in the yard. The dog attacks Hook but is driven off by the hawk's sharp talons and beak. Urged on by the farmer, the dog attacks again and again, finally breaking the hawk's neck. The farmer's wife, witness to the spectacle of death, pronounces an ironically banal epitaph: "Oh, the brave bird."

### Themes and Meanings

In the modern fable "Hook," Walter Van Tilburg Clark develops two converging themes that foreshadow more recent writers, such as Edward Abbey, who decry thoughtless human intrusion into an increasingly defiled western landscape. Clark is not an environmentalist in the modern sense of one who supports a cause rooted primarily in an understanding of ecological checks and balances. Rather, he is concerned with the relationship between the development of aesthetic and moral sensibilities.

When flight frees Hook from his microcosmic life of dust and scurrying insects, he ascends over a vibrantly beautiful landscape, transformed by the sweep and range of his vision. At the zenith of Hook's life, the hawk and nature, fused in rhythmic harmony, play out the essential patterns of life, the flow of seasons, birth and death, prey and predator. His flights across the hills and valleys are visual rhapsodies in celebration of nature's beauty. Hook looks down from the sky on a world of which he is an integral part and cries out with fierce joy. Only the farmer's plot of cultivated land strikes a note of visual discord.

The Japanese farmer who effects Hook's destruction is earthbound. Stooped over hoe and plow, his vision is reminiscent of the fledgling Hook's. The hawk that soars above fails to stir the farmer's spirit, to inspire a sense of awe for the sheer beauty of a raptor in flight. The farmer sees only an unwanted threat to his domestic fowl.

After praising the dog for killing the hawk, the farmer raises the lantern so that his wife might better see the dead bird. They view the hawk with superficial curiosity. The farmer's wife exclaims over the bird's bravery, but neither she nor the farmer experience any sense of loss. Neither realize that the coastal valley in which they live is no longer complete. Neither are aware that they have been diminished by the hawk's death.

Clark once remarked that living in harmony with the natural world was the essence of good. Although the farmer and his wife fail this test of life, their failure to live in harmony with nature comes as the result of ignorance rather than intention. Like Hook, the farmer must struggle for survival. He destroys the hawk because he is ignorant of the way in which it lives, but more important is the fact that he fails to see its intrinsic beauty. His world is limited to family and farm; thus he is unable to value anything outside his immediate sphere of experience. His inability to see the beauty in a bird of prey denotes a moral failure. The farmer and his wife, failing to see themselves as a part of their natural surroundings, remain separate from the very land on which they live. This moral distancing from all life but their own renders them ignorant, unfulfilled, and capable of wanton destruction.

## Style and Technique

Clark's work reflects unusual mastery over poetic voice, careful attention to the details of narration, and, above all, an ear finely attuned to the nuances of language. Clark takes a risk telling his tale from the hawk's point of view. Although the narrative voice gains an intimacy otherwise unavailable, he runs the risk of sentimentality. Clark skillfully avoids obvious anthropomorphism by confining Hook's reactions to relatively primordial emotions such as rage, fear, and triumph and carefully maintaining a disinterested narrative tone.

Although not a biologist, Clark is a keen observer of nature, and in depicting Hook, he depicts the hawk as he understands the behavior of raptors. By carefully recording the events of Hook's life with seeming detachment, the narrative voice appears distanced and disinterested. From the first sentence, "Hook, the hawk's child, was hatched in a dry spring among the oaks beside the seasonal river, and was struck from the nest early," the tone appears to be matter-of-fact. There is a fine deception in this presumption, for Clark selects and arranges the details brought before the eye. Nowhere is the deceptively flat narrative voice more economically powerful than in the closing description of the dead hawk: "Between the great sails the light body lay caved and perfectly still." This single sentence provides a summation of themes. The great sails suggest the hawk's majesty, and the light body suggests the delicate fragility of hollow bird bones. Hook lies in perfect stillness, in perfection not to be reawakened. Clearly the poetic power of the narration is not detached, for it inspires both pity and fear. With this sentence, Clark has awakened a terrible sense of loss, of pity not only for the bird but also for its destroyer and ultimately for the human condition.

*David Sundstrand*

# THE HORLA

*Author:* Guy de Maupassant (1850-1893)
*Type of plot:* Horror
*Time of plot:* The late nineteenth century
*Locale:* Near Rouen, France
*First published:* "Le Horla," 1886 (English translation, 1890)

> *Principal characters:*
> THE NARRATOR, a wealthy young man
> THE HORLA, an invisible spirit that the narrator believes
>    originated in Brazil

## The Story

The story unfolds in a series of journal entries written by an anonymous narrator. Over four months, the narrator recounts his growing uneasiness over strange incidents occurring in his country house near Rouen, France. It is apparent that he is a man of considerable wealth. He mentions having several servants, he refers to an idyllic childhood in a large country home, and he enjoys a life of leisure throughout his narrative.

On the evening of May 8, the narrator is delighted to see a Brazilian ship sailing down the Seine. In the days that follow, however, he finds himself afflicted with a strange sense of malaise. He suffers from a slight fever and becomes increasingly depressed. He is convinced that he is facing some unknown misfortune, and his condition worsens whenever he walks along the river or as night approaches. The local doctor who cares for him cannot find a physical reason for his malady.

Soon the narrator reports that he is having nightmares. He dreams that an invisible creature approaches him as he sleeps and tries to strangle him. Each time he has this dream, he awakens in a cold sweat, only to find that he is alone and that his door is still locked. In despair, he leaves his country home and spends several days at Mont Saint-Michel. While he is there, his malady appears to vanish entirely, so he returns to his country estate believing himself cured. Almost immediately, however, both his illness and his nightmares return.

The narrator now believes that an invisible creature enters his bedroom each night, draining the water from the carafe near his bed. After he finds the carafe empty several mornings in a row, the narrator decides to conduct an experiment. Before going to bed each night, he sets out a carafe of water, glasses of milk and wine, a slice of bread, and some strawberries. Then he locks his door and goes to sleep. Each morning, the result is the same: The water and milk are gone; nothing else appears to have been touched.

To determine if it is he himself who drinks the water and milk while he is asleep, the narrator tries one further experiment. He seals the carafe and glass in white muslin and covers his mouth with black lead before going to sleep. When he awakens the next morning, he finds that the water and milk are gone and that the muslin is completely free of any stain. Now convinced that all this proves some kind of supernatural visitation, he flees to Paris.

In Paris the narrator finds that his illness and nightmares vanish. He returns to his earlier belief that his fears were merely the result of an overactive imagination. As a further sign of this skepticism, he dismisses hypnotism as mere trickery until he witnesses his own cousin under the influence of a posthypnotic suggestion. He again begins to wonder whether supernatural phenomena might actually exist,

Returning to his country house once again, he finds that his sense of foreboding gradually returns. The invisible creature even appears to become bolder. One day, the narrator sees a rose snapped from its stem by an invisible hand. Glasses are broken in sealed cupboards. The narrator finds that words he does not intend to say occasionally emerge from his own lips.

Finally, he reads two works that appear to explain these strange phenomena. One account appears in a book detailing the origin and powers of invisible spirits. The other explanation appears in a scientific article about a strange occurrence in Brazil, where entire villages were abandoned when their inhabitants became terrified by unseen phantoms. The narrator now recalls the Brazilian ship that he saw just before his troubles began, and he concludes that a new race of invisible creatures, successors to the human race, is emerging in Rio de Janeiro. One of these spirits, he concludes, was carried to France by ship where it then took residence in his house.

Unable to rid himself of the spirit in any other way, the narrator sets fire to the country home. The screams of his servants reveal that he has neglected to warn anyone of his plans, and all of the servants perish in the blaze. Nevertheless, the narrator is uncertain whether the creature itself has been killed. If it has not, the narrator concludes that his only recourse is suicide.

### Themes and Meanings

Short stories of the Romantic period generally demonstrate one of two contrasting qualities: realism or a preoccupation with fantasy and the supernatural. Guy de Maupassant's "The Horla" skillfully unites both qualities. The tale begins realistically enough with the narrator's account of his stay at a country house and an almost clinical description of his illness. Only gradually does fantasy begin to intrude on this realistic environment. Maupassant's combination of objectivity and horror thus make "The Horla" unusual in the canon of his works. Heavily influenced by the realistic novels of his mentor Gustave Flaubert, Maupassant is best known for stories of social criticism and portrayals of peasant life in Normandy. "The Horla" differs substantially from these stories. Falling midway between the genuine horror of Edgar Allan Poe's short stories and the psychological horror of Henry James's novella *The Turn of the Screw* (1898), "The Horla" combines realism and terror in a manner uncommon in Romantic literature.

The central theme of "The Horla" is well expressed in a statement made by William Shakespeare's character Hamlet: "There are more things in heaven and earth, Horatio, than are dreamt of in your philosophy." Maupassant's narrator first appears as a confirmed skeptic, dismissing the legend of a ghost near Mont Saint-Michel and refusing to believe in hypnosis. By the end of the story, however, he becomes overwhelmed by the supernatural. "The Horla" thus continues a literary theme originating in Euripides' tragedy *Bakchai* (405 B.C.E.; *The Bacchae*, 1781). It displays the world as far stranger than the rational mind can comprehend. Those who resist the power of irrationality end up being destroyed by it.

Maupassant has constructed "The Horla" in such a way that it can be read both as a serious account of a supernatural event and as the record of a deepening insanity. In fact, Maupassant's first draft of this story presents the narrative, not as selections from a diary, but as the testimony of a psychiatric patient. Moreover, the ambiguous ending of the story is intended to leave the reader with questions: Do the narrator's servants die as the result of a mad delusion? Or were they the innocent victims of a man driven to the brink of despair by a power that he cannot understand? However one views the story, it is a strange irony that, shortly after publishing "The Horla," Maupassant himself exhibited increasingly irrational behavior and went insane (probably as the result of syphilis). He spent his last two years in a mental institution.

*Style and Technique*

The use of a first-person narrator is a highly effective means of intensifying the story's horror. The reader becomes a helpless witness to the onset of the narrator's madness (or perhaps to his visitation by a supernatural being). By first establishing the narrator as a sympathetic figure and then involving the reader in his tragedy, Maupassant makes the ending of his story truly horrific. This is particularly important because the deaths of several innocent victims could all too easily have repelled Maupassant's readers.

"The Horla" is an excellent example of Maupassant's compact style. No detail in the work is unnecessary. The Brazilian ship mentioned at the beginning of the story becomes important, for example, when the narrator reads an account of the "mass hallucination" that occurred near Rio de Janeiro. The monk's tale of a ghost appearing near Mont Saint-Michel and the story of a séance in Paris both serve gradually to strip away the narrator's skepticism. By the time that the climax is reached, every detail of the story has been found to play an important role in advancing a sense of horror.

A word of Maupassant's own coinage, "horla" is a pseudo-Portuguese word that the narrator uses to describe the supernatural being that haunts him. Although derived from the French expressions *hors de lui* ("outside of himself") or *hors là* ("outside there"), "horla" also suggests the words *horreur* ("horror"), *horrible* ("horrible"), and *hurler* ("to howl"). The result is to imply that the level of terror in the story cannot be expressed by ordinary words.

*Jeffrey L. Buller*

# MASTERPLOTS II

## SHORT STORY SERIES
### REVISED EDITION

# TITLE INDEX

TITLE INDEX

# TITLE INDEX